Analyzing Global Social Media Consumption

Patrick Kanyi Wamuyu
United States International University – Africa, Kenya

A volume in the Advances in Social Networking
and Online Communities (ASNOC) Book Series

Published in the United States of America by
IGI Global
Information Science Reference (an imprint of IGI Global)
701 E. Chocolate Avenue
Hershey PA, USA 17033
Tel: 717-533-8845
Fax: 717-533-8661
E-mail: cust@igi-global.com
Web site: http://www.igi-global.com

Library of Congress Cataloging-in-Publication Data

Names: Wamuyu, Patrick Kanyi, 1970- editor.
Title: Analyzing global social media consumption / Patrick Kanyi Wamuyu,
    editor.
Description: Hershey : Information Science Reference, 2020. | Includes
    bibliographical references and index. | Summary: "This book presents all
    aspects of Social Media consumption including current trends, practices,
    and newly emerging narratives from a wide range of disciplinary
    perspectives and on both theoretical and empirical research from
    academic researchers and critical practitioners"-- Provided by
    publisher.
Identifiers: LCCN 2020018654 (print) | LCCN 2020018655 (ebook) | ISBN
    9781799847182 (hardcover) | ISBN 9781799857860 (paperback) | ISBN
    9781799847199 (ebook)
Subjects: LCSH: Social media--Research. | Online social networks--Research.
    | Information technology--Social aspects.
Classification: LCC HM742 .A543 2020 (print) | LCC HM742 (ebook) | DDC
    303.48/33--dc23
LC record available at https://lccn.loc.gov/2020018654
LC ebook record available at https://lccn.loc.gov/2020018655

This book is published in the IGI Global book series Advances in Social Networking and Online Communities (ASNOC) (ISSN: 2328-1405; eISSN: 2328-1413)

British Cataloguing in Publication Data
A Cataloguing in Publication record for this book is available from the British Library.

For electronic access to this publication, please contact: eresources@igi-global.com.

Advances in Social Networking and Online Communities (ASNOC) Book Series

Hakikur Rahman

Institute of Computer Management and Science, Bangladesh

ISSN:2328-1405
EISSN:2328-1413

MISSION

The advancements of internet technologies and the creation of various social networks provide a new channel of knowledge development processes that's dependent on social networking and online communities. This emerging concept of social innovation is comprised of ideas and strategies designed to improve society.

The **Advances in Social Networking and Online Communities** book series serves as a forum for scholars and practitioners to present comprehensive research on the social, cultural, organizational, and human issues related to the use of virtual communities and social networking. This series will provide an analytical approach to the holistic and newly emerging concepts of online knowledge communities and social networks.

COVERAGE

- Introduction to Mobile Computing
- Information Policy Overview
- Generation of Municipal Services in Multi-Channel Environments
- Organizational Knowledge Communication and Knowledge Transfer as the Focal Point of Knowledge Management
- Methodologies to Analyze, Design and Deploy Distributed Knowledge Management Solutions
- Leveraging Knowledge Communication in Social Networks
- Meta-data Representation and Management (e.g., Semantic-Based Coordination Mechanisms, Use of Ontologies, etc.)
- Knowledge as Capacity for Action
- Local E-Government Interoperability and Security
- Leveraging Knowledge Communication Networks – Approaches to Interpretations and Interventions

IGI Global is currently accepting manuscripts for publication within this series. To submit a proposal for a volume in this series, please contact our Acquisition Editors at Acquisitions@igi-global.com or visit: http://www.igi-global.com/publish/.

Titles in this Series

For a list of additional titles in this series, please visit:
http://www.igi-global.com/book-series/advances-social-networking-online-communities/37168

Global Perspectives on Social Media Communications, Trade Unionism, and Transnationa Advocacy
Floribert Patrick C. Endong (University of Calabar, Nigeria)
Information Science Reference • © 2020 • 300pp • H/C (ISBN: 9781799831389) • US $195.00

Electronic Hive Minds on Social Media Emerging Research and Opprtunities
Shalin Hai-Jew (Kansas State University, USA)
Information Science Reference • © 2019 • 358pp • H/C (ISBN: 9781522593690) • US $205.00

Hidden Link Prediction in Stochastic Social Networks
Babita Pandey (Lovely Professional University, India) and Aditya Khamparia (Lovely Professional University, India)
Information Science Reference • © 2019 • 281pp • H/C (ISBN: 9781522590965) • US $195.00

Cognitive Social Mining Applications in Data Analytics and Forensics
Anandakumar Haldorai (Sri Eshwar College of Engineering, India) and Arulmurugan Ramu (Presidency University, India)
Information Science Reference • © 2019 • 326pp • H/C (ISBN: 9781522575221) • US $195.00

Modern Perspectives on Virtual Communications and Social Networking
Jyotsana Thakur (Amity University, India)
Information Science Reference • © 2019 • 273pp • H/C (ISBN: 9781522557159) • US $175.00

Exploring the Role of Social Media in Transnational Advocacy
Floribert Patrick C. Endong (University of Calabar, Nigeria)
Information Science Reference • © 2018 • 307pp • H/C (ISBN: 9781522528548) • US $195.00

Online Communities as Agents of Change and Social Movements
Steven Gordon (Babson College, USA)
Information Science Reference • © 2017 • 338pp • H/C (ISBN: 9781522524953) • US $195.00

Social Media Performance Evaluation and Success Measurements
Michael A. Brown Sr. (Florida International University, USA)
Information Science Reference • © 2017 • 294pp • H/C (ISBN: 9781522519638) • US $185.00

701 East Chocolate Avenue, Hershey, PA 17033, USA
Tel: 717-533-8845 x100 • Fax: 717-533-8661
E-Mail: cust@igi-global.com • www.igi-global.com

List of Reviewers

Ana Antunes, *Lisbon Polytechnic Institute, Portugal*
Aslı Aydın, *Istanbul Bilgi University, Istanbul, Turkey*
Phelix Mbabazi Businge, *Kabale University, Uganda*
Stanley Githinji, *United States International University – Africa, Kenya*
Gregory Gondwe, *University of Colorado, Boulder, USA*
David Lomoywara, *SIMElab Africa, Kenya*
Guy-Maurille Massamba, *Arizona State University, USA*
Kelvin Mudavadi, *United States International University – Africa, Kenya*
Japheth Mursi, *University of KwaZulu-Natal, South Africa*
Paula Musuva, *United States International University – Africa, Kenya*
Peterson Mwangi, *United States International University – Africa, Kenya*
Stephen Ndegwa, *Daystar University, Kenya*
Lawrence Nderu, *Jomo Kenyatta University of Agriculture and Technology, Kenya*
Collins Oduor, *United States International University – Africa, Kenya*
Sanjeev Rao, *CSED, TIET, India*
Mamoon Rashid, *Lovely Professional University, India*
Sagorika Singha, *Jawaharlal Nehru University, India*
Ruth Wario, *University of the Free State, South Africa*

Table of Contents

Detailed Table of Contents

Chapter 1
Stavroula Kalogeras, School of Business, University of Plymouth, UK

This study explores how brand cultures can become learning communities and highlights how social networking sites can emerge as social learning platforms by way of content, conversations, and community. The purpose of this chapter is to examine the concept of learning content in online social learning networks that are initiated by a commercial enterprise to provide a competitive advantage while at the same time providing social good. The proposed framework builds a bridge between the organization and the consumer, takes into account Generation Z, and looks at self-development and knowledge consumption as the key benefit. The work considers transmedia storytelling which has emerged in marketing to expand the brand story. The concept of transmedia learning networks and brand-consumer value-competitiveness model is proposed to show the value proposition of knowledge consumption. The work embraces learning communities, introduces the theory of conversationisim, and encourages participation and conversation on a global scale.

Chapter 2
Ishrat Nazeer, School of Computer Science and Engineering, Lovely Professional University, Jalandhar, India
Mamoon Rashid, School of Computer Science and Engineering, Lovely Professional University, Jalandhar, India
Sachin Kumar Gupta, School of Electronics and Communication Engineering, Shri Mata Vaishno Devi University, Jammu, India
Abhishek Kumar, School of Computer Science and IT, Jain University, Bangalore, India

Twitter is a platform where people express their opinions and come with regular updates. At present, it has become a source for many organizations where data will be extracted and then later analyzed for sentiments. Many machine learning algorithms are available for twitter sentiment analysis which are used for automatically predicting the sentiment of tweets. However, there are challenges that hinder machine learning classifiers to achieve better results in terms of classification. In this chapter, the authors are proposing a novel feature generation technique to provide desired features for training model. Next, the novel ensemble classification system is proposed for identifying sentiment in tweets through weighted majority rule ensemble classifier, which utilizes several commonly used statistical models like naive Bayes, random forest, logistic regression, which are weighted according to their performance on historical data, where weights are chosen separately for each model.

This chapter aims to explore the impact of social networking sites (SNS) usage on individual work performance (IP). A literature review revealed contrasting results. A multiple-case study on 15 employees from eight Tunisian firms has been conducted to highlight the SNS effects on IP in the specific context of democratic transition. Data have been collected by semi-structured interviews and coded using the Nvivo 10 software. The analysis shows that, depending on the level of SNS usage, three types of effect are identified on IP at work: positive, negative, or null. This result invites researcher to consider the usage intensity when analyzing SNS effects on IP. Understanding the different types of SNS usage by actors and their effects on IP could help managers to take appropriate decisions to take profit from this usage. This research suggests also that organizational policy moderates the relationship between SNS usage and IP.

As Web 2.0 technologies have turned the Internet into an interactive medium, users dominate the field. With the spread of social media, the Internet has become much more user-oriented. In contrast to traditional media, social media's lack of control mechanisms makes the accuracy of spreading news questionable. This brings us to the significance of fact-checking platforms. This study investigates the antecedents of spreading false news in Turkey. The purpose of the study is to determine the features of fake news. For this purpose, teyit.org, the biggest fact-checking platform in Turkey, has been chosen for analysis. The current study shows fake news to be detectable based on four features: Propagation, User Type, Social Media Type, and Formatting. According to the logistic regression analysis, the study's model obtained 86.7% accuracy. The study demonstrates that Facebook increases the likelihood of news being fake compared to Twitter or Instagram. Emoji usage is also statistically significant in terms of increasing the probability of fake news. Unexpectedly, the impact of photos or videos was found statistically insignificant.

Chapter 5

Yowei Kang, National Taiwan Ocean University, Taiwan
Kenneth C. C. Yang, The University of Texas at El Paso, USA

Social media have been claimed to homogenize human and consumer behaviors around the world – in other words, to make people think, feel, and act alike regardless of national borders. Scholars often debate this claim from either a convergence or a divergence perspective from the marketing and consumer behavior literature. The theoretical foundation will be based on the convergence-divergence debates that postulate universal consumption patterns and values are made possible, due to the industrialization, modernization, technology, and wealth accumulation. The authors use perceptions of online privacy among users of privacy-invasive technologies as an example to discuss why people will think the same about their own privacy could be a myth for the failure to consider the unique socio-cultural characteristics of each nation. This study begins with a global consumption analysis of social media around the world. Then, they examine how privacy concerns may help account for the homogenization or heterogenization trend of global consumer culture. Discussions and implications are provided.

Chapter 6

Patrick Kanyi Wamuyu, United States International University – Africa, Kenya

Despite the growing popularity of social media among Kenyans, there is limited baseline data on the consumption of these platforms by different Kenyan communities based on demographics such as age, gender, education, income, and geolocation. The study set out to fill this gap through a baseline survey on social media consumption in Kenya. The study used a mixed-method approach, involving a survey of 3,269 respondents and 37 focus group discussions. The social media platforms in use are WhatsApp, Facebook, YouTube, Instagram, LinkedIn, and Snapchat. However, the use of social media differs by demographics. Kenyans use social media for entertainment, education, jobs, politics, sports, and social issues. Most Kenyans access social media using phones for 1-3 hours daily. Motivations for using social media include the acquisition of information, entertainment, and social interactions. Most social media users have experienced fake news, cyberbullying, and bombardment with graphic images of sex and advertisements. Kenyans consider social media to be addictive, expensive, and time-wasting.

Chapter 7

José Duarte Santos, Polytechnic of Porto, Portugal
Steffen Mayer, Aschaffenburg University of Applied Sciences, Germany

The purpose of this chapter is the comparison of social media strategy on Twitter and Sina Weibo by the German company Adidas. A successful social media campaign is pushing brand awareness and companies improve their focus on that. Due to the internet censorship of the Chinese government, the social media landscape in China differs from the Western world. Therefore, companies need cultural and linguistic know how to be successful on Chinese platforms like Sina Weibo. The chapter compares how Adidas uses Twitter and Sina Weibo for their marketing purpose. Cultural differences and the local adaption of their social media appearance will be presented.

The digital era has introduced many changes in the consumer marketplace. Social media and especially social networking sites redefined how consumers relate to and behave towards brands, as well as the brand-consumer relationship. Within this context and the heightened resistance to brand communication through traditional media, marketeers are turning to other strategies to connect with their customers and influence their consumer journey. One of these strategies is influencer marketing. In the last years, brands have used social media influencers as endorsers of their products and services, and as brand ambassadors. Digital influencers connect consumers and brands, strengthening their bond and allowing the brand to reach their target in a more natural way to influence the consumer buying process. In this chapter we will provide a narrative review on the role of digital influencers on the consumer decision processes.

The main objective of this chapter is to gain an in-depth understanding of the social media addiction construct. For this purpose, prior studies on social media addiction are reviewed. Based on this review the influence of several personal, social, and situational factors on social media addiction are examined. Firstly, personal factors such as demographic characteristics, personality traits, self-esteem, well-being, loneliness, anxiety, and depression are studied for their impact on social media addiction. Next, the social correlates and consequents of social media addiction are identified, namely need for affiliation, subjective norms, personal, professional, and academic life. Lastly, situational factors like amount of social media use and motives of use are inspected. Following the review of literature an empirical study is made to analyze factors that discriminate addicted social media users from non-addicted social media users on the basis of these different factors.

Online social networks (OSNs) are nowadays an indispensable tool for communication on account of their rise, simplicity, and efficacy. Worldwide users use OSN as a tool for social interactions, news propagation, gaming, political propaganda, and advertisement in building brand awareness, etc. At the same time, many OSN users unintentionally expose their personal information that is used by the malicious users and third-party apps to perform various kind for cyber-crimes like social engineering attacks, cyber espionage, extortion-malware, drug-trafficking, misinformation, cyberbullying, hijacking clicks, identity theft, phishing, mistrusts, fake profiles, and spreading malicious content. This chapter presents an overview of various cyber-crimes associated with OSN environment to gain insight into ongoing cyber-attacks. Also, counter mechanisms in the form of tools, techniques, and frameworks are suggested.

Chapter 11

Gregory Gondwe, University of Colorado at Boulder, USA
Roberta Muchangwe, University of Zambia, Zambia
Japhet Edward Mwaya, St. Augustine University of Tanzania, Tanzania

Although considerable literature has grown around the motivations for social media use and consumption across Africa, there is still a dearth of research on trends of consumption across different cultures and particular demographic environments. Studies that have attempted to explore this field tend to focus on how social media and the internet as a whole have remedied individuals in different ways. Particularly, how social media usage has enhanced participatory governance economically improved people's lives. This chapter offers a rather nuanced synthesis and perception of social media usage and consumption in Zambia that underscores the motivating factors. Two major interpretations are identified: social media consumption that focuses only on the quantity of proliferated online content and social media usage that interrogates the various ways people in Zambia use social media to suit their tastes and needs. The two approaches underscore the debate in this chapter and highlight how most studies have downplayed the distinction between the two.

Chapter 12

Guy-Maurille Massamba, Independent Researcher, USA

This study focuses on the process of institutional change with regard to the capabilities of African political systems to embrace the conditions that instill and support democracy in the context characterized by pervasive social media consumption. The author wonders in what way institutions and individual behaviors can integrate social media in order to consolidate democracy. In other words, is social media-supported democracy sustainable in Africa? The study analyzes the patterns of social media consumption in its functionality for democratic change in Africa. It examines patterns of institutional change on the basis of the impact of social media consumption in African politics. It highlights two theories of institutional change—structured institutional change and evolutionary institutional change—based on their relevance to the impact of social media consumption in African political settings.

Chapter 13

Patrick Kanyi Wamuyu, United States International University – Africa, Kenya

Kenya has a robust blogger community, with hundreds of active bloggers and a variety of stimulating blogs on politics, agriculture, technology, education, fashion, food, entertainment, sports, and travel. The purpose of this chapter was to explore whether Kenyans participate in online discussions and to determine the role of Kenyan bloggers in online communities. Data was collected through a survey of 3,269 respondents aged between 14 and 55 years and social media mining on Twitter using Network Overview, Discovery and Exploration for Excel (NodeXL) API. Survey data was analyzed using descriptive statistics and cross-tabulation while mined data was analyzed for centrality metrics. The study identified Farmers Trend, Ghafla Kenya, KahawaTungu, and Kachwanya as influential blogs in the Kenyan blogosphere and that most Kenyan women read travel and food and fashion blogs while men mostly read sports and politics blogs. This chapter contributes to a better understanding of the Kenyan blogosphere.

The context of demographic aging, combined with the wide dissemination of information and communication technologies (ICT), in the various domains of society defined a set of challenges, potentialities, and limits for seniors (65+). Although there is a positive evolution regarding adhesion and even domestication of ICT by this age segment, namely the internet and digital social networking sites, the literature review presents us with an immature, limited, and fragmented field of study, comprising an immense space of evolution. Aware of the strength, magnitude, and considerable ignorance of the action of seniors in the network society, this chapter intends to map, through a review of the multidisciplinary literature, how the relationship of seniors with ICTs is configured. In addition, usage behavior, as well as the drivers, and the consequences for the elderly of navigating digital social networks are also analyzed.

Social networks such as Twitter contain billions of data of users, and in every second, a large number of tweets trade through Twitter. Sentiment analysis is the way toward deciding the emotional tone behind a series of words that users utilize to understand the attitudes, thoughts, and emotions that are enunciated in online references on Twitter. This chapter aims to determine the user preference of Bitcoin and Ethereum, which are the two most popular cryptocurrencies in the world by using the Twitter sentiment analysis. It proposes a powerful and fundamental approach to identify emotions on Twitter by considering the tweets of these two distinctive cryptocurrencies. One hundred twenty thousand (120,000) tweets were extracted separately from Twitter for each keyword Bitcoin/BTC and Bitcoin/ETC between the period from 12/09/2018 to 22/09/2018 (10 days).

Foreword

It is a commonplace that social media have impacted media and communication around the world in the last decade like no media innovation before. However, our knowledge on how these innovations affect individual behavior, social structures and societies as a whole is still limited. Albeit there is a lot of empirical research in this field, there are reasons to suspect that scientific endeavor on this issue is not evenly distributed around the world. Research budgets are differing globally in a way that does not reflect the potential for digital innovation in different parts of the world. While U.S. elections, for example, spark studies on social media use every two or four years on a large scale, mobile innovations on the basis of digital media tend to emerge also in areas of the world where much less attention of academia can be expected, like in sub-Saharan Africa.

In my home country, Germany, well-established traditional technologies like landline infrastructure have in many fields turned out to be a retarding agent when it comes to digital innovation. In rankings of mobile or highspeed internet connections, it is ranking somewhere around number 30, outrun by countries like Romania, Thailand, China or Bulgaria – which is hurtfully failing to meet German's self-perception as a technological leader in many fields. An even more relevant result of this state of affairs is the fact that Germany may not be the best place to observe groundbreaking innovations in social media.

The result of this imbalance of media development and innovation on one hand and research effort on the other is a skewed image of use and effects of social media appearing in scientific publications around the globe. In this context this book project, which emerged in the vibrant environment of the SIMELab at USIU-Africa in Nairobi, Kenya, is an extremely valuable contribution to global social media research. It assembles studies not only on a broad variety of relevant but still under researched aspects of social media use and research methodology, but also from researchers from Europe, Africa, Asia, US and Australia and thus is an exemplar of how the global social media environment needs to be assessed from science: in a global network of scholars.

Martin Emmer
Freie Universität Berlin, Germany

Preface

Social media has enormously developed in the past decade. From rudimental social media sites offering low-level services to high-tech mobile social media sites and apps with a vast number of services, attracting millions of daily users. Social media was once seen as a communications channel between family, friends, and colleagues at work, but now has transformed all spheres of everyday life from social interactions, news and journalism, food and fashion, entertainment, business, and research with incredible influence on people's lives. Information shared in social media, also attracts the attention of mainstream media, who are not only using the platforms for content sharing but also as vital sources for news stories. It is therefore important to think about where social media is heading and the trends that are defining the current and future generation of users.

Social media sites and apps have also become the new home where families, friends, influencers, brands, and bloggers converge multiple times daily to share updates and communicate. This has made social media a key subject of scholarly, economic, social, cultural, and political debates. The proliferation of internet-enabled mobile devices has led to the rapid uptake of the internet in developing countries, resulting in a continued reconfiguration of ways in which individuals access and use social networking sites and apps. Social media offers free and easy-to-use applications to produce and distribute digital content which has made it possible for individuals to make use of the full potential of the internet globally. However, people consume social media based on the need and satisfaction which that particular media provides. The motivations for the use and consumption of social media is not determined and dictated by the technology, but the applicability of that technology in a particular context.

Social media has been used to empower people on one hand and as a tool for manipulation on the other. Today, there are changes in content creation and consumption in social media with the exploitative use of algorithms for content curation in social media platforms by manipulative actors who seek to spread propaganda, hate, and fake news, interfering with online debates, influencing elections, polarizing societies, and mobilizing extremist groups. Algorithms have also been used to determine the visibility and invisibility of content on social media by filtering, ranking, selecting, and recommending content that gets displayed on the users' news feeds. The role of social media algorithms is augmented by the use of automated actors such as bots and bad actors such as troll factories. However, whatever our views of the good or bad of social media, one thing is certain: it has impacted most aspects of everyday life.

OBJECTIVE OF THE BOOK

This book was motivated by the desire to understand the trends that are defining the current social media use and consumption practices globally. The book provides a holistic insight into a variety of perspectives on social media use for content creation for specific purposes (Use) and the consumption of the existing online content (Consumption) across geographical boundaries. Despite the increase in popularity of social networking sites and related digital media, there is limited data and studies on the use and consumption patterns of the new media by different global communities. Nevertheless, social media has revolutionized how individuals, communities, and organizations create, share, and consume information. Similarly, social media offers numerous opportunities as well as enormous social and economic ills for individuals, communities, and organizations. In less-developed countries, social media has helped individuals, communities, and organizations to leapfrog technological trends and to succeed in online digital content creation and distribution.

Practitioners and researchers require a current holistic understanding of the trends that are defining today's and the future generation of social media users including hate speech, addiction to our digital identities and social media use, anonymity, privacy, social media marketing, entry of new social media channels, changes in social media consumer demands and how all these define the future of content creation and consumption in social media. Social media is broadening fundamentally the opportunities individuals have to gather, discuss, and act on social, scholarly, and political issues in their social environment as well as on a national and global level.

ORGANIZATION OF THE BOOK

Social media has a tremendous influence on the creation, dissemination, and consumption of online content. The material included in this book covers and explores the different aspects of the use and consumption of social media from both behavioral and computational approaches to social media research. The prospective audiences for this book include researchers, academics, practitioners, and students who seek to engage in social media use and consumption. The book provides multiple perspectives on social media use and consumption in an all-inclusive bundle. A brief description of chapter-by-chapter follows:

Chapter 1 looks at the concept of social learning in an online context that is initiated by a commercial enterprise. The interdisciplinary chapter considers the relationship between social networks and social learning cross-culturally and the prospects of value creation via content, community, collaboration, and conversation. It also looks at the use of social networks by brands to increase value and competitiveness for the brand and the consumer by understanding the new generation of consumers who include Generation Z, a group which perceives information visually and prefer personalized online experiences.

Chapter 2 proposes a novel ensemble machine learning for Twitter sentiment analysis classification which can be used to identify sentiment in tweets through a weighted majority rule ensemble classifier. Many machine learning algorithms are available for Twitter sentiment analysis which are used for automatically predicting the sentiment of tweets. However, some challenges hinder machine learning classifiers to achieve better results in terms of classification. This proposed algorithm is based on ensemble approach which will identify sentiment in tweets through a weighted majority rule ensemble classifier, where several commonly used statistical models like Naive Bayes, Random forest, and Logistic regressions are utilized and weighted according to their performance on historical data. The proposed ensemble model can be used for training datasets for the classification of sentiments in Twitter conversations.

Chapter 3 explores the impact of Social Networking Sites (SNS) usage on individual work performance (IP) as literature shows contrasting results. Understanding the different types of SNS usage by actors and their effects on IP could help managers to take appropriate decisions to take profit from this usage. For this chapter, a multiple-case study on 15 employees from eight Tunisian firms has been conducted by semi-structured interviews to highlight the SNS effects on IP in the specific context of democratic transition. The results show that depending on the level of SNS usage, three types of effect are identified on IP at work: positive, negative, or null. This chapter submits that organizational policy moderates the relationship between SNS usage and IP.

Chapter 4 investigates and determines the features of fake news by analyzing teyit.org, which is the biggest fact-checking platform in Turkey. The chapter shows that fake news is detectable based on four features: Propagation, User, Social Media Type, and Formatting. The chapter also demonstrates that Facebook increases the likelihood of news being fake compared to Twitter and Instagram. Similarly, if a news video's accuracy is suspect, its likelihood of being fake is much higher than that of a news item with a photograph, an indication that video usage increases the likelihood that a news item is fake. Emoji usage is statistically significant in terms of increasing the probability of news being fake. The chapter indicates that real users can also spread misinformation, whether deliberate or not and that verified accounts on social media are unreliable in terms of identifying misleading information. However, the chapter does not offer specific solutions for distinguishing fake news items from real ones, but recommends that users' media literacy levels have a vital role in being aware of misleading content on social media.

Chapter 5 uses secondary data to explain global social media consumption trends, define social media privacy concerns, show the relationship between global consumers' privacy concerns and their social media usage behaviors and the understanding of the convergence vs. divergence trend in terms of global social media usage behaviors. This chapter is predominantly centered on a review of the existing literature. This chapter begins with a global consumption analysis of social media around the world. Then, it examines how privacy concerns may help account for the homogenization or heterogenization trend of global social media consumer culture. The chapter's theoretical foundation is based on the convergence-divergence debates that postulate universal social media consumption patterns and values are made possible, due to the industrialization, modernization, technology, and wealth accumulation. The chapter also uses the perceptions of online privacy among users of privacy-invasive technologies as an example to discuss why people will think the same about their privacy could be a myth for the failure to consider the unique socio-cultural characteristics of each nation.

Chapter 6 descriptively investigates social media consumption by different Kenyan communities based on demographics such as age, gender, education, income, and geolocation. The chapter data was collected using a mixed-method approach, involving a survey of 3269 respondents and 37 focus group discussions. The chapter identifies the social media platforms in use among Kenyans to include What-sApp, Facebook, YouTube, Instagram, LinkedIn, and Snapchat. The chapter indicates that Kenyans use social media for entertainment, education, jobs, politics, sports, and social issues, however, the use differs by different demographics. The chapter shows that most Kenyans access social media using phones for 1-3 hours daily and their motivations for using social media are the acquisition of information, entertainment, social interactions, seeking opportunities to do business, and buying and selling items. The chapter also indicates that most social media users in Kenya have experienced fake news, cyberbullying, and bombardment with graphic images of sex and advertisements. Finally, the chapter establishes that Kenyans consider social media to be addictive, expensive, and time-wasting.

Chapter 7 provides a comparison of social media strategy on Twitter and Sina Weibo by the German company Adidas. The chapter posits that, due to the Internet censorship by the Chinese government, the social media landscape in China differs from that in western countries. The chapter compares how Adidas uses Twitter and Sina Weibo for their marketing purpose. The chapter demonstrates the differences in the successful use of social media between China, Germany, and the United States by using Hofstede´s six dimension models. The main differences were noticeable in the categories of "Power Distance", "Individualism" and Hall´s division in "High context" and "Low context". The chapter recommends that companies need cultural and linguistic know-how to be successful on Chinese platforms like Sina Weibo. Even though Adidas uses both Twitter and Sina Weibo platforms successfully, the chapter data analysis shows that the social media usage exhibits similarities and differences on both platforms.

Chapter 8 adopted a literature review approach to provide a narrative on the role of digital influencers on the consumer decision processes. The chapter posits that there is heightened resistance to brand communication through traditional media which has resulted in marketers turning to other strategies to connect with their customers and influence their consumer journey through influencer marketing. Digital influencers act as bridges that connect consumers and brands, strengthening their bond and allowing brands to reach their targets in a more natural way to influence the consumer buying process. The chapter indicates that brands have used digital influencers (also known as social media influencers) as endorsers of their products and services, and as brand ambassadors over the last few years. The chapter concludes that there is a need for more research for a thorough understanding the several types of digital influencers endorsement effects in the consumer journey. Additionally, the chapter suggests that there is a need to differentiate the multiple competing definitions used to refer to these influencers, which include micro celebrities, social media influencers, and digital influencers.

Chapter 9's main focus is to have a comprehensive look at social media addiction construct by identifying empirically the factors discriminating social media addicts from non-addicts. The chapter utilizes the review of literature to identify several personal, social, and situational factors on social media addiction. Firstly, personal factors such as demographic characteristics, personality traits, self-esteem, well-being, loneliness, anxiety, and depression are studied for their impact on social media addiction. Next, the social influencers and consequences of social media addiction are identified, namely the need for affiliation, subjective norms, personal, professional, and academic life. The situational factors like the amount of social media use and motives of use were also inspected. Finally, the chapter concludes with an empirical study that analyzes the factors that discriminate social media addicts from non-addicts on the basis of these different factors and the extent of association between social media usage duration and social media addiction. The chapter then moves to show the relationship between social media addiction and social media use while conversing with others, driving, and listening to lectures were also analyzed.

Chapter 10 aims at understanding various cyber-crimes and vulnerabilities associated with the Online Social Networks (OSNs) environment that may be directly or indirectly accountable for harming the privacy and security of OSN users. OSNs are used as tools for social interactions, news propagation, gaming, political propaganda, and advertisement in building brand awareness, among others. The chapter highlights how OSN users unintentionally expose their personal information that is used by malicious users and third-party apps to perform various kinds of cyber-crimes like social engineering attacks, cyber espionage, extortion-malware, drug-trafficking, misinformation, cyberbullying, hijacking clicks, identity theft, phishing, creation of fake profiles, and spreading malicious content, etc. The chapter also discusses numerous strategies and methods to counter multiple forms of cyber-attacks including tools, techniques, and frameworks. The chapter elaborates that the fundamental reasons for OSN breaches are due to limitations at the system level and at the user/data level. The chapter suggests that for a better and secure OSN environment, counter-mechanisms should be classified as platform-based, and user and message deception-based counter-mechanisms.

Chapter 11 makes a distinction between social media use and consumption to refer to content creation for a particular purpose (Use) and mere consumption of the existing online content (Consumption). The chapter is guided by a key, yet overlooked question about whether most Africans share the same media consumption tendencies with people in western countries. The chapter offers a rather nuanced synthesis and perception of social media usage and consumption in Zambia that underscores the motivating factors. Two major interpretations are identified: Social media consumption that focuses only on the quantity of proliferated online content, and social media usage that interrogates the various ways people in Zambia use social media to suit their tastes and needs. The chapter starts with a proposition that although considerable literature has grown around the motivations for social media use and consumption across Africa, there is still a dearth of research on trends of consumption across different cultures and particular demographic environments. The chapter indicates that the literature on social media use and consumption is often driven by western scholarship despite the use and the reasons for the consumption of social media varying across geographical boundaries.

Chapter 12 explores and discusses social media consumption in African political settings, presenting the effects of change through social media and digital democracy in African particular cases. The chapter analyses the patterns of social media consumption in its functionality for democratic change in Africa. The chapter posits that unless social media in Africa is supported by an institutional perspective that reinforces transformative capabilities rather than self-interest, and is enacted as an institution rather than an amorphous technology, its relation to digital democracy will be nonconsequential in terms of forward-looking social and political development. The chapter examines patterns of institutional change on the basis of the impact of social media consumption in African politics. The chapter highlights two theories of institutional change—structured institutional change and evolutionary institutional change—based on their relevance to the impact of social media consumption in African political settings. The chapter analyzes the transformative capabilities of social media, in an effort to decipher the institutional significance of the trajectories social media consumption can induce by connecting African societies with the global community through the deployment of their cognitive and structuring capabilities.

Chapter 13 aims to assess whether Kenyans participate in online discussions and the role of Kenyan bloggers in online communities. The chapter shows that blogs are very popular social media platforms among Kenyans where people share topical content online. However, there are clear and significant distinctions in the type of blogs people read based on demographics such as gender, income levels, and geographical location. The chapter illustrates the applicability of social network analysis in determining influence among social media users by using NodeXL to visualize the structure of online conversation on Twitter and identifying prominent opinion leaders in the Kenyan Blogosphere. The chapter concludes that Kenyan bloggers influence social media users in the Kenyan blogosphere while engaging in online discussions using multiple social media platforms.

Chapter 14 reviews multidisciplinary literature with the aim of mapping out how the relationship between seniors and ICTs and, in particular with social media, is configured. The contents of this chapter encompass issues related to the aging problem in Europe (and across the world), articulating the theme of Network Society and ICT with the digital inclusion and literacy of seniors - its benefits and challenges, and discusses the reasons, motivations and effects of the relationship that this group establishes with digital social networks. The chapter suggests that it is relevant to examine seniors' usage of the social networking sites, to understand their differentiated behaviors patterns as much remains to be known regarding the use of the social media in later life as most of the current research on the interaction of the elderly with social media seem to be focused on motives of use and how it affects their lives.

Chapter 15 aims to determine the user preference of Bitcoin and Ethereum, which are the two most popular cryptocurrencies in the world by using Twitter sentiment analysis. The chapter proposes a powerful and fundamental approach to identify emotions on Twitter by considering the tweets of these two distinctive cryptocurrencies. The chapter determines positive, negative, and neutral emotions based on score calculations using sentiment analysis of one hundred twenty thousand (120,000) tweets extracted separately from Twitter for each keyword Bitcoin/ BTC and Bitcoin / ETC between the period from 12/09/2018 to 22/09/2018 (10 days). The chapter concludes that the tweets related to Ethereum have more positive sentiments as compared to the tweets associated with Bitcoin. Conversely, tweets associated with Bitcoin have more negative sentiments than those associated with Ethereum. The chapter articulates the disadvantage of the approach used in that cases of spelling errors in tweets, and the presence of positive and negative words may not produce relevant results because the placement of positive and negative words in the sentences gives different conclusions. The chapter concludes by recommending that future research identifying emotions in sarcastic tweets should be considered.

"Use of digital media and social media are connected to deep-rooting changes of citizens' self-concepts" - *Prof. Dr. Martin Emmer (FU Berlin), during the 2019 International Symposium on Social Media held at USIU-Africa on September 11-12, 2019.*

Acknowledgment

This book includes 15 diverse and globally relevant chapters on social media use and consumption written by knowledgeable, distinguished scholars from many prominent research institutions worldwide. To ensure the quality of the book, all chapters underwent a double-blind review process, meaning that every chapter in this book is a refereed book chapter in the social media use and consumption field. In phase one, all the chapter proposals that were submitted to answer the call were carefully reviewed by the editor in light of their suitability in the area of social media use and consumption and forwarded to expert external reviewers on a double-blind basis. Only chapter submissions with strong and favorable reviews were accepted and the authors requested to submit complete chapters. In phase two, all chapters underwent a double-blind review process. The chapter reviewers were invited based on their sustained scholarship in this field. I would like to extend my gratitude to the reviewers who contributed their time and expertise to this book.

I also wish to thank my fellow authors for their unique contributions to this book. For the authors who also served as referees; I appreciate your willingness to carry out this double task. Without your contribution, this book would not have become a reality.

Special thanks and acknowledgement also goes to Prof. Dr. Martin Emmer, Institute for Media and Communication Studies of Freie Universität Berlin, Founding Director of the Weizenbaum Institute for the Networked Society, who contributed to the Foreword.

Patrick Kanyi Wamuyu
United States International University – Africa, Kenya

Chapter 1
Social Entrepreneurship, Smart Brands, and Epic Social Learning Networks:
Content, Community, and Communication

Stavroula Kalogeras
https://orcid.org/0000-0002-5028-0413
School of Business, University of Plymouth, UK

ABSTRACT

This study explores how brand cultures can become learning communities and highlights how social networking sites can emerge as social learning platforms by way of content, conversations, and community. The purpose of this chapter is to examine the concept of learning content in online social learning networks that are initiated by a commercial enterprise to provide a competitive advantage while at the same time providing social good. The proposed framework builds a bridge between the organization and the consumer, takes into account Generation Z, and looks at self-development and knowledge consumption as the key benefit. The work considers transmedia storytelling which has emerged in marketing to expand the brand story. The concept of transmedia learning networks and brand-consumer value-competitiveness model is proposed to show the value proposition of knowledge consumption. The work embraces learning communities, introduces the theory of conversationisim, and encourages participation and conversation on a global scale.

INTRODUCTION

A social entrepreneur is a pioneer in innovation, acting as a change agents to improve approaches and create value that benefit humanity. A social purpose business is important because it provides a framework for businesses to find their own success by helping others and to help change society in a sustainable way. "Social entrepreneurship is an approach by individuals, groups, start-up companies or entrepreneurs, in which they develop, fund and implement solutions to social, cultural, or environmental

DOI: 10.4018/978-1-7998-4718-2.ch001

issues" (PBS Organization). The ability to think differently, adapt to a world which changes rapidly, to find innovative solutions and engage with a large community to change society in a sustainable way is a characteristic of a social enterprise.

This paper explores the notion of learning cultures where social status, values, and activities are centered on the consumption of knowledge. It does not focus on a consumer culture that is defined as a culture where social status, values, and activities are centered on the consumption of commodities and services. In a consumer culture, a large part of what people do, and what people value is subjected around their consumption of material goods. Today, organizations are tasked with providing social good and smart brands are organizations that answer the call to benefit society. These firms make an effort to create positive change in society through their initiatives. Smart brands, in addition to selling products or services, offer knowledge consumption via digital media platforms. The platforms may be existing social media platforms, learning management systems, or some combination of newly developed or traditional forms. The space of communication is widening to create meaning-making potential by way of social conversations and social learning networks. Learning is a social act, and through conversation and social interaction among participants, learning can be achieved. Furthermore, collaboration has been associated with retention and comprehension, and social networking sites and interactive experiences encourage emotional engagement that can lead to deeper connections with the brand.

Social learning is learning that takes place through social interaction between peers. The theory of social learning contends that people learn from one another, via observation, imitation, and modeling. The theory has often been called a bridge between behaviorist and cognitive learning theories because it encompasses attention, memory, and motivation (Bandura, 1977). Basically, social learning involves the participation of others. To be considered social the process must demonstrate that a change in understanding has taken place in the individuals involved; demonstrate that this change goes beyond the individual and becomes situated within wider social units or communities of practice; and occur through social interactions and processes between actors within a social network (Reed et al., 2010).

The paper looks at social learning that is initiated by a commercial organization on digital media platforms. The primary aim of this study is to introduce the concept of social learning in an online context that is initiated by a commercial enterprise. The interdisciplinary research considers: (1) The relationship between social networks and social learning cross culturally, (2) The prospect of value creation via content, community, collaboration, and conversation, (3) The requirements of Generation Z, (4) The opportunity for self-development and knowledge consumption by way of transmedia touchpoints, (5) The use of social networks by brands to increase value and competitiveness for the brand and the consumer, (6) The theory of conversationisim. There are many components to the interdisciplinary study that need consideration when moving from theory to practice.

The following section contains the literature review and is organized around the following themes: Brand culture and meaning-making, Generation Z, Smart brands, The spaces in-between and unitive experiences, collective consciousness, brand identity and holistic branding, brand competitiveness and customer value, and the conclusion. Based on the theoretical framework derived is a brand-consumer value- competitiveness proposition. The work concludes by discussion, and identifying a promising direction for research and practice in the future.

THEORETICAL BACKGROUND

Conceptual Paper and Literature Review Methodology

This is a conceptual paper based on a new idea and the literature review supports it. By definition, a conceptual paper must present an original concept, but it does not require original data. Conceptual papers synthesizes knowledge from previous work, connect new dots, or even look at the spaces in-between to formulate an idea and present it in a new context. Saunder writes:

The current paradigm in science training and practice is facts/evidence-based. As scientists, we're trained not to have opinions and to control context out of experiments. For peer review, we're trained to identify standards of study design, statistical analyses, presentation and formatting etc. But there are very few standards for judging someone else's ideas. It's easy to subconsciously revert to subjective opinion and critique conceptual papers based on personal views/experience on the topic. Scientific disciplines grow from new concepts, ideas, theories and expert opinions, not just data. (Saunder, 2018)

The work provides value as it presents an original concept that can be relevant and sustainable. Hirshcheim argues in his journal article "Some guidelines for the Critical Review of Conceptual Papers:" Too many researchers…seem to think that any non-empirical paper is simply an essay and devoid of deeper scholarship. Nothing could be further from the truth. More than once I have received comments from reviewers claiming a paper is nothing more than an essay, implying essays are little more than opinions. But aren't all papers "opinions" in one form or another?" 2008: 432.

It is well-known that non-empirical research plays an important role in the academic community by giving researchers a place to start the process to create new areas of research. Non-empirical researchers are known to create theories that are not based on previous research and these theories can also be tested at the present or in the future. "The dividing line between empirical and non-empirical methods is marked by scholars' approach to knowledge gain (i.e., epistemology). Scholars using non-empirical methods consider that reflection, personal observation and authority/experience are just as valuable for knowledge acquisition as empirical data" (Matthes et al., 2017:1). Also, scholarship may include both non-empirical and empirical, or one can follow after the other, as proposed in this paper.

The work consists of non-empirical research, which sets the foundation for the interdisciplinary study that consists of large amounts of information that requires discussion before empirical data is obtained. First, a search of the existing literature was conducted to select the primary themes. Second, the references of the selected papers and the citations were reviewed. Third, the selected papers were classified according to their content. The search of the existing literature was done on the Internet, Google Scholar and Scopus using a combination of keywords: transmedia, storytelling, branding, marketing, social networking, social learning, advertising, holistic branding, identity, digital leadership, competitiveness, and non-empirical research. The papers that were selected from journals, conferences, or online sources were based on the content and not on the dates. The articles gathered were 6718 and then reduced to 513 based on limitations such as source, language, duplication, or accessibility. After scanning titles and abstracts 40 works were accepted that narrowed in on the topic to support brand consumer value through social learning and community. As global connectivity increases, generational shifts play an important role and have more implications for companies. This paper looks to the future and opens up discussion for the evolution of consumerism that can benefit humanity on many levels.

Brand Culture and Meaning-Making

Well-managed organizations have a story to tell whether that is the back-story of how the organization was started, or whether it is an advertisement promoting a product through branded entertainment. Branding has evolved to include storytelling practice but it needs to do more, and it has the potential to do so by addressing the in-between spaces and needs of the market both thoroughly and profoundly. The in-between space or what can be considered the third space is between the organization and consumer.

An organization's brand identity is created and packaged; however, real identity lies between the brand and the consumer. Humans are connected to each other and to brands because they have an emotional response and universal connection on many core beliefs. Branding is about capturing the consumer's heart while advertising was invented to announce that a product or service existed, as well as to promote the unique features. Unlike today, without social networks, the organization had no way to communicate with the consumer until they developed advertising. In the past ads were full of claims and hard sell messages that did not treat the consumer as an intelligent being. Steve Jobs argued, "people don't know what they want until you show it to them" (Goodreads.com).

Perhaps humans do not know what they want because they are bombarded by traditional advertising and branding that tends to feed the ego. When humans are shown an excessive amount of media messages they can lose focus of their true sense of being and well-being through the action of consumerism. Kenton argues (2018), "Consumerism is the theory that a country that consumes goods and services in large quantities will be better off economically. Sometimes, consumerism is referred to as a policy that promotes greed" (6 April 2018) and it is often attributed to over-consumption where people have a lack of self-concept and meaning in their lives. Therefore, organizations must do a better job meeting their consumers need for community and interaction.

Monty (2018) in his article, Reclaiming Humanity in Business argues:

While advertising is still a necessary part of the content ecosystem, we need to find a better way to meet the expectations of consumers. The decades old, twice-broken model of advertising is outdated, and we need to wake up to the fact that people are on social sites to interact, not to be advertised to. Perhaps it means a more hands-on style with a focus on community rather than advertising. There's value in creating connections and leveraging relationships, especially when we have products and services that people genuinely care about or want to tell others about. (27 July 2018)

It is important for brands to highlight community and connections rather than merely product information. "A product is anything that can be offered to a market to satisfy a want or need, including physical goods, services, experiences, events, persons, places, properties, organizations, information, and ideas" (Kotler & Keller, 2015). The brand of the future will provide the consumer with a product of information and ideas, such as enlightening content, and conversations lead by great thinkers for human growth and development. Geertz, an influential cultural anthropologist of the latter twentieth century, argues, "We are not a species concerned with mere transactions. We are creatures of meaning" (Geertz, 1973: 8). Consumers are not simply choosing the best or the cheapest products anymore. They are choosing brands that have the right meaning.

Generation Z

Generation Z has never seen the world without the Internet. They have an affinity to digital communication, absorb a plethora of information, search the Internet for information, and use social media. They are clearly different from the generation before them. It is important to understand the various generations in relation to consumption and their characteristics are highlighted below:

Baby boomers, born from 1940 to 1959, were immersed in the post–World War II context and are best represented by consumption as an expression of ideology. Gen Xers (born 1960–79) consumed status, while millennials (born 1980–94) consumed experiences. For Generation Z (loosely, people born from 1995 to 2010), as we have seen, the main spur to consumption is the search for truth, in both a personal and a communal form. This generation feels comfortable not having only one way to be itself. Its search for authenticity generates greater freedom of expression and greater openness to understanding different kinds of people. (Francis and Hoefel, 2018)

Technology and images play a key role with Generation Z. "Generation Z perceives information visually, so marketing campaigns that are targeted at gen Zers revolve around story telling, explainer videos, and other forms of visualization" (Robertson, 2018), and they prefer personalized experiences. According to Francis and Hoefel (2018), the search for truth is the root of their behavior which is best defined by the exhibit below:

Figure 1. The Search for the truth is at the root of all Generations Z's behavior

Generation Z believe in dialogue to solve conflict and improve the world. They make decisions analytically and pragmatically and that is why Gen Z is known as the "True Gen." Furthermore, the study states:

Companies should be attuned to three implications for this generation: consumption as access rather than possession, consumption as an expression of individual identity, and consumption as a matter of ethical concern. Coupled with technological advances, this generational shift is transforming the consumer landscape in a way that cuts across all socioeconomic brackets and extends beyond Gen Z, permeating the whole demographic pyramid. (Francis and Hoefel, 2018)

Generation Z needs leadership, spirituality, community and context. White (2017) contends:

They are not simply living in and being shaped by a post-Christian cultural context. They do not even have a memory of the gospel. The degree of spiritual illiteracy is simply stunning. ... [Second], they are leaderless. Little if any direction is coming from their families, and even less from their attempts to access guidance from the internet. Online learning communities may be the way to reach them. (White, 2017: 52)

In light of this information organizations must rethink how they deliver value to their future consumers and are challenged to the task of great leadership.

Leading means wading through tough conversations and conversations can lead to positive connections; however, conversations are on the decline with texting and messaging. Proposed in this work is the theory of conversationisim, which states that the universe will be a better place with communication that encourages unity and prosperity for all citizens by way of thoughtful conversation and contemplation, rather than a narrow focus to increase profits from physical products. The work argues for learning communities and conversations led by great thinkers as the new model of knowledge consumption, well-being, and prosperity for all. Leaders must come to understand that the new generation seeks truth; community, personalized experiences, and meaning that originate from a well told story. As a consumer-brand unit, storytelling can create deep connections between the consumer and the brand where learning can take place. Scolari believes, "the brand is a device that can produce a discourse, give it meaning, and communicate this to an audience" (2009: 588).

Transmedia Storytelling and Smart Brands

The conceptual paper bridges the spaces in-between the brand and the consumer and the spaces between consumer-to-consumer via a story making process. Transmedia storytelling is a perfect companion to building a brand. "Transmedia storytelling is the practice of designing, sharing, and participating in a cohesive story experience across multiple traditional and digital delivery platforms - for entertainment, advertising and marketing, or social change" (McIntyre, 2020). A transmedia story stems from the organization and the learning content is a natural extension of the brand. A multifaceted story offers more engagement with the consumer, creating more customer-brand connections, which can fill more spaces with meaning. Research has shown that the best way to create meaning between brand and consumer is through a story (Olenski, 6 April 2018). According to Danetz, storytelling is key for establishing an emotional connection with the brand, breaks through all the noise and competition and assists with greater personalization (Danetz quoted in Olenski, 6 April 2018) which addresses Generation Z. Story making via transmedia can strengthen the bond and lead to positive attitudes, associations, relevance, and even unity. Transmedia narratives or multiplatform stories are essential to create a culture, brand the organization, and then align the content and the conversations for the learning community to engage with meaning exchange.

Branding is a strategy designed by companies to help people to quickly identify the organization and their products or services, and brands give consumers a reason to choose their products over the competitions. Brands are human artifacts, and as such, they must connect on the human factor. Smart brands put people first and have the potential to aid people with self-mastery and even identity formation. Elliott and Wattanasuwan contend, "people no longer consume for merely functional satisfaction, but consumption becomes meaning-based, and brands are often used as symbolic resources for the construction and maintenance of identity" (cited in Schroder and Saltzer-Morling, 2006: 13). An organization that can offer an excellent product or service while focusing on people and their purpose will be the brand the leads in the future.

The branding process provides meaning to a specific company, and its products or services by creating and shaping a brand in the consumers' minds. Brand equity exists when deep emotional relationships are formed between the organization and the consumer. In their influential book, Groundswell: Winning in a World Transformed by Social Technologies, Liand Bernoff states "your brand is whatever your customers say it is" (2008: 78) and if this is the case, marketers must focus on building positive brand associations and trust with their consumers. People will trust a brand if it is reliable, consistent, and honest.

The Harley Davidson Corporation, Nike, and Apple are great examples of branded cultures; however, the brands that will succeed in the future will be branded learning, training and development cultures that encompass a critical consciousness on an epic scale. The brands that already have strong cultures will have an easier time expanding into intelligent learning communities by thought leaders leading the conversations and offering their expertise. There are opportunities for organizations to become brand evangelists for the people and not for the company and can still make profits indirectly by giving back to society. It is in the space in-between the brand and the consumer where the smart brand can make meaning, connection, collaboration, community, and even profits.

The Spaces In-Between and Unitive Experiences

The research addresses the feasibility of creating unity by branding the spaces in-between and looks at the meaning-making that can be derived from these spaces. Human beings negotiate their lives in-between the spaces that are formed by institutions, systems, countries, nations, nationality, societies, gender, politics, religion, rules, regulation, daily lives, celebration, reality, and fiction, etc. The space in-between or the third space is the place that has not been addressed by the brand, or can be fully controlled by the brand. I consider the spaces in-between two points as the spaces that have not been categorized or labeled and where the frames are wide open for new interpretation, perspective, meaning, influence, and even truth.

The concept of in-betweenness was first discussed in my book, Transmedia Storytelling and New Era of Media Convergence in Higher Education where a diasporas narrative was introduced. Similarly, according to Hahn (2012) and the new brand culture model, "We are not limited to the traditional choices offered by the culture we were born into and this is where contemporary anthropologists see brands taking on a new and intriguing role" (Hahn, 2012: 11) and here lies the opportunity.

The spaces in-between is the place where systems and organizations cannot control the breathing and thinking of human beings; however, it is in these spaces that organizations can focus on growth in the form of content, community and collaboration. Branding is about people and the argument set forth is that smart brands must consider people and elevate them through knowledge. It is in the spaces in-between where humans can benefit from connection, respecting the ideas of others, while providing support to one another to further their growth and ultimately the growth of the universe. In the third space social responsibility and justice can be obtained.

A brand's identity is created, packaged, and delivered to consumers by an organization (Nandan, 2005). If a brand's image and identity are in sync, then this can strengthen consumers' brand loyalty (Nandan, 2005). An organization that can help people understand their true identity rather than the organization's brand identity could provide more value to the customer. Further, the organization could assist in strengthening the consumer to grow into their selfhood and discover their whole self, not just the ego self that consumerism and materialism foster.

In the spaces in-between one can also go beyond an individual preference to reach a deeper appeal. Rohr from the Center for Action and Contemplation argues:

So much of our lives are dictated by our preferences, what we like and don't like. We all naturally gravitate toward what we find attractive, and there's nothing inherently wrong with that. But we need to be aware that there are things deeper than our preferences. If we do not recognize that, we will follow them addictively and never uncover our soul's deeper desires. Often the very things that don't appeal to us have the most to teach us spiritually. (Rohr, 20 May 2019)

Rhor's comments are to some extent similar with Steve Jobs as people do not knowing what they want or even need. With message overload that is directed to our superficial selves, there is no wonder that humans do not think deeper.

In general, businesses are not in the practice of human development or even spirituality. However, the evidence shows that Generation Z needs guidance from trustworthy leadership on spiritual growth, but they are not the only generation who requires self development and mastery. The human race has been barraged by the messages of the media and people have moved away from the deeper and more important aspects of life. Currently, organizations focus on social media marketing when they can become social learning enterprise by passing on knowledge and information that helps people develop and have compassion for one another. There is a strong indication that the brand that guides people to their true nature rather than have people conform to an image of who they ought to be will be the brand that succeeds in the future.

Brands should be accountable, and consumers have the power to hold corporations accountable for the lack of social justice. Frankl states, "Between stimulus and response there is space. In that space is our power to choose our response. In our response lies our growth and our freedom" (brainyquote.com, n.d.). Similarly, between stimulus and response there is space for interconnectedness, community building, and meaning-making while embracing differences and acknowledging commonness.

Collective Consciousness

Western culture considers money, power, production, and consumption as a framework for status and freedom. Moreover, marketing and advertising convince consumers to buy the latest version of everything. Greed which is not considered a capital sin anymore widens the gap between the rich and the poor. According to the Soul's Poor Folk report, in the U.S., "the 400 wealthiest Americans now own more wealth than the bottom 64 percent of the U.S. population (or 204 million people)" and "nearly 41 million Americans live below the poverty line" (Anderson, et. al, 2017: 9). Every human being has worth and value, and brands that recognize this will provide more than the necessities for living, and not just by way of products or services, but through filling the gaps in the spaces in-between with more value – by uplifting every human being to a new level of consciousness that provides unity, harmony, and freedom for all. Richard Rohr from the Center for Action and Contemplation explores the dualistic mind:

The dualistic mind, upon which most of us were taught to rely, is simply incapable of the task of creating unity. It automatically divides reality into binary opposites and does most of its thinking inside this limited frame. It dares to call this choosing of sides "thinking" because that is all it knows how to do. "Really good" thinking then becomes devising a strong argument for our side's superiority versus another country, race, group, political party, or religion. It seems we must have our other! We struggle to know who we are except by opposition and exclusion. (Rohr, 2 June 2019)

The dualistic mind is the adversary to human prosperity and compassion for one another. When people come together beyond their ego, unselfishly, with compassion and understanding to achieve a larger purpose, which is rich in consciousness, and unity, then a collective consciousness can emerge. Similarly, the brand and the consumers are one in the same – a living entity, which needs one another to survive. A quote by ThichNhatHanh states it well: "We are here to awaken from the illusion of our separateness" (Spring 2015). Humans are interconnected whether we like it or not, and community is about linking differentiation and diversity where the consumers would experience the smart brands not only through product packaging, advertising, slogans, and mascots but through transmedia learning networks that unite holistically.

Brand Identity and Holistic Branding

Approaching a brand from a holistic perspective means knowledge of identity as a person and organization. Organizations can communicate by visual, verbal and emotional identity from the truth of their being. And meaning can be achieved by considering the identity factors that have been highlighted below:

- *Organizational Identity. Organizational identity is defined as a set of statements that organization members perceive to be central, distinctive, and enduring to their organization (Albert &Whetten, 1985). The "organizational identity is (a) what is taken by employees to be the central attributes of the organization; (b) what makes the organization distinctive and therefore unique from other organizations in the eyes of the employees; and (c) what is perceived by employees to be enduring or continuing, regardless of objective changes in the organizational environments. The three characteristics described above suggest that organizations with a strong identity have central attributes, are distinctive from other organizations and remain the same for longer periods" (cited in Marjon 2006).*
- *Personal Identity. Personal identity is the concept one develops about themselves that evolves over the course of their lives. John Locke contends that "one's personal identity extends only so far as their own consciousness" (Piccirillo, 2010, n.p.), and therefore, common identity must be considered.*
- *Common Identity. Common identity is what all humans have in common – the essence of being, oneness. "Our sickness or "sin" is the illusion of separateness, a completely mistaken identity which is far too small and too boundaried," (Rhor, 2 June 2019) and therefore, "adopting a common identity is the key to tearing down cultural divisions and working toward reconciliation."* (Cleveland, 2013: 117-178).
- The Third Identity. The third identity introduced here is when the personal identity aligns with the common identity and the organizational identity for higher and universal good.

A brand must understand that it is human and as such it must connect on the human factor. The smart brand unites consumers via community building and at the level of the third space. The third space is the collective consciousness, encompassing the good for all of mankind. The third space shows people who they are versus who they ought to be and provides thoughtful conversations and knowledge as consumption. In the online space, social marketing becomes social good, and social networking becomes learning networks that help increase intelligence and wellbeing for all who are connected to Internet technology. The third space can unite people on a deeper level around interests, hobbies, causes, education, spiritual growth, self development, and even self-mastery. The unitive experience brings people together on similar interests with the concept of oneness in the milieu. The social learning concept presented could offer both free entry points to conversations and paid services for learning content. There are a plethora of adaptable versions organizations could use to build value to the brand.

The section above was both philosophical and theoretical, and discussed the concept of branding across culture. Branding via learning networks, especially targeting Generation Z is recommended. Generation Z is interested in co-creating a culture of meaning and smart brands via online communities can offer this experience. In the next section a framework is discussed and a model is presented to show the value of transmedia learning networks for the organization and the consumer. The following section provides a framework for practice. A brand-consumer value proposition and competitiveness factor designed for transmedia learning platforms and networks is argued for business practice.

CONCEPTUAL FRAMEWORK

Organizations are pressed to adopt customer value strategies in order to grow profits and ensure long-term success and even survival. The discourse proposes a model that increases competitiveness for brand and consumer around social learning networks. Competitiveness has become a major concern for businesses, and it is an important topic in management and marketing disciplines. Competitiveness is the ability to compete successfully with other companies or to secure a competitive advantage (Baumann et al., 2017).

Numerous companies in the digital age offer platform business models that create value by connecting different users. In strategy research, competitive advantage can be obtained by superior value creation and performance by the platform's user network (Peteraf and Barney, 2003). Often organizations offer a competitive advantage by providing value to consumers through a better product, service, or price point. In marketing terms, there are two aspects to customer value, and they are desired and perceived value. *Desired value* refers to what customers' desire in a product or service. *Perceived value* is the benefit that a customer believes s/he received from the product or service (Morar 2013). Likewise, proposed here is the construct of *needed value* which refers to what consumers need but don't know it, as Rhor and Jobs alluded to earlier in the paper. The inclusion of 'needed value' can add to the brand-consumer value proposition. An organization can increase competitiveness by offering learning content and discourse which can be considered a 'needed value'.

The literature on marketing concurs that brand equity is the commercial value that derives from consumer perception of the brand name while the brand value is the financial worth of the brand. However, marketing literature does a poor job linking brand equity with brand value and how the customer benefits. The figure below shows how transmedia learning networks offer value and competitiveness for both the organization and the consumer. The learning network is the initial point of knowledge distribution, giving the firm more value and competitive edge. Similarly, the customer receives knowledge which makes them more competitive in the marketplace. The model below explicitly includes the benefit to the consumer and the competitive gain the consumer receives from their interaction with the brand:

Shown in the figure, above is only the value and competitiveness exchange between brand and consumer; however, there can be more consumer-to-consumer interactions and value exchanges overall. An

Figure 2. Transmedia learning networks and brand-consumer value- competitiveness

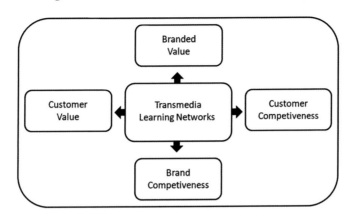

important characteristic of platform specific networks is the value they create for a user increases with the total number of users (Cennamo & Santalo, 2013; Edelman, 2015). Furthermore, social learning networks initiated by brands that already have a higher competitive advantage will more likely be successful over brands that are less successful or competitive.

A brand needs to continuously innovate, as well as consider both the brand and the consumer in terms of value and competitiveness. According to Aaker (1991), brand associations, which sit deep in the customer's mind, build and create positive attitudes and feelings towards brands in the minds of customers that can improve brand image. The positive attitudes and good feelings that consumers have about brands may be the foundation of how accepting they are to learning initiatives in a competitive marketplace.

DISCUSSION

The paper examined how a brand culture can evolve to become a learning culture where learning happens in relation to one another through communication, content, and community. The primary goal of this research was to introduce the concept of social learning via brand-consumer relations. The proposed framework builds a bridge between the organization and the consumer, takes into account Generation Z, and looks at self-development and knowledge consumption. The concept of *Transmedia Learning Networks and Brand-Consumer Value-Competitiveness* model was proposed to show the value proposition of knowledge consumption. The work embraces learning communities, introduces the theory of conversationisim, and encourages participation and conversation on a global scale.

There is a correlation between social learning and social networks that can be put into practice holistically because the social platforms and the cross-cultural communication already exist. Social learning can build and expand on the content, communication, and collaboration model found in online communities. The fundamental nature is value and competitiveness through meaning-making and knowledge consumption for all participants. Transmedia learning opens the gateway to knowledge construction and self-development, unifying people on topics of interest. The transmedia approach can offer learning content that aligns with the brand on different platforms using the affordance of each medium, creating knowledge communities and participatory experiences. The brand story can also be communicated through transmedia marketing. In essence, all the interactions on the various platforms can be considered a form of marketing with a cause.

RECOMMENDATIONS

Non-empirical research plays an important part in academia by giving researchers a place to start the process of carving out scientific facts in new areas of study, and this conceptual paper is simply the beginning. In the future research is required that investigates how transmedia storytelling can support brands and their products and services. Also, more research is required on how smart brands can incorporate social learning into business practice and whether they will work on a local or global scale. Furthermore, research is needed to support the content, community and communication model introduced here and how to measure the value to the consumer, as well as add it to the customer lifetime value metrics of the business. Focus groups, questionnaires, and surveys are some of the tools that could provide additional insight on the way forward. Global considerations are local-language interfaces, customer service and sales support systems, regulatory considerations, and adapting content and marketing to the local needs. Academics and practitioners would need to unite to find the best way forward. Businesses need to be involved to test how commercially viable and profitable the smart brand concept could be to their organizations.

CONCLUSION

It is vital that brands understand the new generation of consumers and the cultural shift that is taking place. Smart brands that focus on leveraging the computer-mediated environment will have the most potential for success. Brand management will need to consider the brand's audience and objectives to be successful in the future. Digital leadership requires the creation of smart brands that will benefit from being fully expressed in everything they do and communicate. An organization that can offer an excellent product and service, as well as focus on people and their holistic development will be the brand that leads forward. Learning networks and conversations of meaning will be the most vital product a brand creates for humanity.

REFERENCES

Aaker, D. A. (1991). *Managing brand equity: Capitalizing on the value of a brand name*. Free Press.

Albert, S., & Whetten, D. A. (1985). Organizational identity. *Research in Organizational Behavior, 7*, 263–295.

Anderson, S., Bayard, M., Bennis, P., Cavanagh, J., Dolan, K., Koshgarian, L., Noffke, A., Pizzigati, S., & Sarkar, S. (2017). *The Souls of Poor Folk: Auditing America 50 Years After the Poor People's Campaign Challenged Racism, Poverty, the War Economy/Militarism and Our National Morality*. Retrieved from https://www.poorpeoplescampaign.org/audit/

Bandura, A. (1977). *Social Learning Theory*. General Learning Press.

Baumann, C., Hoadley, S., Hamin, H., & Nugraha, A. (2017). Competitiveness vis-à-vis service quality as drivers of customer loyalty mediated by perceptions of regulation and stability in steady and volatile markets. *Journal of Retailing and Consumer Services, 36*, 62–74. doi:10.1016/j.jretconser.2016.12.005

Cennamo, C., & Santalo, J. (2013). Platform competition: Strategic trade-offs in platform markets. *Strategic Management Journal, 34*(11), 1331–1350. doi:10.1002mj.2066

Cleveland, C. (2013) *Disunity in Christ: Uncovering the Hidden Forces that Keep Us Apart*. InterVarsity Press.

Edelman, D. C. (2015). How to launch your digital platform. *Harvard Business Review, 93*(4), 91–97.

Enterprising Ideas. (n.d.). *What is a Social Entrepreneur*. PBS Foundation. Retrieved from http://www.pbs.org/now/enterprisingideas/what-is.html

Francis, T., & Hoefel, F. (2018, November). *'True Gen': Generation Z and its Implications for Companies*. Retrieved from https://www.mckinsey.com/industries/consumer-packaged-goods/our-insights/true-gen-generation-z-and-its-implications-for-companies

Frankl, V. E. Quotes. (n.d.). BrainyQuote.com. Retrieved from https://www.brainyquote.com/quotes/viktor_e_frankl_160380

Gabriel, R. (n.d.). *What Is Oneness?* Retrieved from https://chopra.com/article/what-oneness

Geertz, C. (1973). *The Interpretation of Cultures*. Basic Books.

Grandio, M., & Bonaut, J. (2012). Transmedia audiences and television fiction: A comparative approach between skins (UK) and El Barco (Spain). *Participations, 9*(2), 558.

Hahn, D. (2012). *The New Brand Culture Model*. Retrieved from https://www.liquidagency.com/brand-exchange/new-brand-culture-model/Whitepaper

Hirshcheim, R. (2008). Some Guidelines for the Critical Reviewing of Conceptual Papers. *Journal of the Association for Information Systems, 9*(8), 432–441. doi:10.17705/1jais.00167

Jobs, S. Quotes (n.d.). *Quotable Quotes*. Goodreads.com. Retrieved from https://www.goodreads.com/quotes/988332-some-people-say-give-the-customers-what-they-want-but

Johnson, W. (2015). *Floating Sangha Takes Root Early days in Plum Village with ThichNhatHanh*. Retrieved from https://tricycle.org/magazine/floating-sangha-takes-root/

Kalogeras, S. (2014). *Transmedia Storytelling and the New Era of Media Convergence in Higher Education*. Palgrave Macmillan. doi:10.1057/9781137388377

KentonW. (2018). *Consumerism*. Retrieved from https://www.investopedia.com/terms/c/consumerism.asp

Kinder, M. (1991). *Playing with Power in Movies, Television, and Video Games: From Muppet Babies to Teenage Mutant Ninja Turtles*. University of California Press. doi:10.1525/9780520912434

Li, C, & Bernoff, J. (2008 April 21). *Harvard Business School Press (1805) Groundswell: Winning in a World Transformed by Social Technologies.* Academic Press.

Long, G. (2007). *Transmedia Storytelling. Business, aesthetics and production at the Jim Henson Company* (Master's dissertation). MIT. Retrieved from http://cms.mit.edu/research/thesis/GeoffreyLong2007.pdf

Matthes, J., Potter, R., & Davis, C. (2017). *Empirical and Non-Empirical Methods.* Retrieved from: https://www.researchgate.net/publication/309922961_Empirical_and_Non-Empirical_Methods

McIntyre, S. (2020). *Key Concept - What is Transmedia Storytelling?* Retrieved from: https://www.coursera.org/lecture/transmedia-storytelling/key-concept-what-is-transmedia-storytelling-sRicJ?authMode=signup&redirectTo=%2Flearn%2Ftransmedia-storytelling%3Faction%3Denroll

Monty, S. Brand Quarterly. (2018 July 27). *Reclaiming Humanity In Business.* http://www.brandquarterly.com/reclaiming-humanity-business

Morar, D. D. (2013). An overview of the consumer value literature – perceived value, desired value. *Marketing From Information to Decision, 6,* 169–186.

Nandan, S. (2005). An exploration of the brand identity-brand image linkage: A communications perspective. *Journal of Brand Management, 12*(4), 264–278. doi:10.1057/palgrave.bm.2540222

Olenski, S. (2018). *Storytelling, Brands And Some Words Of Wisdom.* Retrieved from https://www.forbes.com/sites/steveolenski/2018/04/06/storytelling-brands-and-some-words-of-wisdom/#6c3335cb5ae1

Peteraf, M. A., & Barney, J. B. (2003). Unraveling the resource-based tangle. *Managerial and Decision Economics, 24*(4), 309–323. doi:10.1002/mde.1126

Piccirillo, R. A. (2010). *The Lockean Memory Theory of Personal Identity: Definition, Objection, Response.* Retrieved from: http://www.inquiriesjournal.com/articles/1683/the-lockean-memory-theory-of-personal-identity-definition-objection-response

Reed, M. S., Evely, A. C., Cundill, G., Fazey, I., Glass, J., Laing, A., Newig, J., Parrish, B., Prell, C., Raymond, C., & Stringer, L. C. (2010). What is Social Learning? *Ecology and Society, 15*(4), r1. doi:10.5751/ES-03564-1504r01

Robertson, S. (2018). *Generation Z Characteristics & Traits That Explain The Way They Learn.* Retrieved from https://info.jkcp.com/blog/generation-z-characteristics

RohrR. (2019a, June 2). *One in Love.* Retrieved from https://cac.org/one-in-love-2019-06-02/

RohrR. (2019b, May 20). *The Psalms.* Retrieved from https://cac.org/the-psalms-2018-05-20/

Saunders, M. (2018). *Ecology is Not a Dirty Word. How do you review a conceptual paper?* Retrieved from https://ecologyisnotadirtyword.com/2018/06/21/how-do-you-review-a-conceptual-paper

Schroder, J. E., & Saltzer-Morling, M. (2006). *Brand Culture.* Routledge. doi:10.4324/9780203002445

Scolari, C. (2009). Transmedia Storytelling: Implicit consumers, narrative worlds, and branding in contemporary media production. *International Journal of Communication, 3,* 586–606.

White, J. E. (2017). *Meet Generation Z: Understanding and Reaching the New Post-Christian World.* Baker Books.

Witting, M. (2006). *Relations Between organizational identity, identification, and organizational objectives: An empirical study in municipalities.* Academic Press.

Chapter 2
Use of Novel Ensemble Machine Learning Approach for Social Media Sentiment Analysis

Ishrat Nazeer

School of Computer Science and Engineering, Lovely Professional University, Jalandhar, India

Mamoon Rashid

(iD) https://orcid.org/0000-0002-8302-4571

School of Computer Science and Engineering, Lovely Professional University, Jalandhar, India

Sachin Kumar Gupta

School of Electronics and Communication Engineering, Shri Mata Vaishno Devi University, Jammu, India

Abhishek Kumar

School of Computer Science and IT, Jain University, Bangalore, India

ABSTRACT

Twitter is a platform where people express their opinions and come with regular updates. At present, it has become a source for many organizations where data will be extracted and then later analyzed for sentiments. Many machine learning algorithms are available for twitter sentiment analysis which are used for automatically predicting the sentiment of tweets. However, there are challenges that hinder machine learning classifiers to achieve better results in terms of classification. In this chapter, the authors are proposing a novel feature generation technique to provide desired features for training model. Next, the novel ensemble classification system is proposed for identifying sentiment in tweets through weighted majority rule ensemble classifier, which utilizes several commonly used statistical models like naive Bayes, random forest, logistic regression, which are weighted according to their performance on historical data, where weights are chosen separately for each model.

DOI: 10.4018/978-1-7998-4718-2.ch002

INTRODUCTION TO SENTIMENT ANALYSIS

In the current world of technology everyone is expressive in one or other way. People want to express their opinions about various issues be it social, political, economic or business. In this process social media is helping people in a great way. Social networking sites like Facebook, twitter, WhatsApp and many others thus become a common tool for people to express themselves. Analyzing the opinions expressed by the people on different social networking sites to get useful insights from them is called social media analytics. The insights gained can then be used to make important decisions. Among all the networking sites twitter is becoming most powerful wherein people express their opinions in short textual messages called tweets. Analyzing the tweets to retrieve insight information is called twitter sentiment analysis (SA) or opinion mining. Sentiment analysis classifies the sentiment of a tweet into three classes of positive negative and neutral (Ahuja, Ret al. 2019). Twitter sentiment analysis is helping the modern world in a great way as an example SA can help a company in knowing the customer reviews about a particular product and will help customers to select the best product based on opinion of people.

Figure 1 shows five main steps required in Sentiment Analysis.

Figure 1. General steps in Twitter sentiment analysis process

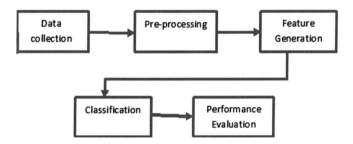

1. **Data Collection**: Process of SA begins by collecting the tweets from twitter using Application Programming Interface (API). API will allow us to interact with the twitter and extract the tweets in a programmatic way. The extracted tweets are then used for further processing,
2. **Pre-Processing**: Data preprocessing is done to remove extra features from the tweets. It decreases the size of tweets and makes them suitable for classification (Rane, A et al. 2018). The feature that are removed include following:
    a. The user name which is preceded by @ symbol.
    b. The retweets which are preceded by RT.
    c. Hashtags denoted by #.
    d. Slang words are replaced with words of equivalent meanings.
3. **Feature Extraction**: Feature extraction steps are responsible for extracting the features from the tweets. Different types of features are there like twitter specific features (includes features like hashtags, retweets, user names, URL), textual features (includes feature like length of tweet and length of words, emoticons, number of question marks), Parts Of Speech (features like nouns, verbs, adverbs, adjectives etc.), Lexicon Based features (comparison of positive and negative word percentages)(Permatasari, R. Iet al. 2018).

4. **Classification**: This step is responsible for determining whether the tweet expresses a positive, negative or neutral sentiment. There are three main approaches to classify the sentiment of a tweet they are, machine learning approach, lexicon based approach and deep learning approach. All these methods classify the polarity of the tweet with varying accuracy levels.

5. **Performance Evaluation**: This step is useful in determining the accuracy of the particular classifier used in the classification stage of the process. Performance is usually determined in terms of accuracy, precision, recall, and f-measure (Gamal, D et al. 2019).

Classification of Sentiment Analysis

Sentiment analysis is done at three different levels they are as follows:

1. **Document Level:** In document level sentiment analysis a document is analysed and the review got from it is classified as being positive negative or neutral. In document level sentiment analysis each document expresses opinion on a single entity (1 from proposal page).

2. **Sentence Level:** In sentence level sentiment analysis a sentence rather than a document is analyzed and classified as being positive negative or neutral. Sentences can be of two types subjective (sentence with opinion) or objective (sentence with factual knowledge). In sentence level classification the type of sentence is first identified and then if it contains an opinion it is classified (Behdenna, Set al. 2018).

3. **Aspect Level:** In aspect level sentiment analysis each aspect of a tweet or sentence is classified individually. The process first identifies the entity and its aspects then classifies the identified aspects.

Use of Twitter Micro-blogging for Sentiment Analysis

Twitter has become an important source of knowledge for people. It acts as a platform where people express themselves using short text messages called tweets. Sentiment analysis is mostly performed on twitter data because of the following reasons:

- It is the most popular micro-blogging site.
- It has 240+ million active users.
- About 500 million tweets are generated each day.
- Tweets are small in length and thus easy to analyze.
- It has variety of users.

Challenges in Twitter Sentiment Analysis

The task of sentiment analysis on twitter data is most challenging. The most common challenges associated with twitter sentiment analysis are as follows:

1. Use of highly unstructured and non-grammatical language in tweets.
2. Use of slang words.
3. Use of sarcasm in tweets.

4. Use of words which have subjective context in one sentence and objective in another.
5. Use of negative words to oppose the sentiment of tweet.
6. Use of acronyms and abbreviations.
7. Use of out of vocabulary words.

INTRODUCTION TO MACHINE LEARNING

Machine learning is a branch of artificial intelligence that gives machines the ability to learn from their own experience without being programmed. Machine learning is trying to impart human learning in computers. Humans learn by reasoning while computers learn by using algorithms. Based on the approach of learning used algorithms are classified into following general categories.

- **Supervised Learning**: Supervised learning algorithms are fed with a labelled dataset. Labelled dataset contains both input and output. The algorithm uses this dataset to train itself. After the training is over the algorithm is tested on a testing dataset, which is similar in dimensions to the training dataset, for predication or classification.
- **Unsupervised Learning**: Unsupervised learning algorithms are fed with an unlabeled dataset. Unlabeled dataset contains only input data and no information about the outputs. The algorithm has to learn by itself as no training is involved (Portugal, I et al. 2018). The algorithm classifies the data based on similarities or differences or patterns present in it.
- **Semi Supervised Learning**: Semi supervised learning algorithms are fed with a labelled dataset which is not complete and has missing information. The algorithm although goes through training but has to learn by itself as well because of the missing information (Portugal, I et al. 2018).
- **Reinforcement Learning**: Reinforcement learning is based on rewards. In this type of learning if algorithm makes a correct decision it is rewarded else it is punished. This type of learning is mostly used in game playing. In game playing if the algorithm makes a correct move the step will be repeated and learned however if an incorrect move is made then the step won't be repeated.

Overview of Machine Learning Classifiers

The different types of machine learning algorithms are given below:

- **Naive Bayes**: Naive Bayes algorithm is a statistical model of classification based on conditional probability. Conditional probability defines the probability of an event given that some other event has already occurred. The formula of Naive Bayes is given by:

$$P\big(H \,/\, X\big) = \frac{P\big(X \,/\, H\big)P\big(H\big)}{P\big(X\big)}$$

- **Support Vector Machine (SVM):** SVM classifier is mostly used for binary classification as shown in Figure 2. SVM is based on the construction of a hyperplane which acts as decision boundary between the two classes to be classified. The hyperplane is defined by w*x+b=0. Where w is the weight vector and b is the bias. Data point with w*x+b>=0 will be classified into a positive category and if w*x+b<0 then it is classified into a negative category (B, V et al. 2016).

Figure 2. Binary classification using SVM
(Mubaris NK, 2017)

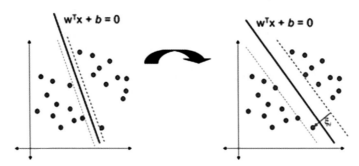

- **Random Forest**: Random forest algorithm builds a multitude of decision trees from the given dataset as shown in Figure 3. It then uses the result of each tree to find the class of data point using majority voting method (Rane, Aet al. 2018).

Figure 3. Illustration of Random forest
(Brendan Tierney, 2018)

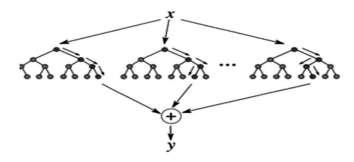

- **Decision Tree**: Decision tree algorithm works by constructing a decision tree from the given data. Each node of the tree represents the attribute of data and branch represents the test on attributes. Leaf nodes of the tree represent the final classes. Decision tree is constructed using the information gain of each node. Figure 4 shows the decision tree constructed for the shown dataset.

- **K Nearest Neighbour (KNN)**: KNN classifier can be used for classification and regression and its illustration is shown in Figure 5. It is based on similarity index. The algorithm first identifies

Figure 4. Classification of data set using Decision tree classifier
(Upasana Priyadarshiny, 2019)

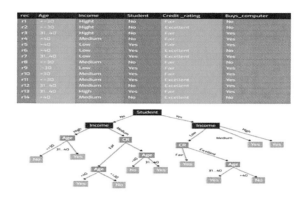

the K nearest neighbors of a data point using a distance measure like Euclidian distance. The data point is then assigned to the class that is most common among its K neighbours.

Figure 5. Classification of a data point using KNN classifier
(Avinash Navlani, 2018)

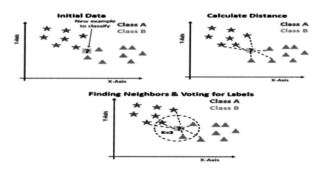

- **K Means Clustering**: K means clustering is an unsupervised learning technique. In this algorithm each data point is assigned to a cluster to which it resembles the most. The grouping of data points in clusters is shown in Figure 6. K represents the number of distinct clusters formed (Dey, A. 2016)

Applying Machine Learning Classifiers for Twitter Analysis

Machine learning involves a set of methods used to identify the features of text. Machine learning enables a computer to learn from the patterns of data and experiences. Thus the computer needs not be programmed explicitly. Machine learning has been successfully used in twitter sentiment classification. Machine learning classifiers have shown a good rate of accuracy in sentiment classification. Some of the recent works done on twitter sentiment analysis are mentioned below.

Figure 6. Grouping of data points into three different clusters
(Arun Manglic, 2017).

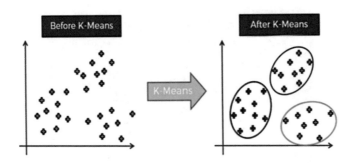

(Nanda, Cet al. 2018) used machine learning algorithms on movie review tweets to classify the tweets into positive and negative. The algorithms used were Support Vector Machine (SVM) and Random Forest (RF). An accuracy of 91.07 and 89.73 was achieved by RF and SVM respectively. (Rathi, M et al. 2018) used an ensemble machine learning algorithm. Ensemble was created by using merging SVM and Decision Tree (DT) algorithms. The algorithm achieved an accuracy of 84% which was greater than the accuracy provided by the individual SVM and DT. (El-Jawad, M. H. A et al. 2018) compared different machine learning and deep learning algorithms. They developed a hybrid model using Naive Bayes, Decision Tree, Convolution Neural Network (CNN) and Recurrent Neural Network (RNN). The model gives an accuracy of 83.6%. (Arti et al. 2019) used Random Forest algorithm on tweets related to Indian Premier League 2016. The classifier achieved an accuracy of 81.69%. (Alrehili, A et al. 2019) combined Naive Bayes, SVM, Random Forest, Bagging and Boosting to create ensemble algorithm for the customer reviews about a product. (Naz, S et al. 2018) used sentiment analysis on SemEval twitter dataset. The machine learning algorithm was SVM which uses multiple features of data to perform better accuracy. (Goel, A et al. 2016) used Naive Bayes algorithm to classify a movie review twitter dataset. (Jose, R et al. 2016) combined machine learning classification approach with lexicon based sentiment classification. The authors combined SentiWordNet classifier, Naive bayes classifier and hidden Markov model classifier to achieve better accuracy.An attempt to fetch twitter data has been done by (Rashid, M et al. 2019). This research used Hadoop distributed file system for storage of data which were fetched with the help of flume. Decision Tree and Naïve Bayes classifiers were used for sentiment analysis. The clustering approach has been used for managing web news data in (Kaur, S et al. 2016). This research has used Back Propagation Neural Network and K-Means Clustering for classifying the news data.

DATA EXTRACTION AND FEATURE SELECTION

When twitter sentiment analysis is done using machine learning approach, feature extraction plays an important role. Features represent the information that can be extracted from the data. Features define the unique property of a data sample. In Machine Learning the feature of data are projected on a higher dimensional feature space. To achieve better accuracy in classification higher dimensional data needs to be mapped onto low dimensional feature space. Feature extraction acts as a dimensional reduction technique. Each machine learning classifier uses most appropriate feature set to classify the sentiment of tweet as positive, negative or neutral (Avinash, M et al. 2018).

El-Jawad, M. H. A *et al.*, (2018) in their study divides features into following categories.

1. **Bag of Words (BOW):** BOW is basically a feature representation technique wherein tweets are commonly converted into an array of numbers. It first learns all the words present in a tweet and then describes the presence of words in a tweet. BOW uses ngram_range as a parameter. ngram range represents number of words taken together. Range can be 1 (unigram), 2 (bigram) or multiple.

2. **Lexicon Based Feature:** In this feature representation technique a comparison is made between percentage of positive and negative words present in a tweet. Positive words include words like good, great, excellent etc. Negative words include words like bad, poor, dangerous etc.

3. **Parts of Speech Feature Representation:** In this feature representation technique the count of nouns, verbs, adverbs, adjectives present in the tweet is determined. By identifying each word of tweet as a different POS it becomes easy to get the context in which each word is used thus helping in analyzing the sentiment of tweet.

4. **Emoticon Based Feature Representation:** Emoticons are used in tweets to represent the feeling an individual has related to a particular event. The number of emoticons present in each tweet represents its feature set. Emoticon based features have been used by many researchers to effectively classify the tweets.

Feature Selection

Feature selection technique is used to select the relevant features and eliminate the irrelevant ones from a tweet. It thus helps in reducing the feature dimensionality of a data set. Lower dimensional feature space provides better accuracy in classification. There are different feature selection methods some of them are discussed below.

1. 1. **Information Gain (IG):** Information gain is used to measure dependencies between the class and the feature. If dependencies are present we select the feature else not. If x is a feature and c1 and c2 are the two classes then the information gain is given by:

$$IG(x) = -\sum_{j=1}^{2} P(C_j) \log\left(P(C_j)\right) + P(x) \sum_{j=1}^{2} P(C_j \mid x) \log\left(P(C_j \mid x)\right)$$
$$+ P(\overline{x}) \sum_{j=1}^{2} P(C_j \mid \overline{x}) \log\left(P(C_j \mid \overline{x})\right)$$

2. 2. **Chi- Square:** Chi square is used when tweets contain categorical features. Chi square is used calculated between feature and the class. The features with best chi-square scores are selected. Chi–square is calculated as follows

$$c^2 = \sum_{i=1}^{k} \left| \frac{\left(O_i - E_i\right)^2}{E_i} \right|$$

Here O denotes the observed frequency, E denotes expected frequency and "i" denotes "ith" position in the contingency table. Expected frequency is the number of expected observations of class when there is no relationship between the feature and the target class and observed frequency is the number of observations of class.

3. **Minimum Redundancy method:** in this method of feature selection the features which are highly dependent on class and minimally dependent on other features are selected. It is also called as Minimum Redundancy Maximum Relevance feature selection. If two features possess redundant information then if only one is selected it does not affect the classification accuracy much.

Training and Testing Machine Learning Classifier for Twitter Sentiment Analysis

Once the data is pre-processed and ready, the next step is train this data to classifier for model preparation. However to evaluate the performance of model, it is very important to split the given data into training and test parts where the performance will be evaluated later by comparing the predictions from machine learning model with that of the target values in outcome variable of testing data. In some cases, separate datasets are to be used for training and tests purposes which is critical in correctly assessing the performance of classifier. The training and testing datasets. Keeping this challenge under consideration, we can use same dataset for training and testing iterations. The concept of k-fold cross validation is to be used where the data is divided into k units or blocks and then classifier is trained for all units except one unit which is to be used for testing purposes and later this process is repeated for all other units. If the value of K is equal to the number of observations, then this process is called as leave one out cross validation. Leave out one validation is turning biased for large value of K. However 10 fold cross validation is always a good choice (Hastie, T et al. 2009).

PROPOSAL OF NOVEL ENSEMBLE MACHINE LEARNING FOR TWITTER SENTIMENT ANALYSIS

In classical machine learning approach a single classifier is applied on the training data at once for classification. This produces different results of accuracy for different classifiers on same training dataset. Moreover if we have a set of classifiers all of which are providing a good accuracy result on same training dataset. Choosing a single classifier will not give us best and generalized results on unseen data. Thus using a single classifier will not help in selecting a best classifier among the competing ones. Also it is difficult to say which realization of a particular classifier will be best set to training data. All of these problems were solved by ensemble learning. Ensemble learning is a Machine Learning methodology in which different base models are combined to produce an optimal classification model. The optimal classification model formed is known as Ensemble classifier. Ensemble classifier combines output of different models to give best and generalized results in classification. The general ensemble classification approach is shown in Figure 7.

The outputs of different base classifiers are combined in multiple ways to get the final prediction. The different approaches by which the outputs of base classifiers can be combined are;

Figure 7. General ensemble classification approach

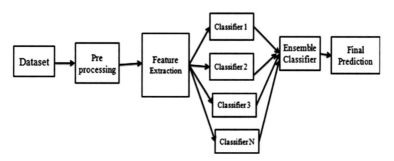

1. **Majority Voting:** In majority voting method the prediction is made by each base classifier. These predictions are deemed as votes. The final output of the ensemble classifier will be the prediction that is most common among the individual classifier predictions. For example if we are using three classifiers in the ensemble if two classifiers are predicting the tweet as positive and one as negative the final output of ensemble will be positive. Majority voting method is shown in Figure 8.

Figure 8. Majority voting method to classification using Ensemble classifier

2. **Maximum Probability:** In maximum probability rule the individual predictions of base classifiers are averaged. The final output of the ensemble classifier is the class with maximum average value. In case of Twitter Sentiment Analysis for each tweet probability of positive as well negative class is calculated. The ensemble classifier then finds the average of probabilities of all classes of each classifier and the class with maximum probability is assigned to the tweet. Maximum probability rule of ensemble classification is shown in Figure 9.

3. **Weighted Average:** Weighted average method is similar to the maximum probability rule however in weighted average rule the base models are assigned with some weights. The weights are given according to the importance of each predictive model. The models which are more effective for a particular dataset will be assigned with larger weights and the models which are less effective are assigned comparatively smaller weights.

The algorithm for ensemble classification is as follows.

Figure 9. Maximum Probability method to classification using Ensemble classifier

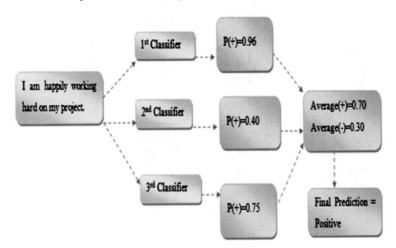

ALGORITHM

Step 1: Extraction of data from twitter using twitters API.

Step 2: Pre-processing the data to remove unwanted symbols and words which are of no use in predicting the sentiment of the tweet.

Step 3: Extracting the features from preprocessed tweets using Bag of Words technique.

Step 4: Applying each individual classifier on the extracted features to get individual predictions.

Step 5: Using majority voting technique on the individual predictions to get the final prediction by ensemble classifier.

Step 6: Output the sentiment of the tweet.

CONCLUSION AND FUTURE DIRECTIONS

In this chapter, the authors proposed novel machine learning approach for the sentiment analysis classification. This proposed algorithm is based on ensemble approach which will identify sentiment in tweets through - Weighted Majority Rule Ensemble Classifier where several commonly used statistical models like Naive Bayes, Random forest, Logistic regression will be utilized and weighted according to their performance on historical data and weights will be chosen separately for each model. In future, this proposed ensemble model will be used for training datasets for the classification of sentiments. This model will also be extended by the application of optimization algorithms for further refining the feature set for better results of classification in sentiment analysis.

REFERENCES

Ahuja, R., Chug, A., Kohli, S., Gupta, S., & Ahuja, P. (2019). The Impact of Features Extraction on the Sentiment Analysis. *Procedia Computer Science, 152*, 341–348. doi:10.1016/j.procs.2019.05.008

Alrehili, A., & Albalawi, K. (2019). Sentiment Analysis of Customer Reviews Using Ensemble Method. *2019 International Conference on Computer and Information Sciences (ICCIS)*. 10.1109/IC-CISci.2019.8716454

Arti, D. K. P., & Agrawal, S. (2019). An Opinion Mining for Indian Premier League Using Machine Learning Techniques. *2019 4th International Conference on Internet of Things: Smart Innovation and Usages (IoT-SIU)*. doi: 10.1109/iot-siu.2019.8777472

Avinash, M., & Sivasankar, E. (2018). A Study of Feature Extraction Techniques for Sentiment Analysis. *Advances in Intelligent Systems and Computing Emerging Technologies in Data Mining and Information Security*, 475–486. doi:10.1007/978-981-13-1501-5_41

B., V., & M., B. (2016). Analysis of Various Sentiment Classification Techniques. *International Journal of Computer Applications, 140*(3), 22–27. doi:10.5120/ijca2016909259

Behdenna, S., Barigou, F., & Belalem, G. (2018). Document Level Sentiment Analysis: A survey. *EAI Endorsed Transactions on Context-Aware Systems and Applications*, *4*(13), 154339. doi:10.4108/eai.14-3-2018.154339

Dey, A. (2016). Machine learning algorithms: A review. *International Journal of Computer Science and Information Technologies*, *7*(3), 1174–1179.

El-Jawad, M. H. A., Hodhod, R., & Omar, Y. M. K. (2018). Sentiment Analysis of Social Media Networks Using Machine Learning. *2018 14th International Computer Engineering Conference (ICENCO)*. doi: 10.1109/icenco.2018.8636124

Gamal, D., Alfonse, M., El-Horbaty, E.-S. M., & Salem, A.-B. M. (2019). Implementation of Machine Learning Algorithms in Arabic Sentiment Analysis Using N-Gram Features. *Procedia Computer Science*, *154*, 332–340. doi:10.1016/j.procs.2019.06.048

Goel, A., Gautam, J., & Kumar, S. (2016). Real time sentiment analysis of tweets using Naive Bayes. *2016 2nd International Conference on Next Generation Computing Technologies (NGCT)*. doi: 10.1109/ngct.2016.7877424

Hastie, T., Tibshirani, R., Friedman, J., & Franklin, J. (2005). The elements of statistical learning: Data mining, inference and prediction. *The Mathematical Intelligencer*, *27*(2), 83–85. doi:10.1007/BF02985802

Jose, R., & Chooralil, V. S. (2016). Prediction of election result by enhanced sentiment analysis on twitter data using classifier ensemble Approach. *2016 International Conference on Data Mining and Advanced Computing (SAPIENCE)*. 10.1109/SAPIENCE.2016.7684133

Kaur, S., & Rashid, E. M. (2016). Web news mining using Back Propagation Neural Network and clustering using K-Means algorithm in big data. *Indian Journal of Science and Technology*, *9*(41). Advance online publication. doi:10.17485/ijst/2016/v9i41/95598

Manglic, A. (2017). *Artificial Intelligence and Machine/Deep Learning*. Retrieved from http://arun-aiml. blogspot.com/2017/07/k-means-clustering.html

Mubaris, N. K. (2017). *Support Vector Machines for Classification*. Retrieved from https://mubaris. com/posts/svm

Nanda, C., Dua, M., & Nanda, G. (2018). Sentiment Analysis of Movie Reviews in Hindi Language Using Machine Learning. *2018 International Conference on Communication and Signal Processing (ICCSP)*. 10.1109/ICCSP.2018.8524223

Navlani, A. (2018). *KNN Classification using Scikit-learn*. Retrieved from https://www.datacamp.com/community/tutorials/k-nearest-neighbor-classification-scikit-learn

Naz, S., Sharan, A., & Malik, N. (2018). Sentiment Classification on Twitter Data Using Support Vector Machine. *2018 IEEE/WIC/ACM International Conference on Web Intelligence (WI)*. 10.1109/WI.2018.00-13

Permatasari, R. I., Fauzi, M. A., Adikara, P. P., & Sari, E. D. L. (2018). Twitter Sentiment Analysis of Movie Reviews using Ensemble Features Based Naïve Bayes. *2018 International Conference on Sustainable Information Engineering and Technology (SIET)*. 10.1109/SIET.2018.8693195

Portugal, I., Alencar, P., & Cowan, D. (2018). The use of machine learning algorithms in recommender systems: A systematic review. *Expert Systems with Applications, 97*, 205–227. doi:10.1016/j.eswa.2017.12.020

Priyadarshiny, U. (2019). *How to create a Perfect Decision Tree*. Retrieved from https://dzone.com/articles/how-to-create-a-perfect-decision-tree

Rane, A., & Kumar, A. (2018). Sentiment Classification System of Twitter Data for US Airline Service Analysis. *2018 IEEE 42nd Annual Computer Software and Applications Conference (COMPSAC)*. doi:10.1109/compsac.2018.00114

Rashid, M., Hamid, A., & Parah, S. A. (2019). Analysis of Streaming Data Using Big Data and Hybrid Machine Learning Approach. In *Handbook of Multimedia Information Security: Techniques and Applications* (pp. 629–643). Springer. doi:10.1007/978-3-030-15887-3_30

Rathi, M., Malik, A., Varshney, D., Sharma, R., & Mendiratta, S. (2018). Sentiment Analysis of Tweets Using Machine Learning Approach. *2018 Eleventh International Conference on Contemporary Computing (IC3)*. 10.1109/IC3.2018.8530517

Silva, N. F. D., Hruschka, E. R., & Hruschka, E. R. (2014). Tweet sentiment analysis with classifier ensembles. *Decision Support Systems, 66*, 170–179. doi:10.1016/j.dss.2014.07.003

Tierney, B. (2018). *Random Forest Machine Learning in R, Python and SQL - Part 1*. Retrieved from https://blog.toadworld.com/2018/08/31/random-forest-machine-learning-in-r-python-and-sql-part-1

Chapter 3
Digital Social Networking Use Effect on Individual Job Performance

Marwa Mallouli Ben Zouitina
Faculty of Economics and Management of Sfax, Tunisia & PRISME Laboratory, Tunisia

Zouhour Smaoui Hachicha
PRISME Laboratory, Faculty of Economics and Management of Sfax, Tunisia

ABSTRACT

This chapter aims to explore the impact of social networking sites (SNS) usage on individual work performance (IP). A literature review revealed contrasting results. A multiple-case study on 15 employees from eight Tunisian firms has been conducted to highlight the SNS effects on IP in the specific context of democratic transition. Data have been collected by semi-structured interviews and coded using the Nvivo 10 software. The analysis shows that, depending on the level of SNS usage, three types of effect are identified on IP at work: positive, negative, or null. This result invites researcher to consider the usage intensity when analyzing SNS effects on IP. Understanding the different types of SNS usage by actors and their effects on IP could help managers to take appropriate decisions to take profit from this usage. This research suggests also that organizational policy moderates the relationship between SNS usage and IP.

INTRODUCTION

The social networking sites (SNS) usage has recently become one of the most social popular activities around the world (Ifinedo, 2016; Cao et al., 2018). Their penetration is expanding in all geographic areas. All continents are affected. SNS have the highest penetration rate in North America with 70% and 53% in Western Europe compared to a penetration rate of 40% in North Africa and 24% in South Asia (Statista, 2019). In 2019, Facebook site comes out on top with a monthly number of 2.45 billion active users. Indeed, there are 1.013 billion visitors in Asia, 387 million in Europe, 247 million in North America and 802 million in the rest of the world (Coëffé, 2020). These few figures show the extent

DOI: 10.4018/978-1-7998-4718-2.ch003

of SNS phenomenon, which constitutes an emerging field of study. Various aspects related to SNS usage have attracted researchers' attention. However, most of these previous researches were mainly conducted in educational institutions and used students as subjects (Charoensukmongkol, 2014; Köffer et al., 2014). The study of the impact of SNS usage in organizations constitutes a little explored field (Charoensukmongkol, 2014).

Recently, SNS such as Facebook, Twitter and LinkedIn have become essential for companies (Corre, 2011). These platforms help employees to communicate, cooperate, and get information or document. Also, they allow to create a social structure and an information transfer between employees (Heidemann et al., 2012). The impact of SNS usage on employee's work is one of the major managers' concerns (IACE, 2016). Besides, the access to different SNS by employees during working time is expanding (Nazir et al., 2016). There is a debate about SNS usage value for organization members. North (2010), Van Zyl (2010) and Ashraf and Javed (2014) found that social networking platforms can lead to difficulties associated with interference between function- related activities and social media activities. Others authors concluded that SNS can improve employee work performance (Hassan et al., 2011; Xi Zhang et al., 2015; Nazir et al., 2016; Kishokumar, 2016). In addition, the SNS impact on IP has been studied in different contexts such as the United States (Moqbel et al., 2013), Greece (Leftheriotis & Giannakos, 2014) and China (Cao et al., 2016). The question of SNS usage in Arabic countries has not yet been investigated (Mallouli et al., 2017). Particularly, democratic transition countries, like Tunisia employed some information control models including social media to ensure opinions' harmonization (Koch, 2015). These practices may affect the way SNS are used by employees.

This research introduces SNS use as a potential determinant of IP at the workplace. On the one hand, the study of this relation is motivated by the increasingly intensive use of these tools in the contemporary organizational context (Charoensukmongkol, 2014; Leftheriotis & Giannakos, 2014; Xi Zhang et al., 2015; Kishokumar, 2016). On the other hand, this choice is driven by the controversial result presented in studies investigating the relationship between SNS usage and IP (Wickramasinghe & Nisaf, 2012; Moqbel et al., 2013).

Therefore, we address the following question: What is the impact of SNS usage at work on individual job performance?

First, this chapter aims to present an overview of key concepts namely SNS, usage and individual performance. Second, the relationship between SNS usage and individual performance is clarified. Then, the methodological choices related to the qualitative study research are described. Finally, the data analysis results are detailed.

THEORETICAL BACKGROUND AND CONCEPTUAL FRAMEWORK

Media Synchronicity Theory (MST)

In this chapter, the Media Synchronicity Theory (MST) presented by Dennis and Kinney (1998) was mobilized to explain the impact of SNS usage on IP at work. Synchronicity of the media means that two people work together on the same task, at the same time and have shared concentration (Chevrin, 2006).

For Dennis and Kinney (1998), MST states that work tasks are based on a communication process which is composed of two fundamental processes. It is mainly about the information transmission process, maintained by media with low synchronicity and convergence process, based on media of high synchronicity requiring an understanding of exchanged information (Karoui & Dudezert, 2010). This theory provides a reference framework to study the importance of social media use in improving communication and therefore performance at work (Cao et al., 2012). Cao et al. (2016) used it to study the influence of social media (including SNS) on IP. MST is often used in SNS literature to explain how the use of these tools influences job performance (Nkwe & Cohen, 2017). According to the latter authors, MST suggests that SNS provide employees with a means of communication allowing them to achieve useful synchronizations for their work.

MST states that IP at work is enhanced if individuals use the media to perform ambiguous tasks that require many interpretations (Dennis et al., 2008). According to these authors, the synchronously used media allows employees to meet at the same time (chat, audio, video and conference), coordinate, interact with useful messages and focus on the task achievement (Dennis et al., 2008).

Social Networking Sites and Their Uses

The terms such as "service" or " site " have been used interchangeably by researchers to refer to SNS (Zhang & Leung, 2014). For example, Schneider et al. (2009), Kluemper and Rosen (2009) and Park and Cho (2012) perceived SNS as communities. Stenger et al. (2010) consider that SNS represent a breeding ground on which communities can appear, but without confusing them. Boyd and Ellison (2007) agree with this distinction and developed a definition that has been widely adopted in SNS researches (Mallouli et al., 2017). For this authors SNS refer to a "Web-based service", that allows users to: (1) construct a public or semi-public profile within a bounded system, (2) articulate a list of other users with whom they share a connection, (3) view and browse their list of connections and those made by others within the system. Beer (2008) and Stenger et al. (2010) proceeded to the determination of a fourth property, which helps to distinguish by a simple question the SNS from social computation by considering the practices and uses of each one of them: (4) base their attractiveness essentially on the first three points and not on a particular activity.

In this chapter, the definition of Cetinkaya and Rashid (2018) is selected. According to these authors, SNS are websites that allow building online relationships between organizations, their employees, customers and stakeholders in order to ensure an ongoing dialogue. This definition was chosen because it is inclusive. It discusses the main features of SNS: SNS are online sites, SNS allow connection to concerned members, SNS enable the creation and exchange of content.

The SNS usage have generated a lot of research for more than a decade (Edosomwan et al., 2011). When many authors try to synthesize the concept of usage (Cigref 2004; Bachelet 2004; Ouni 2005; Fourati Ennouri 2016), they pose the confusion problem between different employed terms to designate it. In the literature, this concept is used to refer at the same time to use, practice or appropriation (Millerand, 1998). Several authors distinguish the usage from use by highlighting that these two terms refer to different logics (Massit Folléa, 2002; Badillo & Pélissier, 2015). Use refers to the user's manual handbook (Kane, 2013). En revanche, selon Fauré (2008), le concept d'usage est souvent confondu avec celui de pratique). However, usage represents the actual practices of technology that can be evaluated over time depending on the individual or collective use of the tool (Fourati Ennouri, 2016).

In literature, usage and practice are either used interchangeably, or distinguished as practice. Usage is more restrictive and refers to the simple use (Badillo & Pélissier, 2015). Furthermore, the concept of practice is more elaborated and covers not only the use of the techniques but also directly or indirectly individuals' behaviors, attitudes and representation relate to the tool.

Appropriation is a new concept close to usage. According to Kane (2013), it can be defined as the progressive construction of usage and how it was included in the everyday.

In this chapter, we selected the definition proposed by Proulx (2001). He considers usage as a complex phenomenon resulting in interactions between human actors and technical devices and corresponds to what they actually do with these objects and technical devices. This definition avoids the trap of double determinism. It considers the effective action of technology in society, and emphasizes the used technical objects by people.

Individual Job Performance Concept

Since job performance is one of the dependent variables interesting companies, research in this area strives to reach a consensus on their definitions and conceptions on individual-level (Vigan et al., 2014).

Historically, job performance is a concept that has generated much debate, without being clearly defined, conceptualized and without producing exploitable empirical results (Campbell, 1990; Viswesvaran 1993; Motowidlo 2003; Charbonnier et al., 2007; Impelman, 2007; Charbonnier - Voirin & Roussel, 2012). First, when treating individual performance concept, researchers focused only on tools and indicators used in companies to measure productivity and products or services quality offered (Charbonnier et al., 2007; Koopmans et al., 2011; Charbonnier-Voirin & Roussel, 2012). Second, to clarify this concept, authors studied individual determinants of performance namely human factors that can explain job performance. For example, motivation, satisfaction, involvement, etc. (Pauvers et al., 2006; Charbonnier et al., 2007 ; Koopmans et al., 2011 ; Basit & Hassan, 2018).

The theoretical concept of "individual performance at work" has been enriched and developed at the beginning of the 19th century (Campbell, 1990; Borman & Motowidlo, 1993; Van Dyne et al., 1995; Motowidlo, 2003, etc.). For Campbell (1990), individual job performance is a "multidimensional behavioral construct" which deals with "a set of *behaviors* or *actions* which are relevant to the organization objectives and which can be measured in terms of skill level and contributions to objective" (Charbonnier et al., 2007). According to this definition, job performance is perceived as the organization expected behavior and action (Demerouti et al., 2014; Jalil et al., 2015). Only behaviors relevant to the organization's objectives are used to determine work performance. Besides, only the measured actions are considered as a constituent of individual performance (Campbell et al., 1993; Sonnentag & Frese, 2003). Furthermore, various authors like Borman and Motowildo (1993) and Motowildo (2003) have not considered that action and behavior are the unique constituents of individual job performance concept (Sonnentag & Frese, 2003). For Motowidlo (2003), individual job performance is a multidimensional construct that deals with a "set of individual's behaviors or actions contributing to the achievement of organization's objectives", and can be measured by skill level and contributions to objectives (Charbonnier et al., 2007). Motowidlo (2003) highlighted a difference between behavior and performance. Behavior is what employees do and performance is the value expected by the company, and reflects what employees do (Carppentier et al., 2015). Behavioral aspects and expected actions (results) do not overlap. Thus, "if we only assess the individual results, we can ignore the situational factors that help or hinder job employee performance. For example, availability and quality of equipment and resources, strategic and operational decisions beyond personal control, market context" (Charbonnier et al., 2007). In this context, Charles-Pauvers et al. (2006) proposed a new definition in which a person can be judged to be successful even if he has failed to achieve his objectives and the reasons for his failure are completely out of his control (Charles-Pauvers et al., 2007). So, individual performance is "the behavior that organization values and expects from its employees. It represents an aggregated set of discrete behaviors that would positively influence the achievement of organizational objectives, like productivity, creativity, profitability, growth, quality, customer satisfaction, etc."

In this chapter, the definition proposed by Charles-Pauvers et al. (2007) is adopted because it was initially proposed to fill the gaps identified in the definitions advanced by Campbel (1990) and Motowildo (2003), two reference authors in individual performance field.

In recent years, the SNS usage has upset the traditional labor practices (Issa et al., 2014 and Cetinkaya and Rashid, 2018). A review of the literature revealed that few articles illustrate the influence of SNS usage on IP (Leftheriotis & Giannakos, 2014; Xi Zhang et al., 2015; Kishokumar, 2016, Brooks & Callif, 2017; Cao et al., 2018) but provide a controversial result.

MAIN FOCUS OF THE CHAPTER: EFFECTS OF DIGITAL SOCIAL NETWORKING SITES ON IP

SNS usage impact on IP feeds a considerable number of researches and continues to be studied in different geographical zones. There are a few studies which were conducted in Asian countries, like China, Pakistan, Sri Lanka and Thailand (Wickramasinghe & Nisaf, 2012; Charoensukmongkol, 2014; Ashraf & Javed, 2014; Balasuriya & Jayalal, 2015; Xi Zhang et al., 2015). American, European and African countries are also interested in this subject (Ferreira & Plessis, 2009; Ali-Hassan et al., 2015). Researchers studying SNS usage effect on IP at work show three types of results. A first group of researchers, like Bennett et al. (2010), Hassan et al. (2011), Munene and Nyaribo (2013), Charoensukmongkol (2014), Shami and Chen (2014), Leftheriotis and Giannakos (2014), Xi Zhang et al. (2015), Nazir et al. (2016) and Kishokumar (2016) found that SNS influence positively employees' job. For Chou et al. (2013), the employee who is more interested in Facebook have the highest professional performance.

Leftheriotis and Giannakos (2014) interviewed 1799 employees from insurance sector. They found that SNS improve collaboration, knowledge sharing and increase productivity among workers. Nazir et al. (2016) questioned 100 Pakistani employees. Their results showed that SNS are often used by HR departments. For example, employee can use the Facebook page for announcing training, meeting, etc. Shami and Chen (2014) studied the effect of social media usage on IP of 75,747 employees of a large IT global company over 3 years. They found that these tools usage was positively associated with performance ratings.

Other authors, like Ferreira and Plessis (2009), North (2010), Van Zyl (2010), Moqbel et al. (2013), Ashraf and Javed (2014), Brooks and Callif (2017) and Zivnuska et al. (2019) supported that SNS can lead to negative spillover effects. However, while SNS increase employee performance by improving internal collaboration, capturing new ideas, responding to work-related issues, and enhancing collaborative learning (Bennett et al., 2009; Van Zyl, 2010; Aguenza & MatSom, 2012; Wickramasinghe & Nisaf, 2012), they can create some difficulties associated with interference between function-related activities and social media. SNS tools can be used during working hours for a personal purpose: exchanging and broadcasting photos, sharing music, videos, etc. (Chen et al., 2008; Ferreira and Plessis, 2009; Wickramasinghe & Nisaf, 2012; Brooks & Callif, 2017; Cao et al., 2018).

Brooks and Callif (2017) explored the social media usage effects on IP of 415 Turkish working professionals from 42 IT companies. They investigated how using social media could induce technostress to users and damage employee performance. Their results indicated that social media tools have direct negative effect on job performance. For these authors, social medias such as Facebook, Twitter and LinkedIn force employees to engage in their uses and complete simultaneously their work tasks, which means managing concurrently multiple streams of information. Cao et al. (2018) examined the effects of excessive social media usage on individual performance through an online questionnaire distributed to 230 Chinese working professionals who use social media in organizations. They revealed that these tools generate negative perceptions and psychological strain to employees at work. Excessive social media usage influences negatively cognition and emotions of employees and expends their time and energy. So, these tools reduce IP.

Zivnuska et al. (2019) explored the impact of social media usage and employees' IP through a questionnaire distributed to 326 working professionals in United States. They found that these used tools at workplace can lead to employee's addiction, which affects negatively IP. However, Meesela et al. (2013), Balasuriya and Jayalal (2015) and Cao et al. (2016) concluded that the SNS usage does not affect worker performance. Cao et al. (2016) studied the impact of using SNS on employee performance by interviewing 379 Chinese employees. For these authors, SNS can only influence work performance through social capital and knowledge transfer. For Balasuriya and Jayalal (2015), the SNS impact on individual performance is explored by interviewing 37 employees from different companies in Sri Lanka. According to them, the lack of this relationship can be explained by the age. The employees were young (under 25 years). They established boundaries separating their professional and personal life. For these authors, culture could also play a role in explaining this relationship. Moreover, the employees are not interested in exchanging work-related information by using social networking tools. Thus, they choose improving their work through classroom training or live discussions.

In order to understand the impact of the SNS usage on Tunisian employees work performance, we adopted a qualitative approach. The methodological choices relating to the approach and research instrument used are presented in the following.

REASERCH METHODOLOGY

Data Collection Tool

To explore the relationship between SNS usage and it impact on IP, a qualitative approach was conducted by studying multiple cases. This approach is particularly adopted in this research because it allows to investigate a recent phenomenon (Benbasat et al., 1987; Yin, 1994; Triki, 2010; Karoui et al., 2014). Qualitative methods provide an overview of interviewer's behavior concerning a predefined subject (Corre, 2011). Case study was conducted in this research because it helps to develop a detailed and profound description of the subject (Taddei, 2009). In addition, SNS usage in democratic transition context is little explored, particularly in the Tunisian one (Mallouli et al., 2016). Data was collected by using semi-directive interview. This technique allows the researcher to understand the organizational practices and interviewee's experiences (Wacheux, 1996) concerning the impact of SNS usage on work performance.

Data was collected over a period of five months; from July 2017 to November 2017. The unit of analysis is the individual. Interviewees are working in eight Tunisian companies from commercial sector which is one of the most dynamic sectors in Tunisia (Abdelaziz & Trabelsi, 2009). The choice of the individual as unit of analysis does not exclude the contribution of each organization in the presentation of information relating to our studied problematic. This research presents an embedded case study. It adopts the typology proposed by Yin (1994). This is a study that covers several companies and each one includes a number of interviewees.

The collected data have been analyzed through content analysis (Miles & Huberman, 2003). Content analysis method has been often used to transcribe interviews (Andreani, 2005). In this research, it was made using "NVivo 10" software. Miles and Huberman (2003) propose to analyze the collected data through codes reflecting the key variables of study. The coding unit adopted is the paragraph which is often considered as the privileged analysis unit in case studies (Paillé, 2006).

Sampling

The population of the study consisted of the number of employees that visited social network for the period under study.

Tables 1 and 2 present the companies studied and the interviewees' profiles that constitute the units of analysis.

Table 1. Presentation of companies

Surveyed Companies	Activity / Sector	Interviewees' Position	Interviewees' ID
Company 1	Insurance agency	Branch Manager	1
Company 2	Control agency (insurance)	Control Manager	2
Company 3	Commercial company (Clothings)	Owner Manager	3
Company 4	Accounting company	Accountant	4
Company 5	IT company	Project Manager Engineer Service Agent Developer Agent	5 6 7 8
Company 6	Power pole installation company	Human Resources Director	9
Company 7	Food products marketing company	Commercial director Purchasing Director Purchasing assistant Cash Manager	10 11 12 13
Company 8	Accounting and auditing company	Accountant Audit Manager	14 15

The interviewees should fulfil the following criteria: being an executive worker in a Tunisian company, having connectivity in workplace and using at least one SNS.

15 interviews were conducted. Data collection stopped at the 15th interview because increasing their number would not provide any additional information to what was conveyed earlier (Mlaiki, 2012).

The administered interview guide addresses two main themes: usage of SNS and individual job performance.

Table 2. Presentation of interviewees' profiles

Parameters	Measures	Respondents' Number
Gender	Male Female	11 4
Age	20-30 31-40 41-50 >50	6 4 2 3
Education	Incomplete college or university Bachelor's degree Diploma Master's degree Docotorate degree	2 2 6 4 1
Work experience	1 year 2-5 years 6-10 years ⩾ 11 years	2 4 3 6

RESULTS AND DISCUSSION

The different usage of SNS by respondents during working hours are first studied in order to highlight their impact on individual performance.

Description of SNS Usage at Work

Respondents' speech analysis enables to classify usage into professional and personal.[1] Most used SNS by interviewees are Facebook, Instagram and LinkedIn. Table 3 describes the identified usage in the workplace.

The results revealed that the interviewees focus more on informational usage that generate a significant exchange of information in order to facilitate their job.

Despite of the specific usage to each case, the interviewees tend to exchange information with superiors, subordinates and colleagues to perform their work effectively. Word or PDF documents, are shared as "template documents ", used to perform a new task. They also include photos, videos, instructions / orders addressed to subordinates to settle remote new case or discuss new contract.

Similarly, all interviewees develop some personal usage of SNS: to follow news, find old friends, start discussions, communicate about events, post articles or pictures, program outing, follow associative activities, etc.

Based on content analysis, it is possible to conclude that professional usage outweigh personal usage. Despite the fact that, "the use of social media at work for personal reasons is becoming the norm" (Brooks & Callif, 2017), previous research has focused on the study of professional usage. For the rest of this chapter, usage concept will be studied without distinguishing between professional and personal usage. In the literature, the boundary between this two categories is still unclear and intangible (Roudaut & Jullien, 2017).

Table 3. SNS usage by interviewees

Interviewees	Used Tools	Professional Usage	Personal Usage
Interviewee 1	Facebook Messenger	Informational exchanges with: ●General management: cars' photos; scanned statements. ●Subordinates: Videos; contacts; discussion.	●News Search
Interviewee 2	Facebook Messenger	Informational exchanges with: ●Subordinates: contracts' copies; car registration document.	●Recognition of new friends; sharing photos; communication about an event.
Interviewee 3	Facebook Messenger Instagram	●Informational use: fashion, competitors offers, customer feedback.	●News search; discussion; sharing photos.
Interviewee 4	Facebook	●Informational use: scanned documents (ID card, affiliation); model documents: works certificate, illness certificate.	●Discussions with friends; news search.
Interviewee 5 Interviewee 6 Interviewee 7 Interviewee 8	Facebook Messenger LinkedIn	Informational exchanges with: ●Subordinates planning discussions; tracking application blocking. ●Candidates (CV, motivation letter).	●News search; organizing outings; consulting job offers.
Interviewee 9	Facebook Messenger	Informational exchanges with: ●Suppliers: discussing prices; discounts; order tracking; materials' availability. ●Colleagues: discussing construction sites progress.	●Discussions with friends; news search.
Interviewee 10 Interviewee 11 Interviewee 12 Interviewee 13	Facebook Messenger	Informational exchanges with: ●Subordinates: ask permission; confirm sales prices; wonder about status stock. ●Colleagues: ask for reservation hotel. ●Customers: exchange an account statement or a discharge.	●News search; following sports activities; sharing photos (travel).
Interviewee 14 Interviewee 15	Facebook Messenger LinkedIn	Informational exchanges with: ●Colleagues: instructions; information about new laws and regulations. ●Assistants: invoice; withholding tax; pointing status. ●Candidates: job offers (LinkedIn)	●Discussions with friends; news search; following associative activities; pprogramming outings; publishing photos.

Effects of SNS Usage on individual Performance at Work

Daily SNS usage by interviewees during their working hours is presented in the table below. Interviewees characterized by low SNS usage are presented at first followed by those with average usage. Interviewees who have shown an intensive usage are finally listed. The first column of the table presents the interviewees. The second gives an assessment level of usage. The third column presents the statement dealing with the impact of SNS usage on individual job performance. An assessment of this impact is mentioned in the fourth column.[2]

Interviewees appreciate differently the impact of SNS usage on their individual performance at work. The distribution of respondents according to their level of use reveals three types of behavior.

The first group includes interviewee (4). He makes a low usage of SNS which does not influence his work performance. He believes that this kind of tools keeps losing the concentration of its users

Table 4. Effects of SNS usage on individual job performance

Interviewees	Level of Usage	Main Statements	Evaluation
Accountant (4)	Low usage	« For me, Facebook has no impact on my efficiency or my work pace ».	No impact
Branch Manager (1)	Average usage	« By connecting regularly on Facebook, I think that I'm up-to-date with what happens in other competing agencies ».	Positive impact
Human Resources Director (9)	Average usage	« A 10-minute beack on Facebook allows me to work 2 hours without interruption ».	Positive impact
Commercial director (10)	Average usage	« Through Messenger, several private discussions have been triggered with my clients by sending messages directly to settle disagreement in the privacy ».	Positive impact
Purchasing Director (11)	Average usage	« Facebook allows me (...) to be up to date in order to execute efficiently suppliers choice and to be more cost efficient ».	Positive impact
Purchasing assistant (12)	Average usage	« Messenger allows me to share valuable information (...), I gave my opinion about the solvency of one of my clients to the commercial assistant, to make him decide to sell him or not on credit ».	Positive impact
Cash Manager (13)	Average usage	« Although I use SNS secretly, these tools allow me to follow information published by my suppliers (...) in order to attend useful trainings and seminars related to my work ».	Positive impact
Accountant (14)	Average usage	« Messenger improves my individual performance in a quantitative and qualitative way ».	Positive impact
Audit Manager (15)	Average usage	« Facebook helped me to attend an interesting training, to solve problems, to ask for help ».	Positive impact
Project Manager (5)	Average usage	« SNS allowed me to choose my collaborators and work with the best skills ».	Positive impact
Developer (8)	Average usage	« LinkedIn enhances my creative abilities and improves my job performance ».	Positive impact
Engineer (6)	Intensive usage	« I spend a long time in discussion with my family on Messenger, I also look some sports videos on Facebook ».	Negative impact
Service Agent (7)	Intensive usage	« Sometimes Facebook distracts me from my mission, (...) I use Facebook during my work hours, to chat with my friends, program coffee or exchange jokes ».	Negative impact
Control Manager (2)	Intensive usage	« All the time, I want to use SNS to discuss about things which are not related to my work ».	Negative impact
Owner Manager (3)	Intensive usage	« When I Feel motivated by feedback and positive comments on my Facebook page, I strive to invent new features or improvements to my work (…). I follow my customers, their expectation, etc. ».	Positive impact

from the first five minutes. According to him, Facebook hinders intellectual and physical fulfillment like, visual fatigue, headaches. It affects the users' ability of evolving and learning due to the inequity between professional and private time. This current result is similar to the findings of Balasuriya and Jayalal (2015) and Cao et al. (2016), in their finding. These authors concluded that SNS doesn't affect worker performance.

The second group of interviewees is characterized by an average SNS usage. For these interviewees, this tools use seems to influence positively their individual performance. Employees in this group report using SNS in managing unpredictable situations to adapt easily. SNS make it possible to disseminate new offers before the others, analyze, transmit messages and respond effectively. According to respondents, Facebook led to a new way of working in line: make purchasing decisions, observe providers' pages, conduct online conversations with customers, answer questions; claim or receive compliments, develop a professional intelligence, etc.

The examination of respondents ' statements in this group shows that Messenger is an effective tool to establish free calls and conduct interactive discussions with colleagues. It leads to solve problems in time. Interviewees also believe that using LinkedIn has a positive effect on their individual work. This use seems to improve their knowledge to invest in new products and propose innovative solutions.

This result is identified in previous studies. Indeed, Hassan et al. (2011), Kamsan (2013), Charoen-sukmongkol (2014), Leftheriotis and Giannakos (2014) and Xi Zhang et al. (2015), indicate that SNS can improve collaboration and communication between colleagues, solve work problems and enhance learning process in service firms. These tools can help employees to build their professional networks and obtain work-related information and feedback (Zivnuska et al. 2019). In addition, kwahk and Park (2016) argued that social media allows different members to learn from each other's personal experiences through sharing knowledge to make right decisions and improve transactive memory.

Many studies focus on the relation between SNS usage and individual performance without highlight-ing the differentiated effect according to different levels of usage. The current results are similar to Cao et al. (2018), in their finding that the excessive usage of SNS could reduce work performance of 230 Chinese employees operating in various sectors (finance, industry, health, IT, etc.). For these authors, this result is due to information and communication overload and employees' stress feeling. Zivnuska et al. (2019) claimed that the excessive social media usage contributes to addictive, behaviors at the expense of other interesting activities at work. For these authors, excessive use of social media leads to wasting time and energy and impacts negatively employees' ability to perform well.

An exception is nevertheless advanced by the owner manager (3) who claims to improve his individual performance by making an intensive SNS usage. Since SNS are used as the main tools at work, they would have the same effects as other technologies and information systems. For Aldebert and Gueguen (2013), the intensive and innovative usage of these technologies by the manager, makes it possible to develop more efficient operating procedures and improve information management. Indeed, according to Ngongang (2014), by adopting this kind of technology, owner tries to exploit his skills and knowledge in favor of behaviors that go beyond the objectives of his work. He strives to manage relationships with customers and suppliers. He involves in all aspects of his business management and spends a lot of time exploiting his expertise.

The interviewees in the third group engage in intensive SNS usage. For this category, the use of SNS seems to have negative results on individual performance. Respondents who connect mostly on these tools does not finish their work on time.

Interviewees (2), (6) and (7) believe that their usage of SNS at work decreases their individual perfor-mance. For them, since these tools allow them to distract themselves and get out from the work context, they negatively influence their recuperation pace after each break. Similarly, Chen et al. (2008), Ferreira and Plessis (2009), and Wickramasinghe and Nisaf (2012) stated that SNS are often used during office work hours for personal purposes. For example, to broadcast photos and online music or videos. Hence, this deviant usage may distract employees from their work and may result to reduce their individual performance.

An exception is nevertheless identified by the owner manager (3). It is a case described as atypical. Although he made an intensive usage of SNS, his performance is positive. Miles and Huberman (2003, p.486) recommend to analyze in depth what is present in this case and missing or different in other standard cases. The owner manager (3) claims that his use of SNS is conducted all day long. These tools offer him a free opportunity to manage his company Facebook page, publish models and ask questions to his customers (share reviews and comments). His speech analysis shows that Facebook allows him to strengthen his company presence on social networks websites and look at marketing programs at lower cost. It seems that the effect of SNS usage on work performance depends on the job position occupied. As an owner, the use of this manager seems to be purely devoted to work and not be bothered with counter-produced effects.

SOLUTIONS AND RECOMMENDATIONS

In exploring the relationship between SNS usages and IP, organizational policy concept emerges from the empirical analysis. It involves either restrictions or permissions from the top management to the use of SNS by employees.

According to interviewees statements analysis, the permission to SNS usage seems to improve the IP of respondents (1); (3); (9) (14) and (15). Branch Manager (1) states that "... There is no restriction regarding to this usage. Besides, there was no follow-up, no condition, nothing, everything is allowed! I know very well that my subordinates are responsible ...". However, the accountant (4) permitted SNS usage, but in a controllable manner. The interviewee said that "... During the weekends, I consult the computers of my employees to look at the histories and see their SNS usage duration...". Finally, the interviewees (2); (4); (5); (6); (7); (8); (10); (11); (12) and (13) register some restrictions on the SNS usage during working time. Administration officers have blocked their access to Facebook, Messenger, Instagram, LinkedIn and Twitter.

Our analysis shows that some employees use their personal devices such as smartphones to bypass firewalls, as a reaction to restrictions. From their smartphones, employees exchange useful information to their work, because they are aware of the usefulness of their usage and its positive contribution to their performance at work.

Our findings show that different levels of SNS usage induce different effects on individual performance. In order to limit negative effects of usage on IP and promote positive ones, regulating usage level could be one mean of action for managers. It could improve the collective intelligence of connected members to develop sharing knowledge, ideas, opinions, questions, etc. The management of the SNS usage time could reduce the problems of users' loss of concentration or fatigue and the excessive use, which often outweighs professional responsibilities. Managers should regulate the way these tools should be used by specifying concerned functions, time of use, etc.

This research could guide managers in their decisions relating to the usage of these tools during working hours. It reveals indications in favor of a formal expression of the rights and duties relating to the use of SNS at work. The development of a charter governing this usage by internal collaborators could therefore be considered. As Moqbel et al. (2013) note, it is recommended that managers approach the possibility of adding the use of SNS to their practices to enhance employees IP.

This research results could help managers to understand and better master SNS usage and effects. According to Azouz (2014), managers do not really know how reacting to SNS use by their employees.

FUTURE RESEARCH DIRECTIONS

This work can serve as a basis for continuing future research studying the relationship between SNS use and employee work performance. Our results remain contextual and cant' be generalized. Thus, future research can be carried out using a quantitative method through a questionnaire.

This research investigates the direct impact of the SNS usage on job work performance. Other future research could study this relationship indirectly through the intermediation of other variables such as social capital, job satisfaction, organizational commitment (Wickramasingh & Nisaf, 2012; Moqbel et al., 2013; Ali- Hassan et al., 2015).

CONCLUSION

The main objective of this chapter is to highlight the effects of SNS usage on individual performance at work. It tries to identify the different usage of these networks by 15 Tunisian interviewees. Interviewees' statements were classified in a decreasing order according to levels of SNS usage. This classification allowed to define three levels of usage usage related to three groups. The first group, which is characterized by low usage, felt that SNS tools did not influence IP at work. The second group is described by an average use of SNS which positively influences IP. Respondents in the third group report heavy use of SNS which seems to have negative effect on IP.

Beyond these results, some contributions and research limitations can be advanced. Concerning the theoretical contributions, firstly, this research aims at clarifying the term of SNS and individual job performance to examine the ambiguities related to these concepts. It also tries to expose the debates that they generate. In addition, the literature has provided little research studying the effects of SNS on work performance, this chapter contributes to shed light on the question, thus enriching SNS research. It discusses the results according to the intensity of the usage.

This research shows that different levels of SNS usage induce different effects on individual performance. Moderated usage seems to be favorable for exchange behaviors, communication, executed tasks and consequently for the individual performance.

Finally, in practice, our results could guide managers in their decisions regardless SNS usage in workplace. Thus, this chapter sensitizes leaders on the importance of measuring degree of SNS usage (excessive or moderate) in order to introduce adequate control practices.

The main limitation of this research is related to the small number of interviewees. It would be interesting to expand the sample to study this phenomenon. This work can be used as a basis to study the organizational policy governing SNS usage in terms of total or partial authorization.

REFERENCES

Abdelaziz, H., & Trabelsi, H. (2009). *Les effets d'une libéralisation dans les secteurs des services en Tunisie*. Institut Tunisien de la Compétitivité et des Études Quantitatives.

Aguenza, B. B., & Som, A. P. M. (2012). A Conceptual Analysis of Social Networking and its Impact on Employee Productivity. *IOSR Journal of Business and Management, 1*(2), 48–52. doi:10.9790/487X-0124852

Ashraf, N., & Javed, T. (2014). Impact of social networking on employee performance. *Business Management and Strategy, 5*(2), 139–150. doi:10.5296/bms.v5i2.5978

Bachelet, C. (2004). *Usages des TIC dans les organisations, une notion à revisiter?* In 9e Colloque de l'AIM.

Badillo, P. Y., & Pélissier, N. (2015). Usages et usagers de l'information numérique. Renouvellement des problématiques et nouveaux enjeux pour les SIC. *Revue française des sciences de l'information et de la communication*, (6).

Balasuriya, U. C., & Jayalal, S. (2015, August). *Impact of social network usage on the job performance of IT professionals in Sri Lanka*. In *2015 Fifteenth International Conference on Advances in ICT for Emerging Regions (ICTer)* (pp. 214-219). IEEE. 10.1109/ICTER.2015.7377691

Basit, A., & Hassan, Z. (2018). The Impact of Social Media Usage on Employee and Organization Performance: A Study on Social Media Tools Used by an IT Multinational in Malaysia. *Journal of Marketing and Consumer Behaviour in Emerging Markets, 1*(7), 48–65.

Beer, D. D. (2008). Social network (ing) sites… revisiting the story so far: A response to danah boyd & Nicole Ellison. *Journal of Computer-Mediated Communication, 13*(2), 516–529. doi:10.1111/j.1083-6101.2008.00408.x

Benbasat, I., & Zmud, R. W. (1999). Empirical research in information systems: The practice of relevance. *Management Information Systems Quarterly, 23*(1), 3–16. doi:10.2307/249403

Bennett, J., Owers, M., Pitt, M., & Tucker, M. (2010). *Workplace impact of social networking*. Property Management. doi:10.1108/02637471011051282

Borman, W. C., & Motowidlo, S. J. (1997). Task performance and contextual performance: The meaning for personnel selection research. *Human Performance, 10*(2), 99–109. doi:10.120715327043hup1002_3

Boyd, D. M., & Ellison, N. B. (2007). Social network sites: Definition, history, and scholarship. *Journal of Computer-Mediated Communication, 13*(1), 210–230. doi:10.1111/j.1083-6101.2007.00393.x

Brooks, S., & Califf, C. (2017). Social media-induced technostress: Its impact on the job performance of it professionals and the moderating role of job characteristics. *Computer Networks, 114*, 143–153. doi:10.1016/j.comnet.2016.08.020

Campbell, J. P. (1990). M*odeling the performance prediction problem in industrial and organizational psychology*. Academic Press.

Campbell, J. P., Gasser, M. B., & Oswald, F. L. (1996). The substantive nature of job performance variability. *Individual Differences and Behavior in Organizations, 258*, 299.

Cao, X., Wang, P., Chaudhry, S., Li, L., Guo, X., Vogel, D., & Zhang, X. (2016). Exploring the influence of social media on employee work performance. *Internet Research, 26*(2), 529–545. doi:10.1108/IntR-11-2014-0299

Cao, X., Yu, L., Liu, Z., & Wang, J. (2018). Excessive social media use at work. *Information Technology & People*.

Cetinkaya, A. S., & Rashid, M. (2018). *The Effect of Social Media on Employees' Job Performance: The mediating Role of Organizational Structure*. Academic Press.

Charbonnier, A., Silva, C. A., & Roussel, P. (2007). *Vers une mesure de la performance contextuelle au travail de l'individu: étude exploratoire*. XVIIIème congrès de l'AGRH.

Charbonnier-Voirin, A., & Roussel, P. (2012). Adaptive performance: A new scale to measure individual performance in organizations. *Canadian Journal of Administrative Sciences/Revue Canadienne des Sciences de l'Administration, 29*(3), 280-293.

Charles-Pauvers, B., Comeiras, N., Peyrat-Guillard, D., & Roussel, P. (2006). *Les déterminants psychologiques de la performance au travail*. Un bilan des connaissances et proposition de voies de recherche.

Charoensukmongkol, P. (2014). Effects of support and job demands on social media use and work outcomes. *Computers in Human Behavior, 36*, 340–349. doi:10.1016/j.chb.2014.03.061

Chen, I. Y. (2008). A social network-based system for supporting interactive collaboration in knowledge sharing over peer-to-peer network. *International Journal of Human-Computer Studies, 66*(1), 36–50. doi:10.1016/j.ijhcs.2007.08.005

Chevrin, V. (2006). *L'interaction Usagers/Services, multimodale et multicanale: une première proposition appliquée au domaine du e-Commerce* (Doctoral dissertation). Lille 1.

Chou, H. T. G., Hammond, R. J., & Johnson, R. (2013). How Facebook might reveal users' attitudes toward work and relationships with coworkers. *Cyberpsychology, Behavior, and Social Networking, 16*(2), 136–139. doi:10.1089/cyber.2012.0321 PMID:23276260

Cigref. (2004). MUSTIC - Métiers et usages des TIC. *La recherche au Cigref, 1*, 17-35.

Coëffé. (2019). *Le média des professionnels du digital*. https://www.blogdumoderateur.com/chiffres-facebook/

Corre, M. (2011). *Les réseaux sociaux dans une stratégie de communication d'une grande entreprise*. Academic Press.

Demerouti, E., Bakker, A. B., & Leiter, M. (2014). Burnout and job performance: The moderating role of selection, optimization, and compensation strategies. *Journal of Occupational Health Psychology, 19*(1), 96–107. doi:10.1037/a0035062 PMID:24447224

Dennis, A. R., & Kinney, S. T. (1998). Testing media richness theory in the new media: The effects of cues, feedback, and task equivocality. *Information Systems Research, 9*(3), 256–274. doi:10.1287/isre.9.3.256

Edosomwan, S., Prakasan, S. K., Kouame, D., Watson, J., & Seymour, T. (2011). The history of social media and its impact on business. *The Journal of Applied Management and Entrepreneurship, 16*(3), 79–91.

Ferreira, A., & Du Plessis, T. (2009). Effect of online social networking on employee productivity. *South African Journal of Information Management, 11*(1), 1–11. doi:10.4102ajim.v11i1.397

Fourati Ennouri, M. (2016). Usages de la banque en ligne et qualité des échanges Entreprises–Banques. In AIMS, XXVe Conférence Internationale de Management Stratégique.

Girard, A., & Fallery, B. (2009). *Réseaux Sociaux Numériques: revue de littérature et perspectives de recherche*. Université Montpellier.

Hassan, H., Nevo, D., & Wade, M. (2015). Linking dimensions of social media use to job performance: The role of social capital. *The Journal of Strategic Information Systems, 24*(2), 65–89. doi:10.1016/j.jsis.2015.03.001

Heidemann, J., Klier, M., & Probst, F. (2012). Online social networks: A survey of a global phenomenon. *Computer Networks, 56*(18), 3866–3878. doi:10.1016/j.comnet.2012.08.009

IACE. (2016). *La Tunisie en transformation: l'impératif Digital*. les journées de l'entreprise.

Ifinedo, P. (2016). Applying uses and gratifications theory and social influence processes to understand students' pervasive adoption of social networking sites: Perspectives from the Americas. *International Journal of Information Management, 36*(2), 192–206. doi:10.1016/j.ijinfomgt.2015.11.007

Impelman, K. (2007). *How does personality relate to contextual performance, turnover, and customer service?* University of North Texas.

Jahn, B., & Kunz, W. (2012). How to transform consumers into fans of your brand. *Journal of Service Management, 23*(3), 344–361. doi:10.1108/09564231211248444

Jalil, S. W., Achan, P., Mojolou, D. N., & Rozaimie, A. (2015). Individual characteristics and job performance: Generation Y at SMEs in Malaysia. *Procedia: Social and Behavioral Sciences, 170*, 137–145. doi:10.1016/j.sbspro.2015.01.023

Jouët, J. (1993). Pratiques de communication et figures de la médiation. Réseaux. *Communication-Technologie-Société, 11*(60), 99–120.

Kane, O. (2013). *Les usages des TIC entre analyse sociotechnique et théories de l'appropriation: état de la littérature*. Les enjeux de la communication. Libreville: Presses universitaires du Gabon, 23-42.

Karoui, M., Dudezert, A., & Leidner, D. E. (2015). Strategies and symbolism in the adoption of organizational social networking systems. *The Journal of Strategic Information Systems, 24*(1), 15–32. doi:10.1016/j.jsis.2014.11.003

Kishokumar, R. (2016). Influence of social networking in the work place on individual job performance: Special reference to the financial sector in Batticaloa District. *International Journal of Engineering Research and General Science, 4*(6), 22–34.

Kluemper, D. H., & Rosen, P. A. (2009). Future employment selection methods: Evaluating social networking web sites. *Journal of Managerial Psychology*, *24*(6), 567–580. doi:10.1108/02683940910974134

Koch, O. (2015). Les médias dans les «transitions démocratiques»: état des lieux et prospective. *Questions de communication*, (28), 211-229.

Köffer, S., Ortbach, K. C., & Niehaves, B. (2014). Exploring the relationship between IT consumerization and job performance: A theoretical framework for future research. *Communications of the Association for Information Systems*, *35*(1), 14. doi:10.17705/1CAIS.03514

Koopmans, L., Bernaards, C. M., Hildebrandt, V. H., Schaufeli, W. B., de Vet Henrica, C. W., & van der Beek, A. J. (2011). Conceptual frameworks of individual work performance: A systematic review. *Journal of Occupational and Environmental Medicine*, *53*(8), 856–866. doi:10.1097/JOM.0b013e318226a763 PMID:21775896

Kwahk, K. Y., & Park, D. H. (2016). The effects of network sharing on knowledge-sharing activities and job performance in enterprise social media environments. *Computers in Human Behavior*, *55*, 826–839. doi:10.1016/j.chb.2015.09.044

Leftheriotis, I., & Giannakos, M. N. (2014). Using social media for work: Losing your time or improving your work? *Computers in Human Behavior*, *31*, 134–142. doi:10.1016/j.chb.2013.10.016

Leidner, D., Koch, H., & Gonzalez, E. (2010). Assimilating Generation Y IT New Hires into USAA's Workforce: The Role of an Enterprise 2.0 System. *MIS Quarterly Executive*, *9*(4).

Lorenzo-Romero, C., Constantinides, E., & Alarcón-del-Amo, M.-C. (2011). Consumer adoption of social networking sites: Implications for theory and practice. *Journal of Research in Interactive Marketing*, *5*(5), 170–188. doi:10.1108/17505931111187794

Mallouli, M., Hachicha, Z. S., & Chaabouni, J. (2016). *Réseaux Sociaux Numériques: état de l'art*. AIM.

Mallouli, M., Hachicha, Z. S., & Chaabouni, J. (n.d.). Management Research on Social Networking Sites: State of the Art and Further Avenues of Research. EJISE, 20(2), 128–141.

Massit-Folléa, F. (2002). Usages des Technologies de l'Information et de la Communication: acquis et perspectives de la recherche. *Le Français dans le monde*, 8-14.

Miles, M. B., & Huberman, A. M. (2003). *Analyse des données qualitatives*. De Boeck Supérieur.

Millerand, F. (2008). *Usages des NTIC: Les approches de la diffusion, de l'innovation et de l'appropriation* (1ère partie). *Commposite*, *2*(1), 1–19.

Moqbel, M., Nevo, S., & Kock, N. (2013). Organizational members' use of social networking sites and job performance. *Information Technology & People*, *26*(3), 240–264. doi:10.1108/ITP-10-2012-0110

Mostafa, M. M. (2013). More than words: Social networks' text mining for consumer brand sentiments. *Expert Systems with Applications*, *40*(10), 4241–4251. doi:10.1016/j.eswa.2013.01.019

Motowidlo, S. J., & Van Scotter, J. R. (1994). Evidence that task performance should be distinguished from contextual performance. *The Journal of Applied Psychology*, *79*(4), 475–480. doi:10.1037/0021-9010.79.4.475

Munene, A. G., & Nyaribo, Y. M. (2013). Effect of social media pertication in the workplace on employee productivity. *International Journal of Advances in Management and Economics*, *2*(2), 141–150.

Nazir, Iqbal, & Kanwal, Nasir & Abid. (2016). Effect of Social Media on Employee's Performance: A Study, in Corporate Sector of Pakistan. *International Review of Basic and Applied Sciences*, *4*(9).

Nkwe, N., & Cohen, J. (2017). *Impact* Of Social Network Sites On Psychological And Behavioural Outcomes In The Work-Place: A Systematic Literature Review. *Association for Information Systems AIS Electronic Library (AISeL)*, 6-10.

North, M. (2010). An evaluation of employees' attitudes toward social networking in the workplace. *Issues in Information Systems*, *11*(1), 192–197.

Ones, D. S., Viswesvaran, C., & Schmidt, F. L. (1993). Comprehensive meta-analysis of integrity test validities: Findings and implications for personnel selection and theories of job performance. *The Journal of Applied Psychology*, *78*(4), 679–703. doi:10.1037/0021-9010.78.4.679

Ouni, A. (2008). *L'élaboration de modèles et d'outils pour l'analyse et la conception des usages des outils de travail collaboratif en entreprise* (Doctoral dissertation).

Paillé, P., & Mucchielli, A. (2016). L'analyse qualitative en sciences humaines et sociales (4th ed.). Armand Colin.

Park, H., & Cho, H. (2012). Social network online communities: Information sources for apparel shopping. *Journal of Consumer Marketing*, *29*(6), 400–411. doi:10.1108/07363761211259214

Proulx, S. (2001). Usages des technologies d'information et de communication: reconsidérer le champ d'étude. *Émergences et continuité dans les recherches en information et communication*, 10-13.

Rispal, M. H. (2002). *La méthode des cas*. De Boeck Supérieur. doi:10.3917/dbu.hlady.2002.01

Roudaut, K., & Jullien, N. (2017). Les usages des outils de réseau social par des salariés: Des registres privés et professionnels individualisés. Terminal. *Technologie de l'information, culture & société*, (120).

Schmidt, F. L., & Hunter, J. (2004). General mental ability in the world of work: Occupational attainment and job performance. *Journal of Personality and Social Psychology*, *86*(1), 162–173. doi:10.1037/0022-3514.86.1.162 PMID:14717634

Schneider, F., Feldmann, A., Krishnamurthy, B., & Willinger, W. (2009, November). Understanding online social network usage from *a* network perspective. In *Proceedings of the 9th ACM SIGCOMM conference on Internet measurement* (pp. 35-48). 10.1145/1644893.1644899

Shami, N. S., Nichols, J., & Chen, J. (2014). Social media participation and performance at work: a longitudinal study. In Proceedings of the SIGCHI conference on human factors in computing systems (pp. 115-118). doi:10.1145/2556288.2557417

Sonnentag, S., & Frese, M. (2002). Performance concepts and performance theory. *Psychological Management of Individual Performance*, *23*(1), 3-25.

Sophia Van Zyl, A. S. (2009). The impact of Social Networking 2.0 on organisations. *The Electronic Library*, *27*(6), 906–918. doi:10.1108/02640470911004020

Statista. (2019). *Médias sociaux et contenu généré par les utilisateurs.* https://fr.statista.com/statistiques/570930/reseaux-sociaux-mondiaux-classes-par-nombre-d-utilisateurs/

Stenger, T., & Coutant, A. (2010). Les réseaux sociaux numériques: des discours de promotion à la déðnition d'un objet et d'une méthodologie de recherche. *HERMES-Journal of Language and Communication in Business,* (44), 209-228.

Triki, A. (2010). *Epistémologie & méthodologie de la recherche: théories et applications en marketing et en gestion.* Academic Press.

Van Dyne, L., Koh, C., Ng, K. Y., Templer, K. J., Tay, C., & Chandrasekar, N. A. (2007). Cultural intelligence: Its measurement and effects on cultural judgment and decision making, cultural adaptation and task performance. *Management and Organization Review, 3*(3), 335–371. doi:10.1111/j.1740-8784.2007.00082.x

Wacheux, F. (1996). Méthodes qualitatives et recherche en gestion. *Economica.*

Wickramasinghe, V., & Nisaf, M. S. M. (2013). Organizational policy as a moderator between online social networking and job performance. *Vine, 43*(2), 161–184. doi:10.1108/03055721311329945

Yin, R. K. (1994). *Case study research Design and methods* (2nd ed.). Sage Publications.

Zhang, X., Gao, Y., Chen, H., Sun, Y., & de Pablos, P. O. (2015). Enhancing Creativity or Wasting Time?: The Mediating Role of Adaptability on Social Media-Job Performance Relationship. In PACIS (p. 230). Academic Press.

Zhang, Y., & Leung, L. (2015). A review of social networking service (SNS) research in communication journals from 2006 to 2011. *New Media & Society, 17*(7), 1007–1024. doi:10.1177/1461444813520477

Zivnuska, S., Carlson, J. R., Carlson, D. S., Harris, R. B., & Harris, K. J. (2019). Social media addiction and social media reactions: The implications for job performance. *The Journal of Social Psychology, 159*(6), 746–760. doi:10.1080/00224545.2019.1578725 PMID:30821647

ADDITIONAL READING

Boyd, D. M., & Ellison, N. B. (2007). Social network sites: Definition, history, and scholarship. *Journal of Computer-Mediated Communication, 13*(1), 210–230. doi:10.1111/j.1083-6101.2007.00393.x

Brooks, S., & Califf, C. (2017). Social media-induced technostress: Its impact on the job performance of it professionals and the moderating role of job characteristics. *Computer Networks, 114,* 143–153. doi:10.1016/j.comnet.2016.08.020

Cao, X., Wang, P., Chaudhry, S., Li, L., Guo, X., Vogel, D., & Zhang, X. (2016). Exploring the influence of social media on employee work performance. *Internet Research, 26*(2), 529–545. doi:10.1108/IntR-11-2014-0299

Cao, X., Yu, L., Liu, Z., & Wang, J. (2018). Excessive social media use at work. *Information Technology & People.*

Cetinkaya, A. S., & Rashid, M. (2018). *The Effect of Social Media on Employees' Job Performance: The mediating Role of Organizational Structure.*

Leftheriotis, I., & Giannakos, M. N. (2014). Using social media for work: Losing your time or improving your work? *Computers in Human Behavior, 31*, 134–142. doi:10.1016/j.chb.2013.10.016

Mallouli, M., Hachicha, Z. S., & Chaabouni, J. (2016). *Réseaux Sociaux Numériques: état de l'art.* AIM, Paris. Mallouli, M., Hachicha, Z. S., & Chaabouni, J. Management Research on Social Networking Sites: State of the Art and Further Avenues of Research. *EJISE, 20*(2), 128–141.

Wickramasinghe, V., & Nisaf, M. S. M. (2013). Organizational policy as a moderator between online social networking and job performance. *Vine, 43*(2), 161–184. doi:10.1108/03055721311329945

KEY TERMS AND DEFINITIONS

Average Usage: SNS usage of 30 minutes to two hours.
Individual Job Performance: Employee's ability to achieve the objectives attached to his work.
Intensive Usage: SNS usage exceeds 2 hours.
Low Usage: SNS usage less than 30 minutes.
Negative Impact: Perceived negative impact of the SNS usage during working hours.
Positive Impact: Perceived positive impact of the SNS usage during working hours.
SNS Usage: Corresponds to the use of social networking platforms by employees at work.
Social Networking Sites: A special type of social media that allow the sharing of content between users with common interests.

ENDNOTES

[1]   In this table, the authors describe the identified usage in the workplace. For the cases studied, two types of SNS usage were noted: personal usage of SNS or professional usage of SNS.

[2]   The distribution of interviewees in three groups according to the use duration is inspired from the literature (Hanna et al., 2017). In our case, a low usage refers to less than 30 minutes usage, an average usage is relative to an interval of 30 minutes to two hours, and an intensive usage exceeds 2 hours.

Chapter 4
Detecting Fake News on Social Media:
The Case of Turkey

Esra Bozkanat
Kırklareli Üniversitesi, Turkey

ABSTRACT

As Web 2.0 technologies have turned the Internet into an interactive medium, users dominate the field. With the spread of social media, the Internet has become much more user-oriented. In contrast to traditional media, social media's lack of control mechanisms makes the accuracy of spreading news questionable. This brings us to the significance of fact-checking platforms. This study investigates the antecedents of spreading false news in Turkey. The purpose of the study is to determine the features of fake news. For this purpose, teyit.org, the biggest fact-checking platform in Turkey, has been chosen for analysis. The current study shows fake news to be detectable based on four features: Propagation, User Type, Social Media Type, and Formatting. According to the logistic regression analysis, the study's model obtained 86.7% accuracy. The study demonstrates that Facebook increases the likelihood of news being fake compared to Twitter or Instagram. Emoji usage is also statistically significant in terms of increasing the probability of fake news. Unexpectedly, the impact of photos or videos was found statistically insignificant.

INTRODUCTION

Because Web 2.0 technologies turned the Internet into an interactive medium, users have since dominated the field. With the spread of social media, the Internet has become much more user-oriented. In contrast to traditional media, the lack of control mechanisms in social media makes us question the accuracy of spreading news.

According to a report from We Are Social (2019), Hootsuite (2020), and Digital (2019), the world currently has 3.484 billion active social media users all over. Given that the number of people, saying that all users have the same education level or the same media literacy level is completely unrealistic. Therefore, users are distinctly affected by the separate content they are exposed to. At times they can

DOI: 10.4018/978-1-7998-4718-2.ch004

question the reality of what they see or read, and other times they for some reason are likely to accept the information on social media without question.

The time spent by Internet users on social networking sites in one day is gradually increasing. While a user spent 90 minutes a day on social networks in 2012, this period increased to 144 minutes in 2019 (Statista, 2019a). This is quite a long time. Given the time people spend on social media, encountering fake content seems likely. While an ordinary social media user can be exposed to fake news at any time, some users are more disadvantaged. According to multi-participation research, older individuals are less successful than young people in distinguishing facts and opinions (FullFact, 2019).

Statista's (2018) report states, "As of March of 2018, around 52 percent of Americans felt that online news websites regularly report fake news stories in the United States. Another 34 percent of respondents stated believing online news websites to occasionally report fake news stories." In addition, a study showed that news with the fake flag had no effect on judgments about truth; flagging headlines as false did not influence users' beliefs. Users maintain their belief in news that aligns with their political opinions (Moravec, Minas, & Dennis, 2018). In Europe, people stated online social networks, video hosting sites, and podcasts to be the most unreliable sources of news and information (Statista, 2018). In Turkey, 53% of people stated users to be able to distinguish between fact and fiction and to not support a social media ban. 66% of people rely on social media companies to ensure the authenticity of shared content in times of crisis (Statista, 2019b). This brings us to the significance of fact-checking mechanisms.

When considering these reasons, fact-checking services in the online environment become vital for millions of people. Their services are expanding and increasing day by day. The Reporters' Lab (2020) at Duke University holds a database of fact-checking services. According to that database, 316 fact-checking platforms exist all around the world. Of these, 217 are currently active and 89 are inactive. There are many well-known fact-checking services in the world. For instance, Africa check is a platform that verifies the news from Kenya, Nigeria, South Africa, and Senegal, as well as every other country. Chequeado is a Spanish fact-checking service. The site does not have an English version. It confirms news regarding economics, health, justice, education, and more. Full Fact is the UK's independent fact-checking service. Teyit.org is Turkey's biggest fact-checking platform. All four sites adjust their sites accordingly when a global issue occurs. For instance, in the days when this research was written, fake news about the COVID-19 epidemic (Coronavirus) had started to spread on social media, and these four platforms added a confirmation section about coronavirus to their website.

The reason the number of Fact-checking services is so high is that real and fake news are indistinguishable in the post-truth era. This research provides suggestions for eliminating this uncertainty by identifying the features of fake news. The study's purpose is to determine the features of fake news in Turkey. For this purpose, the website Teyit.org, a Turkish fact-checking platform, has been chosen for statistical analysis. Previous studies have focused on only one or two features of fake news, such as likes and users (Tacchini, Ballarin, Vedova, Moret, & Alfaro, 2017), inter-user engagement (Ruchansky, Seo, & Csi, 2017), stance classification (Thorne, Chen, Myrianthous, Pu, Wang, & Vlachos, 2017), linguistics (Shu, Sliva, Wang, Tang, & Liu, 2017), and visual features (Yang, Zheng, Zhang, Cui, Li & Yu, 2018). This study differs from previous studies as it combines all the features of fake news. Therefore, the current study differs from other studies in the literature in terms of revealing different antecedents of fake news and fills a gap by showing how fake news can be identified.

This study makes a fivefold contribution. Thus, the paper is organized as follows: The first section summarizes the brief history of fake news in mainstream media and on social media respectively. Then it presents some explanations on the rise of fact-checking services. The second part shows the landscape of fake news propagation and the results from previous studies on fake news detection. The third section reveals the research method, the fourth section is presenting the study's results and the fifth section is the conclusion.

BACKGROUND: A BRIEF HISTORY OF FAKE NEWS BEFORE THE INTERNET

Fake news is defined to be news that is deliberately wrong and could misguide readers (Allcott & Gentzknow, 2017, p. 213). Although fake news is considered to come up with digital communication, rumor and false stories have probably been around among people since ancient times through word of mouth. In times before the pre-printing press, information was usually limited to privileged groups. Thus, controlling information was much easier. However, the invention of the printing press initiated a post-printing press era in which literate people had the opportunity to manipulate information. Printed knowledge became accessible in various formats. Therefore, dispersing information became easier. The first printed fake news samples belong to Edgar Allan Poe. He wrote a hoax newspaper in 1844 (Burkhardt, 2017, pp.5–6) with many stories in the newspaper that later turned out to be fake news (Poe, 1844). Then, the mass-media era emerged. The most popular mass media of the period was the radio and newspapers. Orson Welles (1938) had a broadcast called *Orson Welles's War of the Worlds*. That broadcast caused public panic and showed that people could easily become injured by fake news even without attempting to cheat the public. Fake news was applied by Edward Bernays (1930s). He promoted smoking as a sign of independence among women (John & Opdycke, 2011) and also published fake news in newspapers telling that smoking is healthy for throats (Brandt, 2012).

Fake news is hardly new, and the historical perspective has been elucidative (Gorbach, 2018). The International Center for Journalists (IJFJ, 2018, pp. 3–4) prepared the ecology for clarifying fake news. According to the report, the use of fake news in events that have deeply affected world history can be summarized as follows: from 1914-1918, propaganda played an essential role in World War I's "Your country needs YOU" campaign); in 1917 the Russian Revolution used catchy slogans and punchy colors; in 1933 Joseph Goebbels helped establish the Reich's Ministry of Public Enlightenment and Propaganda; in 1938 Orson Welles had his War of the Worlds radio drama; from 1939-1945, World War II used Nazi Propaganda and Holocaust denial; from 1955-1975, the US propaganda program used for the Vietnam War; in 1965 came the 30th of September Movement in Indonesia with Suharto's forces using anti-communist propaganda; from 1947-1991 was the Cold War and international broadcasting; from 1972-1990s was South Africa's propaganda war; 1983 saw an April Fools interview where Boskin had fake story about a jester who became king; in 1996, and the Daily Show began airing in the US, a satire and self-described "fake news" TV program. The New York Times covered weapons of mass destruction in its papers in 2002 and then apologized for these reports after the Iraq War started. Finally, the Internet era has come, and fake news has reached a new level as it allows user-generated content to flow.

Fake News in the User-Generated Content (UGC) Era

Web 2.0 technology led to a permanent revolution with the inclusion of user interactions. Users are no longer simply content consumers; they are also producers. This feature of Web 2.0 has empowered users. In a way, they are now the gatekeepers of information and in charge of deciding what is going to be on the Internet as well as at the same time what they are going to consume. However, assuming all users to be well-intended would be an unrealistic basis.

One recent study says, "User-Generated Content (UGC) on social media platforms suffers from a lack of professional gatekeepers to monitor this content" (Afify, Eldin, Khedr, & Alsheref, 2019, p.1). According to the study, most online users fall into the trap of being misdirected by the rapid spread of misinformed news. Users accept the information coming from fake news without verifying it, which prevents them from making right decisions about their social lives and social policies (Afify et al., 2019). As understood from that study, users are vulnerable in the face of fake-news flow, which at the same time causes them to be vulnerable because fake news deliberately produces misleading information.

In the Internet era, fake news has been defined as "fabricated information that mimics news media content in form but not in organizational content or intent" (Lazer, Benkler, Berinsky, Greenhill, Öeczer & Zittrain, 2018, p. 1095).

One of the oldest fake news sites is the 1998 online edition of Onions, a USA-based news satire. Their stories had been taken as fact for a long time. Between 2003-2011 during the Iraq War, the declaration in the news that biological weapons were being produced was never independently verified. The propaganda tactics of a former Iraqi diplomat, Muhammed Saeed al-Sahhaf, were so colorful that he became called "Comical Ali". In 2013, Australian media outlets published fake press releases (International Center for Journalists, 2018, pp. 6–7).

Perhaps the most popular online fake news scandal is the 2016 US presidential election. Buzzfeed broke the story of fake news during the elections with the headline "Hyperpartisan Facebook Pages Are Publishing False and Misleading Information at an Alarming Rate." According to analyses from Buzzfeed (2016), "three big right-wing Facebook pages published false or misleading information 38% of the time during the period analyzed, and three large left-wing pages did so in nearly 20% of posts." Academic research conducted after the presidential election also found the results to have been influenced by fake news. A study examined the rate of exposure to fake news on Twitter and found that commitment to the news with a fake origin was highly intense (Grinberg, Joseph, Friedland, Swire-Thompson & Lazer, 2019). Another study suggested that Clinton and Trump's supporters had been affected in different ways from fake news. While Clinton supporters were influenced by the fake spread of traditional center and left-leaning news, the cause was reversed for Trump supporters who influenced the dynamics of the spread of fake news (Bovet & Makse, 2019). Given that Donald Trump won the election against Hillary Clinton, some sense of how fake news affects the elections can be understood. However, other studies have found fake news to have limited effects (Spenkuch & Toniatti, 2016). Even though conservative voters are more inclined to share fake news from fake domains, sharing itself is generally rare (Guess, Nagler, & Tucker, 2019; Wasserman & Madrid-Morales, 2019; Wasserman, 2020; Ahinkorah, Ameyaw, Hagan Junior, Seidu & Schack, 2020).

Following the U.S elections, scandals has become synonymous with 2017 Kenya's elections. Social media has become an indispensable tool in Kenya's politics, used by political leaders to spread false information in political campaigns (Mutahi & Kimari, 2017). Even though Lynch, Willis, and Cheeseman (2018) stated that no targeted advertisements were used on Facebook in the 2017 Kenyan presidential election, Cambridge Analytica has reported that it had a role not only in 2016 US election but also in 2013 and 2017 Kenya election (Karunian, Halme & Söderholm, 2019).

Nevertheless, in the age of post-truth, the reality is more intertwined with the reality in media than ever before. Moreover, social media's reality has replaced actuality. Thus, verifying the news and fact-checking services have become more crucial nowadays.

The Rise of Fact-Checking Services and Teyit.org

In this era defined as post-truth, fake news flows in an irrepressible way that cannot be controlled on social media. Social media has turned into a fake world that includes both those who generate fake news and everyone who clicks the share button without checking its accuracy. The fact that misinformation circulates more than real news from time to time has become a fact of the post-truth era within which we live. One activity that intends to stop this situation is fact-checking services.

Fact-checking services' nature is volunteer-based. Thus, it is not a government initiative or a non-profit organization's intervention. Namely, just as some users are willing to share fake news on social media, others are uncomfortable with this. Although classification is difficult in an environment with numerous fact-checking platforms, Brandtzaeg and Føolstad (2017) indicated that these services can be divided into three parts: general political/public statements, online rumors/hoaxes, and specific topics, controversies, and conflicts (narrowly scoped issues and events).

Probing the history of the relatively new fact-checking platforms' emergence is effective for being able to understand these services. According to a study conducted at Duke University, the number of fact-checking sites was 59 in 2014, with 44 being active. The study stated 27 of the sites to have started in 2012. In 2012 alone, 27 more sites were added to the platform, making a big leap. During that time, the largest fact-checking services were gathered in Europe (21 sites) and North America (15 sites; Reporters Lab, 2014). The number of sites continued to increase in the following years. From 2014-2018, figures tripled, reaching 149. That number was 64 in 2015 and 96 in 2016. 2017 showed a total of 114 services. Every year, the numbers grow apace (Reporters Lab, 2018). In 2019, this number reached 188, with the biggest spurt being in Asia (Reporters Lab, 2019). The actual worldwide total is probably higher than ever.

"The Rise of Fact-Checking Sites in Europe" Report (2016) included Turkey. According to that report, 34 political fact-checking services are active between Ireland and Turkey (Graves & Cherubini, 2016). One of these fact-checking platforms is Teyit.org. Turkey has more than one Internet fact-checking platform. Table 1 shows the popularities of all platforms in Turkey, and Teyit.org is the best-known fact-checking service.

Table 1. Fact-Checking platform's engagement numbers

Fact-Checking Platforms	Instagram Followers	Youtube Subscribers
Teyit.org	139K	3.3K
Malumatfurus.org	39.2K	-
Doğruluk Payı.com	33.5K	16.7K

Teyit.org was established in 2016 to detect suspicious news in mainstream media and social media, to conduct research based on evidence related to these, and to deliver verified information to social-media users. Teyit.org made a deal with Facebook in 2018 and became Turkey's third-party verification organization of Facebook news. Within the scope of this collaboration, Teyit.org marks unfounded news on Facebook and leads the analysis published on the site; Facebook attempts to limit the reach of fake news to users by reducing access (Teyit.org, 2020). Teyit.org is a member of the International Fact-Checking Network (IFCN), a signatory to the International Fact-Checking Network's Code of Principles, and a partner of First Draft News. In addition, "Teyit is financially supported by European Union and embassy funds granted to non-governmental organizations, public institutions, and private enterprises as well as by personal contributions, public reliefs and by generating income through collaborations with several institutions to sustain their broadcast, develop their human resources and to continue offering procurement service." (Teyit.org, 2020, p. About Us).

Teyit.org has a working principle. In addition to being one of Facebook's third-party confirmation partners, they also confirm news reported as notifications. They follow a methodology for verifying the news: *1) Scanning*: The work begins with scanning suspicious news. Here, the biggest helpers are the followers. Users who are unsure of the accuracy of the information they encounter on the Internet send an average of 32 unique suspicious information alerts per day to Teyit via Facebook, Twitter, Whatsapp, and e-mail. The site has a notification button where people can send a suspicious post and have its authenticity confirmed. *2) Selecting and prioritizing*: Verifiable claims are chosen according to their importance and prevalence (virality) in normal times, with additional criteria for urgency in times of crisis. The criteria involve prioritizing what is common among multiple news outlets and can be listed as follows. *a.) Virality*: being on the agenda of Internet users and having received a certain amount of shares. The criterion of vulnerability can differ according to the social media channel where the suspicious news is spread. *b.) Significance*: Individuals, communities, groups, systems, rights, or content that may affect democracy. *c.) Urgency*: the nature of emotional breakdowns, social anger, and fear that arise in times of crisis; it should be confirmed quickly even if it is not viral. *d.) Crisis moment*: Periods of raised emotions, traumatic events, polarization in society, increased hate speech related to events, election periods, systemic changes, and natural/human disasters). *3) Research and evidence*: At least two pieces of evidence are revealed that indicate the correctness or inaccuracy of the alleged investigation. These pieces of evidence can be verified and must have been obtained from the resources available to all users. The evidence must confirm one other with no discrepancies. *4) Writing and Publishing*: In any analysis published on Teyit.org, a certain structure is monitored as required by the public's right to information. Misleading techniques that aim to increase access by hiding information are avoided. The resources collected and analyses prepared under the internal verification processes are read and checked by at least two editors other than the author who wrote the analysis. This control has two stages. In the first stage, the evidence is checked for accuracy and consistency. In the second stage, the simplicity of the narration is examined; is the narration constructed in a way that minimizes any rebound effects? How is its spelling? Teyit.org also considers objections regarding news after the verification processes are completed and gives its interlocutors the right to respond (Teyit, 2020).

Teyit.org is an impact-oriented, non-profit social enterprise. According to their website, it has currently confirmed 1,389 news pieces, and this number increases incrementally every day (Teyit, 2020).

LITERATURE REVIEW

The Spread of Fake News

Today, misinformation propagation is inevitable on social media. As the speed of the spread of fake news in social media is explicit, academics are very eager to study the issue. Therefore, fake news, hoaxes, frauds, deceptions, and misleading news have been studied in the literature quite often over the past years. In fact, between 2003 and 2017, academic articles have defined fake news with the following words: news satire, news parody, fabrication, manipulation, advertising, and propaganda (Tandoc, Lim, & Ling, 2018).

An impressive study was conducted in 2018 on fake news propagation and examined 126,000 pieces of news tweeted by 3 million people between 2006 and 2017. Some of those tweets were true while others were fake. Users shared fake and real news 4.5 million times, and it spread to millions of people. In the study, the authors classified tweets as true or false using six fact-checking services named snopes. com, politifact.com, factcheck.org, truthorfiction.com, hoax-slayer.com, and urbanlegends. about.com. As a result, the study noticed fake news to spread much easier, faster, and deeper than real news. According to the study, fake news is more novel than real news, which means novel news is more likely to be shared (Vosoughi, Roy, & Aral, 2018). Thus, as fake news spreads, it causes more and more people to be misinformed. Other findings have supported the same propagation pattern. Fake news spreads differently from real news. Misinformation spreads within five hours of the first time being shared (Zhao, Sano, Levy, Takayasu & Havlin, 2018).

The reason why fake news spreads fast is that users are overly eager to share fake news. Therefore, knowing users' motivations in sharing fake news would be substantial. Reviewing the literature can explain many of the reasons for sharing motivations. For instance, a study showed online trust, self-disclosure, FoMO (Fear of Missing Out), and fatigue to positively relate to sharing fake news. However, online comparisons have a negative relationship with fake-news sharing (Talwar, Dhir, Kaur, Zafar, & Alrasheedy, 2019).

Habits for sharing fake news are especially hazardous when aimed at public health. A study stated the information circulating on common diseases in social media to be misleading and to have been shared 451,271 times from 2012 to 2017. Misleading health information on social media is a possible threat to public health (Waszak, Kasprzycka-Waszak, & Kubanek, 2018). Culture can be a reason for the accelerated distribution of fake news. A very current study stated culture to have the most significant impact on fake-news distribution. Additionally, age, gender, and education have an equal impact on fake news being accepted (Rampersad & Althiyabi, 2020).

Every fake post has a source post. This source could have been produced deliberately, but its spread is intentional. Users can spread a source post rapidly if they think it might be true, funny, interesting, or useful. Sometimes, users share fake news for no particular reason. One study (Wilson & Umar, 2019) concluded that despite awareness of fake news, wakefulness is limited in terms of the concern for verifying information before sharing. In particular, matters related to politics or crises undergo more fake news than any other issue. Given that someone intentionally produces the source post, their user characteristics can be expected to differ from certain angles. Yet, the study presented the opposite, demonstrating most source fake tweets to have been posted by ordinary users and to frequently include a link to non-trustworthy web sites. Aside from this, fake posts often undergo small modifications during their spread (Jang, Geng, Li, Xia, Huang, Kim & Tang, 2018).

Some societal moments may drive fake news distribution. One study conducted in Turkey (Çömlekçi, 2020) revealed that fact-checking platforms expand their services during elections. Given that one in four Americans visited a fake news web site just in one month in the 2016 presidential elections (Guess, Nyhan, & Reifler, 2018) and that political fake news spreads much faster than fake news about terrorism, natural disasters, science, urban legends, or financial information (Vosoughi et al, 2018), fact-checking services should reasonably take action during elections. Political party supporters produce fake news with various visual or montage videos to mislead opposing party voters. That forces fact-checking services to determine the news.

To prevent the spread of fake news, the number of conscious social media users should increase. Çömlekçi (2019) underlined that civil society initiatives established for verification are insufficient by themselves, stating individual awareness and increased levels of digital media literacy to be equally important. Research conducted by Africa Check, Chequeado, and Full Fact also suggested that real success comes with digital literacy (FullFact, 2019).

A user cannot be expected to distinguish between what is fake and true without being able to identify certain features of fake news.

Detecting Fake News

Identifying fake news requires very detailed analyses, and exploring the repetitive patterns in fake news requires more than human talent; often the human eye and mind are insufficient. When reviewing the current literature in detail as a method, the dominance of computer systems and data mining techniques has been noticed. (Zhang, Gupta, Kauten, Deokar, & Qin, 2019; Vishwakarma, Varshney, & Yadav, 2019). Bondielli and Marcelloni (2019) stated machine learning, deep learning, and computational fact-checking techniques to be different approaches for detecting fake news. Additionally, Granik & Mesyura (2017) underlined artificial intelligence (AI) as a convenient method for addressing fake news identification. Other than that, studies have presented the subject from different perspectives and provided a rich flow of information to the field. One of these studies claimed identifying fake news by writing style to be possible. Scholars have shown that linguistic features make distinguishing regular documents from deceptive ones feasible, with an accuracy of 96.6% (Afroz, Brennan, & Greenstadt, 2012). Other research with the same purpose presented the determinants for identifying fake news. The paper noticed source, headline, body text, images/videos, linguistics, and user features to be able to offer insights about the accuracy of news (Shu et al, 2017).

Can a meticulous user detect fake news by its headline? Fake-news producers use various patterns to attract user attention. Yet, uncovering the pattern is not as easy as one assumes. One study claimed the features of simple and carefully selected titles accurately identify fake news. The authors used logistic classifications with an accuracy of 99.4% (Aldwairi & Alwahedi, 2018).

Identifying the common features of fake-news generators can be used to analyze fake news. Although this is quite difficult, some findings have been obtained. Fake-news writers are prone to use more unnecessary conjunctions and articles (e.g., the, that, she, of) than honest users. Fake users generate more pronouns and adverbs, while real users use more nouns and adjectives (Ahmed, Traore, & Saad, 2017).

Fascinating and controversial entities are used more in fake news (Vicario, Quattrociocchi, Scala, & Zollo, 2019). If the content of news contains unrealistic information and mentions miraculous facts, the news is likely to be false. Predicting that fake news on difficult-to-verify topics spreads more easily is not difficult. Information that cannot be confirmed spreads rapidly in anticipation of verification. Discovering the qualities of misleading news is not limited to the above features. The current study offers a new and unique model.

METHOD

Users post many posts constantly; examining of this user-generated content (UGC) can propose insights into and the determinants of fake news. The study aims to determine the factors that affect the probability of news being fake; the study has preferred binomial logistic regression in the analyses. The Hosmer and Lemeshow test shows the model to be suitable for logistic regression ($p > 0.05$). The study uses whether the news is real or fake as the dependent variable v. If the news is real, $v = 1$, and if the news is fake, $v = 0$. The study's explanatory variables affecting the probability of news being fake are: propagation, user features, social media type, and format features.

Our model is as follows:

Fake news (*FN*) is equated in the following function:

$$FN = \alpha_0 + \beta_1 Proparagation + \beta_2 Users\ features + \beta_3\ social\ media\ type + \beta_4 Formatting \qquad (1)$$

Extracting the Features

Before extracting the features, recurring news patterns were determined on teyit.org. Therefore, the characteristics of each news item could be obtained completely. News features as extracted are based as follows:

- **Propagation.** This feature is about engagement. It shows the number of likes and shares.
- **User type.** User characteristics are determined by the number of followers, anonymity, and fake/real account.
- **Social Media Type.** This feature determines which social media account type spreads fake news: Facebook, Twitter or Instagram.
- **Formatting.** This feature determines the formatting characteristics of the news such as writing quality (misspelled words, misused punctuation), strong sentiment (capitalized words and punctuation marks), and usage of hash-tags, source posts, photos, or videos.

Data Collection

After extracting the features, data were collected from the website Teyit.org's records dating between January 2017 and March 2020. The data collection is based on the method of content analysis using the categories of *propagation*, *user type*, *social media type*, and *formatting*. The web site has a particular section where they collect fake and real news. Therefore this section has been used for the item check. While collecting data, if a news item (*NI*) has one of the above listed features, $NI = 1$; if not, $NI = 0$. Therefore, the data are obtained as discontinuous variables. Between the mentioned dates, 497 news items have been accessed. While 437 items are fake, 62 have had their news validated.

The site has a layout that categorizes fake and real news separately. When monitoring the site regularly, news is seen to have been checked almost every day. The platform classifies the news they check as fake or real and stores it on the site. The news that has been confirmed as true or false on the site constitutes the data set of the research.

Certain limitations have occurred during the data collection period. As the news goes further back, accounts that were recognized to have spread fake news get suspended. As accessing the number of followers of a suspended user or knowing how far their news had spread is not possible, these data have been excluded from the analysis. Therefore, the number of news items obtained in 40 months is 497.

Figure 1. The research model obtained based on the extracted features

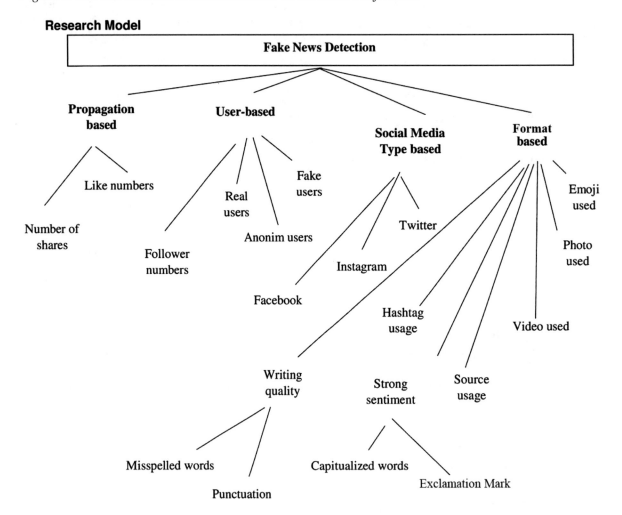

The aim of the study is to determine the features that increase the probability that a news item is fake. For this purpose, the research question has been determined as "Which features of the news increase the probability of new being fake?" The categories obtained during the data collection have been statistically analyzed in the following section, which affects the probability of news being fake.

RESULTS

This section has two parts. The first part demonstrates the descriptive statistics of the case. The second part shows the logistic regression analysis.

Descriptive Statistics

First, statistics regarding the sum of fake and real news items will be shared.

Statistics Regarding All Shared News

According to the descriptive analyses, 497 news items in total have been analyzed, of which 433 (87%) are fake and 64 (12.8%) are real. Of the 497 examined accounts, 311 (62.4%) are anonymous users, six (1.2%) are fake users (bots), and 181 (36.3%) are real users. The number of verified accounts overall is 105 (21.1%).

Among all the news items, the number spread using Twitter is 321 (64.5%), the number spread using Facebook is 172 (34.5%), and the number spread using Instagram is 5 (1%). Usage of misspelled words and incorrect punctuation are noticed in 151 (30.3%) news items. Emoji usage occurred in 92 (18.4%) news items. Only 44 (8.8%) of the shared news items referred to a source; 365 (73%) of the 497 news items were shared using an image, while the number of items shared using a video was less (78, or 15%).

Statistics of Fake News

Descriptive statistics of fake news are as follows. Of the 433 accounts that cause the spread of fake news, 272 (62.7%) belong to anonymous users, 6 (1.4%) to fake users (bots), and 156 (35.9%) belong to real users. Social media users (59%) prefer to share anonymously, especially regarding disputable content. If the content shared is controversial, the rate of users who share anonymously increases by 320% (Zhang & Kizilcec, 2014). Preferring to spread fake news from anonymous accounts as opposed to real accounts is due to how it allows people to not to take responsibility for explaining why they shared fake news.

According to the findings of the current research, the most common type of social media in which fake news is spread is Twitter (263 items, or 60.4%), 166 items (38.2%) are from Facebook, and 5 items (1.2%) are from Instagram. This means users prefer to diffuse fake news on Twitter. According to one study (Vosoughi et al, 2018), Twitter is the platform where fake news spreads the fastest.

Misuse of spelling/punctuation was determined in 141 (32.5%) fake news items. Emojis were used in 89 (20.5%) shared fake news items. One of the methods chosen more often when spreading fake news is the use of capital letters, exclamation marks, or multiple question marks. This occurred in 140 (32.3%) fake news items.

One feature used to make fake news more widespread is hashtags. Hashtags have the feature of listing everything written about the subject when clicked on it. Therefore, the word used in a hashtag spreads easier. In this study, hashtags were used in 58 (13.4%) fake news items. Even referencing a source in a news article may not change the fact that it is fake news. 24 of the shared fake news items (5.5%) spread containing a reference.

Fake images spread through social media have the potential to manipulate, distress, and deceive public opinions. The findings from this study demonstrate that photos/videos have been included in fake news. Photos have been included in 313 fake news items (72.1%). Less so, videos have been embedded in 74 news items (17%). How people evaluate image credibility is significant. Participants Internet skills, photo-editing experience, and social media use have been found to be important predictors in assessing image reliability (Shen, Kasra, Pan, Bassett, Malloch, & O'Brein, 2019).

Propagation Mean Statistics

The average number of shares for fake news is 5,612.87, and the average number of likes is 6,999.48. The average number of followers for accounts with fake news is 2,792,968. The average number of

Table 2. Propagation numbers for fake news

News		Number of Shares	Number of likes	Number of Followers
Real	*M*	2,671.77	6,285.41	647,810.89
	n	64	64	64
	SD	3,063.298	8,072.138	929,637.973
Fake	*M*	5,612.87	6,999.48	2,792,967.52
	n	433	433	431
	SD	23,660.488	1,653.748	48,159,972.614
Total	*M*	5,234.14	6,907.53	2,515,613.94
	n	497	497	495
	SD	22,130.258	14,891.454	44,939,130.014

shares for real news is 2,672, and the average number of likes is 6,285. The average number of followers for accounts spreading real news is 647,811. Fake news has greater averages for number of shares and number of likes. The average number of followers is also higher for fake news. More than one reason may exist for why fake news spreads more than real news. One reason for the spread of fake news is bot accounts. Additionally, 20.5% of fake news spreads from verified accounts. Accounts that actively spread false information are more likely to be bots. Automated accounts are particularly active in the early spreading stages of viral posts and tend to target effective users. (Shao, Ciampaglia, Varol, Flammini, & Mencze, 2017).

Misinformation propagation is more common through videos. On average, fake news is more frequently disseminated through videos. While the average for number of fake news being shared through photos is 5,512, the average for number of fake news being shared with video is 8,213.

While the average for number of fake news shared on Twitter is 2,137.22, the average for number of likes is 8,432.97. While the average for number of fake news shared on Facebook is 11,170.39, the average for number of likes is 4,846.62. These figures show Twitter users to be more into liking than sharing. In contrast, Facebook users are more likely to share fake news than to like them. Lastly, the type of account with the highest average number of fake news shares is anonymous accounts ($\mu = 7,648.25$).

As the type of account type is a categorical variable, being an anonymous account has been used as the reference category for this variable. For the categorical variable of social media type on which the news spreads (Facebook, Twitter, Instagram), Twitter has been determined as the reference category. In addition to these variables, writing quality, emoji usage, strong sentiment, hashtag usage, source usage, photo usage, and video usage have been added to the model. The model was tested and obtained an accuracy rate of 86.7 %.

According to the results from the binomial logistic regression analysis, the spread of news as a post from Facebook significantly increases the probability of the news being fake when compared being spread from Twitter. According to the results of another study in supports of this finding, Facebook is a critical vector for exposure to fake news, and fact-checking results reach almost no target audience there (Guess et al, 2018). Fake news has a higher share rate on Facebook (Silverman & Alexander, 2016).

A news article with low writing quality increases the likelihood of it being fake news an additional 10%. Emoji usage in a news article significantly increases the probability of it being fake. Referring to a source in the news significantly reduces the likelihood of it being fake news. Although photo/video usage

Table 3. Logistic regression results

	B	SD	Wald	df	p
Fake user	19.238	15,205.719	.000	1	.999
Real user	.258	.311	.690	1	.406
Instagram Post	19.813	17,705.106	.000	1	.999
Facebook Post	1.699	.474	12.845	1	.000
Writing Quality	.671	.393	2.914	1	.088
Emoji usage	1.262	.623	4.103	1	.043
Strong Sentiment	.296	.381	.603	1	.437
Hashtag Usage	.523	.459	1.296	1	.255
Source Usage	-1.578	.366	18.557	1	.000
Photo Usage	-.233	.443	.277	1	.599
Video Usage	1.053	.667	2.496	1	.114
Constant	1.291	.463	7.789	1	.005

The variables entered in Step 1 are: Fake user, Real user, Instagram Post, Facebook Post, Writing Quality, Emoji usage, Strong Sentiment, Hashtag usage, Source usage, Photo usage, Video usage

in a news item is expected to have a significant effect on the probability of fake news, these variables have not been found to be statistically significant.

CONCLUSION AND DISCUSSION

Identifying fake news has become a vital matter in the post-truth era. Fact-checking services are expanding their efforts and have adopted a social mission. This study analyzes news items that have been checked on Teyit.org, a pivotal fact-checking platform in Turkey by extracting the features of fake news. The study has investigated the antecedents that increase the likelihood of a news item being fake. The study shows that fake news can be detected based on four factors: propagation, user type, social media type, and formatting. According to the analysis, the study's model has obtained an accuracy of 86.7%. The study demonstrates that Facebook increases the likelihood of news being fake compared to Twitter and Instagram. Accordingly, if a news video's accuracy is suspect, its likelihood of being fake is much higher than that of a news item with a photograph. Increased fake news on Facebook in this study corroborates previous studies (Buchanan & Benson, 2019; Pourghomi, Safieddine, Masri, & Dordevic, 2017).

Emoji usage is statistically significant in terms of increasing the probability of news being fake. Ge & Herring (2018) found that emojis can work like verbal utterances and shape relationships using textual propositions. Thus, using emojis to spread fake news might be pragmatically useful. Unexpectedly, the impact of photos or videos on whether a news item is fake or not has been found to be statistically insignificant.

According to the current study, one outstanding result is that video usage increases the likelihood that a news item is fake. In the analyzed sample, the vast majority of video news items were fake. Using visuals has been shown to be a significant tool of manipulation for fake news propagation. Various visual and statistical features have been extracted for verifying the news (Zhiwei, Juan, Yongdong, Jianshe, & Qi, 2017). Fake news generators prefer to propagate fake news with videos.

Misspellings and improper punctuation were determined in 32.5% of the fake news items. The finding suggests that the news that spreads without grammatical errors also has a risk of being false. Referencing a source might be a clue for verification. Another result of the study is about user type. According to the results, real users can also spread misinformation, whether deliberate or not. Therefore, verified accounts on social media are unreliable in terms of identifying misleading information. The study has also concluded that, with respect to anonymous accounts in terms of account type, whether it is real or fake has no significant effect on the possibility of fake news.

Nevertheless, these results have no certainty for detecting whether a news item is fake or true. Taken together, these findings suggest that being media literate has a role. The study's findings indicate that some features may increase the likelihood of news being fake; however, the study does not offer specific solutions for distinguishing fake news items from real ones. Therefore, users' media literacy levels have a vital role in being aware of misleading content on social media.

This research contributes a new perspective to the literature on fake news as it reveals the premises of misinformation on social media by investigating news items' accuracy through user type (fake user, real user), media type (Instagram, Facebook, Twitter), writing quality, emoji usage, strong sentiment, hashtag usage, source usage, Photo usage, and video usage.

Limitations and Future Studies

This study displays the likelihood of whether news spreading in Turkey is fake or not through four categories using the website Teyit.org. However, using more categories may undoubtedly increase the accuracy level of whether a news item is false or not. Teyit.org may be the biggest, but it is not the only fact-checking platform in Turkey. Namely, this study may be enhanced by analyzing additional fact-checking services to see if the number of categories changes or not.

Detecting and declaring the features of fake news are not enough to combat misinformation. Social media offers a two-way platform. Therefore, the side users have on social media is crucial in the post-truth era. This study did not focus on the side social media users have. Future research may investigate the impact users' media literacy levels have on detecting and propagating fake news.

REFERENCES

Afify, E. A., Eldin, A. S., Khedr, A. E., & Alsheref, F. K. (2019). User-Generated Content (UGC) Credibility on Social Media Using Sentiment Classification. *FCI-H Informatics Bulletin*, *1*(1), 1–19.

Afroz, S., Brennan, M., & Greenstadt, R. (2012, May). *Detecting hoaxes, frauds, and deception in writing style online*. Paper presented at the meeting of IEEE Symposium on Security and Privacy. 10.1109/SP.2012.34

Ahinkorah, B. O., Ameyaw, E. K., Hagan Junior, J. E., Seidu, A. A., & Schack, T. (2020). Rising above misinformation or fake news in Africa: Another strategy to control COVID-19 spread. *Frontiers in Communication*, *5*, 45.

Ahmed, H., Traore, I., & Saad, S. (2017). Detecting opinion spams and fake news using text classification. *Security and Privacy*, *1*(1), e9. doi:10.1002py2.9

Aldwairi, M., & Alwahedi, A. (2018). Detecting fake news in social media networks. *Procedia Computer Science*, *141*, 215–222. doi:10.1016/j.procs.2018.10.171

Allcott, H., & Gentzkow, M. (2017). Social media and fake news in the 2016 election. *The Journal of Economic Perspectives*, *31*(2), 211–236. doi:10.1257/jep.31.2.211

Bondielli, A., & Marcelloni, F. (2019). A Survey on Fake News and Rumour Detection Techniques. *Information Sciences*, *497*, 38–55. Advance online publication. doi:10.1016/j.ins.2019.05.035

Bovet, A., & Makse, H. A. (2019). Influence of fake news in Twitter during the 2016 US presidential election. *Nature Communications*, *10*(1), 1–14. doi:10.103841467-018-07761-2 PMID:30602729

Brandt, A. M. (2012). Inventing conflicts of interest: A history of tobacco industry tactics. *American Journal of Public Health*, *102*(1), 63–71. doi:10.2105/AJPH.2011.300292 PMID:22095331

Brandtzaeg, P., & Følstad, A. (2017). Trust and Distrust in Online Fact-Checking Services. *Communications of the ACM*, *60*(9), 65–71. doi:10.1145/3122803

Burkhardt, J. M. (2017). History of Fake News. *Library Technology Reports*, *53*(8), 5–9.

BuzzFeed News. (2016). *Hyperpartisan Facebook Pages Are Publishing False And Misleading Information At An Alarming Rate*. Retrieved from https://www.buzzfeednews.com/article/craigsilverman/partisan-fb-pages-analysis#.pulP7wZbl

Çömlekçi, M. F. (2019). Sosyal Medyada Dezenformasyon Ve Haber Doğrulama Platformlarının Pratikleri (Disinformation On Social Media And Practices Of Fact-Checking Platforms). *Gümüşhane Üniversitesi İletişim Fakültesi Elektronik Dergisi*, *7*(3), 1549–1563.

Çömlekçi, M. F. (2020). *Combating Fake News Online: Turkish Fact-Checking Services. In Navigating Fake News, Alternative Facts, and Misinformation in a Post-Truth World*. IGI Global.

FullFact. (2019). *Who is most likely to believe and to share misinformation?* Retrieved from https://fullfact.org/media/uploads/who-believes-shares-misinformation.pdf

Ge, J., & Herring, S. C. (2018). Communicative functions of emoji sequences on Sina Weibo. *First Monday*.

Gorbach, J. (2018). Not Your Grandpa's Hoax: A Comparative History of Fake News. *American Journalism*, *35*(2), 236–249. doi:10.1080/08821127.2018.1457915

Granik, M., & Mesyura, V. (2017, May). *Fake news detection using naive Bayes classifier*. Paper presented at the meeting of First Ukraine Conference on Electrical and Computer Engineering (UKRCON). 10.1109/UKRCON.2017.8100379

Graves, L., & Cherubini, F. (2016). *The rise of fact-checking sites in Europe*. Reuters Institute, University of Oxford.

Grinberg, N., Joseph, K., Friedland, L., Swire-Thompson, B., & Lazer, D. (2019). Fake news on Twitter during the 2016 US presidential election. *Science*, *363*(6425), 374–378. doi:10.1126cience.aau2706 PMID:30679368

Guess, A., Nagler, J., & Tucker, J. (2019). Less than you think: Prevalence and predictors of fake news dissemination on Facebook. *Science Advances, 5*(1), eaau4586.

Guess, A., Nyhan, B., & Reifler, J. (2018). Selective exposure to misinformation: Evidence from the consumption of fake news during the 2016 US presidential campaign. European Research Council, 9.

IJCF. (2018). *A short guide to the history of 'fake news' and disinformation.* Retrieved from https://www. icfj.org/sites/default/files/2018-07/A%20Short%20Guide%20to%20History%20of%20Fake%20News%20 and%20Disinformation_ICFJ%20Final.pdf

Jang, S. M., Geng, T., Li, J. Y. Q., Xia, R., Huang, C. T., Kim, H., & Tang, J. (2018). A computational approach for examining the roots and spreading patterns of fake news: Evolution tree analysis. *Computers in Human Behavior, 84*, 103–113. doi:10.1016/j.chb.2018.02.032

Jin, Z., Cao, J., Zhang, Y., Zhou, J., & Tian, Q. (2016). Novel visual and statistical image features for microblogs news verification. *IEEE transactions on multimedia, 19*(3), 598-608.

John, B., & Opdycke, L. M. (2011). The evolution of an idea. *Journal of Communication Management, 15*(3), 223–235. doi:10.1108/13632541111150998

Karunian, A. Y., Halme, H., & Söderholm, A. M. (2019). Data Profiling and Elections: Has Data-Driven Political Campaign Gone Too Far? *Economic Perspectives, 28*(2), 6.

Lazer, D. M. J., Baum, M. A., Benkler, Y., Berinsky, A. J., Greenhill, K. M., Menczer, F., & Zittrain, J. L. (2018). The science of fake news. *Science, 359*(6380), 1094–1096. doi:10.1126cience.aao2998 PMID:29590025

Lynch, G., Willis, J., & Cheeseman, N. (2018). Claims about Cambridge Analytica's role in Africa Should be Taken with a Pinch of Salt. *The Conversation.*

Moravec, P., Minas, R., & Dennis, A. R. (2018). *Fake News on Social Media: People Believe What They Want to Believe When it Makes No Sense at All.* Kelley School of Business Research Paper (18-87).

Mutahi, P., & Kimari, B. (2017). The impact of social media and digital technology on electoral violence in Kenya. *IDS.*

Poe, E. A. (1844). *"The Balloon Hoax," published 1844, reprinted in PoeStories.com.* Retrieved from https://poestories.com/read /balloonhoax

Pourghomi, P., Safieddine, F., Masri, W., & Dordevic, M. (2017, May). How to stop spread of misinformation on social media: Facebook plans vs. right-click authenticate approach. In *2017 International Conference on Engineering & MIS (ICEMIS)* (pp. 1-8). IEEE.

Rampersad, G., & Althiyabi, T. (2020). Fake news: Acceptance by demographics and culture on social media. *Journal of Information Technology & Politics, 17*(1), 1–11. doi:10.1080/19331681.2019.1686676

Reporters Lab. (2014). *Duke Study Finds Fact-Checking Growing Around the World.* Retrieved from https://reporterslab.org/duke-study-finds-fact-checking-growing-around-the-world/

Reporters Lab. (2018). *Fact-Checking Triples Over Four Years.* Retrived from https://reporterslab.org/ fact-checking-triples-over-four-years/

Reporters Lab. (2019). *Number Of Fact-Checking Outlets Surges To 188 İn More Than 60 Countries.* Retrieved from https://reporterslab.org/tag/fact-checking-census/

Reporters Lab. (2020). *Global Fact-Checking sites.* Retrived from https://reporterslab.org/fact-checking/

Ruchansky, N., Seo, S., & Csi, Y. L. (2017). A hybrid deep model for fake news detection. In *Proceedings of the 2017 ACM on Conference on Information and Knowledge Management*, (pp. 797–806). ACM. 10.1145/3132847.3132877

Shao, C., Ciampaglia, G. L., Varol, O., Flammini, A., & Menczer, F. (2017). *The spread of fake news by social bots.* arXiv preprint arXiv:1707.07592

Shen, C., Kasra, M., Pan, W., Bassett, G. A., Malloch, Y., & O'Brien, J. F. (2019). Fake images: The effects of source, intermediary, and digital media literacy on contextual assessment of image credibility online. *New Media & Society, 21*(2), 438-463.

Shu, K., Sliva, A., Wang, S., Tang, J., & Liu, H. (2017). Fake News Detection on Social Media. *ACM SIGKDD Explorations Newsletter, 19*(1), 22–36. doi:10.1145/3137597.3137600

Silverman, C., & Alexander, L. (2016). *Fake news had more share on Facebook than mainstream news, How teens in the balkans are duping trump supporters with fake news.* Buzzfeed News.

Spenkuch, J. L., & Toniatti, D. (2016). *Political advertising and election outcomes.* Kilts Center for Marketing at Chicago Booth–Nielsen Dataset Paper Series, 1-046.

Statista. (2018). *Fake news in Europe - Statistics & Facts.* Retrieved from https://www.statista.com/topics/5833/fake-news-in-europe/

Statista. (2018). *Media Usage.* Retrieved from https://www.statista.com/statistics/649234/fake-news-exposure-usa/

Statista. (2019a). *Opinions on social media bans to prevent fake news in Europe 2019.* Retrieved from https://www.statista.com/statistics/1088148/fake-news-and-social-media-bans-in-europe/

Statista. (2019b). *Daily time spent on social networking by internet users worldwide from 2012 to 2019.* Retrieved from https://www.statista.com/statistics/433871/daily-social-media-usage-worldwide/

Tacchini, E., Ballarin, G. D., Vedova, M. L., Moret, S., & de Alfaro, L. (2017). *Some like it hoax: Automated fake news detection in social networks.* arXiv preprint arXiv:1704.07506

Talwar, S., Dhir, A., Kaur, P., Zafar, N., & Alrasheedy, M. (2019). Why do people share fake news? Associations between the dark side of social media use and fake news sharing behavior. *Journal of Retailing and Consumer Services, 51*, 72–82. doi:10.1016/j.jretconser.2019.05.026

Tandoc Jr, E. C., Lim, Z. W., & Ling, R. (2018). Defining "fake news" A typology of scholarly definitions. *Digital Journalism, 6*(2), 137-153.

Teyit.org. (2020). Retrieved from https://teyit.org/about/

Thorne, J., Chen, M., Myrianthous, G., Pu, J., Wang, X., & Vlachos, A. (2017). Fake news stance detection using stacked ensemble of classifiers. *Proceedings of the 2017 EMNLP Workshop: Natural Language Processing meets Journalism*, 80–83. 10.18653/v1/W17-4214

Vicario, M. D., Quattrociocchi, W., Scala, A., & Zollo, F. (2019). Polarization and Fake News. *ACM Transactions on the Web*, *13*(2), 1–22. doi:10.1145/3316809

Vishwakarma, K. D., Varshney, D., & Yadav, A. (2019). Detection and Veracity analysis of Fake News via Scrapping and Authenticating the Web Search. *Cognitive Systems Research*, *58*, 217–229. Advance online publication. doi:10.1016/j.cogsys.2019.07.004

Vosoughi, S., Roy, D., & Aral, S. (2018). The spread of true and false news online. *Science*, *359*(6380), 1146–1151. doi:10.1126cience.aap9559 PMID:29590045

Wasserman, H. (2020). Fake news from Africa: Panics, politics and paradigms. *Journalism*, *21*(1), 3-16.

Wasserman, H., & Madrid-Morales, D. (2019). An exploratory study of "fake news" and media trust in Kenya, Nigeria and South Africa. *African Journalism Studies*, *40*(1), 107-123.

Waszak, P. M., Kasprzycka-Waszak, W., & Kubanek, A. (2018). The spread of medical fake news in social media–the pilot quantitative study. *Health Policy and Technology*, *7*(2), 115-118.

We are Social. (2019). *Digital in 2019*. Retrived from https://wearesocial.com/blog/2019/01/digital-2019-global-internet-use-accelerates

Wilson, F., & Umar, M. A. (2019). The Effect of Fake News on Nigeria's Democracy within the Premise of Freedom of Expression. *Global Media Journal*, *17*(32), 1–12.

Yang, Y., Zheng, L., Zhang, J., Cui, Q., Li, Z., & Yu, P. S. (2018). *TI-CNN: Convolutional neural networks for fake news detection*. arXiv preprint arXiv:1806.00749

Zhang, C., Gupta, A., Kauten, C., Deokar, A. V., & Qin, X. (2019). Detecting Fake News for Reducing Misinformation Risks Using Analytics Approaches. *European Journal of Operational Research*, *279*(3), 1036–1052. Advance online publication. doi:10.1016/j.ejor.2019.06.022

Zhang, K., & Kizilcec, R. F. (2014, May). *Anonymity in social media: Effects of content controversiality and social endorsement on sharing behavior*. Paper presented at the meeting of Eighth International AAAI Conference on Weblogs and Social Media.

Zhao, Z., Zhao, J., Sano, Y., Levy, O., Takayasu, H., Takayasu, M., & Havlin, S. (2018). *Fake news propagate differently from real news even at early stages of spreading*. arXiv preprint arXiv:1803.03443

ADDITIONAL READING

Ajao, O., Bhowmik, D., & Zargari, S. (2018). *Fake News Identification on Twitter with Hybrid CNN and RNN Models*. Paper presented at the meeting of the 9th International Conference on Social Media and Society - SMSociety '18. 10.1145/3217804.3217917

Janze, C., & Risius, M. (2017, January). *Automatic Detection of Fake News on Social Media Platforms.* Paper presented at the meeting of *PACIS* (p. 261).

Mustafaraj, E., & Metaxas, P. T. (2017, June). *The fake news spreading plague: was it preventable?* IPaper presented at the meeting of *the 2017 ACM on web science conference* (pp. 235-239). 10.1145/3091478.3091523

Thorne, J., Chen, M., Myrianthous, G., Pu, J., Wang, X., & Vlachos, A. (2017, September). Fake news stance detection using stacked ensemble of classifiers. In *Proceedings of the 2017 EMNLP Workshop: Natural Language Processing meets Journalism* (pp. 80-83). 10.18653/v1/W17-4214

KEY TERMS AND DEFINITIONS

Fact-Checking Services/Platforms: The new phenomenon where news items' accuracy are verified.

Fake News: News generated by social media users to damage an agency, entity, or person intentionally.

Disinformation: Disinformation entails the propagation or assertion of false, mistaken, or misleading information in an intentional mislead.

Misinformation: This term defined as false, mistaken, or misleading information.

Misleading Information: Encapsulating concept used for fake news/disinformation on social media.

User-Generated Content (UGC): Content that is produced and circulated by Internet users yet is not checked by any authority.

Chapter 5
Will Social Media and Its Consumption Converge or Diverge Global Consumer Culture?

Yowei Kang
(iD) https://orcid.org/0000-0002-7060-194X
National Taiwan Ocean University, Taiwan

Kenneth C. C. Yang
(iD) https://orcid.org/0000-0002-4176-6219
The University of Texas at El Paso, USA

ABSTRACT

Social media have been claimed to homogenize human and consumer behaviors around the world – in other words, to make people think, feel, and act alike regardless of national borders. Scholars often debate this claim from either a convergence or a divergence perspective from the marketing and consumer behavior literature. The theoretical foundation will be based on the convergence-divergence debates that postulate universal consumption patterns and values are made possible, due to the industrialization, modernization, technology, and wealth accumulation. The authors use perceptions of online privacy among users of privacy-invasive technologies as an example to discuss why people will think the same about their own privacy could be a myth for the failure to consider the unique socio-cultural characteristics of each nation. This study begins with a global consumption analysis of social media around the world. Then, they examine how privacy concerns may help account for the homogenization or heterogenization trend of global consumer culture. Discussions and implications are provided.

DOI: 10.4018/978-1-7998-4718-2.ch005

INTRODUCTION

The Rise of Social Media Ecosystem

Advances in contemporary Information-Communication Technologies (ICTs) are predicted to increase connectivity among consumers and lead to their spending behaviors (Ozturk & Cavusgil, 2019). The term, ICTs, often refer to technologies such as the Internet, World Wide Web, mobile technologies, even smart TV that have included social shaping and consequences (Dutton, 2001; Irion & Helberg, 2017). Recently, the popular Chinese mobile app, Tiktok, has been said to collect users' location, social media contacts, age, and phone contact information (Luna, 2020). These technological developments have led to the rise of a global market where consumers are exposed to similar lifestyles (Frith & Mueller, 2003 cited in Choi & Ferle, 2004; *We Are Social*, 2020). Social media, like many of these contemporary technological innovations, has been claimed to affect consumer behaviors (Voramontri & Klieb, 2019). In a similar vein, social media are likely to homogenize global human and consumer behaviors around the world--- in other words, to make people think, feel, and act alike regardless of national borders (De Mooij, 2019). This claim is in line with what many media and communication scholars have proposed to emphasize the role of media on the emergence and homogenization of global culture (Mustapha, Azeez, & Wok, 2005).

According to Statista (2018, May), the number of social media users around the world has grown from 0.97 billion in 2010, 2.14 billion in 2015, to 2.96 billion in 2020. The number is expected to grow to 3.09 billion in 2021 (Statista, 2018, May). The average worldwide penetration rate of social media has reached 49% (*We Are Social*, 2020) to generate potential and widespread impacts on society. *We Are Social* (2020) has also reported the global Internet users have surpassed over 4.5 billion, while the number of social media users around the world is 3.8 billion, suggesting the rapid rise of social media to influence human society to the extent that the Internet has created. The social media ecosystem is composed of various interconnected applications, including blogs, consumer opinion platforms, micro-blogging sites, social networking sites (Han et al., 2019). The rapid development of social media ecosystem has led some industry pundits to observe the homogenization among social media companies that offer overlapping features in their respective applications (Morgan, 2016).

According to *We Are Social* (2020), the most popular social platform is Facebook, with its global users of 2,449 million users, followed by *YouTube* (2,000 millions), *WhatApps* (1,640 millions), *Facebook Messenger* (1,300 millions), *Weibo/WeChat* (1,151 millions), *Instagram* (1,000 millions), *Douyin/Tiktok* (800 millions), and *QQ* (from China) (731 millions). A report by eBizMBA (2017) observes that the top five most popular social media platforms, on the basis of estimated unique monthly visitors, are *Facebook*, *YouTube*, *Twitter*, *Instagram*, and *LinkenIn* (cited in Koohang, Paliszkiewicz, & Goluchowski, 2018).

The growing importance of social media as part of contemporary human experiences is also attributed to their widespread applications in many marketing activities (Burton, Mueller, Gollins, & Walls, 2017; Grewal, Stephen, & Coleman, 2019; Ham, Leee, Hayes, & Bae, 2018). These scholars have observed that social media have played an essential role as part of the integrated marketing communication platforms to foster relationships with consumers by providing entertaining and informative contents (Burton et al., 2017). For example, Grewal et al. (2019) employ five experiments to examine whether product postings on social media can reveal consumers' own identity to help marketers increase their subsequent purchase intention. Other marketing researchers have also explored the underlying motivations that consumers simulcast branded contents across different social media platforms (Ham et al., 2018). Their study attempts to examine whether pre-existing social relationships can account for consumers' sharing behaviors (Han et al., 2018).

The rapid diffusion of social media has become a global phenomenon (Kolb, 2008) and is likely to influence the behaviors of their global users. Social media giants such as *Facebook* has 37.2% of its users from Asia, 18.8% from Latin America and Caribbean, 17.4% from Europe, 13.3% from North America, 8.0% from Africa, 4.4% from Middle East, and 1.0% from Australia and Oceania (Internet World Stats, 2017). Another popular social media platform, *Twitter*, aims to become "a global town square" for its 300 million monthly global active users in 2014 (Leetaru, 2015). As of January 2020, the top three countries with the most *Twitter* users are the U.S. (59.35 million), Japan (47.75 million), and the U.K. (16.7 million) (Statista, 2020, January). Other countries with *Twitter* presence include Saudi Arabia (14.35 million), Russia (9.46 million), and Malaysia (3.86 million). The global presence of these social media platforms evidently has suggested a globalization and convergence trend. Nevertheless, China has presented a strong case of divergence because its own version of *Sina Weibo* (similar to *Twitter*) (Duan & Dholokia, 2015), *Youku* or *Tencent* (from China) (similar to *YouTube*), *WeChat* (from China) (similar to *Facebook*), *DouYin* (from China) (similar to *Tiktok*) (Kantar China, 2018).

Despite the technology-enhanced convergence or divergence trends around the world, various factors may contribute these developments (Ozturk & Cavusgil, 2019). For example, Ozturk and Cavusgil (2019) observe that technological influence is likely to contribute to the convergence of consumer behaviors while sociocultural factors (such as cultural diversity) may inhibit the convergence trend. The dynamic between these factors is important to caution scholars not to fall into the technology-deterministic prediction. This study will focuses on one of the socio-cultural factors (i.e., the perceptions of privacy) and explain this variable may be used to account for the convergence or divergence trend in the marketing and consumer behavior literature (De Mooij, 2003; Ozturk & Cavusgil, 2019). Specifically, research questions to guide this study are below:

RQ1: What is global social media consumption trend?

RQ2: What is the definition of social media privacy concerns?

RQ3: What is the relationship between global consumers' privacy concerns and their social media usage behaviors?

RQ4: How will this study help explain the convergence vs. divergence trend in terms of global social media usage behaviors?

BACKGROUND

Understanding Global Social Media Consumption Behaviors

To answer the first research question, an extensive review of secondary data was used to provide descriptions of global social media consumption behaviors. A recent Pew Research Center survey of social media users in the U.S. reports that almost 75% use one of the eight social media platforms such as *Facebook*, *Instagram*, *LinkedIn*, *Pinterest*, *Snapchat*, *Twitter*, *WhatsApp*, or *YouTube*) (Smith & Anderson, 2018, cited in Bright, Logan, English, Kingman, & Lyons, 2019). Younger generation tends to use *Snapchat*, *Instagram*, and *Twitter*; they are frequent users of these technologies (Smith & Anderson, 2018, cited in Bright et al., 2019). In the same survey, it is also found that, on a regular basis, most consumers use an average of three social media apps (Smith & Anderson, 2018, cited in Bright et al., 2019). In terms of total minutes spent on social media daily, fifteen minutes are spent in 2008, while 26 minutes are spent in 2010, indicating an 11% increase (McKinsey & Company, 2010).

Because of the global presence of these social media platforms, marketers have increasingly surveyed what consumers around the world have used them (McKinsey & Company, 2011). McKinsey & Company (2011) studied more than 100,000 consumers (aged between 13 and 64+ years old) from China, Europe, India, and North America in 2010 and identified two major segments of digital technology users.

The *Digital Media Junkies* segment are characterized as "extensive users of all things digital (video, music, etc.) across devices" (McKinsey & Company, 2011, p. 3). On the other hand, the *Digital Communicators* segment is described as "more focused on social networking, texting and email" (McKinsey & Company, 2011, p. 3). Overall, digital media are an essential part of these consumers' lives (McKinsey & Company, 2011). Other sub-segments in the McKinsey & Company's report (2011) also include *Video Digerati, Gamers, Professionals, On-the-go Workers,* and *Traditionalist.* While these global consumer segments have all integrated digital media into many areas of their lives, their attitudes toward digital technology and their adoption behaviors have varied. For example, the *Digital Media Junkies* are eager and early adopters of digital technologies (average age of 28 years old), while *On-the-go Workers* and *Traditionalists* are about 41 and 48 years old (McKinsey & Company, 2011).

Globally, in terms of gender distribution, share of global social media users are often found to be balanced with a tilt toward males (55%) (*We Are Social*, 2020). In North and South Americas, female (48%) users are more than males (52%), while in Central America, the percentage between males and females is balanced at 50% (*We Are Social*, 2020). In Western Europe, 49% of social media users is females, while 51% is males (*We Are Social*, 2020). In Eastern Asia, 48% is females, while 52% is males (*We Are Social*, 2020). In Africa, female users are far less than males; in Northern, Western, and Middle Africas, about 38% is females, while over 60% is males (*We Are Social*, 2020). Reports on country-specific social media consumption behaviors also are abundant in both academic and industry research. For example, Duan and Dholakia (2015) use an interpretive content analysis to study *Weibo* postings and conclude that these social media have transformed traditional consumer values by demonstrating the gradual shift to materialism and hedonism values.

The emergence of global digital media users has prompted scholars to study different variables that may help develop more effective marketing campaigns. Global multinational corporations are particularly interested in learning about consumer behavior and cultural changes after the widespread use of the Internet and social media (Choi & Ferle, 2004). For example, in current marketing literature, scholars have discussed variables such as engagement (Dessart, 2017; Pentina, Guilloux, & Micu, 2018), sharing behaviors (Han et al., 2018), and herding (Li & Wu, 2018) have been treated as universal variables that can be applied to study global social media users. Scholars often debate this claim from either a convergence or a divergence perspective from the marketing and consumer behavior literature. We use perceptions of online privacy among users of *privacy-invasive technologies* as an example. Afterwards, we examine the global consumption analysis of social media around the world. Then, we study how privacy concerns may help account for the homogenization or heterogenization trend of global consumer culture.

MAIN FOCUS OF THE CHAPTER

Concerns about misusing personal information have been an important issue among global digital media users (*We Are Social*, 2020) and many ICT researchers (Irion & Helberg, 2017). In a survey of global Internet users aged between 16 and 64 in 2020, 64% has expressed they are concerned about how companies utilize their personal information (*We Are Social*, 2020). Countries in the Central and Southern Americas are most concerned about this issue: Columbia (80%), Brazil (79%), and Mexico (79%) (*We Are Social*, 2020). Eastern Asian countries are less concerned: South Korea (40%) and Japan (40%) (*We Are Social*, 2020).

The concerns about protecting personal information and privacy are particularly important for social media users because a lot of personal information is shared and posted online (Arora & Scheiber, 2017; Burkell, Fortier, Yueng, Wong, & Simpson, 2014), and frequently without the acknowledgement of many users. Burkell et al. (2014) point out that personal information is often shared among so-called "Facebook friends", even though users are not expected to interact with these individuals with "weak ties" (Burkell et al., 2014, p. 975). People who are not supposed to receive personal information about a user can accidentally receive updates because the social networking functions that many social media have enabled. Social media users often adjust their own privacy settings on these social media platforms to protect their own privacy (Burkell et al., 2014). Although privacy is an issue that many scholars place a lot of emphasis, qualitative data from focus group and interview methods have shown that for young people from less affluent demographic segments in Brazil and India have confirmed that these informants have difficult time conceptualizing and describing this abstract concept (Arora & Scheiber, 2017). A similar findings of generational differences can be found among Generation Millennials (Futton & Kirby, 2017). This consumer segment feels protecting their personal information from individuals or government agencies is far more important than from commercial entities (Futton & Kurby, 2017). These findings confirm the authors' speculation that the perceptions of privacy are contingent on social-cultural factors. Jacobs and Li (2017) study the media institutions and systems in China, U.K., and U.K. to examine how political systems could affect Internet policy narratives are framed.

Privacy Concerns and Social Media Consumption

The term, privacy, has been around even far before the arrival of social media. ICTs and other connected devices often incur privacy concerns (Irion & Helberger, 2017) and demand the protection of personal data (Walden & Woods, 2011). Privacy issues are often inter-connected with national security and personal data protection concerns (Irion & Helberger, 2017). Researchers have explained the management of an individual privacy relies on their own decision-making process by which they will evaluate uncertainty about what their privacy-related behaviors could lead to and how they prefer different consequences. In general, the concept of privacy refers to "the "right to be let alone" (Warren & Brandeis, cited in Chung & Paynter, 2002, n.p.). Others have defined privacy as "the moral right of individuals to avoid intrusion into their personal affairs by third parties' (Chaffey et al., 2009, p.139, cited in O'Brien & Torres, 2012, p. 64). When information can be linked to a particular individual, it will be considered personal (Mills, 2008, cited in O'Brien & Torres, 2012, p. 64). Digital technologies such as social media have made the collection, distribution, and selling of personal information easier. The loss of control over personal information is said to be central to the concept of privacy (van Dyke et al., 2007, cited in O'Brien & Torres, 2012, p. 65). Types of privacy invasion include the tracking of web site visits, email addresses, credit card theft, and the selling of confidential personal information to third parties, etc. (Chung & Paynter, 2002). On the other hand, Koohang, Paliszkiewicz, and Goluchowski (2018) focus on whether users believe they have full control of their personal information as part of privacy concern dimensions. Some of these examples include the lack of control over collection and usage of personal information, errors related to the information, improper access, and unauthorized access and usage (Refer to Koohang et al., 2018 for details).

Intuitively privacy concerns should be a major issue for many social media users. Empirical data has confirmed the concerns about whether Facebook could invade personal privacy is among the top 5 reasons for users to exit this platform (Roper, 2020). While privacy is a major concerns among many social media users, Sheehan (2002) finds that 50% of consumers are pragmatic about privacy, while 1/4 of consumers is either not or highly concerned about privacy. Her email survey concludes that concerns about privacy are based on situations and demographic variables (such as age and education) also predict how consumers perceive privacy online (Sheehan, 2002). Older and less educated consumers are found not to feel concerned about their privacy (Sheenhan, 2002). Rütten (2016) further introduces users' generation as a predictive variable and finds that Millennial and Non-Millennial Facebook users perceive their privacy and security differently. The survey of 337 participants confirms that their age has a moderating effect on their perceptions of privacy and security (Rütten, 2016).

To examine the characteristics of privacy in the age of social media, Heyman, de Wolf, and Pierson (2014) propose two types of privacy to understand the concept of social media privacy: "privacy as subject" and "privacy as object." The first category of social media privacy refers to "the management of information about one's identity *vis-a`-vis* the other users" (Heyman et el., 2014, p. 18). The second category, "privacy as object," is also equivalent of "lateral or social privacy" when "users are not seen by other users" but their behavior insights are analyzed through algorithms to generate monetary profits (Heyman et el., 2014, p. 18). Koohang et al. (2018) has developed the term, *social media privacy concerns (SMPC)* that is defined as "[t]he degree to which a user is concerned about a social media site's practices and procedures relating to his or her personal information. The SMPCs include collection, secondary usage, errors, improper access, control and awareness" (p. 1210).

The study of privacy is important to many marketing researchers and practitioners because of its relationship to social media usage (Fox & Royne, 2018, cited in Hunter & Taylor, 2018). Hunter and Taylor (2018) also point out the biggest hurdle in studying privacy related to social media lies in variations in how people define and perceive privacy. Because the global diffusion of social media around the world, this issue can be particularly important because the socio-cultural variations among countries. This methodological problem will worsen after considering how marketers have been using personal information to develop personalized services and contents (Gal-Or, Gal-Or, & Penmetsa, 2018). These categorizations and definitions of social media have allowed scholars to examine further many important issues related to users' privacy concerns. For this study, we reasons that concerns over an individual's online privacy have been well documented not only in the academic literature (Xu, Dinev, & Smith 2011; Lom, Too, Sulaiman, & Adam 2018), but also the popular press (Friesland 2018). Due to the rapid diffusion of social media technologies, it seems reasonable to assume that global consumers affected by these privacy-invasive technologies will think, feel, and act the same toward online privacy concerns. Empirical data have lent support to this claim of homogenization effects. For example, in the 2016 KMPG survey, 55% of consumers around the world report that they decide against buying online due to privacy concerns. The top concerns among these global consumers are the misuse of personal data for unwanted marketing, the monetization of personal data to a 3rd party user, and the lack of cyber-security system (KMPG, 2016).

Theoretical Framework

Researchers have used various methodologies to study if social media users' privacy concerns may affect their consumption and usage behaviors (Lipps & Eppel, 2017). For example, Lipps and Eppel (2017) employed a grounded theory methodology to identify four types of information-sharing behaviors: privacy fatalists, privacy optimists, privacy pragmatists, and privacy victims. These categories of social media usage behaviors lend support to the relationship between social media consumption behaviors and privacy concerns. To support our argument on the possible relationship between global consumer culture of social media consumption and privacy concerns, we further examine social media users' concerns over different types of online privacy in different circumstances in different countries.

This study will rely on the proposition by De Mooij (2019) and other consumer behavior researchers (Mitry & Smith, 2009) when they contend that universal consumption patterns and values are made possible, due to the industrialization, modernization, technology, and wealth accumulation. As Mitry and Smith (2009) argue that "consumer convergence [is] as a reduction in the differences of consumer product selection within a specified population, and therefore a growing similarity of preference. Total fulfilment of convergence would be identity" (p. 316). De Mooij's (2019) proposition is supported by Duan and Dholakia's (2015) empirical study on how social media usage has transformed Chinse value systems from "suppressing desire, delaying gratification and thriftiness" (p. 409). Their study also found the value systems of elite and grass-root Chinese also converge as a result of social media usage (Duan & Dholakia, 2015). However, some scholars have paradoxically claimed that advances in technologies have actually made people more divergent, allowing individual consumers to cultivate their own taste and develop their own media consumption behaviors (De Mooij, 2019).

The rise of a global marketplace has led many to speculate that the homogenization of economic systems will cause the same trend in consumer behaviors, value systems, demographics, among the few (De Mooij, 2003; Mitry & Smith, 2009; Ozturk, 2016; Ozturk & Cavusgil, 2019). De Mooij's (2003) seminal study linking the adoption of media technologies (such as telephones and television sets) in Europe does not provide empirical evidence to support an over-arching converging trend. Her study further observes the co-existence of convergence and divergence trends in many European countries after considering time-series data (De Mooij, 2003). In spite of these inconclusive observations, information-communication technologies (ICTs), to some extent, has the effects of transforming global consumer behaviors. Duan and Dholakia's (2015) study of Chinese social media users lends some support to the convergence trend. Ozturk (2016), on the other hand, studies if the homogenization of consumer spending is found over time across different countries. His empirical analysis has confirmed that a converging pattern in consumer spending can be found as a result of increasing similarities of needs and wants among global consumers (Ozturk, 2016).

A survey by Pew Research Center (2019) on mobile media examines 11 emerging economies (such as Lebanon, Tunisia, South Africa, India, Venezuela, the Philippines, etc.) and observe mobile technology has diffused globally. Only 6% of the adults do not use mobile phone at all (Pew Research Center, 2019). Despite the convenience of mobile technology, many of consumers from these less affluent countries have expressed expense, poor telecommunications infrastructure, and the availability of ancillary equipment (such as a charging station) will affect their adoption behavior of this technology (Pew Research Center,

2019). For example, 51% of the survey participants has expressed that device cost is a major hurdle to their adoption decision, followed by the complexity of device (43%), lack of mobile service (18%), and no apps in their own language (12%) (Pew Research Center, 2019). It is also noteworthy that 29% of the participants mentions that information security is also a big concern (Pew Research Center, 2019).

However, some marketing scholars have argued that local culture is likely to defy the converging trend and become "the main source of divergence" (Ozturk & Cavusgil, 2019, p. 294). Some scholars have found that convergence might not be as prevalent even with the same ethnic group that is supposed to have the same cultural background (de Mooij & Beniflah, 2017). Existing demographic variables (such as age and nativity) may play significant roles in explain these differences (de Mooij & Beniflah, 2017). Unlike the convergence perspective, the divergence line of thinking argues that entities, nations, and organizations will become more heterogeneous as a result of macro-level factors (Ozturk & Cavusgil, 2019) such as national cultural characteristics (De Mooij, 2003, 2019) and value systems (Ozturk & Cavusgil, 2019). Economists who studied the role of technology in global convergence and divergence (Sadik, 2008) have argued that financial system, productivity, interest rate, and many economic factor may also explain these trends.

Recently, scholars have further proposed a more comprehensive the convergence-divergence-crossvergence (henceforth, CDC) framework to take into consideration different converging or diverging behaviors among global consumers (Ozturk & Cavusgil, 2019). The concept of crossvergence (Ralston et al., 1997; Ralston, 2008, cited in Ozturk & Cavusgil, 2019, p. 295) refers to "an alternative to convergence and divergence perspectives. It refers to the blending of different cultural values in cross-cultural managerial settings" (Ralston et al., 1997; Ralston, 2008, cited in Ozturk & Cavusgil, 2019, p. 295).

In addition to pointing out the homogenization or heterogenization phenomena among global consumers, many scholars have focused on what causes them. Related to the present study on social media will be the "technological influences" as brought up by Ozturk and Cavusgil (2019) to explain the role of ICTs as the facilitator of convergence. They reason that these technological advances help promote democracy and human rights by challenging government's censorship (Ozturk & Cavusgil, 2019). Economically, ICTs can also help poor countries to grow and reduce income gaps among countries, leading to income convergence (Ozturk & Cavusgil, 2019). The global diffusion of social media is likely to exercise the same level of technological influences on consumer behaviors.

Research Method

To answer the four research questions above, the authors have relied on on secondary data research (Johnston, 2014) to analyze data available to researchers to explain global social media consumption trend (RQ1), the definitions of social media privacy concerns (RQ2), the relationship between global consumers' privacy concerns and their social media usage behaviors (RQ3), and the understanding of the convergence vs. divergence trend in terms of global social media usage behaviors (RQ4). Hakim (1982) defines secondary analysis as "any further analysis of an existing dataset which presents interpretations, conclusions or knowledge additional to, or different from, those presented" (cited in Johnston, 2014, p. 620). Johnston (2014) details the procedures in conducting secondary data research by the development of research questions, the identification of available data sources, and the assessment of these data sources.

The authors have used "Social Media Privacy", "Privacy", "Privacy Concerns" or "Usage Behaviors" to search Google to identify useful secondary data. The authors will rely on credible industry reports such as KMPG's (2016) data on online privacy perceptions and industry reports by eConsultancy, Eurobarometer, Selligent Marketing Cloud, Pew Research Center, Statista, and *We Are Social* that provide information to answer the proposed research questions. The selection of these data sources is based on its reliability as the well-accepted data sources in the industry as well as academic researchers.

Findings

In the previous section, the authors have explained the global social media consumption trend (RQ1) and the definitions of social media privacy (RQ2), the findings presented in this section will focus on the rest of two research questions (RQ3-RQ4). In terms of the relationship between global consumers' privacy concerns and their social media usage behaviors (RQ3), according to *We Are Social* (2020), the worldwide average of concerns about personal information misuse is about 64%. Countries that are very concerned about this problem, including Columbia (80%), Brazil (79%), Mexico (79%), Spain (73%), Argentina (71%), India (71%), and Romania (70%) (*We Are Social*, 2020). Countries with less than 50% are concerned about this problem include Japan (40%), South Korea (40%), and Sweden (47%) (*We Are Social*, 2020).

According to KMPG's (2016) global survey, over 55% of global consumers has indicated privacy concerns will affect whether they will purchase from a business. One of the major dimensions in social media privacy is a sense of user control over their own personal information (Koohang et al., 2018; O'Brien & Torres, 2012). Globally, only 10% believe they can fully control over how businesses use and handle their personal data (KMPG, 2016). Survey participants from most countries have rated a sense of control of their privacy is far more important than any potential convenience as a result of data sharing (KMPG, 2016). In the same report, a majority (82%) of users share their reservation about the sale of personal data to third party vendors in exchange for benefits such as convenience, home delivery, price comparison, and speed in online shopping (KMPG, 2016). In line with Sheehan (2002), perceptions of privacy are also based on circumstances. The data by KMPG (2016) show that, while the sharing of demographic information (such as education, ethnicity, and gender) causes less concern, fewer than 20% of participants are willing to share more sensitive information such as medical records (13%), address (14%), and location (16%) with businesses. Do not track mechanisms are used by about 1/3 of the survey participants to protect their own privacy (KMPG, 2016). Evidently, users' privacy concerns are universal among global consumers and their perceptions about what information should be protected also shows a homogeneous and converging trend.

On the other hand, country-specific KMPG's data (2016) seems to indicate that countries do vary as to the perceived importance of privacy, suggesting a potentially divergent inclination, due to national cultural characteristics (De Mooij, 2003). Over one-third of consumers from China (39%), India (35%), and Singapore (32%) are the most concerned about their own online privacy, when compared with those from other countries (KMPG, 2016). Malaysian consumers (62%) are most optimistic about online privacy in 10 years, compared with 42% for China and 51% for India (KMPG, 2016), further refuting the claim that global consumers will think and feel like about online privacy simply as a result of the technology.

Morth (2014) reports a survey done in U.K. and concludes that security and online privacy are considered important among British users. Almost 90% of British users admits that they are concerned about their own privacy (Morth, 2014). More than 1/3 of the survey participants indicate that they are "always" and "frequently" worried about protecting their own privacy (Morth, 2014). In terms of what is most likely to cause their privacy concerns, sharing personal information among businesses (60%) tops the list, followed by online tracking to receive targeted ads and contents (54%), privacy policies of social media companies (27%), privacy policies of search engine companies (21%), government surveillance (20%), and mobile tracking by businesses (19%) (Morth, 2014).

The Eurobarometer report by European Commission (2011) has also found that 44% of the European participants are concerned about the misuse of personal information without their knowledge, while 38% are worried about the sale of private information to third party vendors (cited in Heyman, De Wolf, & Pierson, 2014, p. 19). In the same report, 32% are concerned about identity theft, and 28% has expressed concerns about commercial offers not permitted by them (cited in Heyman, et al., 2014, p. 19). More recent data on 5,000 European consumers from Belgium, France, Germany, Italy, Netherlands, Spain, and United Kingdom are reported by Selligent Marketing Cloud (2020). The study observes that 71% of survey participants agree that personalization is very important, and 51% of them is willing to share personal information to obtain personalized consumer experiences (Selligent Marketing Cloud, 2020). Nevertheless, 74% have agreed that privacy is more important than personalized consumer experiences, while 41% agree that they will reduce social media usage as a result of privacy concerns (Selligent Marketing Cloud, 2020).

Compared with the European data, Pew Research Center's survey of 4,272 adults (2019) reports that the majority of American consumers are concerned how their personal data will be collected by the government (64%) and the businesses (79%) (Auxier & Rainie, 2019). About seventy-seven percent of U.S. consumers are aware of the personalized marketing practices using their own personal data collected by the businesses (Auxier & Rainie, 2019). In terms of this type of privacy-invasive business practices, 81% of the U.S. consumers believe the benefits are not sufficient when considering the potential risks (Auxier & Rainie, 2019). A large number of Americans has little or no control over their personal information collected by either the government (84%) or the businesses (81%) (Auxier & Rainie, 2019).

To answer the last research question (RQ4), in terms of the convergence vs. divergence trend in terms of global social media usage behaviors, the global survey of 24 countries and 6,900 consumers has addressed some of the problems in comparing cross-national data (KMPG International, 2016). Situation-based privacy concerns offer the best insights into how countries converge or diverge. Privacy concerns are abundant among online shoppers cross-nationally among 74% of Malaysian, 72% of Finnish, and 70% of Singaporean consumers (KMPG International, 2016), suggesting the widespread privacy impacts of online shopping activities. Contrary to the converging effects, some other activities are showing diverging effects. In terms of the geo-location use by taxi companies, while 78% of India consumers are fine, but only 22% of Danish consumers are comfortable with this privacy-invasive practice (KMPG International, 2016). Similarly, while 60% of Chinese consumers are fine with personalized billboard advertising, only 22% of Japanese consumers support the practice (KMPG International, 2016). These data indicate both converging and diverging effects of ICTs.

One of the limitations of the secondary research is to locate comparable cross-national data. The large-scale data by KMPG International (2016) offers a good set of data to examine if new ICTs may generate converging or diverging effects on cross-national users' perceptions of privacy. The authors particularly focus on whether people will thoroughly review privacy polices when it comes to setting up a social media profile (i.e., the yellow line in Figure 1). In spite of the global diffusion of social media, consumers from countries in this survey actually diverge in their behaviors. While U.K. (14%) and Ireland (14.5%) are similar in terms of their thoroughness in reading privacy policies, over 20% of Swedish consumers will read, while only 10% of Germans will do the same (KMPG International, 2016). Russia (5%), India (5%), South Africa (5%), Brazil (1%), and New Zealand (4.5%) are least concerned about the privacy policies, while Japanese (15%) and U.S.(10%) consumers are concerned, suggesting the divergence may occur across continents (Refer to Figure 1).

Figure 1. The level of thoroughness in reading privacy policies by activity types

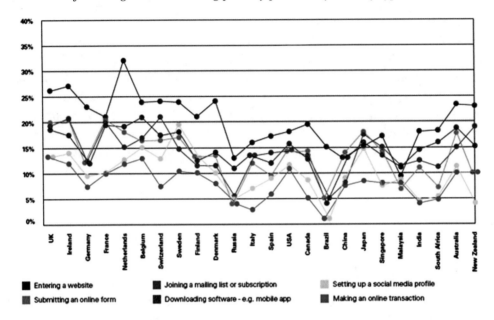

On the other hand, a detailed examination of KMPG's data also suggest that some countries have consistently shown a lower concern for privacy across different types of ICT-enabled activities. For example, Germany has a consistently low score in terms of joining a mailing list or subscription (8%), setting up a social media profile (10%), submitting an online form (12%), downloading software (12%), and making an online transaction (12%), with an exception of entering a website (24%) (KMPG International, 2016). The same phenomena can be observed in Russia, Malaysia, and Brazil, suggesting overall converging trends of privacy perceptions in these four countries (KMPG International, 2016) (Refer to Figure 1).

Discussions

The above global and country data on concerns about privacy present an interesting case of how consumers perceive privacy issues related to technologies. While global consumers have become aware of the potential threats to personal privacy in the age of new media, country variations exist in terms of privacy control, use of private personal information, and actors of privacy invasion. As Ozturk and Cavusgil (2019) point out "[t]he convergence versus divergence debate has persistently presented a puzzle in the scholarly literature" (p. 294). The bi-polarity of convergence vs. divergence debates is likely to render any meaningful interpretation and understanding of the global and country-specific data on privacy concerns possible. As a result, some scholars have introduced the convergence-divergence-crossvergence (CDC) framework that was developed to discuss the value variations and transformation among the headquarter and subsidiaries in an international business research setting to explain "seemingly incomplete explanations of the previously proposed convergence and divergence perspectives" (Ralston, 2008, p. 27). The emphasis on the importance of values in each country can be extended to this study.

Information-communication technologies (ICTs) are likely to contribute cultural convergence of global social media users, despite the similarities in the media consumption behaviors among South Korea and American users are not universal, suggesting the coexistence of convergence and divergence phenomena (Choi & Ferle, 2004). Using the same value transformation and blending mechanism found in crossvergence line of research (Ralston, 2008), it can be argued that new media technologies such as social media are likely to blend with local cultural and value characteristics (De Mooij, 2003) when it comes to how users may perceive privacy issues. As Ozturk and Cavusgil (2019) argue, the crossvergence framework "captures a transitional state of convergence and divergence perspectives" (p. 296). Mostly importantly, Ozturk and Cavusgil (2019) reason that "convergence is driven by technological influence, whereas divergence is driven by sociocultural influence" (p. 296).

While social media platforms are diffused globally (except in China where its own social media platforms thrive) and creates a global social media culture, country-unique sociocultural influence (as explained in Ozturk and Cavusgil, 2019) may offer some explanations about why consumers from different countries vary in their privacy perceptions. Trepte, Reinecke, Ellison, Quiring, Yao, and Ziegele (2017) propose their "privacy calculus" approach to account for whether social media users decide to relinquish their control over personal information depends on how they evaluate the risks and benefits. On the basis of a cross-national survey data of over 1,600 participants from Germany, the Netherland, the U.K., the U.S., and China, their empirical data confirms the importance of cultural factors that may explain the divergence trend. The uncertainty avoidance index (Hofstede, 1991) is the most important predictor to affect social media users' risk and benefit calculation, leading to their determination of how to control their own personal information (Trepte et al., 2017). Their empirical data confirms a higher level of uncertain avoidance negatively predict users' willingness to accept privacy risks and share personal information (such as uploading personal photos) (Trepte et al. 2017). Individualism, another cultural dimension (Hofstede, 1991) is also found to be negatively associated with willingness to avoid risks; in other words, those consumers from a high individualistic culture tend to believe it is less important to avoid risks (Trepte et al. 2017). The above discussions support a more dynamic perspective of various macro-level factors (i.e., sociocultural and technological influences) in terms of how they account for a global convergence trend of privacy concerns with diverging perspectives affected by cultural dimensions.

RECOMMENDATIONS, LIMITATIONS, AND FUTURE DIRECTIONS

To conclude this study, the discussions of convergence and divergence begin with the anecdotal belief that globalization will lead to the homogenization of consumer needs, wants, and their subsequent purchase behaviors (De Mooij, 2003). Because consumers' privacy concerns are evidently affected by both micro- and macro-level factors (such as users' demographics or national cultural characteristics), the phenomenon helps understand the technology-enhanced convergence and divergence trends around the world.

The study of privacy perceptions among cross-cultural consumers are important for a variety of reasons. First, the growing applications of personalized marketing communication messages rely heavily on the collection, analysis, and monetization of personal private information. Many platforms have relied on many privacy-invasive technologies (such as cookies or locational trackings) to generate data to help online advertisers to deliver highly personalized ads, with severe privacy implications (Gal-Or, Gal-Or, & Penmetsa, 2018). Learning the homogenization or heterogenization of media users in terms of their willingness to give up personal control of private information has the practical importance to develop an effective digital advertising campaign (Gal-Or et al., 2018). It also affects the survival of these online advertising platforms because a higher fee can be charged by most differentiating platforms (Gal-Or et al., 2018).

This study applies the convergence and divergence theoretical framework (De Mooij, 2003) with the integration of the latest crossvergence concept (Ozturk & Cavusgil, 2019; Ralston, 2008) to study the privacy perceptions among global social media users. However, the study is limited by the reliance on secondary research data. However, as a research methodology, it has the limitations of dataset availability and comparative data parameters. Secondly, the concepts of convergence or divergence is very comprehensive and its broad nature of these concepts have its limitations (Ozturk & Cavusgil, 2019). Furthermore, consumers' perceptions of privacy are often affected by the news events. For example, Facebook's privacy scandal (Corcoran, 2018) or news about government surveillances have often caused the increase of privacy concerns among both U.K. and U.S. users (Auxier & Rainie, 2019; Morth, 2014). Thirdly, new privacy-invasion technologies (such as geo-tagging in mobile devices) may also present challenges to study privacy concerns as the convergence and divergence phenomena (eMarketer.com, 2020; Friedland & Sommer, 2010) because of the geographical variations in terms of mobile diffusion (Pew Research Center, 2019). Lastly, new technologies unavoidably will generate new type of privacy concept. For example, Such and Criado (2018) propose the concept of multiparty privacy in social media that can be expanded to study similar issues in cloud-based file sharing and collective intelligence.

REFERENCES

Acquisti, A., Brandimarte, L., & Loewenstein, G. (2015). Privacy and human behavior in the age of information. *Science*, *347*(6221), 509–514. doi:10.1126cience.aaa1465 PMID:25635091

Arora, P., & Scheiber, L. (2017). Slumdog romance: Facebook love and digital privacy at the margins. *Media Culture & Society*, *39*(3), 408–422. doi:10.1177/0163443717691225 PMID:29708133

Auxier, B., & Rainie, L. (2019, November 15). Key takeaways on Americans' views about privacy, surveillance and data-sharing. *Pew Research Center*. Retrieved on March 22, 2020 from https://www.pewresearch.org/fact-tank/2019/2011/2015/key-takeaways-on-americans-views-about-privacy-surveillance-and-data-sharing/

Bright, L. F., Logan, K., English, A., Kingman, J., & Lyons, K. (2019). *Social media fatigue and the advertising industry: How are consumers, clients, and content creators dealing with the pressure to be constantly connected?* Paper presented at the American Academy of Advertising Conference, Dallas, TX.

Burkell, J., Fortier, A., Yeung, L. L., Wong, C., & Simpson, J. L. (2014). Facebook: Public space, or private space? *Information Communication and Society*, *17*(8), 974–985. doi:10.1080/1369118X.2013.870591

Choi, S. M., & Ferle, C. L. (2004). Convergence across American and Korean young adults: Socialisation variables indicate the verdict is still out. *International Journal of Advertising*, *23*(4), 479–506. doi:10.1080/02650487.2004.11072896

Chung, W., & Paynter, J. (2002). Privacy Issues on the Internet. *Proceedings of the 35th Hawaii International Conference on System Sciences*. 10.1109/HICSS.2002.994191

Corcoran, K. (2018, March 28). Facebook is overhauling its privacy settings in response to the Cambridge Analytica scandal. *Business Insider*. Retrieved on March 31, 2018 from https://www.businessinsider.com/facebook-overhauls-privacy-settings-after-cambridge-analytica-scandal-2018-2013

De Mooij, M. (2003). Convergence and divergence in consumer behaviour: Implications for global advertising. *International Journal of Advertising*, *22*(2), 183–202. doi:10.1080/02650487.2003.11072848

De Mooij, M., & Beniflah, J. (2017). Measuring cross-cultural differences of ethnic groups within nations: Convergence or divergence of cultural values? The case of the United States. *Journal of International Consumer Marketing*, *29*(1), 2–10. doi:10.1080/08961530.2016.1227758

Dessart, L. (2017). Social media engagement: A model of antecedents and relational outcomes. *Journal of Marketing Management*, *33*(5-6), 375–399. doi:10.1080/0267257X.2017.1302975

Duan, J., & Dholakia, N. (2015). The reshaping of Chinese consumer values in the social media era: Exploring the impact of Weibo. *Qualitative Market Research*, *18*(4), 409–426. doi:10.1108/QMR-07-2014-0058

Dutton, W. (2001). Computers and Society. International Encyclopedia of the Social & Behavioral Sciences, 2480-2487.

eMarketer.com. (2020, March 2). *How Privacy Concerns Are Changing the World of Location Data*. Retrieved on March 22, 2020 from https://www.emarketer.com/content/how-privacy-concerns-are-changing-the-world-of-location-data

Friedland, G., & Sommer, R. (2010, August). Cybercasing the Joint: On the Privacy Implications of Geo-Tagging. *HotSec'10: Proceedings of the 5th USENIX conference on Hot topics in security*.

Fulton, J. M., & Kibby, M. D. (2017). Millennials and the normalization of surveillance on Facebook. *Continuum: Journal of Media & Cultural Studies, 31*(2), 189-199. Advance online publication. doi:10.1080/10304312.10302016.11265094

Gal-Or, E., Gal-Or, R., & Penmetsa, N. (2018, September). The Role of User Privacy Concerns in Shaping Competition Among Platforms. *Information Systems Research*, *29*(3), 698–722. doi:10.1287/isre.2017.0730

Grewal, L., Stephen, A. T., & Coleman, N. V. (2019). When posting about products on social media backfires: The negative effects of consumer identity signaling on product interest. *JMR, Journal of Marketing Research*, *56*(2), 197–210. doi:10.1177/0022243718821960

Hakim, C. (1983). *Secondary analysis in social research: A guide to data sources and methods with examples*. Allen & Unwin.

Ham, C.-D., Lee, J., Hayes, J. L., & Bae, Y. H. (2019). Exploring sharing behaviors across social media platforms. *International Journal of Market Research*, *61*(2), 157–177. doi:10.1177/1470785318782790

Heyman, R., Wolf, R. D., & Pierson, J. (2014). Evaluating social media privacy settings for personal and advertising purposes. *Info, 16*(4), 18-32.

Hofstede, G. H. (1991). *Cultures and organizations: Software of the mind*. McGraw-Hill.

Hunter, G. L., & Taylor, S. A. (2020). The relationship between preference for privacy and social media usage. *Journal of Consumer Marketing, 37*(1), 43–54. doi:10.1108/JCM-11-2018-2927

Internet World Stats. (2017, June). Facebook users in the world. *Internet World Stats*. Retrieved on March 20, 2020 from https://internetworldstats.com/facebook.htm

Irion, K., & Helberger, N. (2017). Smart TV and the online media sector: User privacy in view of changing market realities. *Telecommunications Policy, 41*(3), 170–184. doi:10.1016/j.telpol.2016.12.013

Jacobs, R. N., & Li, M. (2017). Culture and comparative media research: Narratives about Internet privacy policy in Chinese, U.S., and UK newspapers. *Communication Review, 20*(1), 1–25. doi:10.108 0/10714421.2016.1271641

Johnston, M. P. (2014). Secondary Data Analysis: A Method of which the Time Has Come. *Qualitative and Quantitative Methods in Libraries, 3*, 619–626.

Kantar China. (2018, September 5). China social media landscape 2018. *Kantar China*. Retrieved on March 20, 2020 from https://www.chinainternetwatch.com/26502/social-media-22018/

KMPG. (2016, November 7). *Companies that fail to see privacy as a business priority risk crossing the 'creepy line'*. KMPG. Retrieved on June 23, 2019 from https://home.kpmg/sg/en/home/media/ press-releases/2016/2011/companies-that-fail-to-see-privacy-as-a-business-priority-risk-crossing-the-creepy-line.html

KMPG International. (2016). *Creepy or cool? Staying on the right side of the consumer privacy line*. Retrieved on March 22, 2020 from https://home.kpmg.com/sg/en/home/insights/2016/2011/crossing-the-line.html

Kolb, G. (2008, May 29). Social media as a global phenomenon: Recent discoveries. *Corporate Communications Compass*. Retrieved on March 20, 2020 from http://ccc.georgkolb.com/?p=2020

Koohang, A., Paliszkiewicz, J., & Goluchowski, J. (2018). Social media privacy concerns: Trusting beliefs and risk beliefs. *Industrial Management & Data Systems, 118*(6), 1209–1228. doi:10.1108/ IMDS-12-2017-0558

Leetaru, K. H. (2015, August 27). Who's doing the talking on Twitter? *The Atlantic*. Retrieved on March 20, 2020 from https://www.theatlantic.com/international/archive/2015/2008/twitter-global-social-media/402415/

Lips, A. M. B., & Eppel, E. A. (2017). Understanding and explaining online personal information-sharing behaviours of New Zealanders: A new taxonomy. *Information Communication and Society, 20*(3), 428–443. doi:10.1080/1369118X.2016.1184697

Luna, M. D. (2020, July 14). Should you delete TikTok? Why some experts think the app is a privacy threat. *Houston Chronicle*. Retrieved on July 14, 2020 from https://www.chron.com/news/houston-texas/article/Should-you-delete-TikTok-Is-the-popular-app-a-15407966.php

McKinsey & Company. (2011, May). *The world gone digital: Insights from McKinsey's Global iConsumer Research*. New York: McKinsey & Company.

McKinsey & Company. (2012, January). *The Young and the Digital: A Glimpse into Future Market Evolution*. New York: McKinsey & Company.

Mitry, D. J., & Smith, D. E. (2009). Convergence in global markets and consumer behaviour. *International Journal of Consumer Studies*, *33*(3), 316–321. doi:10.1111/j.1470-6431.2009.00746.x

Morgan, E. (2016, September 6). *Homogenization of social media*. Retrieved on March 9, 2020 from https://morganandco.com/homogenization-social-media/

Morth, D. (2014). 89% of British internet users are worried about online privacy: report. *eConsultancy*. Retrieved on March 16, 2020 from https://econsultancy.com/2089-of-british-internet-users-are-worried-about-online-privacy-report/

Mustapha, L. K., Azeez, A. L., & Wok, S. (2011, September). *Globalization, Global Media and Homogenization of Global Culture: Implications for Islam and Muslims*. Paper presented at the National Seminar on New Media and Islamic Issues: Challenges and Opportunities, Organized by Department of Communication, CERDAS & ISTAC, IIUM.

O'Brien, D., & Torres, A. M. (2012, April). Social networking and online privacy: Facebook users' perceptions. *Irish Journal of Management*, *31*(2), 63.

Ozturk, A. (2016, February 26-28). Global Convergence of Consumer Spending Behavior: An Empirical Examination. *2016 AMA Winter Educators' Proceedings*.

Ozturk, A., & Cavusgil, S. T. (2019). Global convergence of consumer spending: Conceptualization and propositions. *International Business Review*, *28*(2), 294–304. doi:10.1016/j.ibusrev.2018.10.002

Pew Research Internet Project. (2019, June 12). *Mobile Technology Fact Sheet*. Washington, DC: Pew Research Internet Project. Retrieved on March 14, 2020 from https://www.pewresearch.org/internet/fact-sheet/mobile/

Ralston, D. A. (2008, January-February). The crossvergence perspective: Reflections and projections. *Journal of International Business Studies*, *39*(1), 27–40. doi:10.1057/palgrave.jibs.8400333

Roper, W. (2020, March 3). *Privacy concerns fuel facebook exodus*. Statista. Retrieved on July 14, 2020 from https://www.statista.com/chart/21018/top-reasons-people-leave-facebook/

Rütten, L. (2016). Facebook user perceptions of privacy and security on Facebook, between Millennials and Non-Millennials. *Political Science*. Retrieved on July 14, 2020 from https://www.semanticscholar.org/paper/Facebook-user-perceptions-of-privacy-and-security-R%C3%BCtten/f878ebd1ffb358a2068e88f-fa9a84c71769a924e

Sadik, J. (2008). Technology adoption, convergence, and divergence. *European Economic Review*, *52*(2), 338–355. doi:10.1016/j.euroecorev.2007.02.005

Selligent Markteting Cloud. (2020). *Selligent Global Connected Consumer Index* (2nd ed.). Selligent Markteting Cloud. Retrieved on March 19, 2020 from Retrieved on March 19, 2020 from https://www.selligent.com/resources/analyst-reports/selligent-global-connected-consumer-index/arconsumerindexus

Statista. (2018, May). *Number of global social media users 2010-2021*. Statista. Retrieved on March 19, 2020 from https://www.statista.com/statistics/278414/number-of-worldwide-social-network-users/

Statista. (2020, January). *Countries with the most Twitter users 2020*. Statista. Retrieved on March 20, 2020 from https://www.statista.com/statistics/242606/number-of-active-twitter-users-in-selected-countries/

Such, J. M., & Criado, N. (2018, August). Multiparty privacy in social media. *Communications of the ACM*, *61*(8), 74–81. doi:10.1145/3208039

Trepte, S., Reinecke, L., Ellison, N. B., Quiring, O., Yao, M. Z., & Ziegele, M. (2017, January-March). *A Cross-Cultural perspective on the privacy calculus. Social Media + Society*, 1-13.

Voramontri, D., & Klieb, L. (2019, January). Impact of social media on consumer behaviour. *International Journal of Information and Decision Sciences, 11*(3), 209-233. Advance online publication. doi:10.1504/IJIDS.2019.101994

Walden, I., & Woods, L. (2011). Broadcasting privacy. *Journal of Medicine and Law*, *3*(1), 117–141. doi:10.5235/175776311796471323

Xu, H., Dinev, T., Smith, J., & Hart, P. (2011, December). Information privacy concerns: Linking individual perceptions with institutional privacy assurances. *Journal of the Association for Information Systems*, *12*(12), 798–824. doi:10.17705/1jais.00281

ADDITIONAL READING

Baruh, L., Secinti, E., & Cemalcilar, Z. (2017). Online privacy concerns and privacy management: A meta-analytical review. *Journal of Communication*, *67*(1), 26–53. doi:10.1111/jcom.12276

Bellman, S., Johnson, E. J., Kobrin, S. J., & Lohse, G. L. (2004). International differences in information privacy concerns: A global survey of consumers. *The Information Society, 20*(5), 313-324. *DOI, 3*. Advance online publication. doi:10.1080/01972240490507956

Blumber, A. J., & Eckersle, P. (2009, August). *On Locational Privacy, and How to Avoid Losing it Forever*. San Francisco, CA: Electronic Frontier Foundation. Retrieved from. Retrieved on March 16, 2020 from http://kelsocartography.com/blog/?p=3536

Bridwell, S. A. (2007). The dimensions of locational privacy. In H. J. Miller (Ed.), *Societies and Cities in the Age of Instant Access* (pp. 209–225). Springer. doi:10.1007/1-4020-5427-0_14

Burstein, A., & Bercu, J. (2017, January). Stress testing the US privacy framework. *InterMEDIA*, *44*(4), 18–21.

Callanan, C., Jerman-Blažic, B., & Blažic, A. J. (2016). User awareness and tolerance of privacy abuse on mobile Internet: An exploratory study. *Telematics and Informatics*, *33*(1), 109–128. doi:10.1016/j. tele.2015.04.009

Cottrill, C. D. (2011). Location privacy: Who protects? *Journal of the Urban and Regional Information Systems Association / URISA*, *23*(2), 49–59.

Dinev, T., & Hart, P. (2004). Internet privacy concerns and their antecedents: Measurement validity and a regression model. *Behaviour & Information Technology, 23*(6), 413-422. *DOI, 4.* Advance online publication. doi:10.1080/01449290410001715723

Dinev, T., & Hart, P. (2005-2006, Winter). Internet Privacy Concerns and Social Awareness as Determinants of Intention to Transact. *International Journal of Electronic Commerce*, *10*(2), 7–29. doi:10.2753/ JEC1086-4415100201

Electronic Frontier Foundation (EFF). (2019). Privacy. San Francisco, CA: Electronic Frontier Foundation. Retrieved on March 16, 2020 from https://www.eff.org/issues/privacy

EPIC. (n.d.). *Locational privacy*. Retrieved on March 16, 2020 from https://epic.org/privacy/location/

Executive Office of the President, President's Council of Advisors on Science and Technology (2014, August). *Report to the President: Big Data and Privacy: A Technological Perspective*. Washington, D.C.: EPIC.

Inmobi. (2013, February). *Global mobile media consumption reaching millennials*. Retrieved on March 16, 2020 from https://www.inmobi.com/blog/2013/02/27/global-mobile-media-consumption-reaching-millennials/

Krumm, J. (2008). *A Survey of Computational Location Privacy*. Redmond, Washington: Microsoft. Retrieved on March h16, 2020 from https://www.microsoft.com/en-us/research/wp-content/uploads/2016/12/ computational-location-privacy-preprint.pdf

Merkovity, N., Imre, R., & Owen, S. (2015). Homogenizing social media - affect/effect and globalization of media and the public sphere. In Media and Globalization: Different Cultures, Societies, Political Systems (pp. 59-71). New York: Maria Curie-Sklodowska University Press (under Columbia University Press).

Minch, R. P. (2004, January 5-8). *Privacy Issues in Location-Aware Mobile Devices*. Paper presented at the Proceedings of the 37th Hawaii International Conference on System Sciences.

Mitry, D. J., & Smith, D. E. (2009). Convergence in global markets and consumer behaviour. *International Journal of Consumer Studies*, *33*(3), 316–321. doi:10.1111/j.1470-6431.2009.00746.x

Nielsen. (2017, March 2). Millennials on millennials: A look at viewing behavior, distraction and social media stars. *Nielsen*, Retrieved on March 14, 2020 from https://www.nielsen.com/us/en/insights/ article/2017/millennials-on-millennials-a-look-at-viewing-behavior-distraction-social-media-stars/

Pasternak, O., Veloutsou, C., & Morgan-Thomas, A. (2017). Self-presentation, privacy and electronic word-of-mouth in social media. *Journal of Product and Brand Management*, *26*(4), 415–428. doi:10.1108/ JPBM-04-2016-1150

Thornthwaite, L. (2018). Social media and dismissal: Towards a reasonable expectation of privacy? *The Journal of Industrial Relations, 60*(1), 119–136. doi:10.1177/0022185617723380

Tucker, C. E. (2013). Social networks, personalized advertising, and privacy controls. *JMR, Journal of Marketing Research, 51*(5), 546–562. doi:10.1509/jmr.10.0355

Xu, H., & Teo, H. H. (2004, December). *Alleviating consumer's privacy concern in location-based services: A psychological control perspective.* Paper presented at the Proceedings of the 25th International Conference on Information Systems, Washington, DC.

Xu, H., & Teo, H. H. (2005). *Privacy considerations in location-based advertising.* Paper presented at the Designing Ubiquitous Information Environments: Socio-Technical Issues and Challenges. IFIP — The International Federation for Information Processing, Boston, MA. 10.1007/0-387-28918-6_8

KEY TERMS AND DEFINITIONS

Consumer Behavior: Refers to the study of the decision-making process (at individual, group, organizational, societal, or national levels) to purchase, consumption, and disposal of a product or a service. The field emerges in 1940s and 1950s as a sub-field in the marketing research.

Convergence: A term that is originally introduced by Marieke de Mooij into the discussion of consumer behavior research in early 2000s. The main thesis of this concept is that, as global consumer income increases across national borders, consumer values and behaviors will become the same (or homogenized) as a result of converging technology development.

Crossvergence: A term used in the convergence-divergence-crossvergence (CDC) framework and refers to a different perspective (from the convengence and divergence).

Divergence: A concept that postulates the globalization of international trade and the convergence of information-communication technologies, on the contrary, will lead to the differentiation and heterogenization of consumer values and behaviors across national borders.

Ecosystem: A biological term that describes a community of living organisms, and by extension, of different entities. The term has been stretched to study different operators/players/companies in a specific industry to describe the arrangement of major and minor players in the industry.

KPMG: A global conglomerate made up different individual firms that offers advisory, financial auditing, and tax services. As one of the four largest auditing firms in the world, KPMG is made of a network of companies in 147 countries and employs over 219,000 employees.

Primary Research Methods: A group of research methods that are planned and executed by researchers or their equivalents to collect first-hand data to answer research questions or problems. Primary research methods usually include in-depth interview, surveys, experiments, focus group, observation, ethnographic, social listening, and text mining methods.

Privacy Concerns: A term that refers to an emotional state of consumers when they are worried about the potential infringement on their rights to be let alone, or their freedom from outside interference or intrusion without their prior consent.

Secondary Research Methods: A research method that relies on existing or already published documents to generate insights into an object of research. The technique refers to a synthesis of existing data, a meta-analysis of published journal articles, or a comparison of past studies. The term is often used in comparison with primary research methods that rely on a researcher's original investigation of a phenomenon.

Social Media: A group of Internet or mobile-delivered social networking service applications that allow people to share personal information and connect with others to establish and maintain interpersonal relationships. Popular social media include Facebook, Instagram, Snapchat, and Twitter.

Chapter 6
Social Media Consumption Among Kenyans:
Trends and Practices

Patrick Kanyi Wamuyu

https://orcid.org/0000-0002-4241-2519

United States International University – Africa, Kenya

ABSTRACT

Despite the growing popularity of social media among Kenyans, there is limited baseline data on the consumption of these platforms by different Kenyan communities based on demographics such as age, gender, education, income, and geolocation. The study set out to fill this gap through a baseline survey on social media consumption in Kenya. The study used a mixed-method approach, involving a survey of 3,269 respondents and 37 focus group discussions. The social media platforms in use are WhatsApp, Facebook, YouTube, Instagram, LinkedIn, and Snapchat. However, the use of social media differs by demographics. Kenyans use social media for entertainment, education, jobs, politics, sports, and social issues. Most Kenyans access social media using phones for 1-3 hours daily. Motivations for using social media include the acquisition of information, entertainment, and social interactions. Most social media users have experienced fake news, cyberbullying, and bombardment with graphic images of sex and advertisements. Kenyans consider social media to be addictive, expensive, and time-wasting.

BACKGROUND

Social Media has revolutionized how individuals, communities, and organizations create, share, and consume information. Social networks have also helped people to communicate, breaking down the geographical barriers which restricted instant communication thus permitting successful social media-facilitated collaboration. However, many social media users are also faced with emerging challenges associated with the dark side of social media use. These include ethical and privacy violation issues, data abuse and misuse, the credibility of social media content, hate speech, fake news, and bot-driven interactions. Social media has also been associated with social and economic ills including family disin-

DOI: 10.4018/978-1-7998-4718-2.ch006

tegration, dented reputations, and facilitation of terrorism. Social Media include SMS-based messaging platforms (e.g. WhatsApp, Facebook Messenger, WeChat), blogging platforms (e.g. WordPress, Blogger), social networking sites (e.g. Facebook, LinkedIn, Xing), Microblogs (e.g. Twitter, Tumblr), community media sites (e.g. Instagram, Snapchat, Flickr, YouTube, Dailymotion), wiki-based knowledge-sharing sites (e.g. Wikipedia), Social news aggregation sites and websites of news media (e.g. Buzzfeed, Huffington Post, Tuko News), Social Bookmarking sites (e.g. del.icio.us, Digg), social curation sites (e.g. Reddit, Pinterest) and websites by traditional news organizations, forums, mailing lists, newsgroups, social question and answer sites (e.g. Quora), user reviews (e.g. Yelp, Amazon) and location-based social networks (e.g. Foursquare).

Information and Communications Technologies (ICT) in Kenya have grown rapidly since the Internet was first launched in the early 1990s. Kenya is described as the Silicon Savanah owing to its dynamic ICT sector that has seen the development of globally acclaimed applications such as M-Pesa and Ushahidi. Ushahidi (https://www.ushahidi.com/) is an open-source platform that allows collection of distributed data via SMS, email or web and visualize it on a map or timeline from the public for use in crisis response. M-Pesa (https://www.safaricom.co.ke/personal/m-pesa) is a mobile money transfer service, payments and micro-financing service, in Kenya. Social media has become a key aspect in Kenyan public discourse, facilitating online discussions while at the same time being a key subject of scholarly, socio-cultural, economic, and political debates. Despite the growing popularity of social media platforms, there is limited baseline data on the consumption of the digital media by different Kenyan communities.

Statement of the Problem

Several studies have studied distinct use of different social media platforms including, Twitter (Tully, & Ekdale, 2014) and Facebook (Wamuyu, 2018). The Kenya Audience Research Foundation (KARF, 2020) has also been conducting media consumption audits/surveys since 2007 for their clients, with a focus on traditional media and its audiences. Nendo (Nendo, 2020) observes the use of the internet, apps, websites and social media by businesses in Kenya and providing statistical insights to enterprises in form of infographics. Studies have also explored the use of social media in different sectors of the Kenyan economy such as banking (Njeri, 2014; Njoroge & Koloseni, 2015), journalism (Nyamboga, 2014; Media Council of Kenya, 2016), community development (Murungi, 2018; Ndlela & Mulwo, 2017), advertising and marketing (Mwangi & Wagok, 2016; Aluoch, 2017) and in post-election crisis (Makinen & Kuira, 2008; Ogola, 2019).There is no data on research or a baseline survey on social media in Kenya despite its wide usage and consumption. Therefore, the study set out to fill this research gap by conducting a baseline survey on Social Media consumption in Kenya to identify the patterns of social media usage among Kenyans as well the factors motivating their use of social media.

Research Questions

The proliferation of internet-enabled mobile devices has led to the rapid development of social networking sites, resulting in a continued reconfiguration of ways in which individuals or groups access and use social media platforms. Nevertheless, little is known on how different social media platforms are relevant to diverse groups of people in Kenya based on demographics such as age, gender, education level, geographical location and income. The study was guided by the following questions: (1) what are the major Social Media sites and apps used by Kenyans?; and (2) what are the motivations behind use of social media among Kenyans? The study draws from a nationwide survey on social media consumption patterns among different demographic segments, conducted between December 2018 and March 2019. The survey sampled 3,269 respondents aged between 14 and 55 years.

Significance of the Study

The study provides the missing and much-needed baseline data on social media use among Kenyans based on different demographics. The results of this study contribute to literature on social media use in Kenya since no similar research had been carried out to measure social media use among Kenyans based on different demographics such as age, gender, education level, geographical location, and income. The study has also identified key statistics on social media users in Kenya. These statistics could be used by government, academic institutions and enterprises in the formulation of informed business strategies in order to better reach an identified target audience for improved service delivery, communication, and marketing strategies. For example, the time of the day when most Kenyans are online, could be used to identify the best time to post on social media for a target audience when the engagement rates are higher. Additionally, these statistics can be further used to develop issue-based policies, provide insights for academic inquiries, specific economic development strategies, among others.

The results also highlight the rural-urban digital divide, with most social media users in the rural areas accessing social media using cyber cafés. This could be used by the government to develop policies to address the issues pertaining to social, economic, and political empowerment. There is also a need for the government, individuals and organizations to disseminate their information through the social media, as one of the main motivations of social media use for a majority of Kenyans is the acquisition of information.

From the focus group discussions, the results indicate that individuals use social media when solving life problems. Many people have made their decisions on matters politics, personal relations, careers, and life based on social media conversations.

The paper is structured into six sections. Section 1 is the introduction, Section 2 is the literature review, and Section 3 is an elaboration on the study's research methodology, including the design and development of the survey instrument and the focus group discussion guide. Sections 4, 5, and 6 cover the study results, discussion of the study's empirical findings and the success of the study, highlighting its theoretical and practical implications, limitations and suggestions for further research, respectively.

LITERATURE REVIEW

Globally, the use of social media platforms is increasing exponentially. People use social networks such as Facebook, Twitter, and Instagram for the sole purpose of entertainment and maintaining contacts with their friends' list (Narula & Jindal, 2015). This section introduces use of social media platforms along with the motivations for using social media.

Usage of Social Media Platforms

Social media comprises of communication sites that facilitate relationship forming between users from diverse backgrounds, resulting in a rich social structure (Kapoor *et al.,* 2018). Many people are aware of the ever-mushrooming social media platforms such as Facebook, twitter, WhatsApp, LinkedIn, Instagram, TikTok, among many others (Hedman & Djerf-Pierre, 2013). According to a cross-sectional survey conducted by Alhabash and Ma (2017) among college students (N=396) which explored differences between Facebook, Twitter, Instagram, and Snapchat in terms of intensity of use, time spent daily on the platform, and use motivations, findings showed that participants spent the most time daily on Instagram, followed by Snapchat, Facebook, and Twitter, respectively. Alhabash and Ma's (2017) study also indicated that the students had the highest use intensity on Snapchat and Instagram (nearly equally), followed by Facebook and Twitter. In regard to use motivations, Snapchat took the lead in five of the nine motivations assessed by Alhabash and Ma (2017).

He, Wang, Chen, and Zha (2017) note that social media has become an online platform for businesses to market products/services and to manage customer relationships. Many small businesses have in the recent past joined the social media use bandwagon. Nawaz and Mubarak (2015) examined the adoption of social media in Sri Lankan enterprises and found that Facebook and Twitter were being used by the tourism product suppliers for advertisement and promotional purposes. Young (2017) examined how and why nonprofit human service organizations (HSOs) are using social media and found that these organizations are generally satisfied with social media use primarily to promote their organization's brand with even limited resources. Similarly, Hou and Lampe (2015) note that social media platforms are increasingly adopted by small nonprofit organizations (NPOs) to help them meet their public engagement goals. Leonardi (2015) indicates that use of enterprise social networking technologies can increase the accuracy of people's knowledge of "who knows what" and "who knows whom" at work.

Social media is known to facilitate escapism among people from some things in life. Hunt, Marx, Lipson and Young (2018) performed an experimental study to investigate the potential causal role that social media plays in the well-being of students. During the experiment, Hunt *et al.,* (2018) monitored 143 undergraduates at the University of Pennsylvania, where one group of the study participants were randomly assigned limited access to Facebook, Instagram and Snapchat and only allowed to use 10 minutes, per platform, per day, while the other group was allowed to use social media as usual for three weeks. The study results indicated that the limited use group showed significant reductions in loneliness and depression over the three-week study period as compared to the control group. A similar study conducted among secondary school students and teachers in Embu, Kenya, by Nyagah, Asatsa and Mwania (2015), showed that social media has an influence on how teenagers connect with each other and which in the long run affects their self-esteem.

The global use of social media has surpassed 3.5 billion users as of July 2019 (Social, 2019), an indication that 46 percent of the world's total population is using social media. In the Philippines, individuals spend approximately three hours and fifty-seven minutes every day on social media, making the country the global leader in social media usage (Social, 2019). In contrast, Poushter, Bishop and Chwe (2018) indicate that only less than half of Germany's population use social media. Statista's 2018 report revealed that in 2016, 38 percent of individuals in the EU-28 used social networks daily. The country with the highest share of daily social media use was Denmark, where 59 percent of the population actively engaged on social media platforms on a daily basis. Kenya has a very dynamic ICT sector, however, there is no baseline data on use of social media in Kenya despite its wide usage and consumption. Wamuyu (2017) notes that the existing digital divide, characterized by a lack of computer literacy skills, low internet access, and inadequate ICT infrastructure may be the reasons behind the low social media use among low-income urban communities. In response to this, the author sought to address the following question: Therefore, the author sought to address the following question:

RQ1: What are the major social media platforms used by Kenyans?

Under this question, several more specific sub-questions were asked.

1. What are the social media platforms used by Kenyans?
2. What do Kenyans use social media platforms for?
3. How frequently do Kenyans access social media platforms?
4. How do Kenyans access social media platforms?
5. Where do Kenyans access social media platforms?
6. How much time do Kenyans spend on social media platforms per day?
7. What time of the day do Kenyans use social media platforms?

Motivations for Using Social Media

In today's world, individuals spend several hours every day accessing and using social media platforms for social interactions, news, entertainment, and searching for information. Brandtzæg and Heim (2015) posit that people use social networks to get in contact with new people, to keep in touch with their friends, and general socializing. Studies have identified a number of factors motivating use of social media which include entertainment, information seeking, personal utility and convenience (Al-Menayes, 2015; Lampe, Ellison, & Steinfield, 2006), social surveillance or voyeurism (Mäntymäki & Islam, 2016), and self-promotion and exhibitionism (Belk, 2013; Mäntymäki & Islam, 2016). Whiting and Williams (2013) identified 10 motivations for using social media: social interaction, information seeking, passing time, entertainment, relaxation, communicatory utility, convenience utility, expression of opinion, information sharing, and surveillance or knowledge about others. Lee and Ma (2011) show that information seeking, socializing, and status seeking are the motivations for users sharing news on social media sites.

While Jung and Sundar (2016) found that people over 60 years old used Facebook for social bonding, social bridging, and as a vehicle for responding to family member requests, Joinson (2008) identified a set of eight different motivations college going students have for using Facebook, such as social connection, shared identities, photographs, content, social investigation, social network surfing, entertainment-related content, and status updates. Smock, Ellison, Lamp and Wohn (2011) studied motivations for using different features of Facebook and concluded that there are nine motives for using Facebook. These motives include habitual pastime, wanting to be part of a cool and new trend, entertainment, information sharing, escapism, companionship, professional advancement, social interaction, and meeting new people. Park, Kee and Valenzuela (2009) posit that individuals have different motivations to join Facebook groups. Some people join Facebook groups to look cooler and develop their careers, while others join the groups for socializing, entertainment needs or because they feel pressured by their friends and feel that joining these Facebook groups will boost their social standing among friends (Valenzuela, 2009).

Dhaha and Igale (2013) indicate that the motives for using Facebook among Somali youth are virtual companionship escape, interpersonal habitual entertainment, information seeking, self-expression, and passing time. In a study conducted among US adults, Lin, Lee, Jin and Gilbreath (2017) identified Facebook users' motivations as socialization, entertainment and information seeking as compared to Pinterest users whose motivations were entertainment, information seeking, and self-status seeking. Tartari (2015) identified seven motivations for Facebook use among Albanian students which included virtual companionship escape, interpersonal habitual entertainment, self-description, self-expression, information seeking, passing time, and the establishment of a new online reality that they desire, not where they actually live in.

By studying how students from University of Alabama used Twitter before, during and after a tornado disaster in April 2011, Maxwell (2020), identified four motivations for using Twitter which included the need to socialize, to entertain, to gain status or to gather information. Other studies have identified motivations to use Twitter to include information sharing and social interaction, of information seeking, mobilization, and public expression (Liu, Cheung, & Lee, 2010; Park, 2013). A review of four scholarly works done by Coursaris, Yun and Sung (2010) identified entertainment, relaxation/escape, social interaction, and information seeking as the motivations for using Twitter. Greenwood (2013) suggests that the motives for most Twitter and Facebook users are to pursue fame and to feel valued. A study among Kuwait college students identified the motivations to use Snapchat as passing time, self-expression, self-presentation, and entertainment, while the motivations for using Twitter are self-presentation, entertainment, and social interaction, with the motivations for using Instagram including passing time, social interaction, self-presentation, and entertainment (Alsalem, 2019).

Other studies have also identified motivations for using most of the world's popular social media tools. Mull and Lee (2014) identified five motivations for Pinterest usage, which included fashion, creative projects, virtual exploration, organization, and entertainment. Huang and Su (2018) posit that motivations for using Instagram are seeking social validation, social interactions and diversion. Marcus (2015) indicates that the primary motive for Facebook posts is to establish relationships with others, whereas Instagram is more for personal use and mostly for people who are looking to get praise and likes which gives users a unique sense of satisfaction.

The motivations to use YouTube include to contribute content, including liking content, sharing a link with friends and uploading content, viewing content uploaded by others, need for relaxation and entertainment, and to meet needs for information and learning (Rosenthal, 2018; Klobas *et al.,* 2018). Klobas et al., (2018) found that Malaysian university students were strongly motivated to use YouTube for entertainment, information and learning. Myrick (2015) shows that one of the motivations to watch YouTube is to improve personal mood. Studies have also shown that the users of WhatsApp are mainly motivated by cost, entertainment, leisure, sense of community, immediacy, and intimate communication (Karapanos, Teixeira & Gouveia, 2016; Church & de Oliveira, 2013). Motivations for YouTube users also include expressing opinions and making their voice heard among their peers, entertainment and information-seeking (Hanson & Haridakis, 2008).

Zhang and Pentina (2012) identified the motivations for Chinese users of Weibo as information seeking, social connection, to facilitate their professional development, fulfill emotional needs, reciprocate by helping other users with advice and information, enhance their social status, express oneself, and interact with the site and other users. Hwang and Choi (2016) identified the motivations for using Sina Weibo among Chinese college students as information-gathering, followed by accessibility to celebrity, social connection, self-presentation and entertainment. Lien and Cao (2014) indicates that Chinese WeChat users' motivations are entertainment, sociality and information. Basak and Calisir (2014) identified seven motivations among LinkedIn users in Turkey which included self-promotion, group activities, job and job affairs, finding old and new friends easily, follow up, profile viewer data, and professional networking. In a study on the motives of accessing political candidate profiles on MySpace, Ancu and Cozm (2009) derived three motivations which included social interaction, information seeking and guidance, and entertainment. An online survey among the users of the social news website Reddit.com showed that the Redditors' motivations are socializing/community building, status-seeking and entertainment (Moore & Chuang, 2017).

While the above studies have identified a number of factors motivating use of social media in different countries and in diverse social, cultural and economic settings, their findings may not generalize to the Kenyan setting. The focus of this study was to examine whether the findings from past studies could be generalized to the Kenyan setting. Therefore, the author sought to address the following question:

RQ2: What are the motivations behind using social media among Kenyans?

This study investigated the following five motivations to use social media among Kenyans.

1. Acquiring information (news, knowledge, exploration);
2. Entertainment and pleasure (emotional experiences);
3. Personal identity (personal stability, social status, need for self-respect);
4. Social interactions with family members, friends and connection with the outside world;
5. To escape some things (release tension, shifting attention from unpleasant happenings).

RESEARCH METHODOLOGY

The researchers used a mixed study approach, which involved collecting both quantitative (survey) and qualitative (focus group discussions) data in two phases. Focus group discussions were used as a complementary method to the survey. Descriptive analysis was completed for the quantitative data and thematic analysis was used for the qualitative data. Use of focus group discussions resulted in the collection of in- depth data which could not have been obtained if only a survey had been used. For example, the emergence of two new motivations of using social media, namely seeking business opportunities through social media and buying and selling on social media were only realized from focus group discussions as the survey only had the commonly known motivations from the literature.

Data collection in phase one was achieved through a baseline survey to collect data on the social media usage patterns among Kenyans. The baseline survey was accomplished using a hand-delivered questionnaire. The questionnaire consisted of open-ended and closed-ended questions to measure individual social media use patterns, motivations to using social media as well as demographic questions. The participants were assured of their anonymity and confidentiality, and informed that their participation in the study was voluntary.

Phase two data was collected using focus group discussions aimed at getting the insights on the survey participants' reflections on their social media and internet use experiences and motivations. The focus group discussion sessions lasted for 120 minutes (2 hours). During each focus group meeting, 60 minutes were used for the focus group discussion guide while the other 60 minutes were for introductions, closing remarks and refreshments. Each focus group discussion had 6 to 10 participants and a moderation team (the moderator and the assistant) whose members had shared tasks.

The target population was stratified into five groups based on ages to enable a comparative analysis on social media consumption patterns. The five strata have been designed in accordance with the socio-demographic characteristics. The five strata are as follows:

- 14 to 20 years old - These constitute the high school level students that access to internet and social media during holiday period and were born in the digital media environment.
- 21 to 25 years old - These constitute college-level students and were also born in the digital media environment.
- 26 to 35 years old - These constitute early career workers and were born in a non-digital media environment but they use it.
- 36 to 45 years old - These constitute the middle-to-late career workers who mostly learnt to use digital media when they were adults.
- 46 years and above – These constitute seniors who have historically been late adopters of technology compared to the younger population.

For purposes of obtaining a representative sample, the study divided the country along the former eight administrative provinces – Nairobi, Coast, Central, Western, Nyanza, Eastern, Rift Valley, and North Eastern for purposes. From each of the former provinces, the county with the highest access to Internet was selected for data collection based on the level of internet penetration data from the Kenyan Integrated Household Budget Survey, Kenya National Bureau Statistic (KNBS, 2016). The eight counties selected were Nairobi (Nairobi Province), Mombasa (Coast), Meru (Eastern), Bungoma (Western), Mandera (North Eastern), Trans Nzoia (Rift Valley), Kisumu (Nyanza), and Nyeri (Central).

From the selected counties, one urban and one rural location with Internet penetration as per KNBS 2016 report were selected for data collection. The locations selected for data collection except Nairobi were as follows: Central (Nyeri Town and Naro Moru); Coast (Mombasa City and Changamwe); Eastern (Meru Town and Kathera); North Eastern (Mandera Town and Banissa), Nyanza (Kisumu City and Nyando); Rift Valley (Kitale Town and Kiminini); and Western (Bungoma Town and Kanduyi). However, since there is no distinction between urban and rural areas in Nairobi, the capital city was subdivided according to the socio-economic demographics used by the KNBS as follows: lower income, lower middle-income, middle-income, and high-income. Specifically, for lower income, the data was collected in (Mathare, Kangemi, Kawangware, Mukuru Kwa Njenga, Mukuru Kwa Reuben, Laini Saba, Korogocho, Kariobangi North, Dandora I through V, Kayole and Kiamaiko. For lower middle, the data was collected in Umoja I through III, Kariobangi South, Imara Daima, Riruta, Githurai, Kahawa West, Zimmerman, Mwiki, Kasarani, Njiru, Ruai, Komarock, Savannah, and Eastleigh. In middle-income, the neighborhoods were Parklands, Highridge, Mountain View, Lang'ata, South C, Nyayo Highrise, Nairobi West, Woodley, and Westlands. Runda, Kitisuru, Kileleshwa, Muthaiga, Karen, and Kilimani represented high-income neighborhoods.

RESULTS AND ANALYSIS

Baseline Survey

The nationwide survey of social media consumption patterns among different demographic segments was conducted between December 2018 and March 2019. The survey sampled 3,269 respondents aged between 14 and 55 from eight counties drawn from Kenya's former eight administrative provinces – Nairobi, Coast, Central, Western, Nyanza, Eastern, Rift Valley, and North Eastern. From the sample of

3,269, 3,166 questionnaires were fully answered – representing a health response rate of 96.9%. The data from the 3,166 respondents was used to answer research question one.

RQ1 (1): What Are the Social Media Platforms Used by Kenyans?

Use of Social Media Platforms in Kenya

Figure 1 captures a snapshot of social media platform use by Kenyans. The vast majority of Kenyans almost equally use WhatsApp (89.4%) and Facebook (89.3%). The third most used social media is YouTube (51.6%) followed by Instagram (39.4%). Both LinkedIn and Snapchat are the least popular platforms in Kenya at 9.3% and 9.1% respectively.

Figure 1. Social Media use in Kenya

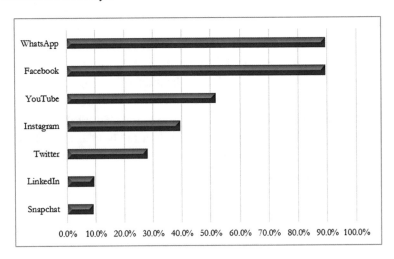

Social Media Use by Age

From Figure 2, the most active age group on social media is 26-35 years, while the least active are those aged above 46 years. Facebook is mostly used by 26-35 year-olds (34.6%) and least used by those 46 years and above (4.6%). Twitter is mostly used by those of 26-35 years (39.3%) and least used by 46 years and above (4.8%). When it comes to WhatsApp, it is also commonly used by Kenyans aged 26-35 years. Instagram is most used by 21-25 year-olds at 38.7% and least used by those beyond 46 years (2.8%). Similarly, Snapchat is also mostly used by those aged 21-25 (36.6%). YouTube is most used by 26-35 year-olds (34.1%) and least used by 46 years and above. LinkedIn is most used by 26-35 year-olds (43.7%) and least used by those 46 years and above.

Use of Social Media by Gender

The men in Kenya are generally more active on social media platforms compared to the women (see Figure 3). They lead in all the social media platforms as active users. The preferred social media plat-

Figure 2. Social Media use by Age

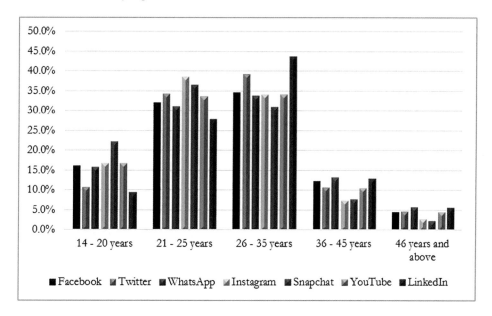

forms among men include LinkedIn (67.8%) and Twitter (67.0%), with Snapchat being the least preferred platform, which is used by 52.5% of men, compared to 47.5% of women who had Snapchat as one of their preferred social media platforms.

The women reported the least use of LinkedIn, at 32.2%. as shown in Figure 3. It is conspicuous that while men use LinkedIn the most, women use it the least, with the reverse being true when it comes to Snapchat.

Figure 3. Use of Social Media by Gender

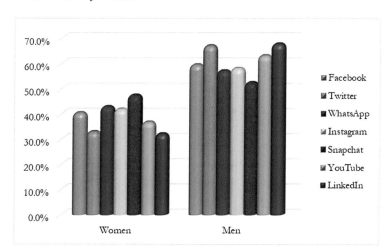

Use of Social Media by Geo-Location

Majority of Kenyans in the rural areas use Facebook (47.9%), WhatsApp (46.8%) and YouTube (44.2%), as compared to a majority of urban residents who use LinkedIn (70.3%), Snapchat (64.2%), Instagram (58.2%) and Twitter (56.8%) as shown in Figure 4.

Figure 4. Use of Social Media by Geo-Location

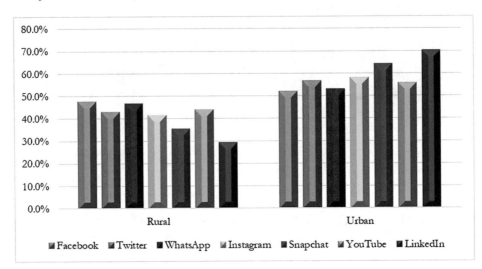

Use of Social Media by Income

A majority of low-income earners in Kenya are using WhatsApp (29.43%), YouTube (29.74%), Twitter (29.37%) and Facebook (29.28%), as compared to a majority of high-income earners who use LinkedIn (51.0%), Twitter (37.2%), YouTube (28.7%) and Instagram (27.3%), as shown in Figure 5. Most of the middle-income earners use LinkedIn (54.6%), Twitter (29.7%), Snapchat (27.8%), and YouTube (24.4%).

Use of Social Media by Income in Nairobi

In Nairobi, the majority of residents live in urban slums. Thus, those who live in informal settlements or the low-income residential areas use Facebook (30%) and WhatsApp (25%) as their social media platforms of choice as indicated in Figure 6. The middle-income residents of Nairobi mostly use LinkedIn (44.5%), Snapchat (29.8) and Twitter (29.7%). However, the lower middle-income population in Nairobi use YouTube (47.6%), WhatsApp (46.0%) and Instagram (45.6%). The high-income Nairobi residents mostly use LinkedIn YouTube and Twitter as shown in Figure 6.

Use of Social Media Platforms by Education Level

From Figure 7, the use of Facebook is more common among those with high school and college levels of education. Among those with higher education levels (undergraduate and graduate), the most common

Figure 5. Use of Social Media by Income

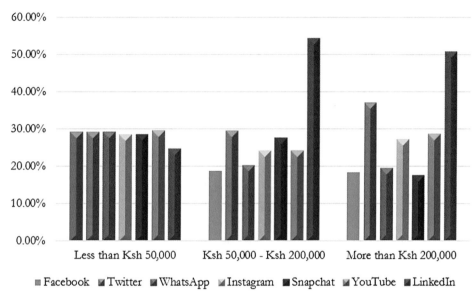

social media platform is LinkedIn. In the primary school category, Facebook tops at 8.5%, followed by WhatsApp and YouTube. For high school graduates, the most prevalent platform is Facebook (34.5%) followed by YouTube (32.3%). WhatsApp is third with 31.4%. However, among those with college-level education, WhatsApp is the most preferred platform (40.6%). The second most popular social media platform among those with college-level education is Instagram (40.4%) followed by Snapchat (40.0%). Other popular platforms among those with college-level education are Facebook (39.4%), YouTube (39.1%), and Twitter (38.5%). For the undergraduate category, the leading social media platform in use

Figure 6. Use of Social Media by income levels in Nairobi

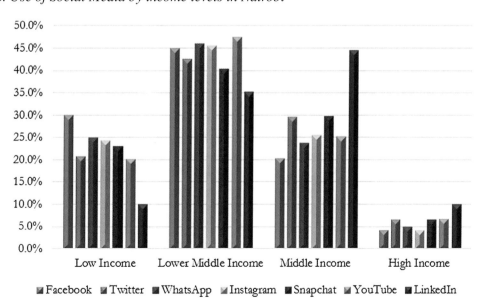

is LinkedIn (36.8%) followed by Twitter (32.1%). Similarly, LinkedIn is the mostly used social media platform among those with Masters and Doctorate level degrees (19.5%). Coming a distant second is Twitter (6.4%) followed by Snapchat (5.0%). Overall, there is heavy use of social media platforms among those with college-level education, while the least usage of social media platforms is among the primary school graduates.

Figure 7. Social Media Use by Education Level

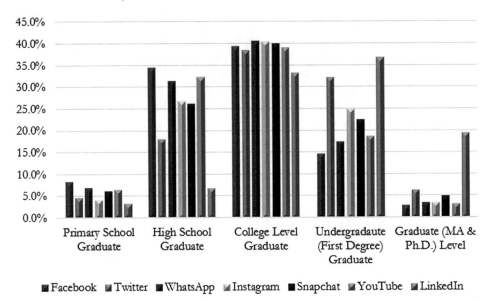

RQ1 (2): What Do Kenyans Use Social Media Platforms For?

Most Kenyans use social media platforms for entertainment, education, jobs, politics, sports, and social issues as shown in Figure 8. LinkedIn (42.1%) and YouTube (38.2%) are the social media platforms mostly used for educational issues. YouTube (74.4%), Instagram (68.9%) and Snapchat (67.3%) are frequently used for entertainment. WhatsApp is mostly used for social issues (89.4%) while LinkedIn is commonly used for job-related issues (61.9%) and education matters (42.1%). Facebook is mostly used for social (65.3%) and entertainment (60.0%) issues. Twitter is used for both social (50.2%) and political (35.1%) issues. The issues the respondents used social media for is a clear indication that people use social media to solve their life problems, make decisions and create identities.

RQ1 (3): How Frequently Do Kenyans Access Social Media Platforms?

Frequency of Accessing Social Media

Social media users in Kenya are highly engaged with the platforms, with most Kenyans accessing more than one social media platform daily as indicated in Figure 9. The data on social media platform use shows that 89.3% of WhatsApp users use the platform daily, with 9.2% accessing it weekly, while 1.4%

Figure 8. Issues of Focus in Using Social Media

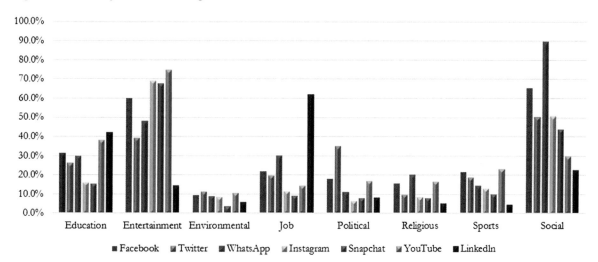

use it less often. 80.7% Facebook users visit the site daily, 15.8% use the platform weekly, while 3% say they visit the site less often. 63.6% of YouTube users visit the site daily, another 29.8% say they use it a few days a week, while 5.7% say they use the use the video-sharing platform less often. Almost half (48.7%) of Snapchat users are on the platform daily, with 27.7% who say they check in weekly, while 8.5% visit Snapchat less often than that. 54.6% of Twitter users visit the site daily, another 32.4% say they visit a few days a week, while 9.2% say they check Twitter less often. 59.8% of Instagram users visit the site every day.

Figure 9. Frequency of Accessing Social Media

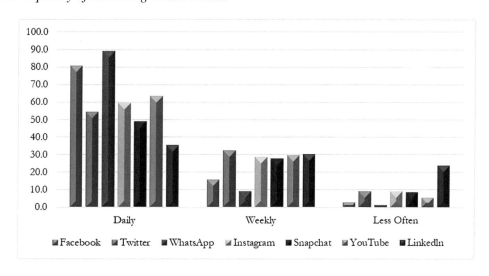

RQ1 (4): How Do Kenyans Access Social Media Platforms?

Devices Used to Access Social Media

According to the survey data, most social media platform users in Kenya used their phones to access their preferred platforms. According to the survey, 78.6% of respondents stated that they accessed the platforms using mobile phones. Almost all WhatsApp (97.5%) and Facebook (96.2%) users accessed the platforms using mobile phones as shown in Figure 10. However, 40.2% and 16.5% of respondents indicated that they accessed LinkedIn using laptops and desktops respectively.

Figure 10. Devices Used to Access Social Media

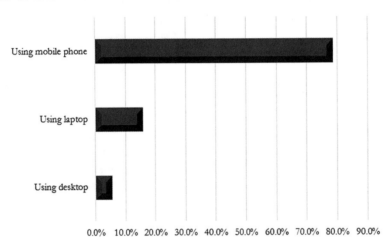

RQ1 (5): Where Do Kenyans Access the Social Media Platforms?

Physical Location of Accessing Social Media

People access social media from different physical locations, including at home (85.5%), public hotspots (23.3%), offices (22.1%) and cyber cafés (14.5%) as shown in Figure 11.

Physical Location of Accessing Social Media in Different Geo-locations

A majority of Kenyans in the rural areas and those living in low-income urban areas still value and use the services of a cyber café (53.1%). However, most of the urban population access social media from the offices (58.1%) and the public hotspots (57.7%), as indicated in Figure 12.

Physical Location of Social Media Access by Income in Nairobi

Even though Internet access charges are comparatively low compared to many African countries, Internet access is still expensive in Kenya. A majority of the middle-income (42.2%) Kenyan population use the

Figure 11. Physical Location of Accessing Social Media

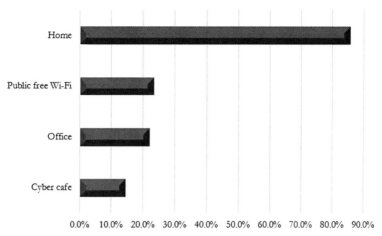

Figure 12. Physical Location of Accessing Social Media in different Geo-locations

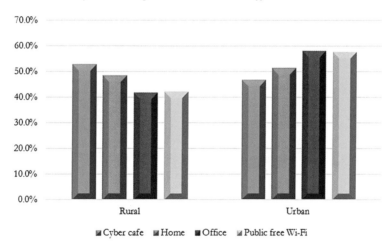

office internet to access social media platforms, while the lower middle-income (49%) take advantage of readily available public Wi-Fi provided in the malls, training institutions and the entertainment spots to access their preferred social media platforms. The people living in low-income (36.1%) urban areas still value and use the services of a cyber café as shown in Figure 13.

Physical Location of Social Media Access by Gender

From Figure 14, the physical location of social media access varies among gender. Women are more likely to access social media at home (43%) or on public Wi-Fi (41%), and men are more likely to prefer accessing social media at the offices (60.1%) or at cyber cafés (66.4%).

Figure 13. Physical Location of Social Media Access by Income in Nairobi

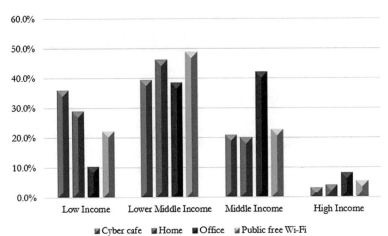

Figure 14. Physical Location of Social Media Access by Gender

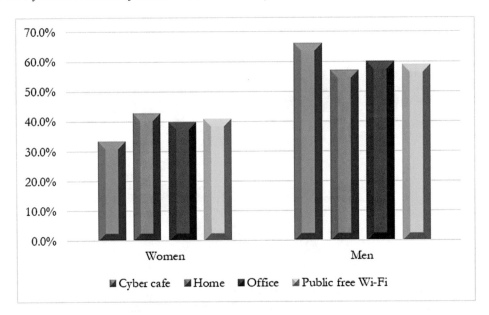

RQ1 (6): How Much Time Do Kenyans Spend on Social Media Platforms per Day?

Daily Time Spent on Social Media

On average, a vast majority of Kenyans spend more than one hour daily on social media platforms. 19.4% of social media users in Kenya spend more than three hours interacting through the social media on a daily basis as shown in Figure 15.

Figure 15. Daily time spent on Social Media

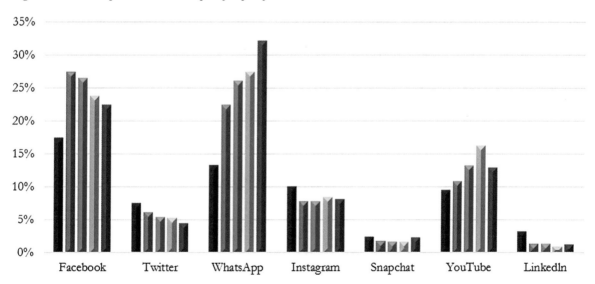

86% of WhatsApp users, 73% of Facebook users and 43% of YouTube users spend more than 1 hour online everyday as shown in Figure 16, while 60% of WhatsApp users, 46% of Facebook users and 29% of YouTube users spend more than 2 hours online everyday as shown in Figure 16.

Figure 16. Time spent online on specific platforms

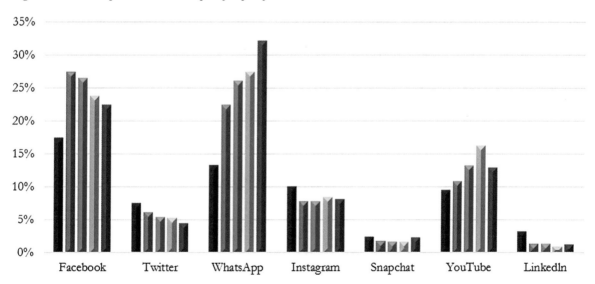

Daily Time Spent on Social Media by Gender

Figure 17 indicates that most Kenyan men spend more time on various social media platforms available to them than women. For example, in a typical day most men (61%) spend more than two hours on social media daily as compared to 39% of women.

Figure 17. Daily Time Spent on Social Media by Gender

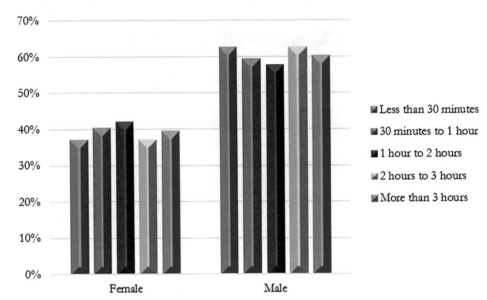

Daily Time Spent on Social Media by Geolocation

60% of the urban population in Kenya use social media platforms for more than 2 hours daily as compared to 40% of the people living in the rural areas who use social media for more than 2 hours on daily basis. A majority of the rural population spend between 1 and 2 hours on social media daily as shown in Figure 18.

Figure 18. Daily Time Spent on Social Media by Geolocation

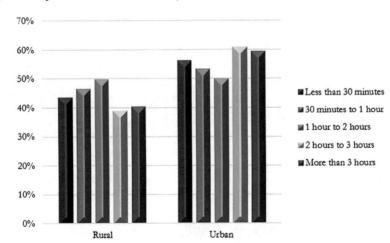

Daily Time Spent on Social Media by Age

Figure 19 shows that Kenyans of the ages between 21 and 35 (age brackets of 21-25 years and 26-35 years) are the most active users of social media available in the country. The data on the time spent on social media by age shows that the people the between the ages of 21 and 35 years spend an average of 2 hours per day on social media platforms. 37% of the 21-25 year-olds spend more than 3 hours a day on social media.

Figure 19. Daily Time Spent on Social Media by Age

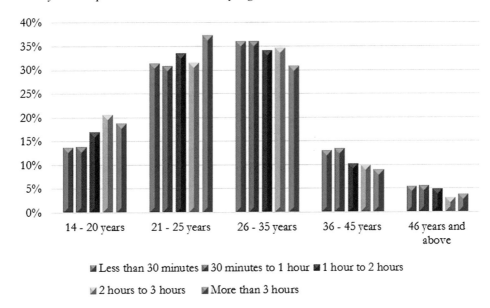

Daily Time Spent on Social Media by Income

Figure 20 shows that Kenya's middle-income group are the most active users of social media platforms in Kenya. 53% of the lower middle-class spend more than 3 hours a day on social media.

Daily Time Spent on Social Media by Education

Figure 21 shows that the college-level graduates spend much more time on social media than any other category of the education group. 41% of the respondents who were college-level graduates spent more than three hours on social media daily, while another 44% spent 2-3 hours on social media a day.

Figure 20. Daily Time Spent on Social Media by Income

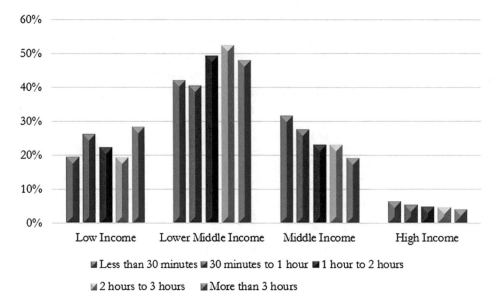

RQ1 (7): What Time of the Day Do Kenyans Use Social Media Platforms?

Time of the Day Spent on Social Media

Both night and evening hours are the times of the day when a majority of Kenyans spend most of their time on various social media platforms (see Figure 22). This could be attributed to the fact that these are the times of the day when most of Kenyans are at home after their day's work. Kenyans also spend

Figure 21. Daily Time Spent on Social Media by Education

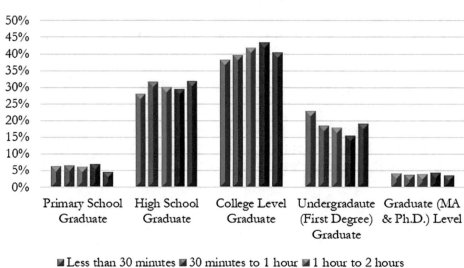

Figure 22. Time of the day Spent on Social Media

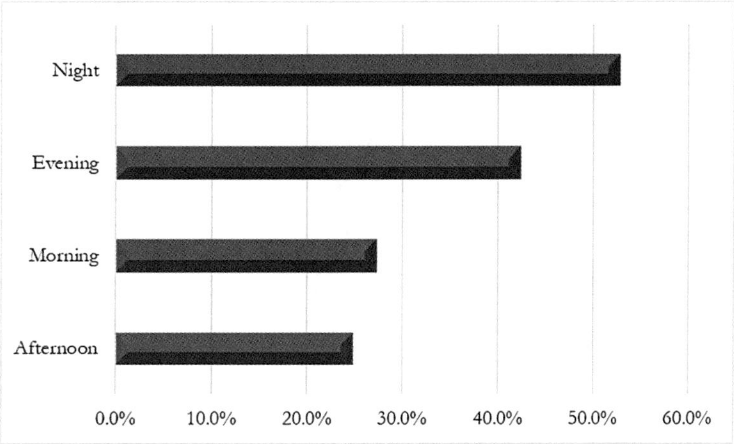

a considerable amount of time in the morning hours on the social media platforms – which could be the period before they get busy with their daily routines.

Time of the Day Spent on Social Media by Gender

When analyzed by gender (see Figure 23), a majority of the Kenyan men (63.9%) spend more time on social media in the mornings, while most women (41.6%) spend their time on the social media platforms in the evenings.

Figure 23. Time of the day Spent on Social Media by Gender

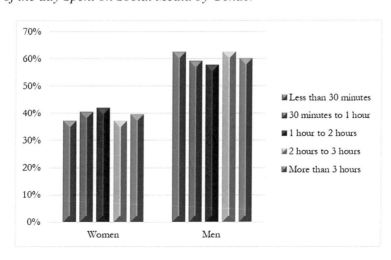

Figure 24. Time of the day Spent on Social Media by Age

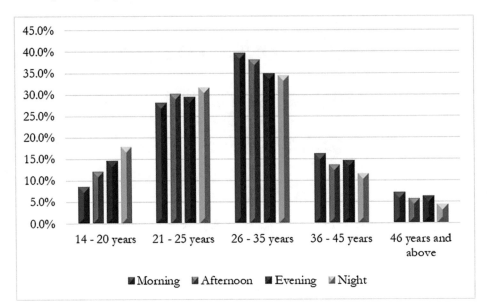

Time of the Day Spent on Social Media by Age

From Figure 24, a majority of the age groups including 26-35 years, 36-45 years and 46 years and above, spend a lot of time on various social media platforms during the morning hours. They also spend a substantial amount of time on social media during afternoon and evening hours. Kenyans in the age groups 14-20 years and 21-25 years spend most of time on social media platforms at night.

Figure 25. Time of the day Spent on Social Media by Geolocation

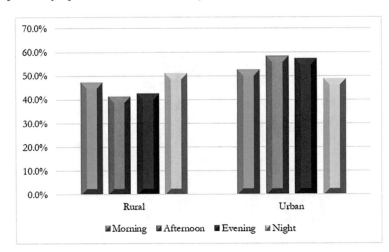

Time of Day Spent on Social Media by Geolocation

Figure 25 indicates that Kenyans residing in rural areas mostly spend their time on social media platforms at night (51.2%) and in the morning (47.3%) hours. On the other hand, Kenyans in urban areas spend most of their time on social media during the afternoon and evening hours.

RQ2: What Are the Motivations Behind Using Social Media Among Kenyans?

As indicated in Figure 26, the vast majority of Kenyans' motivations for using social media are acquiring information (31%), entertainment (28%) and social interactions (24%).

Figure 26. Motivations for using social media platforms

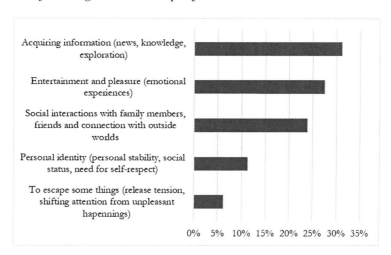

Motivations to Use Specific Social Media Platforms

Among the five motivations for using the social media platforms sought (information acquisition, entertainment, social interactions, personal identity, and escaping social realities), Facebook and WhatsApp are the mostly used for social interactions with family members, friends and connection with the outside world, while Instagram, Snapchat, and YouTube are commonly used for entertainment and pleasure (emotional experiences) and to escape societal realities (release tension, shifting attention from unpleasant happenings). On the other hand, Twitter and LinkedIn are used in creating personal identity (personal stability, social status, need for self-respect) and acquiring information (news, knowledge, exploration) as indicated in Figure 27.

Motivations to Use Specific Social Media Platforms by Different Age Groups

As shown in Figure 28, the motivations for using social media among the young people aged 14-20 years old is entertainment and pleasure (emotional experiences) while the motivations for using the internet for

Figure 27. Motivations to use specific social media platforms

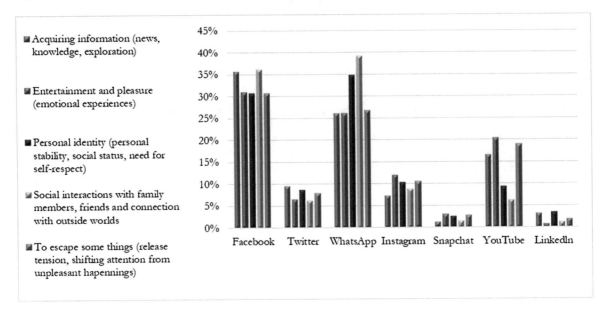

the 21-25 year-olds is to escape things (release tension, shifting attention from unpleasant happenings) and acquiring information (news, knowledge, exploration). For the population aged 26-35 years, the motivations to use social media are acquiring information (news, knowledge, exploration) as compared to those aged more than 36 years, whose motivations to use social media are social interactions.

Figure 28. Motivations to use specific social media platforms by different age groups

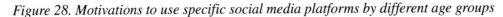

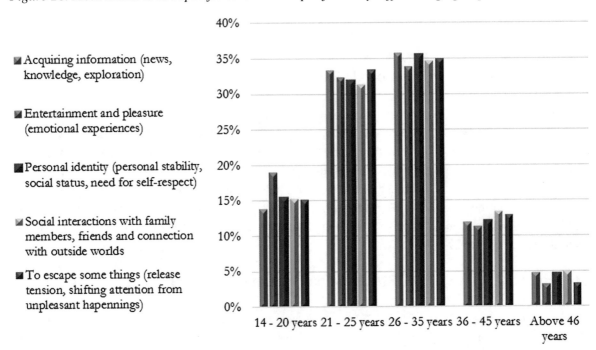

Motivations to Use Specific Social Media Platforms by Different Gender

Most men use social media for personal identity (personal stability, social status, need for self-respect) (64%), and acquiring information (news, knowledge, exploration) (62%). Kenyan women use social media to escape some things in society (release tension, shifting attention from unpleasant happenings) (44%) and entertainment and pleasure (emotional experiences) (41%), as shown in Figure 29.

Figure 29. Motivations to use specific social media platforms by different gender

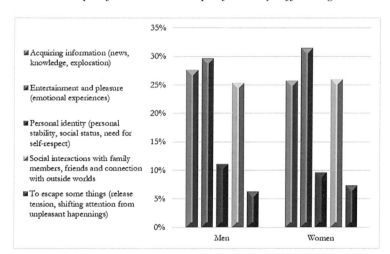

Focus Group Discussions

The study held thirty-seven focus group discussions with 258 participants in four different counties to probe participants' social media consumption. From the focus group discussions, thirteen main themes on use of internet and social media emerged: Dating (1%), Pornography (1%) Games (2%), Religion (2%), Fashion (2%), Politics (2%), Job related issues (4%), Sports (8%), Information (8%), Education (14%), Communication (15%), and Socializing (19%).

A majority of the participants indicated that at a personal level, they have experienced unpleasant experiences while using social media including fake news, cyberbullying, bombardment with graphic images of sex, and advertisements. From the focus group discussions with those aged 14-20 years and 21-25 years, the common recurring challenges associated with social media included social media being very addictive, very expensive, and time-consuming. However, the two age groups, 14-20 years and 21-25 years, also pointed out that social media creates opportunities for people to break out of boredom, to get other people's opinions on matters of interest, and to influence other people's religious beliefs.

The use of groups in social media was also a common theme among different age brackets. Social media groups are niche-specific forums where individuals share information on matters of common interest. Among the focus group discussions held in low-income areas, most social media users were members of different social media groups. The social media groups were to help the group members get updates on what is happening in their neighborhoods. One such a group is the Mathare Forum (https://

web.facebook.com/Mathare-forum-773578946016362/?_rdc=1&_rdr), which had several of its members participating in three of this study's four focus group discussions held in Mathare slums. The members of social media groups such as the Mathare Forum noted that being a member of such a group is fulfilling.

Production and consumption of social media content were widespread among the focus group participants. News content consumption and contribution through social media was prevalent among the study participants. There was a high consumption of news on social media by respondents aged 26-35 years old and 36-45 years old. Video consumption and engagement on social media was the most preferred form of social media entertainment for those aged 14-20 years and 21-25 years old. Consumption of political content on social media was more common with the participants who were more than 45 years old. Among the study participants aged 14-20 years old, there were many passive consumers of social media content who were only viewing or reading social media content without contacting others or contributing.

From the focus group discussions, there was evidence of positive and negative consequences of social media content consumption. 43% of the focus group discussions' participants indicated that social media consumption has in the past influenced their actions, such as making decisions on politics, relationships and religion an indication that individuals use social media conversations to solve their life problems. The participants did draw connections between their decision making and social media consumption. The participants also indicated that creation and the consumption of social media content could lead to lose of several hours per day on less useful activities especially if one had several connections and interests online.

From the focus group discussions, two new motivations for using social media emerged. They are (i) Seeking business opportunities through social media and (ii) buying and selling on social media.

- **Seeking business opportunities:** A number of participants indicated that they use social media to reach out to potential customers and that they have been able to cultivate personal business contacts by directly messaging customers through the social media. Twenty-two study participants were using social media to promote their home businesses, to create online presence and to increase their business' visibility using Instagram, Twitter and Facebook.
- **Buying and selling on social media:** Six participants said that they have been able to directly target their customers, including their friends and followers, in a cheap and effective way and to sell their farm produce even before they harvest through Facebook and WhatsApp.

DISCUSSION

A majority of Kenyans use social media platforms on daily basis. The most commonly used social media platforms are WhatsApp, Facebook, YouTube, Instagram, LinkedIn, and Snapchat. However, the use of social media differs in platforms used by age, gender, geolocation, and levels of income. Most young Kenyans use Instagram and Snapchat while older people prefer Facebook and LinkedIn. Kenyan men use LinkedIn and Twitter while females prefer using WhatsApp and Snapchat. The people living in low-income residential areas in Nairobi use Facebook, WhatsApp, and Instagram while the residents of the middle and higher-income areas of Nairobi mostly use LinkedIn, Twitter, and YouTube. Kenyans in the rural areas mostly use Facebook, WhatsApp, and YouTube as compared to a majority of urban residents who use LinkedIn, Snapchat, Instagram, and Twitter. There are several less developed technological infrastructures in the rural areas which prevent the use of high- resource demanding social media platforms such as Snapchat and Instagram. The use of Facebook, WhatsApp, and YouTube in the rural areas could be attributed to free complimentary services offered by the telecommunications service providers.

Kenyans use social media platforms for entertainment, education, jobs, politics, sports, and social issues. LinkedIn is used for educational and job-related issues. YouTube is used for educational and entertainment issues while WhatsApp is mostly used for social issues. Facebook is mostly used for social and entertainment issues while Twitter is used for both social and political issues. More than half of the Kenyans who use WhatsApp, YouTube, Twitter, and Instagram access these platforms daily. Most of the users of these social media access the platforms using mobile phones. Most Men also access social media from cyber cafés. Most Kenyans spend 1-3 hours on social media every day. People living in urban centers access their social media platforms from their offices and public hotspots while the residents of rural areas mostly access their social media from cyber café. Most Kenyans have transitioned from accessing the internet from cyber café and offices into using mobile phones, hence most people access social media platforms at home. However, a majority of Kenyan in the rural areas and those living in low-income urban areas still value and use the services of a cyber café. Most urban population also access their social media from the offices and the public Wi-Fi. This explains why there is less activities on social media during the weekends and why most social media users post their weekend activities on Monday morning. This could be attributed to two things: One, the fact that most of the people living in urban areas are working and hence they can access the social media using the office internet; and two, in most urban areas, there is the provision and availability of open public Wi-Fi hotspots in eateries, malls and learning institutions.

Kenyans use the internet and social media platforms for dating, watching pornography, playing games, religious matters, fashion, politics, work-related issues, sports, acquiring information, education, communication, and socializing. The motivations for using social media include acquiring information, entertainment, and social interactions. Facebook and WhatsApp are the mostly used for Social interactions while Instagram, Snapchat, and YouTube are commonly used for Entertainment and to escape societal realities. Twitter and LinkedIn are used for creating a personal identity and acquiring information. Social media also influences how Kenyans make decisions on politics, relationships, and religion. Even though social media creates opportunities for people to break out of boredom, to get other people's opinions on matters of interest, and to influence other people's religious beliefs, most users have experienced unpleasant experiences such as fake news, cyberbullying, and bombardment with graphic images of sex and advertisements. Kenyans also consider social media to be addictive, expensive, and time-wasting.

CONCLUSION

This paper has provided an overview of the uses of social media platforms in Kenya and the motivations for using social media platforms among Kenyans based on diverse demographics such as age, gender, education levels, income levels, and geographical locations. The use of digital technology tends to reflect, reproduce, and amplify existing inequalities. The communities living in the rural areas and urban slums are often at a disadvantage when it comes to social media access due to infrastructural challenges such a lack of electricity and high-speed internet connectivity through the fiber cable to home or nearby rural-urban centers. This lack of infrastructure to facilitate internet and social media platforms is reflected in the number, size, and range of social media platforms accessed by the rural population, therefore, the use of social media platforms seems to reflect and amplify the existing social inequalities. But, the creation and consumption of social media content continue to be part of the Kenyan online community.

ACKNOWLEDGMENT

The author acknowledges the support of the National Research Fund, Kenya under Grant NRF/1/ MMC/418 and SIMElab Africa, a project hosted by the School of Science at USIU-Africa and funded by the US Embassy in Nairobi.

REFERENCES

Al-Menayes, J. J. (2015). Motivations for Using Social Media: An Exploratory Factor Analysis. *International Journal of Psychological Studies*, *7*(1), 43–50. doi:10.5539/ijps.v7n1p43

Alhabash, S., & Ma, M. (2017). A tale of four platforms: Motivations and uses of Facebook, Twitter, Instagram, and Snapchat among college students? *Social Media+Society, 3*(1), 1-13.

Alouch, L. D. (2017). *Social Media Marketing and Business Growth of Commercial Banks in Kenya* (Master Thesis). School of Business, Department of Business Administration, University of Nairobi.

Alsalem, F. (2019). Why Do They Post? Motivations and Uses of Snapchat, Instagram and Twitter among Kuwait College Students. *Media Watch*, *10*(3), 550–567. doi:10.15655/mw/2019/v10i3/49699

Ancu, M., & Cozma, R. (2009). Myspace politics: Uses and gratifications of befriending candidates. *Journal of Broadcasting & Electronic Media*, *53*(4), 567–583. doi:10.1080/08838150903333064

Basak, E., & Calisir, F. (2014). Uses and Gratifications of LinkedIn: An Exploratory Study. *Proceedings of the World Congress on Engineering 2014, 2*.

Belk, R. W. (2013). Extended self in a digital world. *The Journal of Consumer Research*, *40*(3), 477–500. doi:10.1086/671052

Brandtzæg, P. B., & Heim, J. (2009). Why People Use Social Networking Sites. In A. A. Ozok & P. Zaphiris (Eds.), Lecture Notes in Computer Science: Vol. 5621. *Online Communities and Social Computing. OCSC 2009*. Springer. doi:10.1007/978-3-642-02774-1_16

Church, K., & de Oliveira, R. (2013). What's up with WhatsApp?: Comparing mobile instant messaging behaviors with traditional SMS. *Proceedings of the 15th International Conference on Human-Computer Interaction with Mobile Devices and Services*, 352-361. 10.1145/2493190.2493225

Coursaris, C. K., Yun, Y., & Sung, J. (2010). *Twitter Users vs. Quitters: A Uses and Gratifications and Diffusion of Innovations approach in understanding the role of mobility in microblogging*. Paper presented at the Mobile Business and 2010 Ninth Global Mobility Roundtable (ICMB-GMR), 2010 Ninth International Conference. 10.1109/ICMB-GMR.2010.44

Dhaha, I. S. Y., & Igale, A. B. (2013). Facebook usage among Somali youth: A test of uses and gratifications approach. *International Journal of Humanities and Social Science*, *3*(3), 299–313.

Greenwood, D. N. (2013). Fame, Facebook, and Twitter: How attitudes about fame predict frequency and nature of social media use. *Psychology of Popular Media Culture, 2*(4), 222–236. doi:10.1037/ppm0000013

Hanson, G., & Haridakis, P. (2008). Users Watching and Sharing the News: A Uses and Gratifications Approach. *The Journal of Electronic Publishing: JEP, 11*(3). Advance online publication. doi:10.3998/3336451.0011.305

He, W., Wang, F. K., Chen, Y., & Zha, S. (2017). An exploratory investigation of social media adoption by small businesses. *Information Technology Management, 18*(2), 149–160. doi:10.100710799-015-0243-3

Hedman, U., & Djerf-Pierre, M. (2013). The social journalist: Embracing the social media life or creating a new digital divide? *Digital Journalism, 1*(3), 368–385. doi:10.1080/21670811.2013.776804

Hou, Y., & Lampe, C. (2015, April). Social media effectiveness for public engagement: Example of small nonprofits. In *Proceedings of the 33rd annual ACM conference on human factors in computing systems* (pp. 3107-3116). 10.1145/2702123.2702557

Huang, Y., & Su, F. S. (2018). Motives for Instagram Use and Topics of Interest among Young Adults. *Future Internet, 10*, 77.

Hunt, M. G., Marx, R., Lipson, C., & Young, J. (2018). No more FOMO: Limiting social media decreases loneliness and depression. *Journal of Social and Clinical Psychology, 37*(10), 751–768. doi:10.1521/jscp.2018.37.10.751

Hwang, H. S., & Choi, E. K. (2016). Exploring Gender Differences in Motivations for Using Sina Weibo. *Transactions on Internet and Information Systems (Seoul), 10*(3), 1429–1441.

Joinson, A. M. (2008). Looking at, looking up or keeping up with people?: Motives and use of Facebook. *Proceedings of the Twenty-Sixth Annual SIGCHI Conference on Human Factors in Computing Systems 2008*, 1027-1036. 10.1145/1357054.1357213

Jung, E. H., & Sundar, S. S. (2016). Senior citizens on Facebook: How do they interact and why? *Computers in Human Behavior, 61*, 27–35. doi:10.1016/j.chb.2016.02.080

Kapoor, K. K., Tamilmani, K., Rana, N. P., Patil, P., Dwivedi, Y. K., & Nerur, S. (2018). Advances in social media research: Past, present and future. *Information Systems Frontiers, 20*(3), 531–558. doi:10.100710796-017-9810-y

Karapanos, E., Teixeira, P., & Gouveia, R. (2016). Need fulfillment and experiences on social media: A case on Facebook and WhatsApp. *Computers in Human Behavior, 55*, 888–897. doi:10.1016/j.chb.2015.10.015

Kenya Audience Research Foundation. (2020). *KARF Media Establishment Survey Highlights.* https://www.karf.or.ke/research/

Kenya National Bureau of Statistics. (2016). *Kenya Integrated Household Budget Survey (KIHBS) March 2016.* http://www.knbs.or.ke/

Klobas, J. E., McGill, T. G., Moghavvemi, S., & Paramanathan, T. (2018). Compulsive YouTube usage: A comparison of use motivation and personality effects. *Computers in Human Behavior, 87*, 129–139. doi:10.1016/j.chb.2018.05.038

Lampe, C., Ellison, N. B., & Steinfield, C. (2006). A face(book) in the crowd: Social searching vs. Social browsing. In *Proceedings of the 2006 20th Anniversary Conference on Computer Supported Cooperative Work* (pp. 167–170). 10.1145/1180875.1180901

Lee, C. S., & Ma, L. (2011). News sharing in social media: The effects of gratifications and prior experience. *Computers in Human Behavior, 28*(2), 331–339. doi:10.1016/j.chb.2011.10.002

Leonardi, P. M. (2015). Ambient awareness and knowledge acquisition: Using social media to learn 'who knows what' and 'who knows whom'. *Management Information Systems Quarterly, 39*(4), 747–762. doi:10.25300/MISQ/2015/39.4.1

Lien, H. C., & Cao, Y. (2014). Examining WeChat users' motivations, trust, attitudes, and positive word-of-mouth: Evidence from China. *Computers in Human Behavior, 41*, 104–111. doi:10.1016/j.chb.2014.08.013

Lin, J.-S., Lee, Y.-I., Jin, Y., & Gilbreath, B. (2017). Personality Traits, Motivations, and Emotional Consequences of Social Media Usage. *Cyberpsychology, Behavior, and Social Networking, 20*(10), 615–623. doi:10.1089/cyber.2017.0043 PMID:29039699

Liu, I. L. B., Cheung, C. M. K., & Lee, M. K. O. (2010). Understanding Twitter usage: What drive people continue to tweet. PACIS 2010 Proceedings, 928–939.

Makinen, M & Kuira, W. M. (2008). Social Media and Post-Election Crisis in Kenya. *Information & Communication Technology – Africa, 13*.

Mäntymäki, M., & Islam, A. K. M. N. (2016). The Janus face of Facebook: Positive and negative sides of social networking site use. *Computers in Human Behavior, 61*, 14–26. doi:10.1016/j.chb.2016.02.078

Marcus, S. R. (2015). 'Picturing' ourselves into being: Assessing identity, sociality and visuality on Instagram. *Proceedings of the International Communication Association Conference*.

Maxwell, M. E. (2012). *Motivations to tweet: a uses and gratifications perspective of twitter use during a natural disaster* (Master's thesis). Department of Advertising and Public Relations, University of Alabama.

Media Council of Kenya. (2016). *The Impact of Digital Technologies and Internet on Media and Journalism in Kenya*. United Nations Office at Nairobi.

Moore, C., & Chuang, L. (2017). Redditors Revealed: Motivational Factors of the Reddit Community. *Proceedings of the 50th Hawaii International Conference on System Sciences*, 2313-2322. 10.24251/HICSS.2017.279

Mull, I. R., & Lee, S. E. (2014). "PIN" pointing the motivational dimensions behind Pinterest. *Computers in Human Behavior, 33*, 192–200. doi:10.1016/j.chb.2014.01.011

Murungi, K. M. (2018). Influence of Social Media to Community Development: Lessons from Kenya. *International Journal of Social Science and Technology, 3*(6), 1–18.

Mwangi, M. W., & Wagok, J. (2016). Effect of Social Media on Performance of Advertisement Business in the Mainstream Media in Kenya: A Survey of Leading Media Groups in Kenya. *International Journal of Economics. Commerce and Management*, *IV*(4), 159–177.

Myrick, J. G. (2015). Emotion regulation, procrastination, and watching cat videos online: Who watches Internet cats, why, and to what effect? *Computers in Human Behavior*, *52*, 168–176. doi:10.1016/j.chb.2015.06.001

Narula, S., & Jindal, N. (2015). Use of social network sites by AUMP students: A comparative study on Facebook, Twitter and Instagram usage. *Journal of Advanced Research*, *2*(2), 20–24.

Nawaz, S. S., & Mubarak, K. M. (2015). Adoption of Social Media Marketing By Tourism Product Suppliers: A Study in Eastern Province Of Sri Lanka. *European Journal of Business and Management*, *7*(7), 448–455.

Ndlela, M. N., & Mulwo, A. (2017). Social media, youth and everyday life in Kenya. *Journal of African Media Studies*, *9*(2), 277–290. doi:10.1386/jams.9.2.277_1

Nendo. (2020). *Nendo 2020 Digital Report*. https://www.nendo.co.ke/2020dtr

Njeri, M. W. (2014). *Effect of Social Media Interactions on Financial Performance of Commercial Banks in Kenya* (Master Thesis). School of Business, Department of Finance, University of Nairobi.

Njoroge, C., & Koloseni, D. (2015). Adoption of Social Media as Full-Fledged Banking Channel: An Analysis of Retail Banking Customers in Kenya. *International Journal of Information and Communication Technology Research*, *5*(2), 1–12.

Nyagah, V. W., Asatsa, S., & Mwania, J. M. (2015). Social Networking Sites and their Influence on the Self Esteem of Adolescents in Embu county, Kenya. *Journal of Educational Policy and Entrepreneurial Research*, *2*(1), 87–92.

Nyamboga, E. N. (2014). Social Media in Kenyan Journalism: Benefits, Opportunities and Challenges. *IOSR Journal of Humanities and Social Science*, *19*(12), 89–94. doi:10.9790/0837-191248994

Ogola, G. (2019). What would Magufuli do? Kenya's digital "practices" and "individuation" as a (non) political act. *Journal of Eastern African Studies: the Journal of the British Institute in Eastern Africa*, *13*(1), 124–139. doi:10.1080/17531055.2018.1547263

Park, C. S. (2013). Does Twitter motivate involvement in politics? Tweeting, opinion leadership, and political engagement. *Computers in Human Behavior*, *29*(4), 1641–1648. doi:10.1016/j.chb.2013.01.044

Park, N., Kee, K. F., & Valenzuela, S. B. (2009). Being immersed in social networking environment: Facebook groups, uses and gratifications, and social outcomes. *Cyberpsychology & Behavior*, *12*(6), 729–733. doi:10.1089/cpb.2009.0003 PMID:19619037

Poushter, J., Bishop, C., & Chwe, H. (2018). Social media use continues to rise in developing countries but plateaus across developed ones. Pew Research Center, 22.

Rosenthal, S. (2018). Motivations to seek science videos on YouTube: Free-choice learning in a connected society. *International Journal of Science Education*, *8*(1), 22–39.

Smock, A. D., Ellison, N. B., Lampe, C., & Wohn, D. Y. (2011). Facebook toolkit: A uses and gratification approach to unbundling feature use. *Computers in Human Behavior, 27*(6), 2322–2329. doi:10.1016/j.chb.2011.07.011

Social, W. A. (2019). Global Social Media Users Pass 3.5 Billion. *Global Digital Reports.* https://wearesocial.com/blog/2019/07/global-social-media-users-pass-3-5-billion

Statista. (2018). *Social media usage in Europe - Statistics & Facts.* https://www.statista.com/topics/4106/social-media-usage-in-europe/

Tartari, E. (2015). Facebook usage among Albanian Students: A Test of uses and Gratifications Theory. *EDULEARN15 Proceedings,* 3774-3779.

Tully, M., & Ekdale, B. (2014). Sites of playful engagement: Twitter hashtags as spaces of leisure and development in Kenya. *Information Technologies and International Development, 10*(3), 67–82.

Wamuyu, P. K. (2017). Closing the digital divide in low-income urban communities: A domestication approach. *Interdisciplinary Journal of e-Skills and Lifelong Learning, 13,* 117-142.

Wamuyu, P. K. (2018). Leveraging Web 2.0 technologies to foster collective civic environmental initiatives among low-income urban communities. *Computers in Human Behavior, 85,* 1–14. doi:10.1016/j.chb.2018.03.029

Whiting, A., & Williams, D. (2013). Why people use social media: A uses and gratifications approach. *Qualitative Market Research, 16*(4), 362–369. doi:10.1108/QMR-06-2013-0041

Young, J. A. (2017). Facebook, Twitter, and blogs: The adoption and utilization of social media in nonprofit human service organizations. *Human Service Organizations, Management, Leadership & Governance, 41*(1), 44–57. doi:10.1080/23303131.2016.1192574

Zhang, L., & Pentina, I. (2012). Motivations and Usage Patterns of Weibo. *Cyberpsychology, Behavior, and Social Networking, 6*(15), 312–317. doi:10.1089/cyber.2011.0615 PMID:22703037

Chapter 7
Social Networks and Cultural Differences:
Adidas's Case on Twitter and Sina Weibo

José Duarte Santos
https://orcid.org/0000-0001-5815-4983
Polytechnic of Porto, Portugal

Steffen Mayer
Aschaffenburg University of Applied Sciences, Germany

ABSTRACT

The purpose of this chapter is the comparison of social media strategy on Twitter and Sina Weibo by the German company Adidas. A successful social media campaign is pushing brand awareness and companies improve their focus on that. Due to the internet censorship of the Chinese government, the social media landscape in China differs from the Western world. Therefore, companies need cultural and linguistic know how to be successful on Chinese platforms like Sina Weibo. The chapter compares how Adidas uses Twitter and Sina Weibo for their marketing purpose. Cultural differences and the local adaption of their social media appearance will be presented.

INTRODUCTION

Marketing is a well-developed method and is constantly changing its rules according to the needs and developments being held in and around it. To establish itself, it has begun adopting new paradigms of business (Saravanakumar & SuganthaLakshmi, 2012). The rapid development of the Internet is producing new ways to connect with the customer. One of the new forms of advertisement is Social Media. Bonnie Sainsbury, who is a Canadian influencer says: "Social media will help you build up loyalty of your current customers to the point that they will willingly, and for free, tell others about you" (e-Clincher, 2015). A blog, post or tweet can be twisted and viewed by millions almost for free and enables companies to make their own interest content that viewers will follow.

DOI: 10.4018/978-1-7998-4718-2.ch007

With the help of the Internet, social media campaigns can be launched globally. As a result, companies are able to increase their brand awareness around the world. Whereas famous social media platforms like Twitter, Facebook or Instagram are famous in most of the countries, it can not be used in one of the most important markets in the world. China has draconian internet restrictions and is blocking most of the western social media platforms. As a result, western marketing campaigns are stopping right at the Chinese border. However, the restriction has supported the development of Chinese social media platforms like Sina Weibo. This platform varies much from their western counterparts. Logically, they need specific advertisement approaches to be successful in the Chinese market. So, this work is based on one central research question: the presence of a brand on the social network Sina Weibo implies adjustments compared to the presence on the Twitter network?

The terms Social Media, Web 2.0, Social Media Marketing and Microblog will be described to set the framework of the article. Second, social media platforms Twitter and Sina Weibo will be described and differences will be exposed. Besides technical differences on the platform, the article also shows cultural differences by analyzing the United States of America, Germany, and China. Communication is always a matter of culture and needs to be adapted according to the target market. Furthermore, the paper introduces the company Adidas with its most important business categories. One of the main parts of the article is the usage analyzation of Twitter and Sina Weibo. Part of the analysis is the structure, frequency of posts, the use of mediums, content, design, language, and the use of models and celebrities.

BACKGROUND

Social Media and Web 2.0

The term Web 2.0 was introduced by Tim O´Reilly and defines the business revolution in the computer industry. The change is due to the movement of the internet as a platform and the attempt to understand the rules of success for this platform. The aim is to build applications that harness network effects to get better the more people use them. Internet users are no longer limited to a one-sided communication flow in which companies only inform through websites. Web 2.0 effects online users by how many things they can do, interact, combine, remix, upload and customize for themselves (Shuen, 2018).

The term social media refers to all posts in the form of text, pictures, videos or audio which are created in order to get an interaction. Therefore, social media is connecting technology, content, and creativity to achieve a communicational exchange on a virtual platform (Hettler, 2012). Besides the information exchange, Weinberg, Ladwig and Pahrmann (2012) focus on the fact that social media enables communication without geographical boundaries and at every time. The values of social media sites are their users and the content which users are sharing. This term of information is referred as user-generated content.

Social media platforms can be divided into three groups (Kreutzer, 2018):

1.   Communication: blogs, micro-blogs, private and business social networks, Messenger;
2.   Cooperation between user: wiki, rating portal;
3.   Content-sharing: text-sharing, foto-sharing, video-sharing, audio-sharing.

Social Media Marketing

In the today's world, companies change their marketing strategy from being product-centric to being customer-centric and relationship-driven (Sheth, Sisodia, & Sharma, 2000). Social Media Marketing (SMM) is a tool that supports that trend.

SMM is used to describe the use of social media platforms for the purpose of marketing. Akar and Topçu (2011) has defined SMM as the promotion of the company and its products through social media. On the other hand, Drury (2008) describes the increase of brand awareness among consumers through the word of mouth principle as a purpose of SMM. For Tuten and Soloman (2017), SMM is the utilization of social media platforms to create, communicate, deliver, and exchange offerings that has value for an organization´s stakeholder. While the first definitions have a concentrated focus on the classical promotion of the company, Assaad and Gómez (2011) sees SMM as a great opportunity to talk with the customer on a personal level. Therefore, those social networking sites should be considered as an additional channel with unique characteristic and not like a traditional marketing tool. For them, SMM is an effective means of getting vital information that is essential to the success of the business.

Microblogs

This paper will focus on the use of Microblogs. Therefore, it is important in order to describe the term in detail. Microblogs are an established form in the group of social media platforms with a broad interest in consumers and companies. They differ from traditional blogs in that its content is typically smaller in file size. Mostly, the length of a text message is limited to less than 200 characters and focusses on the exchange of short sentences, individual images or video links (Kaplan & Haenlein, 2011). The limitation is also the main factor of their success story and they are are typically used for crisis management, journalism, or politics (Aichner & Jacob, 2015; Mendoza, Poblete & Castillo, 2010). The biggest and most famous microblogging provider in Western countries is Twitter, whereas in China Sina Weibo is the most popular platform (Kreutzer, 2018).

What Is the Success Story of Microblogs?

First, microblogs create a concept called ambient awareness. The theory describes the feeling of closeness and intimacy a person gets by reading through various several small tweets of one blogger. Due to that ambient awareness, microblogs result in a relatively high level of social presence, that can be achieved between two individuals, and media richness, defined as the amount of information that can be transmitted in a given time interval (Daft & Lengel, 1986).

The second reason behind the popularity of microblogs is the unique type of communication. When a person decides that a tweet of another person is relevant, he can become a follower of that person. Following means, the user is getting all new posts of the person he decides to follow (Cha, Haddadi, Benevenuto & Gummadi, 2010). In many cases, the content of tweet may be read and immediately forgotten, but in other cases the post might be seen so relevant that the user chooses to retweet the post. Tweet is a message that the user receives from a person he follows and directly forward to his own followers (Weinberg et al., 2012). The initial tweet can be forwarded from one user to another and can transform from a simple piece of information to a word-of-mouth phenomenon (Kaplan & Haenlein, 2011).

The third reason for its popularity is the motivation of a user to get additional information about the tweeted subject because the tweet with its limited characters can not fully describe the topic. By using short URL´s, microblogging messages become similar to traditional ads, which motivate users to click on it (Kaplan & Haenlein, 2011). The "click-through" can positively affect consumer behaviour (Manchanda, Dubé, Goh & Chintagunta, 2006).

Marketing Strategies of Companies Based on Microblog

Microblogs have a huge potential for companies to get the customer brand opinion, improve the relationship and communication with the customer and solve customers problems. Therefore, companies can use microblogs as a brand promotional tool. The brand image has a significant influence on customers buying decisions (Malik et al., 2013). Microblog messages contain much information about brands including brand sentiment, product experience and customer satisfaction (Sui & Yang, 2010).

The companies can use that information flow to increase their brand awareness, creating an official microblog account and publishes news and information about their product and activities via it. It is important that a company follows a clear strategy on how to present itself on a microblog platform (Kreutzer, 2018). The published information can impress the customers and engage them to receive more relevant information and intensify the brand image (Sui & Yang, 2010). For the right communication, companies have to safe all rights of their brand name (Kreutzer, 2018).

The content of a post is very important and has to be attractive to the customer. Therefore, companies should provide exclusive information about their products, their company or their industry. Moreover, they should attract customers by exclusive offers (limited and attractive in terms of price) and exclusive services (preview for new offers or new products). Those exclusive contents will bind customers closer to the company. The reason for that is, that customer will check the postings on the microblog frequently if they believe they will only receive the information through that channel (Kreutzer, 2018).

Microblogs are very suitable for big companies in order to start a community with their fans. In such a community, the company can directly or indirectly talk with its clients about the company or new offers. Moreover, companies can use those platforms to launch customer service and answer customer questions or complaints. The answers will be posted publicly and force the customer service to work quickly, respectful and solution-oriented and will result to a better customer service level (Kreutzer, 2018; Sui & Yang, 2010).

Twitter

Twitter can be categorized as a microblog and was founded in 2006 in San Francisco (Arceneaux & Weiss, 2010). It enables the user to post short messages to individuals who have chosen to follow the sender. Retweeting the post engages the follower to participate in the conversation (Burton, Dadich & Soboleva, 2013). A post is limited by Twitter to 280 characters (Geier & Gottschling, 2019). The platform is not just limited to text messages. Moreover, Twitter enables its users to use pictures, videos or quoting other posts. Through the use of "@" in their own post, users can refer to other accounts like a company or a private person (Hettler, 2012). The use of hashtags is also very popular on Twitter. It serves to refer to certain topics without the need to explain them. Hashtags are linked to posts with the same hashtag to help to connect a variety of different posts about the same topic. Users who have an interest in a topic can use the search function of Twitter for looking up a hashtag. (Weinberg et al., 2012). The importance of Twitter has increased tremendously in our society based on the use of celebrities. The best example is the sitting US president Donald Trump who announces his political agenda on a daily basis on Twitter (Stolee & Caton, 2018).

In the first quarter of 2019, Twitter had 330 million active monthly users (Twitter, 2019). Moreover, Twitter generated 4.17 billion visitors on their webpage (SimilarWeb, 2019). 27 percent of all users are from the US, followed by Japan with 14 percent (SimilarWeb, 2019). In comparison to other social media platforms, Twitter is not used from a specific age group. The difference in the daily use of a 16-year-old person compared to a 49-year-old varies by only 4 percent (Brown, 2017). Besides Twitter, other microblogs exist but they play a niche role and are mostly in financial difficulties (Hettler, 2012). Therefore, Twitter can be described as the most important microblogging platform for the western world.

Social Media in China and Sina Weibo

China is by far the number one of internet users. In 2018, 828.51 million people in China used the Internet (Statista, 2020). Moreover, China has the world´s most active environment for social media. Almost every Internet user in China uses social media. The Chinese internet is also a unique place. Western social media is not taking place in China. The country has blocked the world´s four most visited websites: Google, Facebook, Youtube and Twitter and also denied other western social media platforms access to the Chinese market (Wang, 2016). In reality, most Chinese internet users do not really notice the absence of western social media because the country has accustomed themselves to indigenous websites. Today, China has a grown and unique social media landscape. Social media in China is experiencing a massive growth without copying the western equivalents. Instead, they are new creations customized for the Chinese culture, habits, and behaviour (He & Pedraza, 2015). Some of the social media innovations are even leading the global trend of media development. Chinese platforms live in a complicated and competitive environment and face quick changes. All in all, the Chinese social media platforms can be defined as unique, complex fragmented and local (He & Pedraza, 2015).

Sina Weibo is one of the most famous social network sites in China and has become a crucial medium to share information like breaking news, social events and products (Lei et al., 2018). The microblogging platform was launched in 2009 and has grown rapidly to influence millions of internet users in China. It can be described as the Chinese version of Twitter (Nooruddin & Zhang, 2012). In July 2019, almost 600 million unique devices have visited Sina Weibo (Statista, 2019), which is nearly two times more visitors than Twitter (330 million).

Chinese use microblogging platforms like Sina Weibo to get credible information about current events or news. The reason for that is, that microblogging sites allow to spread informations quickly (Liu, 2016). As already mentioned, Weibo is often compared to Twitter. Besides that, Weibo might be more social in terms of openness of network, applications and multimedia choices (Chen & Zhang, 2011). In the early days, Weibo had a limit of 140 characters but has removed this limit in January 2016 by by allowing users to post up to 2.000 characters (Hlee, Cheng, Koo & Kim, 2017). Weibo allows their users to follow others, comment on other´s weibos and click the "zan" button which is similar to a "like" button in western social media, and add weibos to the personal gallery (Hlee et al., 2017). Moreover, users can integrate graphical emoticons, pictures, music, and videos to their weibos (Guan et al., 2014). Comparable to Twitter is the use of hashtags which enable users to find weibos and news (Hlee et al., 2017).

An advantage of Sina Weibo is their cooperation with the big online market place Alibaba. Sina Weibo has connectivity to Alibaba which enables companies to sell their products through the microblogging page. They also invented their own payment system "Weibo Payment" in order to make the purchasing progress quicker and more efficient (Havinga, Hoving & Swagemakers, 2016).

Each social media platform in China attracts specific users with different characteristics (Sullivan, 2012). Consumers who favour Sina Weibo tend to be in higher income brackets, earning more than 1.300$ a month, and they are much more likely to live in big cities (Chiu, Lin & Silverman, 2012). Very interesting for companies is the Enterprise-Version of Sina Weibo. It enables companies to analyze their followers (age, gender, regional differences). Those data can be used for further marketing strategies. Furthermore, Sina Weibo offers marketing tools which enable organisations to get in conversations with their follower and start online surveys (Liu, 2016). Companies can send private messages to either a specific percentage of followers or to all of them. The messages can be used to get customer attention, send them prize competitions, or interesting news in order to increase the interest to follow the company (Liu, 2016). Like Twitter, Weibo also requires a specific strategy of how to operate on the platform. In general, the plan is relatively similar. Companies should use hashtags cleverly, create a fan base, post relevant and interesting topics, take the respond of the followers serious. Weibo has to be seen as an influential marketing tool with all the different aspects it offers(Chen & Zhang, 2011).

A great challenge for using Sina Weibo is the cultural difference entrepreneurs have to face. A European or American company can not post or interact with their follower in the same way they are used in their home market. The Chinese culture has different rules and defines different taboo on topics like humour, erotic, politics and religion. This cultural framework can deviate extremely to the western usage. To be successful in the Chinese social media world, companies have to hire social media workers with explicit cultural competence about the Chinese culture. Companies should also consider to post in mandarin and therefore hire a Chinese speaking employee (Svensson, 2014).

Cultural Diferences

While the explosive growth of social media is a phenomenon across many countries, the way people use the platform and their reason for doing so may vary according to their social and cultural milieu (Kim, Sohn & Choi, 2011). Therefore, it is necessary to adopt a deeper look at the cultural differences of China compared to the United States and Germany as a benchmark.

Hofstede, which is a leading expert on cultural studies, defines culture as a collective programming of the mind that distinguished the members of one group or category of people from others (Hofstede, 2011). Moreover, Hofstede (2011) is dividing culture into six dimensions which are: Power Distance, Uncertainty Avoidance, Individualism vs. Collectivism, Masculinity vs Feminity, Long Term vs Short Term Orientation, Indulgence vs Restraint. The chapter will focus only on two of the six Hofstede dimensions which are power distance and individualism vs collectivism.

According to Hofstede, power distance explains how societies deal with inequalities and hierarchies in terms of social status, wealth and power. In a culture with a high-power distance, less powerful members of an organization accept and expect that power is made available unequally (Hofstede, 2011). In a society with low power distance, equality is treasured and authorities are often challenged (Fi & McNeal, 2001). In terms of marketing, consumer in a high-power distance country has a tendency to use expensive, luxurious symbols and high-status appeals such as celebrity endorsement to highlight power, wealth, and elitism. In contrast, low power distance countries prefer down-to-earth appearances with normal persons (Albers-Miller & Gelb, 1996). It is noted, that China has a very high score of 80, whereas Germany and the US only score 35 and 40 points. That illustrates that Chinese culture extreme values power distance.

Individualism describes a society in which everyone is only looking after himself and his family. Independence, individuality, and self-realization have a great importance. Moreover, actions are determined by personal goals and individual welfare. In comparison, a collectivistic side is a culture in which people are integrated into a robust, family-extended group which stays loyal and oppose other groups. The goals of a community and collectivistic welfare take precedence over personal achievement. Furthermore, they live in a "we" society in which interdependence with others is valued. (Hofstede, 2011). A collectivistic society is more likely to share content within its group (Ji et al., 2010). Social media appearances should respect the difference between individualism and collectivism. A collectivistic country appreciates collectivistic appeals like popularity, collective benefits, and group achievement, and less individualistic approaches like uniqueness or the promotion of adventures (Cheong, Kim & Zheng, 2010). According to the graph, China can be categorized as a collectivistic culture. Germany is tending to be more individualistic, whereas the United States can be characterized as strongly individualistic.

Another factor which is not described in the six dimensions model of Hofstede is the difference in communication. Hall (1973) states, that human communication always follows cultural and contextual patterns. Furthermore, Hall (1989) divides cultures into high context and low context depending on the amount of information transmitted at the moment of communication. The general term of context can be described as the information that surrounds an event and must be known in order to understand the meaning of an event or subject. A high context message is one in which most of the information is already in the person, while very little is explicitly transmitted in the message. Those cultures do not require or expect in-depth background information because they keep themselves informed about everything having to do with the people who play a significant role in their life. In contrast, in a low context message, the mass of the information is vested in the explicit code. For our article it is important to know that China is clarified as a high context culture whereas Germany and the United States are a low context culture. Low context people compartmentalize their personal relationships and many other aspects of day-to-day life. As a consequence, each time they interact with others they need detailed background information (Hall & Hall, 2001). In other words, low context communication tends to be more direct, is less focussing on context, and contains more factual information (Gudykunst, 2004; Kim, Cole & Gould, 2009). In comparison, high context communication is more indirect and ambiguous, favouring metaphors and symbols and is less understandable to persons who are outside the group (Kim et al., 2009). Societies which favour a low context communication style use rational cues such as product features, the functional value of a product or references to competing brands to promote a product. On the other side, high context cultures talking in a more direct and implicit way about a product or a brand (Gudykunst, 2004). They use a persuasive communication style which is more likely to use emotional appeals and symbolic association with a celebrity or lifestyle (Tsai & Men, 2012). For example, Chinese advertisements feature values that are symbolic and suggestive of human emotions. Moreover, web sites are more likely to offer information about consumers connection to their community (Lee, Geistfeld & Stoel, 2007). In high context cultures, the news are transmitted colourful, inspirational and in an interesting way. Pathos and entertainment are preferred (Corduan, 2018). Furthermore, high-context cultures prefer special graphics, design elements, and colourful background design. Users in those cultures place more emphasis on the appearance of posts, are less focused, and therefore prefer a variety of content types.

Companies operating in a high context should focus on building a relationship with the customer through the soft-sell approach (Pollay, 1983). Consumers in China focus on the intangible aspects of advertising messages. Of great importance is the aesthetic and entertainment values, rather than product features and benefits (Mooij, 2018). A successful way to transport good feelings and create a happy atmosphere is the use of celebrities and the approach of an emotional appealing (Johansson, 1994).

METHODOLOGY

The data analysis in this chapter is based on a quantitative approach, whereby the researcher obtained the data from observing the last 40 social media posts posted by Adidas company on Twitter and Sina Weibo. The observation of the posts was made during the month of November 2019. By counting specific characteristic the author was able to put the observation into a quantitative perspective and present the results. The variables analyzed were structure of account network, topic of the post, design of the post, language of the post, diversity of the post and cooperation with celebrities.

ADIDAS BACKGROUND

Adidas was founded in 1949 by Adi Dassler in the small German city Herzogenaurach. Today, it is a multinational corporation that designs and manufactures shoes, clothing, and accessories. It is the largest sportswear manufacturer in Europe and the second-largest in the world (Kreutzer, 2018). The brand has a long history and deep-rooted sports connection with a diverse portfolio of major global sports. Today, Adidas is one of the most recognized and iconic global brands. The company's mission is to be the best sports brand in the world by designing, building and selling the best sport products in the world, with the best service and experience and in a sustainable way (Adidas, 2018). In 2018, Adidas generated worldwide sales of 21.915 billion Euros (increase of 3.3% to 2017), 7.1 billion Euros were generated in China (increase of 14.9% to 2017) (Adidas, 2018).

Brand Adidas is divided into the following sub-brands (Adidas, 2019):

- Adidas Sport: sportswear for professionals
- Adidas Original: A lifestyle brand marked by the iconic Trefoil logo.
- Adidas Core: sportswear for everyone
- Reebok Running: innovative technologies for high-performance runners
- Reebok Training: specialized products of fitness
- Reebok Classics: sportive fitness clothes for the daily life

In 2019, Adidas has over 57000 employees and produced over 900 million sports and sports lifestyle products. Sales of 21.015 billion Euros were generated in 2018 by Adidas.

RESULTS

Network Presence of Adidas

Adidas Original has established themselves successfully in the western and Chinese microblogging platform. They have a structured and successful social media strategy by adapting to both regions. While addressing a wide customer range on Twitter, they focus especially on the Chinese culture on Sina Weibo. Language, colours, celebrities, and models are customized for Chinese preferences. Furthermore, Adidas is able to maintain its core values and recognition in both markets. They do adapt but do not change their branding. This is noticeable by having the same profile picture and the slogan "Three Stripes. Past. Present. Future" on both platforms.

Adidas states that their Original sub-brand is a main driver of their global success. The sub-brand has verified accounts on Twitter and Sina Weibo with millions of followers and will be used for the following comparison. Adidas Original´s Twitter account is addressing the users globally, whereas the Sina Weibo account is posting specifically for the Chinese market. This must be taken into consideration for the following analysis. According to the 2018s annual report, Adidas believes that possible changes in customer demands might be high. One reason is the quick changes in demand for fashion. Therefore, it is necessary to identify fashion trends. Social media interaction with the customer helps to spot changing fashion preferences (Adidas, 2018).

Today, the Twitter Account of Adidas Original has 4.07 million followers and cumulative 17,500 tweets. Retweets are included. The account was founded in February 2009 and has a global focus. In comparison, the Adidas Original Account of Sina Weibo has currently 2.46 million followers and 4,600 posts. Adidas posts regularly on Twitter and Sina Weibo. In this article, the last recent 40 posts of both platforms were analysed. Adidas needed 105 days for 40 posts on Twitter, whereas they needed only 73 days on Sina Weibo. Adidas is posting more frequently on Sina Weibo (1.8 days/post) than on Twitter (2.6 days/post). Table 1 presents the variables compared.

Table 1. Comparison of adidas on Twitter and Sina Weibo

Variable	Twitter	Sina Weibo
Followers	4.07 million	2.46 million
Posts	17500	4600
Number of days to make 40 publications	105	73
Range of days per post	2.6	1.8

Source: authors

Structure of Account Network

The structure of their Twitter and Sina Weibo account is relatively similar. Both platforms use the same Adidas Original logo as their profile picture and the slogan "Three Stripes. Past. Present. Future" in their profile description. Furthermore, both websites use their cover picture to promote the newest fashion advertisements. Currently, both sides are presenting the new shoe collection on their cover picture. In the profile description of Sina Weibo, Adidas connects the user to other Adidas communities at Sina Weibo and to the external social network Douban. In contradiction, Adidas is not using links on their Twitter profile.

A visible contrast is the use of colours. The cover picture of Twitter is kept mainly white and makes a subtle but classy impression. In contrast, Adidas Original uses for Sina Weibo a very colourful background to promote their shoes. For using a cover picture at Sina Weibo Adidas needs to be a verified company.

Topic of the Post

One of the most important aspects of analysing a post is the topic which it is addressing. Every post is establishedof a different purpose. Promoting a product, a new collection, presenting new information about the company or just telling a story. Interesting content is bounding the customer closer to the company´s profile. Big differences in the online topics were noticeable during the last 40 posts on both platforms. On Twitter, Adidas Original is focussing primarily on their shoe collection. More than 70% of their posts present the newest footwear and only 10% of the posts are promoting the street wear collections. The missing 20% are dealing with presenting the latest cooperation, telling a story, or dealing with diverse topics.

In contradiction, Adidas Original diversificate the topics on Sina Weibo. 43% of their posts are presenting the newest footwear and 38% promote the street wear collection. Likewise to Twitter, the final 20% is presenting the latest cooperation, telling a story or presenting diverse topics.

Design of the Post

By addressing the follower on social media, the design of the post is an important factor. Especially the used colour have to attract the users and reflect cultural standards. It is noted, that Adidas Original uses more colour for their posts on Sina Weibo than on Twitter. Most of the posts on Twitter are comparable to the left picture. The shoe is in front of a white and simple background. No colours that might distract the consumer from the product is visible. In contrast, Adidas uses colourful pictures on Sina Weibo. Most of the pictures offer a full range of different colours. The product is not part of the main focus. More than 80% of all pictures on Twitter show a subtle background, while Adidas posts more than 60% with a colourful one.

Language of the Post

The language on both platforms is different and adapted to the target market. On Twitter, Adidas is communicating for a global performance in english, whereas on Sina Weibo the used language is mandarin. However, the name of the shoes are not translated and remains in English. In order to compare the text messages, the post has to concern a similar topic. One good example is the promotion of the "YEEZY" collections that are also optically very similar. Adidas is keeping their messages on Twitter very short. They only introduce the shoe model and the date for the sales launch. The writing style is direct, offers factual information and therefore focus on a low-context culture.

On Sina Weibo, Adidas is using more text to interact with with their customer. They start the conversation with the question "What´s the matter, let´s talk outside the clouds Ù" After that, they introduce the name of the shoe collection and present details about the used materials or the weight. The date of sales launch is presented with the information that the collection is limited. Furthermore, they describe the shoe with the statement: "The iconic mid sole makes you feel like walking through the clouds" which refers to the first sentence of the post.

Diversity of the Post

When looking at the posts on Sina Weibo, it is noticeable that the majority of the models and beauty bloggers are from Asia. In contradiction, Adidas uses ethnically diverse models on Twitter. However, this result is understandable, and it makes sense that the Chinese market to select models with which the target group can identify with. Twitter is used globally. Therefore, Adidas hoes to have to address all different ethnicities with the goal that no one feels excluded.

Cooperation With Celebrities

As an outfitter to numerous famous athletes, sport teams and sports organizers, Adidas has gained international significance. According to their own annual report, they focus on promotional partnerships and brand marketing activities (digital advertising, point of sales) (Adidas, 2018).

Adidas´s brand awareness was achieved mainly through promotional partnerships. Adidas is sponsoring sporting events and equipping major football teams or athletes such as Lionel Messi or Aaron Rodgers. Marketing through promotional partnerships with famous athletes has been a tradition since the company´s foundation and is, therefore, an important factor in increasing Adidas brand awareness (Heiden, 2015). Moreover, Adidas also focus on non-sports celebrities such as American musician Kanye West and Pharrell Williams to expand the brand reach. In collaboration with Kanye West, Adidas Original created the "YEEZY" collection, which is very successful internationally (Yang, 2019). In October 2019, Adidas Original advertised the New "YEEZY BOOST 700" shoe and the Pharrell Williams collection on Twitter. Each of both posts has more than 1.400 likes which are a significant difference in other Twitter posts from Adidas Original. But, Adidas is not promoting the campaign with pictures or mentions of Kanye West and Pharell Williams. The collection "YEEZY" stands for itself. One exception is the announced collaboration of Pharrel William´s Human Race with Nigo´s Human Made. For that advertisement, they used pictures of both designers to promote the new campaign. These types of cooperation are also suitable for the Chinese market. However, it is necessary to work with personalities who have a high reputation in China. As a result, Adidas is partnering with Chinese celebrities and public figures. One of the newest campaigns on Sina Weibo is promoting the shoe "Adidas Continental 80" in cooperation with the Chinese actress and singer Yang Mi. She can be considered as a superstar on Sina Weibo with more than 105,6 million followers. The post was liked 107.900 times and reposted more than 77.000 times. The figures are ten times higher than normal Adidas Original posts. Adidas is working closely together with celebrities. Almost every post is linked with a famous person like Lu Han (musician) with 60 Mio followers or Angela Yeung Wing (model) with 101 Mio followers. The "YEEZY" collection was the only posts that were not linked with a star.

The following table summarizes for the variables analyzed the differences between the two social networks.

Table 2. Major differences in Adidas' presence on social networks Twitter and Sina Weibo

Variable	Twitter	Sina Weibo
Structure of account network	Cover picture essentialy white	Cover picture colourful background
Topic of the post	Focussing primarily on their shoe collection	Diversificating the topics
Design of the post	Few colors	Full range of different colours.
Language of the post	English	Mandarin, but the name of the shoes are not translated; more text
Diversity of the post	Ethnically diverse models	Beauty bloggers from Asia
Cooperation with celebrities	Partnering with famous athletes and non-sports celebrities	Partnering with chinese celebrities and public figures

Source: authors

DISCUSSION

The symbolism of color and the importance that people give varies between countries and is an element that marketing and in particular marketing on social networks can not belittle, to achieve go against the culture of the country. This situation is explored by Adidas on the cover of social networks and also in the number of colors used in the creation of posts.

Adidas Original is implementing the recommendations from the literature. By keeping their posts simple on Twitter they use the method that is favouring low context cultures. Sina Weibo is used in China which is categorized as a high-context culture. Consequently, they utilize colourful pictures, and special graphics and design elements in order to be adapted to the taste of the culture.

The theme of the post is more concentrated on the social network Twitter, than on the social network Sina Weibo. By using an inspirational and symbolic writing style, the post appeals perfectly to high-context cultures. Moreover, the aesthetic of a post is really important for a high-context culture. Therefore, Adidas uses the symbol of a cloud as an additional design element to increase the optical impression. The writing language used on Twitter - English - goes against a more global presence, but that in the case of China, the company felt the need to go against the local culture, using Mandarin, bearing in mind that language is one of the maximum expressions of a culture.

Also the use of personalities, incorporating in its communication Chinese celebrities and public figures, reveals that in the social network Sina Weibo, the company seeks to meet a local communication. On Twitter the diversity of nationalities is a reality, as well as the area of activity of these people, which demonstrates that there is a preference to be as comprehensive as possible, which fits into the transversality of various cultures. The difference in the diversity of the post, which in the social network Sino Weibo bet on beauty bloggers from Asia reinforces the focus of the Adidas brand on Asian culture.

CONCLUSION

Since introducing Web 2.0, Social media has become an effective tool for communication without geographical boundaries at every time. Companies benefit from that development by using social media marketing. This form of marketing contributes to interact with the customer on a personal level, increase brand awareness and push the success of the company. Microblogs are a form of social media platform which is limiting the length of text messages. Their success story is built on several aspects. By creating ambient awareness the users feel a closeness and intimacy between themselves. Moreover, the unique type of communication through the function of resending posts can create a mass word-of-mouth phenomenon and motivate a user to get additional information on a specific topic. Companies have discovered the potential of microblogs and developed them as a brand promotional tool. Increasing communication with their customers, creating a community, inform about the newest products are some of the information a company shares on microblogs. The most famous microblog in the western world is Twitter with 330 million active monthly users.

Companies face difficulties when entering the Chinese social media markets. Famous western platforms like Facebook or Twitter are blocked by the government. As a result, China has developed its own unique social media landscape customized to the local culture. The most famous equivalent to Twitter is Sina Weibo with almost 600 million visitors per month. For a successful social media performance in China, companies need to understand the culture. Therefore, the article showed the differences between China, Germany, and the United States by using Hofstede´s six dimension models. The main differences were noticeable in the categories "Power Distance", "Individualism" and Hall´s division in "High context" and "Low context".

Company Adidas Original uses both social media platforms successfully. The analyse of their social media usage showed similarities and differences in both platforms. The structure, company profile and profile picture is relatively similar. Furthermore, both platforms use their cover picture for the newest product promotions. Commonly, the use of pictures or videos is also spread. However, social media team of the company is adapting its online presence on the market. In general, Adidas is posting more frequently on Sina Weibo (1,8 posts/day) than on Twitter (2,6 posts/day). By focussing on street wear on Twitter the focus of the microblogging platform is set differently to Sina Weibo which also concentrates on the street wear collection. Another adaption that both platforms do is on the design and the used language. On Twitter, Adidas provides only the main product information and focus on the design of the post on the product, whereas they do a different approach on Sina Weibo. By focussing on the use of a high-context culture, the language is more inspirational and provides more information. Moreover, the design can be described as more colourful.

Adidas uses the cooperation with celebrities differently on Twitter and Sina Weibo. With the help of celebrities, Adidas creates its own collections which they promote on Twitter. One of the famous product lines is called "YEEZY" that is promoted by models and not by the celebrities themselves. The promotional strategy on Sina Weibo is differently. First, Adidas collaborates only with celebrities known in China. Secondly, they use the reputation of the star by putting them in the main focus of their post. In Summary, Adidas is able to present the company on both platforms successfully. By adapting to the cultural standards they ensure that the followers can identify with the brand without losing their core values and brand recognition.

The study is positioned as exploratory and we consider that it provides some indications for the development of more structured and in-depth studies, namely on the elements that were analyzed in the two social networks and which contribute to check for differences in content and presentation, including graphics. It has several limitations, such as the mode used for the selection of posts, the number of posts used and the criteria used in the choice of the elements considered to analyze the post.

REFERENCES

Adidas. (2018). *Adidas annual report, 2018*. Retrieved from https://report.adidas-group.com/fileadmin/user_upload/adidas_Annual_Report_GB-2018-EN.pdf

Adidas. (2019). *Company brands*. Retrieved from https://www.adidas-group.com/en/brands/adidas/

Aichner, T., & Jacob, F. (2015). Measuring the degree of corporate social media use. *International Journal of Market Research, 57*(2), 257–276. doi:10.2501/IJMR-2015-018

Akar, E., & Topçu, B. (2011). An examination of the factors influencing consumers' attitudes toward social media marketing. *Journal of Internet Commerce, 10*(1), 35–67. doi:10.1080/15332861.2011.558456

Albers-Miller, N. D., & Gelb, B. D. (1996). Business advertising appeals as a mirror of cultural dimensions: A study of eleven countries. *Journal of Advertising, 25*(4), 57–70. doi:10.1080/00913367.1996.10673512

Arceneaux, N., & Weiss, A. S. (2010). Seems stupid until you try it: Press coverage of Twitter, 2006-9. *New Media & Society, 12*(8), 1262–1279. doi:10.1177/1461444809360773

Assaad, W., & Gómez, J. M. (2011). Social network in marketing (social media marketing) opportunities and risks. *International Journal of Managing Public Sector Information and Communication Technologies, 2*(1), 13.

Brown, K. M. (2017). *Anteil der mehrmals täglichen Nutzer von ausgewählten soizalen Netzwerken nach Altersgruppen weltweit im Jahr 2016*. Retrieved from https://de.statista.com/statistik/daten/studie/680253/umfrage/mehrmals-taegliche-nutzung-von-sozialen-netzwerken-nach-altersgruppen/

Burton, S., Dadich, A., & Soboleva, A. (2013). Competing voices: Marketing and counter-marketing alcohol on Twitter. *Journal of Nonprofit & Public Sector Marketing, 25*(2), 186–209. doi:10.1080/10495142.2013.787836

Cha, M., Haddadi, H., Benevenuto, F., & Gummadi, K. P. (Eds.). (2010). Measuring user influence in twitter: The million follower fallacy. *Fourth international AAAI conference on weblogs and social media*.

Chen, S., Zhang, H., Lin, M., & Lv, S. (2011, December). Comparision of microblogging service between Sina Weibo and Twitter. In *Proceedings of 2011 International Conference on Computer Science and Network Technology* (Vol. 4, pp. 2259-2263). IEEE. 10.1109/ICCSNT.2011.6182424

Cheong, Y., Kim, K., & Zheng, L. (2010). Advertising appeals as a reflection of culture: A cross-cultural analysis of food advertising appeals in China and the US. *Asian Journal of Communication, 20*(1), 1–16. doi:10.1080/01292980903440848

Chiu, C., Lin, D., & Silverman, A. (2012). *China's social-media boom*. McKinsey & Company.

Corduan, A. (2018). *Social media als instrument der kundenkommunikation*. Springer. doi:10.1007/978-3-658-22317-5

Daft, R. L., & Lengel, R. H. (1986). Organizational information requirements, media richness and structural design. *Management Science, 32*(5), 554–571. doi:10.1287/mnsc.32.5.554

Drury, G. (2008). Opinion piece: Social media: Should marketers engage and how can it be done effectively? *Journal of Direct, Data and Digital Marketing Practice*, *9*(3), 274–277. doi:10.1057/palgrave.dddmp.4350096

e-Clincher. (2015). *43 Of The Best Social Media Marketing Quotes*. Retrieved from https://eclincher.com/blog/43-of-the-best-social-media-quotes/

Geier, A., & Gottschling, M. (2019). Wissenschaftskommunikation auf Twitter? Eine Chance für die Geisteswissenschaften! *Mitteilungen des Deutschen Germanistenverbandes*, *66*(3), 282–291. doi:10.14220/mdge.2019.66.3.282

Guan, W., Gao, H., Yang, M., Li, Y., Ma, H., Qian, W., Cao, Z., & Yang, X. (2014). Analyzing user behavior of the micro-blogging website Sina Weibo during hot social events. *Physica A*, *395*, 340–351. doi:10.1016/j.physa.2013.09.059

Gudykunst, W. B. (2004). Bridging differences: *Effective intergroup communication. Sage (Atlanta, Ga.)*.

Hall, E. T. (1973). *The slient language*. Anchor.

Hall, E. T. (1989). *Beyond culture*. Anchor.

Hall, E. T., & Hall, M. R. (2001). Key concepts: Underlying structures of culture. *International HRM: Managing diversity in the workplace*, 24-40.

Havinga, M., Hoving, M., & Swagemakers, V. (2016). Alibaba: a case study on building an international imperium on information and E-Commerce. In R. T. Eden (Ed.), *Multinational Management: a casebook ons Asis's global market leaders* (pp. 13–32). Springer. doi:10.1007/978-3-319-23012-2_2

He, X., & Pedraza, R. (2015). Chinese social media strategies: Communication key features from a business perspective. *El Profesional de la Información*, *24*(2), 200–209. doi:10.3145/epi.2015.mar.14

Heiden, A. (2015). *Sponsoring im Profifußball: Das Beispiel adidas*. Bacherol Master Publishing.

Hettler, U. (2012). *Social media marketing: Marketing mit Blogs, sozialen Netzwerken und weiteren Anwendungen des Web 2.0*. Gebundenes Buch.

Hlee, S., Cheng, A., Koo, C., & Kim, T. (2017). The difference of information diffusion for Seoul tourism destination according to user certification on Sina Weibo: Through data crawling method. *International Journal of Tourism Sciences*, *17*(4), 262–275. doi:10.1080/15980634.2017.1384131

Hofstede, G. (2011). Dimensionalizing cultures: The Hofstede model in context. *Online Readings in Psychology and Culture*, *2*(1), 8. doi:10.9707/2307-0919.1014

Ji, M. F., & McNeal, J. U. (2001). How Chinese children's commercials differ from those of the United States: A content analysis. *Journal of Advertising*, *30*(3), 79–92. doi:10.1080/00913367.2001.10673647

Ji, Y. G., Hwangbo, H., Yi, J. S., Rau, P. P., Fang, X., & Ling, C. (2010). The influence of cultural differences on the use of social network services and the formation of social capital. *International Journal of Human-Computer Interaction*, *26*(11-12), 1100–1121. doi:10.1080/10447318.2010.516727

Johansson, J. K. (1994). The sense of "nonsense": Japanese TV advertising. *Journal of Advertising, 23*(1), 17–26. doi:10.1080/00913367.1994.10673428

Kaplan, A. M., & Haenlein, M. (2011). The early bird catches the news: Nine things you should know about micro-blogging. *Business Horizons, 54*(2), 105–113. doi:10.1016/j.bushor.2010.09.004

Kim, H., Coyle, J. R., & Gould, S. J. (2009). Collectivist and individualist influences on website design in South Korea and the US: A cross-cultural content analysis. *Journal of Computer-Mediated Communication, 14*(3), 581–601. doi:10.1111/j.1083-6101.2009.01454.x

Kim, Y., Sohn, D., & Choi, S. M. (2011). Cultural difference in motivations for using social network sites: A comparative study of American and Korean college students. *Computers in Human Behavior, 27*(1), 365–372. doi:10.1016/j.chb.2010.08.015

Kreutzer, R. T. (2018). *Social-Media-Marketing kompakt: Ausgestalten, Plattformen finden, messen, organisatorisch verankern.* Springer Gabler. doi:10.1007/978-3-658-21147-9

Lee, M. S., Geistfeld, L. V., & Stoel, L. (2007). Cultural differences between Korean and American apparel web sites. *Journal of Fashion Marketing and Management, 11*(4), 511–528. doi:10.1108/13612020710824571

Lei, K., Liu, Y., Zhong, S., Liu, Y., Xu, K., Shen, Y., & Yang, M. (2018). Understanding user behavior in sina weibo online social network: A community approach. *IEEE Access: Practical Innovations, Open Solutions, 6*, 13302–13316. doi:10.1109/ACCESS.2018.2808158

Liu, Y. (2016). *Social Media in China.* Springer Gabler. doi:10.1007/978-3-658-11231-8

Malik, M. E., Ghafoor, M. M., Iqbal, H. K., Ali, Q., Hunbal, H., Noman, M., & Ahmad, B. (2013). Impact of brand image and advertisement on consumer buying behavior. *World Applied Sciences Journal, 23*(1), 117–122.

Manchanda, P., Dubé, J.-P., Goh, K. Y., & Chintagunta, P. K. (2006). The effect of banner advertising on internet purchasing. *JMR, Journal of Marketing Research, 43*(1), 98–108. doi:10.1509/jmkr.43.1.98

Mendoza, M., Poblete, B., & Castillo, C. (2010, July). Twitter under crisis: Can we trust what we RT? In *Proceedings of the first workshop on social media analytics* (pp. 71-79). 10.1145/1964858.1964869

Mooij, M. (2018). *Global marketing and advertising: Understanding cultural paradoxes* (5th ed.). SAGE Publications Limited.

Nooruddin, Z., & Zhang, L. (2012). *7 Steps to Weibo Success.* Retrieved from https://www.chinabusinessreview.com/7-steps-to-weibo-success/

Pollay, R. W. (1983). Measuring the cultural values manifest in advertising. *Current Issues and Research in Advertising, 6*(1), 71-92.

Saravanakumar, M., & SuganthaLakshmi, T. (2012). Social media marketing. *Life Science Journal, 9*(4), 4444–4451.

Sheth, J. N., Sisodia, R. S., & Sharma, A. (2000). The antecedents and consequences of customer-centric marketing. *Journal of the Academy of Marketing Science, 28*(1), 55–66. doi:10.1177/0092070300281006

Shuen, A. (2018). *Web 2.0: A Strategy Guide: Business thinking and strategies behind successful Web 2.0 implementations*. O'Reilly Media.

SimilarWeb. (2019). *Twitter.com - Visits weltweit 2019 | Statista*. Retrieved from https://de.statista.com/statistik/daten/studie/1021439/umfrage/anzahl-der-visits-pro-monat-von-twittercom/

Statista. (2019). *Apps - Top 20 nach Anzahl der Unique Devices in China 2019 | Statista*. Retrieved from https://de.statista.com/statistik/daten/studie/894126/umfrage/beliebteste-apps-nach-anzahl-der-unique-visitors-in-china/

Statista. (2020). *Number of internet users in China from December 2008 to December 2018*. Retrieved from http:// https://www.statista.com/statistics/265140/number-of-internet-users-in-china/

Stolee, G., & Caton, S. (2018). Twitter, Trump, and the Base: A Shift to a New Form of Presidential Talk? *Signs and Society (Chicago, Ill.)*, *6*(1), 147–165. doi:10.1086/694755

Sui, Y., & Yang, X. (2010, June). Article. In *Second International Conference on Communication Systems, Networks and Applications* (*Vol. 1*, pp. 164-167). IEEE.

Sullivan, J. (2012). A tale of two microblogs in China. *Media Culture & Society*, *34*(6), 773–783. doi:10.1177/0163443712448951

Svensson, M. (2014). Voice, power and connectivity in China's microblogosphere: Digital divides on SinaWeibo. *China Information*, *28*(2), 168–188. doi:10.1177/0920203X14540082

Tsai, W.-H., & Men, L. R. (2012). Cultural values reflected in corporate pages on popular social network sites in China and the United States. *Journal of Research in Interactive Marketing*, *6*(1), 42–58. doi:10.1108/17505931211241369

Tuten, T. L., & Solomon, M. R. (2017). Social media marketing. *Sage (Atlanta, Ga.)*.

Twitter. (2019). *Anzahl der monatlich aktiven Nutzer von Twitter weltweit vom 1. Quartal 2010 bis zum 1. Quartal 2019 (in Millionen)*. Retrieved from https://de.statista.com/statistik/daten/studie/232401/umfrage/monatlich-aktive-nutzer-von-twitter-weltweit-zeitreihe/

Wang, X. (2016). *Social media in industrial China*. UCL Press. doi:10.2307/j.ctt1g69xtj

Weinberg, T., Ladwig, W., & Pahrmann, C. (2012). *Social Media Marketing: Strategien für Twitter, Facebook & Co*. O'Reilly.

Yang, J. (2019). Cheap Wheat Adidas-apmkingstrack. com. *American Journal of Industrial and Business Management*, *9*(3), 720–726.

Chapter 8
The Role of Social Media Influencers on the Consumer Decision-Making Process

Ana Cristina Antunes

https://orcid.org/0000-0001-8983-2062

School of Communication and Media Studies, Lisbon Polytechnic Institute, Portugal

ABSTRACT

The digital era has introduced many changes in the consumer marketplace. Social media and especially social networking sites redefined how consumers relate to and behave towards brands, as well as the brand-consumer relationship. Within this context and the heightened resistance to brand communication through traditional media, marketeers are turning to other strategies to connect with their customers and influence their consumer journey. One of these strategies is influencer marketing. In the last years, brands have used social media influencers as endorsers of their products and services, and as brand ambassadors. Digital influencers connect consumers and brands, strengthening their bond and allowing the brand to reach their target in a more natural way to influence the consumer buying process. In this chapter we will provide a narrative review on the role of digital influencers on the consumer decision processes.

INTRODUCTION

The digital era has witnessed considerable changes in the consumer marketplace. Some of these changes have been introduced by the rise and massive use of social media by individuals. Nowadays, social media has become, as Duffett (2017) claims, an indispensable part of life in contemporary societies, deeply intertwined in our daily activities.

Its pervasiveness in multiple spheres of society has extended to businesses and consumers. Social media and especially social networking sites (SNS) redefined how consumers relate to and behave towards brands, as well as the balance of power in the brand-consumer relationship. Their consumer

DOI: 10.4018/978-1-7998-4718-2.ch008

journey has also been altered, from information search to post-purchase, under this ever-present influence of social media.

In their continuous effort to adapt to consumer changes, businesses have altered their marketing strategies, using digital channels to better reach their targets, although many businesses have little in-depth knowledge about SNS such as Facebook, Twitter, YouTube, Instagram, or Pinterest (Whiting et al., 2019). It is in this digital context of transformation that businesses are increasingly using influencer marketing, moving away from celebrities as endorsers, and instead relying on social media opinion leaders, often referred as social media influencers or digital influencers (e.g., Abidin, 2015; Freberg et al., 2011; Uzunoğlu & Kip, 2014).

Attending to the relevance that social media influencer communication has recently gained for brands and consumers, in this chapter we will review the existing literature on the field of influencer marketing, highlighting the role of social media influencers on the consumer decision processes. We initially proceed to the description and characterization of these digital influencers, as well as present the main characteristics that enhance their influence on consumers. We then review the existing evidence on the role of social media influencers on each phase of consumer decision journey.

DEFINITION AND CHARACTERIZATION OF SOCIAL MEDIA INFLUENCERS

Social media influencers are do-it-yourself social media users that create their own digital persona, are content generators and have the capacity to attract and build a sizable audience overtime (e.g., Lou & Yuan 2019; Marwick, 2010; Turner, 2006). They can attract and mobilize their audience's attention throughout time, strategically sharing information through posts, pictures and messages to boost their popularity (e.g., Hearn & Schoenhoff, 2016; Marwick, 2016; Ruiz-Gomez, 2019). Abidin (2015) adds their engagement with their audiences and their orientation to monetize their social media activity when she defines them as "everyday, ordinary Internet users who accumulate a relatively large following on blogs and social media through the textual and visual narration of their personal lives and lifestyles, engage with their following in digital and physical spaces, and monetize their following by integrating 'advertorials' into their blog or social media posts" (p. 1). Yet, one must note that only social media users with the right kind of social capital of interest for brands can monetize (Zulli, 2018).

Opinion leaders have been described as socially active individuals, interconnected in the social system (Rogers, 1995), a notion that can be extended to the digital world. Indeed, digital opinion leadership is seen, first and foremost, as a social practice that involves an ongoing carefully constructed self-presentation to be consumed by others, by an audience of fans, and popularity is maintained through a continuous process of fan management (Marwick & boyd, 2011). But not only social: Pöyry et al. (2019) go one step further, by defending that it is a technosocial practice, where social media influencers have constantly to deal with the pressure of being likeable, credible and interesting for their fans, as well as economically profitable and, at the same time, they have to assimilate and adapt to the changing technological affordances of the digital platforms.

At the core of this notion is the idea of interpersonal influence: these digital content creators have the ability to influence, to persuade and to shape the opinions, attitudes and behaviors of their followers through regular content production and distribution and ongoing interaction on social media (e.g., Enke & Borchers, 2018; Freberg et al., 2011; Gorry & Westbrook, 2009).

It is this power to influence their audiences that makes them valuable for brands. In the last years, we have wittedness marketeers' resort to influencer marketing in their marketing strategies, using social media influencers as digital ambassadors or endorsers of brands. This is acknowledged by Freberg et al. (2011), when they define social media influencers as a third-party endorser with the ability to shape their audiences' attitudes through social media. Endorser is a term that has been used to describe celebrities but is now also applied to social media influencers. An endorser, according to McCracken (1989) is "any individual who enjoys public recognition and who uses this recognition on behalf of a consumer good by appearing with it in an advertisement" (p. 310).

As Choi and Rifon (2012) defend, celebrity endorsement has been extensively studied and its positive effects on consumer attitudes and behaviors are well documented in extant literature (e.g., Amos et al., 2008; Bergkvist & Zhou, 2016; Erdogan, 1999). This is not the case for digital influencer endorsement, an area that is still in its infancy and where much remains to be known. Albeit this, nowadays marketeers are relying less on celebrities and more on social media influencers. According to Lokithasan et al. (2019), marketeers believe that digital influencers improve brand sentiment, allow reaching a large number of consumers in short time, and provide authentic storytelling. Their value for brands relies not only in this far-reaching impact and viral growth potential (De Veirman et al., 2017) but also in their ability to increase sales and engagement (e.g., Jaakonmäki et al., 2017; Sudha & Sheena, 2017). Carter (2016) and Weiss (2014) add that influencer marketing can, in some ways, be more effective than other marketing strategies in the sense that it allows a more targeted reach, an ability to focus on specific target markets that otherwise would be difficult. Thus, identifying and selecting influencers for a given brand is a relevant issue. This selection by a brand is determined by multiple factors, such as their popularity (Forbes, 2016) or reachability through the number of followers (e.g., De Veirman et al., 2017), and the number of hits they receive in social media channels (Freberg et al., 2011). Their self-presentation skills and ability to draw attention to themselves (Ruiz-Gomez, 2019), their distinctive self-branding (Carter, 2016), and ability to offer a unique selling proposition (Khamis et al., 2017) are also relevant aspects for this selection. Ruiz-Gomez (2019) adds their social capital, which precedes economic capital and can determine the value for potential brand endorsements.

One of the factors that has increased the popularity of these endorsers is the marketeers' belief that social media influencers can play a relevant role on the consumer journey. As Batra and Keller (2016) defend, a brand can use these influencers, together with other marketing tools in "more powerful ways to move consumers more quickly along their decision journey or funnel than was ever possible before" (p. 122).

According to Li et al. (2014) the most powerful factor that can affect the consumer's attitude towards a social media influencer are the consumer's associations and perceptions of that specific influencer. This implies that the main characteristics ascribed to social media influencers can influence the consumer's journey and, therefore, must be examined in this chapter.

In this context, Armano (2011) considers the existence of six critical "pillars", six significant factors when examining the question of influence. These pillars are 1) Reach, related to the size and potency of a social media influencer "social graph", attending to the ability of digital platforms to distribute ideas, opinions and perspectives. The more digital platforms the social media influencer uses, the higher the reach; 2) Proximity, that is the ability of the individuals to influence those close to them, even if their reach is limited; 3) Expertise, since the perceived expertise in topics or subject matters establishes influence. Social media influencers are considered as experts that add value to the social system; 4) Relevancy, which affects how much influence one has the potential to yield within a community; 5) Credibility, that is established by the activities of social media influencers through their thoughts, actions and what they generate; and 6) Trust: that is critical in the effectiveness of influencing a thought, behavior or action.

Empirical evidence supports the attribution of these set of characteristics to social media influencers. Several studies reveal that SNS users perceive these influencers as experts, and as credible and trustworthy sources (e.g., Chapple & Cownie, 2017; Djafarova & Rushworth, 2017). Social media influencers are even perceived by their followers as more credible and trustworthy sources than celebrities (e.g., De Veirman et al., 2017; Djafarova & Rushworth, 2017; Sertoglu et al., 2014). Audiences also acknowledge a higher similarity and wishful identification with influencers than celebrities, making the formers more effective as endorsers (e.g. Schouten et al., 2019). Gräve (2017) argues that social media influencers are also more effective than celebrities as endorsers when they have a high level of familiarity with their audience, especially on platforms like Instagram and YouTube, where people deliberately choose to follow their activities and influencers are considered as a part of the digital community.

Some components of the influencers' credibility, such as attractiveness and perceived similarity (to their followers), also play a relevant role in this equation. Physical attractiveness seems to cast a "halo effect" over the general impressions on attractive individuals, biasing judgements on other attributes in a positive direction (e.g., Forgas & Laham, 2017). Previous research suggests that, amongst other aspects, it has a positive impact on consumer behavior (e.g., Erdogan 1999; Liu et al, 2010), even in children (e.g., Vermeir & Sompel, 2014). In the digital realm, Djafarova and Rushworth (2017) found that, for some users, attractiveness and the quality of posted photos are two of the reasons to follow Instagram influencers. Attractiveness also stimulates positive consumers attitudes (Lim et al., 2017), specifically positive attitudes towards a brand (Torres et al., 2019). Both social media influencer attractiveness and perceived similarity (to their followers) are positively related to followers' trust in influencer-generated branded posts, which subsequently influence brand awareness (Lou & Yuan, 2019). Similarity also relates with familiarity. According to the findings of Gräve (2017), when there is a high level of familiarity between social media influencers and their fans, the former is considered as more trustworthy and similar to oneself than celebrities.

Adopting a different angle of research, De Veirman et al. (2017) developed two experimental studies to examine the impact of Instagram influencers' number of followers and influencers' followers/followees ratio. Their findings suggest that popular Instagram influencers are perceived as more likeable, but if the influencer follows very few accounts, this can negatively impact popular influencers' likeability. Likeability appears to be such a relevant factor that De Veirman et al. (2017, p. 799) suggest that for a brand "to increase the message's impact one should search for the most likeable, credible influencer who has a high value as an opinion leader".

Many other studies examined the characteristics of social media influencers that distinguish them from celebrities and from other social media users. In their seminal study, Freberg et al. (2011) analyzed their core specific attributes and found that they are perceived as outspoken, smart, ambitious, productive, and poised. Social media influencers are least likely perceived as self-pitying or indecisive (Freberg et al., 2011).

Social media influencers are also perceived as more authentic than celebrities (e.g., Abidin, 2015; Duffy, 2017; Lim et al., 2017). Publishing what appears to be their own personal experiences helps to distinguish social media influencers from celebrities, who often serve their audiences with carefully crafted fantasies, and from other influencers, since they offer something that is unique to their followers (Abidin, 2015; Cotter, 2018; Duffy, 2017). Whereas traditional celebrities tend to maintain their distance and build hierarchical relationships with their fans, social media influencers create an impression of authenticity, that helps them to cultivate a sense of intimacy, accessibility, proximity and relatability, which constitute the basis of affective relationships with their followers (e.g., Abidin, 2015; Cotter, 2019; Duffy, 2017; Marwick, 2016).

Based on a quantitative study with 808 followers of an Instagram fashion influencer account, Casaló et al. (2020) suggest that originality and uniqueness stand as crucial factors to become or to be recognized as an opinion leader on Instagram. Their study also reveals that digital opinion leadership is positively related to consumer behavioral intentions both towards the influencer (intention to interact in the account and recommend it) and towards the fashion industry, that is, the intention to follow the fashion advice posted (Casaló et al., 2020).

Another dimension for understanding social media influencer effects and their interest as endorsers for brands is congruence, at two different levels: 1) the match or fit between the influencer and a product and/or brand (the match-up hypothesis) and 2) the congruence between the digital influencer personality characteristics and the consumers' Self.

The relevance of the match-up hypothesis (i.e., the match between a celebrity and the product or the brand being endorsed) is widely acknowledged as an explanation for celebrity endorsement effectiveness (e.g., Kahle & Homer, 1985; Till & Busler, 1998, 2000; Wright, 2016). The notion behind this hypothesis is that a good match between the celebrity attractiveness or expertise and the product or brand is more effective than a poor match (Choi & Rifon, 2012). Törn (2012) defends, on the other hand, that this match-up between the endorser and the brand is more relevant for new brands. According to his study, selecting a brand-incongruent celebrity endorser for an established brand can generate more favorable brand attitudes, more brand interest, higher purchase intentions, and more positive word-of-mouth communication.

The scarce studies that examine this question in the case of social media influencers (not celebrities) have focused in the congruence (not incongruence) between the digital endorser and the brand. So far, the match-up hypothesis seems to be a relevant factor for explaining social media influencers success as endorsers (e.g., Djafarova & Rushworth, 2017; Torres et al., 2019). To substantiate this effect, Schouten et al. (2019) defend that the associative link between the product and the social media endorser may be easily established on account of their successful self-branding as experts on a particular domain of interest and of their regular content production and sharing of product information with their followers. Empirical evidence suggests that product-social media endorser fit enhances positive attitudes towards an ad (Schouten et al., 2019) and towards a brand (Torres et al., 2019).

Congruence can be also examined in the scope of the endorser-consumer relationship. This refers to congruence between personalities and/or Self dimensions (e.g., self-concept, self-image). The effectiveness of celebrities' endorsement seems to be related with the consumers' ideal self-image (Choi & Rifon, 2012). When a consumer perceives a celebrity endorser as possessing an image close to his or her ideal self-image, the consumer develops a more positive attitude towards the ad and greater purchase intentions (Choi & Rifon, 2012). This facet of endorsement remains underresearched in the case of social media influencers. Yet, preliminary evidence from Casaló et al. (2020) suggests that the perceived ðt between the influencer's persona displayed in his/her account(s) and the consumer's personality strengthens their influence on their followers, increasing the intention to follow the influencer advice.

CLASSIFICATION OF SOCIAL MEDIA INFLUENCERS

There are numerous typologies of digital influencers depending on several factors, such as their status, practices, or their impact and presence in specific social media platforms, but the most popular classification is related to audience size, that is, their number of followers (e.g., Bullock, 2018; Coursaris et al., 2018; Ruiz-Gomez, 2019; Zulli, 2018). There is an ongoing discussion on the academic literature regarding audience size, on what constitutes a large number of followers and how many levels of classification should be employed, as can be seen in Table 1.

Table 1. Overview of several classifications of social media influencers based on the number of followers

Author(s)/Year	Number of Levels	Classification	Number of Followers
De Veirman et al. (2017)	2	High number of followers Moderate	21.2K 2.1K
Lammers (2018)	3	Megainfluencers, Macroinfluencers Microinfluencers	More than 1M 10K-1M 500 to 10K
SanMiguel et al. (2018)	4	Celebrity influencers Megainfluencers, Macroinfluencers Microinfluencers	More than 1M More than 1M 10K-1M 1K to 10K
Schouten et al. (2019)	2	Traditional / Celebrity Social media influencers	More than 1 M 10K or less
Vodák et al. (2019)	4	Megainfluencers, Macroinfluencers Microinfluencers Nanoinfluencers	More than 1M 100k to 1M 1K to 100k Less than 1K
Kay et al. (2020)	2	Macroinfluencers Microinfluencers	More than 100K More than 10K
Britt et al. (2020)	2	Megainfluencers Microinfluencers	More than 1 M 10K or less
Campbell & Farrell (2020)	5	Celebrity influencers Megainfluencers, Macroinfluencers Microinfluencers Nanoinfluencers	More than 1M + enjoy public recognition outside social media More than 1M 100k to 1M 10K to 100k 0 to 10K

Although we do not intend to provide an exhaustive review on this subject, a brief analysis of Table 1 reveals a lack of consensus on this classification and even on the number of followers associated with some types (e.g., the range of followers of nano, micro and macroinfluencers varies between researchers).

The practitioners' perspective can offer some clarity, even if the number required to be in one tier or another differs according to the social media platform (Kay et al. 2020; Ruiz-Gomez, 2019). The most popular classifications vary between three and four levels and imply a hierarchy and key differences in recognition and monetization opportunities (Ruiz-Gomez, 2019). Many practitioners employ a three-level classiõcation distinguishing microinfluencers, macroinfluencers and megainfluencers (e.g., Bullock, 2018; Porteous, 2018), while others add a fourth level - nanoinfluencers (e.g., Foxwell, 2020; Ismail, 2018).

Each of these types of social media influencers can be beneficial for brands, although their differential impact on the consumer journey has not been sufficiently addressed and warrants further research. According to Coursaris et al. (2018) microinfluencers may be perceived as more authentic and trustworthy than megainfluencers, since the last may arise consumer skepticism about the sincerity of their endorsements. Comparing mega and micro beauty and fashion social media influencers, Britt et al. (2020) found that microinfluencers are more central to two-way dialogue within their own networks, while megainfluencers garner more affect, indicating that they can generate a higher level of trust than microinfluencers.

SOCIAL MEDIA INFLUENCERS AND THE CONSUMER DECISION-MAKING PROCESS

There are numerous consumer decision-making models based on the assumption that there are a set of sequential, well defined stages consumers are said to go through during their consumer journey. One of the most popular assumes five stages in the consumer decision-making process: need recognition, information search, alternative evaluation, purchase and post-purchase. This õve-stage buying decision process model is a widely used tool for marketers to gain a better understanding about their customers and their consumer behavior (Comegys et al., 2006).

In this chapter we will review the role of social media influencers on each of the five steps. For clarification purposes, we will review the existing evidence on each stage separately.

Need Recognition

The buying process begins with need recognition (sometimes referred to as problem recognition), that is primarily related to the individuals' motives, and needs. During this stage the consumer becomes aware that something is missing, that there is an unmet need or motive, which results from a gap between the person actual state and the desired state (e.g., Sethna & Blythe, 2016). So far, this stage has received scarce attention within the scope of influencer marketing. In a qualitative study, Aranha and Miranda (2019) found that some followers, when seeing the product being used by social media influencers, imagine themselves using those products and feel the need to buy it. Lutkenhaus et al. (2019) assume that the digital dialogue between influencers and their fans can either implicitly or explicitly raise awareness, increase exposure and make audiences more receptive to information about a speciõc issue. Therefore, it is possible that by merely publishing content regarding a given product or service or recommending their use on their social media accounts, social media influencers can raise awareness on a given product and create a sense of need on their followers.

Information Search

Information search is the process by which we survey the environment to gather appropriate data to make a consumption decision (Solomon, 2018). When searching for information, consumers may do it internally and externally. Internal search is memory-related. External main information sources fall, according to Kotler et al. (2019), into four groups: 1) Personal sources, which include family, friends, neighbors and acquaintances; 2) Commercial sources, which include advertising, websites, salespeople and packaging; Public sources, including mass media and consumer-rating organizations; and 4) Experiential sources, which involve handling, examining and using the product.

Personal sources are of the utmost importance for consumers, that trust them above other sources, as noted by Cooley and Parks-Yancy (2019). Albeit this, in recent years we have witnessed a trend, that of a consumer that actively seeks information when needed (Batra & Keller, 2016), especially online.

Consumers are also increasingly using social media to gather product or brand information on which to base their decisions (Casaló et al., 2020). Social media grants easy access to large amounts of information on all kinds of different products from very diverse sources, some of them deemed more reliable and trustworthy than the seller (e.g., Bronner & de Hoog, 2014; Chapple & Cownie, 2017; Lou & Yuan, 2019). Therefore, user generated content like recommendations or reviews are researched, read and considered by consumers that want to make the right purchase decision. However, it is important to note that the different SNS are not equally used for all product categories. There is a tendency to use Instagram for apparel information, while YouTube is most relevant to gather information on cosmetic and hair products (Cooley & Parks-Yancy, 2019). On what concerns fashion, social media influencers serve as role models and sources of information and inspiration for their female followers, generating new needs (SanMiguel et al., 2018).

In this stage of the consumer decision making process the social media influencers can act as information providers, contributing to word of mouth (WOM) and electronic word of mouth (eWOM) on a product, service or brand. WOM is considered as one of the most influential factors on consumer behavior (Daugherty & Hoffman, 2014) and the most important information source about products and services for consumers' decisions (Huete-Alcocer, 2017; Litvin et al., 2008) and influencers have the ability to create WOM and eWOM. Social media influencers, as opinion leaders, are considered an important source of word-of-mouth communication because they credible, trustworthy and have knowledge and expertise that can guide the decision making of followers (e.g., Djafarova & Rushworth, 2017; Rahman et al., 2014). As Casaló et al. (2020) refer, by following the social media accounts of social media influencers, consumers can get up-to-date and important information from someone who is considered to have a great degree of credibility (De Veirman et al., 2017), an extensive involvement (Rahman et al., 2014) with that topic, and more personalized advice, by comparison to marketeer-generated content (Yadav et al., 2013). On other hand they also indirectly create WOM in both traditional media and social media inactives (Liu et al., 2013).

Social media influencers can be effective in this and other stages of the consumer decision making process as long as they are perceived as possessing the characteristics previously described. Indeed, Evans et al. (2017) study indicates that when the consumer understands that a given post is advertising, and they also remember a disclosure in that content (i.e., a clear reference that it is a sponsored or paid ad) there is a signiðcant negative impact on attitudes and intention to spread eWOM, eventually because the credibility of the inñuencer is diminished.

In this context not only the producer, but also the content, assumes relevance. For instance, consumers engage with fashion and beauty influencers for valued information, not for affect laden messages (Britt et al., 2020). The combination of both influencer and contents characteristics are significantly related with the perceived usefulness of the content (Racherla & Friske, 2012). Influencers' generated content is perceived as useful, since it reduces the effort of search for more information on products and services and increases the probability of a better choice by the consumer (Yadav et al., 2013). The combined effect of influencer-generated posts' informative value, with some components of influencer credibility, can positively affect followers' trust in influencer-generated branded posts, which in turn affects brand awareness (Lou & Yuan, 2019).

The influencer generated content has also to be unique and original, fresh, authentic, engaging and personal (Jaakonmäki et al., 2017; Luoma-aho et al., 2019; Tolson, 2010), to capture the attention of viewers in a consistent manner (Ruiz-Gomez, 2019) and allow the audience to consider the interaction more individual, quick and intimate (boyd & Ellison, 2007). The content can be customized to make it more appealing and desirable for followers who will read it later (Song & Yoo, 2016).

Yet, one must note that despite prior research suggests that celebrities and social media influencers can have a positive impact as information providers on raising product awareness, consumers still trust more endorsements from people whom they know personally, as the study of Cooley and Parks-Yancy (2019) reveals.

Alternative Evaluation

After acquiring information about the products, the consumers compare and evaluate the relevant options from the existent alternatives, to be able to choose a product (Solomon, 2018). Prior research on celebrity or expert endorsement effects has shown that consumers are more likely to produce a positive evaluation on products and brands endorsed by opinion leaders deemed as experts, credible, and trustworthy (e.g., Erdogan, 1999). Regarding social media influencers as endorsers, empirical evidence is still scant. Yet, the study of Casaló et al. (2020) provides some clues regarding their effect on this process. Their findings suggest that digital opinion leadership exerts an influence on the intention to follow the advice provided, that is, the extent that individuals will follow, take into account and put into practice the suggestions of the opinion leader. This implies that subsequent phases of the consumer decision making process, such as the evaluation of the different alternatives or product purchase, can be influenced by the information provided by the social media influencer. It is important to note that social media and other information sources grant consumers more control over the evaluation process, but the use of social media tends to lengthen the evaluation stage (Lindsey-Mullikin & Borin, 2017), and requires a lighter but more frequent exposure to products, services and brands information (Campbell & Farrell, 2020).

Purchase Decision

In this stage, a decision is made regarding the product the consumer is going to buy. This step involves multiple sub-decisions from the consumer, like the price range, the point of sale to be chosen, time and volume of purchase, and method of payment. (Comegys et al., 2006).

So far, the literature as focused on the effects of the characteristics of these influencers, previously described, on purchase intentions. However, studies have not yet provided conclusive evidence regarding the effects of social media influencers on this stage.

A majority of studies found an increased purchase intent (e.g., Djafarova & Rushworth, 2017; Lim et al., 2017; Schouten et al,, 2019; Sertoglu et al., 2014; Sokolova & Kefi, 2020), while other studies did not found a significant direct effect of influencers on these intentions (Cooley & Parks-Yancy, 2019; Johansen & Guldvik, 2017).

Inconsistent findings were also noted across studies when examining specific characteristics of these endorsers and purchase intentions. Credibility seems to be positively related to purchase intentions in the studies of Chapple and Cownie (2017), Djafarova and Rushworth (2017) and Sokolova and Kefi

(2020). On the other hand, Lou and Yuan (2019) and Lim et al. (2017) results suggest that none of the source credibility dimensions examined in their studies positively and significantly influenced purchase intentions.

Trustworthiness appears to be an important variable for explaining why social media influencers are more effective as endorsers than celebrities, attending to the results of Schouten et al. (2019). By contrast, influencer trustworthiness negatively influenced brand awareness and purchase intentions in the study of Lou and Yuan (2019).

Regarding attractiveness, findings from Torres et al. (2019) suggest that purchase intentions are positively influenced by the digital influencer's attractiveness (including both likeability and familiarity), while in the study of Lim et al. (2017) source attractiveness of social media influencers failed to influence consumers' purchase intentions.

Prior research has systematically overlooked two important steps when examining social media influencers endorsement: their impact on the actual decision to buy and on the purchase behavior.

But one must draw a difference between purchase decision, purchase behavior and purchase intention. A popular theory in social psychology, the Theory of Reasoned Action (Ajzen & Fishbein, 1980; Fishbein & Ajzen, 1975), postulates that behavioral intentions are antecedents of the actual behaviors. In the consumer behavior area, the purchase intention can be defined as the consumers' intention to buy a product in the future (e.g., Hsu & Tsou, 2011). This willingness to purchase a given product or service may be considered the main predictor of actual purchase behavior. But even if a consumer develops an intention to buy a product, this does not mean that he/she will buy that product. Several factors can come between the decision and purchase intention; other factors may later affect whether an actual purchase is made or not (Solomon, 2018).

Attending to the inconclusive findings on the role of social media influencers on this stage and the sole focus on purchase intention, more research is needed to fully understand the impact of the different types of social media influencers on this specific stage, their differences from other types of endorsers, and their influence across product categories and social media platforms.

Postpurchase

The postpurchase phase involves the consumption experience and the decision whether the product/service bought meets (or even exceeds) the consumer previous expectations (Solomon, 2018). It concerns both consumer satisfaction and postpurchase action, either in the form of WOM and eWOM or even complaint behavior, if previous expectations were not met (e.g., Comegys et al., 2006; Solomon, 2018).

Despite its relevance of this phase for brands for its influence on brand loyalty, the effects of social media influencers on this phase of the consumer journey remains under researched. At this purpose, Forbes (2016) suggests that if the product or service performance is similar to the experience shared by the social media influencer, it is more likely that the consumer feels that he/she has purchased the most suitable product. Yadav et al. (2013) add a possible double effect that may derive from the brand's use of social media influencers: an increase in brand loyalty and an increase in the followers' loyalty towards the social media influencer, in the sense that these consumers will continue to follow their future advices and recommendations regarding products, services, and brands.

CONCLUDING REMARKS

Nowadays, brands have been trying to find more effective ways to reach their targets and communicating their products and services. Influencer marketing is a part of their marketing strategies but with a recent change: the introduction of new actors, the so-called social media influencers. This has become a trend for practitioners and academia is trying to keep pace with these practices and examine their impact in marketing, advertising and consumer behavior. Yet, as Schouten et al. (2019) note, research on digital influencers endorsements is "still in its infancy" (p. 260), and a careful analysis of the existing literature reveals a limited body of knowledge, with numerous gaps and biases in this emerging field.

Conceptually, there are multiple competing definitions regarding these influencers, that enhance different aspects and provide different descriptions of the same (or a similar) reality. Even the terms to name them vary, from microcelebrities, to social media influencers and digital influencers, without a proper clarification of the proximity or differentiation between these terms.

The theoretical framework also varies, and it is usually imported from other areas.

Focusing on the role and impact of social media influencers on consumer decision processes, it is possible to observe this is a field of study that is gathering some interest on researchers. Despite the limited research on this subject, social media influencers seem to be relevant for inspiration, information search, and for developing positive attitudes towards a brand and favorable purchase intentions, although their role on the actual purchase and in the post-purchase phases need to be scrutinized. More research is required for a thorough understanding on the several types of digital influencers endorsement effects in the consumer journey.

REFERENCES

Abidin, C. (2015). Communicative intimacies: Influencers and perceived interconnectedness. *Ada: A Journal of Gender, New Media, and Technology, 8.*

Ajzen, I., & Fishbein, M. (1980). *Understanding attitudes and predicting social behavior.* Prentice-Hall.

Amos, C., Holmes, G., & Strutton, D. (2008). Exploring the relationship between celebrity endorser effects and advertising effectiveness: A quantitative synthesis of effect size. *International Journal of Advertising, 27*(2), 209–234. doi:10.1080/02650487.2008.11073052

Aranha, E., & Miranda, S. (2019). *O papel dos influenciadores digitais no processo de intenção de compra* [The role of digital influencers on the buying intention process]. Novas Edições Académicas.

Armano, D. (2011, January 18). *Pillars of the new influence.* https://hbr.org/2011/01/the-six-pillars-of-the-new-inf

Bergkvist, L., & Zhou, K. Q. (2016). Celebrity endorsements: A literature review and research agenda. *International Journal of Advertising, 35*(4), 642–663. doi:10.1080/02650487.2015.1137537

boyd, d., & Ellison, N.B. (2007). Social network sites: Definition, history, and scholarship. *Journal of Computer-Mediated Communication, 13*(1), 210–230.

Britt, R. K., Hayes, J. L., Britt, B. C., & Park, H. (2020). Too big to sell? A computational analysis of network and content characteristics among mega and micro beauty and fashion social media influencers. *Journal of Interactive Advertising, 20*(2), 111–118. doi:10.1080/15252019.2020.1763873

Bronner, F., & de Hoog, R. (2014). Social media and consumer choice. *International Journal of Market Research, 56*(1), 51–71. doi:10.2501/IJMR-2013-053

Bullock, L. (2018, July 31). How to evaluate and partner with social media influencers *Social Media Examiner*. https://www.socialmediaexaminer. com/partner-social-media-influencers/

Campbell, C., & Farrell, J. R. (2020). More than meets the eye: The functional components underlying influencer marketing. *Business Horizons, 63*(4), 469–479. doi:10.1016/j.bushor.2020.03.003

Carter, D. (2016). Hustle and brand: The sociotechnical shaping of influence. *Social Media & Society, 2*(3), 1–12.

Casaló, L. V., Flavián, C., & Ibáñez-Sánchez, S. (2020). Influencers on Instagram: Antecedents and consequences of opinion leadership. *Journal of Business Research, 117*, 510–519. doi:10.1016/j. jbusres.2018.07.005

Chapple, C., & Cownie, F. (2017). An investigation into viewers' trust in and response towards disclosed paid-for-endorsements by YouTube lifestyle vloggers. *Journal of Promotional Communications, 5*, 110–136.

Choi, S. M., & Rifon, N. J. (2012). It is a match: The impact of congruence between celebrity image and consumer ideal self on endorsement effectiveness. *Psychology and Marketing, 29*(9), 639–650. doi:10.1002/mar.20550

Comegys, C., Hannula, M., & Väisänen, J. (2006). Longitudinal comparison of Finnish and US online shopping behavior among university students: The five-stage buying decision process. *Journal of Targeting. Measurement and Analysis for Marketing, 14*(4), 336–356. doi:10.1057/palgrave.jt.5740193

Cooley, D., & Parks-Yancy, R. (2019). The effect of social media on perceived information credibility and decision making. *Journal of Internet Commerce, 18*(3), 249–269. doi:10.1080/15332861.2019.1595362

Cotter, K. (2019). Playing the visibility game: How digital influencers and algorithms negotiate influence on Instagram. *New Media & Society, 21*(4), 895–913. doi:10.1177/1461444818815684

Coursaris, C. K., Van Osch, W., & Kourganoff, C. (2018). Designing the medium and the message for sponsorship recognition on social media: The interplay of influencer type, disclosure type, and consumer culture. SIGCHI 2018 Proceedings.

Daugherty, T., & Hoffman, E. (2014). eWOM and the importance of capturing consumer attention within social media. *Journal of Marketing Communications, 20*(1-2), 82–102. doi:10.1080/13527266. 2013.797764

De Veirman, M., Cauberghe, V., & Hudders, L. (2017). Marketing through Instagram influencers: The impact of number of followers and product divergence on brand attitude. *International Journal of Advertising, 36*(5), 798–828. doi:10.1080/02650487.2017.1348035

Djafarova, E., & Rushworth, C. (2017). Exploring the credibility of online celebrities' Instagram profiles in influencing the purchase decisions of young female users. *Computers in Human Behavior, 68,* 1–7. doi:10.1016/j.chb.2016.11.009

Duffett, R. (2017). Influence of social media marketing communications on young consumers' attitudes. *Young Consumers, 18*(1), 19–39. doi:10.1108/YC-07-2016-00622

Duffy, B. E. (2017). *(Not) getting paid to do what you love.* Yale University Press. doi:10.12987/yale/9780300218176.001.0001

Enke, N., & Borchers, N. S. (2018). Von den zielen zur umsetzung: Planung, organisation und evaluation von influencer-kommunikation [From objectives to implementation: Planning, organizing and evaluating influencer communication]. In A. Schach & T. Lommatzsch (Eds.), *Influencer relations: Marketing und PR mit digitalen meinungsführern* (pp. 177–200). Springer. doi:10.1007/978-3-658-21188-2_12

Erdogan, B. Z. (1999). Celebrity endorsement: A literature review. *Journal of Marketing Management, 15*(4), 291–314. doi:10.1362/026725799784870379

Ertekin, Z., & Atik, D. (2012). Word-of-mouth communication in marketing: An exploratory study of motivations behind opinion leadership and opinion seeking. *ODTÜ Gelisme Dergisi, 39,* 323–345.

Evans, N. J., Phua, J., Lim, J., & Jun, H. (2017). Disclosing Instagram influencer advertising: The effects of disclosure language on advertising recognition, attitudes, and behavioral intent. *Journal of Interactive Advertising, 17*(2), 138–149. doi:10.1080/15252019.2017.1366885

Fishbein, M., & Ajzen, I. (1975). *Belief, attitude, intention, and behavior: An introduction to theory and research.* Addison-Wesley.

Forbes, K. (2016). Examining the beauty industry's use of social influencers. *Elon Journal of Undergraduate Research in Communications, 7*(2), 78–87.

Forgas, J. P., & Laham, S. M. (2017). Halo effects. In R. F. Pohl (Ed.), *Cognitive illusions* (2nd ed., pp. 276–290). Routledge.

Foxwell, B. (2020, February 17). *A guide to social media influencers: Mega, macro, micro, and nano.* https://blog.iconosquare.com/guide-to-social-media-influencers/

Freberg, K., Graham, K., McGaughey, K., & Freberg, L. A. (2011). Who are the social media influencers? A study of public perceptions of personality. *Public Relations Review, 37*(1), 90–92. doi:10.1016/j.pubrev.2010.11.001

Gorry, G. A., & Westbrook, R. A. (2009). Academic research: Winning the internet confidence game. *Corporate Reputation Review, 12*(3), 195–203. doi:10.1057/crr.2009.16

Gräve, J.-F. (2017). Exploring the perception of influencers vs. traditional celebrities: Are social media stars a new type of endorser? In *Proceedings of the 8th International Conference on Social Media & Society* (#SMSociety17). Association for Computing Machinery. 10.1145/3097286.3097322

Hearn, A., & Schoenhoff, S. (2016). From celebrity to influencer: Tracing the diffusion of celebrity value across the data stream. In P. D. Marshall & S. Redmond (Eds.), A companion to celebrity (pp. 194-212). Wiley.

Hsu, H. Y., & Tsou, H. T. (2011). Understanding customer experiences in online blog environments. *International Journal of Information Management*, *31*(6), 510–523. doi:10.1016/j.ijinfomgt.2011.05.003

Huete-Alcocer, N. (2017). A literature review of word of mouth and electronic word of mouth: Implications for consumer behavior. *Frontiers in Psychology*, *8*, 1256. doi:10.3389/fpsyg.2017.01256 PMID:28790950

Ismail, K. (2018, December 10). *Social media influencers: Mega, macro, micro or nano*. https://www.cmswire.com/digital-marketing/social-media-influencers-mega-macro-micro-or-nano/

Jaakonmäki, R., Müller, O., & Vom Brocke, J. (2017). The impact of content, context, and creator on user engagement in social media marketing. *Proceedings of the 50th Hawaii International Conference on System Sciences*. 10.24251/HICSS.2017.136

Johansen, I. K., & Guldvik, C. S. (2017). *Influencer marketing and purchase intentions: How does influencer marketing affect purchase intentions?* [Unpublished master thesis]. Norwegian School of Economics, Bergen, Norway.

Kahle, L. R., & Homer, P. M. (1985). Physical attractiveness of the celebrity endorser: A social adaptation perspective. *The Journal of Consumer Research*, *11*(4), 954–961. doi:10.1086/209029

Kay, S., Mulcahy, R., & Parkinson, J. (2020). When less is more: The impact of macro and micro social media influencers' disclosure. *Journal of Marketing Management*, *36*(3-4), 248–278. doi:10.1080/0267257X.2020.1718740

Khamis, S., Ang, L., & Welling, R. (2017). Self-branding, 'micro-celebrity' and the rise of Social Media Influencers. *Celebrity Studies*, *8*(2), 191–208. doi:10.1080/19392397.2016.1218292

Kotler, P., Keller, K. L., Brady, M., Goodman, M., & Hansen, T. (2019). *Marketing management* (4th European Ed.). Pearson Education Limited.

Lammers, M. (2018). Wie unternehmen aus micro-influencern co-marketer machen. In M. Jahnke (Ed.), *Influencer marketing* (pp. 107–126). Springer Gabler. doi:10.1007/978-3-658-20854-7_6

Li, Y.-M., Lee, Y.-L., & Lien, N.-J. (2014). Online social advertising via influential endorsers. *International Journal of Electronic Commerce*, *16*(3), 119–153. doi:10.2753/JEC1086-4415160305

Lim, X. J., Radzol, A. R., Cheah, J., & Wong, M. W. (2017). The impact of social media influencers on purchase intention and the mediation effect of customer attitude. *Asian Journal of Business Research*, *7*(2), 19–36. doi:10.14707/ajbr.170035

Lindsey-Mullikin, J., & Borin, N. (2017). Why strategy is key for successful social media sales. *Business Horizons*, *60*(4), 473–482. doi:10.1016/j.bushor.2017.03.005

Litvin, S. W., Goldsmith, R. E., & Pan, B. (2008). Electronic word-of-mouth in hospitality and tourism management. *Tourism Management*, *29*(3), 458–468. doi:10.1016/j.tourman.2007.05.011

Liu, B. F., Jin, Y., & Austin, L. L. (2013). The tendency to tell: Understanding publics' communicative responses to crisis information form and source. *Journal of Public Relations Research*, *25*(1), 51–67. doi:10.1080/1062726X.2013.739101

Liu, M. T., Shi, G., Wong, I. A., Hefel, A., & Chen, C.-Y. (2010). How physical attractiveness and endorser–product match-up guide selection of a female athlete endorser in China. *Journal of International Consumer Marketing*, *22*(2), 169–181. doi:10.1080/08961530903476238

Lokithasan, K., Simon, S., Jasmin, N. Z., & Othman, N. A. (2019). Male and female social media influencers: The impact of gender on emerging adults. *International Journal of Modern Trends in Social Sciences*, *2*(9), 21–30. doi:10.35631/IJMTSS.29003

Lou, C., & Yuan, S. (2019). Influencer marketing: How message value and credibility affect consumer trust of branded content on social media. *Journal of Interactive Advertising*, *19*(1), 58–73. doi:10.108 0/15252019.2018.1533501

Luoma-aho, V., Pirttimäki, T., Maity, D., Munnukka, J., & Reinikainen, H. (2019). Primed authenticity: How priming impacts authenticity perception of social media influencers. *International Journal of Strategic Communication*, *13*(4), 352–365. doi:10.1080/1553118X.2019.1617716

Lutkenhaus, R. O., Jansz, J., & Bouman, M. P. (2019). Tailoring in the digital era: Stimulating dialogues on health topics in collaboration with social media influencers. *Digital Health*, *5*, 1–11. doi:10.1177/2055207618821521 PMID:30729023

Marwick, A. (2010). *Status update: Celebrity, publicity and self-branding in Web 2.0* [Unpublished doctoral dissertation]. New York University.

Marwick, A. (2016). You may know me from Youtube: (Micro-)celebrity in social media. In P. D. Marshall & S. Redmond (Eds.), A companion to celebrity (pp. 333-350). Wiley.

Marwick, A., & boyd. (2011). To see and be seen: Celebrity practice on Twitter. *Convergence*, *17*(2), 139–158. doi:10.1177/1354856510394539

McCracken, G. (1989). Who is the celebrity endorser? Cultural foundations of the endorsement process. *The Journal of Consumer Research*, *16*(3), 310–321. doi:10.1086/209217

Porteous, J. (2018, June 20). *Micro inñuencers vs macro inñuencers, what's best for your business?* https://www.socialbakers.com/blog/micro-inñuencers-vs-macro-inñuencers

Pöyry, E. I., Pelkonen, M., Naumanen, E., & Laaksonen, S.-M. (2019). A call for authenticity: Audience responses to social media influencer endorsements in strategic communication. *International Journal of Strategic Communication*, *13*(4), 336–351. doi:10.1080/1553118X.2019.1609965

Racherla, P., & Friske, W. (2012). Perceived 'usefulness' of online consumer reviews: An exploratory investigation across three services categories. *Electronic Commerce Research and Applications*, *11*(6), 548–559. doi:10.1016/j.elerap.2012.06.003

Rahman, S. U., Saleem, S., Akhtar, S., Ali, T., & Khan, M. A. (2014). Consumers' adoption of apparel fashion: The role of innovativeness, involvement, and social values. *International Journal of Marketing Studies*, *6*(3), 49–64. doi:10.5539/ijms.v6n3p49

Rogers, E. M. (1995). *Diffusion of innovations* (4th ed.). Free Press.

Ruiz-Gomez, A. (2019). Digital fame and fortune in the age of social media: A classification of social media influencers. *aDResearch ESIC, 19*, 8-29.

SanMiguel, P., Guercini, S., & Sádaba, T. (2018). The impact of attitudes towards influencers amongst millennial fashion buyers. *Studies in Communication Sciences, 18*, 439–460.

Schouten, A. P., Janssen, L., & Verspaget, M. (2019). Celebrity vs. influencer endorsements in advertising: The role of identification, credibility, and product-endorser fit. *International Journal of Advertising, 39*(2), 258–281. doi:10.1080/02650487.2019.1634898

Sertoglu, A. E., Catli, O., & Korkmaz, S. (2014). Examining the effect of endorser credibility on the consumers' buying intentions: An empirical study in Turkey. *International Review of Management and Marketing, 4*(1), 66–77.

Sethna, Z., & Blythe, J. (2016). *Consumer behavior*. Sage (Atlanta, Ga.).

Sokolova, K., & Kefi, H. (2020). Instagram and YouTube bloggers promote it, why should I buy? How credibility and parasocial interaction influence purchase intentions. *Journal of Retailing and Consumer Services*, 53.

Solomon, M. (2018). *Consumer behavior: Buying, having, and being* (12th ed.). Pearson Education.

Song, S., & Yoo, M. (2016). The role of social media during the pre-purchasing stage. *Journal of Hospitality and Tourism Technology, 7*(1), 84–99. doi:10.1108/JHTT-11-2014-0067

Sudha, M., & Sheena, K. (2017). Impact of influencers in consumer decision process: The fashion industry. *Journal of Indian Management, 14*(3), 14–30.

Till, B. D., & Busler, M. (1998). Matching products with endorsers: Attractiveness versus expertise. *Journal of Consumer Marketing, 15*(6), 576–586. doi:10.1108/07363769810241445

Till, B. D., & Busler, M. (2000). The match-up hypothesis: Physical attractiveness, expertise, and the role of fit on brand attitude, purchase intent, and brand beliefs. *Journal of Advertising, 29*(3), 1–13. doi:10.1080/00913367.2000.10673613

Tolson, A. (2010). A new authenticity? Communicative practices on YouTube. *Critical Discourse Studies, 7*(4), 277–289. doi:10.1080/17405904.2010.511834

Torres, P., Augusto, M., & Matos, M. (2019). Antecedents and outcomes of digital influencer endorsement: An exploratory study. *Psychology and Marketing, 36*(12), 1267–1276. doi:10.1002/mar.21274

Turner, G. (2006). The mass production of celebrity: 'Celetoids', reality TV and the 'demotic turn'. *International Journal of Cultural Studies, 9*(2), 153–165. doi:10.1177/1367877906064028

Uzunoğlu, E., & Kip, S. M. (2014). Brand communication through digital influencers: Leveraging blogger engagement. *International Journal of Information Management, 34*(5), 592–602. doi:10.1016/j.ijinfomgt.2014.04.007

Vermeir, I., & Sompel, D. (2014). Assessing the what is beautiful is good stereotype and the influence of moderately attractive and less attractive advertising models on self-perception, ad attitudes, and purchase intentions of 8–13-year-old children. *Journal of Consumer Policy, 37*(2), 205–233. doi:10.100710603-013-9245-x

Vodak, J., Cakanova, L., Pekar, M., & Novysedlak, M. (2019). Influencer marketing as a modern phenomenon in reputation management. *Managing Global Transitions, 17*(3), 211–220.

Weiss, R. (2014). Influencer marketing: How word-of-mouth marketing can strengthen your organization's brand. *Marketing Health Services, 34*(1), 16–17. PMID:24741762

Whiting, A., Williams, D. L., & Hair, J. (2019). Guest editorial. *Qualitative Market Research, 22*(2), 90–93. doi:10.1108/QMR-08-2018-0098

Wright, S. A. (2016). Reinvestigating the endorser by product matchup hypothesis in advertising. *Journal of Advertising, 45*(1), 26–32. doi:10.1080/00913367.2015.1077360

Yadav, M. S., Valck, K. D., Hennig-Thurau, T., Hoffman, D. L., & Spann, M. (2013). Social commerce: A contingency framework for assessing marketing potential. *Journal of Interactive Marketing, 27*(3), 311–323. doi:10.1016/j.intmar.2013.09.001

Zulli, D. (2018). Capitalizing on the look: Insights into the glance, attention economy, and Instagram. *Critical Studies in Media Communication, 35*(2), 137–150. doi:10.1080/15295036.2017.1394582

Chapter 9
Understanding Social Media Addiction Through Personal, Social, and Situational Factors

Ozge Kirezli
Yeditepe University, Turkey

Asli Elif Aydin
 https://orcid.org/0000-0002-9145-386X
Istanbul Bilgi University, Turkey

ABSTRACT

The main objective of this chapter is to gain an in-depth understanding of the social media addiction construct. For this purpose, prior studies on social media addiction are reviewed. Based on this review the influence of several personal, social, and situational factors on social media addiction are examined. Firstly, personal factors such as demographic characteristics, personality traits, self-esteem, well-being, loneliness, anxiety, and depression are studied for their impact on social media addiction. Next, the social correlates and consequents of social media addiction are identified, namely need for affiliation, subjective norms, personal, professional, and academic life. Lastly, situational factors like amount of social media use and motives of use are inspected. Following the review of literature an empirical study is made to analyze factors that discriminate addicted social media users from non-addicted social media users on the basis of these different factors.

INTRODUCTION

Internet has dramatically changed the communication patterns of individuals. It has become a pervasive part of consumers' lives such that, researchers heightened their attention to understand the positive and negative effects of internet on human life. Certainly, several positive outcomes of internet can be counted as; providing easy access to information and leveraging early learning (Reid et al, 2016; Bauer, Gai, Kim, Muth, & Wildman, 2002), providing chances for widening social surroundings (Hampton & Well-

DOI: 10.4018/978-1-7998-4718-2.ch009

man, 2003; Katz & Aspden, 1997; Rheingold, 1993) and improving psychological mood via creating opportunities for social contact and support (Reid et al, 2016; Chen, Boase, &Wellman, 2002; Kang, 2007). However, some potential negativities also emerged namely; decreasing level of social contact of individuals (Kim & Harikadis, 2009; Sanders, Field,Diego, & Kaplan, 2000; Kraut,Patterson, Landmark, Kielser,Mukophadhyaya, & Scherlis, 1998; Stoll, 1995; Turkle, 1996), causing loneliness and eventually, clinical depression (Young & Rogers, 1998). These negativities especially intensified as individuals' frequency and duration of internet increased specifically in the cases of addiction.

Internet addiction has gained substantial interest by both mental health professionals and academic researchers. "Addiction" term, actually, is based on biological and psychological dependence of a physical item. The Diagnostic and Statistical Manual of Mental Disorders (DSM) is the most well-known and appreciated source for addiction related terms, but behavioral addictions are not listed in mental disorders according to psychiatric literature. Recognizing this gap in the field, Goldberg (1996) established "internet addiction disorder" term for excessive human-machine interaction. Goldberg(1996) supported his argument by referring how the four components of addiction also exist in internet addiction, as well. These four components are; tolerance (increasing the engagement level to reach previous improved mood states), withdrawal (feeling discomfort when the behavior is prohibited), negative life outcomes (neglecting social, educational or work related issues), and craving (increasing the level of intensity) (Kim & Harikadis, 2009; Goldberg, 1996). In time, three more components are added to the four existing components namely; salience (being preoccupied with the behavior), mood modification (using this to alleviate psychological state) and relapse (fail to control the behavior) (Kim & Harikadis, 2009; Griffiths, 1998).

A growing wave of researchers supported the notion of using addiction term to characterize high dependence of certain behaviors especially among the youth (Kuss & Griffiths, 2011; Young, 2004; Lemon, 2002; Orford, 2001; Shaffer, 1996; Griffiths, 1998; Peele 1985). Moreover, the recent edition of "Diagnostic and Statistical Manual of Mental Disorders" recognized gambling as an addiction and listed digital game addiction as a potential behavioral addiction (American Psychiatric Association, 2013). Likewise a number of various behavioral addictions have been examined such as; internet addiction, social media addiction, digital game addiction (Keepers, 1990) and smartphone addiction (Savci & Aysan, 2017). This chapter focuses on social media addiction. Although in the literature there exist different terminology to explain this phenomenon, specifically problematic social media/Facebook use (Kırcaburun et al., 2019; Shensa et al., 2017), social networking addiction (Griffiths et al., 2018; Monacis et al., 2017; Wang et al., 2015) and compulsive social media usage (Dhir et al., 2018; Aladwani et al., 2017), social media addiction term is used deliberately to reach consistency within the work.

This chapter aims to understand "social media addiction" concept by examining its correlates. Moreover, it contributes to social media addiction literature in two ways. First of all, it provides a comprehensive look to social media addiction by discussing a variety of factors, which are beneficial for academicians' to be used for further research. Secondly, with an empirical study, factors discriminating social media addicts from non-addicts are identified.

SOCIAL MEDIA ADDICTION: EN EMERGING TREND

At the present time, the dramatic role of social media on communicational patterns cannot be underestimated. Even though, social media use provides many benefits such as of eroding distance between people, easing and speeding up the interaction, even changing the formal communicational patterns in the business life, excessive use of social media can be problematic as it potentially harms social and psychological life of individuals (Karaiskos et al., 2010; Kuss & Griffiths, 2011). It has become almost a social obligation for individuals to check their social media updates, even when they are walking, shopping, listening to a lecture, and driving (Sriwilai & Charoensukmongkol, 2015). People engage in social media for a variety of reasons, specifically to play games, to fill waiting times, to communicate, to share their "self" and to respond to other "selves" (Andreassen et. al, 2017; Allen, Ryan, Gray, McInerney, &Waters, 2014; Ryan, Chester, Reece, & Xenos, 2014). Enjoyment gained through social media can stimulate a strong habit which occasionally transforms into an irresistible urge (Longstreet & Brooks, 2017). This urge to make frequent checks or updates in social media, has a potential to turn into a compulsive disorder, which might be harmful for academic, professional and social life of individuals (Karaiskos et al., 2010). In that perspective, Andreassen and Pallasen (2014, p.4054) defined social media addiction as "being overly concerned about social media, driven by an uncontrollable motivation to log on to or use social media, and devoting so much time and effort to social media that it impairs other important life areas".

Coining the term "social media addiction" brought about two burdens. The first one is about differentiating addicts from non-addicts, whereas the second one is about constituting the criteria for distinguishing the addicts. In 2012, Andreassen and her colleagues developed a new scale entitled Bergen Facebook Addiction Scale (BFAS), using Facebook's position of being a pioneer in social media. In this scale, there exist six main characteristics of addictions, prevailed in Facebook addiction. These characteristics are identified as; salience (continuous preoccupation with Facebook), tolerance (incremental engagement with Facebook to reach prior mood escalating effect), mood modification (using Facebook for mood alleviation), relapse (failed attempts of limiting or prohibiting Facebook use), withdrawal (feeling anxious without Facebook) and conflict (excessive Facebook use causing social, academic or work related problems) (Andreassen et al., 2013, 2012; Wilson et al., 2010). Hence this characterization was the first attempt to distinguish extreme or enthusiastic users and addicts, since it is not only increasing the amount of time spent for social media, but the incremental and possibly detrimental effect on individuals' life. In addition, this characterization provided further insights about the progressive nature of addiction as checking the concept in six dimensions in continuous basis, rather than dichotomous addict or non-addict basis.

FACTORS RELATED TO SOCIAL MEDIA ADDICTION

In the literature, the effects of variety of personal, social and situational factors on social media addiction has been explored. Several studies categorized the related factors as either antecedents or consequences yet majority of the analyses are made based on correlations. Therefore, this chapter intends to present the influential factors altogether to better examine potential antecedent or consequential effects.

Personal Factors

Demographic Characteristics

A substantial amount of research examined the role of demographic characteristics on the prevalence of social media addiction (Marino et al., 2018; Andreassen et al 2016; Van Deursen et al., 2015; Kuss et al., 2014; Koç & Gulyagci, 2013). Within this stream of research, gender's effect on social media addiction is well examined. There exist three main perspectives which explain gender's role on social media addiction. The first one advocates that women are more vulnerable to addictive usage of social media compared to men due to their heightened interest in social activities (Andreassen, 2015; Van Deursen, Bolle, Hegner, & Kommers, 2015; Kuss et al. 2014; Turel et al., 2014; Griffiths et al., 2014; Andreassen et al., 2013; Moreau et al., 2015). Kuss et al. (2014) suggested the idea that both men and women have the tendency to become technology addicts, however males are more interested in gaming, pornography and gambling, whereas women favor social media, texting and online shopping (Maraz et al., 2015; Van Deursen et al., 2015; Andreassen et al., 2013). The second view, emerged as gender having a minimal role in explaining social media addiction (Beyens, Frison, & Eggermont, 2016; Lee, 2015). The third view, interestingly, suggests that men are more likely to be addicted to social media compared to women (Çam& Isbulan, 2012; Ryan et al., 2014). Thus, gender's role on social media addiction seems to be an unresolved issue, hence needs further empirical data to reach conclusive findings.

Compared to gender, age seems to have a greater impact on overall demographic characteristics. Research indicated that young individuals have higher scores in social media addiction compared to older individuals (Andreassen et al., 2012; Kuss et al., 2014). This phenomenon might be explained by new generations' easy adaptation to technology and simply embracing the state of being "constantly online" (Prensky, 2001), their tendency to develop their self via a virtual identity in social media freely (Andreassen, 2015; Mazzoni & Iannone, 2014) and their readiness to use social platforms as effective entertainment and leisure activities (Allen et al., 2014).

Another significant demographic variable is defined as individuals' relationship status. Research shows that people, not in a relationship, are more prone to social media addiction (Kuss et al., 2014). Also some studies interpret this fact with, how social media can serve as a medium to meet new people as to create or nurture relations with potential partners (Andreassen, Torsheim, & Pallesen, 2014; Ryan et al., 2014).

Self Esteem

A number of studies investigate the association between social media usage frequency and self-esteem. These studies report a negative relationship between duration of time spent on social media and self-esteem (Kalpidou, Costin,& Morris, 2011; Vogel et al., 2014). Studies also corroborated that for adolescents a negative relationship exists between intensity of social media use and individuals' self-esteem (Valkenburg, Peter, & Schouten, 2006; Woods & Scott, 2016; Ingólfsdóttir, 2017). As for tracing the relationship between self-esteem and addictive type of behaviors, notable amount of research indicated that, individuals having low level of self-esteem are more inclined to engage in addictive type of behaviors (BaÂnyai et al., 2017; Andreassen et al., 2017; Baturay & Toker, 2016; Malik & Khan, 2015; Eraslan-Capan, 2015; Marlatt et al., 1988). There exist three probable explanations about self-esteem's role on social media addiction. The first one argues that, individuals having low self-esteem have negative feelings towards themselves, and social media addiction serves as an escape strategy to suppress this stress and anxiety (Błachnio et al., 2016; De Cock et al., 2014; Bozoglan, Demirer, & Sahin, 2013; Baumeister, 1993; Swann, 1996). The second one suggests that, people use social media to strengthen their self-esteem (Peele, 1985; Steinfield, Ellison, & Lampe, 2008; Gonzales & Hancock, 2011). Gonzales and Hancock (2011) use the term of "selective self-presentation" as how people carefully select the media by highlighting the most positive and appealing slices of their life. The third one is, related to individuals having delicate self-esteem as having extreme awareness of what the environment thinks about them and embracing social media as avoiding real human contact (Eraslan Çapan, 2015). Social media serves as a magical digital channel for individuals to remove the uncomfortable feeling of one-to-one communication with others, especially for those having insufficient social skills (Boyce & Parker, 1989).

In contrary with these views, Blachnio et al. (2016) propose that, it is not only individuals with low self-esteem that use social media addictively, but people with high levels of self-esteem use social media in an addictive manner, as well. These people are motivated to sustain their social bonds via social media, and extend their social circle by being active in social media. Marino et al. (2018) interpret the overall relationship between self-esteem and social media use referring to the social compensation theory. According to that people with high self-esteem boost their self-esteem via social media presence and people with low self-esteem, use social media as a way to compensate their deficiency.

Personality Traits

In the literature, personality is widely characterized through the Five-Factor Model (Caprara, Barbaranelli, Borgogni, & Perugini, 1993; Caprara, Barbaranelli, & Livi, 1994; Marino et al., 2018). According to this model, there exist five dimensions in personality, which are extroversion, agreeableness, conscientiousness, neuroticism and openness. Extraversion refers to the quantity of social interaction, the individual prefers. It gives critical hints about sociability and emotional expression level of individuals. It is believed that, introverted individuals (scoring low in extroversion dimension) mostly engage in social media to compensate the stability of their social life (Amichai-Hamburger, Wainapel, & Fox, 2002; Bodroza & Jovanovic, 2016). On the contrary, Andreassen et al. (2012) argued that extroverted people are more inclined to be social media addicts, as a result of their motivation to sustain their sociability. Perhaps, the most comprehensive view came from Kuss and Griffiths (2010), indicating that extrovert people engage in social media for social boost, whereas introvert people engage in social media for improving social well-being. Agreeableness refers to the quality of social interaction, as how kind, emphatic and helpful the individual is towards others. Individuals scoring high in agreeableness, excessively use social media to convey their relational achievements to stay connected to the others (Marshall, Lefringhausen, & Ferenczi, 2015). However, there exist studies claiming insignificant relations between agreeableness trait and social media addiction (Lee, 2015; Błachnio et al., 2017). Further a negative relationship is also found which indicates that a high agreeableness score potentially results with lower social media addiction tendency (Andreassen et al., 2013; Bodroza & Jovanovic, 2016). Conscientiousness trait is related to being organized, competent, goal-driven and having self-discipline. Those, scoring high in this dimension, either favor organizing tools of social media as facilitators or enjoy accelerating number of friends (Amichai-Hamburger & Vinitzky, 2010). However, there also exist intriguing reverse relationship suggestions, which suggest that highly conscientious people avoid social media since social media is seen as a disturbing activity (Wilson et. al., 2010; Andreassen et al., 2012; Andreassen et al., 2013; Lee, 2015; Bodroza & Jovanovic, 2016; Błachnio et al., 2017). Neuroticism reflects individuals' incapacity to deal with anxiety and stress. Hence, it is usually taken as an indicator for emotional (in) stability. According to literature, neuroticism is evident in addictive type of behaviors (Andreassen et al., 2012; Tang, Chen, Yang, Chung, & Lee, 2016; Marino et al. 2018). Neurotic people are articulated as heavy social media users to alleviate their mood due to emotional instability (Marino et. al., 2018), to pursue emotional support via this online channel (Andreassen et. al, 2012). Likewise, Ross et al. (2009) believed neuroticism plays a significant role in information sharing tendency of people in social media. Last dimension is openness, which symbolize how ready the individuals are to embrace novelty in their life. Individuals, who are high in openness to experience, are frequently labeled as information searchers or sharers in the social media. Thus, this information concern, make these people vulnerable for excessive use and potentially addictive behavior (Hughes, Rowe, Batey, & Lee, 2012).

Loneliness

Loneliness is also among the potential antecedents of social media addiction. According to an empirical study with a sample size of 1193, active social media users expressed they felt less lonely and gained social support after they used social media, compared to passive social media users (Wilson, Gosling, & Graham, 2012). People, who have low social skills (McKenna and Bargh, 2000) or feel socially incompetent (Kubey et al., 2001) might feel more relaxed and comfortable with online activities. Loneliness is also matched with other addictive activities such as consumption of drugs (Grunbaum, Tortolero, Weller, & Gingiss, 2000) and alcohol (Loos, 2002; Medora & Woodward, 1991). In that perspective, heavy dependence on internet and social media to cope with loneliness might cause social media addiction (Caplan, 2002, 2003; Davis, 2001).

Well-being

One factor that is examined as a negative correlate of social media addiction is individuals' well-being. It is suggested that meaningless time on Facebook dampens individuals' morale (Sagioglou & Greitemeyer, 2014). Besides, compared to non-addicts, those who are addicted to social media score lower on subjective happiness and subjective vitality (Uysal, Satici, & Akin, 2013). Moreover, it is indicated that procrastination due to social media use has a damaging effect on general well-being (Meier, Reinecke, & Meltzer, 2016). A study which examined the impact of instantaneous and prolonged Facebook use, reveal that increased usage of Facebook lessens individuals' well-being (Kross et al., 2013). A negative relationship is also demonstrated between Facebook addiction and satisfaction with life (Błachnio, Przepiorka, & Pantic, 2016; Satici & Uysal, 2015). Likewise, a decrease in social media use enhances satisfaction with life (Hinsch, & Sheldon, 2013).

Anxiety and Depression

In the literature, depression and anxiety are related to social media addiction in two aspects. The first aspect is figured as anxiety/depression's role as an antecedent, whereby people feeling more anxious or depressed spend more time in social media and decrease the level of communication with their social circle (Pantic,2014; Kraut et al. 2002). Block et al. (2014) reported that depressed individuals use media (internet, tv and social media) more frequently than regular people. Likewise, Clayton, Osborne, Miller, and Oberle (2013) referred anxiousness as an important antecedent of emotional connectedness to social media.

The second aspect is visualized as a consequence, as of social media addiction's detrimental effect on producing more depressed and anxious individuals (Shensa et al., 2017; Moreno et al., 2011). Addictive use of internet increases depression symptoms (Gámez-Guadix, 2014). Specific to social media domain, it is also found that excessive use of social media correlates with increased likelihood of depression (Moreau et al., 2015; Lin et al., 2016). Another study also reported increased levels of anxiety and depression as a result of increased social media usage for adolescents (Woods & Scott, 2016). Similarly, it is revealed that social media addiction contributes to emotional burn out through the use of emotional strategies of coping with stress (Sriwilai & Charoensukmongkol, 2016). Social media addiction may also lead to physical health issues (Andreassen, 2015). For instance, both overall state of health and sleep quality deteriorate with social media addiction (Atroszko, 2018). Additionally, it is indicated that excessive use of social media results in delayed bedtimes and rising times (Andreassen, et al., 2012).

In sum, social media addiction is perceived as a significant contributor to depression, especially in youth, according to a substantial number of research (Younnes et al., 2016; Levenson et al., 2016; Liu et al., 2016; Block et al., 2014; Feinstein et al., 2012; Moreno et al., 2011; Desjarlais & Willoughby, 2010; Mihajlović et al., 2008). On the other hand, studies also tried to validate the potential positive effects of social media on human spirit. Interestingly, McDougall et al. (2016) initiated that social media might produce benefits as fueling social support to remove depression, yet he argued that social media did not nurture depressive symptoms, but let people share their inner world and start almost like a primitive therapy for these people. In that vein, excessive social media users or social media addicts do not necessarily in all cases, suffer from depression and anxiety. Eventually, the relationship between social media, depression and anxiety seem ambiguous, in terms of whether addictive social media causing these negative feelings or negative feelings lead individuals to addictive social media use.

Social Factors

Need for Affiliation / Social Enhancement

Need for affiliation is described as the individuals' inclination to develop and maintain social relationships (Veroff, Reuamn & Feld, 1984; Murray, 1938). Seeking social approval or belongingness is a natural drive, since people show considerable energy for social interaction to satisfy the need for appreciation and affection. Yet, human interaction is not limited to face-to-face contact, writing letters once was the main practice for engaging in distant relationships (Lansing & Heyns, 1959). Thanks to advances in communication technologies, internet and social media acts as an efficient tool for individuals' contact with their friends. Ample amount of studies underlined people's enthusiasm for social connectedness as the major reason of social media use (Valentine, 2013; Kuss & Griffiths, 2011; Sheldon, 2009; Joinson, 2008; Raacke & Bonds-Raacke, 2008). In the studies, validating the correlation between individuals' need for affiliation and internet communication, respondents expressed that web based communication is deeper and more pleasant than face-to-face interaction (Peter & Valkenburg, 2006; Caplan, 2003). Similarly, it was argued that, need for affiliation is a strong motivator for new generation to take place in social media due to frequency and quality of communication they develop with others (Chuang & Nam, 2007). The type of interaction is different in social media, such as receiving and sending comments, writing on the wall of others, number of shares, likes and so on. This reciprocity produces a virtual community for those people, whereby they can satisfy the need for affiliation. In that vein, online social networking can be beneficial for social functioning (Burke, Marlow, & Lento, 2010; Ellison, Steinfield, & Lampe, 2007; Steinfield, Ellison, & Lampe, 2008). Furthermore, the individual can create and develop the desired "self", which serves the need for affiliation, as well (Gibbs, Ellison, & Heino, 2006). Even so, having such a convenient, cheap and easy communication tool seems promising, it comes with a cost. It is interesting to reveal that, individuals excessively using social media might turn into socially isolated individuals in real life (Allen et al., 2014). When taken with facilitating demographic characteristics (being young and having no relationship), need for affiliation via social media can evolve to social media addiction, whereby the individual experiences an alienation in real social settings and escapes to virtual world for social gratification (Shen &Williams, 2010; Valkenburg & Peter, 2009; Mesch, 2001).

Subjective Norms

Subjective norms are defined as individuals' perception of the type of conduct that is expected from them within a group (Davis, 1989; Cialdini, Kallgren & Reno, 1991). It is a more lenient form of group pressure, which creates an obligation to act suitably (Marino et al., 2016). Studies support the notion that, especially in youth, subjective norms can have both positive and negative impacts (Venkatesh et al., 2003; Borsari & Carey, 2003; Pozzoli & Gini, 2013). Rabaai et al. (2018) suggested that subjective norms might function in two ways. The first one is due to rapid adoption of technology especially in younger generation, individuals feel like they have to be present in social media, even though they do not have a certain desire (Lewis et al., 2012). Even more, Olowu and Seri (2012) state that existence in social media might be for just suppressing the social pressure of "have to be there, have to be online". In that sense, adolescents seem more vulnerable to seize social media just for approval due to peer influence. The second impact emerges, when the individuals observe how their social circle experience and enjoy social media, they feel the strong need to feel alike (Huang et al., 2014). Compared to previous trigger, hereby not solely being online in social media motivates the person, but seeks to actively participate in conversations and events for the purpose of enriching social life and not missing out on joyful events. If individuals become heavily anxious about their social life performance, they fear of social exclusion (Blackwell et al., 2017). In that perspective, fear of missing out might promote individuals increased social media use. Fear of missing out is defined as a type of fear when individual thinks other people are enjoying their time without him/her (Przybylski, Murayama, DeHaan, &Gladwell, 2013).

Personal, Professional and Academic Life

The influence of social media use on real life relationships are also examined within this stream of research. When individuals use social media excessively their relationships with friends and family are damaged since they dedicate less time to their social environment (Zheng & Lee, 2016). Studies also demonstrate detrimental effects of social media addiction on romantic relationships such that a positive association between addiction and romantic detachment along with betrayal exists (Abbasi, 2018, 2019).

Social media addiction may also lead to problems in individuals' professional life. Firstly, individuals declare a slightly negative impact of social media use on their job performance (Andreassen, Torsheim, & Pallesen, 2014). On the other hand, it is indicated that excessive use of social media use impedes individuals' work conduct (Zheng & Lee, 2016). It is further revealed that social media addiction hinders job performance as a result of social media induced distraction and negative affect (Moqbel, & Kock, 2018). Parallel to that a decline in job performance is shown due to addiction based work-family life imbalance and emotional exhaustion (Zivnuska et al., 2019). Finally, addiction to social media is shown to influence job satisfaction negatively as well (Choi, 2018).

The impact of use of social media on academic performance also received some scholarly interest. First of all, it is shown that those who use Facebook spend less time studying compared to those who do not use Facebook (Kirschner & Karpinski, 2010). Furthermore, it is indicated that as the frequency of Facebook use increase, the overall GPA of students decrease (Junco, 2012). Parallel to that, multitasking social media while studying is shown to be negatively related to overall GPA (Junco& Cooten, 2012; Lau, 2017). It is also demonstrated that individuals, who show symptoms of social media addiction, performed poorly in their academic studies (Al-Menayes, 2015).

Situational Factors

Amount of Use

Social media addiction, just like the other addictions, can be assessed in an incremental basis on a continuum. As it can be expected, the higher amount of time the individual uses social media, the likelihood to get addicted increases (Widyanto & McMurran, 2004; Leung, 2004). Yet, prior research supported that problematic social media users tend to spend more time rather than regular users, signaling significant positive relationship between two concepts (Hormes et al., 2014). However, studies distinguishing excessive social media usage and social media addiction, state that amount of use might not indicate problematic/addictive social media use, in all cases (Pontes et al., 2015; Griffiths, 2010). By making this distinction, emphasis is put on the availability of negative consequences. If the individual does not suffer from negative outcomes (e.g. delay in daily chores, feelings of insecurity or discomfort when deprived from social media etc.) then the individual is not considered addicted (Griffiths, 2010). In sum, addicts use social media frequently; however, excessive users (referring to the quantitative data) do not necessarily always show addictive symptoms. In that manner, apart from the quantitative approach, the qualitative nature of the time spent on social media needs to be explored.

Motives

Motives leading to excessive or addictive usage of social media might be numerous. Studies proposed various motives for social media usage; fulfilling relational needs (interaction, affection, approval, self-expression) or fulfilling media related entertainment needs (learning new things, leisure activity, using applications and tools) (Charney & Greenberg, 2002; Ebersole, 2000; Ferguson & Perse, 2000; Kaye & Johnson, 2004; Papacharissi & Rubin, 2000). It was suggested that, if the individual is aware of the motives that lead them to excessive or addictive usage of social media, that would reduce the potential manifestation of the negative outcomes (Song, LaRose, Eastin, & Lin, 2004). A growing body of research indicated that people that are using social media for social goals (socialization, companionship and social interaction) and lightening mood (escapism, feel good effect, passing time) are more likely to be addicts (Bodroza & Jovanovic, 2016; Koc & Gulyagci, 2013; Tang et al., 2016; Sharifah et al., 2011; Dhaha, 2013; Masur et al., 2014). Similarly, Ryan et al. (2016) stressed social media's effect on emotional life of individual as repairing mood or overcoming boredom besides social motives. The motivational model for social media, is characterized as having two dimensions; positive / negative valence (enhancing positive mood, or repairing negative mood) and internal / external resource (satisfying one's own internal needs or others') (Marino et. al., 2016; Bischof-Kastner et al., 2014). Consequently, four motives emerge, namely enhancement, coping, conformity and social. Enhancement refers to positive valence and internal source, meaning that individuals with this motive aim to improve positive feelings for them. Coping refers to negative valence and internal source, meaning people wish to escape from negative feelings via social media. Conformity refers to negative valence and external source, which is related to using social media to overcome social pressure. Social motive is related to use social media with the aim of improving social interaction with existing or potential friends (Marino et. al., 2016; Bischof-Kastner et al., 2014).

THE STUDY

The objective of the empirical study is to gain a better understanding of social media addiction. For this purpose a comparison of addicted social media users and non-addicted social media users are made based on a number of factors. First, the study examines the relationship between social media addiction and motives underlying social media use. Second, the impact of person characteristics such as loneliness and life satisfaction on social media addiction is investigated in the study. The influence of individuals' judgments regarding their satisfaction with their lives and participants' subjective feelings of social seclusion on the degree of their social media addiction is also examined. Moreover, the extent of association between social media usage duration and social media addiction is inspected. Finally, the relationship between social media addiction and social media use while conversing with others, driving, listening to lectures is also analyzed.

METHOD

Data

The empirical study for this chapter is conducted in Turkey. It is stated that Turkey is one of the top twenty countries based on time spent each day on social platforms (GlobalWebIndex, 2019). Accordingly, the tendency to use social media in a problematic manner is quite high in Turkey. The data is collected from a sample of college students. Social media use is most widespread among the young; hence the age base of the sample is deemed appropriate.

Undergraduate students of Business Department of three major universities in Istanbul, Turkey are invited to the study. Students are incentivized to participate to the study with bonus credit offerings. A total of 269 students completed a web-based survey. The survey took on average 10 minutes to complete. 11 students did not own a social media account. Therefore, they were removed from the sample. Moreover, 23 students failed to answer correctly to an attention test and hence were removed. Consequently, 235 participants were retained in the final sample.

Measures

Social Networking Addiction

To assess participants' level of social media addiction Bergen Social Networking Addiction Scale (Andreassen et al., 2012) was employed. The scale includes six items corresponding to six main dimension of addiction namely salience (prominence of social media use in individuals' thinking), mood modification (social media use improving mood), tolerance (increasing amount of social media use to experience the same effects), withdrawal (presence of negative feelings when social media is not used), conflict (negative impact of social media use on studies/work), and relapse (returning to earlier use of social media after exercising self-restraint). Participants' were asked to indicate how often they experienced the mentioned thoughts, feelings and behaviors during the past year. They responded using a five-point scale ranging from (1) very rarely to (5) very often. A summated score of 6 to 30 marks the extent of social networking addiction. The Cronbach's alpha of the scale was 0.75 for the current sample.

Motives for Using Social Media

As a measure of participants' motives underlying social media, the 16-item Motives for Using Social Media Scale (Marino et al. 2016) was included in the study. The scale assesses four key motives namely; enhancement (to improve positive feelings by using social media), coping (to reduce negative feelings by using social media), conformity (to conform to peer group norms by using social media), and social (to improve relationships with friends). Participants' were asked to indicate how often they used social media for each motive on a five-point scale ranging from (1) never or almost never to (5) always or almost always. Higher scores on this scale indicate stronger motives. The Cronbach's alpha of the scale was 0.91.

Loneliness

The trait loneliness was assessed using eight-item Loneliness Scale developed by Hays and DiMatteo (1987). The scale assesses individuals' feelings of social isolation. Participants were asked to indicate to what extent they agree with the statements on a four-point scale ranging from (1) never to (4) always. Those who obtain a high score on this scale were considered to feel lonely. The Cronbach's alpha of the scale was 0.73.

Satisfaction with Life

In order to measure participants' satisfaction with their lives the Life Satisfaction Scale developed by Diener et. al. (1985) was employed. The scale comprises five items that assess a cognitive appraisal of individuals' satisfaction with their lives. Participants were asked to indicate to what extent they agree with the statements on a four-point scale ranging from (1) strongly disagree to (4) strongly agree. The Cronbach's alpha of the scale was 0.78.

Social Media Use Duration

The measure for Social Media Use Duration was adapted from Facebook use duration scale of Brailovskaia et al. (2019). The scale is adapted by substituting the Facebook term with social media. One item assessed frequency of social media use on a 6-point scale ranging from (1) less than once a day to (6) ten times a day or more. Another item assessed length of social media usage period on a 7-point scale ranging from (1) less than five minutes to (7) more than 180 minutes. The average frequency and length of social media use for this sample was 5.01(SD=1.21) and 4.83 (SD=1.52), respectively.

A combined measure for social media use duration was also calculated by taking the average of two Z-transformed scores of both measures.

Improper Use of Social Media

In order to assess improper use of social media a three-item scale is developed for this study. Items related to the tendency to use social media while conversing with others, driving and attending a lecture are included. Participants were asked to indicate to how frequently they engaged in the behaviors reported in the statements on a four-point scale ranging from (1) never to (4) always. The Cronbach's alpha of the scale was 0.6.

Demographics

Participants' age, gender and relationship status were included in the questionnaire. The mean age of the sample was 20.77 (SD=3.35). 40 percent of the participants were female and 34 percent of the whole sample was in a relationship.

Analysis and Results

Initially mean values, standard deviations and bivariate correlations of the study constructs are computed (Table 1). The average summated social media addiction score for the sample is 16.16 (SD = 5.04) out of a possible 30 points.

Table 1. Descriptives and Correlation coefficients between constructs

	A	B	C	D	E	F	G	H	I
A. Social Media Addiction	1								
B. Life Satisfaction	-0.02	1							
C. Loneliness	0.18**	-0.17**	1						
D. Social Motive	0.40**	0.10	0.15*	1					
E. Enhancement Motive	0.54**	0.10	0.13	0.56**	1				
F. Conformity Motive	0.46**	-0.04	0.32**	0.40**	0.42**	1			
G. Coping Motive	0.62**	-0.1	0.20**	0.43**	0.51**	0.39**	1		
H. Composite duration	0.51**	0.12	0.01	0.39**	0.51**	0.21**	0.32**	1	
I. Improper use	0.52**	0.09	0.11	0.38**	0.45**	0.35**	0.40**	0.39**	1
Mean	16.16	4.62	1.92	3.33	3.05	1.77	2.88	0.00	2.28
Standard deviation	5.04	1.05	0.43	1.12	1.01	0.98	1.22	0.88	0.83

* p< 0.05
** p< 0.01

A multiple regression analysis is made to examine the predictors of social media addiction. The variables of the study explained 54% of the variance of social media addiction (Table 2). Multicollinearity among the variables is inspected based on bivariate correlations and variance inflation factors. It is seen that there is no multicollinearity since all correlation coefficients are below 0.7 and variance inflation factors for all variables are below 3 (Hair et al., 2006). According to the results of the multiple regression analysis significant variables are social media use duration (β=0.25), enhancement motive (β=0.13), conformity motive (β=0.18), coping motive (β=0.34), and improper use (β=0.19). The other variables are not significant.

Table 2. Regression analysis for social media addiction

	B	Std. Error	β	t	Sig.
(Constant)	8.38	2.28		3.67	0
Composite duration	1.42	0.31	0.25	4.65	0.00
Life satisfaction	-0.14	0.23	-0.03	-0.63	0.53
Loneliness	0.35	0.55	0.03	0.63	0.53
Social motive	-0.35	0.26	-0.08	-1.35	0.18
Enhancement motive	0.64	0.32	0.13	2.02	0.04
Conformity motive	0.93	0.27	0.18	3.43	0.00
Coping motive	1.40	0.23	0.34	6.09	0.00
Improper use	1.16	0.32	0.19	3.66	0.00
Age	-0.08	0.07	-0.05	-1.13	0.26
Gender	0.79	0.47	0.08	1.69	0.09
Relationship Status	-0.21	0.48	-0.02	-0.43	0.67

R^2: 0.57
Adjusted R^2: 0.54
Std. Error of the Estimate: 3.37
$F_{(df1,df2)}$: $F(11,223)=27.35$
*p<0.05; **p<0.01

Next, a logistic regression analysis is made with the same variables to predict the likelihood of being addicted to social media. In order to distinguish addicted individuals, having a minimum score of three or more for at least four of the six items is required, following Andreassen et al. (2012)'s approach. A dummy variable, which takes the value 1 for addicted individuals, is created for the analysis. Based on that a total of 113 participants fit this criteria and hence were categorized as addicted individuals.

The logistic model is statistically significant (χ^2 (11, N = 235) = 106.56, p < 0.05) which suggests that differences between addicted and non-addicted individuals can be identified. Hosmer - Lemeshow test is employed to assess goodness of fit for the logistic regression. The p-value, which is greater than 0.05, indicates no significant difference between the expected and the observed data. 77% of the cases are correctly classified by the model. Four variables are significant namely; social media use duration, conformity motive, coping motive, and improper use. According to that, individuals, who used social media for longer durations are 2.01 times more likely to be addicted (p = 0.01). Moreover, using social media with conformity motive and coping motive increase the chances of being addicted with odds ratios of 2.09 (p < 0.01) and 1.94 (p < 0.01) respectively. Lastly, improper use of social media increase the odds of being addicted with a ratio of 1.87 (p = 0.01).

Table 3. Logistic regression analysis predicting likelihood of being addicted to social media

Variables	B	S.E.	Wald	df	Sig.	Exp(B)	95% C.I. for Exp(B)	
							Lower	Upper
Composite duration	0.70	0.26	7.36	1	0.01	2.01	1.21	3.33
Life satisfaction	0.01	0.18	0.01	1	0.94	1.01	0.71	1.45
Loneliness	0.47	0.44	1.10	1	0.29	1.59	0.67	3.81
Social motive	-0.12	0.19	0.38	1	0.54	0.89	0.61	1.29
Enhancement motive	0.03	0.23	0.02	1	0.89	1.03	0.66	1.62
Conformity motive	0.74	0.23	10.33	1	0.00	2.09	1.33	3.28
Coping motive	0.66	0.18	14.19	1	0.00	1.94	1.37	2.74
Improper use	0.63	0.25	6.35	1	0.01	1.87	1.15	3.05
Age	-0.09	0.06	2.38	1	0.12	0.91	0.81	1.02
Gender	0.02	0.36	0.00	1	0.96	1.02	0.50	2.05
Relationship Status	-0.39	0.38	1.03	1	0.31	0.68	0.32	1.43
Constant	-3.38	1.88	3.23	1	0.07	0.03		

Hosmer-Lemeshow
$\chi2$: 5.66
Sig.: 0.69
N: 235

DISCUSSION

Firstly, the empirical study supported that the degree of social media addiction increases with increased duration of use. The composite index of frequency and length of social media use significantly predict social media addiction. This finding corroborates findings of prior studies which show a significant link between time spent on the internet and internet addiction (Leung, 2004) as well as a significant link between amount of daily online presence and Facebook addiction (Przepiorka, & Blachnio, 2016; Brailovskaia, Margraf, & Köllner, 2019).

Secondly, the study point out that neither life satisfaction nor loneliness determines social media addiction. Even though prior research demonstrated that individuals who are socially secluded seek interactions through online mediums (McKenna & Bargh, 2000), and that a positive relationship exists between state of loneliness and internet addiction (Kubey et al., 2001; Kim & Haridakis, 2009), findings demonstrate no significant relationship between loneliness and social media addiction. Moreover, earlier studies indicate positive relationship between social media addiction and life satisfaction (Błachnio, Przepiorka & Pantic, 2016; Longstreet & Brooks, 2017). Current study does not support these findings. One probable account for this discrepancy is that life satisfaction is a general concept which encapsulates global evaluations of every dimension of life. Therefore, judgments about life in general might not be a driver of social media addiction.

Regarding the motivation of social media use, results indicated that conformity and coping motives distinguish between addicted and non-addicted users. Those, who used social media to reduce their negative feelings or to conform to peer norms, are more likely to get addicted. Moreover, enhancement motive is found to be a significant predictor of social media addiction. Even though enhancement does not discern addicts from non-addicts, the motive to improve positive feelings increase degree of social media addiction. Lastly social motive does not determine social media addiction since majority of the users' main drive in social media use is to improve relationships with friends. Accordingly, social motive becomes a generic purpose for all users.

Another finding demonstrated that those who use social media improperly are more likely to get addicted to social media. Those, who compulsively check their social media feeds during lectures, while driving or having a conversation with others, are more likely to be addicted. This finding demonstrates the detrimental effects of social media addiction and hence is valuable. Further studies might investigate the impact of improper use on social interactions as well as performance of daily tasks.

Finally, the findings reveal that gender does not discern likelihood of being addicted to social media. It is shown that only marginally significant differences exist on extent of social media addiction between men and women. Specifically, the extent of social media addiction is slightly higher for women than for men. Prior studies report conflicting findings regarding the role of gender in predicting social media addiction (Çam & Isbulan, 2012; Griffiths et al., 2014; Wang et al., 2015). Our study also does not clarify the influence of gender on social media addiction. Furthermore, neither age nor relationship status predict social media addiction. The age range of the current sample is rather narrow due to student based sampling. Thus, it is unsurprising that age does not predict social media addiction with this sample. Regarding the relationship status, it is shown that being addicted to social media does not depend on being in a relationship or being single. This finding contradicts earlier work which demonstrated that individuals who are not in a relationship have higher levels of social media addiction (Andreassen et al., 2017). Still, the authors of that study also report that the impact of being in a relationship on social media addiction is rather small, almost negligible.

CONCLUSION

In this chapter, social media addiction construct is discussed extensively, starting with the facilitating conditions that cause social media addiction to become an emerging trend especially with the young generation. Diverse perspectives from psychology, psychiatry, and social psychology are reviewed to indicate conceptual differences and grasp the theoretical underpinning. Then, the influences of most significant personal, social and situational variables are presented. Prior work, which investigate the impact of these factors on social media addiction along with the impact of social media addiction on some of these factors, are assessed. Regarding the personal variables; demographics, self-esteem, personality traits, loneliness, well-being, anxiety and depression are studied as they received the most scholarly interest. For the social factors; need for affiliation/social enhancement, subjective norms, and personal/ professional/ academic life are scrutinized. Lastly, situational factors are investigated such as individuals' amount of social media use and motives leading people to social media use.

In order to better understand the impact of these defined factors, an empirical study is designed. Using a sample of university students, the predictors of social media addiction are examined. The study highlighted four major findings. The first one is, as anticipated, there exist a significant relationship between amount of social media usage and social media addiction. In that perspective, for future studies, the qualitative nature of that time might be studied by examining the amount spent for leisure (game etc.),interpersonal relation (texting, replying and so on) or gathering information (about others, events, news). The second finding demonstrates how loneliness and life satisfaction might be irrelevant factors to determine addictive type of behaviors. The literature proposes conflicting results; hence further examination is needed on the effect of these predictors. The third outcome validates, how the nature of the motives to use social media might produce social media addiction. Conformity and coping motives are stated as crucial contributors to social media addiction. Meaning that, individuals using social media to alleviate their negative mood or conform to social circle's norms have the tendency to get addicted. The forth finding supports the view that, a close relationship exists between improper use of social media while doing other staff (in the lecture, reading, driving etc.) and social media addiction. Finally, contrary to some of the prior research, the findings did not support the demographic characteristics effect on social media addiction. Even so, demographic factors need further examination perhaps on a wider and heterogeneous sample. The findings of the current study contributes to the social media addiction literature, in a both corroborating and contradicting manner with prior work. As a result, it is evident that this stream of research is at its infancy and more research is imperative.

As popularity of social media grows, recognizing adverse effects of social media addiction becomes essential. Compulsive use of social media has several negative correlates however majority of the studies in this domain are cross-sectional. Even though a number of relationships are depicted with these studies, causal inferences can not be made. There is a pressing need for longitudinal research, which will provide insight into the negative consequences of social media addiction. Understanding the direction of the relationship between social media addiction and variables such as depression, anxiety, and self-esteem is necessary.

REFERENCES

Abbasi, I. S. (2018). The link between romantic disengagement and Facebook addiction: Where does relationship commitment fit in? *The American Journal of Family Therapy*, *46*(4), 375–389. doi:10.108 0/01926187.2018.1540283

Abbasi, I. S. (2019). Social media addiction in romantic relationships: Does user's age influence vulnerability to social media infidelity? *Personality and Individual Differences*, *139*, 277–280. doi:10.1016/j. paid.2018.10.038

Al-Menayes, J. J. (2015). Social media use, engagement and addiction as predictors of academic performance. *International Journal of Psychological Studies*, *7*(4), 86–94. doi:10.5539/ijps.v7n4p86

Aladwani, A. M., & Almarzouq, M. (2016). Understanding compulsive social media use: The premise of complementing self-conceptions mismatch with technology. *Computers in Human Behavior*, *60*, 575–581. doi:10.1016/j.chb.2016.02.098

Allen, K. A., Ryan, T., Gray, D. L., Mclnerney, D. M., & Waters, L. (2014). Social media use and social connectedness in adolescents: The positives and the potential pitfalls. *The Australian Educational and Developmental Psychologist*, *31*(1), 18–31. doi:10.1017/edp.2014.2

American Psychiatric Association. (2013). *Diagnostic and Statistical Manual for Mental Disorders* (5th ed.). American Psychiatric Association.

Amichai-Hamburger, Y., Wainapel, G., & Fox, S. (2002). On the Internet no one knows I'm an introvert": Extroversion, neuroticism, and Internet interaction. *Cyberpsychology & Behavior, 5*(2), 125–128. doi:10.1089/109493102753770507 PMID:12025878

Andreassen, C. S. (2015). Online social network site addiction: A comprehensive review. *Current Addiction Reports, 2*(2), 175–184. doi:10.100740429-015-0056-9

Andreassen, C. S., Griffiths, M. D., Gjertsen, S. R., Krossbakken, E., Kvam, S., & Pallesen, S. (2013). The relationship between behavioral addictions and the five-factor model of personality. *Journal of Behavioral Addictions, 2*(2), 90–99. doi:10.1556/JBA.2.2013.003 PMID:26165928

Andreassen, C. S., & Pallesen, S. (2014). Social network site addiction – An overview. *Current Pharmaceutical Design, 20*(25), 4053–4061. doi:10.2174/13816128113199990616 PMID:24001298

Andreassen, C. S., Pallesen, S., & Griffiths, M. D. (2017). The relationship between addictive use of social media, narcissism, and self-esteem: Findings from a large national survey. *Addictive Behaviors, 64*, 287–293. Advance online publication. doi:10.1016/j.addbeh.2016.03.006 PMID:27072491

Andreassen, C. S., Torsheim, T., Brunborg, G. S., & Pallesen, S. (2012). Development of a Facebook addiction scale. *Psychological Reports, 110*(2), 501–517. doi:10.2466/02.09.18.PR0.110.2.501-517 PMID:22662404

Andreassen, C. S., Torsheim, T., & Pallesen, S. (2014). Use of online social network sites for personal purposes at work: Does it impair self-reported performance? *Comprehensive Psychology, 3*(1), 18. doi:10.2466/01.21.CP.3.18

Atroszko, P. A., Balcerowska, J. M., Bereznowski, P., Biernatowska, A., Pallesen, S., & Andreassen, C. S. (2018). Facebook addiction among Polish undergraduate students: Validity of measurement and relationship with personality and well-being. *Computers in Human Behavior, 85*, 329–338. doi:10.1016/j.chb.2018.04.001

Bányai, F., Zsila, Á., Király, O., Maraz, A., Elekes, Z., Griffiths, M. D., Andreassen, C. S., & Demetrovics, Z. (2017). Problematic social media use: Results from a large-scale nationally representative adolescent sample. *PLoS One, 12*(1), e0169839. doi:10.1371/journal.pone.0169839 PMID:28068404

Baturay, M. H., & Toker, S. (2017). Self-esteem shapes the impact of GPA and general health on Facebook addiction: A mediation analysis. *Social Science Computer Review, 35*(5), 555–575. doi:10.1177/0894439316656606

Bauer, J. M., Gai, P., Kim, J-H., Muth, T., & Wildman, S. (2002). *Broadband: Benefits and policy challenges*. A report prepared for Merit Network, Inc.

Baumeister, R. F. (1993). Understanding the inner nature of low self-esteem: Uncertain, fragile, protective, and conflicted. In *Self-esteem* (pp. 201–218). Springer. doi:10.1007/978-1-4684-8956-9_11

Beyens, I., Frison, E., & Eggermont, S. (2016). "I don't want to miss a thing": Adolescents' fear of missing out and its relationship to adolescents' social needs, Facebook use, and Facebook related stress. *Computers in Human Behavior, 64*, 1–8. doi:10.1016/j.chb.2016.05.083

Bischof-Kastner, C., Kuntsche, E., & Wolstein, J. (2014). Identifying problematic Internet users: Development and validation of the Internet Motive Questionnaire for Adolescents (IMQ-A). *Journal of Medical Internet Research, 16*(10), e230. doi:10.2196/jmir.3398 PMID:25299174

Błachnio, A., Przepiorka, A., & Pantic, I. (2016). Association between Facebook addiction, self-esteem and life satisfaction: A cross-sectional study. *Computers in Human Behavior, 55,* 701–705. doi:10.1016/j.chb.2015.10.026

Blackwell, D., Leaman, C., Tramposch, R., Osborne, C., & Liss, M. (2017). Extraversion, neuroticism, attachment style and fear of missing out as predictors of social media use and addiction. *Personality and Individual Differences, 116,* 69–72. doi:10.1016/j.paid.2017.04.039

Block, M., Stern, D. B., Raman, K., Lee, S., Carey, J., Humphreys, A. A., ... Blood, A. J. (2014). The relationship between self-report of depression and media usage. *Frontiers in Human Neuroscience, 8,* 712. doi:10.3389/fnhum.2014.00712 PMID:25309388

Bodroža, B., & Jovanović, T. (2016). Validation of the new scale for measuring behaviors of Facebook users: Psycho-Social Aspects of Facebook Use (PSAFU). *Computers in Human Behavior, 54,* 425–435. doi:10.1016/j.chb.2015.07.032

Borsari, B., & Carey, K. B. (2003). Descriptive and injunctive norms in college drinking: A meta-analytic integration. *Journal of Studies on Alcohol, 64*(3), 331–341. doi:10.15288/jsa.2003.64.331 PMID:12817821

Boyce, P., & Parker, G. (1989). Development of a scale to measure interpersonal sensitivity. *The Australian and New Zealand Journal of Psychiatry, 23*(3), 341–351. doi:10.1177/000486748902300320 PMID:2803146

Bozoglan, B., Demirer, V., & Sahin, I. (2013). Loneliness, self-esteem, and life satisfaction as predictors of Internet addiction: A cross-sectional study among Turkish university students. *Scandinavian Journal of Psychology, 54*(4), 313–319. doi:10.1111jop.12049 PMID:23577670

Brailovskaia, J., Margraf, J., & Köllner, V. (2019). Addicted to Facebook? Relationship between Facebook Addiction Disorder, duration of Facebook use and narcissism in an inpatient sample. *Psychiatry Research, 273,* 52–57. doi:10.1016/j.psychres.2019.01.016 PMID:30639564

Burke, M., Marlow, C., Lento, T., Fitzpatrick, G., Hudson, S., Edwards, K., & Rodden, T. (2010). proceedings of the SIGCHI Conference on Human Factors in Computing Systems. *Social Network Activity and Social Well-Being,* 1909-1912.

Çam, E., & Isbulan, O. (2012). A new addiction for teacher candidates: Social networks. *The Turkish Online Journal of Educational Technology, 11,* 14–19.

Caplan, S. E. (2002). Problematic Internet use and psychosocial well-being: Development of a theory-based cognitive-behavioral measurement instrument. *Computers in Human Behavior, 18*(5), 553–575. doi:10.1016/S0747-5632(02)00004-3

Caplan, S. E. (2003). Preference for online social interaction: A theory of problematic Internet use and psychosocial well-being. *Communication Research, 30*(6), 625–648. doi:10.1177/0093650203257842

Caprara, G. V., Barbaranelli, C., Borgogni, L., & Perugini, M. (1993). The "Big Five Questionnaire": A new questionnaire to assess the five factor model. *Personality and Individual Differences*, *15*(3), 281–288. doi:10.1016/0191-8869(93)90218-R

Caprara, G. V., Barbaranelli, C., & Livi, S. (1994). Mapping personality dimensions in the Big Five model. *European Review of Applied Psychology*, *44*(1), 9–15.

Charney, T., & Greenberg, B. S. (2002). Uses and gratification of the Internet: Communication, technology and science. In C. Lin & D. Atkin (Eds.), *Communication, technology and society: New media adoption and use* (pp. 379–407). Hampton Pres.

Chen, W. J., Boase, J., & Wellman, B. (2002). The Global villagers: Comparing Internet users and uses around the world. In B. Wellman & C. Haythornthwaite (Eds.), *The Internet in Everyday Life* (pp. 74–113). Blackwell. doi:10.1002/9780470774298.ch2

Choi, Y. (2018). Narcissism and social media addiction in workplace. Journal of Asian Finance. *Economics and Business*, *5*(2), 95–104.

Chung, D., & Nam, C. S. (2007). An analysis of the variables predicting instant messenger use. *New Media & Society*, *9*(2), 212–234. doi:10.1177/1461444807072217

Cialdini, R. B., Kallgren, C. A., & Reno, R. R. (1991). A focus theory of normative conduct: A theoretical refinement and reevaluation of the role of norms in human behavior. In Advances in Experimental Social Psychology (Vol. 24, pp. 201–234). Academic Press. doi:10.1016/S0065-2601(08)60330-5

Clayton, R. B., Osborne, R. E., Miller, B. K., & Oberle, C. D. (2013). Loneliness, anxiousness, and substance use as predictors of Facebook use. *Computers in Human Behavior*, *29*(3), 687–693. doi:10.1016/j.chb.2012.12.002

Davis, F. (1989). Perceived usefulness, perceived ease of use, and user acceptance of information technology. *Management Information Systems Quarterly*, *13*(3), 319–339. doi:10.2307/249008

Davis, R. A. (2001). A cognitive–behavioral model of pathological Internet use. *Computers in Human Behavior*, *17*(2), 187–195. doi:10.1016/S0747-5632(00)00041-8

De Cock, R., Vangeel, J., Klein, A., Minotte, P., Rosas, O., & Meerkerk, G. J. (2014). Compulsive use of social networking sites in Belgium: Prevalence, profile, and the role of attitude toward work and school. *Cyberpsychology, Behavior, and Social Networking*, *17*(3), 166–171. doi:10.1089/cyber.2013.0029 PMID:24111599

Desjarlais, M., & Willoughby, T. (2010). A longitudinal study of the relation between adolescent boys and girls' computer use with friends and friendship quality: Support for the social compensation or the rich-get-richer hypothesis? *Computers in Human Behavior*, *26*(5), 896–905. doi:10.1016/j.chb.2010.02.004

Dhaha, I. S. Y. (2013). Predictors of Facebook addiction among youth: A structural equation modeling (SEM). *Journal of Social Sciences (COES&RJ-JSS)*, *2*(4), 186-195.

Dhir, A., Yossatorn, Y., Kaur, P., & Chen, S. (2018). Online social media fatigue and psychological wellbeing—A study of compulsive use, fear of missing out, fatigue, anxiety and depression. *International Journal of Information Management*, *40*, 141–152. doi:10.1016/j.ijinfomgt.2018.01.012

Diener, E. D., Emmons, R. A., Larsen, R. J., & Griffin, S. (1985). The satisfaction with life scale. *Journal of Personality Assessment*, *49*(1), 71–75. doi:10.120715327752jpa4901_13 PMID:16367493

Ebersole, S. (2000). Uses and gratifications of the Web among students. *Journal of Computer-Mediated Communication*, *6*(1), 0. doi:10.1111/j.1083-6101.2000.tb00111.x

Ellison, N. B., Steinfield, C., & Lampe, C. (2007). The benefits of Facebook "friends:" Social capital and college students' use of online social network sites. *Journal of Computer-Mediated Communication*, *12*(4), 1143–1168. doi:10.1111/j.1083-6101.2007.00367.x

Eraslan-Capan, B. (2015). Interpersonal sensitivity and problematic Facebook use in turkish university students. *The Anthropologist*, *21*(3), 395–403. doi:10.1080/09720073.2015.11891829

Feinstein, B. A., Bhatia, V., Hershenberg, R., & Davila, J. (2012). Another venue for problematic interpersonal behavior: The effects of depressive and anxious symptoms on social networking experiences. *Journal of Social and Clinical Psychology*, *31*(4), 356–382. doi:10.1521/jscp.2012.31.4.356

Ferguson, D., & Perse, E. (2000). The World Wide Web as a functional alternative to television. *Journal of Broadcasting & Electronic Media*, *44*(2), 155–174. doi:10.120715506878jobem4402_1

Gámez-Guadix, M. (2014). Depressive symptoms and problematic Internet use among adolescents: Analysis of the longitudinal relationships from the cognitive–behavioral model. *Cyberpsychology, Behavior, and Social Networking*, *17*(11), 714–719. doi:10.1089/cyber.2014.0226 PMID:25405784

Gibbs, J. L., Ellison, N. B., & Heino, R. D. (2006). Self-presentation in online personals: The role of anticipated future interaction, self-disclosure, and perceived success in Internet dating. *Communication Research*, *33*(2), 152–177. doi:10.1177/0093650205285368

Global Web Index. (2019). *Digital vs. Traditional Media Consumption'2019*. Retrieved February 28, 2020, from Global web index: https://www.globalwebindex.com/hubfs/Downloads/Digital_vs_Traditional_Media_Consumption-2019.pdf

Goldberg, I. (1996). *Internet addiction disorder*. Retrieved March 3, 2008, from http//www.cog.brown.edu/brochures/people/duchon/humor/internet.addiction.html

Gonzales, A. L., & Hancock, J. T. (2011). Mirror, mirror on my Facebook wall: Effects of exposure to Facebook on self-esteem. *Cyberpsychology, Behavior, and Social Networking*, *14*(1-2), 79–83. doi:10.1089/cyber.2009.0411 PMID:21329447

Griffiths, M. (1998). Internet addiction: does it really exist? In J. Gackenbach (Ed.), *Psychology and the Internet: Interpersonal, interpersonal and intranspersonal applications* (pp. 61–75). Academic Press.

Griffiths, M. D. (2010). The role of context in online gaming excess and addiction: Some case study evidence. *International Journal of Mental Health and Addiction*, *8*(1), 119–125. doi:10.100711469-009-9229-x

Griffiths, M. D., Kuss, D. J., & Demetrovics, Z. (2014). Social networking addiction: An overview of preliminary findings. In K. P. Rosenberg & L. C. Feder (Eds.), *Behavioral addictions: Criteria, evidence, and treatment* (pp. 119–141). Academic Press. doi:10.1016/B978-0-12-407724-9.00006-9

Grunbaum, J. A., Tortolero, S., Weller, N., & Gingiss, P. (2000). Cultural, social, and intrapersonal factors associated with substance use among alternative high school students. *Addictive Behaviors*, *25*(1), 145–151. doi:10.1016/S0306-4603(99)00006-4 PMID:10708330

Hair, J. F., Black, W. C., Babin, B. J., Anderson, R. E., & Tatham, R. L. (2006). *Multivariate data analysis* (Vol. 6). Pearson Prentice Hall.

Hampton, K. N., & Wellman, B. (2003). Neighboring in netville: How the Internet supports community and social capital in a wired suburb. *City & Community*, *2*(4), 277–311. doi:10.1046/j.1535-6841.2003.00057.x

Hays, R. D., & DiMatteo, M. R. (1987). A short-form measure of loneliness. *Journal of Personality Assessment*, *51*(1), 69–81. doi:10.120715327752jpa5101_6 PMID:3572711

Hinsch, C., & Sheldon, K. M. (2013). The impact of frequent social Internet consumption: Increased procrastination and lower life satisfaction. *Journal of Consumer Behaviour*, *12*(6), 496-505. doi:10.1002/cb.1453

Hormes, J. M., Kearns, B., & Timko, C. A. (2014). Craving F acebook? Behavioral addiction to online social networking and its association with emotion regulation deficits. *Addiction (Abingdon, England)*, *109*(12), 2079–2088. doi:10.1111/add.12713 PMID:25170590

Hosmer, D. W., & Lemeshow, S. (2000). *Applied Logistic Regression*. John Wiley & Sons, Inc., doi:10.1002/0471722146

Huang, L. Y., Hsieh, Y. J., & Wu, Y. C. J. (2014). Gratifications and social network service usage: The mediating role of online experience. *Information & Management*, *51*(6), 774–782. doi:10.1016/j.im.2014.05.004

Hughes, D. J., Rowe, M., Batey, M., & Lee, A. (2012). A tale of two sites: Twitter vs. Facebook and the personality predictors of social media usage. *Computers in Human Behavior*, *28*(2), 561–569. doi:10.1016/j.chb.2011.11.001

Ingólfsdóttir, H. R. (2017). *The relationship between social media use and self-esteem: gender difference and the effects of parental support* (Doctoral dissertation).

Joinson, A. N. (2008). Looking at, 'looking up' or 'keeping up with' people? Motives and uses of Facebook. *Proceeding of the SIGCHI Conference on Human Factors in Computing System*.

Junco, R. (2012). Too much face and not enough books: The relationship between multiple indices of Facebook use and academic performance. *Computers in Human Behavior*, *28*(1), 187–198. doi:10.1016/j.chb.2011.08.026

Junco, R., & Cotten, S. R. (2012). No A 4 U: The relationship between multitasking and academic performance. *Computers & Education*, *59*(2), 505–514. doi:10.1016/j.compedu.2011.12.023

Kalpidou, M., Costin, D., & Morris, J. (2011). The relationship between Facebook and the well-being of undergraduate college students. *Cyberpsychology, Behavior, and Social Networking*, *14*(4), 183–189. doi:10.1089/cyber.2010.0061 PMID:21192765

Kang, S. (2007). Disembodiment in online social interaction: Impact of online chat on social support and psychosocial well-being. *Cyberpsychology & Behavior, 10*(3), 475–477. doi:10.1089/cpb.2006.9929 PMID:17594274

Karaiskos, D., Tzavellas, E., Balta, G., & Paparrigopoulos, T. (2010). P02-232-Social network addiction: A new clinical disorder? *European Psychiatry, 25*, 855. doi:10.1016/S0924-9338(10)70846-4

Katz, J. E., & Aspden, P. (1997). A nation of strangers? *Communications of the ACM, 40*(12), 81–86. doi:10.1145/265563.265575

Kaye, B. K., & Johnson, T. J. (2004). Web for all reasons: Uses and gratifications of Internet components for political information. *Telematics and Informatics, 21*(3), 197–223. doi:10.1016/S0736-5853(03)00037-6

Keepers, G. A. (1990). Pathological preoccupation with video games. *Journal of the American Academy of Child and Adolescent Psychiatry, 29*(1), 49–50. doi:10.1097/00004583-199001000-00009 PMID:2295578

Kim, J., & Haridakis, P. M. (2009). The role of Internet user characteristics and motives in explaining three dimensions of Internet addiction. *Journal of Computer-Mediated Communication, 14*(4), 988–1015. doi:10.1111/j.1083-6101.2009.01478.x

Kırcaburun, K., Kokkinos, C. M., Demetrovics, Z., Király, O., Griffiths, M. D., & Çolak, T. S. (2019). Problematic online behaviors among adolescents and emerging adults: Associations between cyberbullying perpetration, problematic social media use, and psychosocial factors. *International Journal of Mental Health and Addiction, 17*(4), 891–908. doi:10.100711469-018-9894-8

Kirschner, P. A., & Karpinski, A. C. (2010). Facebook® and academic performance. *Computers in Human Behavior, 26*(6), 1237–1245. doi:10.1016/j.chb.2010.03.024

Koc, M., & Gulyagci, S. (2013). Facebook addiction among Turkish college students: The role of psychological health, demographic, and usage characteristics. *Cyberpsychology, Behavior, and Social Networking, 16*(4), 279–284. doi:10.1089/cyber.2012.0249 PMID:23286695

Kraut, R., Kiesler, S., Boneva, B., Cummings, J., Helgeson, V., & Crawford, A. (2002). Internet Paradox Revisited. *The Journal of Social Issues, 58*(1), 49–74. doi:10.1111/1540-4560.00248

Kraut, R., Patterson, M., Landmark, V., Kielser, S., Mukophadhyaya, T., & Scherlis, W. (1998). Internet paradox: A social technology that reduces social involvement and psychological well-being? *The American Psychologist, 53*(9), 1017–1031. doi:10.1037/0003-066X.53.9.1017 PMID:9841579

Kross, E., Verduyn, P., Demiralp, E., Park, J., Lee, D. S., Lin, N., ... Sueur, C. (2013). Facebook use predicts declines in subjective well-being in young adults. *PLoS One, 8*(8), e69841. doi:10.1371/journal.pone.0069841 PMID:23967061

Kubey, R. W., Lavin, M. J., & Barrows, J. R. (2001). Internet use and collegiate academic performance decrements: Early findings. *Journal of Communication, 51*(2), 366–382. doi:10.1111/j.1460-2466.2001.tb02885.x

Kuss, D. J., & Griffiths, M. D. (2011). Online social networking and addiction—A review of the psychological literature. *International Journal of Environmental Research and Public Health, 8*(9), 3528–3552. doi:10.3390/ijerph8093528 PMID:22016701

Lansing, J. B., & Heyns, R. W. (1959). Need affiliation and frequency of four types of communication. *Journal of Abnormal and Social Psychology, 58*(3), 365–372. doi:10.1037/h0045906 PMID:13653887

Lau, W. W. (2017). Effects of social media usage and social media multitasking on the academic performance of university students. *Computers in Human Behavior, 68,* 286–291. doi:10.1016/j.chb.2016.11.043

Lee, E. B. (2015). Too much information: Heavy smartphone and Facebook utilization by African American young adults. *Journal of Black Studies, 46*(1), 44–61. doi:10.1177/0021934714557034

Lemon, J. (2002). Can we call behaviors addictive? *Clinical Psychologist, 6*(2), 44–49. doi:10.1080/13284200310001707411

Leung, L. (2004). Net-generation attributes and seductive properties of the Internet as predictors of online activities and Internet addiction. *Cyberpsychology & Behavior, 7*(3), 333–348. doi:10.1089/1094931041291303 PMID:15257834

Levenson, J. C., Shensa, A., Sidani, J. E., Colditz, J. B., & Primack, B. A. (2016). The association between social media use and sleep disturbance among young adults. *Preventive Medicine, 85,* 36–41. doi:10.1016/j.ypmed.2016.01.001 PMID:26791323

Lin, L. Y., Sidani, J. E., Shensa, A., Radovic, A., Miller, E., Colditz, J. B., & Primack, B. A. (2016). Association between social media use and depression among U.S. young adults. *Depression and Anxiety, 33*(4), 323-331. . doi:10.1002/da.22466

Liu y Lin, B. A. (2016). Association between social media use and depression among US young adults. *Depression and Anxiety, 33*(4), 323–331. doi:10.1002/da.22466 PMID:26783723

Longstreet, P., & Brooks, S. (2017). Life satisfaction: A key to managing internet & social media addiction. *Technology in Society, 50,* 73–77. doi:10.1016/j.techsoc.2017.05.003

Loos, M. D. (2002). The synergy of depravity and loneliness in alcoholism: A new conceptualization, and old problem. *Counseling and Values, 46*(3), 199–212. doi:10.1002/j.2161-007X.2002.tb00213.x

Malik, S., & Khan, M. (2015). Impact of facebook addiction on narcissistic behavior and self-esteem among students. *JPMA. The Journal of the Pakistan Medical Association, 65*(3), 260–263. PMID:25933557

Maraz, A., Eisinger, A., Hende, B., Urbán, R., Paksi, B., Kun, B., Kökönyei, G., Griffiths, M. D., & Demetrovics, Z. (2015). Measuring compulsive buying behaviour: Psychometric validity of three different scales and prevalence in the general population and in shopping centres. *Psychiatry Research, 225*(3), 326–334. doi:10.1016/j.psychres.2014.11.080 PMID:25595336

Marino, C., Gini, G., Vieno, A., & Spada, M. M. (2018). A comprehensive meta-analysis on problematic Facebook use. *Computers in Human Behavior, 83,* 262–277. doi:10.1016/j.chb.2018.02.009

Marino, C., Vieno, A., Moss, A. C., Caselli, G., Nikčević, A. V., & Spada, M. M. (2016). Personality, motives and metacognitions as predictors of problematic Facebook use in university students. *Personality and Individual Differences, 101,* 70–77. doi:10.1016/j.paid.2016.05.053

Marlatt, G. A., Baer, J. S., Donovan, D. M., & Kivlahan, D. R. (1988). Addictive behaviors: Etiology and treatment. *Annual Review of Psychology*, *39*(1), 223–252. doi:10.1146/annurev.ps.39.020188.001255 PMID:3278676

Marshall, T. C., Lefringhausen, K., & Ferenczi, N. (2015). The Big Five, self-esteem, and narcissism as predictors of the topics people write about in Facebook status updates. *Personality and Individual Differences*, *85*, 35–40. doi:10.1016/j.paid.2015.04.039

Masur, P. K., Reinecke, L., Ziegele, M., & Quiring, O. (2014). The interplay of intrinsic need satisfaction and Facebook specific motives in explaining addictive behavior on Facebook. *Computers in Human Behavior*, *39*, 376–386. doi:10.1016/j.chb.2014.05.047

Mazzoni, E., & Iannone, M. (2014). From high school to university: Impact of social networking sites on social capital in the transitions of emerging adults. *British Journal of Educational Technology*, *45*(2), 303–315. doi:10.1111/bjet.12026

McDougall, M. A., Walsh, M., Wattier, K., Knigge, R., Miller, L., Stevermer, M., & Fogas, B. S. (2016). The effect of social networking sites on the relationship between perceived social support and depression. *Psychiatry Research*, *246*, 223–229. doi:10.1016/j.psychres.2016.09.018 PMID:27721061

McKenna, K. Y. A., & Bargh, J. A. (2000). Plan 9 from cyberspace: The implication of the Internet for personality and social psychology. *Personality and Social Psychology Review*, *4*(1), 57–75. doi:10.1207/S15327957PSPR0401_6

Medora, N. P., & Woodward, J. C. (1991). Factors associated with loneliness among alcoholics in rehabilitation centers. *The Journal of Social Psychology*, *131*(6), 769–779. doi:10.1080/00224545.1991.9924664 PMID:1667810

Meier, A., Reinecke, L., & Meltzer, C. E. (2016). "Facebocrastination"? Predictors of using Facebook for procrastination and its effects on students' well-being. *Computers in Human Behavior*, *64*, 65–76. doi:10.1016/j.chb.2016.06.011

Mesch, G. S. (2001). Social relationships and Internet use among adolescents in Israel. *Social Science Quarterly*, *82*(2), 329–339. doi:10.1111/0038-4941.00026

Mihajlović, G., Hinić, D., Damjanović, A., Gajić, T., & Dukić-Dejanović, S. (2008). Excessive internet use and depressive disorders. *Psychiatria Danubina*, *20*, 5–14. PMID:18376325

Monacis, L., De Palo, V., Griffiths, M. D., & Sinatra, M. (2017). Social networking addiction, attachment style, and validation of the Italian version of the Bergen Social Media Addiction Scale. *Journal of Behavioral Addictions*, *6*(2), 178–186. doi:10.1556/2006.6.2017.023 PMID:28494648

Moqbel, M., & Kock, N. (2018). Unveiling the dark side of social networking sites: Personal and work-related consequences of social networking site addiction. *Information & Management*, *55*(1), 109–119. doi:10.1016/j.im.2017.05.001

Moreau, A., Laconi, S., Delfour, M., & Chabrol, H. (2015). Psychopathological profiles of adolescent and young adult problematic Facebook users. *Computers in Human Behavior*, *44*, 64–69. doi:10.1016/j.chb.2014.11.045

Moreno, M. A., Jelenchick, L. A., Egan, K. G., Cox, E., Young, H., Gannon, K. E., & Becker, T. (2011). Feeling bad on Facebook: Depression disclosures by college students on a social networking site. *Depression and Anxiety*, *28*(6), 447–455. doi:10.1002/da.20805 PMID:21400639

Murray, H. A. (1938). *Explorations in Personality*. Oxford University Press.

Olowu, A. O., & Seri, F. O. (2012). A study of social network addiction among youths in Nigeria. *Journal of Social Science and Policy Review*, *4*, 62–71.

Orford, J. (2001). *Excessive appetites: A psychological view of addictions* (2nd ed.). Wiley.

Pantic, I. (2014). Online social networking and mental health. *Cyberpsychology, Behavior, and Social Networking*, *17*(10), 652–657. doi:10.1089/cyber.2014.0070 PMID:25192305

Papacharissi, Z., & Rubin, A. M. (2000). Predictors of Internet use. *Journal of Broadcasting & Electronic Media*, *44*(2), 175–196. doi:10.120715506878jobem4402_2

Peele, S. (1985). *The Meaning of Addiction*. Lexington Books.

Peter, J., & Valkenburg, P. M. (2006). Adolescents' exposure to sexually explicit material on the Internet. *Communication Research*, *33*(2), 178–204. doi:10.1177/0093650205285369

Pontes, H. M., Kuss, D. J., & Griffiths, M. D. (2015). Clinical psychology of Internet addiction: A review of its conceptualization, prevalence, neuronal processes, and implications for treatment. *Neuroscience and Neuroeconomics*, *4*, 11–23.

Pozzoli, T., & Gini, G. (2013). Why do bystanders of bullying help or not? A multidimensional model. *The Journal of Early Adolescence*, *33*(3), 315–340. doi:10.1177/0272431612440172

Prensky, M. (2001). Digital natives, digital immigrants part 1. *On the Horizon*, *9*, 1–6.

Przepiorka, A., & Blachnio, A. (2016). Time perspective in Internet and Facebook addiction. *Computers in Human Behavior*, *60*, 13–18. doi:10.1016/j.chb.2016.02.045

Przybylski, A. K., Murayama, K., DeHaan, C. R., & Gladwell, V. (2013). Motivational, emotional, and behavioral correlates of fear of missing out. *Computers in Human Behavior*, *29*(4), 1841–1848. doi:10.1016/j.chb.2013.02.014

Raacke, J., & Bonds-Raacke, J. (2008). MySpace and Facebook: Applying the uses and gratifications theory to exploring friend-networking sites. *Cyberpsychology & Behavior*, *11*(2), 169–174. doi:10.1089/cpb.2007.0056 PMID:18422409

Rabaa'i, A. A., Bhat, H., & Al-Maati, S. A. (2018). Theorising social networks addiction: An empirical investigation. *International Journal of Social Media and Interactive Learning Environments*, *6*(1), 1–24. doi:10.1504/IJSMILE.2018.092363

Reid Chassiakos, Y., Radesky, J., Christakis, D., Moreno, M. A., & Cross, C. (2016). Children and Adolescents and Digital Media. *Pediatrics*, *138*(5), 1–18. doi:10.1542/peds.2016-2593 PMID:27940795

Rheingold, H. (1993). *The virtual community: Homesteading on the electronic frontier*. Addison Wesley.

Ross, C., Orr, E. S., Sisic, M., Arseneault, J. M., Simmering, M. G., & Orr, R. R. (2009). Personality and motivations associated with Facebook use. *Computers in Human Behavior*, 25(2), 578–586. doi:10.1016/j.chb.2008.12.024

Ryan, T., Chester, A., Reece, J., & Xenos, S. (2014). The uses and abuses of Facebook: A review of Facebook addiction. *Journal of Behavioral Addictions*, 3(3), 133–148. doi:10.1556/JBA.3.2014.016 PMID:25317337

Ryan, T., Reece, J., Chester, A., & Xenos, S. (2016). Who gets hooked on Facebook? An exploratory typology of problematic Facebook users. *Cyberpsychology (Brno)*, 10(3). Advance online publication. doi:10.5817/CP2016-3-4

Sagioglou, C., & Greitemeyer, T. (2014). Facebook's emotional consequences: Why Facebook causes a decrease in mood and why people still use it. *Computers in Human Behavior, 35*, 359-363. . doi:10.1016/j.chb.2014.03.003

Sanders, C. E., Field, T. M., Diego, M., & Kaplan, M. (2000). The relationship of Internet use To depression and social isolation among adolescents. *Adolescence, 35*, 237–242. PMID:11019768

Satici, S. A., & Uysal, R. (2015). Well-being and problematic Facebook use. *Computers in Human Behavior, 49*, 185-190. doi:10.1016/j.chb.2015.03.005

Savci, M., & Aysan, F. (2017). Technological addictions and social connectedness: Predictor effect of internet addiction, social media addiction, digital game addiction and smartphone addiction on social connectedness. *Dusunen Adam: Journal of Psychiatry & Neurological Sciences*, 30(3), 202–216. doi:10.5350/DAJPN2017300304

Shaffer, H. J. (1996). Understanding the means and objects of addiction: Technology, the Internet and gambling. *Journal of Gambling Studies*, 12(4), 461–469. doi:10.1007/BF01539189 PMID:24234163

Sharifah, S. S., Omar, S. Z., Bolong, J., & Osman, M. N. (2011). Facebook addiction among female university students. *Revista De Administratie Publica Si Politici Sociale*, 3(7), 95.

Sheldon, P. (2009). Maintain or develop new relationships. Gender differences in Facebook use. *Rocky Mountain Communication Review*, 6(1), 51–56.

Shen, C., & Williams, D. (2011). Unpacking time online: Connecting internet and massively multiplayer online game use with psychosocial well-being. *Communication Research*, 38(1), 123–149. doi:10.1177/0093650210377196

Shensa, A., Escobar-Viera, C. G., Sidani, J. E., Bowman, N. D., Marshal, M. P., & Primack, B. A. (2017). Problematic social media use and depressive symptoms among US young adults: A nationally-representative study. *Social Science & Medicine, 182*, 150–157. doi:10.1016/j.socscimed.2017.03.061 PMID:28446367

Song, I., LaRose, R., Eastin, M., & Lin, C. (2004). Internet gratifications and Internet addiction: On the uses and abuses of new media. *Cyberpsychology & Behavior*, 7(4), 384–394. doi:10.1089/cpb.2004.7.384 PMID:15331025

Sriwilai, K., & Charoensukmongkol, P. (2016). Face it, don't Facebook it: Impacts of social media addiction on mindfulness, coping strategies and the consequence on emotional exhaustion. *Stress and Health*, *32*(4), 427–434. doi:10.1002mi.2637 PMID:25825273

Steinfield, C., Ellison, N. B., & Lampe, C. (2008). Social capital, self-esteem, and use of online social network sites: A longitudinal analysis. *Journal of Applied Developmental Psychology*, *29*(6), 434–445. doi:10.1016/j.appdev.2008.07.002

Stoll, C. (1995). *Silicon snake oil*. Doubleday.

Swann Jr, W. B. (1996). *Self-traps: The elusive quest for higher self-esteem*. WH Freeman/Times Books/ Henry Holt & Co.

Tang, J. H., Chen, M. C., Yang, C. Y., Chung, T. Y., & Lee, Y. A. (2016). Personality traits, interpersonal relationships, online social support, and Facebook addiction. *Telematics and Informatics*, *33*(1), 102–108. doi:10.1016/j.tele.2015.06.003

Turel, O., He, Q., Xue, G., Xiao, L., & Bechara, A. (2014). Examination of neural systems sub-serving Facebook "addiction". *Psychological Reports*, *115*(3), 675–695. doi:10.2466/18.PR0.115c31z8 PMID:25489985

Turkle, S. (1996). Virtuality and its discontents: Searching for community in cyberspace. *The American Prospect*, *24*, 50–57.

Valentine, O. A. (2013). Uses and gratifications of Facebook members 35 years and older. In *The Social Media Industries* (pp. 188–212). Routledge.

Valkenburg, P. M., & Peter, J. (2009). Social consequences of the Internet for adolescents: A decade of research. *Current Directions in Psychological Science*, *18*(1), 1–5. doi:10.1111/j.1467-8721.2009.01595.x

Valkenburg, P. M., Peter, J., & Schouten, A. P. (2006). Friend networking sites and their relationship to adolescents' well-being and social self-esteem. *Cyberpsychology & Behavior*, *9*(5), 584–590. doi:10.1089/ cpb.2006.9.584 PMID:17034326

Van Deursen, A. J. A. M., Bolle, C. L., Hegner, S., & Kommers, P. A. M. (2015). Modeling habitual and addictive smartphone behavior: The role of smartphone usage types, emotional intelligence, social stress, self-regulation, age, and gender. *Computers in Human Behavior*, *45*, 411–420. doi:10.1016/j. chb.2014.12.039

Venkatesh, V., Morris, M. G., Davis, G. B., & Davis, F. D. (2003). User acceptance of information technology. *Management Information Systems Quarterly*, *27*(3), 425–478. doi:10.2307/30036540

Veroff, J., Reuman, D., & Feld, S. (1984). Motive in American men and women across the adult life span. *Developmental Psychology*, *20*(6), 1142–1158. doi:10.1037/0012-1649.20.6.1142

Vogel, E. A., Rose, J. P., Roberts, L. R., & Eckles, K. (2014). Social comparison, social media, and self-esteem. *Psychology of Popular Media Culture*, *3*(4), 206–222. doi:10.1037/ppm0000047

Wang, C. W., Ho, R. T., Chan, C. L., & Tse, S. (2015). Exploring personality characteristics of Chinese adolescents with internet-related addictive behaviors: Trait differences for gaming addiction and social networking addiction. *Addictive Behaviors, 42,* 32–35. doi:10.1016/j.addbeh.2014.10.039 PMID:25462651

Widyanto, L., & McMurran, M. (2004). The psychometric properties of the internet addiction test. *Cyberpsychology & Behavior, 7*(4), 443–450. doi:10.1089/cpb.2004.7.443 PMID:15331031

Wilson, K., Fornasier, S., & White, K. M. (2010). Psychological predictors of young adults' use of social networking sites. *Cyberpsychology, Behavior, and Social Networking, 13*(2), 173–177. doi:10.1089/cyber.2009.0094 PMID:20528274

Wilson, R. E., Gosling, S. D., & Graham, L. T. (2012). A review of Facebook research in the social sciences. *Perspectives on Psychological Science, 7*(3), 203–220. doi:10.1177/1745691612442904 PMID:26168459

Woods, H. C., & Scott, H. (2016). #Sleepyteens: Social media use in adolescence is associated with poor sleep quality, anxiety, depression and low self-esteem. *Journal of Adolescence, 51,* 41–49. doi:10.1016/j.adolescence.2016.05.008 PMID:27294324

Younes, F., Halawi, G., Jabbour, H., El Osta, N., Karam, L., Hajj, A., & Khabbaz, L. R. (2016). Internet addiction and relationships with insomnia, anxiety, depression, stress and self-esteem in university students: A cross-sectional designed study. *PLoS One, 11*(9), e0161126. doi:10.1371/journal.pone.0161126 PMID:27618306

Young, K. S. (2004). Internet addiction: A New Clinical Phenomenon and Its Consequences. *The American Behavioral Scientist, 48*(4), 402–415. doi:10.1177/0002764204270278

Young, K. S., & Rogers, R. C. (1998). The relationship between depression and Internet addiction. *Cyberpsychology & Behavior, 1*(1), 25–28. doi:10.1089/cpb.1998.1.25

Zivnuska, S., Carlson, J. R., Carlson, D. S., Harris, R. B., & Harris, K. J. (2019). Social media addiction and social media reactions: The implications for job performance. *The Journal of Social Psychology, 159*(6), 746–760. doi:10.1080/00224545.2019.1578725 PMID:30821647

Chapter 10
Online Social Networks Misuse, Cyber Crimes, and Counter Mechanisms

Sanjeev Rao

(iD) https://orcid.org/0000-0001-7338-1930

Thapar Institute of Engineering and Technology, India

Anil Kumar Verma

Thapar Institute of Engineering and Technology, India

Tarunpreet Bhatia

Thapar Institute of Engineering and Technology, India

ABSTRACT

Online social networks (OSNs) are nowadays an indispensable tool for communication on account of their rise, simplicity, and efficacy. Worldwide users use OSN as a tool for social interactions, news propagation, gaming, political propaganda, and advertisement in building brand awareness, etc. At the same time, many OSN users unintentionally expose their personal information that is used by the malicious users and third-party apps to perform various kind for cyber-crimes like social engineering attacks, cyber espionage, extortion-malware, drug-trafficking, misinformation, cyberbullying, hijacking clicks, identity theft, phishing, mistrusts, fake profiles, and spreading malicious content. This chapter presents an overview of various cyber-crimes associated with OSN environment to gain insight into ongoing cyber-attacks. Also, counter mechanisms in the form of tools, techniques, and frameworks are suggested.

INTRODUCTION

The outburst of the World Wide Web is the most productive and expedient ways to find and distribute information. The Web 2.0 has emerged from "read-only web" to "read-write web" constitutes tools such as podcasting, blogging, tagging, RSS feed, social bookmarking, social networking platforms, web content

DOI: 10.4018/978-1-7998-4718-2.ch010

voting etc. With the start of Web 2.0, the media becomes very dynamic and used as blogs, messenger services, websites, social networking sites etc. to provide vast applications such as communication, news, entertainment, businesses, gaming, marketing and advertisement, live-streaming, job search, dating, education, healthcare etc. Among many social media tools, the popularity and usage of OSNs have increased at an incredible rate and becomes an essential tool for every OSN user worldwide. The main focus of this chapter is towards OSNs and its associated cyber-crimes. (Anderson, 2016). In figure 1, the relationship between web 2.0, social media and online social networks is mentioned.

Figure 1. Relationship between web 2.0, social media and OSNs

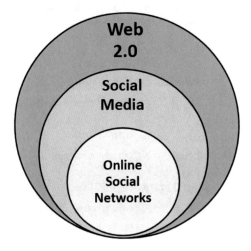

In OSNs, the developers and designers have given much focus on the design and features. However, less emphasis is provided on the privacy and security of OSN users. So this has become a wide area of research and has fascinated the interest of many research scholars. In this chapter, authors aim is to provide valuable understandings regarding the social media ecosystem, various cyber-crimes and vulnerabilities associated with OSNs, and security mechanisms to prevent such attacks.

ONLINE SOCIAL MEDIA ECOSYSTEM

Online social media ecosystem is used as a vehicle for communication and is based on 3C's, i.e. creation, curation, and consumption. The content on the social media ecosystem can be self-created/owned in the form for posts, page, and blogs etc., paid media in the form advertisement and earned media in the form of spam and viral messages etc. In figure 2, the Social media ecosystem (Sharma et al., 2020) is mentioned. Social media ecosystem consists of numerous entities represented as different forms of media, social media content used (text, audio, video, real-time and on-demand etc.), various types of users, usage, computing platform, personalization and management and so forth.

Figure 2. Social Media Ecosystem
(Sharma et al., 2020)

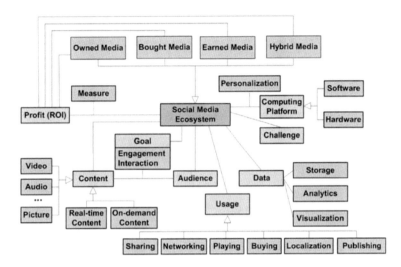

ONLINE SOCIAL NETWORK - MODEL AND SERVICES

OSN is a web-based tool that offers many as web-based services to the OSN user such as profile creation, adding friends/follower, content creation and sharing etc.

OSN platforms such as Facebook, Twitter, and LinkedIn etc. use social network services (SNS) to perform a set of operations (Cutillo et al., 2010). The three-layered architecture of Social Network Model is shown in figure 3.

Figure 3. The three-layered architecture of OSN model

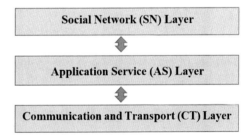

Social network services can be described by a three-layered model with specific tasks as follows:

1. Social Network (SN) Layer: Constructs the digital representations of members and their connections. This layer offers two classes of functions to each member depending on their social communications. Real-time communications management functions such as chats, posts, phone calls, emails and tweets etc. are managed by first class. In contrast, relationship management functions

such as profile access rights, reputation administration and friend requests etc. are controlled by second class.

2. Application Service (AS) Layer: Establishes the application infrastructure supervised by OSN platforms. This layer implements SN layer functions such as data storage, network and communication services. The essential functions managed by this layer are data retrieval, indexing, data access control and shift control to other servers in case of failures etc.

3. Communication and Transport (CT) Layer: Characterizes the communication and transport internet services governed by one or more network service providers.

The conversations on OSNs is in the form of posts, comments, likes, dislikes, tags, sharing posts, followers, following, etc. The applications of OSNs are marketing, news, advertising, promotions, product reviews, knowing public opinion in political elections, online learning, growing business reputation, disaster management, healthcare, professional network, crowdsourced content and recommender systems, etc. (Fire et al., 2014; Penni, 2017). The growing use of OSNs leads to the accretion of massive multimedia data that generates other issues such as data storage, data management, and data analyses. In building social trust among online users, sometimes the innocent users expose their personal information to strangers and third-party applications. Later personal information could be revealed and abused maliciously to perform various illegal cyber activities (Bilge et al., 2009; Gangavarapu et al., 2020). The unlawful practices such as data stealing, ransomware, false accounts, spamming, invading viruses, phishing, cyberbullying and sexual assault, and fake reviews, etc. performed by malicious users and hackers (Persia & D'Auria, 2017).

Some critical facts collected from (Kemp, 2020) about the usage and consumption of social media and OSN worldwide are mentioned as follows:

1. The total number of internet users is 4.57 billion, with a rise of 7 percent recorded since last year.
2. Mobile users around the world have consumed approximately 40 billion gigabytes of mobile data every month during Quarter 4, 2019.
3. The total number of users on social media crossed 3.81 billion, with an 8 percent increase since April 2019.
4. The most used OSN sites worldwide are Facebook, Twitter, Instagram, and WhatsApp etc.
5. Facebook has the highest number of active users, and this is approximately 2.5 billion monthly active users.
6. Social media users invest approximately 2 hours and 24 minutes on social networks and messaging applications.
7. In India, advertisers will now reach 280 million users on Facebook, 20 million more since January 2020.

CYBER-CRIMES AND VULNERABILITIES IN OSNs

OSNs are used as the best tool by masses for communication and transferring information. The OSN websites/mobile applications are consumed by OSN users' in many forms such as communication, news, marketing, healthcare, matrimonial applications, professional networking, gaming, messenger, travelling, and recommender systems etc. At the same time, these OSN environments and its applications are misused by many users, hackers, and other cybercriminals etc. for performing crimes such as social engineering attacks, spreading spam campaigns, misinformation, fraud, identity theft, fake news, rumors, and phishing URL's, etc. Mitre Attack offered a publicly accessible knowledge base in the form of an attack matrix to counter cyber-attacks, threats, vulnerabilities, etc. (MITRE Corporation, 2019). The Open Web Applications Protection Project (OWASP) study has found top-ten vulnerabilities on the Web (Watson & Zaw, 2018).

The various types of cyber-crimes associated with OSNs are classified as follows:

1. Cyber Crimes in OSN - Attacks, Threats, and Frauds
2. OSN vulnerabilities

Cyber-Crimes in OSN

Cyber-crime is a criminal act involving a computer and the Internet. Cyber-crime could be a threat to the individuals and the financial health of an individual or a nation. Cybercrime does not recognize any territorial boundaries, borders or distances. Cyber Crime is a broad term that covers other security terms such as cyber-attacks, cyber threats, and cyber frauds.

Cyber-attacks are a type of offensive techniques used by individuals or organizations to attack computer information systems, computer networks and personal computer devices by various types of unauthorized activities such as data theft, hacking, phishing, ransomware etc.

Cyber-threats are the vulnerabilities exploited by threat actors to harm any individual or organization. Threat actors are mainly cybercriminals, hacktivists, terrorist groups, thrill-seekers and advanced persistent threat (APT) (Humayun et al., 2020; Prasad & Rohokale, 2020b).

Cyber-fraud is cyber-crime in which the attackers first build an in-person association with other potential victims on social networks to obtain the information of the victim. Later they use this information and information extracted from victim's profiles to do criminal activities such as data theft, fraudulent transactions, spamming, identity theft etc. (Apte et al., 2018; Ramalingam & Chinnaiah, 2018).

Some of the important cyber-crimes (attacks, threats and frauds) are listed below:

1. Social Engineering Attacks: It is an art of manipulating people that results in a user being deceived by unintentionally breaching security protocols into accessing confidential information. The main vectors of Social engineering attacks are phishing, vishing (voice phishing), smishing (SMS phishing), impersonation, baiting, pharming etc. (Chiew et al., 2018; Salahdine & Kaabouch, 2019).
2. Phishing: It is a form of social engineering attack used to obtain personal and confidential information for illegal purposes, by masking online communication as a trusted individual. Phishers can quickly analyze the information freely available on OSN sites such as Facebook, Twitter etc. to increase the accuracy rate of a phishing attack (Chiew et al., 2018; Humayun et al., 2020).
3. Malware Attack: It is a program code used to perform phishing attack in the form of trojan, ransomware, botnets, remote access trojan (RAT) and spyware etc. Malicious links containing malware once clicked and successfully downloaded on targets machine can perform various cyber-crime such as misleading the user, stealing personal details, demanding ransom etc. (Brown & Hermann, 2020; Ramkumar et al., 2016).
4. Extortion/Ransomware Attack: It is a type of malware attack that is used for extortion, in which attacker locks/encrypts data on target's machine and demands a ransom to decrypt or unlock the file

or device to run again. Scareware ransomware used by pirated apps or antiviruses to threat target with issues/viruses and demands online payment to repair the issues. The cost of ransomware attacks in 2019 was $7.5 billion (Crane, 2020). Recently the British Health care system was targeted with WannaCry ransomware (Bijitha et al., 2020).

5. Cyber Espionage: In general, it is the act of collecting confidential information, without the consent of any individual, group, organization and government etc. using proxy servers, hacking and malware, spywares etc. Cyber espionage is also used to perform corporate surveillance and government espionage. Corporate espionage is done to damage the financial image of the organization by stealing the organization's vital information such as research, patents, new products/services, customer's databank, employee's confidential data etc. In contrast, government espionage is done to steal trade secrets, army operations, planning etc. Secret agencies perform cyber espionage to detect terrorist attacks, riots etc. by extracting and analyzing associated data from social networks (Herrmann, 2019; Libicki, 2018).

6. Impersonation using Fake/Clone Profiles or Bots: Fake/Cloned profiles and artificial intelligence-based social bots can be used to impersonate users, control user profiles, disseminating spam messages, profile browsing, fake reviews, messaging, and marketing and advertisements etc. (Cresci et al., 2017). Fake profiles can be used to post fake reviews, market promotions in bulk to increase the product's sale incomes or service offerings. Malicious users generate many fake/cloned accounts to reach a larger number of trustworthy users and communities for performing cyber-crimes. (Persia & D'Auria, 2017; Ramalingam & Chinnaiah, 2018).

7. Spam Fake Reviews/Comments: Spam is unwanted content spread on social network platforms in the form of malware, pornography links, messages, advertisements, fake reviews/comments by spammers, fake profiles and bots etc. Spam is a serious problem that is directly or indirectly linked in spreading other cyber-crimes such as phishing, misinformation, fake news, opinion biasing etc. (Adewole et al., 2017; Ferrara, 2019). Social networks are often misused to distribute spamming content through fake celebrities and business profiles, promotional threads or even via the social network's advertisement platforms. Crowdturfing is the phenomenon in which massive numbers of individuals are hired to assign nominal work to a specific challenge such as tagging photos, putting fake ratings or comments etc.(T. Wang et al., 2013).

8. Spambots: Spambots are the self-governing internet program which sends spam to a large number of users on online social media. A spambot may first accumulate email addresses from various sources such as websites, blogs, chatrooms, Newsgroups, and Special Interest Group (SIG) posts etc.(Cresci et al., 2017; Hayati et al., 2009)

9. Misinformation: In this crime unauthentic information in the form of fake news, rumor, and fake comments etc. are created and propagated on social network platforms to alter the public perceptions during elections, product buying etc. The deceptive content can quickly be disseminated to masses through fake accounts, crowdsourcing accounts, and through artificial enabled social bots etc. (Qi et al., 2018). Cyber-criminals perform other attacks such as phishing, click-baiting, session hijacking, fake news, child pornography etc. with the spread of misinformation (Fazil & Abulaish, 2018; Patil & Patil, 2018). Misinformation can also be propagated through socwares.

10. Socware: OSN users usually come across malicious websites /third party apps/ links etc. in the form of text, links, ads, clickbait, news, etc. Through clicking on the link and downloading the socware, the socware will immediately execute actions such as transmitting ransomware, spam, etc. to another user in the network without user permission. The study showed that 49% of OSN

users and 40 million messages were exposed to socware attacks (Rahman et al., 2012b; Thejas et al., 2019).

11. Click Baiting: Click baiting is another form of attack that is usually done on OSNs, online blogs, news, video links, reviews etc. Cybercriminals lure users into clicking on some news headlines that may redirect users to some other webpage that has no connection with the news headlines to generate huge revenues from redirected links/advertisements (Salahdine & Kaabouch, 2019).

12. Cyber Bullying: Cyberbullying attack is made to harass OSN users especially children, teenagers and young girls by pornographic links/images, vulgar videos, blackmailing, and violent content etc. to their OSNs environment etc. (Herrmann, 2019; Kumar et al., 2018). In the field of video games, cyberbullying is widespread. Gaming and web platforms notice an increase of 39 percent in attacks in early 2020 (Crane, 2020). Offensive comments of all sorts are thrown to receivers around the world in both text and voice chat. The effects of cyberbullying are lifelong disorders such as anxiety, panic, anger, depression etc. (Ioannou et al., 2018). The other criminal activities performed by online predators are sexual harassment, sexting (sending sexual messages), revenge porn, stalking, catphishing (luring someone into a relationship with fake profiles), trolling, impersonation etc.(Fire et al., 2014; Prasad & Rohokale, 2020b).

13. Hijacking Clicks: Cybercriminals performs clickjacking attack by luring users to click on some link or button, text, image etc. to which the user is not intended to click. Once the link is clicked, attackers can hijack their OSN session to do fraudulent crimes. Likejacing and cursorjacking are other variants of clickjacking. Likejacking works mainly on Facebook, whereas cursorjacking can be used to redirect the user's attention to other links which the attacker wants to click on (Thejas et al., 2019).

14. Cloning/Profile Squatting Attack: Cloned fake user profiles that look very similar to a legitimate user profile of the victim is used to send friend requests to victim's network to build a trust relationship and to extract other required information. Later this information is used to perform other forms of crimes such as spamming, fake reviews, bullying, humiliation, affecting social image and brand value of product etc. (Bilge et al., 2009; Shan et al., 2013).

15. Attribute Inference Attack: Cybercriminals, social network provider, advertiser and third party applications etc. in OSNs use machine learning-based recommender systems to perform privacy attack on OSN users by stealing their confidential data such as their location, images, taste, behaviours, preferences etc. of for direct marketing, product endorsements, selling data to other advertisers etc. The attackers may carry out additional attacks such as spear phishing, and cloning attacks inferred attributes might also be used by the attacker or other parties who concluded it from on multiple OSNs, etc., which may lead to increased privacy and security issues. (Zhenqiang Gong & Liu, 2018).

16. Man-In-The-Middle (MITM)/Eavesdropping Attack: In such attacks, attackers brought themselves into a two-party exchange. When the traffic gets interrupted, the attacker can explore and steal confidential data. Attackers attack the victims through unprotected public Wi-Fi and malware breaches (Libicki, 2018).

17. Botnets: Bots and botnets are rampant on OSNs. A botnet is a web of internet-connected computers, with one or more bots in execution. Botnets may be used to conduct Distributed Denial-of-Service (DDoS) attacks, steal data, submit spam and enable the system and its links to be exploited by the intruder (Zhang et al., 2018).

18. Distributed Denial of Service (DDoS) Attack: A DDoS attack is a fraudulent effort to stop a targeted website, device or network's usual traffic by flooding the target or its surrounding systems with a flood of Internet traffic. The most frequent DDoS attacks are smurf attack, teardrop attack, TCP synchronizes flood attack and buffer overload etc. Many popular OSNs are exposed to such organized attacks performed by bots, Sybil identities, fake and compromised accounts etc. (Kayes & Iamnitchi, 2017; Prasad & Rohokale, 2020a). In the year 2019, approximately 8.4 million DDoS attacks reported (NETSCOUT, 2019). Sybil identities are the multiple fake accounts in OSNs. In a Sybil attack, a malicious user obtains various fake identities and pretends to be multiple distinct nodes in the system to perform crime activities (Al-Qurishi et al., 2017).

19. Face Recognition: OSN face recognition software/applications are used as face authentication tools to authenticate OSN users. The massive amount of freely available profile pictures are used by attackers to build a biometric database that can be later used to perform threats to biometric systems in exploring any OSN user details without his consent. Extracted images database and deep learning techniques can be used to create synthetic media known as deep fakes. (Korshunov & Marcel, 2018; Sabir et al., 2019).

20. Location Privacy Threat: OSN users generally share their current and future location using geotag while performing any activity on OSN environment. Such information can be utilized by criminals and stalkers to play out a deceitful action that may make considerable harm such as extortion, theft at home or workplaces, physical assault, and so on. (Costa et al., 2013; Nalinipriya and Asswini, 2016).

OSN Vulnerabilities

OSN Vulnerabilities relates to the weakness of any application, software, website etc. that can be misused by any threat actors to gain unauthorized access to OSN resources and commit various types of cyber-crimes. The Open Web Applications Security Project (OWASP) report listed top-ten web vulnerabilities (Watson & Zaw, 2018). OSN is a large environment and usually susceptible to cyber-crimes and vulnerabilities such as weak passwords, server misconfigurations, cross-site-scripting (XSS), SQL injection, social data aggregators, flooding, spamming, fake/cloned profile, Identity theft, phishing and malware attacks etc. (Rodríguez et al., 2020). Some of the common vulnerabilities are weak login passwords, unauthentic third-party apps/browser extensions, puppetnets with malware, and spam propagation etc. Some of the important OSN vulnerabilities are listed below:

1. Cross-Site Scripting (XSS) Attack: XSS is the vulnerability explored by the attackers using social engineering technique, in which attackers send malicious script built-in JavaScript (*.js) or any other scripting language from the browser on the victim's computer through web applications such as email, OSN posts, chat boxes, messengers, SMS, blogs etc. Once the script gets executed successfully on the victim's computer, the attacker takes control of the machine, hijack session to do fraudulent activities. Attacks like malware, ransomware, hijacking clicks and like-jacking etc. are part of XSS attacks that are triggered by clicking on some hidden link or through third-party cookies in the form of like buttons, links, tags or scripts etc. to steal personal and login details of users (Faghani & Nugyen, 2017; Rodríguez et al., 2020).

2. SQL Injection Vulnerability: SQL injection is a well-known security vulnerability to a database powered online applications and smartphone applications. It is a loophole in the software applica-

tion where computer criminals secretly add structured Query Language (SQL), NoSQL commands to web-form input text artifacts to gain access to confidential data and other services in databases (Khanna & Verma, 2018). The SQL injection aims to attack remotely on the database to modify records, execute denial of service (DoS) assault, access database schemes, unauthorized access to the database, fingerprinting etc. Piggybacked queries, union queries, stored protocols, timing attacks and blind injections, tautologies etc. are some unsafe SQL injections (Sadeghian et al., 2013). 42% of the most widespread flaws were recognized as SQL injections (Crane, 2020). Recently in the year 2017, companies like NextGEN, Airsoft GI were targeted by cybercriminals using SQL injection (Almarabeh & Sulieman, 2019).

3. Server Misconfigurations Vulnerabilities: When a part of a web server becomes susceptible to attack due to coding flaws, insecure configuration and misconfigured HTTP headers. For better security system tools, application software and antivirus must be configured appropriately and upgraded. Some of the attacks that aim misconfiguration vulnerability are directory listing, brute force, SQL injection, XSS, and forceful browsing etc. (Humayun et al., 2020).

4. Browser Vulnerabilities: Browser extensions are currently an integral part of web browsers and offer numerous functionalities such as web page customization, application debugging, language conversion, downloads of media files etc. These become very vulnerable to OSNs when they capture and track user activities such as web history analysis to display advertisements, login details, third party cookies to obtain confidential information such as IP address, login details etc. The unauthentic third-party extensions function with untrusted web, so attackers may use them to execute different cyber-attacks (Cao & Caverlee, 2015; Humayun et al., 2020; Schewe & Thalheim, 2019).

5. Social Network Aggregator (SNA) Vulnerability: Social Network Aggregator (SNA) such SocConnect, Flock, XeeMe, Hootsuite etc. are the web-based tools/applications used to manage various OSNs user account on a common SNA platform as shown in figure 4. Upon logging in to the SNA account, users can access their social network accounts via a standard interface without having to log in to each OSN site individually. The connection between the user and the SNA is established initially, then between the SNA and the linked OSN accounts. The communication is carried out using Open APIs supported by the different OSNs. The aggregated data can be utilized for content, comparison, relationships and process aggregation etc. (Virmani et al., 2014). Weak SNA authentication leads to higher vulnerability and contributes to other cyber-crimes, such as identity theft, loss of privacy and providing a more comprehensive database for cybercriminals to exploit (Kamran, 2016; Y. Wang & Ma, 2014).

COUNTER MECHANISMS

The previous section mentioned various attacks/threats related to OSN that may be directly or indirectly accountable for harming the privacy and security of OSN users. CIA triads (Confidentiality, Integrity, and Availability) for information security play a significant role in ensuring secure OSN environment (Guo et al., 2020). The fundamental reasons for OSN breaches/attacks are due to limitations at the system level and user/data level.

For a better and secure OSN environment, counter mechanisms are classified as follows:

Figure 4. Data aggregation through Social Network Aggregator (SNA)

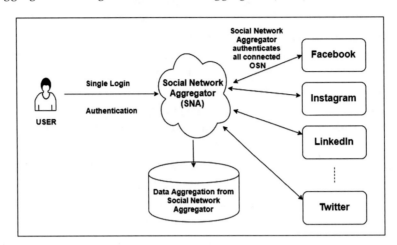

1. System/Platform based counter mechanisms
2. User and message deception-based counter mechanisms

System/Platform Based Counter Mechanisms

OSN networks are more susceptible to cyber-attacks and vulnerabilities, such as hacking, intrusion, ransomware attacks, server misconfigurations, DDOS attacks, XSS attacks, SQL injections, man-in-middle attacks and vulnerable third-party applications etc. Developers, designers and administrators will protect OSN users and their privacy from possible cyber-crimes and vulnerabilities in the network.

Some of the significant existing counter mechanisms implemented at the system/platform level are mentioned below:

1. Secure User Authentication and Communication Mechanisms: Authentication restricts cyber-criminal from having access to hijacked accounts and posting misinformation. For secure logins, multi-factor user authentication mechanisms can be applied such as two-factor authentication (2FA), cryptographic functions, channel-based, ID-based and biometric-based authentication counter mechanisms can be incorporated (Ferrag et al., 2020). The service provider ensures that all client-server communication is encrypted using secure HTTPS platforms (Oukemeni et al., 2019).
2. Network Security Protocols: Network security protocols are designed primarily to prohibit any unauthorized access, application, service or device from accessing data from the network. Such protocols ensure the confidentiality and integrity of the data travelling through an interface. Also, network security protocols describe mechanisms and methodologies for protecting network data against any unauthorized threat to access or extract the contents of data. Network security protocols usually utilize cryptography and encryption techniques to protect the data so that they can only be decrypted with a specific cipher, cryptographic key, mathematical formula or a blend of all of them. Some of the prevalent network security protocols include Secure Hypertext Transfer Protocol (HTTPS), Secure Socket Layer (SSL), Secure File Transfer Protocol (SFTP) and OAuth 2.0 protocol to give access to API endpoints (Kayes & Iamnitchi, 2017).

3.   Trust Modeling: Trust in OSNs is made-up of hard trust and soft trust fundamentally. The hard trust is based on a cryptographic mechanism, and soft trust is based on social control via the concept of recommendation protocols. Trust Modeling consisting abstraction, establishment, derivation and evaluation combined with hybrid trust models would result in building more secure OSN environment (Lin et al., 2004; Sherchan et al., 2013).

4.   Privacy of OSN users can be preserved using privacy-preserving protocols such as homomorphic encryption and decryption algorithms.

5.   Incorporating secure protocols for profile search and attribute-based encryption algorithms for providing better access and control mechanisms.

6.   Safeguarding OSN user accounts using spoofing control mechanisms.

7.   Allow only authenticated and trustworthy applications in OSN environment.

8.   User awareness about OSN's existing and new policies, privacy settings and content sharing etc.

9.   Installation of updated Antivirus, Intrusion detection system (IDS), Firewalls and other virus scanning software/tools to avoid OSN systems from various cyber-crimes and vulnerabilities.

10. Monitoring and investigating OSN systems for any suspicious activities.

User and Message Deception-Based Counter Mechanisms

OSN users face several threats covered under this category such as ransomware, identity theft, impersonation, fake and cloned profile, compromised accounts, fake reviews, misinformation and spambots etc.

Some of the essential existing counter mechanisms to deal with the user and message deception are mentioned below:

1.   Ransomware Detection: Crypto-ransomware is a form of malware that encrypts user accounts, deletes the original data and demands for ransom to get the stolen records back online. The ransomware attack can be detected using honeypots/files, CryptoStopper, CISCO Advanced Malware Protection (AMP), ShieldFS, R-locker (Gómez-Hernández et al., 2018), RAPTOR (Quinkert et al., 2018), RAPPER (Alam et al., 2018), CryptoDrop, McAfee Ransomware Interceptor, Avast Premier Behavior Shield, TShark or Wireshark to trace input/output operations, Bitdefender Anti-Ransomware tool behaviour analysis and traffic analysis tools etc. (Berrueta et al., 2020; Bijitha et al., 2020; Genç et al., 2019; Wolf, 2017).

2.   Spam and Fake Reviews/Comments Detection: Spammers took advantage of sharing spam content on OSNs due to a large number of active online users and less spread time. Spam can be detected using existing techniques such as honeypot, filtering methods based on the list such as blacklist, whitelist, greylist, etc. These methods are not competent enough to work with due to the changing nature of spam and spammers. Ensemble methods, machine learning and deep learning related approaches are used in recent works to evaluate the information, behavior, suspicious connections, etc., and are much more reliable than filtering approaches (Lalitha et al., 2018; Mehmood et al., 2018; Wu et al., 2018).

3.   Phishing Detection: Phishing attacks can be detected and prevented using Anti-phishing methods or tools such as WarningBird URL detection system is used to identify phishing URLs in OSN environment (Lee & Kim, 2013), blacklist methods (Wu et al., 2017), visual similarity (Fu et al., 2018), PhishAri technique (Liew et al., 2019), rule-based heuristics (Apruzzese et al., 2018), and behaviour analysis to detect spam URLs (Cao & Caverlee, 2015) etc. Some researchers have used

supervised and unsupervised machine learning algorithms such as KNN (K Nearest Neighbor), SVM (Support Vector Machine), C4.5, K-means, and DBSCAN, etc. (Gangavarapu et al., 2020; Liew et al., 2019).

4. Cloned Profile Detection: Attackers steal user's profile picture and other valuable details from one OSN and build a fake profile on any other OSN to gain the confidence of real user's friends, to propagate spam or malicious content later. The researchers developed various methods to counter this attack. They analyzed the same profiles in terms of the same attributes, the similarity of relationship networks, node similarity, graph similarity measures etc. The CloneSpotter technique was developed to identify cloning attacks using the user's login IP addresses (Kamhoua et al., 2017; Zare et al., 2020).

5. Fake Profile Detection: Fake accounts are among OSN 's favourite ways of spreading spam, malicious content, cyberbullying, and other illegal activities. The popular methods for Fake Profile detection literature are divided into three categories: machine learning-based, crowdsourcing, and graph-based etc. (Adewole et al., 2017; Ramalingam & Chinnaiah, 2018). DeepScan model detects malevolent accounts using g long short-term memory (LSTM) and neural networks (Gong et al., 2018).

6. Sybil Detection: Sybils are the multiple fake accounts in OSN, many counter mechanisms developed in the form of tools, protocols, algorithms etc. The user authentication mechanisms should be stronger to avoid such attacks. The counter mechanisms are Random Walk (RW) methods (Jia et al., 2017), Loop Belief Propagation (LBP) methods, SybilScar (B. Wang et al., 2017), SybilGuard protocol, SybilLimit protocol, SybilInfer defense algorithm, SumUp Sybil defense system, SybilRank tool, and SybilRadar (Al-Qurishi et al., 2017; Ramalingam & Chinnaiah, 2018).

7. Socware and Malware Detection: Socware is a new kind of attack for distributing spam and malware on OSN 's social walls. Facebook OSN is more vulnerable to socware attacks (Rahman et al., 2012b). The counter mechanisms to detect socware attacks are MyPagekeeper application in Facebook OSN, which analyzes the registered user's OSN wall and news feed for detecting socware. Another such application is Facebook's Rigorous Application Evaluator (FRAppE) that was used to identify malevolent activities on Facebook (Lokare et al., 2016; Rahman et al., 2012a; Ramkumar et al., 2016).

8. Cyberbullying Detection: Cyberbullying covers many types of threats and crimes done using Internet and OSNs. Cyberbullying involves child abuse, revenge porn, blackmailing, pornography, social and mental harassment etc. Cyberbullying on OSNs and gaming platforms is done using offensive comments, malicious posts, vulgar videos etc. Such offensive comments and cyberbullying can be detected using concepts of data mining, Machine learning, ensemble methods, deep learning, Information retrieval (IR) techniques, genetic algorithms for optimization and Natural language processing (NLP) etc. In existing literature researchers have used sentiment analysis, text-mining, fuzzy rules and part of speech tagging (POS) for extracting and analyzing cyberbullying content in OSN posts, comments, messages etc. (Ioannou et al., 2018; Vyawahare & Chatterjee, 2020). Authors in (Singh et al., 2019) detected aggression using deep leaning based Convolutional Neural Network (CNN) and Long Short Term Memory networks (LSTMs).

9. Bot/Spambot Detection: Bots have been used extensively for numerous benefits and malicious activities such as fake-news, rumors, spam and misinformation on web and OSNs. Spambots are a kind of artificial intelligence that enabled web robots that spread spam automatically on OSNs. Recent work done for a bot or spambot detection includes tools, frameworks and methods such

as BotorNot (Davis et al., 2016), BotWalk (Minnich et al., 2017), DeBot (Chavoshi et al., 2017), Bot-Hunter (Beskow & Carley, 2018), Retweet-Buster (RTbust) (Mazza et al., 2019); DNA based Social Fingure printing (Cresci et al., 2018) and detect me if you can (Alhosseini et al., 2019) etc.

FUTURE RESEARCH DIRECTIONS

After a thorough study on cyber-crimes and their counter mechanisms, many key research possibilities have been established that can be further explored:

- Privacy and security of mobile OSNs.
- Efficient detection of crowdsourcing, crowdturfing and spammers in OSNs.
- Opinion Mining.
- Trust computation and management.
- Decentralized and blockchain based OSN systems.
- User authentication and access control mechanisms.
- Analysis of user behaviour and streaming suspicious activities.
- Information diffusion models.
- Recommender systems.
- Resource management etc.

CONCLUSION

OSNs are tools that offer promising new connectivity opportunities. But it also provides opportunities to cyber adversaries to participate in malicious activities. In this paper, extensive study of cyber-crimes and vulnerabilities is outlined that exist on OSN environments. Later we also discussed numerous strategies and methods to counter multiple forms of cyber-attacks. The counter mechanisms are grouped into two groups, i.e. platform-based, user and message deception-based counter mechanisms. Finally the paper concludes with several significant research directions that would be valuable for readers and aspiring researchers.

REFERENCES

Adewole, K. S., Anuar, N. B., Kamsin, A., Varathan, K. D., & Razak, S. A. (2017). Malicious accounts: Dark of the social networks. *Journal of Network and Computer Applications, 79*(September), 41–67. doi:10.1016/j.jnca.2016.11.030

Al-Qurishi, M., Al-Rakhami, M., Alamri, A., AlRubaian, M., Rahman, S. M. M., & Hossain, M. S. (2017). Sybil defense techniques in online social networks: A survey. *IEEE Access: Practical Innovations, Open Solutions*, 5, 1200–1219. doi:10.1109/ACCESS.2017.2656635

Alam, M., Bhattacharya, S., Mukhopadhyay, D., & Chattopadhyay, A. (2018). *RAPPER: Ransomware Prevention via Performance Counters*. http://arxiv.org/abs/1802.03909

Alhosseini, S. A., Najafi, P., Tareaf, R. B., & Meinel, C. (2019). Detect me if you can: Spam bot detection using inductive representation learning. *The Web Conference 2019 - Companion of the World Wide Web Conference, WWW 2019*, 148–153. 10.1145/3308560.3316504

Almarabeh, H., & Sulieman, A. (2019). The impact of Cyber threats on Social Networking Sites. *International Journal of Advanced Research in Computer Science*, *10*(2), 1–9. Advance online publication. doi:10.26483/ijarcs.v10i2.6384

Anderson, P. (2016). Web 2.0 and beyond: Principles and technologies. In *Web 2.0 and Beyond: Principles and Technologies*. CRC Press. doi:10.1201/b12087-20

Apruzzese, G., Colajanni, M., Ferretti, L., Guido, A., & Marchetti, M. (2018). On the effectiveness of machine and deep learning for cyber security. *International Conference on Cyber Conflict, CYCON*, 371–389. 10.23919/CYCON.2018.8405026

Apte, M., Palshikar, G. K., & Baskaran, S. (2018). Frauds in Online Social Networks. *RE:view*, 1–18. doi:10.1007/978-3-319-78256-0_1

Berrueta, E., Morato, D., Magana, E., & Izal, M. (2020). Open Repository for the Evaluation of Ransomware Detection Tools. *IEEE Access: Practical Innovations, Open Solutions*, *8*, 65658–65669. doi:10.1109/ACCESS.2020.2984187

Beskow, D. M., & Carley, K. M. (2018). *Bot-hunter: A Tiered Approach to Detecting & Characterizing Automated Activity on Twitter*. http://www.casos.cs.cmu.edu/publications/papers/LB_5.pdf

Bijitha, C. V., Sukumaran, R., & Nath, H. V. (2020). A survey on ransomware detection techniques. *Communications in Computer and Information Science, 1186*, 55–68. doi:10.1007/978-981-15-3817-9_4

Bilge, L., Strufe, T., Balzarotti, D., & Kirda, E. (2009). *All your contacts are belong to us*. doi:10.1145/1526709.1526784

Brown, S. S., & Hermann, M. G. (2020). *Black Spots in Cyberspace?* doi:10.1057/978-1-137-49670-6_7

Cao, C., & Caverlee, J. (2015). Detecting Spam URLs in Social Media via. *The Behavior Analyst*, 703–714. doi:10.1007/978-3-319-16354-3_77

Chavoshi, N., Hamooni, H., & Mueen, A. (2017). DeBot: Twitter bot detection via warped correlation. *Proceedings - IEEE International Conference on Data Mining, ICDM*. 10.1109/ICDM.2016.86

Chiew, K. L., Yong, K. S. C., & Tan, C. L. (2018). A survey of phishing attacks: Their types, vectors and technical approaches. In *Expert Systems with Applications* (Vol. 106, pp. 1–20). Elsevier Ltd., doi:10.1016/j.eswa.2018.03.050

Crane, C. (2020). *The Definitive Cyber Security Statistics Guide for 2020 - Security Boulevard*. https://securityboulevard.com/2020/05/the-definitive-cyber-security-statistics-guide-for-2020/

Cresci, S., Di Pietro, R., Petrocchi, M., Spognardi, A., & Tesconi, M. (2018). Social Fingerprinting: Detection of Spambot Groups Through DNA-Inspired Behavioral Modeling. *IEEE Transactions on Dependable and Secure Computing*, *15*(4), 561–576. doi:10.1109/TDSC.2017.2681672

Cresci, S., Spognardi, A., Petrocchi, M., Tesconi, M., & Di Pietro, R. (2017). The paradigm-shift of social spambots: Evidence, theories, and tools for the arms race. *26th International World Wide Web Conference 2017, WWW 2017 Companion*, 963–972. 10.1145/3041021.3055135

Cutillo, L. A., Manulis, M., & Strufe, T. (2010). Security and Privacy in Online Social Networks. In *Handbook of Social Network Technologies and Applications*. doi:10.1007/978-1-4419-7142-5_23

Davis, C. A., Varol, O., Ferrara, E., Flammini, A., & Menczer, F. (2016). *BotOrNot: A system to evaluate social bots*. doi:10.1145/2872518.2889302

Ferrag, M. A., Maglaras, L., Derhab, A., & Janicke, H. (2020). *Authentication schemes for smart mobile devices: threat models, countermeasures, and open research issues*. doi:10.100711235-019-00612-5

Ferrara, E. (2019). The history of digital spam. In Communications of the ACM (Vol. 62, Issue 8, pp. 82–91). Association for Computing Machinery. doi:10.1145/3299768

Fire, M., Goldschmidt, R., & Elovici, Y. (2014). Online social networks: Threats and solutions. *IEEE Communications Surveys and Tutorials*, *16*(4), 2019–2036. doi:10.1109/COMST.2014.2321628

Fu, Q., Feng, B., Guo, D., & Li, Q. (2018). Combating the evolving spammers in online social networks. *Computers & Security*, *72*, 60–73. doi:10.1016/j.cose.2017.08.014

Gangavarapu, T., Jaidhar, C. D., & Chanduka, B. (2020). Applicability of machine learning in spam and phishing email filtering: Review and approaches. *Artificial Intelligence Review*, 1–63. doi:10.100710462-020-09814-9

Genç, Z. A., Lenzini, G., & Sgandurra, D. (2019). On deception-based protection against cryptographic ransomware. Lecture Notes in Computer Science, 11543, 219–239. doi:10.1007/978-3-030-22038-9_11

Gómez-Hernández, J. A., Álvarez-González, L., & García-Teodoro, P. (2018). R-Locker: Thwarting ransomware action through a honeyfile-based approach. *Computers & Security*, *73*, 389–398. doi:10.1016/j.cose.2017.11.019

Gong, Q., Chen, Y., He, X., Zhuang, Z., Wang, T., Huang, H., Wang, X., & Fu, X. (2018). DeepScan: Exploiting Deep Learning for Malicious Account Detection in Location-Based Social Networks. *IEEE Communications Magazine*, *56*(11), 21–27. Advance online publication. doi:10.1109/MCOM.2018.1700575

Guo, Z., Cho, J., Chen, I., Sengupta, S., Hong, M., & Mitra, T. (2020). Online Social Deception and Its Countermeasures for Trustworthy Cyberspace: A Survey. *ACM Computing Surveys*, *1*(1). http://arxiv.org/abs/2004.07678

Hayati, P., Chai, K., Potdar, V., & Talevski, A. (2009). HoneySpam 2.0: Profiling web spambot behaviour. Lecture Notes in Computer Science, 5925, 335–344. doi:10.1007/978-3-642-11161-7_23

Herrmann, D. (2019). Cyber Espionage and Cyber Defence. In Information Technology for Peace and Security (pp. 83–106). Springer Fachmedien Wiesbaden. doi:10.1007/978-3-658-25652-4_5

Humayun, M., Niazi, M., Jhanjhi, N. Z., Alshayeb, M., & Mahmood, S. (2020). Cyber Security Threats and Vulnerabilities: A Systematic Mapping Study. *Arabian Journal for Science and Engineering*, *45*(3), 3171–3189. doi:10.100713369-019-04319-2

Ioannou, A., Blackburn, J., Stringhini, G., De Cristofaro, E., Kourtellis, N., & Sirivianos, M. (2018). From risk factors to detection and intervention: A practical proposal for future work on cyberbullying. *Behaviour & Information Technology, 37*(3), 258–266. doi:10.1080/0144929X.2018.1432688

Jia, J., Wang, B., & Gong, N. Z. (2017). Random Walk Based Fake Account Detection in Online Social Networks. *Proceedings - 47th Annual IEEE/IFIP International Conference on Dependable Systems and Networks, DSN 2017*, 273–284. 10.1109/DSN.2017.55

Kamhoua, G. A., Pissinou, N., Iyengar, S. S., Beltran, J., Kamhoua, C., Hernandez, B. L., Njilla, L., & Makki, A. P. (2017). Preventing Colluding Identity Clone Attacks in Online Social Networks. *Proceedings - IEEE 37th International Conference on Distributed Computing Systems Workshops, ICDCSW 2017*, 187–192. 10.1109/ICDCSW.2017.64

Kamran, S. (2016). Privacy in the age of social networking. In *Information Security Management Handbook* (6th ed., Vol. 5, pp. 55–66). CRC Press. doi:10.1201/b11250-8

Kayes, I., & Iamnitchi, A. (2017). Privacy and security in online social networks: A survey. *Online Social Networks and Media, 3–4*(4), 1–21. doi:10.1016/j.osnem.2017.09.001

Kemp, S. (2020). *Digital around the world in April 2020 - We Are Social.* https://wearesocial.com/blog/2020/04/digital-around-the-world-in-april-2020

Khanna, S., & Verma, A. K. (2018). Classification of SQL injection attacks using fuzzy tainting. *Advances in Intelligent Systems and Computing, 518*, 463–469. doi:10.1007/978-981-10-3373-5_46

Korshunov, P., & Marcel, S. (2018). *DeepFakes: a New Threat to Face Recognition? Assessment and Detection.* http://arxiv.org/abs/1812.08685

Kumar, R., Reganti, A. N., Bhatia, A., Maheshwari, T., & Rao, B. (2018). Aggression-annotated Corpus of Hindi-English Code-mixed Data. *Proceedings of the Eleventh International Conference on Language Resources and Evaluation (LREC 2018).* https://www.aclweb.org/anthology/L18-1226

Lalitha, L. A., Hulipalled, V. R., & Venugopal, K. R. (2018). Spamming the mainstream: A survey on trending Twitter spam detection techniques. *Proceedings of the 2017 International Conference On Smart Technology for Smart Nation, SmartTechCon 2017*, 444–448. 10.1109/SmartTechCon.2017.8358413

Lee, S., & Kim, J. (2013). Warning bird: A near real-time detection system for suspicious URLs in twitter stream. *IEEE Transactions on Dependable and Secure Computing, 10*(3), 183–195. doi:10.1109/TDSC.2013.3

Libicki, M. C. (2018). Drawing inferences from cyber espionage. *International Conference on Cyber Conflict, CYCON*, 109–121. 10.23919/CYCON.2018.8405013

Liew, S. W., Sani, N. F. M., Abdullah, M. T., Yaakob, R., & Sharum, M. Y. (2019). An effective security alert mechanism for real-time phishing tweet detection on Twitter. *Computers & Security, 83*, 201–207. doi:10.1016/j.cose.2019.02.004

Lin, C., Varadharajan, V., Wang, Y., & Mu, Y. (2004). On the design of a new trust model for mobile agent security. Lecture Notes in Computer Science, 3184, 60–69. doi:10.1007/978-3-540-30079-3_7

Lokare, R., Kumari, K. W. S. N., Yadav, U., Borge, S., & Shinkar, D. V. (2016). *FRAppE Detecting Malicious Facebook Applications*. Academic Press.

Mazza, M., Cresci, S., Avvenuti, M., Quattrociocchi, W., & Tesconi, M. (2019). *RTbust: Exploiting Temporal Patterns for Botnet Detection on Twitter*. http://arxiv.org/abs/1902.04506

Mehmood, A., On, B. W., Lee, I., Ashraf, I., & Sang Choi, G. (2018). Spam comments prediction using stacking with ensemble learning. *Journal of Physics: Conference Series*, *933*(1). Advance online publication. doi:10.1088/1742-6596/933/1/012012

Minnich, A., Chavoshi, N., Koutra, D., & Mueen, A. (2017). BotWalk: Efficient adaptive exploration of twitter bot networks. *Proceedings of the 2017 IEEE/ACM International Conference on Advances in Social Networks Analysis and Mining, ASONAM 2017*. 10.1145/3110025.3110163

MITRE Corporation. (2019). *Matrix - Enterprise | MITRE ATT&CK®*. https://attack.mitre.org/matrices/enterprise/

NETSCOUT. (2019). *Threat Intelligence Report - Powered by ATLAS | NETSCOUT*. https://www.netscout.com/threatreport?ls=PR-MKTG&lsd=pr-021820-5

Oukemeni, S., Rifà-Pous, H., & Puig, J. M. M. (2019). Privacy analysis on microblogging online social networks: A survey. In ACM Computing Surveys (Vol. 52, Issue 3, pp. 1–36). Association for Computing Machinery. doi:10.1145/3321481

Persia, F., & D'Auria, D. (2017). A survey of online social networks: Challenges and opportunities. *Proceedings - 2017 IEEE International Conference on Information Reuse and Integration, IRI 2017*, 614–620. 10.1109/IRI.2017.74

Prasad, R., & Rohokale, V. (2020a). *BOTNET*. doi:10.1007/978-3-030-31703-4_4

Prasad, R., & Rohokale, V. (2020b). Cyber Threats and Attack Overview. In *Cyber Security: The Lifeline of Information and Communication Technology. Springer Series in Wireless Technology* (pp. 15–31). Springer. doi:10.1007/978-3-030-31703-4_2

Quinkert, F., Holz, T., Hossain, K. T., Ferrara, E., & Lerman, K. (2018). *RAPTOR: Ransomware Attack PredicTOR*. http://arxiv.org/abs/1803.01598

Rahman, M. S., Huang, T. K., Madhyastha, H. V., & Faloutsos, M. (2012a). FRAppE: Detecting malicious facebook applications. *CoNEXT 2012 - Proceedings of the 2012 ACM Conference on Emerging Networking Experiments and Technologies*, 313–324. 10.1145/2413176.2413213

Rahman, M. S., Huang, T. K., Madhyastha, H. V., & Faloutsos, M. (2012b). Efficient and scalable socware detection in online social networks. *Proceedings of the 21st USENIX Security Symposium*, 663–678.

Ramalingam, D., & Chinnaiah, V. (2018). Fake profile detection techniques in large-scale online social networks: A comprehensive review. *Computers & Electrical Engineering*, *65*(3), 165–177. doi:10.1016/j.compeleceng.2017.05.020

Ramkumar, G., Vigneshwari, S., & Roodyn, S. (2016, August 2). An enhanced system to identify mischievous social malwares on Facebook applications. *Proceedings of IEEE International Conference on Circuit, Power and Computing Technologies, ICCPCT 2016*. 10.1109/ICCPCT.2016.7530271

Rodríguez, G. E., Torres, J. G., Flores, P., & Benavides, D. E. (2020). Cross-site scripting (XSS) attacks and mitigation: A survey. *Computer Networks*, *166*, 106960. doi:10.1016/j.comnet.2019.106960

Sabir, E., Cheng, J., Jaiswal, A., AbdAlmageed, W., Masi, I., & Natarajan, P. (2019). Recurrent Convolutional Strategies for Face Manipulation Detection in Videos. *Proceedings of the IEEE Conference on Computer Vision and Pattern Recognition Workshops*, 80–87. http://arxiv.org/abs/1905.00582

Sadeghian, A., Zamani, M., & Abdullah, S. M. (2013). A taxonomy of SQL injection attacks. *Proceedings - 2013 International Conference on Informatics and Creative Multimedia, ICICM 2013*, 269–273. 10.1109/ICICM.2013.53

Salahdine, F., & Kaabouch, N. (2019). Social engineering attacks: A survey. In Future Internet (Vol. 11, Issue 4, p. 89). MDPI AG. doi:10.3390/fi11040089

Schewe, K.-D., & Thalheim, B. (2019). Web Information Systems Engineering. In Design and Development of Web Information Systems (Vol. 2). Springer International Publishing. doi:10.1007/978-3-662-58824-6_12

Shan, Z., Cao, H., Lv, J., Yan, C., & Liu, A. (2013). Enhancing and identifying cloning attacks in online social networks. *Proceedings of the 7th International Conference on Ubiquitous Information Management and Communication, ICUIMC 2013*, 1–6. 10.1145/2448556.2448615

Sharma, V. D., Yadav, S. K., Yadav, S. K., & Singh, K. N. (2020). Social media ecosystem: Review on social media profile's security and introduce a new approach. In *Lecture Notes in Networks and Systems* (Vol. 119, pp. 229–235). Springer. doi:10.1007/978-981-15-3338-9_27

Sherchan, W., Nepal, S., & Paris, C. (2013). A survey of trust in social networks. *ACM Computing Surveys*, *45*(4), 1–33. doi:10.1145/2501654.2501661

Singh, V., Varshney, A., Akhtar, S. S., Vijay, D., & Shrivastava, M. (2019). Aggression Detection on Social Media Text Using Deep Neural Networks. *October*, 43–50. doi:10.18653/v1/w18-5106

Thejas, G. S., Boroojeni, K. G., Chandna, K., Bhatia, I., Iyengar, S. S., & Sunitha, N. R. (2019). Deep learning-based model to fight against Ad click fraud. *ACMSE 2019 - Proceedings of the 2019 ACM Southeast Conference*, 176–181. 10.1145/3299815.3314453

Virmani, C., Pillai, A., & Juneja, D. (2014). Study and analysis of social network aggregator. *ICROIT 2014 - Proceedings of the 2014 International Conference on Reliability, Optimization and Information Technology*, 145–148. 10.1109/ICROIT.2014.6798314

Vyawahare, M., & Chatterjee, M. (2020). Taxonomy of Cyberbullying Detection and Prediction Techniques in Online Social Networks. *Advances in Intelligent Systems and Computing*, *1049*, 21–37. doi:10.1007/978-981-15-0132-6_3

Wang, B., Zhang, L., & Gong, N. Z. (2017). SybilSCAR: Sybil detection in online social networks via local rule based propagation. *Proceedings - IEEE INFOCOM*. Advance online publication. doi:10.1109/INFOCOM.2017.8057066

Wang, T., Wang, G., Li, X., Zheng, H., & Zhao, B. Y. (2013). Characterizing and detecting malicious crowdsourcing. *Computer Communication Review, 43*(4), 537–538. doi:10.1145/2534169.2491719

Wang, Y., & Ma, J. (2014). *Mobile Social Networking and Computing: A Multidisciplinary Integrated Perspective*. CRC Press. https://dl.acm.org/doi/book/10.5555/2721424

Watson, C., & Zaw, T. (2018). *OWASP Automated Threat Handbook*. doi:10.1023/A:1020392231924

Wolf, J. (2017). *Ransomware Detection*. Academic Press.

Wu, T., Liu, S., Zhang, J., & Xiang, Y. (2017). Twitter spam detection based on deep learning. *ACM International Conference Proceeding Series*. 10.1145/3014812.3014815

Wu, T., Wen, S., Xiang, Y., & Zhou, W. (2018). Twitter spam detection: Survey of new approaches and comparative study. *Computers & Security, 76*, 265–284. doi:10.1016/j.cose.2017.11.013

Zare, M., Khasteh, S. H., & Ghafouri, S. (2020). Automatic ICA detection in online social networks with PageRank. *Peer-to-Peer Networking and Applications*, 1–15. doi:10.100712083-020-00894-6

Zhang, J., Zhang, R., Zhang, Y., & Yan, G. (2018). The rise of social botnets: Attacks and counter-measures. *IEEE Transactions on Dependable and Secure Computing, 15*(6), 1068–1082. doi:10.1109/TDSC.2016.2641441

Zhenqiang Gong, N., & Liu, B. (2018). Attribute Inference Attacks in Online Social Networks. *ACM Trans. Priv. Secur, 21*(3). Advance online publication. doi:10.1145/3154793

ADDITIONAL READING

Al-Hamami, A. H., & Al-Saadoon, G. M. W. (2014). Handbook of research on threat detection and countermeasures in network security. In *Handbook of Research on Threat Detection and Countermeasures in Network Security*. IGI Global., doi:10.4018/978-1-4666-6583-5

Crane, C. (2020). The Definitive Cyber Security Statistics Guide for 2020 - Security Boulevard. https://securityboulevard.com/2020/05/the-definitive-cyber-security-statistics-guide-for-2020/

Cutillo, L. A., Manulis, M., & Strufe, T. (2010). Security and Privacy in Online Social Networks. In Handbook of Social Network Technologies and Applications., doi:10.1007/978-1-4419-7142-5_23

ENISA. (2019). *ENISA Threat Landscape Report 2018 15 Top Cyberthreats and Trends*. Issue January., doi:10.2824/622757

Kamran, S. (2016). Privacy in the age of social networking. In *Information Security Management Handbook* (6th ed., Vol. 5, pp. 55–66). CRC Press., doi:10.1201/b11250-8

Latah, M. (2020). Detection of Malicious Social Bots: A Survey and a Refined Taxonomy. *Expert Systems with Applications*, *151*, 113383. doi:10.1016/j.eswa.2020.113383

MITRE Corporation. (2019). Matrix - Enterprise | MITRE ATT&CK®. https://attack.mitre.org/matrices/enterprise/

Prasad, R., & Rohokale, V. (2020). Cyber Threats and Attack Overview. In *Cyber Security: The Lifeline of Information and Communication Technology. Springer Series in Wireless Technology*. Springer.

Sherchan, W., Nepal, S., & Paris, C. (2013). A survey of trust in social networks. *ACM Computing Surveys*, *45*(4), 1–33. doi:10.1145/2501654.2501661

Watson, C., & Zaw, T. (2018). OWASP Automated Threat Handbook. doi:10.1023/A:1020392231924

KEY TERMS AND DEFINITIONS

Advanced Persistent Threat (APT): It is a broad term used to describe an attack campaign in which an intruder, or team of intruders, establishes an illicit, long-term presence on a network, to mine highly sensitive data and are significantly more complicated.

Application Programming Interface (API): It is an intermediate software that enables two applications to speak to each other. You're using an API any time while using an app like Facebook, sending an instant message, or monitoring the weather on your screen. As a consumer, you just observe one interface; however, in the background, numerous applications are cooperating utilizing APIs.

Artificial Intelligence: It is the science and engineering of making intelligent machines. Artificial intelligence (AI) makes it possible for machines to learn from experience, adjust to new inputs and perform human-like tasks. Examples of AI-based personal assistant are Siri, Google Assistant, Cortana, Bixby, etc.

Child Pornography: Any visual depiction of sexually explicit conduct involving a child which includes a photograph, video, digital or computer-generated image indistinguishable from an actual child and an image created, adapted, or modified but appeared to depict a child.

Cookie: A cookie is a small amount of data generated by a website and saved by your web browser. Its purpose is to store preferences and other information for the visited webpages.

Cybersecurity: Cybersecurity refers to the set of technologies, processes, and practices designed to safeguard networks, devices, programs, and data from attack, threats, or unauthorized access.

Cyberspace: Cyberspace, is supposedly "virtual" world/network created by links between computers, Internet-enabled devices, servers, routers, and other components of the Internet's infrastructure.

Denial-of-Service (DOS) Attack: A denial of service (DoS) event is a cyber-attack in which hackers make a machine, online service, or network resource unavailable to its intended users.

Fake News: News headlines and stories that have no factual basis but are presented as facts. The spreading of untrue facts online or through Social Networking Sites that may influence readers' opinions, voting choices, and election outcomes.

Hacktivism: Derived from the words 'Hack' and 'Activism', hacktivism is the act of hacking, or breaking into a computer system. The person who performs an act of hacktivism is known as a hacktivist.

Intrusion Detection System (IDS): It is a type of security software system that monitors network traffic and alerts the administrators for any suspicious, malicious activities or security policy violations.

JavaScript: It is an object-oriented scripting language commonly used to create interactive effects within web applications.

Machine Learning: Machine learning is an application of artificial intelligence (AI) that provides systems with the ability to learn and improve from experience without being explicitly programmed automatically.

Malicious Code: Malicious code is the term used to describe any code in any part of a software system or script that is intended to cause undesired effects, security breaches or damage to a system.

Spyware: A software that installs itself on the computer and starts monitoring your online behavior without user permission is known as spyware.

Stalking: Stalking is unwanted surveillance by an individual or group toward another person, invading their privacy, and that may result in a potential safety threat.

Uniform Resource Locator (URL): It is used to denote or refer to any resource on the internet.

Chapter 11
Motivations for Social Media Use and Consumption in Zambian Online Platforms

Gregory Gondwe
https://orcid.org/0000-0001-7444-2731
University of Colorado at Boulder, USA

Roberta Muchangwe
University of Zambia, Zambia

Japhet Edward Mwaya
St. Augustine University of Tanzania, Tanzania

ABSTRACT

Although considerable literature has grown around the motivations for social media use and consumption across Africa, there is still a dearth of research on trends of consumption across different cultures and particular demographic environments. Studies that have attempted to explore this field tend to focus on how social media and the internet as a whole have remedied individuals in different ways. Particularly, how social media usage has enhanced participatory governance economically improved people's lives. This chapter offers a rather nuanced synthesis and perception of social media usage and consumption in Zambia that underscores the motivating factors. Two major interpretations are identified: social media consumption that focuses only on the quantity of proliferated online content and social media usage that interrogates the various ways people in Zambia use social media to suit their tastes and needs. The two approaches underscore the debate in this chapter and highlight how most studies have downplayed the distinction between the two.

DOI: 10.4018/978-1-7998-4718-2.ch011

INTRODUCTION

The proliferated social media usage and online content creation and consumption that have emerged in the wake of technological advancements in much of sub-Saharan Africa, are often hailed to have improved the general lifestyles of the people (Wamuyu, 2018; 2017; Wahila et. al. 2018; Wyche & Baumer, 2017; Akakandelwa & Walunita, 2017). Such arguments have become ubiquitous and almost inescapable to the literature on social media in Africa, therefore, revolutionizing and posing as a hallmark for theoretical frameworks that wave through the cultural fabrics of social media in Africa. On the other hand, media practitioners and other political elites are alleged to indulge in practices that produce media agenda and propaganda content that has greater influence on social media consumers (Madrid-Morales, et. al. 2020). While these assumptions have been substantially justified, the existing arguments are still patterned on the western models that are meant to promote the positive influence of social media in Africa. As a result, the actual practices and social media consumption tendencies of the people in most sub-Saharan countries are ignored and characterized as similar to other tendencies across the globe. In other words, as Traber (1989, cited in Mfumbusa, 2006) had asserted, Africans and their media are "foreign bodies in the cultural fabric of Africa" (p. 259).

Unfortunately, literature on social media use and consumption is often driven by western scholarship. For example, the effects of the Arab springs were made prominent by western scholarship, and later snowballed across all continents regarding the influence of social in mitigating change through youth empowerment (Howard & Duffy, 2011). Further compounding arguments can also be seen in how the notion of 'Fake news' has been brought to prominence after the 2016 US presidential election. Facebook and WhatsApp are the most widely used social media platforms in Africa. However, there is still a dearth of research on the two because of their diminish effects in most western countries. At most, Twitter and Instagram are the most used social media platforms in developing countries, therefore attracting a myriad of scholarship even in Africa. This emphasis ignores the role of Facebook and WhatsApp in Africa and the innovations that most Africans are making through these platforms. This paper, therefore, situates the study in Zambia, while addressing the challenges and the gaps in literature that accompany the study of social media use and consumption in most sub-Saharan African countries. The study addresses issues of usage and consumption while drawing and mapping out various reasons for consumption and use that have been innovated in Africa and for African, so as to address the needs of the people. In other words, we highlight the way people in sub-Saharan Africa have transformed the traditional social media usage and consumption to meet the needs and demands of their everyday lifestyles. Overall, the chapter contributes to the literature by methodologically and theoretically expanding the scope on the motivations for social media use in Africa.

FRAMING THE QUESTION

Debates about social media engagement and participation that have emerged in the wake of proliferated advanced technological tools in much of sub-Sahara Africa often take a Manichean prism. A schism exists between those that perceive social media as skewing the behaviors of people that actively participate online (Kubheka, 2017; Ephraim, 2013; Burton & Mutongwizo, 2009) versus those that see it as a panacea to a number of things, including participatory democracy (Bosch, 2017; Wamuyu, 2017; Nyamnjoh, 2015; Chatora, 2012). Such a prism extends to the current debates on 'fake news' and the questions of whether social media could be blamed for such (Wasserman & Madrid-Morales, 2019) – therefore, alleging that platform owners I indulge in practices that tend to exacerbate homophily and polarizations across political and tribal affiliations. Against such a backdrop is the question of the kind of content published and whether people do actually believe and consume it whenever it comes to their disposal. For example, in an experimental study involving Zambia and Tanzania's social media platforms, Gondwe (2018) observed that people in these two countries were skeptical about most stories from social media, and that their participation in the consumption of online content did not entail believability and trustworthiness.

Such arguments leave a gap in literature about why people in Zambia choose to participate in social media. Is it because everyone is on social media? Is it for social status or do they do it with an intention of gaining something vital? This chapter is, therefore, aimed at examining the perceptions that Zambians have about social media in general. Particularly, the authors hope to examine how they perceive and consume content from social media sources. The paper also makes distinction between social media use and consumption to refer to content creation for a particular purpose (Use) and mere consumption of the existing online content (consumption). In other words, the distinction is respectively rooted sender – receiver relationship. Other extended factors include gadget use, such as money sending apps with less regard to social interactions. Overarchingly, the author asks a key, yet overlooked question about whether most Africans share the same media consumption tendencies with people in western countries. The significance of this study lies in giving us an opportunity to understand the phenomenon of social media consumption behaviors, not only in Zambia, but across most African countries. Essentially, the author addresses the following questions:

RQ:1: What leads one to join a social media platform?

Rationale: This question will address two main themes: Having an account with a social media platform and joining a closed group on social media platforms. Hypothetically, the author argues that most people will join these platforms for status reason – and that the common narrative would be to catch-up with friends. A number of studies have justified this argument. Particularly, Charney & Greenberg (2001) who identified some among the motivations for social media as being identity. There is still the dearth of research that addressed motivations in Zambia, and intently, sub-Saharan Africa.

RQ2: How do social media participants perceive other participants in 'closed groups' platforms?

Rationale: Under this question, we assert that most individuals are in groups encompassing people they do not know or whose members they have little trust of. Hypothetically, the author argues that their membership is just for information and catharsis. There is a plethora of such studies particularly those done by Kaye (2007), Johnson and Kaye (2003), Witte and Howard (2003). While these studies address various motivational categories, their findings might not be generalized, especially in African settings. It is the aim of this study to examine whether their findings do apply in the African settings.

RQ3: How do individuals in online closed groups perceive the messages shared and discussed at length on those platforms?

Rationale: Essentially, the author asserts that because people do not know most individuals in those platforms, there is less information they trust as true from those online platforms. Their participation online does not entail believability and trust for the message. In this case, we argue that most social media consumption in Zambia does not extend beyond the seeing of the message. In other words, most social media messages do not translate into action.

SITUATING SOCIAL MEDIA USE AND CONSUMPTION IN AFRICA

Most scholars in the field of media and communication who attempt to study the social media phenomenon, and the motivation for using and consuming online content, tend to pay attention to mass effects, particularly how social media influences audience social behavior. From the christening of the Arab uprising (Breuer, Landman, and Farquhar, 2015) as a technological revolutionary event, through the most recent cases of 'Fake news in Africa' (Wasserman, 2020; Wasserman & Madrid-Morales, 2018) the ideas of the effects of social media content have been the overriding factors. By and large, these and other similar studies tend to suggest that many people in sub-Saharan Africa, decades after independence, are no different from other people around the world, when it comes to how social media content affects them. This assumption is driven by the argument that most people in sub-Saharan Africa still rely on western news sources for what Kasoma (1995) referred to as 'real news'. They tend to trust news from the western media more than from their local media (Gondwe, 2018).

As Mfumbusa (2006) observes, the local media and their content are seen as inept and partisan, low and dwindling (p. 260), therefore, leading to a perception and conclusion that the local media has hit a nadir, and the sense of euphoria that surrounds the advent of the "African" media seems to have proven evanescent among its audience. Such an understanding emerges not only from the pioneering studies of social media in the United States, but also the subsequent studies in Africa that employed western approaches to the problems of Africa. While acknowledging this fact, and the argument that technology as a whole has infiltrated our lives and become an extension of our bodies (McLuhan, 1964), it is also necessary to acknowledge that most works have gone into the use of digital technologies and their applications for human and social change (Adu-kumi, 2016). These perceptions ignore how some African cultures transform technology, not only in physical form but also mentally to fit their needs.

Social Media Use vs Consumption in Zambia

Studies about social media in Africa tend to take a media effect approach. The schism that distinguish them is based on the fact that one takes a positive approach, and the other takes a negative one. As indicated above, almost all studies that present a positive perception tend to dwell on how technology has been used to influence positive social behaviors both physically and psychologically. Wahila et. al. (2018), for example, examine how social media content supported nursing students in Zambia, both at a practicle and mental level. Similarly, Chatora (2012) also examined how physical social media platforms encouraged political participation. Negative perceptions include studies done especially in some parts of Africa such as Kenya and South Africa. For example, Ndiege, Okello, & Wamuyu (2020) explored how social media influenced and perpetuated cyberbullying among university students in Kenya. Adu-kumi (2016), on the other hand, explored how WhatsApp is considered a platform for venting sexual expressions among university students. The venting in this case is not perceived in terms of catharsis but as a platform for defying cultural and societal norms.

These arguments, however, ignore the idea that although technology and social media have proven to have great influence, their main purpose is to satisfy the needs of humans in their own contextual environments. Particularly there is a need to observe social forces that shape technology usage and consumption tendencies that are usually informed by economic, cultural, political, religious and social determinants. Proponents of such arguments assert that technology at all levels is not an extension of human agency in the sense that it cannot determine the cultural and social output of societies and people (William, 1983). In one of his recent studies, Wasserman (2020) argues that online information whether 'real' or 'fake' should not be understood outside its particular context of production and consumption, but by taking account of the local specificities. Particularly, he argues that "The phenomenon of 'fake news', the discourses that surround it and responses by audiences and the journalistic community have to be understood within the particular social, cultural and political context" (p.3). This is necessary because although the quantity of usage might be the same, the contextual usage and the processing of the consumed online content would vary based on the contextual factors that shape the significance of the situation.

Motivation for Using and Consuming Social Media Content

Generally, a myriad of studies have been done on the motivations for social media use and consumption. As technology advances, studies also emerge to adapt to the changing faces of the internet. Since the 1990s, there have been a growing body of research on the use of the internet. For example, James et. al., 1995, Fuentes, 2000, Papacharissi & Rubin, 2000, and Kaye & Johnson, 2004 address the reasons why users turned to those interactive online sources. Kaye (2007) extended this to identify other motivation categories. While these categories are important, it is necessary to measure and understand whether they address the situations that might be relevant for the Zambian situation and sub-Sahara as a whole.

There is still a dearth of research on the motivation for social media use and consumption in sub-Saharan Africa, let alone Zambia. Studies that exist tend to connect motivations to generic ideas of entertainment, escape and social interaction needs, and simply to pass time (Mambwe, 2019; Daka, et.al. 2017; Charney & Greenberg, 2001; Ferguson & Perse, 2000). Other studies have attributed motivation to identity formation (Turkle, 1999) and guidance needs (Kaye, 2007). Information seeking is equally singled out as a motivation for using and consuming internet or social media content. Eid & Al-Jabri (2016) asserts that social media content provides the latest news and analysis by people with inside knowledge, some of which is glossed over or omitted by the traditional media that is mostly owned by the government or elite members of society. Further, Akakandelwa & Walubita (2017) observe that "worldwide, digital consumers are now spending an average of 1 hour and 58 minutes per day on social networks and messaging. This number has increased by over 20 minutes since 2012 (Chaffey, 2016). Studies examining use of media among college students suggest that students spend between 30 to 60 minutes of social networking (Jacobsen & Forste, 2010; Pempek, Yermolayeva, & Calvert, 2009). The estimated daily median time spent on social media by older adolescents was 28 minutes (Jelenchick, Eickhoff & Moreno, 2013)". Most of these studies point to anecdotal evidence about the motivations for social media use. They draw their arguments from Kaye (2005) who analyzed 28 reasons for accessing online content. Accordingly, the author pointed to sic main factors: convenience, information seeking, media check, personal fulfilment, political surveillance, social surveillance, and expressions/affiliation. While these arguments seem to be exhausted, their strength is limited to a smooth-running media where individuals fully exercise their press freedom. This leaves a gap in literature on consumers from countries with less media freedom.

Measuring Social Media Use and Consumption

Pre-existing scales for measuring general media use and gratification are still relevant when measuring social media use and consumption today. However, several methods that include both qualitative and quantitative approaches have been used. For example, Bellamy and Walker (1990) developed 12 gratification categories that have remained essential and pinnacles for subsequent studies. Over the years some other studies have emerged to either expand or summarize them to fit their framework of research or context. Notably, Kaye and Johnson (2004) expanded the 12 categories to 62 items to fit the internet age. However, the 62 items were later summarized to explain the blog motivation phenomenon.In 2007 Kaye further summarized the 62 motivational items that were perceived as applicable to study the internet into 10 categories which she labeled as Presentation characteristics (to refer to characteristics of the internet that are not found anywhere else); Personal fulfillment (to refer to the personal gratification that individuals get from accessing certain online platforms); Expression/Affiliation (to refer to the connection that the internet brings about); Information seeking (associated with the quest knowledge for various needs); Intellectual/Aesthetic fulfillment (the desire not only to seek a variety of information, but to learn something new from seeking that information); Anti-traditional media sentiment (similar to revolting to traditional media); Guidance/opinion seeking (referring for the quest for support and validation of participants' opinions); Convenience (the easy accessibility of the platforms – i.e. it is easy to access news from *Mwebantu Media* on Facebook that watching TV or buying a newspaper); Political Surveillance (giving users the ability to track politicians); and Fact Checking (the ability to quickly verify and compare accounts of news and information and check the accuracy of traditional media).

In sub-Saharan Africa, however, research media use and consumption, as defined in this study is still scanty. Most studies that exist tend to focus on the physical use of the internet and its gadgets – and to a large extent, focusing on issues of health, particularly HIV/AIDS (Phiri & Junior, 2018; Mwalimu, Malauzi, & Mwiinga, 2017) advertising (Ndlela & Mulwo, 2017; Wamuyu, 2017; Zhang & Mao, 2016) and tourism (Mkono, 2017a, 2018b); Mostert, 2016). Although categories like personal fulfillment, expression/affiliation, information seeking, intellectual/aesthetic fulfillments, anti-traditional media sentiments, guidance, and most probably political surveillance probably resonate with the Zambian, and sub-Saharan context as a whole, most studies tend to ignore these roles. Particularly, studies tend to ignore the role and the influence that the audience have in the process of crowd sourcing, and the audience' ability to create the agenda of the online content (Some, et.al. 2019; Gondwe, 2017). Fashoro & Bernard (2017) provide a closely related study that explores the motivations for the adoption of social media for public participation in municipal activities. According to the findings of their study, three main items underscore the relevance and motivation for the use of social media: Surveillance, diversion/personal fulfillment through entertainment, and convenience (p. 108). While this study does provide relevant scales, it limits these scales to political and civic duties alone. Regardless, most of these measures have been found to provide valid and reliable scales that are adaptable to various media and technologies.

This study, therefore, employed the same measures through surveys that were posted on various online platforms nested on Facebook. This was done over a period of three months (December, 2019 to March, 2020). We also sent survey questionnaires to random active participants on social media platforms and requested them to invite other participants after they filled the survey. There was a $10 raffle ticket to be won by one of the lucky respondents. Second, we assessed the participants' motivations for using social media with an open-ended question that asked respondents to list at least five (5) separate reasons they used social media. Third, we coded the motivations for using social media using a multistep approach. Generally, this approach involved the reading and categorization of each response based on words and phrases. Nvivo 12 software was leveraged for this process. Fourth, we developed categories by grouping similar responses together and then labeling each group as a motivation item. Fifth, we grouped the items into broader motivational blocks based on meanings through an iteration process. These items were coded with two trained coders, yielding Krippendorff's alphas of 89.7 and 87.8.

FINDINGS

This study set out to understand why people in Zambia use and consume social media content. On set, we differentiated 'Use' vs 'Consumption' to emphasize quality vs quantity. The main aim was to argue that just as the use of social media varies across geographical boundaries, so are the reasons for consumption. We received an overwhelming total number of 5894 participants that were willing to participant from a population of more than 300 thousand possible participants. However, only 2681 (48.5%) participants met the criteria after responding to the important open-ended questions. Of the 2681 respondents, 71.3% indicated that their motivations by the desire to counteract government propaganda, 13% were motivated by anti-traditional media sentiments, 7% were motivated by the desire for personal fulfillment, usually entertainment and connections, 6% indicated that they use it for information seeking and guidance, 1.7% for convenience, and 1% indicated that they use it for intellectual/aesthetic fulfillments.

Particularly, most respondents indicated that they would share information even if they knew it was fake just for either fun or see how others would react to that. Others indicated that they consumed and shared information so as to compare with news coming from the government media. As one indicated, "relying on government news media is toxic, so getting something else from somewhere, regardless of whether that information is true or false is healthier". Second, those that indicated information seeking as their motivation justified that social media had a wide range of information that provided viable information. And those that indicated intellectual fulfillment argued that social media had somethings new to offer. Convenience simply referred to accessibility and user friendliness. It also referred to the easiness in accessing data, i. e. on their phones, while in bed and at a minimal mobile internet fee. Table 1 below presents a summary of the findings.

DISCUSSION

This chapter set out to offer a rather nuanced synthesis and perception of social media usage and consumption in Zambia. The main aim was to differentiate the meanings of use vs consumption of social media, and to determine the motivations for using and consuming online/social media content in Zambia, and probably sub-Saharan Africa at large. There is no doubt that social media use and consumption are among the most studied phenomena. However, almost all the studies take a generic approach that combines both usage and consumption while aggregating consumption as a criterion for usage and subsequent gratification. The conclusions made in these studies tend to also end in a similar way in which

Table 1. Motivations for the use and consumption of social media in Zambia

N0. of Items	Percentage	Motivation
1911	**71.3%**	**Counteracting Government Propaganda***
1123		- Govt. is biased so social media gives a different perspective
647		- Fact checking government stories
141		- To expose government lies
		- To see the weaknesses of our politicians and other leaders
349	**13%**	**Anti-Traditional media sentiments**
218		- Access information, I cannot find in traditional media
87		- Traditional media is biased
44		- Traditional media owned/controlled by government
187	**7%**	**Personal Fulfillment/Entertainment**
91		- I find a lot entertainment on social media platforms
66		- I have been more connected by social media
63		- I feel relaxed when using social media
		- Interesting content
161	**6%**	**Information Seeking**
101		- Social media provides a wide variety of opinions
56		- Helps keep up with current events
9		- Research/work/school
		- Scientific and technical information digested
46	**1.7%**	**Convenience**
19		- Data easily accessed viable mobile phone
13		- Almost free or cheap to get information
9		- Information accessed at anytime
5		- I can make contributions to the content
27	1%	**Intellectual Aesthetic fulfillments**
		- I get news ideas from social media platforms
		- Sometimes there are some intellectual debates
		- Social media explains issues better
		- Free access to expert ideas

*** Unique items revealed by the study and not present in previous studies

social media consumption in sub-Saharan Africa is equated to other parts of the world. This by itself tends to ignore the contributions that the theory of users and gratification offers. As noted, the theory asserts that people consume their media based on the need and satisfaction which that particular media provides (McQuail, 2010; West & Turner, 2007; Ruggiero, 2000; McQuail, 1994; Katz, Blumler, & Gurevitch, 1974). This implies that although technology is the same, the motivations for use and consumption will be determined and dictated not by technology, but the applicability of that technology in a particular context. Studies done in most African countries about mobile usage are a textbook example of the people of sub-Saharan Africa have managed to transform mobile phones, that are mostly used for communication (the purpose designed for), into online banking (Phiri & Banda, 2019; Mwiya et. al. 2017; Mulenga, 2017). In a similar way, western media use and consume social media for many various reasons – little for political discussions or for counteracting government propaganda as this study asserts.

This study was able to demonstrate through responses from open-ended question that most of the motivations suggested by other studies are true. However, there are other important motivations that might range from one geographical location to the other. For example, in Zambia, where press freedom is perceived to be dwindling (2020, World Press Freedom index - https://rsf.org/en/ranking_table) the aggregate findings suggest that most people's motivation to use social media stem from the biased information that they get from traditional media. As indicated, many argued that social media was the only platform that allowed for diversity of thought. In other words, social media use and consumption was largely driven by the quest to have other opinions outside government-driven propaganda. Although not statistically significant in comparison, the second opinion suggested that the motivations were driven by people's anti-traditional media related sentiments. In other words, the participants held that traditional media was mostly controlled and sometimes owned by the elite who were in the forefront of creating the agenda. Accordingly, most participants found it useful that they were able to participate in content creation and even commenting on the content they either agreed or disagreed with. These findings contribute to the understanding of the motivations for using social media not only in Zambia, but in most sub-Saharan Africa by uncovering some overlooked reasons that might only be prevalent in Africa. Mfumbusa's (2006) argument that the neo-multiparty media, considered as traditional, and accused of mediocrity, sensational and focusing on non-issues (Djokotoe, 2004) is more substantiated in these findings than ever. The respondents in this study indicated that they consider social media platforms as alternatives to traditional media that is mostly run and controlled by the government or elites that are mostly members of the government offices.

CONCLUSION AND RECOMMENDATIONS FOR FUTURE RESEARCH

What this study has presented contributes to the already existing items and categories that motivate people to participate on social media platforms. The study also introduces a new category that most existing studies have ignored. Specifically, the idea that motivations are driven by the desire to bring up some confounders in government propaganda – getting alternative news that counteracts with government propaganda in countries with limited press and media freedom. Second, the study also demonstrates the need for context when studying social media use and consumption. The underlying argument is that most studies in Africa tend to draw frameworks from western scholarship, therefore mimicking the findings so as to conform to the normative standards. In reality, social media use and consumption does not follow the normative standards, as many studies have demonstrated, but that it adapts to the environment. In trying to fit the situations of Africa in normative standards, we miss the core reasons that could explain various hidden phenomena.

The study was posed with certain limitations, particularly with the methodological approaches. Despite the overwhelming responses, sampling procedure makes it hard to generalize the data. Future research should consider employing qualitative approaches such as interviews and online ethnography. Second, further research should focus on the impact or value of user-generated content. This will help provide a better picture and understanding of the motivations for using social media. Third, the construction of the motivational categories, though drawing from Kaye's (2007) study, was subjective. Indeed, intercoder reliability was reached, yet our blocks still lack or could not be tested for reliability. The retrospective look presented in this paper also raises the need to discover what changes have been observed in the time following this study. Overarchingly, studies should continue to introspect the changes that have occurred in social media use and consumption in sub-Saharan Africa as it relates to politics, and especially in countries with limited press freedom. Nonetheless, the future of social media networks in Zambia is that of potential. As observed over the years, Zambia has seen a rise of participants in social network platforms nested on Facebook. Platforms like *Mwebantu Media* and other related platforms hosts more than 100 thousand subscribers, especially the youth (Mambwe, 2017). This makes it more relevant to understand the motivating factors for social media use.

REFERENCES

Adu-Kumi, B. (2016). *Sexuality Going Viral: Using WhatsApp as a Site for Sexual Exploration Among College Students in Ghana* (Doctoral dissertation). University of Oregon.

Akakandelwa, A., & Walubita, G. (2017). Students' Social Media Use and its Perceived Impact on their Social Life: A Case Study of the University of Zambia. *The International Journal of Multi-Disciplinary Research*, *5*(3), 1–14.

Bosch, T. (2017). Twitter activism and youth in South Africa: The case of# RhodesMustFall. *Information Communication and Society*, *20*(2), 221–232. doi:10.1080/1369118X.2016.1162829

Breuer, A., Landman, T., & Farquhar, D. (2015). Social media and protest mobilization: Evidence from the Tunisian revolution. *Democratization*, *22*(4), 764–792. doi:10.1080/13510347.2014.885505

Burton, P., & Mutongwizo, T. (2009). Inescapable violence: Cyber bullying and electronic violence against young people in South Africa. *Centre for Justice and Crime Prevention*, *8*, 1–12.

Chatora, A. (2012). *Encouraging Political Participation in Africa The Potential of Social Media Platforms*. Academic Press.

Daka, H., Jacob, W. J., Kakupa, P., & Mwelwa, K. (2017). *The Use of Social Networks in Curbing HIV in Higher Education Institutions: A Case Study of the University of Zambia*. Academic Press.

Ephraim, P. E. (2013). African youths and the dangers of social networking: A culture-centered approach to using social media. *Ethics and Information Technology*, *15*(4), 275–284. doi:10.100710676-013-9333-2

Fashoro, I., & Barnard, L. (2017, July). Motivations for Adopting Social Media as a Tool for Public Participation and Engagement in Nelson Mandela Bay Municipality. In *Proceedings of the 4th European Conference on Social Media ECSM* (pp. 106-114). Academic Press.

Fuentes, A. (2000). Won't you be my neighbor? *American Demographics*, *22*(6), 60–62.

Gondwe, G. (2017). Are Late Night TV Shows Polarizing Society? Examining the Ambivalence of New Version of Political Partisanship in the United States. *Global Media Journal*, 15.

Gondwe, G. (2018). News Believability & Trustworthiness on African Online Networks: An Experimental Design. *International Communication Research Journal, 53*(2), 51–74.

Howard, P. N., Duffy, A., Freelon, D., Hussain, M. M., Mari, W., & Maziad, M. (2011). *Opening closed regimes: what was the role of social media during the Arab Spring?* Available at SSRN 2595096

James, M. L., Wotring, C. E., & Forrest, E. J. (1995). An exploratory study of the perceived benefits of electronic bulletin board use and their impact on other communication activities. *Journal of Broadcasting & Electronic Media, 39*(1), 30–50. doi:10.1080/08838159509364287

Kubheka, B. (2017). Ethical and legal perspectives on use of social media by health professionals in South Africa. *South African Medical Journal, 107*(5), 386–389. doi:10.7196/SAMJ.2017.v107i5.12047 PMID:28492116

Mambwe, E. (2014). 20 years of internet in Zambia-how has journalism been impacted? African trends. *Rhodes Journalism Review, 2014*(34), 77–80.

Mambwe, E. (2019). Investigating the use and impact of social media in Zambian newsrooms between 2011-2013. *International Journal of Multidisciplinary Research and Development, 6*(4), 30–37.

Mfumbusa, B. F. (2006). Media accountability challenges in sub-Saharan Africa: the limits of self-regulation in Tanzanian newsrooms. *Cross connections: Interdisciplinary communication studies at the Gregorian University*, 259-270.

Mkono, M. (2018). The age of digital activism in tourism: Evaluating the legacy and limitations of the Cecil anti-trophy hunting movement. *Journal of Sustainable Tourism, 26*(9), 1608–1624. doi:10.1080/09669582.2018.1489399

Mkono, M., & Tribe, J. (2017). Beyond reviewing: Uncovering the multiple roles of tourism social media users. *Journal of Travel Research, 56*(3), 287–298. doi:10.1177/0047287516636236

Mostert, C. (2016). Determining the motivating factors for the general use of social media amongst tourists to South Africa. *International Journal of Business and Management Studies, 8*(2), 84–101.

Mulenga, F. K. (2017). *Factors that influence mobile applications (apps) usage in mobile banking in Zambia* (Unpublished Master's thesis). University of Cape Town, Cape Town, South Africa.

Mwalimu, E. C., Mulauzi, F., & Mwiinga, T. M. (2017). *Use of social media among University of Zambia lecturers in teaching and learning*. Academic Press.

Mwiya, B., Chikumbi, F., Shikaputo, C., Kabala, E., Kaulung'ombe, B., & Siachinji, B. (2017). *Examining Factors influencing e-banking adoption: evidence from bank customers in Zambia*. Available at SSRN 2987982

Ndlela, M. N., & Mulwo, A. (2017). Social media, youth and everyday life in Kenya. *Journal of African Media Studies, 9*(2), 277–290. doi:10.1386/jams.9.2.277_1

Nyamnjoh, F. (2015). *New media and religious transformations in Africa*. Indiana University Press.

Papacharissi, Z., & Rubin, A. M. (2000). Predictors of Internet use. *Journal of Broadcasting & Electronic Media, 44*(2), 175–196. doi:10.120715506878jobem4402_2

Phiri, M., & Junior, B. M. (2018). *PA 19-4-0723 Use of social media to provide awareness about medical and social service aid to victims of gender-based violence in Zambia.* Academic Press.

Phiri, M. N., & Banda, D. E. (2019). Investigating Mobile Money Usage Patterns in Zambia: A Case of Mobile Network Operator Systems. *International Journal of Advanced Studies in Computers Science and Engineering*, *8*(2), 13–20.

Some, E., Gondwe, G., & Rowe, E. W. (2019, October). Cybersecurity and Driverless Cars: In Search for a Normative Way of Safety. In *2019 Sixth International Conference on Internet of Things: Systems, Management and Security (IOTSMS)* (pp. 352-357). IEEE.

Wahila, R., Mwape, L., Lyambai, K., & Kabinga-Makukula, M. (2018). Use of social media to support nursing students' learning in Zambia. *Creative Education*, *9*(08), 1237–1251. doi:10.4236/ce.2018.98092

Wamuyu, P. K. (2017). Bridging the digital divide among low income urban communities. Leveraging use of Community Technology Centers. *Telematics and Informatics*, *34*(8), 1709–1720. doi:10.1016/j.tele.2017.08.004

Wamuyu, P. K. (2017, September). Exploring the Use of Global Positioning System (GPS) for Identifying Customer Location in M-Commerce Adoption in Developing Countries. In *International Conference on Information and Communication Technology for Develoment for Africa* (pp. 99-111). Springer.

Wasserman, H. (2020). Fake news from Africa: Panics, politics and paradigms. *Journalism*, *21*(1), 3–16. doi:10.1177/1464884917746861

Wasserman, H., & Madrid-Morales, D. (2019). *An Exploratory Study of "Fake News" and Media Trust in Kenya.* African Journalism Studies. doi:10.1080/23743670.2019.1627230

Wyche, S., & Baumer, E. P. (2017). Imagined Facebook: An exploratory study of non-users' perceptions of social media in rural Zambia. *New Media & Society*, *19*(7), 1092–1108. doi:10.1177/1461444815625948

Zhang, J., & Mao, E. (2016). From online motivations to ad clicks and to behavioral intentions: An empirical study of consumer response to social media advertising. *Psychology and Marketing*, *33*(3), 155–164. doi:10.1002/mar.20862

Chapter 12

Institutionalism, Social Media, and Democracy in Africa:
An Inquiry Into the Potential of Digital Democracy

Guy-Maurille Massamba
Independent Researcher, USA

ABSTRACT

This study focuses on the process of institutional change with regard to the capabilities of African political systems to embrace the conditions that instill and support democracy in the context characterized by pervasive social media consumption. The author wonders in what way institutions and individual behaviors can integrate social media in order to consolidate democracy. In other words, is social media-supported democracy sustainable in Africa? The study analyzes the patterns of social media consumption in its functionality for democratic change in Africa. It examines patterns of institutional change on the basis of the impact of social media consumption in African politics. It highlights two theories of institutional change—structured institutional change and evolutionary institutional change—based on their relevance to the impact of social media consumption in African political settings.

INTRODUCTION

This study is motivated by the following question: in what way social media constitutes a reasonable and reliable support for democracy in Africa. Based on this question I wonder whether the limited influence of social media on democracy in Africa is due to the limited implementation of the policy adopted by the political leadership. The African Information Society Initiative is a framework that upholds an "African digital vision and agenda," and calls for the improvement of communication services and the creation of "a continent-wide information and telecommunication network that will allow for fast and reliable communications to and from the continent" (United Nations Economic Commission for Africa, 2008). Although the use of digital media has increased in Africa, internet access is still limited for many

DOI: 10.4018/978-1-7998-4718-2.ch012

Africans, and in some cases, access is not possible because of internet shutdowns for political reasons. Apart from the limits related to information technology infrastructure, other issues such as regulation impede the development of digital democracy. The study is an exploration of the type of institutional approach most suitable for the deployment of digital democracy in Africa. In other words, it is an inquiry into the institutional framework that could support the enactment of technology through digital democracy in the continent.

Participation in democratic processes reflects the assumption that political involvement gives meaning to one's life and interaction in society. This is facilitated through institutions, which have the necessary mechanisms for regulation and support of individual political behavior. Institutional mechanisms, such as social media and democracy interact with others, guide and strengthen political behavior, and these capabilities cannot achieve their assigned objectives unless they are fully developed and soundly established. The use of social media venues is viewed from an institutional perspective insofar as the practice embedded in them is not merely the repetition of tasks and the consumption of information, and social media are much more than a set of data-producing resources and tools. The exchange and communication taking place through social media venues in the context of digital democracy are loaded with intentionality, that is, the production of, and search for, political, economic and cultural meaning.

In the process of institutional anchoring, Segaard (2017, p. 124) points to congruence as "an important condition of successful communication between voters and politicians." The search for congruence drives the implementation of adequate technological settings and institutional parameters with the purpose to make communications between different political stakeholders effective, and create the institutional and technological conditions for digital democracy to deploy its full potential. That is the underlying concern of this study, which implies the argument that the result of institutional anchoring is a more effective use of technology fostering digital democracy. Would the institutional anchorage of social media venues create the conditions for institutional change in order to make digital democracy a reliable, constructive determinant for social and political development in Africa?

The central argument of this paper is stated as follows: unless social media in Africa are supported by an institutional perspective that reinforces transformative capabilities rather than self-interestedness, and are enacted as institutions rather than amorphous technology, their relation to digital democracy will be nonconsequential in terms of forward-looking social and political development. After the initial step of the literature review focused on the three key concepts of institutionalism, digital democracy, and social media consumption, I delve right into the exploration of social media consumption in African political settings, which reflect the struggle to institute democratic change trough social media. Then I analyze the transformative capabilities of social media, in an effort to decipher the institutional significance of the trajectories social media consumption can induce by connecting African societies with the global community through the deployment of their cognitive and structuring capabilities. Last, based on relevant theories of institutional change I examine the patterns of social media-induced institutional change, presenting the effects of change through social media and digital democracy in African particular cases.

LITERATURE REVIEW

Three concepts stand out in this study and for this reason, they are the focus of this review of literature. They are: institutionalism, digital democracy, and social media. First, institutionalism constitutes a determinant organizing principle that structures political performance and interactions, such as administrative management and democratic practices. Second, digital democracy is the likely result of the intersection of digital communications and political processes, with the important factor of political behavior expressing shared or conflicting objectives asserted through political participation. Last, social media provide mechanisms through interactive communication tools serving as means of expression of political views, intents and behaviors.

Institutionalism

Research on institutionalism covers various fields. Despite multiple orientations and views, the theory on institutionalism has not lost its focus as a logical explanation of the structuration of the practices that characterize human development, including political development, made possible through organizations and various social and political arrangements. It is to such need to ensure certainty in human processes that Olivier Berthod (2016) points to as he focuses on the purposeful meaning of institutions. He develops this notion with an explanation that brings forth the internal constituents that fill and shape the organizations. From his standpoint, organizations are constituted by deeply rooted and far-reaching elements, such as beliefs, rules, values roles and symbols shared by individuals, and which determine their choices individually and through organizations. This explanatory effort contributes to a meaning that recoups what B. Guy Peters (2019, p. 30)) endeavors to capture as he reflects on the elaborate and extensive work by James March and Johan P. Olsen. These authors reassert "the centrality of political values, collective choice, and organizations." According to this perspective, political science, in its analysis of institutions, runs the risk of theoretical deviation if it does not realign the object of its analysis, which is fundamentally structured around collective being. Realigning implies allowing political thought to "integrate individual action with fundamental normative premises" (Peters 2019, p. 30). The deviation has been mostly noted in works that seek to depend on individualistic assumptions that March and Olsen (1984) thought were being used to replace the centrality of such shared standards as values and norms. These are embedded in organizations and can hardly be considered inoperative with regard to individual behavior. In particular, an important warning, among their criticisms of theoretical political science by these authors, denounces the reductionist tendency in political thought, which is "less inclined to ascribe the outcomes of politics to organizational structures and rules of appropriate behavior" (March and Olsen (1984, p. 735). Institutional perspectives derived from this conceptualization emphasize the integration of the social context and individual motives, which is facilitated by the role of political institutions, such as the state in its mutual interaction with society through which they affect each other. Ultimately this prescribes a process for designing political institutions, such as democracy and institutions of social interactions and communication, describing them as operational "collections of standard procedures and structures that define and defend interests" (March and Olsen 1984, p. 738). In its expression of individual interests, human behavior is structured by norms and values shared in society, and is characteristically a factor affecting institutions, and is affected by them.

When this mutual influence is fleshed out in an effort to clearly define the extent to which individuals and structures affect each other and their contribution to each other's life and meaning, one comes across "ontic differentiation," a process identified by Steve Fleetwood (2008), which requires a distinction between the two interacting entities and helps to avoid conflation of individuals and institutions. Fleetwood makes an important clarification, which goes even further as he highlights the irreducibility of social structures and institutions to the subjectivity of individuals. The elucidation rejects "methodological and ontological individualism," in the sense that institutions are here presented as having a distinctive identity, which is "irreducible, in an ontological and/or an explanatory sense, to individuals, to the subjectivity of individuals, and the inter-subjectivity" (Fleetwood 2008, p. 4, taken from a version of the article made available online. See the reference section). In the interaction between individual behavior and institutional framework, it is generally the institutional settings that embed the parameters upon which behavior is regulated. This is a meaning that Scott (2008) presents as the foundational character of institutions that support the structure of human and social activities. Through norms and standards to be cognitively incorporated by individual and social behavior, institutions provide regularities. He argues that "institutions are comprised of regulative, normative, and cultural-cognitive elements that, together with associated activities and resources, provide stability and meaning to social life (Scott 2008, p. 222). The explanation of the foundational character of institutions may not appear complete without pointing out the functional dimension embedded in the functions that norms and values serve to play in institutions. Here the contribution by functionalists of Durkheim's school is appealing because of its focus on positive effects of social institutions as they provide regularities. Whitney Pope presents their views as a school of thought that assumes "a tendency toward system equilibrium," and "views society as a whole composed of interrelated parts (i.e., as a system)" (Pope 1975, p.361). Think, for instance of social positions or political behavior, and social communications, such as social media and view them in light of socially or politically conditioned or defined behavior. They are given substance and function through the activities they create and fulfill while they find support in logical, cognitive, and directional basis in culturally defined elements. This reflection branches into the study of the role of agency and institutions proposed by Samer Abdelnour, Hans Hasselbladh and Jannis Kallinikos (2017), and contributes to the field of institutionalism through the analysis of the relationship between actors and institutions, and the reference to the concept of agency as essentially tied to institutional dynamics operating in particular social settings. For the purpose of this study, what is useful is the conceptualization they make of institutions as defining and organizing realities for individual behavior, be it political, cultural, and social. They view them as pillars.

To the notion of pillar, Abdelnour, Hasselbadh and Kallinikos (2017, p. 1777) also add the concept of "social categories and cultural scripts" to develop the understanding of institutions in contexts. Drawing from explanations by Barley and Tolbert (1997), the authors observe that the system or conditions within which social actors operate and express themselves are intrinsically tied to institutions while they are simultaneously a reflection of contextual determination structuring the social role within the ineluctable interactive context in which agency takes meaning. The simultaneity and conjunction of these two settings are contextually deployed as the condition in which "abstract principles of institutions—such as democracy, markets, hierarchy, etc.—are tailored to and made operable in particular social settings as interpretive schemes, resources and norms" (Addelnour, Hasselbach and Kallinkos 2017, p. 1778). This explains the existence of specified behavior in accordance to particular institutional arrangements and social realities. It is close to the view adopted by historical institutionalism through a focus on path dependence (Fioretos, Falleti, and Sheingate 2016; Thelen 1999), From a sociological standpoint, path dependency justifies the reliance on the empirical conditions under which "political actors extract causal designations from the world around them and these cause-and-effect understandings inform their approaches to new problems" (Thelen 1999, p. 386). According to historical institutionalism, the structure of individual behavior is established through a conjunction of context and rule.

Expanding this view leads to the question of choice as to why individuals and societies establish particular political settings and choose specific means to pursue certain objectives and outcomes (Steinmo 2008). In this light, governments as institutions are structured to set rules, establish norms and conditions, and make policy decisions that strengthen or weaken the capability of forces of production, the determination of democratic and social forces to assert their rights, or access to the means of communication for the expression of civil liberties. Bates, Block, Fayad and Hoeffler (2013) refer to the relationship studied by the new institutionalists between the use of coercion by government and social gains to support the notion that there exists a relationship between democracy and development, based on evidence found by the new institutionalism. This is underscored by the correlation between the type of political forces and political institutions. Bates and his colleagues find evidence of this correlation within the African context in the introduction of democratic institutions resulting from demands by political forces emerging in the 1980s. It is mostly historical institutionalism that such authors as Erdmann, Elischer and Stroh (2011) rely on to assert the importance of "an institution-based examination of African politics." Their two-step approach constitutes first an inquiry whether the framework of historical institutionalism can account for political development in sub-Saharan Africa. Furthermore, using this very paradigm they enquire on its usefulness in terms of explaining the emergence of different types of regimes in Africa. The elaboration of the framework leaves no doubt on the challenges about the temptation of reading African politics through the prism of Western political theory. That is why a reading of the historical development of Africa over time is critical. In order to overcome the difficulty, the authors recognize the importance of analyzing the development of political institutions in Africa in a more systematic way, going beyond ethnographic accounts.

Digital Democracy

With the use of information technologies in the political arena comes virtual political system. The study of this complex interconnecting organization and its requirements has led many an observer to characterize it as "the way that governments and civic societies are in the process of adapting to information technologies, and the structure of political opportunities this creates for active citizenship and civic engagement" (Norris 2001, p. 95; Bekkers 2003; Fountain 2004). It is identified as a virtual organization that has its own complexity as it deploys its webs of interactions and its functions transforming the way the public sector operates (Bekkers 2003). The complexity certainly gives rise to a number of questions about the interest in establishing a virtual political system or a virtual state, its shape and components, its capabilities and internal functioning agencies, as well as the interconnection of its various branches and processes (Fountain 2004). An important basis for this line of inquiry relates to the critical impact of technology on governance.

A transformational approach referred to by Helbig, Gil-Garciá and Ferro (2009) with regard to the incorporation of new technologies in government processes has been used to emphasize the causality assumption implying technology contributes to solving various government issues. Some of the problems noted as finding solution relate to areas of productivity, decision-making practices, decentralization, integration of services. Danziger and Kraemer (1985), for instance, point to the expectation of productivity improvement associated with the use of computer in government. They state that "the processing of information is so central to the work of some professionals, such as planners, stock brokers, accountants and journalists, that the work seems well-suited to productivity gains from computing" (p. 196). The transformational capabilities of information technology have also been touted (Akrivopoulou and Garipidis 2013, p. xvii) with the emergence of e-democracy, presented as "a model of transparency aiming at enhancing the accountability and legitimacy of the democratic institutions". This hope pinned on digital democracy is seen from a taxonomy that highlights new qualities gained by democracy by embracing information and communication technology in government and political systems. Among the trends observed in the classification, one notes enhanced deliberation processes through the incorporation of diverse voices, opinions and political choices and expressions in debates (Akrivopoulou and Garipidis, 2013). These and other researchers (Dubow, Devaux and Manville 2017; Vissers and Stolle 2014; Milakovich 2010) have also explored the potential of digital technology to enhance civic engagement. The prospect has been identified as direct democracy, with the expectation that the ensuing increased popular involvement would contribute to resolving problems of political disinterest.

An additional line of inquiry, followed by Van der Meer, Gelders and Rotthier (2014), involves finding ways to encourage the use of e-government processes to enhance transparency and accountability in the relationship between governments and citizens. In a research on ways for governments to increase transparency and accountability, Halachmi and Greiling (2014) emphasize the need to conceptualize required capabilities in order to foster a sound incorporation of technological tools as managerial instruments enabling efficiency in response to daily public needs. The reasoning behind such a theory reflects the search for means to improve government performance in a way that combine greater openness, transparency and efficiency patterned on private-sector efficiency. The authors term this requirement a balancing challenge for governments, which implies aiming at establishing open governing systems while operating according a model of private sector to increase efficiency. The same interest has been pursued by Madzova, Sajnoski and Davcev (2013) through a comparative study that seeks to decipher the trends and conditions of transformational shifts observed in governments. They note that "some governments have seized the opportunities offered by the new and emerging information and communication technologies to transform government based on democracy, inclusiveness and performance excellency" (p. 159).

Research on digital democracy in Africa shows that the continent has not be left untouched by the global spread of digital technology and its use by governments and civil society. What is critical in the appropriateness of the information and communications technology (ICT) is the way it has been assumed by African government entities and societies as a practical method and transformational capabilities for a more meaningful impact in terms of political development and efficient governance. This is the underlying query that such a research initiative as the one by Dobra (2012), which seeks to unearth the conditions that could either foster or impede the development of democracy through ICT. The author proposes an examination of the "African anthropology of the state and the public sphere" (p. 73), which means engaging in a search for African solutions in order to indigenize ICT and its integration in African ways of life, including political practices. Her contribution seeks to go beyond the focus on technology and infrastructure, which has been the common emphasis in the analysis of the ICT in Africa. This is not an easy task, in light of the unsteady pace of democratic transformation that most African countries have experienced since democratic practices were introduced in the 1990s. It adds a level of complexity in an already challenged context characterized by dwindling political prospects and incomplete institutionalized democratic practices (Norris 2001). Yet this very dissatisfaction with democratic sluggishness constitutes the very reason why Dobra's suggestion makes perfect sense. More broadly, a country's past and political development strongly influences the media environment.

Not only has digital democracy been welcomed by African political forces for the transparency and accountability it is expected to engender, but it has also been adopted by all actors with the hope it would allow increased numbers of people to participate in political issues and play a major role in politics. One of the outcomes of this process has been the strategic view old leaders have had with regard to the new technologies, which they use to strengthen their hold on power. In a study titled Digital Dictatorship versus Digital Democracy in Africa, Ronak Gopaldas (2019) reports on a global trend showing how strongmen and populist rulers resort to new technologies and take advantage of the new media environment. The African context offers propitious conditions to such practice, given the circumstances in which democratic rule is implemented. The author points out the relevance of the concept of digital dictatorship in Africa partly enabled by the relatively early stages of democracy. In addition to the practices by dictators in Africa, the frailty of the new democratic context is also noted in a study by Samantha Fleming (2002), referring to limited citizen participation due to a set of social and economic factors, and by Kersting (2012) who sees disparities in social and economic levels and limited access to ICT infrastructure. The point on economic problems and their impact on access to the internet is given particular emphasis in the analysis of the digital divide by Christian Fuchs and Eva Horak (2008), as they assert that large parts of Africa are affected by global inequality characterized by the distribution of "material wealth and wealth production," which is "more and more based on technology and knowledge" (p. 100). Through a technology-oriented analysis, Bagula and al. (2011) present the structure of the divide as it affects African societies, pointing to the imbalance as a multi-faceted problem that involves different aspects of the issue comprising high costs, electricity infrastructure, and various networking dimensions, such as optical, wireless, mobile, and sensor. Their analysis offers hopeful outcomes, as it indicates a potential evidenced in the continent by the existence of mobile technologies that can be established as the foundation of efforts to eradicate the gap. These technologies include wireless, optical, mobile, and sensor networking.

The potential is not limited to infrastructure, but it can also be expected that spread of information technology gains in Africa will significantly contribute to the development of democracy in Africa. This expectation is at the core of a research conducted by Aletta van Rensburg (2012), and presented in a study of South Africa, Kenya and Zambia. The study embeds the relationship between the internet and democracy in the broader concern with the development of democratic practices in Africa. It posits a positive correlation between the use of internet and the development of democratic culture fostered by public discourse and citizen participation. Furthermore, the process of such development is critically contingent upon the capacity afforded by citizens to to consume and integrate ICTs in the pursuit of their individual and political objectives.

Social Media Consumption

The central place that social media occupy today is the result of change in the news environment and news consumption practices (Bergström and Belfrage (2018) taking place through social network sites. This observation can be applied to the context of political consumption of social media, and attention given to this fact reflects the interest in the relationship between social media and politics. Bergström and Belfrage make the observation even less unambiguous, as they state that "social engagement and a general political interest are usually good predictors of news consumption practices and their explanatory power has increased over time" (p. 585). Factored in the exponential growth of consumption practices in social media is the aspect of interactivity that facilitates the interaction between consumers of various backgrounds and interests instantly sharing and reacting to each other and to many others, and connected through the use of digital technologies (Manning 2014). The interactivity itself is embedded in the technological capabilities that are inherently characteristic of social network sites. This conceptualization captures and relies on a definition of social media that Kaplan and Haenlein (2010) give of social media in a comprehensive statement. They define social media as "a group of Internet-based applications that build on the ideological and technological foundations of Web 2.0 and that allow the creation and exchange of user-generated content" (p. 61).

Given the importance of exchange and technological foundations that constitute the complex in which social media operations take place, the concept of social network sites and their significance come to the fore. boyd and Ellison (2007) provide a definition of social network sites that encompass all key aspects operating in the functioning of social media as connecting tools. According to this definition, social network sites are "web-based services that allow individuals to (1) construct a public or semi-public profile within a bounded system, (2) articulate a list of other users with whom they share a connection, and (3) view and traverse their list of connections and those made by others within the system" (p. 211). Social network sites are seen as crucial venues for political campaigns throughout the globe. Examples abound, which show the use of social media sites by politicians. A few of them can serve as illustration. Carlisle and Patton (2013) note the prominent role played by social network sites, such as Facebook, in the 2008 U.S. presidential campaign. In another case, Biswas, Ingle and Roy (2014) show the importance of social media in elections in India, and they observe the effectiveness of social media as it contributed to the victory of the AamAadmi Party (AAP) or Common Man's Party won power in Delhi in December 2013, and helped to powerfully galvanize volunteers and sympathizers to raise considerable amounts of funds and reach out 3.5 million people before the election. In a comparative analysis of the use of social media in political campaigns in Mexico and Chile, among others, Cárdenas, Ballesteros and Jara (2017) discuss the ways social media have been integrated by political campaigners with varying degrees of success, which reflect historical circumstances and the media environment and institutions, as well as the habits in each country. Chile, for instance, provides a case that substantiates the perspective of this study, which assumes the correlation of the impact of social media on politics with the increasing influence of social media venues in the political sphere. The authors assert that the increase in social media consumption in Chile is apparent through the extensive use in political campaigns. The penetration of social media in politics is undeniable in all parts of the globe, although with different degrees of influence and resulting outcomes. Success in electoral achievements has been widely identified and associated to the way the strategy associated with social media use. However, given the pervasiveness of social media in political settings, failure to achieve intended results can also be attributed not to lack of social media sites and tools, but to the strategic processing of the capabilities inherent in social media applications and tools. In a study of the impact of social media on politics in Malaysia, Gomez (2014) reports on an analysis that attributes the loss of parliamentary majority control by the ruling party, Barisan Nasional, "to the online contents disseminated through blogs, opposition party websites and alternative news portals" (p. 96).

The literature leaves no doubt about the consumption of social media in most areas of human life, including politics. Being a method of political communication endowed with a cognitive dimension that enables to facilitate interactions, and generate and feed information into political campaign, political marketing, and government decision making, social media has become increasingly instrumental in politics. This perspective finds an echo in Carderaro's analysis (2018), which points out that "addressing social media is therefore useful for understanding how political communities use the Internet to create their own channels of communication and contribute to the development of political knowledge" (p. 783). The increase in relevance as a communication tool for political objectives is associated with a shift in public communication, whereby content and knowledge in social media is no longer exclusively produced and managed by leaders or specific actors, such as politicians (Lakkysetty, Deep and Balamurugan 2018). Electoral periods are particularly revealing of the increase in social media consumption (Corchia 2019), as campaigns strive to create momentum and extend their outreach. An important implication is that social media has created the opportunity for anyone to be involved in the political and public sphere. Baker (2009) identifies models of political interaction, the populist and the cyber-salon models, in which the dynamics of interaction are designed, in their particularity, to get everyone involved in the political process or the deliberative discourse with the intent to pursue particular political objectives. An important implication of this development is the heterogeneous character of social media environments (Barnidge et al. 2018) and participants in these processes of political exchange. Social media consumers are not generally homogenous, and this is also the case in the consumption of social media in the political sphere. Social media consumers engage in networks according to their political interests. An illustration of this point is the existence of the variety of topics of interests referred to by Larsson and Hallvard (2012) in their study of the use of trending subjects and hashtags signs in Twitter as a way the network helps consumers to specify and identify with their topics by following threads of online discussion that meet their perceived objectives.

THE USE OF SOCIAL MEDIA IN AFRICAN POLITICAL SETTINGS

Political change in a number of African countries has been associated with the emergence and use of social media. The enthusiasm generated by new technologies has spilled over onto the political realm not only by becoming instruments of political change, but also through their introduction into political processes, behavior and institutions, such as legislative chambers (Hamajoda 2016), electoral campaigns, political advertisements by opposition and government leaders alike, electronic fundraisings (Mano and Ndlela 2020). Online platforms have created and offered a new space for political exchange, and consecutive interactions have fostered strong commitment from numerous participants fighting for change. Beside its structural and technological dimension of providing connectivity and enabling social networking sites for users, social media in Africa have also enabled wide participation in politics from various segments of the population, particularly among youth and women (Jimada 2019). In a study conducted on Kenya, Kamau (2017) established a positive association of reliance on social networking sites with political participation. Though Kamau nuances the influence of social network sites on political participation as lower than one might imagine given the proliferation of digital media, he still describes online activities including campaign information sharing and distribution as catalysts of political participation in Kenya. Similar trends are noted in Nigeria (Madueke 2017), and Zambia (Oginni and Moitui 2015), where political activities by politicians, from government officials and opposition members, and civilians have been enhanced through the use of digital media. The Zambian case is indicative of popular commitment to ensure both increased participation through the use of social media with Facebook and Twitter, and good conditions for electoral processes. Oginni and Moitui point out the existence of a civil society group, Bantu Watch, committed to encouraging participants in electoral processes to use the online link "Zambiaelections" as a platform whereby election-related violence and corruption could be reported.

Other uses of social media have combined political engagement and symbolism in efforts to assert national identity. A particular instance of symbolism is the use of the flag in the Zimbabwean #ThisFlag campaign, which fostered the reclaiming of national identity through the wearing of the national flag and the subsequent discourse that promoted the rights of citizens to demand better development policies and outcomes. This implied entering a political space and using social media as tools to define the political identity of social actors who were marginalized. In addition to the process of identity affirmation, social media were instrumental in efforts to seek inclusion in a political context entirely dominated by members of ZANU ruling party who considered themselves as the only true Zimbabweans and patriots while opposition partisans and supporters were castigated as 'sell-outs' (Karekwaivanane and Mare, 2019, p. 45). Social media have been linked to the emergence and expansion of digital spaces of contention in many African countries, for struggles that defied the construction of differentiated citizenship by dominant powers seeking to classify members of society in terms of their willingness, or lack thereof, to promote the interests of the authoritarian regimes. The case of Zimbabwe shows that the framework of communication provided by social media could be useful to incite commitment and create a narrative in support of the struggle for democracy.

Cases in the Southern African region illustrate the use of social media in the assertions of demands for political, economic and social rights. The typical drive that gives energy to demands is a psychological determination engendered by expectations of better conditions. Demonstrations and protests channel the complexity of choices imbricated in the process of demands for social, economic and political rights that reveal layers of discontent and expectations (Mare 2014). Social media tools are more than simple technical instruments inasmuch as they are embraced as conveyers of the hope and necessity to disentangle the trappings of social and political existence. They denote intents to institute new rules of political behavior and desired systems of social and economic interactions among members of national communities. They generate and support creativity outside the framework of government institutions, and through their inherent versatility they literally give freedom of expression.

The use of social media in oppositional politics in Africa has been the object of increasing attention in the literature and general political observation (Ntuli and Teferra 2017; Thompson, 2011; Oginni 2015; Bosch 2019). Social media have provided democratic movements with additional and efficient tools that have been instrumental to the aggregation and networking of various particular interests and the definition of political and ideological choices. Despite resistance from governing institutions using the same digital tools as opposition forces to counter the democratic push, the movement taking shape and place in the African democratic institutional space are reflected in the surge in institutions set to pursue common purposes and instill consciousness of shared identity (Ogri, Mboso and Adomi 2016). Many social and political activists and concerned Africans eager for change have heeded the appeal both as a commitment to impress their beliefs and values on the collective identity, and a utilitarian adhesion to new communication practices perceived as capable of extending the impact of political and social action. The political conditions that have curtailed democracy in Africa have invigorated social media-activated popular demands through what Sokoloff (2017, p. xii) termed as "confrontational citizenship." The process is a restructuring endeavor that validates and asserts political identity by challenging and disrupting existing corrupt orders and methods of governance prone to negate and undermine opposing forces and marginalized identities through exclusion and exploitation. It establishes the authenticity of institutions to which citizens wish to belong and reconnect through efforts aimed at inducing positive change, renewal or transformation of institutions "to ensure their authority and legitimacy" (Sokoloff, 2017, p. xii).

Social media have contributed to the fertilization of a democratic field that has become a prolific ground for the rise of social movements burgeoning as "emerging counterpublics" with a characteristic definition as "opposition to prevailing norms" (Aslam 2017, p. 16). The widespread use of social media is not exempt of potential crises and conflicts of interest. As some political activists make the choice for radical revolutions to assert their desire for political change, government leaders, using the same tools, are determined to maintain the existing order of things and norms. Northern African revolutions stirred with the help of social media showed radical demands for change in the face of firm government resistance. Social media have contributed to fueling protests with intensity resulting from their capacity to widely and rapidly spread messages, and develop a synergy (Thompson 2011; Ogri, Mboso and Adomi 2016) within a network of followership adhering to the promoted concept and interests. Digital media and democracy have combined in an interdependent manner that boosts their respective capacity to establish and support networks of interaction thrusting human agency into an effort of translating social and political aspirations for political change, development and well-being into institutional norms. Embedded in digital reality that is constantly changing, social media are by nature part of the dynamics driving global cultural transformation.

TRANSFORMATIVE SOCIAL MEDIA

The new media have been heralded for their potential to stir change in a number of areas, including governance, democratic processes, such as elections and political and economic activities. All of these areas have institutional character to which human behavior contributes through the use of media and social interactions. They have provided reason for hope to bring democratic change in African politics. It is difficult to expect transformation by the mere use of technological tools if behaviors and intents are not the drive to cause change. For this reason, expectations have been hauled down with regard to the impact of social media in the African political context. However, despite this cautious observation, an increase in the use of social media in democratic processes is globally noticeable (Baber 2002). Digital communication technologies bring change to the way people communicate and interact. They connect people and create communities as they overcome the constraints that require individuals to be geographically close in order to socially interact (Pfeffer and Carley 2012). With the internet, new communication tools facilitate social mobilization and change ignited through online mobilization and coordination, which result in political conversations of global proportions. Such development reflects the transformative power of social media, which has been touted, for instance, in the popular demands for institutional change and the emergence of new political systems witnessed in North African countries.

The observation of the events surrounding the Arab Spring in the Middle East and North Africa cannot mistake the political change spurred by new media for a regular transition grounded on stable legal and political apparatuses of existing institutions. The regimes in Tunisia and Egypt, known for not being inclined to relinquish power, were strongholds for the ruling oligarchies, and were established on institutional disconnect between the governing entities and the unsteady socioeconomic situations that comprised various social actors. Interconnectivity through new technologies and media has made visible societies and exposed the complex organization of their political and social interactions. Its capability to disseminate information has also allowed societies to open themselves up to ways of disentangling constraining political and social grips. The protests in Tunisia, for instance, were quickly exposed to the world through information dissemination on the Internet on YouTube and Twitter by protesters. The exposed intensification of violent repression by government forces sparked global condemnation of the regime and sympathy from foreign governments. As an article published in *The New York Times* comments, "by many accounts, the new arsenal of social networking helped accelerate Tunisia's revolution, driving the country's 23 years, Zine el-Abidine Ben Ali, into ignominious exile and igniting a conflagration that has spread across the Arab world at breathtaking speed" (*New York Times*, January 30, 2011). The end of the authoritarian regime ushered in institutional change loaded with hopes for a comprehensive transformation of the political system.

The existence of social conditions facilitating public debate and interactions through appropriate networks constitutes the backdrop of institutional arrangements that compound expressed choices and interests. Contrary to traditional mass media, which have been dominated by elites and ruling authoritarian regimes in Africa, the new media have transformed and impacted the social order with the inclusion of citizens hitherto unable to share and communicate due to social status or lack of political power. These social conditions are consistent with the capabilities established by online networks, internet communication settings and platforms. They transmute into what Habermas would call the public sphere, a framework of alternative communication premised on the possibility of debate among citizens, free of government interposition, and working toward shared understanding and hopes about inclusive good governance. The creation of the public sphere and the social conditions on which it is grounded correlate with social rationalization steering the harmonization of social action through communication (Habermas, 1984). It is safe to assert without exaggeration that the public sphere is an extended area of multiform interconnections and interests structured with global dimensions enabling adaptability and mutual influence. Through the public sphere citizens are granted possibilities of informal deliberation. The public sphere combines interest in social development through communicative practice and a reflection on means to strengthen democracy. It contributes to the creation and dynamics of subsystems that engage in, and build on, particular conversations and interactions between social actors dispersed around myriads of locations. The structural changes experienced by subsystems are the results of communicative operations within the global sphere of interactions made possible by new communication technologies. The particularity of each system does not, however, extinguish the inputs from various subsystems and locations made possible by everyday exchange. African societies, local and national, are immersed in conversations that are both contextual and global, and are learning from the global community, just as they contribute to the expansion of shared knowledge.

In the context of social media, contents of online discussions are the creation of participants (Pfeffer and Carley 2012), and African participants bring to the conversation what they experience in their political institutions. Note that in this perspective it is not political history that is transformed since its path precedes the entry of African societies into the global conversation made possible by social media. The object of transformation is the institutional setting in the sense that social change, through intercultural interactions facilitated and impacted by exchange through social media, requires adaptation (Sawyer 2011) of the rules challenging the hegemonic control of the power structures (Miladi 2016). There is an increased density in the communications landscape, coupled with complexity, which is significant of more diverse and engaged participation from individuals and organizations (Engelstad 2017). Access to information is becoming widely available to greater numbers of the global population and more and more people have opportunities to create messages, voice their ideas, and engage in public, even global debates, stimulating widespread collective action. In such a context, the strategic aspect of communication requires efforts to design specific messaging aimed at broadening the public sphere and including more voices in the debate. Within this new and broadened and specifically and rationally designed democratic space, democracy implies not only the structuring of messages to respond to specific interests, but also the consideration of institutional fitness and relevance with its capacity to include and meet people's voiced expectations, intents and interests.

Social media have reinforced the capabilities of social movements to drive institutional change. They open channels through which beliefs, ideas and values are shared. As an institution, media serves to infuse these values while supporting other institutions for the same process, resulting in value and belief transmission and consequential behavior creation, change, and habituation. In this multiple action, media, including social media, affect institutional development and the impact can be observed though the pace of change within the institutions. In some circumstances media can also constitute a barrier to institutional change (Coyne and Leeson 2009). This is significant of the way preferences and interests permeate and affect the system.

SOCIAL MEDIA AND INSTITUTIONAL CHANGE IN AFRICA

What patterns of change are consequential in social media consumption for the consolidation of democratic regime in Africa? How well suited are political systems to the task of coping with the social-media stimulated changes and to demands for democratic consolidation coming from social actors? The question of suitability to the task of coping with social-media stimulated changes in Africa is relevant in light of the push-and-pull dynamics of political change that cause unsteadiness in the process of democratization. The literature on institutional change provides the concept of political creativity as the way to combine order and change relying essentially on the availability of formal rules and roles. The concept is a derivative of what Berk and Galvan call "creative syncretism," which produces "institutional order and change simultaneously (Berk & Galvan, 2013, p. 29). The conceptualization of institutional change by this approach highlights the interplay among various forces endowed with various capabilities in accordance with their social and political place and role in the interactive configuration. In the case of institutional change in Africa, the interplay takes place in the dynamics that sets a face-off between political leaders and democratic forces expressing demands for change and democratic institutions. It gives concrete form to the theory of "structured institutional change" advanced by historical institutionalists focusing on the factors of change, rather than on the resulting situation (Scott, 2014, p. 42). The identification of the factors of change cannot be ignored as it allows to understand how well suited the political systems are to integrating such factors as social media and the democratic demands they trigger.

Being suitable implies seeing social-media induced social and political changes as opportunities rather than threats. An example can be noted in Africa as evidence of a political system showing political creativity. The emerging development state in Rwanda is the result of determined initiatives by Paul Kagame's regime to invest, among other programs, resources in the information and technology infrastructure. The government has also facilitated investment in mobile telephony, and made possible the setting of a national fiber optic infrastructure (Mann and Berry, 2015). This pattern of change is supported by "centralized institutional change" initiated by a "collective-choice process in which rules are explicitly specified by a collective political entity, such as the community or the state" (Coccia, 2018, p. 338). However, despite the Rwandan government's commitment to develop ICT infrastructure, its centralized institutional change and political creativity is by no means associated with the development of a democratic state. The country's democracy index is among non-democratic regimes (IDEA, 2019). The Rwandan case is an example of a government curtailing the democratic benefits of the patterns of learning inherent in the integration of social media in political culture. This is an approach to regime consolidation that strategically shrouds a potential disjuncture between the values promoted by the government and the behavior of social and political actors.

Another approach to institutional change that is present in the African political content animated by social media is related to evolutionary theory. The theory of evolutionary institutional change leans on human creative capacities and learning abilities (Coccia, 2018) that are brought to useful contribution to problem solving. These capabilities instill continued variation that cause social systems, including cultural and political organizations to change. Analysts from this perspective argue that "humans' advanced cognitive capacities contribute to an evolutionary understanding of institutional change" (Lewis and Steinmo, 2012). Cognition constitutes an impetus that stimulates human interest, through learning processes (Peters, 2019) of appropriate behavior (March and Olsen, 1989), in integrating new factors in individual and social development. These cognitive capacities are deployed in the learning process that characterize social media consumption.

The pace of institutional change is specified by Coyne and Leeson in terms of "gradual effect," "punctuation effect" and "reinforcement effect." Gradual effect is the most prevailing situation in African countries where governments have adopted policies of internet control in order to induce marginal institutional change. Internet shutdowns in times of political events, such as election campaigns, have reduced the capability of opponents and political activists to emerge and reach prominence and prevent the impact of their ideas and interests from becoming dominant, and the content of their political narratives from gaining institutional viability. According to CIPESA (2019, p. 4), "internet disruptions are the preserve of African's most authoritarian states." Countries pointed out to support the observation are Algeria, Burundi, the Central African Republic (CAR),3 Cameroon, Chad, DR Congo, Congo (Brazzaville), Egypt, Equatorial Guinea, Gabon, Ethiopia, Libya, Niger, Togo, and Zimbabwe. On the other hand, the hybrid regimes include Uganda, Mali, Morocco, the Gambia and Sierra Leone. The process of regulating social media use through frequent and forceful internet showdowns and censure has the effect of slowing the pace of institutional change.

The second effect, the punctuation effect, occurs when media accelerates widespread institutional change. The two movements, acceleration and complete overtaking, were particularly salient in the Tunisian and Egyptian experiences of social media-activated revolutions. The reinforcement effect, the third effect, which consolidates the gains stemming from institutional change has yet to materialize in post-Arab Spring Tunisia, as it is still dealing with the tasks of rebuilding institutions, which carry the scars of dictatorship. However, materialized instances of the reinforcement effect could be interpreted as such in the enthusiasm and increased political mobilization generated through social media in some African countries. The reinforcement effect has stemmed from the attitude by political leaders to get involved with constituents through social media, implying that they support and consolidate the institutional transformation brought about digital technology. A research on South Africa by Mhlomi and Osunkule (2017) point to the interest that respondents expressed in social media as a facilitator of political and social engagement. This interest has unleashed political activities and has engendered sustained interactions between politicians and civil society. Parliaments have created websites and blogs to communicate with their constituencies. Kenyan politicians use new media to reach their targeted supporters creating campaign messages on social media platforms. The reinforcement effect in Kenya is discernible in the country's national policy framework allowing for the development of ICTs. For Kenyan politicians the infrastructure has the potential of facilitating their engagement with the population. In their article on political marketing in Kenya, Ndavula and Mueni (2014) establish a link that relates developments in technological infrastructure and improved internet access to increased political marketing.

CONCLUSION

It is important to recognize the factors that influence the manner in which information technology is designed, perceived, implemented and used. These factors are significant of the prevailing social, cultural and political context. They relate to the way social actors identify with the social, cultural, cognitive and institutional structures. They determine the design, perception, implementation and use of information technology (Fountain 1995). Social networks and institutional characteristics within the national context have a bearing on technological enactments and the way information is created and shared through social media.

Proponents of historicism might find that too little or no reference is made to the historical development of African societies, and too much emphasis on their current situations given the emergence of such new factors as information technology. I concede that social media as a phenomenon in the field of political development studies constitutes a challenge. However, the history of African societies is not overlooked even in the context of social-media activated path to democracy. The institutional change that is influenced by the integration of social media is a process that relates to historical conditions of particular societies. The critical approach is to find ways to institutionalize social media policies for a sound integration of shared beliefs, norms, and assumptions that have shaped societies. Resistance to social-media activated democracy reflects uncertainty in institutional change at all levels, including social media policies, political demands, and democratic processes. For the standpoint of institutionalism, the effectiveness of multi-faceted institutional change requires that questions be asked about the components and characteristics to be patterned and promoted for institutional setting so as to transcend individual interests and instill regularities in change and political interactions (Peters 2019). The integration of social media as support to democracy is problematic in a number of African countries. In some cases, where policies have promoted such integration, such as Rwanda, Uganda, etc. political behavior reflects ambiguity in terms of norms and values adhered to by political leadership. This indicates disparities and instability in the pursuit of institutional objectives and consolidation of democratic values and norms.

REFERENCES

Abdelnour, Hasselbladh, & Kallinikos. (2017). Agency and Institutions in Organization Studies. *Organization Studies*, *38*(2), 1775-1792. https://journals.sagepub.com/doi/pdf/10.1177/0170840617708007

Akrivopoulou, C., & Garipidis, N. (2013). *Digital Democracy and the Impact of Technology on Governance and Politics: New Globalized Practices*. IGI Global doi:10.4018/978-1-4666-3637-8

Aslam, A. (2017). *Ordinary democracy: Sovereignty and Citizenship Beyond the Neoliberal Impasse*. Oxford University Press. doi:10.1093/acprof:oso/9780190601812.001.0001

Baber, Z. (2002). Engendering or Endangering Democracy? The Internet, Civil Society and the Public Sphere. *Asian Journal of Social Science*, *2*(30), 287–303. doi:10.1163/156853102320405861

Bagula, A., Zennaro, M., Nungu, A., & Nkoloma, M. (2011). Bridging the Digital Divide in Africa: A Technology Perspective. *Conference: 2011 Wireless Communication and Information (WCI 2011) on Digital Divide and Mobile Applications*. https://www.researchgate.net/publication/233817849_Bridging_the_Digital_Divide_in_Africa_A_Technology_Perspective>

Baker, M. (2009). The Impact of Social Networking Sites on Politics. *The Review: A Journal of Undergraduate Student Research, 10*, 72-74. http://fisherpub.sjfc.edu/ur/vol10/iss1/12

Barley, S. R., & Tolbert, P. S. (1997). Institutionalization and structuration: Studying the links between action and institution. *Organization Studies*, *18*(1), 93–117. doi:10.1177/017084069701800106

Barnidge, M., Huber, B., de Zúñiga, H. G., & Liu, J. H. (2018). Social Media as a Sphere for "Risky" Political Expression: A Twenty-Country Multilevel Comparative Analysis. *The International Journal of Press/Politics*, *23*(2), 161–182. doi:10.1177/1940161218773838

Bates, R. H., Block, S. A., Fayad, G., & Hoeffler, A. (2013). The New Institutionalism and Africa. *Journal of African Economies, 22*(4), 499-522. doi:10.1093/jae/ejs031

Bekkers, V. J. J. M. (2003). E-Government and the Emergence of Virtual Organizations in the Public Sector. *Information Polity*, *8*(3/4), 89–102.

Bergström, A., & Belfrage, M. J. (2018). News in Social Media. *Digital Journalism*, *6*(5), 583–598. doi:10.1080/21670811.2018.1423625

Berk, G., & Galvan, D. C. (2013). Processes of Creative Syncretism Experiential Origins of Institutional Order and Change. In G. Berk, D. C. Galvan, & V. Hattam (Eds.), *Political Creativity: Reconfiguring Institutional Order and Change* (pp. 29–54). University of Pennsylvania Press.

Berthod, O. (2016). Institutional Theory of Organizations. In A. Farazmand (Ed.), *Global Encyclopedia of Public Administration, Public Policy, and Governance*. Springer. doi:10.1007/978-3-319-31816-5_63-1

Biswas, A., Ingle, N., & Roy, M. (2014). Influence of Social Media on Voting Behavior. *Journal of Power. Politics & Governance*, *2*(2), 127–155.

Bosch, T. (2019). Social Media and Protest Movements in South Africa. In Social Media and Politics in Africa: Democracy, Censorship and Security. London: Zed Books.

Boyd, d., & Ellison. (2008). Social Networking Sites: Definition, History, and Scholarship. *Journal of Computer-Mediated Communication, 13*(1), 210-230.

Calderaro, A. (2018). Social Media and Politics. In The SAGE Handbook of Political Sociology. Sage. doi:10.4135/9781526416513.n46

Cárdenas, A., Ballesteros, C. & Jara, R. (2017). Redes Sociales y Campañas Electorales en Iberoamérica. Un Análisis Comparativo de los Casos de España, México y Chile. *Cuadernos.info: Comunicación y Medios en Iberoamérica*, (41), 19-40. doi:10.7764/cdi.41.1259

Carlisle, J., & Patton, R. (2013). Is Social Media Changing How We Understand Political Engagement? An Analysis of Facebook and the 2008 Presidential Election. *Political Research Quarterly*, *66*(4), 883–895. doi:10.1177/1065912913482758

CIPESA. (2019). Despots and Disruptions: Five Dimensions of Internet Shutdowns in Africa. *CIPESA: Collaboration on International ICT Policy for East and Southern Africa*.

Coccia, M. (2018). An introduction to the theories of institutional change. *Journal of Economics Library*, *5*(4), 337–344.

Corchia, L. (2019). Political Communication in Social Networks Election Campaigns and Digital Data Analysis: A Bibliographic Review. *Rivista Trimestrale di Scienza dell'Administrazione. Studi di Teoria e Ricerca Sociale*. http://www.rtsa.eu/

Coyne, C. J., & Leeson, P. T. (2009). Media as a Mechanism of Institutional Change and Reinforcement. *Kyklos. International Review for Social Sciences*, *1*(62), 1–14.

Danziger, J. N., & Kraemer, K. L. (1985). Computarized Data-Based Systems and Productivity Among Professional Workers: The Case of Detectives. *Public Administration Review*, *45*(1), 196-209. https://www.jstor.org/stable/3110149?seq=1

Diermeier, D. (2015). Institutionalism and the Normative Study of Politics: From Rational Choice to Behavioralism. *The Good Society, 24*(1), 15-29.

Dobra, A. (2012). The Democratic Impact of ICT in Africa. *Africa Spectrum*, *1*(1), 73–88. doi:10.1177/000203971204700104

Dubow, T., Devaux, A., & Manville, C. (2017). Civic Engagement: How Can Digital Technology Encourage Greater Engagement in Civil Society? *Rand Europe: Perspective, Expert Insights on a Timely Policy Issue*, 1-11. https://www.rand.org/content/dam/rand/pubs/perspectives/PE200/PE253/RAND_PE253.pdf

Dwyer, M., & Molony, T. (2019). Mapping the Study of Politics and Social Media Use in Africa. In *Social Media and Politics in Africa: Democracy, Censorship and Security* (pp. 1–17). Zed Books.

Engelstad, F. (2017). Strategic Communication and Institutional Change. In *Institutional Change in the Public Sphere: Views on the Nordic Model* (pp. 139–159). De Gruyter. doi:10.1515/9783110546330-008

Erdmann, G., Elischer, S., & Stroh, A. (2011). Can Historical Institutionalism Be Applied to Political Regime Development in Africa? *German Institute for Global and Area Studies*. www.jstor.org/stable/resrep07620

Fioretos, O., Falleti, T., Sheingate, A., Fioretos, O., Falleti, T., & Sheingate, A. (2016). Historical Institutionalism in Political Science. In *The Oxford Handbook of Historical Institutionalism* (pp. 3–17). Oxford University Press. https://www.oxfordhandbooks.com/view/10.1093/oxfordhb/9780199662814.001.0001/oxfordhb-9780199662814-e-1

Fleetwood, S. (2008). Institutions and Social Structures. *Journal for the Theory of Social Behaviour*, *38*(3). 241-265. http://citeseerx.ist.psu.edu/viewdoc/download?doi=10.1.1.464.8152&rep=rep1&type=pdf

Fleming, S. (2002). Information and Communication Technologies (ICTs) and Democracy Development in the South: Potential and Current Reality. *EJISDC*, *10*(3), 1–10.

Fountain, J. E. (1995). *Enacting Technology: An Institutional Perspective*. John F. Kennedy School of Government, Harvard University.

Fountain, J. E. (2004). *Prospects for the Virtual State*. Working papers. http://www.j.u-tokyo.ac.jp/coeps/pdf/040710.pdf

Fuchs, C., & Horak, E. (2008). Africa and the Digital Divide. *Telematics and Informatics*, *25*(2), 99–116. doi:10.1016/j.tele.2006.06.004

Gomez, J. (2014). Social Media Impact on Malaysia's 13th General Election. *Asia Pacific Media Educator*, *24*(1), 95–105. doi:10.1177/1326365X14539213

Gopaldas, R. (2019). Digital Dictatorship versus Digital Democracy in Africa. *Policy Insights*, *75*, 1–18.

Habermas, J. (1984). The Theory of Communicative Action.: Vol. 1. *Reason and the Rationalization of Society*. Beacon Press.

Halachmi, A., & Greiling, D. (2014). Transparency, E-Government, and Accountability. *Public Performance & Management Review*, *36*(4), 562–584.

Hamjoda, A. (2016). Embracing New Media in Political Communication: A Survey of Parliamentarians' Attitude and Practices in a Changing Media Landscape in West Africa. *The Electronic Journal on Information Systems in Developing Countries*, *7*(77), 1–10. doi:10.1002/j.1681-4835.2016.tb00566.x

Helbig, N., Gil-García, J. R., & Ferro, E. (2009). Understanding the complexity of electronic government: Implications from the Digital Divide Literature. *Government Information Quarterly*, *26*(1), 89–97. doi:10.1016/j.giq.2008.05.004

IDEA. (2019). *The Global State of Democracy 2019: Addressing the Ills*. Reviving the Promise.

Kamau, S. C. (2017). Democratic Engagement in the Digital Age: Youth, Social Media and Participatory Politics in Kenya. *Communicatio*, *2*(43), 128–146. doi:10.1080/02500167.2017.1327874

Kaplan, A. M., & Haenlein, M. (2010). Users of the World, Unite! The Challenges and Opportunities of Social Media. *Business Horizons*, *53*(1), 59–68. doi:10.1016/j.bushor.2009.09.003

Karekwaivanane, G., & Mare, A. (2019). 'We are not just voters, we are citizens': Social media, the #ThisFlag campaign and insurgent citizenship in Zimbabwe. In Social Media and Politics in Africa: Democracy, Censorship and Security. London: Zed Books.

Kersting, N. (2012). The Future of Electronic democracy. In *Electronic Democracy* (pp. 11-54). Verlag Barbara Budrich. https://www.jstor.org/stable/j.ctvddzwcg.5?seq=1#metadata_info_tab_contents

Kiranda, Y., Mugisha, M., & Ojok, D. (2016). Social media, Political Communication and Campaigning in Uganda: Opportunity or Challenge? In Assessing the Impact of Social Media on Political Communication and Civic Engagement in Uganda. Konrad-Adenauer-Stiftung, Uganda Programme.

Lakkysetty, N., Deep, P., & Balamurugan, J. (2018). Social Media and its Impact on Politics. *International Journal of Advance Research. Ideas and Innovations in Technology*, *4*(2), 2108–2118.

Larsson, A. O., & Hallvard, M. (2012). Studying political microblogging: Twitter Users in the 2010 Swedish Election Campaign. *New Media & Society*, *14*(5), 729–747. doi:10.1177/1461444811422894

Lewis, O. A., & Steinmo, S. (2012). How Institutions Evolve: Evolutionary Theory and Institutional Change. *Polity*, *44*(3), 314–339. doi:10.1057/pol.2012.10

Liebowitz, J., & Beckman, T. (1998). *Knowledge Organizations: What Every Manager Should Know*. St. Lucie Press.

Madzova, V., Sajnoski, K., & Davcev, L. (2013, June). E-Government as an Efficient Tool towards Good Governance: Trends and Comparative Analysis throughout Worldwide Regions and within West Balkan Countries. *Balkan Social Science Review*, *1*, 157–174.

Mann, L., & Berry, M. (2015). Understanding the political motivations that shape Rwanda's emergent developmental state. *New Political Economy*, *21*(1), 119-144.

Manning, J. (2014). Definition and Classes of Social Media. In K. Harvey (Ed.), *Encyclopedia of Social Media and Politics* (pp. 1158–1162). Sage.

Mano, W., & Ndlela, M. N. (2020). Introduction: Social Media, Political Cultures and Elections in Africa. In M. Ndlela & W. Mano (Eds.), *Social Media and Elections in Africa* (Vol. 2, pp. 1–7). Palgrave Macmillan. doi:10.1007/978-3-030-32682-1_1

March, J. G., & Olsen, J. P. (1984). The New Institutionalism: Organizational Factors in Political Life. *The American Political Science Review*, *78*(3), 734–749. doi:10.2307/1961840

March, J. G., & Olsen, J. P. (1989). *Rediscovering Institutions: The Organizational Basis of Politics.* The Free Press.

Mare, A. (2014). Social Media: The New Protest Drums in Southern Africa? In B. Pătruţ & M. Pătruţ (Eds.), *Social Media in Politics. Public Administration and Information Technology* (Vol. 13, pp. 315–335). Springer. doi:10.1007/978-3-319-04666-2_17

Mhlomi, Y., & Osunkule, O. (2017). Social Media and Youth Political Participation in South Africa's 2014 General Election. *Communitas*, *12*(22), 149–158.

Miladi, N. (2016). Social Media and Social Change. *DOMES. Digest of Middle East Studies.*, *1*(25), 36–51. doi:10.1111/dome.12082

Milakovich, M. E. (2010). The Internet and Increased Citizen Participation in Government. *JeDEM - eJournal of eDemocracy and Open Government*, *2*(1), 1-9. https://www.jedem.org/index.php/jedem/article/view/22

Mthokozisi E. N & Teferra, D. (2017). Implications of Social Media on Student Activism: The South African Experience in a Digital Age. *JHEA/RESA, 15*(2), 63-80.

Ndavula, J. O., & Mueni, J. (2014). New Media and Political Marketing in Kenya: The Case of 2013 General Elections. *International Journal of Arts and Commerce*, *6*(3), 69–84.

Ndlela, M. N. (2020). Social Media Algorithms, Bots and Elections in Africa. In Social Media and Elections in Africa, Volume 1. Theoretical Perspectives and Election Campaigns. Palgrave Macmillan.

Norris, P. (2001). *Digital Divide: Civic Engagement, Information Poverty, and the Internet Worldwide.* Cambridge University Press. doi:10.1017/CBO9781139164887

Oginni, S. O., & Moitui, J. N. (2015). Social Media and Public Policy Process in Africa: Enhanced Policy Process in Digital Age. *Consilience. The Journal of Sustainable Development Vol.*, *2*(14), 158–172.

Ogri, E. U., Mboso, A. G. & Adomi, K. O. (2016). Social Media and Participatory Democracy in Africa: A Study of Democratic Transitions in Nigeria and Uganda. *International Journal of Linguistics and Communication, 3*(2), 25-49.

Peters, B. G. (2019). *Institutional Theory in Political Science: The New Institutionalism*. Edward Elgar Publishing.

Petersen, M. B., & Aarøe, L. (2015). Evolutionary Theory and Political Behavior. In R. Scott & S. Kosslyn (Eds.), *Emerging Trends in the Social and Behavioral Sciences* (pp. 1–15). John Wiley & Sons, Inc. doi:10.1002/9781118900772.etrds0125

Petracca, M. P. (1991). The Rational Choice Approach to Politics: A Challenge to Democratic Theory. *The Review of Politics, 2*(53), 289–319. doi:10.1017/S0034670500014637

Pfeffer, J., & Carley, K. M. (2012). Social Networks, Social Media, Social Change. In Advances in Design for Cross-Cultural Activities Part II. Boca Raton: CRC Press.

Pope, W. (1975). Durkheim as a Functionalist. *The Sociological Quarterly, 16*(3), 361–379. doi:10.1111/j.1533-8525.1975.tb00954.x

Riley, E. (2019). Social media, activism and democracy in Senegal. In Social Media and Politics in Africa: Democracy, Censorship and Security. London: Zed Books.

Robertson, P. J., & Tang, S.-Y. (1995). The Role of Commitment in Collective Action: Comparing the Organizational Behavior and Rational Choice Perspectives. *Public Administration Review, 55*(1), 67–80. doi:10.2307/976829

Sawyer, R. (2011). The Impact of New Social Media on Intercultural Adaptation. *Senior Honors Projects*. Paper 242. http://digitalcommons.uri.edu/srhonorsprog/242http://digitalcommons.uri.edu/srhonorsprog/242

Scharpf, F. W. (1991). Political Institutions, Decision Styles, and Policy Choices. In A. Windhoff-Héritier & R. Czada (Eds.), *Political Choice: Institutions, Rules, and the Limits of Rationality* (pp. 53–86). Westview Press.

Scott, W. R. (2008). Lords of the dance: Professionals as institutional agents. *Organization Studies, 29*(2), 219–238. doi:10.1177/0170840607088151

Scott, W. R. (2014). *Institutions and Organizations: Ideas, Interests and Identities*. Sage Publications Ltd.

Segaard, S. B. (2017). The Institutional Anchoring of Social Media Venues as Arenas for Local Political Communication. Perceptions by Voters and Politicians. In F. Engelstad, H. Larsen, J. Rogstad, K. Steen-Johnsen, D. Polkowska, A. S. Dauber-Griffin, & A. Leverton (Eds.), *Institutional Change in the Public Sphere: Views on the Nordic Model* (pp. 118–138). De Gruyter. doi:10.1515/9783110546330-007

Smith, D. (2014). Internet Use on Mobile Phones in Africa Predicted to Increase 20-fold. *The Guardian*. Retrieved from http://www.theguardian.com/world/2014/jun/05/internet-use-mobilephones-africa-predicted-increase-20-fold

Sokoloff, W. W. (2017). *Confrontational Citizenship: Reflections on Hatred, Rage, Revolution, and Revolt*. State University of New York Press.

Steinmo, S. (2008). Historical institutionalism. In D. Della Porta & M. Keating (Eds.), *Approaches and Methodologies in the Social Sciences: A Pluralist Perspective,* (pp. 118-138). Cambridge: Cambridge University Press. https://www.cambridge.org/core/books/approaches-and-methodologies-in-the-social-sciences/historical-institutionalism/B6482BAC0D68CE27AC1DBF6A3AE5A1B9

Thelen, K. (1999). Historical Institutionalism in Comparative Politics. *Annual Review of Political Science, 2*(1), 369–404. doi:10.1146/annurev.polisci.2.1.369

Thompson, R. L. (2012). Radicalization and the Use of Social Media. *Journal of Strategic Security, 4*(4), 167–190. doi:10.5038/1944-0472.4.4.8

Van der Meer, T. G. L. A., Gelders, D., & Rotthier, S. (2014). E-Democracy: Exploring the Current Stage of e-Government. *Journal of Information Policy, 4*, 489–506. doi:10.5325/jinfopoli.4.2014.0489

Van Rensburg, A. H. J. (2012). Using the Internet for Democracy: A Study of South Africa, Kenya and Zambia. Global Media Journal African Edition, 6(1), 93-117.

Vissers, S., & Stolle, D. (2014). The Internet and New Modes of Political Participation: Online Versus Offline Participation. *Information Communication and Society, 17*(8), 937–955. doi:10.1080/1369118X.2013.867356

Windhoff-Héritier, A., & Czada, R. (1991). Introduction. In A. Windhoff-Héritier & R. Czada (Eds.), *Political Choice: Institutions, Rules, and the Limits of Rationality* (pp. 9–26). Westview Press.

KEY TERMS AND DEFINITIONS

Digital Democracy: Participation in political processes through online and internet-based means and tools generally termed as digital technology, with the possibility to directly connect with governments and public administration institutions and affect policy.

Institutional Change: Change in institutions brought about by opportunities or threat to its processes and "established pattern of behavior" (Peters, 2019, p. 42).

Institutionalism: An approach to political, organization, and social activity and processes. Depending on the focus of a particular approach, the term evokes different theories of institutionalism.

Methodological Individualism: An approach derived from rational choice theory, which considers that "everything about society and social action can be reduced to statements about component individuals" (Petracca, 1991, p. 293).

Political Behavior: Political behavior is human behavior that shapes the environment while being shaped by it, through the assertion of political interests, the struggle for power, and the normative structural and institutional configuration. It operates as "behavior seeking to enforce one's interests by pushing the shared sense of regularity into greater alignment with one's interests" (Petersen & Aarøe, 2015, p. 1).

Rational Choice: An institutional theory that stresses utility-maximizing individual choices and decisions. Despite the focus on individual behavior, the theory recognizes that human behavior takes place within institutions.

Transformative Social Media: Structures of exchange and interaction that lead to behavioral and structural change.

Chapter 13

Blogs as Pathways to Information and Influence Within the Kenyan Blogosphere

Patrick Kanyi Wamuyu

(iD) https://orcid.org/0000-0002-4241-2519

United States International University – Africa, Kenya

ABSTRACT

Kenya has a robust blogger community, with hundreds of active bloggers and a variety of stimulating blogs on politics, agriculture, technology, education, fashion, food, entertainment, sports, and travel. The purpose of this chapter was to explore whether Kenyans participate in online discussions and to determine the role of Kenyan bloggers in online communities. Data was collected through a survey of 3,269 respondents aged between 14 and 55 years and social media mining on Twitter using Network Overview, Discovery and Exploration for Excel (NodeXL) API. Survey data was analyzed using descriptive statistics and cross-tabulation while mined data was analyzed for centrality metrics. The study identified Farmers Trend, Ghafla Kenya, KahawaTungu, and Kachwanya as influential blogs in the Kenyan blogosphere and that most Kenyan women read travel and food and fashion blogs while men mostly read sports and politics blogs. This chapter contributes to a better understanding of the Kenyan blogosphere.

INTRODUCTION

Sánchez-Villar, Bigné, and Aldás-Manzano (2017) define blogs as websites where people write about recent events or topics that interest them. Herring et al., (2015, pp.1) define blogs as frequently modified web pages in which dated entries are listed in reverse chronological sequence. Blogs allow individuals and organizations to engage in discussions with the blog authors and readers over time facilitating exchange of ideas and the emergence of individuals who are influencers or opinion leaders. Kenya has a robust blogger community with hundreds of active bloggers. In 2015, the Bloggers Association of Kenya (BAKE) Chairman Kennedy Kachwanya indicated that there were an estimated 15,000 registered blogs

DOI: 10.4018/978-1-7998-4718-2.ch013

in Kenya, with over 3,000 of, these active blogs registered by Kenyans on the WordPress, Blogger and Tumblr platforms (BAKE, 2015, pp. 2).

The Kenyan blogger community is mainly synonymous with political bloggers. This could be attributed to the fact that the Kenyan political blogosphere has over the years been considered antagonistic. It is worth noting that political discourse on Twitter is more likely to be opinionated and often more negative concerning political candidates than that on blogs (Pew Research Center, 2011; Choi, Sang & Park, 2012). However, Kranzberg (1985) contends that technology is not inherently good or bad; nor is it neutral, and as such Kenyans are increasingly turning to blogs for news, information, politics, and entertainment. It has also been said that technology is inherently political and that technologies are compatible with certain political configurations and relationships (Winner, 2009). There is also an assumption that most Kenyans read political blogs than any other kind of blogs, yet, there are many and more stimulating blogs on matters education, fashion, food, entertainment, sports and travel in the Kenyan blogosphere as listed on BAKE's website. There are more readers of the entertainment, educational, business and sports blogs than there are political blog readers.

STATEMENT OF THE PROBLEM

Blogs and bloggers have received a lot of attention from researchers across diverse disciplines such as marketing, information technology, information systems, communication and journalism as they influence most spheres of life. Blogs are sources of opinions and sentiments allowing bloggers to exert influence over the blog readers (Tan & Na, 2013). Karanja (2016) describes bloggers as influential agenda setters. But, to have any influence through social media, one has to know what to share, how to share, where to share, and how often to share. Most Kenyan bloggers know the importance of using multiple social media platforms, and are good in sharing the same message in multiple platforms. On a given day, a blogger prepares and posts a story on their blog, tweets the link, adds the blogpost link on their Facebook page, and creates an Instagram hashtag about the blogpost as well as sharing the post's link in several WhatsApp groups. Bloggers also tend to share blog post content from influential blogs (Tan & Na, 2013). A social media influencer is defined as an independent third-party endorser who shapes audience attitudes through blogs, tweets, and the use of other social media (Freberg, Graham, McGaughey, & Freberg, p. 90).

In the absence of any previous research on the perceived influence of bloggers among the Kenyan online community, this study serves as the basis from which one can examine the Kenyan blogosphere and gain an understanding on whether Kenyans do read online blogs, participate in online debates and to assess how influential Kenyan bloggers are. The study uses betweenness centrality to test whether bloggers act as a bridging agent in social communication networks on Twitter, i.e. if more people depend on the blogger to make connections with other people.

RESEARCH QUESTIONS

The use of social media as a source of information has triggered renewed interest in social media analytics research (Struweg, 2018). For example, identifying the influencers in a given online ecosystem "can be useful in tasks such as planning successful advertising strategies, political campaigning, and identifying terrorist leaders" (Rosenthal & Mckeown, 2017, pp. 1). Identifying influencers in online discussions on social media can be accomplished through an analysis of the graph-based representation of user interactions in a social network or by measuring the impact of the linguistic content of user messages through Social Network Analysis. Social Network Analysis models "relations and associations, developments and dynamic forces in networks and activities on social media platforms" (Struweg, 2018, pp. 3). Blog authors act as leaders who give their opinion, so their influence becomes significant among their readers. The study objectives are (1) to explore whether Kenyans participate in online discussions, (2) to explore the role of the Kenyan bloggers in the online discussions and the entire Kenyan blogosphere by examining the network structure of online discussions on Twitter to identify the opinion leaders who are likely to influence the flow of information. The study was guided by the following questions:

1.   Do Kenyans read online blogs?
2.   Do Kenyans participate in online discussions?
3.   Are Kenyan bloggers opinion leaders (influential actors) in online discussions among social media users?

To answer the three research questions, the study collected data using a baseline survey and an analysis of the graphic representation of a network structure of online discussions among the Kenyan bloggers and their readers on the Twitter social media platform using Network Overview, Discovery and Exploration for Excel (NodeXL). The baseline survey was accomplished using a hand-delivered questionnaire. The Clauset-Newman-Moore cluster algorithm (Clauset, Newman & Moore, 2019) was used to identify groups within online discussions on Twitter, while NodeXL's network visualization of graphic connections was laid out using the Harel-Koren Fast Multiscale Layout Algorithm (Harel & Koren, 2001).

SIGNIFICANCE OF THE STUDY

This study was aimed at investigating whether Kenyans read online blogs and how blogs can facilitate online discussions. It also explored the role of Kenyan bloggers in online discussions and the entire Kenyan blogosphere. The results of this study contribute to the related literature on the reading and use of blogs and the blogging phenomenon in Kenya since no similar research has been carried out. It also contributes to the literature on the applicability of social network analysis in determining influence and influencers among social media users in the Kenyan blogosphere. By demonstrating how to identify influencers among social media users, the study is significant to the companies that use or intend to use blogs as part of their marketing and communications efforts and in the formulation and execution of their influencer marketing strategies to boost their brand exposure. The study also identifies the use of blogs as an efficient way to access essential information and to facilitate online discussions among diverse demographic groups and in a much wider geographical area.

This paper's focus is on the aggregate Kenyan blogosphere as the unit of study. The rest of the paper is organized as follows: Section 2 is a review of the literature, Section 3 describes the methodology, while Section 4 gives the study results. Section 5 has the discussion of the results and Section 6 outlines the study implications, limitations and directions for future research.

LITERATURE REVIEW

This literature review discusses the three key elements of the study which include (i) blogs and the Kenyan blogger community, (ii) online discussions and online opinion leadership and, (iii) the study application tools, Twitter and NodeXL.

Blogs, Bloggers and the Kenyan Bloggers Communities

In today's online world, blogs cover nearly every topic of interest, on any conceivable subject and have become an important source of information for a range of issues. Studies have defined blogs as websites where people write about recent events or topics of their interest (Sánchez-Villar, Bigné, & Aldás-Manzano, 2017; Chesney & Su, 2010). Sánchez-Villar *et al.,* (2017) indicate that a blog's information quality increases its reputation and consequently, reinforces its trustfulness and usefulness. The buyout of the *Ghafla* blog by Ringier Africa in 2016 was noted as a reflection on the growing importance and influence of blogs in Kenya (BAKE, 2016). However, as indicated by Jackson (2001, pp.295), a "vast majority of blogs are probably only read by family and friends, with only a few elite blogs which are read by comparably large numbers".

The Bloggers Association of Kenya (BAKE) was formed in 2011. However, blogging in Kenya started in 2003 when Daudi Were started his blog, mentalacrobatics.com (BAKE, 2015). Kenya's pioneer bloggers were mainly Kenyans in the diaspora writing on varying topics from politics to social commentary. Between January 2016 and July 2018, many of the Kenyan political bloggers were arrested and charged in the courts of law for either publishing false statements likely to cause fear and alarm to the public or by contravening the provisions of Section 29 of the Information and Communication Act. However, their arrests were unusually brief and only served to create public sympathy. A report by the Bloggers Association of Kenya (BAKE, 2016) indicates that at least 60 bloggers were arrested in 2016, as senior government officials looked for ways of legally intimidating bloggers. However, many Kenyan bloggers take sides and online discussions end up becoming ethnically or politically tense. Most Kenyan political bloggers are thought to be fake, or whenever they write, they are seen as dancing to the tune of their highest buyer. However, this has not deterred Kenyans from reading online blogs. Moreover, there are tens of non-political blogs in the Kenyan blogosphere.

Blogs can attract attention and exert considerable influence on individuals, politics, fashion, and consumer goods and also provide an additional cognitive bias that connects online environments with the offline world (Hsu & Lin, 2008; Sánchez-Villar *et al.,* 2017). BAKE (2016, pp. 4) indicates that the monthly blog readership in Kenya in 2016 was 18.1 Million and this was credited to the increase in the number of Kenyans who can access the Internet through their phones and that "blogs are seen by many Kenyans as authentic means to get news and opinions which mainstream media would normally shy away from". Tan and Na, (2013) posit that bloggers' influence can be measured in terms of engagement, persuasion, and persona style. This study sought to assess whether the Kenyan bloggers influence Kenyan social media users based on social network analysis and centrality metrics of online discussions.

Online Discussions

Social media platforms offer opportunities to have online discussions and the creation of productive online communities with the potential for asynchronous online debates. Social media also functions as an alternative medium for citizen communication by facilitating online discussions as witnessed during the post-election crisis in 2008 in Kenya where discussion forums aimed to promote peace and Kenyan unity were created on Flickr.com and relevant video files added on the YouTube.com (Maarit & Kuira, 2008).

Social media platforms are increasingly becoming important forums for public debate and are known to influence individual attitudes and behaviors (Williams, *et al.,* 2015). Lange *et al.,* (2008) indicate that forums and blog posts are among the most popular ways of online discussions. Besides facilitating online discussions, communicating information and opinions, blogs help individuals to establish identity, status, authority, and connections among online communities.

Identifying Online Opinion Leaders on Twitter

Opinion leaders are described as engaged and competent individuals who are viewed as honest and trustworthy by opinion followers, with whom they frequently interact (Turcotte *et al.,* 2015). Opinion leaders are those individuals who are more connected than others and thus are more likely to influence the flow of information by facilitating the dissemination of media messages to audiences. Network analysis techniques have been adopted to explore opinion leaders within the structure of social relationships as opinion leaders take up strategically beneficial positions in a network (Xu et al., 2014). Further, studies have concluded that among Twitter users, there are opinion leaders who influence others and their friends through network participants (Wu et al., 2011; An et al., 2011). However, there is no standard way to identify and define influential users' in online social networks (Mahmoudi, Yaakub & Bakar, 2018). Opinion leadership in this study is measured using in-degree centrality, betweenness centrality, and eigenvector centrality. In-degree centrality is the number of ties received from others and the higher the in-degree centrality of an actor, the more central the actor's position is in the network, greater is the trust, authority, and power (Valente, 2010).

By doing Social Media Analytics on Twitter data, one can be able to identify diverse and useful users' network patterns and intelligence. Conversely, Razis, Anagnostopoulos, and Zeadally (2020) indicate that previous studies have shown that the most active users or those having the most followers in the online social networks are not necessarily the most influential ones. Hence, most online conversations usually have only one or zero influencers (Rosenthal, 2014). Online influencers or opinion leaders (Riquelme & Cantergiani, 2016), play the role of information brokers who pass messages to followers around topics of common interest.

Anger and Kittl (2011) suggest that having a large number of followers does not guarantee high influence among Twitter network users and propose a methodology based on the number of tweets, replies, retweets, and mentions of a user's account. Similarly, Cha *et al.,* (2010) indicate that there are three types of influence in Twitter networks, namely "In-degree" (number of followers), "Retweets" (number of user-generated tweets that have been retweeted) and "Mention" influence (number of times the user is mentioned in other users' tweets). Francalanci and Hussain (2017) created a framework for identifying the top influencers using "both user-level (i.e. followers, following, tweets, lists) and content-based (hashtags, URLs, retweets, favorites, mentions) parameters". Bigonha *et al.,* (2012) proposed a centrality measure that combines betweenness and eigenvector centralities, in-degree, and the follower-followee ratio on graphs of relationships, mentions, replies and retweets. This study utilizes the tweets, replies, retweets, and mentions of a user's account and the user's betweenness and eigenvector centralities, in-degree, and the follower-followee ratio on a Twitter social network graph to identify the top influencers among the Kenyan blogger community.

Twitter

Twitter is considered as one of the most dominant and persuasive social media platforms today (Sanawi, Samani & Taibi, 2017). Twitter is a microblogging site created in 2006. Microblogging is a form of blogging that allows users to send brief text (microposts) updates or micromedia such as photographs or audio clips. Other microblogging services include Plurk, Tumblr, Sina Weibo, and Soup.io. Twitter currently has a text limit of 280 characters as compared to 140 characters per message when it was launched in 2006. Twitter users can also upload photos and short videos. Twitter supports social networking through "friending" or "following" and large-scale sharing and diffusion of information (Bruns & Burgess, 2011). Twitter users use hashtags, which consist of brief keywords or abbreviations with a prefixed hash symbol for effective communication with an ad hoc community sharing the same concerns or topics of interest.

Twitter is commonly used to study online behavior because of its very open application programming interface (API), its search features which allow users to look up tweets and it has a strong hashtag culture which makes it easier gathering, sorting, and expanding searches when collecting data, in addition to Twitter accounts being public (Grandjean, 2016; Ahmed, Bath, & Demartini, 2017; Marwick & Boyd, 2011).

Several previous studies have been carried out using Twitter data. Ch'ng (2015) used Twitter data to find the formation of online communities. Sakaki, Okazaki, and Matsuo (2010) used Twitter data to analyze real-time interaction of events such as earthquakes by considering Twitter users as sensors, while Baek and Kim (2015) explored how an individual participant's role and position affects their information sharing activities within an online community over time. Grandjean (2016) used Twitter to highlight the structure of the online community network's relationships by identifying users whose position is particular while Bravo and Del Valle (2017) used social network analysis techniques on following-follower and mention network in the identification of opinion leaders in Twitter networks.

Several other studies have also studied the use of Twitter in the political domain. These studies include: How political leaders communicate (Aharony, 2012); how politicians use Twitter as a

channel of personal interaction with the electorate (Ignacio Criado et al., 2011); patterns to characterize identities in virtual communities during the Latvian parliamentary elections of 2010 (S̆kilters et al., 2012); parliamentary representatives use of Twitter to disseminate information in Norway (Sæbø, 2011); the role of Twitter in political deliberations in Korea (Kim & Park, 2012); the political usage of Twitter as a tool of impression management among UK MPs (Jackson & Lilleker, 2011); the use of Twitter as a forum for political deliberation (Tumasjan et al., 2011); the use of political community behavior on Twitter to predict political orientation (Mustafaraj & Metaxas, 2010).

NodeXL

The Network Overview, Discovery and Exploration for Excel (NodeXL) is a Microsoft Excel add-in template which allows users to generate social network graphs for social media network analysis and visualization. NodeXL can harvest data from a variety of sources including Twitter, YouTube, Flickr, email, and WWW hyperlinks). NodeXL can analyze Twitter content such as key topics, hashtags, and users' networks. NodeXL is capable of calculating network matrices like "in-degree", "out-degree", "betweenness" and "eigenvector" centralities in the Twitter online social network graph which this study used in identifying influencers among the Kenyan blogger community. NodeXL is developed by the Social Media Research foundation (https://www.smrfoundation.org/nodexl/). Over the years, researchers and marketers have been able to use NodeXL to access to the social network application programming interfaces (APIs) of Flickr, Facebook, YouTube, and Twitter, as well as other third-party graph data importers

Previous studies have been carried out using NodeXL. Hitesh *et al.*, (2018) used NodeXL to analyze social network for a big forensic data, Yep and Shulman (2014) used NodeXL to determine a library's social media audience and Akrouf *et al.*, (2013) used NodeXL to predict social media influence using Flickr users' contacts and YouTube users' comments.

Hanchard (2019) in a blogpost demonstrates how to analyze Facebook and YouTube using NodeXL, while Campbell's (2010) blogpost shows how to visualize email communications using NodeXL. The use of NodeXL in Twitter social media data analytics is evident from past studies such as Ferra and Nguyen's 2017 study on the European migration crisis, Brummette and Fussell Sisco's 2018 study on the Chipotle restaurant chain crisis; and a study by Keib, Himelboim and Han (2018) on the controversial Black Lives Matter in the United Kingdom. When using NodeXL, one can import data on a particular topic from the past seven days and/or a maximum of 18 000 tweets.

METHODOLOGY

Figure 1 provides a schematic overview of the research methodology employed. The study used a quantitative research methodology implemented using a baseline survey and a quantitative network analysis. Data collection was done in two sequential phases. In phase one, the study used hand-delivered questionnaires to collect baseline data on the use of the internet, participation in online discussions, and the use of online blogs. The questionnaire consisted of open-ended and closed-ended questions to get data on individual blog usage patterns, participation in online discussions as well as the demographics. Data was collected from eight counties which included Nairobi, Mombasa, Meru, Bungoma, Mandera, Trans Nzoia, Kisumu, and Nyeri. The participants were assured of their anonymity and confidentiality and informed that their participation in the study was voluntary. The data collected in this phase was analyzed using descriptive statistics and cross-tabulation.

During the second phase, data was collected through social media mining using NodeXL API for quantitative network analysis. The data in this phase was collected by importing network data from Twitter to NodeXL for network analysis and visualization. Struweg (2018) posits that the power of social media continues to increase, hence the need to measure it. However, the challenge on how to measure the power of social media continues unless the available social media analytics tools are more effectively and constantly explored by scholars in different contexts, methodologies, and disciplines. One such tool is the NodeXL, a social media analytics tool that uses advanced 'crawling' capabilities over several social media platforms to capture, analyze, and visualize the social network of available public information.

Three blogs were purposely selected for data collection. Under entertainment, Ghafla Kenya (https://www.ghafla.com/ke, @GhaflaKenya) was selected, for social issues, politics and active citizenship, Kahawa Tungu (https://www.kahawatungu.com/, @*KahawaTungu*) was selected, in addition to an agricultural blog (http://farmerstrend.co.ke/, @*FarmersTrend)* and a technology blog, Kachwanya (https://www.kachwanya.com/, @*Kachwanya*).

Data analysis for this phase was done through a descriptive/exploratory analysis of the social networks. This was achieved using NodeXL social network analysis and the interpretation of the advanced network metrics including betweenness centrality, closeness centrality, and Eigenvector centrality. Wasserman and Faust (1994) posit that in a descriptive/exploratory analysis of a social network, the researcher tries to make sense of a complex structure using various structural features of the network. The analysis was based on influence *metrics* including the activity of the blogs Twitter account (e.g. tweets, re-tweets, replies, mentions), its social degree (e.g. followers, following) and its impact on Twitter (e.g. content diffusion, social acknowledgement etc.). The Twitter data for the study was imported on May 26, 2020 through NodeXL Twitter Importer.

Figure 1.

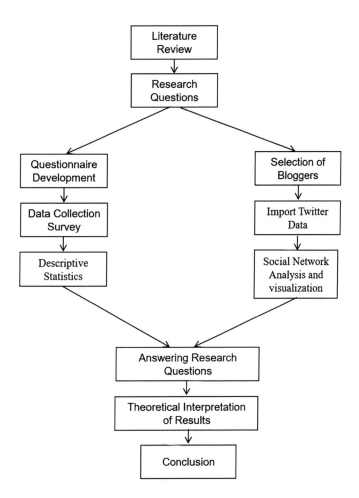

RESEARCH FINDINGS

Findings From the Baseline Survey

The survey sampled 3,269 respondents aged between 14 and 55. From this sample, 3,166 questionnaires were fully answered – representing a health response rate of 96.9%. The data from the 3,166 respondents was used to answer the study research questions.

Research Question 1: Do Kenyans read online blogs?

The study results showed that 74% of the respondents read online blogs. Figure 2 shows the types of online blogs Kenyans read, with entertainment blogs being the most popular. The study data also indicated that 70% of the online blog readers read their favorite blogs daily.

Figure 2. Types of online blogs Kenyans are reading

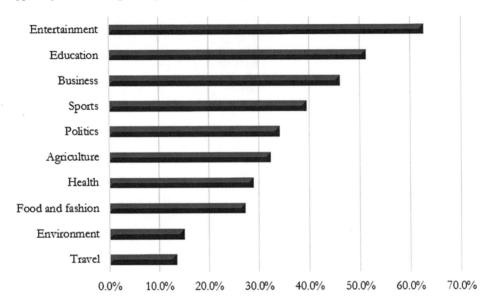

Reading of Blogs by Gender

As indicated in Figure 3, most women are reading food and fashion (62%), and travel (47%) blogs as compared to Kenyan men who mostly read sports (83%), and political (73%) blogs. While most males read sports blogs, very few women read them and whereas most females read food and fashion blogs, very few males read them, which is a direct opposite in the likes and preferences of the two genders regarding the type of online blogs they read.

Reading of Blogs by Geolocation

The rural population mostly read sports (47.5%) and entertainment (45.7%) blogs as compared to the urban residents who mostly read travel (61.6%) and food and fashion (59.2%) blogs. As indicated in Figure 4, most people residing in the rural areas read sports blogs while very few urban residents read the sports blogs, which is a direct opposite in the likes and preferences of the residents of the two different geolocations regarding the type of the online blogs they read.

Figure 3. Reading of Online Blogs by Gender

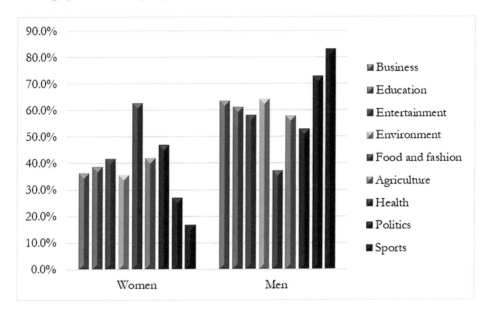

Reading of Blogs by Income

The residents of the low-income areas in Nairobi Mostly read entertainment (31.8%) and sports (27.5%) blogs. The residents of middle-income areas in Nairobi read business (49.5%), food, and fashion (46.9%) blogs as shown in Figure 5. The residents of the high-income residential areas of Nairobi read travel (45.9%) and health (37.7%) blogs.

Figure 4. Reading of Online Blogs by Geolocation

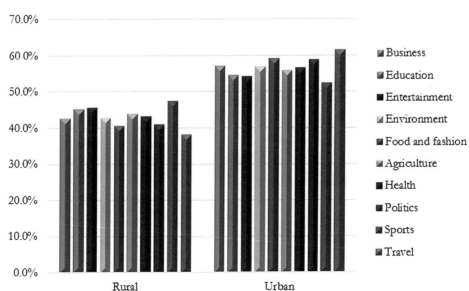

Figure 5. Reading of online blogs by income

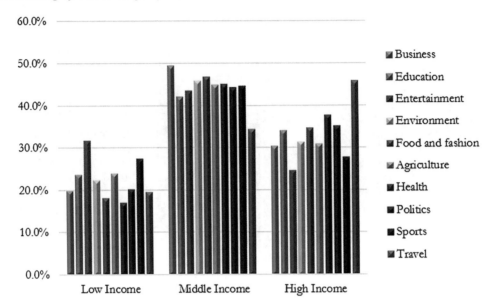

Research Question 2: Do Kenyans participate in online discussions?

Social media is an important part of most of the Kenyans' everyday lives. As such, people use various social media channels for a variety of reasons. One of the emerging area is robust online debates surrounding contemporary issues in the Kenya society. 67% of the study respondents indicated that they have used social media for online debates at least once (see Figure 6).

Figure 6. Kenyans participation in online discussions

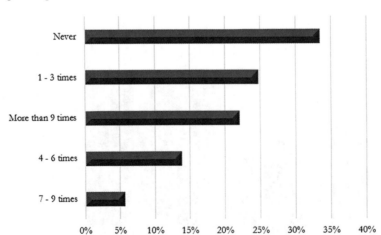

When the respondents were asked whether they have been influenced by their social media contacts, 43% indicated that their decisions have been swayed by their contacts on social media in the following four areas.

1. Politically - shifting from one political party to another.
2. Personal relationships - when making decision regarding personal social relationships.
3. Careers and jobs - when faced tough career decisions, online contacts can help you to regain self-control and make the best choice.
4. Life – when making make decisions while frustrated, the online contacts influences the choice one makes.

Findings From the Twitter Social Network Analysis and Visualization Using NodeXL

To successfully get Twitter social network analysis using NodeXL, one must follow these four steps: (1) Import and clean the data, (2) process the data, (3) calculate and refine the graph metrics (4) interpret the metrics. The study used NodeXL Version: 1.0.1.433.

Research Question 3: Are the Kenyan bloggers opinion leaders (influential actors) in online discussions among social media users?

To answer the research question, the researcher needed to:

1. Identify who are the most central users in Twitter's social networks involving the study blogs
2. Analyze the flow of information among the participants of online discussions involving the study blogs.

Data was collected using NodeXL Twitter Search Network data collector to get tweets having each of the study blogs hashtags, tweets, retweets or mentions. The NodeXL template was tasked to calculate matrices including "in-degree", "out-degree", "betweenness centrality", "density", "clustering coefficient", and "modularity" for each of the study bloggers.

- In-degree is the number of tweets that replied to or mentioned a user in question. In this sense, in-degree can be considered as a measure of popularity.
- Out-degree of a Twitter user account is simply the number of tweets that the user in question replies to or mentions in the network.
- Eigenvector centrality measures a node's connectedness to others who are also well-connected.
- Betweenness centrality describes the role of a node as a bridge or intermediary in the network.
- Closeness centrality. Closeness centrality indicates how much an actor would not be controlled by other actors. The lower the values of closeness centrality, the more central a node is in the network.

For each of the three study bloggers, NodeXL was used to calculate the values of in-degree, out-degree, eigenvector centrality, closeness centrality, and betweenness centrality. The bloggers' Twitter accounts were ranked according to their values of the five metrics among the blogs' network structure.

Network Structure Analysis for the Study Blogs

The network structure was analyzed quantitatively and represented visually using the Clauset-Newman-Moore Cluster layout algorithm and the Harel-Koren Fast Multi-scale layout algorithm, reducing the number of visible elements and minimizing the graphs' visual complexity (Smith, Rainie, Shneiderman, & Himelboim, 2014). This was followed by the calculation of the relevant metrics for each of the vertices. Vertices are nodes in the social network and represent keyword tags or web pages. Finally, the clustering coefficient was calculated and analyzed using a community detection algorithm resulting in visible clusters. Apart from vertices, edges are also a key concept in the social network. Edges are the links involving social interactions such as the hyperlinks. Therefore, an edge connects two vertices together. Edges are represented on a social network graph as a line connecting two vertices.

The FarmersTrend Blog - https://farmerstrend.co.ke/, @FarmersTrend

The mined @*FarmersTrend* network structure contained a total of 898 edges (including 557 unique edges and 341 edges with duplicates) and 144 vertices identified using NodeXL. The edges in this study were

Figure 7. The Betweenness Centrality network structure of '@FarmersTrend'

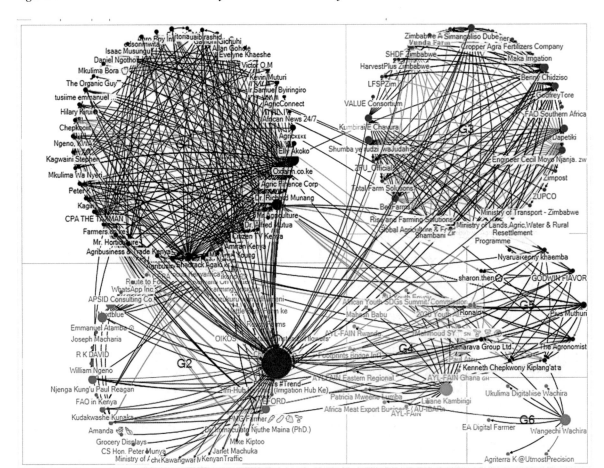

all presented as directed edges. These mined edges included Replies to, Mentions, Retweet, Mentions in Retweet, and Tweets. Figure 7 illustrates the network graph according to the Harel-Koren multiscale layout algorithm, a visual representation of the overall networked data from *@FarmersTrend* showing the clusters and clearly indicating the influencers on the social network. Each circle corresponds to a node or Twitter user, the size and opacity of each user is proportional to their betweenness centrality value, while the color corresponds to sub-communities or clusters automatically identified. The larger circles made of connected nodes represent a group.

Online discussions' influencers in an online social network structure are the users with many "in-degree" and few "out-degree" links. FarmersTrend is number one in the in-degree and number twenty-five in the out-degree an indication of opinion leadership. Higher eigenvector centrality indicates quality connections with other users who are well connected. FarmersTrend has the highest eigenvector among Twitter users in the network structure. "Betweenness and eigenvector centralities have very desirable properties for the location of an influencing potential" (Litterio et al., 2017, pp. 355). A member of the Online Social Network Structure network who simultaneously meets the highest values of both betweenness and eigenvector centrality are classified as influencers, hence the FarmersTrend blog is an influencer among Twitter users in the Kenyan blogosphere. Table 1, provides a summary of the FarmersTrend blog social network graph metrics.

Table 1. Graph metrics for the FarmersTrend

Blog	In Degree	Out Degree	Betweenness Centrality	Closeness Centrality	Eigenvector Centrality	PageRank
@ FarmersTrend	60	11	12219.904	0.005	0.042	7.092

Ghafla Kenya - https://www.ghafla.com/ke, @GhaflaKenya

Ghafla Kenya is a Kenyan entertainment blog. The mined *@GhaflaKenya'* network structure, had a total of 2117 edges (including 355 unique edges and 1762 edges with duplicates) and 307 vertices identified using NodeXL. The edges in this study were all presented as directed edges. These mined edges included Replies to, Mentions, Retweet, Mentions in Retweet, and Tweets. Figure 8 illustrates the network graph representation of the overall networked data from the *@GhaflaKenya*. *@GhaflaKenya* is number one in the in-degree and number sixty-two in the out-degree an indication of opinion leadership. Ghafla also has the highest eigenvector among Twitter users in the network structure. This is an indication that *Ghafla Kenya* satisfies the requirement of an online influencer by Litterio et al., (2017) which indicates that a social media user who simultaneously meets the highest values of both betweenness and eigenvector

Table 2. Graph metrics for the GhaflaKenya

Blog	In-Degree	Out-Degree	Betweenness Centrality	Closeness Centrality	Eigenvector Centrality	PageRank
@GhaflaKenya	215	2	88786.598	0.003	0.045	60.869

centrality is classified an influencer, hence the *Ghafla Kenya* blog is an influencer among Twitter users in the Kenyan blogosphere. Table 2, provides a summary of *Ghafla's* social network graph metrics.

KahawaTungu - https://www.kahawatungu.com/, @KahawaTungu

KahawaTungu is a social issue, politics, and active citizenship blog. The mined '@KahawaTungu' network structure, had a total of 1062 edges (including 613 unique edges and 449 edges with duplicates) and 286 vertices identified using NodeXL. The edges in this study were all presented as directed edges. These mined edges included Replies to, Mentions, Retweet, Mentions in Retweet, and Tweets. Figure 9 illustrates the network graph representation of the overall networked data from the @*KahawaTungu*. One unique feature of the *KahawaTungu* network structure is that there are many isolates. Isolates like to mention or retweet influencers in the network and have low connectivity in the network. @*Kahawa-Tungu* is number one in the in-degree and number thirty sixty in the out-degree an indication of opinion leadership. @*KahawaTungu* also has the highest eigenvector among Twitter users in the network structure. This is an indication that KahawaTungu satisfies the requirement of an online influencer by Litterio et al., (2017) which indicates that a social media user who simultaneously meets the highest

Figure 8. Betweenness Centrality network structure of '@GhaflaKenya'

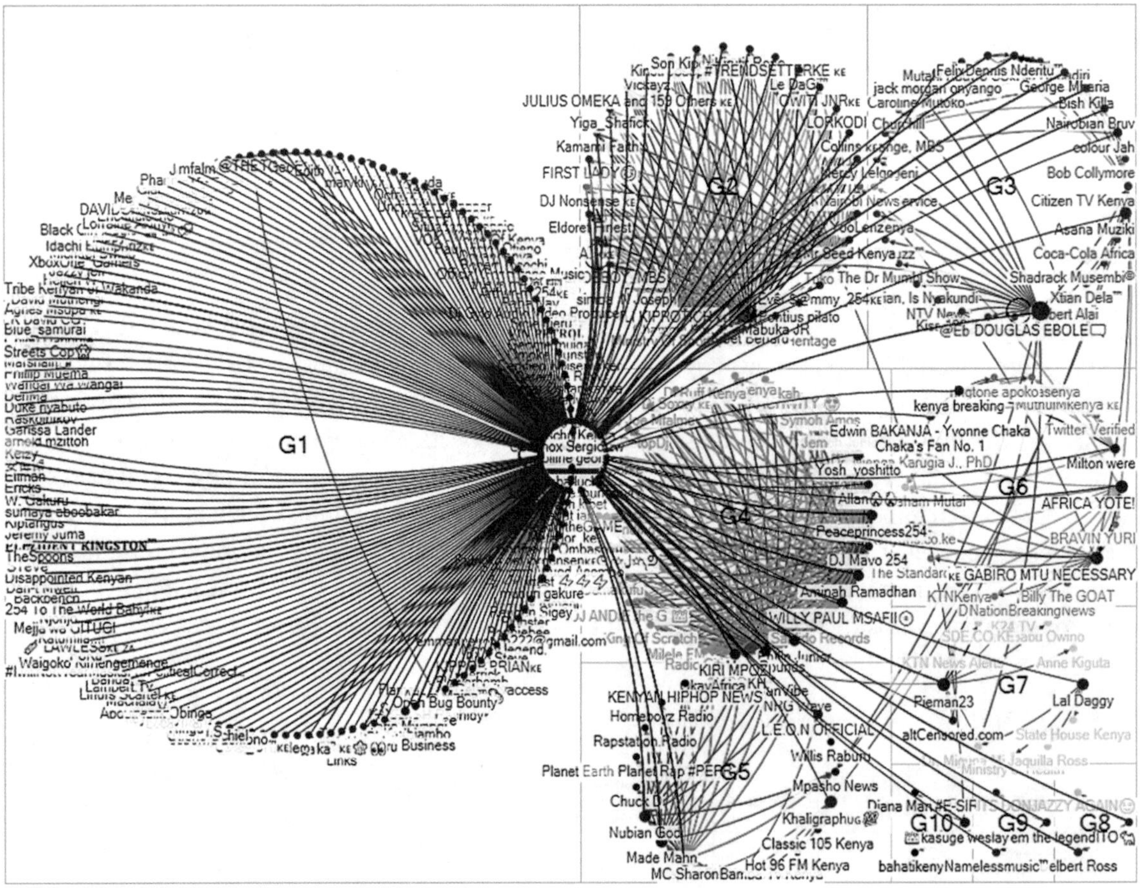

values of both betweenness and eigenvector centrality is classified an influencer, hence *@KahawaTungu* blog is an influencer among Twitter users in the Kenyan blogosphere. Table 3, provides a summary of *KahawaTungu's* social network graph metrics.

Table 3. Graph metrics for the KahawaTungu

Blog	In-Degree	Out-Degree	Betweenness Centrality	Closeness Centrality	Eigenvector Centrality	PageRank
KahawaTungu	225	3	58895.238	0.003	0.040	51.390

Kachwanya - https://www.kachwanya.com/, @kachwanya

Kachwanya as a blog provides tech gadget reviews, business IT news updates, discussions, reviews, and opinions on daily IT and business and innovation trends. The mined *@kachwanya* network structure

Figure 9. The Betweenness Centrality network structure of '@KahawaTungu'

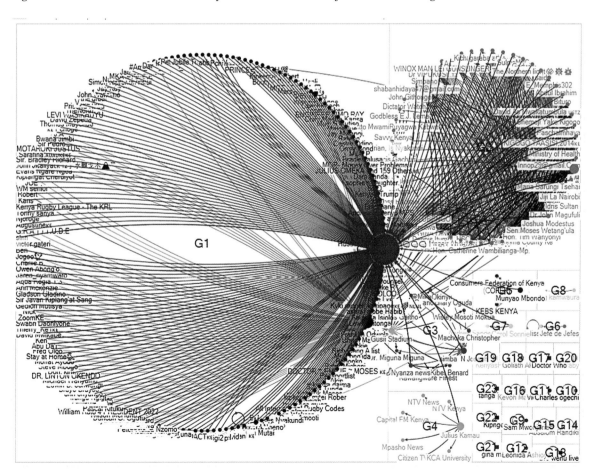

had a total of 1876 edges (including 967 unique edges and 909 edges with duplicates) and 396 vertices identified using NodeXL. The edges in this study were all presented as directed edges. These mined edges included Replies to, Mentions, Retweet, Mentions in Retweet, and Tweets. Figure 10 illustrates the network graph representation of the overall networked data from the *@kachwanya*. *@ kachwanya* is number one in the in-degree and also has the highest eigenvector among the Twitter users in the network structure. This is an indication that *Kachwanya* satisfies the requirement of an online influencer by Litterio et al., (2017) which indicates that a social media user who simultaneously meets the highest values of both betweenness and eigenvector centrality is classified an influencer, hence the *kachwanya* blog is an influencer among Twitter users in the Kenyan blogosphere. Table 4 provides a summary of *kachwanya's* blog social network graph metrics.

Table 4. Graph Metrics for the Kachwanya blog

Blog	In-Degree	Out-Degree	Betweenness Centrality	Closeness Centrality	Eigenvector Centrality	PageRank
@Kachwanya	331	28	144128.770	0.002	0.034	71.987

DISCUSSIONS

Kenyans read a diverse set of online blogs including entertainment, education business, sports, politics, health, agriculture, travel, environment food, and fashion with entertainment blogs being the most read type of blog. The Kenyan bloggers' community is mainly synonymous with political bloggers as most of the passionate and opinionated bloggers are political bloggers. However, the assumption that most Kenyans read political blogs than any other kind of blogs is not correct as the study found that there are many more exciting blogs on matters education, fashion, food, agriculture, entertainment, sports, and travel in the Kenyan blogosphere. Politics blogs rank fifth among the top ten most commonly read blogs in Kenya after entertainment, education, business, and sports blogs.

There are clear and significant distinctions in the type of blogs people read based on demographics such as gender, income levels, and geographical location. While the rural population mostly read the sports and entertainment blogs, urban residents read travel and food and fashion blogs which is a direct opposite in blogs' preferences by the population of these two different geolocations. Based on the gender of blog readers, most women read food, fashion, and travel blogs while men mostly read sports and politics blogs. Residents of low-income neighborhoods in Nairobi mostly read entertainment and sports blogs while those of the middle-income housing estates read business, food, and fashion blogs. The residents of the high-income residential areas read travel and health blogs. Therefore, demographic factors can be a determinant of the blogs people read as the study found dissimilarity in the types of blogs read based by different demographic groups.

By performing social network analysis on social media data mined from the Twitter platform, the study was able to show that the *KahawaTungu* blog is an influencer in the Kenyan blogosphere for the people interested in politics and social issues while *Ghafla Kenya* is an influencer of people interested in entertainment. The study also found that the *Kachwanya* blog influences people who are interested in technologies and innovations while the *FarmTrends* blog influences people interested in agriculture

Figure 10. The Betweenness Centrality network structure of '@kachwanya'

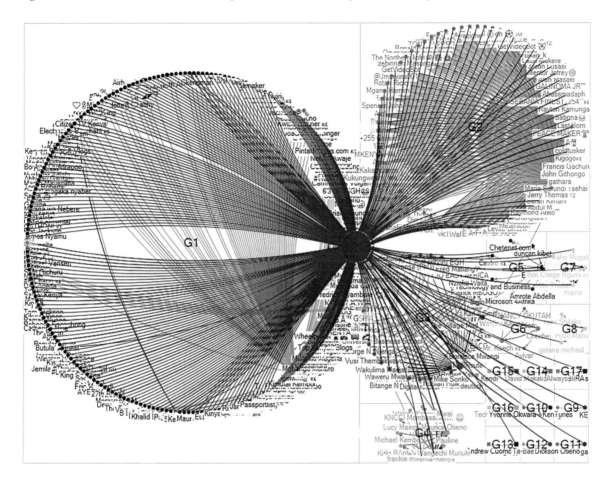

and farming. From the study, Kenyan bloggers influence social media users and engage in online discussions using multiple social media platforms, especially on blogs and Twitter. This is a good reason to trust that Kenyan bloggers can use social media platforms to fight for social justice as many bloggers have done globally.

CONCLUSION

The study has established that social media platforms have become a popular medium for online debates and discussions among Kenyans. Further, the study has shown that blogs are very popular social media platforms among Kenyans where people share topical content online. The study has also illustrated the applicability of social network analysis in determining influence among social media users by using NodeXL to visualize the structure of online conversation on Twitter and identifying prominent opinion leaders in the Kenyan Blogosphere. Identifying social network influencers could be used to raise awareness among a target audience by building conversations on a particular topic of interest. Future studies should seek to compare the influence of individuals across multiple social media platforms to understand whether one individual could have the same level of influence in multiple distinct social media platforms within the same population.

ACKNOWLEDGMENT

The author acknowledges the support of the National Research Fund, Kenya under Grant NRF/1/ MMC/418 and SIMElab Africa, a project hosted by the School of Science at USIU-Africa and funded by the US Embassy in Nairobi.

REFERENCES

Aharony, N. (2012). Twitter use by three political leaders: An exploratory analysis. *Online Information Review*, *36*(4), 587–603. doi:10.1108/14684521211254086

Ahmed, W., Bath, P. A., & Demartini, G. (2017). Using Twitter as a Data Source: An Overview of Ethical, Legal, and Methodological Challenges. In The Ethics of Online Research (Advances in Research Ethics and Integrity, Vol. 2). Emerald Publishing Limited. doi:10.1108/S2398-601820180000002004

Akrouf, S., Meriem, L., Yahia, B., & Eddine, M. N. (2013). Social Network Analysis and Information Propagation: A Case Study Using Flickr and YouTube Networks. *International Journal of Future Computer and Communication*, *2*(3), 246–252. doi:10.7763/IJFCC.2013.V2.161

An, J., Cha, M., Gummadi, K., & Crowcroft, J. (2011). Media landscape in twitter: a world of and political diversity. In *Proceedings of the Fifth International AAAI Conference on Weblogs and Social Media in Barcelona, Spain*. The AAAI Press.

Anger, I., & Kittl, C. (2011). Measuring influence on Twitter, In *Proceedings of the 11th International Conference on Knowledge Management and Knowledge Technologies (i-KNOW '11)*. ACM.

Baek, S. I., & Kim, Y. M. (2015). Longitudinal analysis of online community dynamics. *Industrial Management & Data Systems*, *115*(4), 661–677. doi:10.1108/IMDS-09-2014-0266

Baker, J. R., & Moore, S. M. (2008). Blogging as a social tool: A psychosocial examination of the effects of blogging. *Cyberpsychology & Behavior*, *11*(6), 747–749. doi:10.1089/cpb.2008.0053

Bigonha, C. A. S., Cardoso, T. N. C., Moro, M. M., Gonçalves, M. A., & Almeida, V. A. F. (2012). Sentiment-based influence detection on Twitter. *Journal of the Brazilian Computer Society*, *18*(3), 169–183. doi:10.100713173-011-0051-5

Bloggers Association of Kenya (BAKE). (2015). State of Blogging & Social Media in Kenya 2015 Report. *Bloggers Association of Kenya (BAKE)*.

Bloggers Association of Kenya (BAKE) (2016). State of the Internet in Kenya 2016 Report. *Bloggers Association of Kenya (BAKE)*.

Bravo, R. B., & Del Valle, M. E. (2017). Opinion leadership in parliamentary twitter networks: A matter of layers of interaction? *Journal of Information Technology & Politics*, *14*(3), 263–276. doi:10.1080/1 9331681.2017.1337602

Brummette, J., & Fussell Sisco, H. (2018). Holy guacamole! Framing and the Chipotle contamination issue. *Journal of Communication Management*, *22*(3), 280–295. doi:10.1108/JCOM-08-2017-0085

Bruns, A., & Burgess, J. (2012). Researching News Discussion on Twitter. *Journalism Studies*, *13*(5-6), 801–814. doi:10.1080/1461670X.2012.664428

Campbell, H. (2010, July 4). *Visualizing Email Communications using NodeXL*. Retrieved June 01, 2020, from http://ichromatiq.blogspot.com/2010/07/visualizing-email-communications-using.html

Cha, M., Haddadi, H., Benevenuto, F., & Gummadi, P. K. (2010). Measuring User Influence in Twitter: The Million Follower Fallacy. *Proceedings of the Fourth International Conference on Weblogs and Social Media (ICWSM 2010)*.

Ch'ng, E. (2015). The bottom-up formation and maintenance of a twitter community: Analysis of the# freejahar twitter community. *Industrial Management & Data Systems*, *115*(4), 612–624. doi:10.1108/ IMDS-11-2014-0332

Chesney, T., & Su, D. K. S. (2010). The impact of anonymity on weblog credibility. *International Journal of Human-Computer Studies*, *68*(10), 710–718. doi:10.1016/j.ijhcs.2010.06.001

Choi, M., Sang, Y., & Woo, H. (2014). Exploring political discussions by Korean twitter users A look at opinion leadership and homophily phenomenon. *ParkAslib Journal of Information Management*, *66*(6), 582–602. doi:10.1108/AJIM-11-2012-0089

Clauset, A., Newman, M. E. J., & Moore, C. (2004). Finding community structure in very large networks. *Physical Review. E*, *70*(6), 066111. doi:10.1103/PhysRevE.70.066111

Ferra, I., & Nguyen, D. (2017). #Migrantcrisis: "Tagging" the European migration crisis on Twitter. *Journal of Communication Management*, *21*(4), 411–426. doi:10.1108/JCOM-02-2017-0026

Francalanci, C., & Hussain, A. (2017). Influence-based Twitter browsing with NavigTweet. *Information Systems*, *64*, 119–131. doi:10.1016/j.is.2016.07.012

Freberg, K., Graham, K., McGaughey, K., & Freberg, L. (2011). Who are the social media influencers?: A study of public perceptions of personality. *Public Relations Review*, *37*(1), 90–92. doi:10.1016/j. pubrev.2010.11.001

Grandjean, M. (2016). A social network analysis of Twitter: Mapping the digital humanities community. *Cogent Arts & Humanities*, *3*(1), 1171458. doi:10.1080/23311983.2016.1171458

Hanchard, S. (2019, April 24). *PR and communications network analysis with NodeXL and Netlytic*. Retrieved June 01, 2020, from http://www.dataviz.my/2019/04/24/pr-and-communications-network-analysis-with-nodexl-and-netlytic/

Harel, D., & Koren, Y. (2001). A Fast Multi-Scale Method for Drawing Large Graphs. *Graph Drawing*, 183–196.

Herring, S. C., Scheidt, L. A., Wright, E., & Bonus, S. (2005). Weblogs as a bridging genre. *Information Technology & People, 18*(2), 142–171. doi:10.1108/09593840510601513

Hitesh, S., Hayden, W., Lei, C. & Carl, R. (2018). A New Framework for Securing, Extracting and Analyzing Big Forensic Data. *Journal of Digital Forensics, Security and Law, 13*(2), Article 6.

Hsu, C. L., & Lin, J. C. (2008). Acceptance of blog usage: The roles of technology acceptance, social influence and knowledge sharing motivation. *Information & Management, 45*(1), 65–74. doi:10.1016/j.im.2007.11.001

Ignacio Criado, J., Martı'nez-Fuentes, G., & Silva'n, A. (2011). Social media for political campaigning. Theuse of Twitter by Spanish Mayors in 2011 local elections. In C. G. Reddick & S. K. Aikins (Eds.), *Web 2.0 Technologies and Democratic Governance, Public Administration and Information Technology* (pp. 219–232). Springer.

Jackson, N. (2006). Dipping their big toe into the blogosphere: The use of weblogs by the political parties in the 2005 general election. *Aslib Proceedings, 58*(4), 292–303. doi:10.1108/00012530610687678

Jackson, N., & Lilleker, D. (2011). Microblogging, constituency service and impression management: UK MPs and the use of Twitter. *Journal of Legislative Studies, 17*(1), 86–105. doi:10.1080/13572334.2011.545181

Karanja, J. M. (2016). *Using Blogs to Create a Competitive Advantage: A Case of the Blogging Industry in Kenya* (MBA thesis). USIU-Africa, Nairobi, Kenya. Retrieved from http://erepo.usiu.ac.ke/11732/2826

Keib, K., Himelboim, I., & Han, J. Y. (2018). Important tweets matter: Predicting retweets in the #BlackLivesMatter talk on Twitter. *Computers in Human Behavior, 85*, 106–115. doi:10.1016/j.chb.2018.03.025

Kim, M., & Park, H. (2012). Measuring Twitter-based political participation and deliberation in the South Korean context by using social network and Triple Helix indicators. *Scientometrics, 90*(1), 121–140. doi:10.100711192-011-0508-5

Kranzberg, M. (1986). Technology and History: Kranzberg's Laws. *Technology and Culture, 27*(3), 547. doi:10.2307/3105385

Lange, C., Bojars, U., Groza, T., Breslin, J., & Handschuh, S. (2008). Expressing argumentative discussions in social media sites. *Social Data on the Web (SDoW2008), Workshop at the 7th Int. Semantic Web Conference.*

Maarit, M. & Kuira, M. W. (2008). Social Media and Post-Election Crisis in Kenya. *Information & Communication Technology-Africa, 13.*

Mahmoudi, A., Yaakub, M. R., & Bakar, A. A. (2018). New time-based model to identify the influential users in online social networks. *Data Technologies and Applications, 52*(2), 278–290. doi:10.1108/DTA-08-2017-0056

Mustafaraj, E., & Metaxas, P. (2010). From obscurity to prominence in minutes: political speech and real-time search. *Proceedings of the WebSci10: Extending the Frontiers of Society On-Line.*

Razis, G., Anagnostopoulos, I., & Zeadally, S. (2020). Modeling Influence with Semantics in Social Networks: A Survey. *ACM Computing Surveys, 53*(1), 7.

Riquelme, F., & Cantergiani, P. G. (2016). Measuring user influence on Twitter. *Information Processing & Management, 52*(5), 949–975. doi:10.1016/j.ipm.2016.04.003

Rosenthal, S. (2014). Detecting influencers in social media discussions. *XRDS: Crossroads, 21*(1), 40–45. doi:10.1145/2659889

Rosenthal, S., & Mckeown, K. (2017). Detecting Influencers in Multiple Online Genres. *ACM Transactions on Internet Technology, 17*(2), 12. doi:10.1145/3014164

Sanawi, J., Samani, M. C., & Taibi, M. (2017). #Vaccination: Identifying Influencers in the Vaccination Discussion on Twitter Through Social Network Visualisation. *International Journal of Business and Society, 8*(S4), 718–726.

Sánchez-Villar, J., Bigné, E., & Aldás-Manzano, J. (2017). Blog influence and political activism: An emerging and integrative model. *Spanish Journal of Marketing, 21*(2), 102–116. doi:10.1016/j.sjme.2017.02.002

Sakaki, T., Okazaki, M., & Matsuo, Y. (2010). Earthquake shakes Twitter users: Real-time event detection by social sensors. *World Wide Web (Bussum)*, 851–860.

Smith, M. A., Rainie, L., Shneiderman, B., & Himelboim, I. (2014). Mapping Twitter topic networks: From polarized crowds to community clusters. *Pew Research Center, 20*, 1–56.

Struweg, I. (2018). # Liberty breach: an exploratory usage case of NodeXL Pro as a social media analytics tool for Twitter. *ICMBD Conference Proceedings*, 153-163.

Sæbø, Ø. (2011). Understanding twittere use among parliament representatives: a genre analysis. In *Proceedings of the Third IFIP WG 8.5 International Conference on Electronic Participation*. Springer.

S'kilters, J., Kreile, M., Bojaˉrs, U., Briksˇe, I., Pencis, J., & Uzule, L. (2012). The pragmatics of political messages in Twitter communication. In The Semantic Web: ESWC 2011 Workshops. Springer.

Tan, L. K.-W., & Na, J.-C. (2013). Bloggers' Influence Style within Blog. *Journal of Information Science Theory and Practice, 1*(2), 36–57. doi:10.1633/JISTaP.2013.1.2.3

Tumasjan, A., Sprenger, T. O., Sandncr, P. G., & Welpe, I. M. (2011). Election forecasts with Twitter – how 140 characters reflect the political landscape. *Social Science Computer Review, 29*(4), 402–418. doi:10.1177/0894439310386557

Turcotte, J., York, C., Irving, J., Scholl, R. M., & Pingree, R. J. (2015). News recommendations from social media opinion leaders: Effects on media trust and information seeking. *Journal of Computer-Mediated Communication, 20*(5), 520–535. doi:10.1111/jcc4.12127

Valente, T. W. (2010). *Social Networks and Health: Models, Methods, and Applications*. Oxford University. doi:10.1093/acprof:oso/9780195301014.001.0001

Wasserman, S., & Faust, K. (1994). *Social network analysis: Methods and applications*. Cambridge University Press. doi:10.1017/CBO9780511815478

Williams, H. T. P., McMurray, J. R., Kurz, T., & Lambert, T. H. (2015). Network analysis reveals open forums and echo chambers in social media discussions of climate change. *Global Environmental Change, 32,* 126–138. doi:10.1016/j.gloenvcha.2015.03.006

Winner, L. (2009). Do Artifacts have Politics. In *Readings in the Philosophy of Technology* (pp. 251–263). Rowman & Littlefield Publishers.

Wu, S., Hofman, J. M., Mason, W. A., & Watts, D. J. (2011). Who says what to whom on twitter. In *Proceedings of the 20th International Conference on World Wide Web in Hyderabad.* ACM. 10.1145/1963405.1963504

Xu, W. W., Sang, Y., Blasiola, S., & Park, H. W. (2014). Predicting opinion leaders in twitter activism networks: The case of the Wisconsin recall election. *The American Behavioral Scientist, 58*(10), 1278–1293. doi:10.1177/0002764214527091

Yep, J., & Shulman, J. (2014). Analyzing the library's Twitter network Using NodeXL to visualize impact. *ACRL TechConnect, 75*(4), 177–186.

Chapter 14
Golden Years in Social Media World:
Examining Behavior and Motivations

Sandra Lopes Miranda

School of Communication and Media Studies, Lisbon Polytechnic Institute, Portugal

Ana Cristina Antunes

https://orcid.org/0000-0001-8983-2062

School of Communication and Media Studies, Lisbon Polytechnic Institute, Portugal

ABSTRACT

The context of demographic aging, combined with the wide dissemination of information and communication technologies (ICT), in the various domains of society defined a set of challenges, potentialities, and limits for seniors (65+). Although there is a positive evolution regarding adhesion and even domestication of ICT by this age segment, namely the internet and digital social networking sites, the literature review presents us with an immature, limited, and fragmented field of study, comprising an immense space of evolution. Aware of the strength, magnitude, and considerable ignorance of the action of seniors in the network society, this chapter intends to map, through a review of the multidisciplinary literature, how the relationship of seniors with ICTs is configured. In addition, usage behavior, as well as the drivers, and the consequences for the elderly of navigating digital social networks are also analyzed.

INTRODUCTION

The context of demographic aging on a large scale (in developed and developing countries) combined with the relevant role of networked ICTs in several areas of society, to study the relationship of the senior population with ICTs and with digital social networks takes on particular relevance.

It is undeniable that ICT currently occupies a preponderant place in contemporary societies, and the existing literature conceptualizes and discusses the rapid evolution of advanced high-tech societies in networked information societies, as a new form of social organization (Castells, 2003; Van Dijk, 2005).

DOI: 10.4018/978-1-7998-4718-2.ch014

The expansion and evolution to the web 2.0, associated with interactivity and the concept of network, enabled a more active role for the user, integrating the possibility of content production and interaction, as well as the expansion of the communication modalities, the possibilities of connection and social relationship (O'Reilly, 2007).

But if technological evolution can be assumed as an element that facilitates processes and connections, it can also be a potentiator of social exclusion and a reflection of inequalities in access to benefits (Coelho, 2019). Despite the growth in all age groups, it is older people who least use the internet and digital social networks (Páscoa & Gil, 2015). As Cardoso et al. (2015, p. 359) say, "what a decade ago was an embryonic process has now become a widespread reality". In fact, despite an effort to domesticate ICT, seniors, doubly disadvantaged by patterns of inequality (Coelho, 2019), are further removed from the Internet and social networking sites, so it is urgent to scrutinize the dynamics associated with this phenomenon.

Contents of this chapter encompass issues related to the aging problem in Europe (and across the world), articulating the theme of Network Society and ICT with the digital inclusion and literacy of seniors - its benefits and challenges, and discusses the reasons, motivations and effects of the relationship that this group establishes with digital social networks.

SENIORS AND THE CHALLENGE OF INFORMATION AND COMMUNICATION TECHNOLOGIES (ICT)

Contemporary societies experience a market demographic aging process in developed countries and this global demographic megatrend has inspired studies in different areas of knowledge. According to the World Population Prospects study (United Nations, 2020) - this aging wave that we are experiencing is an unprecedented phenomenon in human history. Today, there are 703 million persons aged 65 years or over in the world. This number is projected to double to 1,5 billion in 2050. In the European Union (EU), ageing population is one of the major challenges that many of its member states must face in the next decade. Enhanced life expectancy and decreasing fertility rates result in an increased number and proportion of older adults. Data provided by the European Commission (2019) estimates that in 2060, 1 in 3 European citizens will be 65 years old or older.

The dual dimension of aging, the individual level and the population level, led to a paradigm shift based on the notion that since life is longer, it must be lived in an "active" way. The challenge launched in 2002 by the World Health Organization (WHO), in the document "Active aging. A policy framework", has appealed to the need to foresee aging from a holistic and optimistic point of view, one that aims at quality of life, to the detriment of a pessimistic view characterized by successive losses both physically, mentally and socially. It is about promoting an active and competent aging based on a series of social and personal conditions that involve commitment to life, making elderly citizens proactive, regulating their quality of life through active participation in economic, civic, technological, cultural or even spiritual issues, and in the definition of social policies (Pinheiro & Areosa, 2018). The challenge is to ensure that aging occurs with quality in all areas and that this stage of life is an asset for society.

As we watch the planetary aging process of the population, we observe the internet drawing on the fabric of our lives (Castells, 2003), acknowledging the inevitability of Information and Communication Technologies (ICT), installed as new modalities of social organization (Van Dijk, 2006), assuming an ubiquitous position in our world, to the point of being essential in the most diverse spheres of our lives.

The preponderance and ubiquity of new technologies means that today there is no option regarding the use or not of technological devices, since the migration from the real to the digital is already an irreversible scenario - after all, all paths will lead to the web!

To Jan van Dijk (2006), the ICT revolution "with little exaggeration, we may call the 21st century the age of networks. Networks are becoming the nervous system of our society, and we can expect this infrastructure to have more influence on our entire social and personal lives them did the construction of roads for the transportation of goods and people in the past" (p. 2).

It is this network society, this screens society (Castells, 2009) that contributed to the modification of the classic models of information dissemination, transformed agents into potential producers, transmitters and receivers of information. In addition, it created new communicational logics, facilitated communicative autonomy (Cardoso, 2009), and made online social networks into new territories that amplify sociability and reconfigure life projects (Alvarenga, Yassuda & Cachioni, 2019). This perspective of the network society is marked by the presence of some authors who try to counter the idea that the internet has come to untie social ties and contribute to the isolation of individuals. For example, Cardoso et al. (2015) argue that social networking sites can enhance the strengthening and multiplication of social ties, and that the combination of face-to-face and virtual relationships should be seen as accumulative and not as substitutes for each other. On the other hand, some of the literature puts the emphasis on the inequalities that ICT has been provoking, assuming that technological innovation accompanies and reproduces previously existing stratification and inequality processes (Hargittai & Hsieh, 2013), and may even promote processes of social polarization (Flores-Gomes, 2019) accentuating the digital divide (Hargittai, 2003). According to Hargittai (2003), as ICT and the internet have been installed as a rising tide in all spheres of society, segments of the population stand out that reveal greater difficulties in their access and use, as is the case of the so-called digital immigrants (Prensky, 2001) namely older generations - a group often excluded from contact with the internet (Coelho, 2019).

As Marc Prensky (2001) explains, "The "digital immigrant accent" can be seen in such things as turning to the Internet for information second rather than first, or in reading the manual for a program rather than assuming that the program itself will teach us to use it. Today's older folk were "socialized" differently from their kids and are now in the process of learning a new language. And a language learned later in life, scientists tell us, goes into a different part of the brain" (p. 2). This means that, when compared to digital natives, late contact with communication mediation technologies makes digital immigrants more distant and with more difficulties in dealing with ICT, removing the possibility of exercising an active and full citizenship, with all the consequences that such deprivation can have on the quality of life and well-being. Van Dijk and Hacker (2003) add that the lack of elementary digital experience and the lack of significant use opportunities (frequency) are also weight factors to take into account the digital divide.

At the limit, we can witness the phenomena of social exclusion as a direct consequence of a digital exclusion (Gil, 2019), since the internet structure develops in open dialogue with the existing economic and social inequalities, and it can not only reproduce these inequalities but also aggravate them (Witte & Mannon, 2010). For Rosa (2001), the obstacle is not so much the aging of the population, but rather the difficulties that societies are experiencing in adjusting to this demographic change, verifying that, in a more or less explicit way, there is an effective discrimination against older people which is mainly due to the outdated knowledge associated with new technologies. Despite the advances, there is clearly a markedly negative societal discourse about the elderly that highlights situations of scientific and technological literacy reproducing the widespread acceptance that this segment does not want or is unable to use the internet (Coelho, 2019; Mauriti, 2004).It is relevant to note that the age-based digital divide comprehends at least two distinct levels. On one hand, this digital divide differentiates between digital and internet users and non-users. Another division is related to the skills and abilities required for ICT use (e.g., Hargittai, 2002). It should be noted that having access to the Internet is not enough to claim that there is an effective digital inclusion. Equally or more important than access is ensuring that individuals have the necessary skills to be able to make proper use of digital resources. As Castells (2012) stated, the reality of info-exclusion goes beyond simple access to the internet. It is necessary to consider all the consequences that of such access. This means that digital literacy and skills cannot be framed in a perspective of mere instrumental use but rather in a social practice, that is, properly framed in a socio-affective-economic-cultural context for users to question the objectives and purposes this 'functionality' and this 'utility' (Gil, 2019). Dias adds, "to include, technologically, it means to apprehend the discourse of technology, not only in terms of execution and qualification, but also in the perspective of the subjects being able to influence the importance and purposes of digital technology itself" (Dias, 2012, p. 59).

According to Coelho (2019), and in harmony with Eurostat data (2016), under the surface of the expansion of the network society seethe dynamics intertwined with generations of inequalities. The distribution of internet use by age groups shows that in the case of individuals aged 65 and over the usage rate is close to 35% (use the internet at least once a week) and only 16% access online social networks. However, despite having an immense margin of progression, it appears that among the older generations the digitization rate has seen a positive evolution since in 2005 61% of the 65-74 year old people in Europe reported never to have used a computer or the internet (Demunter, 2006). Among the non-users, the main reason for not using these technologies is lack of skills (60%) and lack of interest and/or perception of little usefulness of this resource (22%). Rebelo (2013) points out that the lack of interest may be the result of a weak capacity for domestication (Silvestorne, 2003) and adaptation of technology to daily life, needs, habits, sensitivities and values of senior citizens.

It should be noted that, although age is, in itself, an explanatory factor for the digital exclusion, Loos (2012) warns that this issue is much more complex and multidetermined than it might seem at first, being fallacious to look at the elderly as a homogeneous group as individual differences vary as age advances. Recent studies document another digital division within this age group, the so-called grey digital divide, materialized in seniors' interindividual differences on frequency of use of ICT and participation in social media (Friemel, 2016; Lagacé et al., 2016). Besides age, Neves et al. (2013) conclude that a set of other factors influence the use of computers and mobile phones, such as education, that ends up even compensating for age. Variables such as gender and income level should also be considered. When analyzing gender differences in activities developed on the internet, Deursen and Helsper (2015) show that seniors are effectively a very diverse group and that the differences found are also due to education, household composition and attitude towards the Internet. Roberto et al. (2015) consider that the socioeconomic dimension and education should be considered as transversal and structural dimensions to analyze the phenomenon.

In addition, the reduced exposure to ICTs throughout life, the fact that older adults are outside the formal educational pathways, and the sensory and cognitive changes related to the aging process can constitute obstacles to the use of ICTs (Van Deursen & Van Dijk, 2014). In the wake of Loos, for White and Cornu (2011) attitudes, behaviors and usage practices are much more related to the level of motivation and context than to age. Coelho (2019) defends the need to study this reality in the sociological and cultural context where it develops, since the study of the relationship between the media and society must be based on social change and not on technological innovation (Livingstone, 1999). Perol et al. (2015)

add the importance of adding psychological cohort variables (such as cognitive age and technology anxiety) since they have a clear explanatory value in the development of expertise and skills in the elderly.

SENIORS AND SOCIAL MEDIA

Kaplan and Haenlein (2010) define social media as "a group of Internet-based applications that build on the ideological and technological foundations of Web 2.0 and that allow the creation and exchange of user generated content" (p. 61). By facilitating interactive communication and content exchange, this social sharing facilitates the development of social networks online and the creation of links among users and user-generated content in online environments (Obar & Wildman, 2015).

Reports and studies on social media use in later life clearly indicate that seniors are typically behind younger cohorts, regarding the percentage of social media users, number of platforms used and types of uses (Coto et al., 2017; Eurostat, 2019; Khoros, 2020; Pew Research Centre, 2019; Statista, 2020a). Albeit this trend, in the last decade we have witnessed a rising number of senior citizens as social media users, as well as the increasing amount of time spent per day by these users (Hutto et al., 2015; Yang et al., 2016).

In the European Union, and comparing numbers from this decade, while in 2010 18% of those aged between 55-74 years old used chat sites, blogs, or social networking sites, in 2019 this percentage rose to 29% (Eurostat, 2010, 2019). Considering senior citizens, in 2019 almost one fifth (19%) of people aged 65 to 74 years in EU-28 participated and interacted in social networking sites (Eurostat, 2019). Yet, there are significant differences between countries, since this share ranged from 8% in Bulgaria and 9% in Greece to 46% in Denmark. These generic statistics provided by the Eurostat (2019) are valuable but require a cautious analysis, since they blur the boundaries and neglect the specificities of the different social networking sites, uniting them into a single digital information.

Therefore, it is relevant to examine seniors' usage among some of these social networking sites, to understand their differentiated behaviors patterns. Considering the number of active users worldwide, Facebook, Youtube, and Instagram are some of the most popular social networking sites today (Statista, 2020b). When examining the use of these social media platforms by age group, the available data reveals that they are increasingly being used by the older adult population. Figures 1 and 2 show, respectively, the distribution of Facebook and Instagram users worldwide as of April 2020, by age and gender.

As can be observed in Table 1, of the 2.6 billion monthly active Facebook users worldwide, 2.25% are older adults (65+), with a slighter higher percentage of older women (2.4%) than their masculine counterparts (2.1%). Although by comparison with other age groups the 65+ age segment presents the lower percentage of active Facebook users, an analysis of these statistics in the last years suggests that this percentage has been steadily growing.

Instagram has now 1 billion monthly active users (Khoros, 2020) and according to the information contained in Table 2, approximately 1% of these are older adults (65+). According to the worldwide data available in Statista (2020d), there is a slightly higher percentage of older women (1.1%), as compared with men (0.8%), as verified with Facebook.

Country differences are also worth considering. In USA, the Pew Research Center (2019) examined social media platform usage by age and found that in 2018 46% of U.S.65+ adults reported using Facebook while 8% use Instagram. On the contrary, in Brazil more senior citizens (especially more women) use Instagram (2%) instead of Facebook (1.5%) (Statista, 2020e, 2020f). This landscape changes in India,

Figure 1. Distribution of Facebook users worldwide as of April 2020, by age and gender
Source – Statista (2020c)

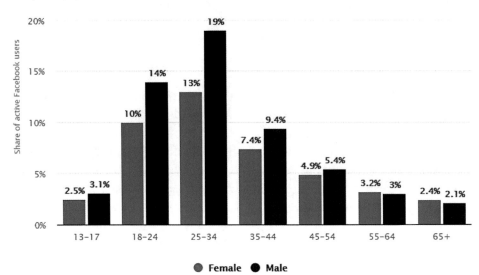

where there is approximately the double of senior men (350000) using Instagram than women (160000), corresponding to 0.2% vs. 0.1% of the population, respectively (NapoleonCat, 2019).

On what concerns Youtube, with more than 2 billion monthly active users (Youtube, n.d.), the 55+ age group seems to be one of the fastest growing YouTube demographics (Omnicore, 2020). In UK and USA, according to We Are Flint (2018) data, older groups use Youtube less than younger counterparts,

Figure 2. Distribution of Instagram users worldwide as of April 2020, by age and gender
Source – Statista (2020d)

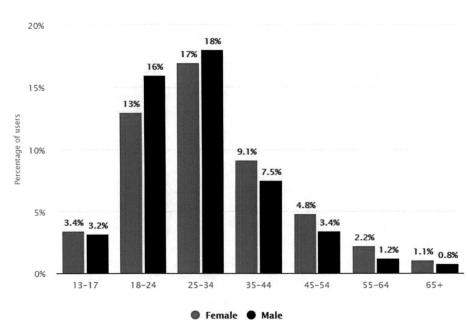

but its usage among older groups is still strong. In UK, 54% of the of 65-74-year-olds and 40% of the 75+ use Youtube. In USA, two thirds (66%) of users between 65-74 years old and 51 percent of people over the age of 75 are watching videos on YouTube, 51% on a daily basis (Pew Research Centre, 2019). In Japan, in 2019 approximately 41% of people between 60-69 years old used this platform, while in Latin America, during 2018, the share of Youtube users aged 61+ was significantly lower (11%) (Statista, 2020g, 2020h).

These sets of data suggest that there are major usage differences across social networking sites, with a marked global preference of seniors regarding Youtube and Facebook to the detriment of Instagram. Seniors social media usage behaviors also differs across countries. This requires further cross-cultural research, to examine and explain these diverse social media practices in later life, as performed in different parts of the world. Nimrod (2017) study has taken this cross-cultural stance in Europe. The results, based on a cross-European survey of 1039 Internet users aged 60 years and up, reveal that older Internet users are more inclined to use traditional mass media than new social media and prefer synchronous to asynchronous mass media. She also identified four subsegments and one of these, labelled *heavy AM* (Asynchronous Media) *users,* made an intense use of social media and was characterized by a relatively high level of education. Hutto et al. (2015) also examined the sociodemographic characteristics of US active older adult Facebook users. According with their findings, these were mostly female younger seniors, educated and with a higher income.

Bearing in mind that, as Castells (2009) points out, the demands of contemporary societies have placed education and lifelong learning as essential tools for personal development, and that social networking sites have become one of the main vehicles for this information, it is natural that seniors feel the need to take advantage of their potential as much as possible. In addition, the affordances available in Web 2.0 (O'Reilly, 2005) silence unidirectional communication and give voice to the bidirectional paradigm, which blurs the production-consumption distinction, resulting instead in an agglutination of both (Hiremath & Kenchakkanavar, 2016). That is, in addition to the number of users has increased exponentially, users have become prosumers (Yen & Dey, 2019). Nowadays, users are not solely passive receivers, but people that active and deliberately intervene in information and content production, give meanings and create digital identities, immersing themselves in a democratic culture of participation by all and for all. Web 2.0 has revolutionized the forms of interaction and communication between people, as well as contributed to their enrichment through discussions in virtual environments.

This digital environment is favorable and adjustable to seniors' needs and motivations. The literature reveals that, for the elderly, adherence to digital social networks is seen as a solution for social isolation, and for entertainment, but also allows the creation of new acquaintances and share of accumulated knowledge and experiences (Balcerzak et al., 2017; Nguyen & Fain, 2015; Nimrod, 2014; Rebelo, 2013; Yang et al., 2016). When investigating the reasons for the use of Facebook by the elderly, Ito (2001, p. 2) claimed that "they don't just look for information on the network, they seek affiliation, support and affirmation", providing support to the thesis that social networking sites "not only have a multiplier effect of contacts with family and friends, but it is also among their users that there are less occurrences of the feeling of being isolated from the world or depressed" (Cardoso et al., 2003, p.179).

According to Erickson (2011), Facebook is seen by older people as a privileged link with friends and family - strengthening (or even recovering) the affective and social bond they have with them, as well as intergenerational relationships. Moreover, digital social networks are a space to recover memories and establish links with the past, enabling reunions and the resumption of lost personal ties and contacts, sometimes for many years (Miranda et al., 2020).

For Barroso et al. (2015), social networking sites are digital tools that enhance the reinforcement and multiplication of social ties through constant dialogue with the past, multiplying contacts with people, friends and family to whom seniors had lost track. They also enable recovering memories of personal history, of places, photographs, music, traditions and experiences. In addition, seniors' adherence to social networking sites should be seen as fostering intergenerational relationships as it makes them more adept at decoding and participating in the world and the dialogues of younger people, but also because social networks socialization is, as a general rule, done by family members or younger friends.

Rebelo (2015) found that factors such as loneliness, the need to occupy free time and to understand what others talk about, in order to be able to participate in conversations and integrate communities, are pointed out as the main motives for older people to join social networking sites. Besides, the presence in a digital social network often leads to sharing and obtaining emotional support that go beyond the virtual domain, either this occurs in person and/or through other channels.

For Coelho (2019), and in harmony with the data of the Network Society in Portugal, there are three major reasons for enrolling in these digital platforms. The first two bring together motives directly associated with online sociability, such as the reinforcement of offline social ties (with people with whom you have regular contact or with people who are far away or who have not seen each other for a long time) and the possibility of sharing content with other people. The second integrates reasons related to the opportunity to build new relationships of sociability (meeting new people) but also avoid social exclusion. The third concerns an interventive participation in society and information dissemination, including the intention to promote events or social and political causes.

Besides seniors' interaction behavior and motives for social media use, some of the research efforts in this area have been focused on examining how social media affects senior citizens lives (Coto et al., 2017).

Fostering social inclusion and the strengthening of social ties are well documented effects of seniors' social media use. Social networking sites seem to have the potential to help facilitate social connectedness (e.g., Hutto et al., 2015), allowing older people to stay in contact and actively participate in society (Coto et al., 2017). Their use by the elderly increases their sense of belonging and perceived social support (Shaw & Gant, 2002; Silvia et al., 2018), as expected by these users (Eggermont et al., 2005). Older users of a social networking site also reported higher levels of social satisfaction than nonusers (Bell et al., 2013). Using digital social networks as a means of communication may even allow older adults with limited mobility to maintain social connections, ultimately contributing to their wellbeing (e.g., Choi & DiNitto, 2013). However, evidence of the relationship between social networking sites use and perceived loneliness in old age is mixed. Some evidence indicates no association between social media use and loneliness (Bell et al., 2013), while other studies found that social networking sites can prevent and/or alleviate social isolation and loneliness (e.g., Aarts et al., 2015; Hutto et al., 2015; Khosravi et al., 2016).

On the other hand, Nimrod (2017) defends that the seniors' digital prosumption enables them to remain not only socially but also mentally active, allowing them to express their interests and strengths. Although there are scarce studies on these subjects, elderly's mental health and cognitive functioning seem to derive several benefits from using social media. When examining diverse social technology uses by the elderly (among which is included the use of social media), Chopik (2016) found that a higher use was associated with a higher subjective well-being, along with other physical and mental health benefits, such as better self-rated health, fewer chronic illnesses, and fewer depressive symptoms. According to his findings, the links between social technology use and health was mediated by reduced loneliness, meaning that social networks can contribute to improve physical and mental health as long as they have the ability to minimize loneliness. On his analysis on how engagement in social media was related to cognitive functioning, specifically with processing speed, inhibitory control, and working memory, Quinn (2018) found a significant improvement in these cognitive domains for a group of older social media users. Results from the experimental study of Myhre et al. (2017) revealed that the elderly that were trained in and used Facebook for eight weeks had a significant increase in executive functioning associated with complex working memory tasks, although social support and other cognitive functions, like processing speed, showed no differential improvement.

Sims et al. (2017) found a positive relationship between ICT use and life satisfaction in later life. Focusing on social media use, Gaia et al. (2020) also identified a positive association between social networking sitess use and life satisfaction in old age. Additionally, seniors seem to be more satisfied with their social roles in life when they are active users of social media (Hutto et al., 2015).

On what concerns empowerment, digital technology is seen by senior citizens both as a tool to disempower and empower (Hill et al., 2015). Barak et al. (2008) argue that social media may contribute to older people's empowerment, while increasing their sense of control and self-efficacy. Disempowerment is related to the recognition that without the appropriate abilities and skills to use it or without adequate measures to tackle anxiety and fear of technology, the digital divide is likely to widen as more services migrate to the virtual world (Hill et al., 2015).

DISCUSSION

While young adults and adults have embraced digital technology, senior citizens are frequently depicted as non-users (e.g., McDonough, 2020; Neves et al., 2018), giving way to the so-called digital divide. Yet, as digital technology evolves and societies are ageing, this age segment has also been changing. Not only older adults show a tendency to evaluate the technology positively (e.g., Mitzner et al., 2018; Neves & Amaro, 2012), but also the internet and social media use among senior citizens has increased significantly in the last years (e.g., Eurostat, 2010, 2019; Khoros, 2020; Pew Research Centre, 2019; Statista, 2020a). Attending to internet and social media potential and its diverse positive consequences for the elderly, combined with the migration of many public and private sector services to an online delivery mode (McDonough, 2020), understanding the adoption and use of digital technology in later life have become pressing issues. The available data suggests that the percentage of elderly users of the most popular social networking sites, such as Facebook, Instagram, and Youtube, has been steadily growing globally.

Albeit this, our comprehension around the antecedents and consequences of social media use and their role in later life is still limited. In a systematic review, Coto et al. (2017) have already identified some research fragilities in this field. Nimrod (2017) also criticizes the fact that many studies that examine internet use in later life treat the internet as a single medium, without differentiating between the various functions and activities it allows. Our analysis of the extant literature reveals a fragmented and atomistic perspective on this senior-social media relationship, focused on understanding their motives of use and social media impact on specific dimensions of seniors' lives (e.g., on the social dimension).

Regarding its antecedents, their social value appears to be one of the main motives of use. Social networking sites are regarded as digital tools that enhance the reinforcement and multiplication of social ties (Barroso et al., 2015; Cardoso et al., 2015) strengthening the affective and social bond with family and friends, but also providing an opportunity to build new relationships and avoid social exclusion (Coelho, 2019). These digital platforms have become spaces to recover memories and establish links with the past, enabling the recovery of lost personal ties and contacts (Miranda et al., 2020). Social media also allows older adults to express themselves and enables an interventive participation in society and information dissemination, including the intention to promote events or social and political causes (e.g., Coelho, 2019; Lin & Chou, 2014). In general, older adults acknowledge that social media improves their digital literacy and skills and promotes opportunities for information search and knowledge sharing, fostering communication exchange and relationship building (Bell et al., 2013; Coto et al., 2017).

There are several studies that have examined the impact of social media use in later life. Such studies focused on several key issues, such as the positive effects of social networking sites on the social sphere, by reducing social isolation, facilitating social connectedness and increasing the sense of belonging and perceived social support (Aarts et al., 2015; Hutto et al., 2015; Shaw & Gant, 2002; Silvia et al., 2018). Their use also seems to benefit physical and mental health, and cognitive functioning (Chopik, 2016; Myhre et al., 2017; Quinn, 2018), although the evidence is still scarce on these matters.

Despite this, the influence of social networking sites on other life dimensions remains under researched. For instance, their impact on quality of life, well-being, and promotion of active aging. More research is also necessary on the role of social networking sites, or other forms of social media, on physical and mental health in later life, as well as on cognitive and affective functioning.

From our point of view, there are other relevant research lines that need to be addressed to better understand the impact of social media in the elderly population. For instance, the negative impact that derives from the use of digital social networks in later life needs to be more carefully examined. Also, when examining the effects of social media on the elderly, researchers have focused on Facebook and the predictors and consequences of its use. Other digital social networks that are being used by the elderly, such as the Instagram and Youtube, among others, received much less attention. The presence and use, by the elderly, of other digital platforms that are included in social media, like virtual communities and blogs, have received even less attention and more research is also necessary on these subjects.

Acknowledging that older adults are a heterogeneous group on what pertains to digital technology and social media use (the so-called grey digital divide), has led researchers to focus on the behavior of a subsegment of this age group. This implies that there is a lack of knowledge on the rest of this age segment, and much remains to be known about the role of digital technology, ICT and social media for the oldest old. Therefore, we call for further research on the antecedents and effects of social media on senior lives, as well as to the development of tools and interventions that increase senior citizens digital literacy and a deepen knowledge regarding ICT and social media use.

CONCLUSION

In the last decades, societies have been witnessing a demographic transformation. The western world, as we know it, is aging. This major change brings new questions and challenges, some of them related to the elderly. This chapter intends to map, through a literature review, how the relationship of seniors with ICT and, in particular with social media, is configured. There is a growing body of evidence of the multiple roles and major contributions of Information and Communication Technologies (ICT) and the internet for children, teens, young adults and adults but much remains to be known regarding the use of the ICT and the internet in later life. On what concerns the interaction of the elderly with social media, the research efforts seem to be focused on motives of use and how it affects their lives.

Future work should be aimed at deepening our comprehension on the many aspects related to ICT, internet and social media use in later life, since this field of study benefits from adopting a more holistic and integrated perspective. With this objective in mind, the factors that promote ICT, the internet and social media use in later life, but also the positive and negative impact of the diverse social media tools on the elderly require further research. This may contribute to the development of strategies and policies aimed for this age segment, as well as guide designers, caretakers and other practitioners in their senior-related activities.

REFERENCES

Aarts, S., Peek, S. T. M., & Wouters, E. J. M. (2015). The relation between social network site usage and loneliness and mental health in community-dwelling older adults. *International Journal of Geriatric Psychiatry, 30*(9), 942–949. doi:10.1002/gps.4241 PMID:25503540

Alvarenga, G. M., Yassuda, M., & Cachioni, M. (2019). Inclusão digital com tablets entre idosos: Metodologia e impacto cognitivo. *Psicologia, Saúde & Doenças, 20*(2), 384–401. doi:10.15309/19psd200209

Balcerzak, B., Kopeć, W., Nielek, R., Kruk, S., Warpe-Chowski, K., Wasik, M., & Wegrzyn, M. (2017). Press F1 for help: Participatory design for dealing with on-line and real-life security of older adults. In *Proceedings of 12th International Scientific and Technical Conference on Computer Sciences and Information Technologies* (Vol. 1, pp. 240-243). 10.1109/STC-CSIT.2017.8098778

Barak, A., Boniel-Nissim, M., & Suler, J. (2008). Fostering empowerment in online support groups. *Computers in Human Behavior, 24*(5), 1867–1883. doi:10.1016/j.chb.2008.02.004

Barroso, C., Ábad, M., & Valle, M. (2015). Mayores e internet: La red como fuente de oportunidades para un envelhecimiento activo. *Media Education Research Journal, 45*(23), 29–36.

Batista, E. B., Silva, L., Moura, L., Queiroz, V., Matos, R., Silva, S., Oliveira, D. (2018). Inclusão Digital como ferramenta ao envelhecimento ativo: um relato de experiência. *Prisma.com, 38.*

Bell, C., Fausset, C., Farmer, S., Nguyen, J., Harley, L., & Fain, W. B. (2013). Examining social media use among older adults. In *Proceedings of the 24th ACM Conference on Hypertext and Social Media* (pp. 158–163). ACM. 10.1145/2481492.2481509

Cardoso, G. (2008). From mass to networked communication: Communicational models and the informational society. *International Journal of Communication, 2,* 587–630.

Cardoso, G., Coelho, A. R., & Costa, A. F. (2015). *A sociedade em rede em Portugal: Uma década de transição.* Campo de Letras.

Cardoso, G., Costa, A. F., Conceição, M., & Gomes, A. (2003). *A sociedade em rede em Portugal.* Campo de Letras.

Castells, E. (2003). *A galáxia da internet.* Jorge Zahar.

Castells, M. (2009). *A sociedade em rede. A era da informação: Economia, sociedade e cultura.* Paz e Terra.

Castells, M. (2012). *Networks of outrage and hope: Social movements in the internet age.* Wiley.

Choi, N. G., & Dinitto, D. M. (2013). Internet use among older adults: Association with health needs, psychological capital, and social capital. *Journal of Medical Internet Research, 15*(5), e97. doi:10.2196/jmir.2333 PMID:23681083

Chopik, W. J. (2016). The benefits of social technology use among older adults are mediated by reduced loneliness. *Cyberpsychology, Behavior, and Social Networking, 19*(9), 551–556. doi:10.1089/cyber.2016.0151 PMID:27541746

Coelho, A. R. (2019). *Seniores 2.0: Inclusão digital na sociedade em rede* [Unpublished doctoral dissertation]. Lisbon University Institute, Lisbon, Portugal.

Coto, M. C., Lizano, F., Rivera, S. M., & Fuentes, J. (2017). Social media and elderly people: Research trends. In G. Meiselwitz (Ed.), *Social computing and social media: Applications and analytics* (pp. 65–81). Springer International Publishing. doi:10.1007/978-3-319-58562-8_6

Demunter, C. (2006). How skilled are Europeans in using the computers and the internet? *Statistics in Focus, 17*, 1–8.

Dias, I. (2012). O uso das tecnologias digitais entre os seniores: Motivações e interesses. Sociologia. *Problemas e Práticas, 68*, 51–77.

Eggermont, S., Vandebosch, H., & Steyaert, S. (2005). Towards the desired future of the elderly and ICT: Policy recommendations based on a dialogue with senior citizens. *Poiesis & Praxis: International Journal of Ethics of Science and Technology Assessment, 4*(3), 199–217. doi:10.100710202-005-0017-9

Erickson, L. B. (2011), Social media, social capital, and seniors: The impact of Facebook on bonding and bridging social capital of individuals over 65. *Proceedings of the 17th Americas Conference on Information Systems (AMCIS 2011).*

European Commission. (2019). *Demography.* https://data.europa.eu/euodp/pt/data/

Eurostat. (2010). *Internet access and use in 2010.* https://ec.europa.eu/eurostat/documents/2995521/5042418/4-14122010-BP-EN.PDF/2276f2ef-a45b-49ef-90ea-8987cbb8cddd

Eurostat. (2019). *Are you using social networks?* https://ec.europa.eu/eurostat/web/products-eurostat-news/-/EDN-20190629-1

Flores-Gomes, G. (2019). *Efeitos de um programa de inclusão digital nas funções cognitivas e qualidade de vida de idosos.* Universidade Federal do Paraná.

Friemel, T. N. (2016). The digital divide has grown old: Determinants of a digital divide among seniors. *New Media & Society, 18*(2), 313–331. doi:10.1177/1461444814538648

Gaia, A., Sala, E., & Cerati, G. (2020). Social networking sites use and life satisfaction: A quantitative study on older people living in Europe. *European Societies*, 1–21. doi:10.1080/14616696.2020.1762910

Gil, H. (2019). A pertinência de uma cidadania digital 65. In *Atas do Seminário Internacional Cidadania Digital.* Instituto de Educação da Universidade de Lisboa.

Hargittai, E. (2002). The second-level digital divide: Differences in people's online skills. *First Monday*, *7*(4). Advance online publication. doi:10.5210/fm.v7i4.942

Hargittai, E. (2003). Informed web surfing: The social context of user sophistication. In P. E. N. Howard & S. Jones (Eds.), *Society online* (pp. 257–274). Sage.

Hargittai, E., & Hsieh, Y. P. (2013). Digital inequality. In W. H. Dutton (Ed.), *The Oxford handbook of internet studies* (pp. 129–150). Oxford University Press.

Hill, R., Betts, L. R., & Gardner, S. E. (2015). Older adults' experiences and perceptions of digital technology: (Dis)empowerment, wellbeing, and inclusion. *Computers in Human Behavior*, *48*, 415–423. doi:10.1016/j.chb.2015.01.062

Hiremath, B. K., & Kenchakkanavar, A. Y. (2016). An alteration of the web 1.0, web 2.0 and web 3.0: A comparative study. *Imperial Journal of Interdisciplinary Research*, *2*(4), 705–710.

Hutto, C. J., Bell, C., Farmer, S., Fausset, C., Harley, L., Nguyen, J., & Fain, B. (2015). Social media gerontology: Understanding social media usage among older adults. *Web Intelligence*, *13*(1), 69–87. doi:10.3233/WEB-150310

Kaplan, A. M., & Haenlein, M. (2010). Users of the world, unite! The challenges and opportunities of Social Media. *Business Horizons*, *53*(1), 59–68. doi:10.1016/j.bushor.2009.09.003

Khoros. (2020). *The 2020 social media demographics guide*. https://khoros.com/resources/social-media-demographics-guide

Khosravi, P., Rezvani, A., & Wiewiora, A. (2016). The impact of technology on older adults' social isolation. *Computers in Human Behavior*, *63*, 594–603. doi:10.1016/j.chb.2016.05.092

Lagacé, M., Charmarkeh, H., Zaky, R., & Firzly, N. (2016). From psychological to digital disengagement: Exploring the link between ageism and the 'grey digital divide'. *Romanian Journal of Communication and Public Relations*, *18*(1), 65–75. doi:10.21018/rjcpr.2016.1.202

LévyP. (1999). *Cibercultura*. Editora 34.

Lin, S.-H., & Chou, W. H. (2014). Developing a social media system for the Taiwanese elderly by participatory design. *Bulletin of Japanese Society for the Science of Design*, *60*(3), 39–48.

Livingstone, D. W. (1999). Exploring the icebergs of adult learning: Findings of the first Canadian survey of informal learning practices. *Canadian Journal for the Study of Adult Education*, *13*(2), 49–72.

Loos, E. (2012). Designing for dynamic diversity: Representing various senior citizens in digital information sources. *The Observatory Journal*, *7*(1), 21–45.

Mauritti, R. (2004). Padrões de vida na velhice. *Analise Social*, *39*(171), 339–363.

McDonough, C. C. (2016). Determinants of a digital divide among able-bodied older adults: Does "feeling too old" play a role? *International Journal of Aging Research*, *3*, 60.

Miranda, S., Antunes, A. C., Machado, A. T., & Gama, A. (2020). Age 2.0: Motivations and brand engagement. *Proceedings of 7th European Conference on Social Media*.

Myhre, J. W., Mehl, M. R., & Glisky, E. L. (2017). Cognitive benefits of online social networking for healthy older adults. *Journal of Gerontology, 72*(5), 752–760. PMID:26984523

NapoleonCat. (2019). *Instagram users in India.* https://napoleoncat.com/stats/instagram-users-in-india/2019/01

Neves, B., & Amaro, F. (2012). Too old for technology? How the elderly of Lisbon use and perceive ICT. *The Journal of Community Informatics, 8*(1), 1–12.

Neves, B. B., Waycott, J., & Malta, S. (2018). Old and afraid of new communication technologies? Reconceptualising and contesting the 'age-based digital divide.'. *Journal of Sociology (Melbourne, Vic.), 54*(2), 236–248. doi:10.1177/1440783318766119

Nimrod, G. (2014). Seniors' online communities: A quantitative content analysis. *The Gerontologist, 50*(3), 382–392. doi:10.1093/geront/gnp141 PMID:19917645

Nimrod, G. (2017). Older audiences in the digital media environment. *Information Communication and Society, 20*(2), 233–249. doi:10.1080/1369118X.2016.1164740

Obar, J. A., & Wildman, S. S. (2015). Social media definition and the governance challenge: An introduction to the special issue. *Telecommunications Policy, 39*(9), 745–750. doi:10.1016/j.telpol.2015.07.014

Omnicore. (2020). *YouTube by the numbers: Stats, demographics & fun facts.* https://www.omnicore-agency.com/youtube-statistics/

Páscoa, G., & Gil, H. (2015). Uma nova forma de comunicação para o cidadão sénior: Facebook. *Revista Kairós Gerontologia, 18*(1), 9–29.

Paúl, C., & Fonseca, A. (2005). *Envelhecer em Portugal.* Climepsi.

Perol, A., Gaitan, J., & Ramos, A. (2015). From digital divide to psycho-digital divide: Elders and online social networks. *Media Education Research Journal, 45*, 57–64.

Pew Research Centre. (2019). *Social media fact sheet.* https://www.pewresearch.org/internet/fact-sheet/social-media/

Pinheiro, O. D., & Areosa, S. (2018). A importância de políticas públicas para idosos. *Revista Brasileira de Assuntos Regionais e Urbanos, 4*(2), 183–193. doi:10.18224/baru.v4i2.6724

Prensky, M. (2001). Digital natives, digital immigrants. *On the Horizon, 9*(5-6), 1–6.

Quinn, K. (2018). Cognitive effects of social media use: A case of older adults. *Social Media and Society, 4*(3), 1–9. doi:10.1177/2056305118787203

Rebelo, A. R. (2013). *Seniores em rede: Motivações para o uso da internet e do Facebook pelos mais velhos* [Unpublished master thesis]. Lisbon University Institute, Lisbon, Portugal.

Rebelo, C. (2015). Utilização da internet e do Facebook pelos mais velhos em Portugal: Estudo exploratório. *Observatorio (OBS*), 9*(3), 129-153.

Roberto, M., Fidalgo, A. & Buckingham, D. (2015). De que falamos quando falamos de infoexclusão e literacia digital? *Perspetivas dos nativos digitais. Observatorio (OBS*), 9*(1), 43-54.

Rosa, M. J. (2012). *O envelhecimento da sociedade portuguesa*. Fundação Francisco Manuel dos Santos.

Shaw, L. H., & Gant, L. M. (2002). In defense of the internet: The relationship between internet communication and depression, loneliness, self-esteem, and perceived social support. *Cyberpsychology & Behavior, 5*(2), 157–171. doi:10.1089/109493102753770552 PMID:12025883

Silverstone, R. (2003). *Media and technology in the everyday life of European societies*. Routledge.

Silvia, F., Scortegagna, S. A., & De Marchi, A. C. B. (2018). Facebook as a social support environment for older adults. *Universitas Psychologica, 17*(3), 1–11. doi:10.11144/Javeriana.upsy.17-3.fsse

Sims, T., Reed, A. E., & Carr, D. C. (2017). Information and communication technology use is related to higher well-being among the oldest-old. *The Journals of Gerontology: Series B, 72*(5), 761-770.

Statista. (2020a). *Average Number of Social Media Accounts per Internet User as of July 2019, by Age Group* [Graph illustration]. https://www.statista.com/statistics/381964/number-of-social-media-accounts/

Statista. (2020b). *Most Popular Social Networks Worldwide as of April 2020, Ranked by Number of Active Users* [Graph illustration]. https://www.statista.com/statistics/272014/global-social-networks-ranked-by-number-of-users/

Statista. (2020c). *Distribution of Facebook Users Worldwide as of April 2020, by Age and Gender* [Graph illustration]. https://www.statista.com/statistics/376128/facebook-global-user-age-distribution/

Statista. (2020d). *Distribution of Instagram Users Worldwide as of April 2020, by Age and Gender* [Graph illustration]. https://www.statista.com/statistics/248769/age-distribution-of-worldwide-instagram-users/

Statista. (2020e). *Distribution of Facebook Users in Brazil as of January 2018, by Age group and Gender* [Graph illustration]. https://www.statista.com/statistics/198923/age-distribution-of-users-facebook-brazil/

Statista. (2020f). *Distribution of Instagram Users in Brazil as of January 2018, by Age Group and Gender* [Graph illustration]. https://www.statista.com/statistics/866268/instagram-user-share-brazil-age/

Statista. (2020g). *Penetration Rate of YouTube among People in Japan as of March 2019, by Age Group* [Graph illustration]. https://www.statista.com/statistics/1071780/japan-youtube-penetration-rate-by-age-group/

Statista. (2020h). *Share of YouTube Users in Latin America in 2018, by Age* [Graph illustration]. https://www.statista.com/statistics/754376/latin-america-usage-penetration-youtube-age/

Tofler, A. (1980). *The third wave*. Think Review.

United Nations. (2020). *World population prospects 2020: Highlights*. https://population.un.org/wpp/Publications/Files/WPP2019_Highlights.pdf

Van Deursen, A. J. A. M., & Helsper, E. J. (2015). The third level digital divide: Who benefits most from being online? In L. Robinson, S. R. Cotten, & J. Schulz (Eds.), *Communication and information technologies annual* (Vol. 9, pp. 29–52). Emerald. doi:10.1108/S2050-206020150000010002

Van Deursen, A. J. A. M., & Van Dijk, J. A. G. M. (2014). The digital divide shifts to differences in usage. *New Media & Society*, *16*(3), 507–526. doi:10.1177/1461444813487959

Van Dijk, J. (2005). The deepening divide: Inequality in the information society. *Sage (Atlanta, Ga.)*.

Van Dijk, J. A. G. M., & Hacker, K. (2003). The digital divide as a complex and dynamic phenomenon. *The Information Society*, *19*(4), 315–326. doi:10.1080/01972240309487

We Are Flint. (2018). *Social 2018 main findings*. https://castfromclay.co.uk/main-findings-social-media-demographics-uk-usa-2018

White, D., & Cornu, A. (2011). Visitors and residents: A new typology for online engagement. *First Monday*, *16*(9). Advance online publication. doi:10.5210/fm.v16i9.3171

Witte, J., & Mannon, S. (2010). *The internet and social inequalities*. Routledge. doi:10.4324/9780203861639

Yang, Y., Yuan, Y., Archer, N. P., & Ryan, E. (2016). Adoption of social media and the quality of life of older adults. In *Proceedings of the 49th Hawaii International Conference on System Sciences (HICSS)*. IEEE Computer Society. 10.1109/HICSS.2016.394

Yen, D., & Dey, B. (2019). Acculturation in the Social Media: Myth or reality? Analysing social-media-led integration and polarisation. *Technological Forecasting and Social Change*, *145*, 426–427. doi:10.1016/j.techfore.2019.04.012

YouTube. (n.d.). *YouTube for press*. https://www.youtube.com/about/press/

Chapter 15
Twitter Sentiment Data Analysis of User Behavior on Cryptocurrencies:
Bitcoin and Ethereum

Hasitha Ranasinghe
Charles Sturt University, Australia

Malka N. Halgamuge
 https://orcid.org/0000-0001-9994-3778
The University of Melbourne, Australia

ABSTRACT

Social networks such as Twitter contain billions of data of users, and in every second, a large number of tweets trade through Twitter. Sentiment analysis is the way toward deciding the emotional tone behind a series of words that users utilize to understand the attitudes, thoughts, and emotions that are enunciated in online references on Twitter. This chapter aims to determine the user preference of Bitcoin and Ethereum, which are the two most popular cryptocurrencies in the world by using the Twitter sentiment analysis. It proposes a powerful and fundamental approach to identify emotions on Twitter by considering the tweets of these two distinctive cryptocurrencies. One hundred twenty thousand (120,000) tweets were extracted separately from Twitter for each keyword Bitcoin/BTC and Bitcoin/ETC between the period from 12/09/2018 to 22/09/2018 (10 days).

DOI: 10.4018/978-1-7998-4718-2.ch015

INTRODUCTION

Figure 1.

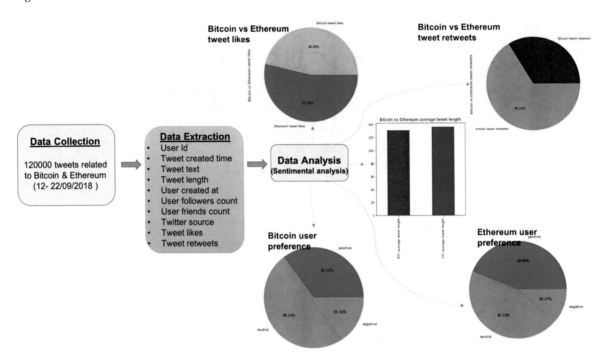

The footstep in big data analysis is to accumulate the data. This is called "data mining" (Hewage et al., 2018). Those data can be from any source. There are lots of data sources where we can collect a huge number of data. Twitter is one of the best sources used in data science. It is also free social networking media that allows users to broadcast tweets. These tweets are known as short messages used to send tweets (short messages) for all kind of reasons such as pride, attention, dullness, help, to become famous etc. The vast majority of users use Twitter for fun, giving a shout out to the world and ensure to distribute ideas within communities. Unlike other social platforms, every user's tweets are entirely public and able to retrieve. Twitter data can be accessed by general public perception and how they sense topics. Twitter's API allows developers to pull data. However, some limitations are included (Wu et al., 2011).

Sentiment analysis is the process of determining the emotional tone behind a series of words that can be used to understand the attitudes, thoughts, and emotions articulated in online references. It is very beneficial in monitoring social media (Singh et al., 2018; Hewage et al., 2018) since it enables us to present broader public opinion about specific topics. It can also be a significant part of market research and approach to customer service.

Cryptocurrency is a digital or virtual currency designed to work as a medium of exchange that uses cryptography for security. Cryptocurrency is also an equivalent electronic currency (Bohr et al., 2018). Bitcoin has a rapid rise in the price of a virtual currency over the past few months. The basis for creating Bitcoin and all subsequent virtual treaties is to address some perceived deficiencies by way of payment being made from one party to another. The most famous cryptocurrency is bitcoin which makes everyone interested in the matter of encryption, because of its unpredictable growth that has become the de facto standard for cryptocurrencies (Kaushal et al., 2017). Although there are various cryptocurrencies, Bitcoin and Ethereum are the most two that lead the market. Bitcoin (BTC) is the first coin, and Ethereum (ETH) becomes the second a few years later. However, Bitcoin and Ethereum have different purposes. Bitcoin is created as a substitute for regular currency; it is a medium for payment transactions and value storage, while Ethereum is developed as a platform to promote peer-to-peer contracts and applications through its currency instruments (Velankar et al., 2018).

Most of the reviewed articles use Twitter API to retrieve data from Twitter while some articles used paid APIs such as Sentiment 140 (Chakraborty et al., 2017; Attarwala et al., 2017). Some articles find out that there is a high correlation between the probabilities of the influence of Twitter users and the probabilities influenced, and most users maintain a sentimental balance in both. Twitter provides the functionality of social networks is used to know if users are exposed to the surroundings in the online social world that control their sentiments. The designed models to learn both sentimental influencing probabilities and influenced probabilities for users and present observations are based on real social network data. For each posted tweet by a user, an emotional analysis is performed to determine its polarity, whether it is positive or negative. After pre-processing the raw data, followed classifiers NB, SVM, N-SVM, ME, KNN, DT are used. Information Gain and Gain Ratio techniques are used for feature reduction. Knowledge enhancer and synonym binder module are applied to enhance the information again. This chapter discusses how to use Twitter data to choose the user preference between Bitcoin and Ethereum, which is useful for people who are new to cryptocurrencies to get ideas before they get involved.

The rest of the chapter is organized, as follows: Section 2 introduces the dataset and materials and methods used. Subsequently, the Tweet comparison results on Ethereum and Bitcoin are presented in Section 3. Section 4 provides a related discussion and potential future improvements in the area, and, finally, the chapter concludes in Section 5.

MATERIAL AND METHODS

Figure 2 illustrates the five significant steps of the research.

Data Collection

Tweepy python library is used to extract data from Twitter. Tweepy library provides methods to access Twitter API. The API class provides access to the entire Twitter RESTful API methods. Each method can accept various parameters and return responses. A Twitter developer account should be created before creating an API. Once Twitter API is created, consumer API keys and access token and secret keys should be provided in python code for authentication. These are unique for each Twitter API. By using the API, 120,000 tweets were extracted separately for each keyword Bitcoin/ BTC and Ethereum/ ETC between 12/09/2018 and 22/09/2018. Tweets were posted for ten days related to topic Bitcoin and Ethereum. Save these data into two CSV file separately.

Figure 2. Procedure of the research

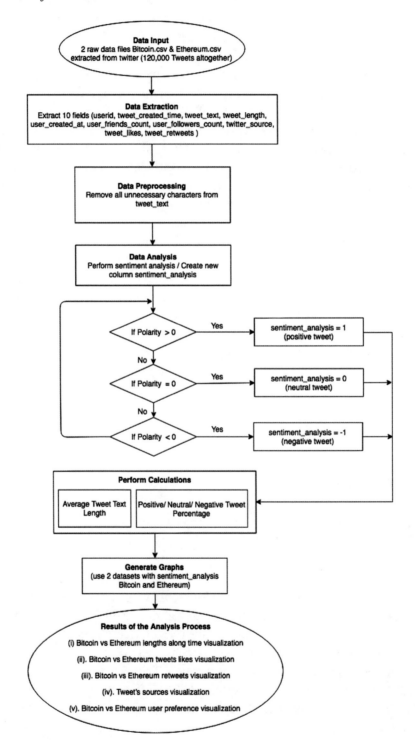

Data Inclusion Criteria

The criteria for data inclusion are Tweepy library which provides access to retrieve many fields for a single tweet. However, only relevant fields needed for this research were extracted. Those fields are given below in-detail.

Table 1. Selected attribute description

Attribute Name	Data Type	Description
user_id	int64	Unique ID for the user
tweet_created_time	object	Tweet created date and time
tweet_text	object	Tweet text
tweet_length	int64	Character length of tweet text
user_created_at	object	Account created date of the user who posted the tweet
user_followers_count	int64	Number of followers of the user
user_friends_count	int64	Number of friends of the user
twitter_source	object	User's source used to post the tweet
tweet_likes	int64	Number of likes for the tweet
tweet_retweets	int64	Number of retweets for the tweet

*Nominal data type represents the text data

Data Analysis

1. Extracted tweets needed to be processed before performing the analysis. The preprocessor and re libraries are used for the pre-processing.
   a. Change all letters to lowercase letters to prevent a repetition of the same words in the feature vector.
   b. <http://>, <https://> and <www.> URL starting with above needed to be removed from the text.
   c. Consecutive whitespaces are replaced to a single whitespace.
   d. Usernames start with @ are removed.
   e. Remove all RT, <'>, <''> quote signs and all non-ASCII codes.
   f. Hashtags # are removed.
2. Sentiment analysis is completed by using the TextBlob library, which is used for textual data processing.

If *polarity > 0*, then *sentiment_analysis = 1*, hence positive tweets
   If *polarity = 0*, then *sentiment_analysis = 0*, hence neutral tweets
   If *polarity <0*, then *sentiment_analysis = -1*, hence negative tweets

3. Sentiment analysis is completed, and a new column "sentiment_analysis" was created for each row.

4. Calculate the percentage of positive, neutral and negative tweets for both Bitcoin and Ethereum datasets.
5. Five observations are created to analyze and compare between Bitcoin and Ethereum.
    a. Bitcoin vs Ethereum lengths along with time visualization
    b. Bitcoin vs Ethereum tweets likes visualization
    c. Bitcoin vs Ethereum retweets visualization
    d. Tweet's sources visualization
    e. Bitcoin vs Ethereum user preference visualization.

Tweet Calculation

Average tweet text length value for both Bitcoin and Ethereum is calculated using

$$\text{Average tweet text length} = \frac{\text{Total tweet length}}{\text{Number of tweets in the dataset}}. \tag{1}$$

Then the Equation (2), (3) and (4) are used to extract the percentages for this study,

$$\text{Positive tweets percentage} = \frac{\text{Positive tweet count of the dataset} \times 100}{\text{Length of the dataset}}, \tag{2}$$

$$\text{Neutral tweets percentage} = \frac{\text{Neutral tweet count of the dataset} \times 100}{\text{Length of the dataset}}, \tag{3}$$

Figure 3. Bitcoin vs Ethereum lengths with time visualization (using 120,000 tweets (Bitcoin and Ethereum) collected during September 2018)

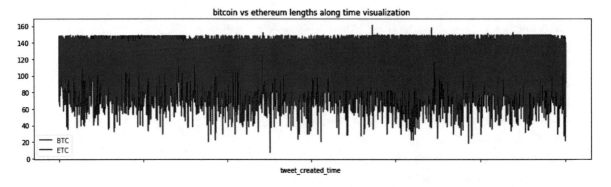

$$\text{Negative tweets percentage} = \frac{\text{Negative tweet count of the dataset} \times 100}{\text{Length of the dataset}}. \tag{4}$$

RESULTS

Bitcoin vs Ethereum Lengths With Time Visualization

Figure 3 represents tweet text lengths which are generated at the beginning of the process when collecting tweets from Twitter API. Lengths are generated before text pre-processing in order to get the correct number of characters for an individual tweet. Figure 2 is obtained with text length with the tweet creation date for both Bitcoin and Ethereum. Tweet lengths of tweets related to Bitcoin show longer values than the tweets related to Ethereum.

Figure 4. Bitcoin and Ethereum average tweet length numerical representation (using 120,000 tweets (Bitcoin and Ethereum) collected during September 2018)

```
Bitcoin average tweet length: 130.68
Ethereum average tweet length: 135.55
```

According to Figure 3, Bitcoin and Ethereum have an average value of 130.68 and 135.55, respectively. It proves that the tweet length of Ethereum is lengthier than the tweet length of Bitcoin.

Figure 5 was obtained for more clarification using the average values of both BTC and ETC.

Bitcoin vs Ethereum Tweets Likes Visualization

Figure 6 shows that the tweet has a similar counter that shows how many people like this tweet. Compared to Facebook, Twitter likes are not to display a list of people who like tweets. The list of likes on the Twitter profile will appear when people like tweets.

When someone likes a tweet, the poster of that particular tweet will be notified. Tweet likes between Bitcoin and Ethereum along their created date are observed. Our results show that in most days, tweets related to Ethereum have obtained more likes than tweets related to Bitcoin.

Figure 7 shows the total amount of likes for each tweet for both Bitcoin and Ethereum. Figure 7 shows the Bitcoin and Ethereum total tweet likes percentage. Bitcoin tweet likes percentage is 46.26%, and Ethereum likes percentage is 53.74% which is higher than Bitcoin. This proves that people have liked tweets related to Ethereum more than Bitcoin.

Figure 5. Bitcoin and Ethereum average tweet length visualization (using 120,000 tweets (Bitcoin and Ethereum) collected during September 2018)

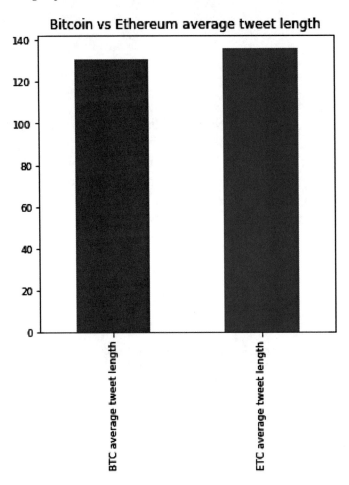

Figure 6. Bitcoin vs Ethereum likes visualization (using 120,000 tweets (Bitcoin and Ethereum) collected during September 2018)

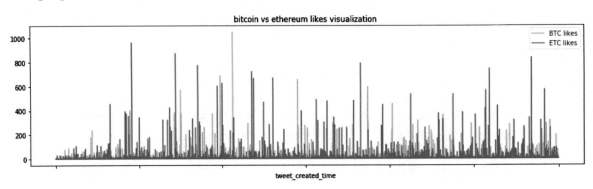

Figure 7. Bitcoin vs Ethereum total tweet likes visualization (using 120,000 tweets (Bitcoin and Ethereum) collected during September 2018)

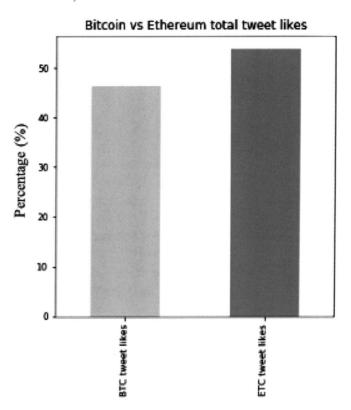

Bitcoin vs Ethereum Retweets Visualization

Retweeting sends another twitter user's tweet to demonstrate the user's followers. For example, in Hashtag, the retweets are a community-based experience on twitter help improve service quality and facilitate the spreading of discussions within people. According to Figure 8, Bitcoin maintains an average number of

Figure 8. Bitcoin vs Ethereum retweets visualization (using 120,000 tweets (Bitcoin and Ethereum) collected during September 2018)

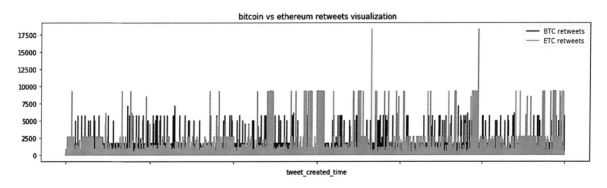

retweets continuously. Nonetheless, the retweet count for tweets related to Ethereum has ups and downs. Somedays the count has risen unexpectedly than ETC. Sudden changes for ETC tell that either new people are getting attraction or the rate of ETC is changing in a way that people feel disappointed. BTC shows stability than ETC between 12/09/2018 and 22/09/2018.Figure 9. Bitcoin vs Ethereum total tweet retweets visualization (using 120,000 tweets (Bitcoin and Ethereum) collected during September 2018)

Figure 9 shows the retweets percentage for both Bitcoin and Ethereum. Bitcoin tweet likes percentage is 33.86%, and Ethereum likes percentage is 66.14% which is higher than Bitcoin. This proves that people have retweeted tweets related to Ethereum more than Bitcoin.

Figure 9.

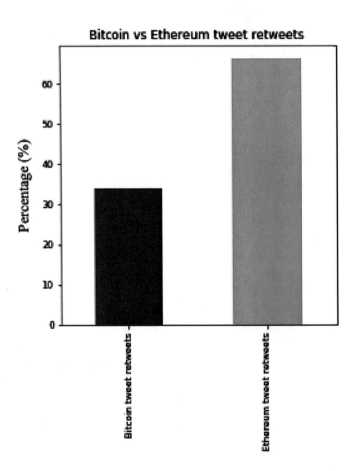

Tweet's Sources Visualization to Post Tweets in Twitter

Figure 10 demonstrates people use a variety of sources to post tweets on Twitter. Our results show the top 5 sources to post tweets on Twitter is recognized as the (i) Twitter web client (42.5%), (ii) Twitter for Android (18.5%), (iii) Twitter for iPhone (8.3%), (iv) Twitter lite (6.4%) and (v) IFTTT (3.9%). Other sources include many other methods such as TRONBEE_Bot, cryptocrown, Gleam Competition App, Twitter Lite, mykurrenciesData, VirtualCoinCap, Buffer, CurrencyBuzzer, CryptoUpdater, Altcoin Freebies, Btct, CR_to_twitter, CryptoTradeBot2, Crypto Gulp Bot, Coin Spectator, Blockchain-Tweet

Figure 10. Tweet's sources to post tweets visualization (using 120,000 tweets (Bitcoin and Ethereum) collected during September 2018).
Here other sources include many other methods such as TRONBEE_Bot, cryptocrown, Gleam Competition App, Twitter Lite, mykurrenciesData, VirtualCoinCap, Buffer, CurrencyBuzzer, CryptoUpdater, Altcoin Freebies, Btct, CR_to_twitter, Crypto-TradeBot2, Crypto Gulp Bot, Coin Spectator, Blockchain-Tweet Bot, CryptoVentures, Zapier.com, WordPress.com, Bitcoins Channel Auto, dlvr.it, StartupUSATato, Hootsuite Inc., medicinetoletitwin, RdemirTwitBot, ZohoTwitterApp, PetroPublisApi, CryptoNewswire, B.A.T Crypto News, AwebAnalysis.

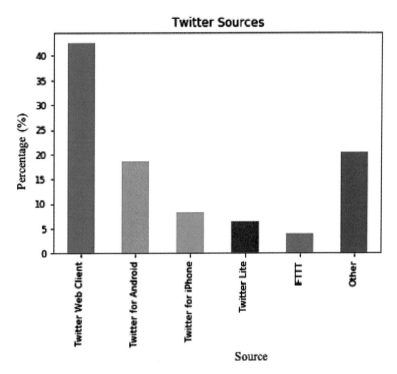

Bot, CryptoVentures, Zapier.com, WordPress.com, Bitcoins Channel Auto, dlvr.it, StartupUSATato, Hootsuite Inc., medicinetoletitwin, RdemirTwitBot, ZohoTwitterApp, PetroPublisApi, CryptoNewswire, B.A.T Crypto News, AwebAnalysis. Most of Twitter users use PCs or desktop computers.

Bitcoin vs Ethereum User Preference Visualization

The sentiment analysis was generated for each tweet in both datasets consists of 120,000 tweets. After performing the sentiment analysis, every tweet is given a value of 1, 0 or -1 depending on its positive, neutral or negative polarity, respectively. Derived values are added as a new column called "*sentiment_analysis*" to both data sets. In order to obtain the percentage of each positive, neutral and negative tweets, three lists of counted tweets for each category are generated. A function called Enumerate, which is a built-in function of Python, is used for this purpose. It allows us to loop over something and have an automatic counter.

According to Figure 11, the positive percentage is 35.12%, and the negative percentage is 15.74%, the positive percentage is 43.9%, and the negative percentage is 10.37%. This demonstrates a high percentage of neutral tweets which is half the users. Those tweets generated 0 in the sentiment analysis. That

Figure 11. Bitcoin and Ethereum user preference visualization (using 120,000 tweets (Bitcoin and Ethereum) collected during September 2018)

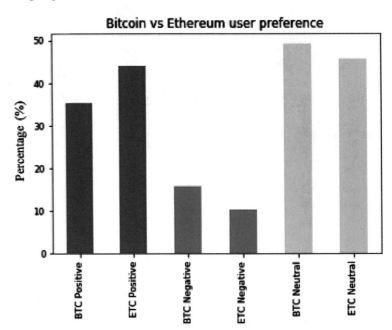

means the positivity or the negativity cannot be decided from those tweets. Our results of this analysis show that people prefer Ethereum more than Bitcoin.

DISCUSSION

The aim of this study is to gain an idea about how users react to Bitcoin and Ethereum in the cryptocurrency world and to observe the user behaviour on both. After comparing these with the values, we will be able to decide the best option within these two based on user preferences. This is a provable source to the public to believe rather than a general article or post on the web. People are used to following what the majority follows. Thus, this research can change the mind of the public and make a difference in both cryptocurrencies.

Cryptocurrency is one of the most secure and trusted digital currencies that the public like today. In a world with a lot of robbers and stealers, we all need to trade in the safest way (Bajpai et al., 2018). Cryptocurrencies provide us with a guarantee that it is an essential source of investment for the present and the future. Another reason for the cryptocurrency becoming extremely challenging is their policy. In terms of cryptocurrency, the user does not want necessary to deal with third parties. This provides people with a sense of wellbeing and safety. The fact that cryptocurrency is a digital currency diminishes the need for third parties.

Findings from previous research conclude some essential features of sentiment analysis. The problem of drawing features/attributes from an input dataset is significant for the sentiment analysis. Dimensionality is high in most cases (Batool et al., 2013; Wankhede et al., 2017). Wankhede et al., (2017) have used Information Gain and Gain Ratio that is two main popular feature reduction techniques. Sentiment quantification plays a significant role in sentimental analysis. However, it faces many challenges. Quantification is still an area of insufficient research because it has not been identified as it can work by itself (Bouazizi et al., 2016). Chakraborty et al. (2017) have used Sentiment 140 API to pull data from twitter. Sentiment140 API service is not free. License fee has to be paid, and it is expensive. The lowest fee will be USD200 per month. The difference of this API in related to other APIs is that it uses classifiers built from machine learning algorithms instead of simple keyword-based algorithms and it provides transparency for the individual classified tweets. Few issues can be raised [8] due to the feedback submitted by students which might affect the ratings of the faculty. Students might submit the form without any interest by putting some random values, and some might give bad feedback due to some personal grudge.

Analysis of the reviewed article confirms that there is a significant gap in some of the published articles (Wu et al., 2011; Wankhede et al., 2017; Adarsh et al., 2018). For the analysis, they do not consider enough number of tweets. A few other studies have taken (Batool et al., 2013; Anto et al., 2016; Bouazizi et al., 2016; Chakraborty et al., 2017; Attarwala et al., 2017; Krishnaveni et al., 2017; Anastasia et al., 2016) enough number of tweets for their research. Accurate results cannot be obtained with a smaller number of data. The disadvantage of this method is that in the case of spelling errors in tweets, the presence of positive and negative words may not produce relevant results because the placement of positive and negative words in the sentence gives different conclusions. Attarwala et al. (2017) have used 27 million tweets. That is a useful dataset for the analysis, although they have to be careful with SVM because it has a limitation in speed and size on both training and testing data. In this research, 120,000 tweets are used for the analysis, which is a considerable amount comparing with the other researches. It will assist in maximizing the accuracy of the results of the research. This chapter investigates the user preference between two worlds most famous cryptocurrencies by using the sentiment analysis technique for Twitter data.

Future research could use the price value of both cryptocurrencies and predict the future impact. It would help readers to understand the value changes of both Bitcoin and Ethereum in the future and decide the best option to use. Moreover, extensive data size should be used to obtain the most accurate results; however, the performance and speed will be impacted when dealing with large data sets.

CONCLUSION

Observing social media is advantageous since it encourages us to disclose more extensive public opinion about particular topics. This chapter proposes a useful approach to distinguish emotions on Twitter by considering the tweets of two types of cryptocurrencies Bitcoin and Ethereum. Determining positive, negative and neutral emotions is based on score calculations using sentiment analysis. Tweets related to Ethereum have more positive sentiments when compared to the tweets associated with Bitcoin and tweets associated with Bitcoin have more negative sentiments than Ethereum. Both have the same number of neutral tweets. The analysis shows that the user preferred Ethereum more than Bitcoin. The top 5 sources to post tweets in Twitter were recognized as the (i) Twitter web client, (ii) Twitter for Android, (iii) Twitter for iPhone, (iv) Twitter lite and (v) IFTTT (3.9%). Most of Twitter users use PCs or desktop computers. One disadvantage of the approach is that in the case of spelling errors in tweets, the presence of positive and negative words may not produce relevent results because the placement of positive and negative words in the sentences gives different conclusions. Hence, in future research identifying emotions in sarcastic tweets should be considered.

REFERENCES

Adarsh, M., & Ravikumar, P. (2018). An Effective Method of Predicting the Polarity of Airline Tweets using sentimental Analysis. *2018 4th International Conference on Electrical Energy Systems (ICEES)*. 10.1109/ICEES.2018.8443195

Anastasia, S., & Budi, I. (2016). Twitter sentiment analysis of online transportation service providers. *2016 International Conference on Advanced Computer Science and Information Systems (ICACSIS)*. 10.1109/ICACSIS.2016.7872807

Anto, M., Antony, M., Muhsina, K., Johny, N., James, V., & Wilson, A. (2016). Product rating using sentiment analysis. *2016 International Conference on Electrical, Electronics, and Optimization Techniques (ICEEOT)*. 10.1109/ICEEOT.2016.7755346

Attarwala, A., Dimitrov, S., & Obeidi, A. (2017). How efficient is Twitter: Predicting 2012 U.S. presidential elections using Support Vector Machine via Twitter and comparing against Iowa Electronic Markets. *2017 Intelligent Systems Conference (IntelliSys)*. 10.1109/IntelliSys.2017.8324363

Bajpai, P. (2018). Bitcoin Vs Ethereum: Driven by Different Purposes. *Investopedia*. Available: https://www.investopedia.com/articles/investing/031416/bitcoin-vs-ethereum-driven-different-purposes.asp

Batool, R., Khattak, A., Maqbool, J., & Lee, S. (2013). Precise tweet classification and sentiment analysis. *2013 IEEE/ACIS 12th International Conference on Computer and Information Science (ICIS)*. 10.1109/ICIS.2013.6607883

Bohr & Bashir. (2014). Who Uses Bitcoin? An exploration of the Bitcoin community. *2014 Twelfth Annual International Conference on Privacy, Security and Trust*.

Bouazizi, M., & Ohtsuki, T. (2016). Sentiment Analysis in Twitter: From Classification to Quantification of Sentiments within Tweets. *2016 IEEE Global Communications Conference (GLOBECOM)*. 10.1109/GLOCOM.2016.7842262

Chakraborty, P., Pria, U., Rony, M., & Majumdar, M. (2017). Predicting stock movement using sentiment analysis of Twitter feed. *2017 6th International Conference on Informatics, Electronics and Vision & 2017 7th International Symposium in Computational Medical and Health Technology (ICIEV-ISCMHT)*. 10.1109/ICIEV.2017.8338584

Hewage, T. N., Halgamuge, M. N., Syed, A., & Ekici, G. (2018, February). Review: Big data techniques of Google, Amazon, Facebook and Twitter. *Journal of Communication, 13*(2), 94–100. doi:10.12720/jcm.13.2.94-100

Kaushal, P., Bagga, A., & Sobti, R. (2017). Evolution of bitcoin and security risk in bitcoin wallets. *2017 International Conference on Computer, Communications and Electronics (Comptelix)*. 10.1109/COMPTELIX.2017.8003959

Krishnaveni, K., Pai, R., & Iyer, V. (2017). Faculty rating system based on student feedbacks using sentimental analysis. *2017 International Conference on Advances in Computing, Communications and Informatics (ICACCI)*. 10.1109/ICACCI.2017.8126079

Singh, A., Halgamuge, M. N., & Mouess, B. (2019). An Analysis of Demographic and Behaviour Trends using Social Media: Facebook, Twitter and Instagram. In *Social Network Analytics: Computational Research Methods and Techniques*. Elsevier. doi:10.1016/B978-0-12-815458-8.00005-0

Velankar, S., Valecha, S., & Maji, S. (2018). Bitcoin price prediction using machine learning. *2018 20th International Conference on Advanced Communication Technology (ICACT)*.

Wankhede, R., & Thakare, A. (2017). Design approach for accuracy in movies reviews using sentiment analysis. *2017 International conference of Electronics, Communication and Aerospace Technology (ICECA)*. 10.1109/ICECA.2017.8203652

Wu, Y., & Ren, F. (2011). Learning Sentimental Influence in Twitter. *2011 International Conference on Future Computer Sciences and Application*. 10.1109/ICFCSA.2011.34

Compilation of References

Aaker, D. A. (1991). *Managing brand equity: Capitalizing on the value of a brand name*. Free Press.

Aarts, S., Peek, S. T. M., & Wouters, E. J. M. (2015). The relation between social network site usage and loneliness and mental health in community-dwelling older adults. *International Journal of Geriatric Psychiatry, 30*(9), 942–949. doi:10.1002/gps.4241 PMID:25503540

Abbasi, I. S. (2018). The link between romantic disengagement and Facebook addiction: Where does relationship commitment fit in? *The American Journal of Family Therapy, 46*(4), 375–389. doi:10.1080/01926187.2018.1540283

Abbasi, I. S. (2019). Social media addiction in romantic relationships: Does user's age influence vulnerability to social media infidelity? *Personality and Individual Differences, 139*, 277–280. doi:10.1016/j.paid.2018.10.038

Abdelaziz, H., & Trabelsi, H. (2009). *Les effets d'une libéralisation dans les secteurs des services en Tunisie*. Institut Tunisien de la Compétitivité et des Études Quantitatives.

Abdelnour, Hasselbladh, & Kallinikos. (2017). Agency and Institutions in Organization Studies. *Organization Studies, 38*(2), 1775-1792. https://journals.sagepub.com/doi/pdf/10.1177/0170840617708007

Abidin, C. (2015). Communicative intimacies: Influencers and perceived interconnectedness. *Ada: A Journal of Gender, New Media, and Technology, 8*.

Acquisti, A., Brandimarte, L., & Loewenstein, G. (2015). Privacy and human behavior in the age of information. *Science, 347*(6221), 509–514. doi:10.1126cience.aaa1465 PMID:25635091

Adarsh, M., & Ravikumar, P. (2018). An Effective Method of Predicting the Polarity of Airline Tweets using sentimental Analysis. *2018 4th International Conference on Electrical Energy Systems (ICEES)*. 10.1109/ICEES.2018.8443195

Adewole, K. S., Anuar, N. B., Kamsin, A., Varathan, K. D., & Razak, S. A. (2017). Malicious accounts: Dark of the social networks. *Journal of Network and Computer Applications, 79*(September), 41–67. doi:10.1016/j.jnca.2016.11.030

Adidas. (2018). *Adidas annual report, 2018*. Retrieved from https://report.adidas-group.com/fileadmin/user_upload/adidas_Annual_Report_GB-2018-EN.pdf

Adidas. (2019). *Company brands*. Retrieved from https://www.adidas-group.com/en/brands/adidas/

Adu-Kumi, B. (2016). *Sexuality Going Viral: Using WhatsApp as a Site for Sexual Exploration Among College Students in Ghana* (Doctoral dissertation). University of Oregon.

Afify, E. A., Eldin, A. S., Khedr, A. E., & Alsheref, F. K. (2019). User-Generated Content (UGC) Credibility on Social Media Using Sentiment Classification. *FCI-H Informatics Bulletin, 1*(1), 1–19.

Afroz, S., Brennan, M., & Greenstadt, R. (2012, May). *Detecting hoaxes, frauds, and deception in writing style online.* Paper presented at the meeting of IEEE Symposium on Security and Privacy. 10.1109/SP.2012.34

Aguenza, B. B., & Som, A. P. M. (2012). A Conceptual Analysis of Social Networking and its Impact on Employee Productivity. *IOSR Journal of Business and Management, 1*(2), 48–52. doi:10.9790/487X-0124852

Aharony, N. (2012). Twitter use by three political leaders: An exploratory analysis. *Online Information Review, 36*(4), 587–603. doi:10.1108/14684521211254086

Ahinkorah, B. O., Ameyaw, E. K., Hagan Junior, J. E., Seidu, A. A., & Schack, T. (2020). Rising above misinformation or fake news in Africa: Another strategy to control COVID-19 spread. *Frontiers in Communication, 5*, 45.

Ahmed, W., Bath, P. A., & Demartini, G. (2017). Using Twitter as a Data Source: An Overview of Ethical, Legal, and Methodological Challenges. In The Ethics of Online Research (Advances in Research Ethics and Integrity, Vol. 2). Emerald Publishing Limited. doi:10.1108/S2398-601820180000002004

Ahmed, H., Traore, I., & Saad, S. (2017). Detecting opinion spams and fake news using text classification. *Security and Privacy, 1*(1), e9. doi:10.1002py2.9

Ahuja, R., Chug, A., Kohli, S., Gupta, S., & Ahuja, P. (2019). The Impact of Features Extraction on the Sentiment Analysis. *Procedia Computer Science, 152*, 341–348. doi:10.1016/j.procs.2019.05.008

Aichner, T., & Jacob, F. (2015). Measuring the degree of corporate social media use. *International Journal of Market Research, 57*(2), 257–276. doi:10.2501/IJMR-2015-018

Ajzen, I., & Fishbein, M. (1980). *Understanding attitudes and predicting social behavior.* Prentice- Hall.

Akakandelwa, A., & Walubita, G. (2017). Students' Social Media Use and its Perceived Impact on their Social Life: A Case Study of the University of Zambia. *The International Journal of Multi-Disciplinary Research, 5*(3), 1–14.

Akar, E., & Topçu, B. (2011). An examination of the factors influencing consumers' attitudes toward social media marketing. *Journal of Internet Commerce, 10*(1), 35–67. doi:10.1080/15332861.2011.558456

Akrivopoulou, C., & Garipidis, N. (2013). *Digital Democracy and the Impact of Technology on Governance and Politics: New Globalized Practices.* IGI Global doi:10.4018/978-1-4666-3637-8

Akrouf, S., Meriem, L., Yahia, B., & Eddine, M. N. (2013). Social Network Analysis and Information Propagation: A Case Study Using Flickr and YouTube Networks. *International Journal of Future Computer and Communication, 2*(3), 246–252. doi:10.7763/IJFCC.2013.V2.161

Aladwani, A. M., & Almarzouq, M. (2016). Understanding compulsive social media use: The premise of complementing self-conceptions mismatch with technology. *Computers in Human Behavior, 60*, 575–581. doi:10.1016/j.chb.2016.02.098

Alam, M., Bhattacharya, S., Mukhopadhyay, D., & Chattopadhyay, A. (2018). *RAPPER: Ransomware Prevention via Performance Counters.* http://arxiv.org/abs/1802.03909

Albers-Miller, N. D., & Gelb, B. D. (1996). Business advertising appeals as a mirror of cultural dimensions: A study of eleven countries. *Journal of Advertising, 25*(4), 57–70. doi:10.1080/00913367.1996.10673512

Albert, S., & Whetten, D. A. (1985). Organizational identity. *Research in Organizational Behavior, 7*, 263–295.

Aldwairi, M., & Alwahedi, A. (2018). Detecting fake news in social media networks. *Procedia Computer Science, 141*, 215–222. doi:10.1016/j.procs.2018.10.171

Alhabash, S., & Ma, M. (2017). A tale of four platforms: Motivations and uses of Facebook, Twitter, Instagram, and Snapchat among college students? *Social Media+Society, 3*(1), 1-13.

Alhosseini, S. A., Najafi, P., Tareaf, R. B., & Meinel, C. (2019). Detect me if you can: Spam bot detection using inductive representation learning. *The Web Conference 2019 - Companion of the World Wide Web Conference, WWW 2019*, 148–153. 10.1145/3308560.3316504

Allcott, H., & Gentzkow, M. (2017). Social media and fake news in the 2016 election. *The Journal of Economic Perspectives, 31*(2), 211–236. doi:10.1257/jep.31.2.211

Allen, K. A., Ryan, T., Gray, D. L., McInerney, D. M., & Waters, L. (2014). Social media use and social connectedness in adolescents: The positives and the potential pitfalls. *The Australian Educational and Developmental Psychologist, 31*(1), 18–31. doi:10.1017/edp.2014.2

Almarabeh, H., & Sulieman, A. (2019). The impact of Cyber threats on Social Networking Sites. *International Journal of Advanced Research in Computer Science, 10*(2), 1–9. Advance online publication. doi:10.26483/ijarcs.v10i2.6384

Al-Menayes, J. J. (2015). Motivations for Using Social Media: An Exploratory Factor Analysis. *International Journal of Psychological Studies, 7*(1), 43–50. doi:10.5539/ijps.v7n1p43

Al-Menayes, J. J. (2015). Social media use, engagement and addiction as predictors of academic performance. *International Journal of Psychological Studies, 7*(4), 86–94. doi:10.5539/ijps.v7n4p86

Alouch, L. D. (2017). *Social Media Marketing and Business Growth of Commercial Banks in Kenya* (Master Thesis). School of Business, Department of Business Administration, University of Nairobi.

Al-Qurishi, M., Al-Rakhami, M., Alamri, A., AlRubaian, M., Rahman, S. M. M., & Hossain, M. S. (2017). Sybil defense techniques in online social networks: A survey. *IEEE Access: Practical Innovations, Open Solutions, 5*, 1200–1219. doi:10.1109/ACCESS.2017.2656635

Alrehili, A., & Albalawi, K. (2019). Sentiment Analysis of Customer Reviews Using Ensemble Method. *2019 International Conference on Computer and Information Sciences (ICCIS)*. 10.1109/ICCISci.2019.8716454

Alsalem, F. (2019). Why Do They Post? Motivations and Uses of Snapchat, Instagram and Twitter among Kuwait College Students. *Media Watch, 10*(3), 550–567. doi:10.15655/mw/2019/v10i3/49699

Alvarenga, G. M., Yassuda, M., & Cachioni, M. (2019). Inclusão digital com tablets entre idosos: Metodologia e impacto cognitivo. *Psicologia, Saúde & Doenças, 20*(2), 384–401. doi:10.15309/19psd200209

American Psychiatric Association. (2013). *Diagnostic and Statistical Manual for Mental Disorders* (5th ed.). American Psychiatric Association.

Amichai-Hamburger, Y., Wainapel, G., & Fox, S. (2002). On the Internet no one knows I'm an introvert": Extroversion, neuroticism, and Internet interaction. *Cyberpsychology & Behavior, 5*(2), 125–128. doi:10.1089/109493102753770507 PMID:12025878

Amos, C., Holmes, G., & Strutton, D. (2008). Exploring the relationship between celebrity endorser effects and advertising effectiveness: A quantitative synthesis of effect size. *International Journal of Advertising, 27*(2), 209–234. doi:1 0.1080/02650487.2008.11073052

An, J., Cha, M., Gummadi, K., & Crowcroft, J. (2011). Media landscape in twitter: a world of and political diversity. In *Proceedings of the Fifth International AAAI Conference on Weblogs and Social Media in Barcelona, Spain*. The AAAI Press.

Anastasia, S., & Budi, I. (2016). Twitter sentiment analysis of online transportation service providers. *2016 International Conference on Advanced Computer Science and Information Systems (ICACSIS)*. 10.1109/ICACSIS.2016.7872807

Ancu, M., & Cozma, R. (2009). Myspace politics: Uses and gratifications of befriending candidates. *Journal of Broadcasting & Electronic Media*, *53*(4), 567–583. doi:10.1080/08838150903333064

Anderson, S., Bayard, M., Bennis, P., Cavanagh, J., Dolan, K., Koshgarian, L., Noffke, A., Pizzigati, S., & Sarkar, S. (2017). *The Souls of Poor Folk: Auditing America 50 Years After the Poor People's Campaign Challenged Racism, Poverty, the War Economy/Militarism and Our National Morality*. Retrieved from https://www.poorpeoplescampaign.org/audit/

Anderson, P. (2016). Web 2.0 and beyond: Principles and technologies. In *Web 2.0 and Beyond: Principles and Technologies*. CRC Press. doi:10.1201/b12087-20

Andreassen, C. S. (2015). Online social network site addiction: A comprehensive review. *Current Addiction Reports*, *2*(2), 175–184. doi:10.100740429-015-0056-9

Andreassen, C. S., Griffiths, M. D., Gjertsen, S. R., Krossbakken, E., Kvam, S., & Pallesen, S. (2013). The relationship between behavioral addictions and the five-factor model of personality. *Journal of Behavioral Addictions*, *2*(2), 90–99. doi:10.1556/JBA.2.2013.003 PMID:26165928

Andreassen, C. S., & Pallesen, S. (2014). Social network site addiction – An overview. *Current Pharmaceutical Design*, *20*(25), 4053–4061. doi:10.2174/13816128113199990616 PMID:24001298

Andreassen, C. S., Pallesen, S., & Griffiths, M. D. (2017). The relationship between addictive use of social media, narcissism, and self-esteem: Findings from a large national survey. *Addictive Behaviors*, *64*, 287–293. Advance online publication. doi:10.1016/j.addbeh.2016.03.006 PMID:27072491

Andreassen, C. S., Torsheim, T., Brunborg, G. S., & Pallesen, S. (2012). Development of a Facebook addiction scale. *Psychological Reports*, *110*(2), 501–517. doi:10.2466/02.09.18.PR0.110.2.501-517 PMID:22662404

Andreassen, C. S., Torsheim, T., & Pallesen, S. (2014). Use of online social network sites for personal purposes at work: Does it impair self-reported performance? *Comprehensive Psychology*, *3*(1), 18. doi:10.2466/01.21.CP.3.18

Anger, I., & Kittl, C. (2011). Measuring influence on Twitter, In *Proceedings of the 11th International Conference on Knowledge Management and Knowledge Technologies (i-KNOW '11)*. ACM.

Anto, M., Antony, M., Muhsina, K., Johny, N., James, V., & Wilson, A. (2016). Product rating using sentiment analysis. *2016 International Conference on Electrical, Electronics, and Optimization Techniques (ICEEOT)*. 10.1109/ICEEOT.2016.7755346

Apruzzese, G., Colajanni, M., Ferretti, L., Guido, A., & Marchetti, M. (2018). On the effectiveness of machine and deep learning for cyber security. *International Conference on Cyber Conflict, CYCON*, 371–389. 10.23919/CYCON.2018.8405026

Apte, M., Palshikar, G. K., & Baskaran, S. (2018). Frauds in Online Social Networks. *RE:view*, 1–18. doi:10.1007/978-3-319-78256-0_1

Aranha, E., & Miranda, S. (2019). *O papel dos influenciadores digitais no processo de intenção de compra* [The role of digital influencers on the buying intention process]. Novas Edições Académicas.

Arceneaux, N., & Weiss, A. S. (2010). Seems stupid until you try it: Press coverage of Twitter, 2006-9. *New Media & Society*, *12*(8), 1262–1279. doi:10.1177/1461444809360773

Armano, D. (2011, January 18). *Pillars of the new influence*. https://hbr.org/2011/01/the-six-pillars-of-the-new-inf

Arora, P., & Scheiber, L. (2017). Slumdog romance: Facebook love and digital privacy at the margins. *Media Culture & Society*, *39*(3), 408–422. doi:10.1177/0163443717691225 PMID:29708133

Arti, D. K. P., & Agrawal, S. (2019). An Opinion Mining for Indian Premier League Using Machine Learning Techniques. *2019 4th International Conference on Internet of Things: Smart Innovation and Usages (IoT-SIU)*. doi: 10.1109/iot-siu.2019.8777472

Ashraf, N., & Javed, T. (2014). Impact of social networking on employee performance. *Business Management and Strategy*, *5*(2), 139–150. doi:10.5296/bms.v5i2.5978

Aslam, A. (2017). *Ordinary democracy: Sovereignty and Citizenship Beyond the Neoliberal Impasse*. Oxford University Press. doi:10.1093/acprof:oso/9780190601812.001.0001

Assaad, W., & Gómez, J. M. (2011). Social network in marketing (social media marketing) opportunities and risks. *International Journal of Managing Public Sector Information and Communication Technologies*, *2*(1), 13.

Atroszko, P. A., Balcerowska, J. M., Bereznowski, P., Biernatowska, A., Pallesen, S., & Andreassen, C. S. (2018). Facebook addiction among Polish undergraduate students: Validity of measurement and relationship with personality and well-being. *Computers in Human Behavior*, *85*, 329–338. doi:10.1016/j.chb.2018.04.001

Attarwala, A., Dimitrov, S., & Obeidi, A. (2017). How efficient is Twitter: Predicting 2012 U.S. presidential elections using Support Vector Machine via Twitter and comparing against Iowa Electronic Markets. *2017 Intelligent Systems Conference (IntelliSys)*. 10.1109/IntelliSys.2017.8324363

Auxier, B., & Rainie, L. (2019, November 15). Key takeaways on Americans' views about privacy, surveillance and data-sharing. *Pew Research Center*. Retrieved on March 22, 2020 from https://www.pewresearch.org/fact-tank/2019/2011/2015/key-takeaways-on-americans-views-about-privacy-surveillance-and-data-sharing/

Avinash, M., & Sivasankar, E. (2018). A Study of Feature Extraction Techniques for Sentiment Analysis. *Advances in Intelligent Systems and Computing Emerging Technologies in Data Mining and Information Security*, 475–486. doi:10.1007/978-981-13-1501-5_41

B., V., & M., B. (2016). Analysis of Various Sentiment Classification Techniques. *International Journal of Computer Applications*, *140*(3), 22–27. doi:10.5120/ijca2016909259

Baber, Z. (2002). Engendering or Endangering Democracy? The Internet, Civil Society and the Public Sphere. *Asian Journal of Social Science*, *2*(30), 287–303. doi:10.1163/156853102320405861

Bachelet, C. (2004). *Usages des TIC dans les organisations, une notion à revisiter?* In 9e Colloque de l'AIM.

Badillo, P. Y., & Pélissier, N. (2015). Usages et usagers de l'information numérique. Renouvellement des problématiques et nouveaux enjeux pour les SIC. *Revue française des sciences de l'information et de la communication*, (6).

Baek, S. I., & Kim, Y. M. (2015). Longitudinal analysis of online community dynamics. *Industrial Management & Data Systems*, *115*(4), 661–677. doi:10.1108/IMDS-09-2014-0266

Bagula, A., Zennaro, M., Nungu, A., & Nkoloma, M. (2011). Bridging the Digital Divide in Africa: A Technology Perspective. *Conference: 2011 Wireless Communication and Information (WCI 2011) on Digital Divide and Mobile Applications*. https://www.researchgate.net/publication/233817849_Bridging_the_Digital_Divide_in_Africa_A_Technology_Perspective>

Bajpai, P. (2018). Bitcoin Vs Ethereum: Driven by Different Purposes. *Investopedia*. Available: https://www.investopedia.com/articles/investing/031416/bitcoin-vs-ethereum-driven-different-purposes.asp

Baker, M. (2009). The Impact of Social Networking Sites on Politics. *The Review: A Journal of Undergraduate Student Research, 10*, 72-74. http://fisherpub.sjfc.edu/ur/vol10/iss1/12

Baker, J. R., & Moore, S. M. (2008). Blogging as a social tool: A psychosocial examination of the effects of blogging. *Cyberpsychology & Behavior, 11*(6), 747–749. doi:10.1089/cpb.2008.0053

Balasuriya, U. C., & Jayalal, S. (2015, August). *Impact of social network usage on the job performance of IT professionals in Sri Lank*a. In *2015 Fifteenth International Conference on Advances in ICT for Emerging Regions (ICTer)* (pp. 214-219). IEEE. 10.1109/ICTER.2015.7377691

Balcerzak, B., Kopeć, W., Nielek, R., Kruk, S., Warpe-Chowski, K., Wasik, M., & Wegrzyn, M. (2017). Press F1 for help: Participatory design for dealing with on-line and real-life security of older adults. In *Proceedings of 12th International Scientific and Technical Conference on Computer Sciences and Information Technologies* (Vol. 1, pp. 240-243). 10.1109/STC-CSIT.2017.8098778

Bandura, A. (1977). *Social Learning Theory*. General Learning Press.

Bányai, F., Zsila, Á., Király, O., Maraz, A., Elekes, Z., Griffiths, M. D., Andreassen, C. S., & Demetrovics, Z. (2017). Problematic social media use: Results from a large-scale nationally representative adolescent sample. *PLoS One, 12*(1), e0169839. doi:10.1371/journal.pone.0169839 PMID:28068404

Barak, A., Boniel-Nissim, M., & Suler, J. (2008). Fostering empowerment in online support groups. *Computers in Human Behavior, 24*(5), 1867–1883. doi:10.1016/j.chb.2008.02.004

Barley, S. R., & Tolbert, P. S. (1997). Institutionalization and structuration: Studying the links between action and institution. *Organization Studies, 18*(1), 93–117. doi:10.1177/017084069701800106

Barnidge, M., Huber, B., de Zúñiga, H. G., & Liu, J. H. (2018). Social Media as a Sphere for "Risky" Political Expression: A Twenty-Country Multilevel Comparative Analysis. *The International Journal of Press/Politics, 23*(2), 161–182. doi:10.1177/1940161218773838

Barroso, C., Ábad, M., & Valle, M. (2015). Mayores e internet: La red como fuente de oportunidades para un envelhecimiento activo. *Media Education Research Journal, 45*(23), 29–36.

Basak, E., & Calisir, F. (2014). Uses and Gratifications of LinkedIn: An Exploratory Study. *Proceedings of the World Congress on Engineering 2014, 2*.

Basit, A., & Hassan, Z. (2018). The Impact of Social Media Usage on Employee and Organization Performance: A Study on Social Media Tools Used by an IT Multinational in Malaysia. *Journal of Marketing and Consumer Behaviour in Emerging Markets, 1*(7), 48–65.

Bates, R. H., Block, S. A., Fayad, G., & Hoeffler, A. (2013). The New Institutionalism and Africa. *Journal of African Economies, 22*(4), 499-522. doi:10.1093/jae/ejs031

Batista, E. B., Silva, L., Moura, L., Queiroz, V., Matos, R., Silva, S., Oliveira, D. (2018). Inclusão Digital como ferramenta ao envelhecimento ativo: um relato de experiência. *Prisma.com, 38*.

Batool, R., Khattak, A., Maqbool, J., & Lee, S. (2013). Precise tweet classification and sentiment analysis. *2013 IEEE/ACIS 12th International Conference on Computer and Information Science (ICIS)*. 10.1109/ICIS.2013.6607883

Baturay, M. H., & Toker, S. (2017). Self-esteem shapes the impact of GPA and general health on Facebook addiction: A mediation analysis. *Social Science Computer Review, 35*(5), 555–575. doi:10.1177/0894439316656606

Bauer, J. M., Gai, P., Kim, J-H., Muth, T., & Wildman, S. (2002). *Broadband: Benefits and policy challenges.* A report prepared for Merit Network, Inc.

Baumann, C., Hoadley, S., Hamin, H., & Nugraha, A. (2017). Competitiveness vis-à-vis service quality as drivers of customer loyalty mediated by perceptions of regulation and stability in steady and volatile markets. *Journal of Retailing and Consumer Services, 36,* 62–74. doi:10.1016/j.jretconser.2016.12.005

Baumeister, R. F. (1993). Understanding the inner nature of low self-esteem: Uncertain, fragile, protective, and conflicted. In *Self-esteem* (pp. 201–218). Springer. doi:10.1007/978-1-4684-8956-9_11

Beer, D. D. (2008). Social network (ing) sites... revisiting the story so far: A response to danah boyd & Nicole Ellison. *Journal of Computer-Mediated Communication, 13*(2), 516–529. doi:10.1111/j.1083-6101.2008.00408.x

Behdenna, S., Barigou, F., & Belalem, G. (2018). Document Level Sentiment Analysis: A survey. *EAI Endorsed Transactions on Context-Aware Systems and Applications, 4*(13), 154339. doi:10.4108/eai.14-3-2018.154339

Bekkers, V. J. J. M. (2003). E-Government and the Emergence of Virtual Organizations in the Public Sector. *Information Polity, 8*(3/4), 89–102.

Belk, R. W. (2013). Extended self in a digital world. *The Journal of Consumer Research, 40*(3), 477–500. doi:10.1086/671052

Bell, C., Fausset, C., Farmer, S., Nguyen, J., Harley, L., & Fain, W. B. (2013). Examining social media use among older adults. In *Proceedings of the 24th ACM Conference on Hypertext and Social Media* (pp. 158–163). ACM. 10.1145/2481492.2481509

Benbasat, I., & Zmud, R. W. (1999). Empirical research in information systems: The practice of relevance. *Management Information Systems Quarterly, 23*(1), 3–16. doi:10.2307/249403

Bennett, J., Owers, M., Pitt, M., & Tucker, M. (2010). *Workplace impact of social networking.* Property Management. doi:10.1108/02637471011051282

Bergkvist, L., & Zhou, K. Q. (2016). Celebrity endorsements: A literature review and research agenda. *International Journal of Advertising, 35*(4), 642–663. doi:10.1080/02650487.2015.1137537

Bergström, A., & Belfrage, M. J. (2018). News in Social Media. *Digital Journalism, 6*(5), 583–598. doi:10.1080/2167 0811.2018.1423625

Berk, G., & Galvan, D. C. (2013). Processes of Creative Syncretism Experiential Origins of Institutional Order and Change. In G. Berk, D. C. Galvan, & V. Hattam (Eds.), *Political Creativity: Reconfiguring Institutional Order and Change* (pp. 29–54). University of Pennsylvania Press.

Berrueta, E., Morato, D., Magana, E., & Izal, M. (2020). Open Repository for the Evaluation of Ransomware Detection Tools. *IEEE Access: Practical Innovations, Open Solutions, 8,* 65658–65669. doi:10.1109/ACCESS.2020.2984187

Berthod, O. (2016). Institutional Theory of Organizations. In A. Farazmand (Ed.), *Global Encyclopedia of Public Administration, Public Policy, and Governance.* Springer. doi:10.1007/978-3-319-31816-5_63-1

Beskow, D. M., & Carley, K. M. (2018). *Bot-hunter: A Tiered Approach to Detecting & Characterizing Automated Activity on Twitter.* http://www.casos.cs.cmu.edu/publications/papers/LB_5.pdf

Beyens, I., Frison, E., & Eggermont, S. (2016). "I don't want to miss a thing": Adolescents' fear of missing out and its relationship to adolescents' social needs, Facebook use, and Facebook related stress. *Computers in Human Behavior, 64,* 1–8. doi:10.1016/j.chb.2016.05.083

Bigonha, C. A. S., Cardoso, T. N. C., Moro, M. M., Gonçalves, M. A., & Almeida, V. A. F. (2012). Sentiment-based influence detection on Twitter. *Journal of the Brazilian Computer Society, 18*(3), 169–183. doi:10.100713173-011-0051-5

Bijitha, C. V., Sukumaran, R., & Nath, H. V. (2020). A survey on ransomware detection techniques. *Communications in Computer and Information Science, 1186*, 55–68. doi:10.1007/978-981-15-3817-9_4

Bilge, L., Strufe, T., Balzarotti, D., & Kirda, E. (2009). *All your contacts are belong to us.* doi:10.1145/1526709.1526784

Bischof-Kastner, C., Kuntsche, E., & Wolstein, J. (2014). Identifying problematic Internet users: Development and validation of the Internet Motive Questionnaire for Adolescents (IMQ-A). *Journal of Medical Internet Research, 16*(10), e230. doi:10.2196/jmir.3398 PMID:25299174

Biswas, A., Ingle, N., & Roy, M. (2014). Influence of Social Media on Voting Behavior. *Journal of Power. Politics & Governance, 2*(2), 127–155.

Błachnio, A., Przepiorka, A., & Pantic, I. (2016). Association between Facebook addiction, self-esteem and life satisfaction: A cross-sectional study. *Computers in Human Behavior, 55*, 701–705. doi:10.1016/j.chb.2015.10.026

Blackwell, D., Leaman, C., Tramposch, R., Osborne, C., & Liss, M. (2017). Extraversion, neuroticism, attachment style and fear of missing out as predictors of social media use and addiction. *Personality and Individual Differences, 116*, 69–72. doi:10.1016/j.paid.2017.04.039

Block, M., Stern, D. B., Raman, K., Lee, S., Carey, J., Humphreys, A. A., ... Blood, A. J. (2014). The relationship between self-report of depression and media usage. *Frontiers in Human Neuroscience, 8*, 712. doi:10.3389/fnhum.2014.00712 PMID:25309388

Bloggers Association of Kenya (BAKE) (2016). State of the Internet in Kenya 2016 Report. *Bloggers Association of Kenya (BAKE).*

Bloggers Association of Kenya (BAKE). (2015). State of Blogging & Social Media in Kenya 2015 Report. *Bloggers Association of Kenya (BAKE).*

Bodroža, B., & Jovanović, T. (2016). Validation of the new scale for measuring behaviors of Facebook users: Psycho-Social Aspects of Facebook Use (PSAFU). *Computers in Human Behavior, 54*, 425–435. doi:10.1016/j.chb.2015.07.032

Bohr & Bashir. (2014). Who Uses Bitcoin? An exploration of the Bitcoin community. *2014 Twelfth Annual International Conference on Privacy, Security and Trust.*

Bondielli, A., & Marcelloni, F. (2019). A Survey on Fake News and Rumour Detection Techniques. *Information Sciences, 497*, 38–55. Advance online publication. doi:10.1016/j.ins.2019.05.035

Borman, W. C., & Motowidlo, S. J. (1997). Task performance and contextual performance: The meaning for personnel selection research. *Human Performance, 10*(2), 99–109. doi:10.120715327043hup1002_3

Borsari, B., & Carey, K. B. (2003). Descriptive and injunctive norms in college drinking: A meta-analytic integration. *Journal of Studies on Alcohol, 64*(3), 331–341. doi:10.15288/jsa.2003.64.331 PMID:12817821

Bosch, T. (2019). Social Media and Protest Movements in South Africa. In Social Media and Politics in Africa: Democracy, Censorship and Security. London: Zed Books.

Bosch, T. (2017). Twitter activism and youth in South Africa: The case of# RhodesMustFall. *Information Communication and Society, 20*(2), 221–232. doi:10.1080/1369118X.2016.1162829

Bouazizi, M., & Ohtsuki, T. (2016). Sentiment Analysis in Twitter: From Classification to Quantification of Sentiments within Tweets. *2016 IEEE Global Communications Conference (GLOBECOM).* 10.1109/GLOCOM.2016.7842262

Bovet, A., & Makse, H. A. (2019). Influence of fake news in Twitter during the 2016 US presidential election. *Nature Communications*, *10*(1), 1–14. doi:10.103841467-018-07761-2 PMID:30602729

Boyce, P., & Parker, G. (1989). Development of a scale to measure interpersonal sensitivity. *The Australian and New Zealand Journal of Psychiatry*, *23*(3), 341–351. doi:10.1177/000486748902300320 PMID:2803146

boyd, d., & Ellison, N.B. (2007). Social network sites: Definition, history, and scholarship. *Journal of Computer-Mediated Communication, 13*(1), 210–230.

Boyd, d., & Ellison. (2008). Social Networking Sites: Definition, History, and Scholarship. *Journal of Computer-Mediated Communication, 13*(1), 210-230.

Boyd, D. M., & Ellison, N. B. (2007). Social network sites: Definition, history, and scholarship. *Journal of Computer-Mediated Communication*, *13*(1), 210–230. doi:10.1111/j.1083-6101.2007.00393.x

Bozoglan, B., Demirer, V., & Sahin, I. (2013). Loneliness, self-esteem, and life satisfaction as predictors of Internet addiction: A cross-sectional study among Turkish university students. *Scandinavian Journal of Psychology*, *54*(4), 313–319. doi:10.1111jop.12049 PMID:23577670

Brailovskaia, J., Margraf, J., & Köllner, V. (2019). Addicted to Facebook? Relationship between Facebook Addiction Disorder, duration of Facebook use and narcissism in an inpatient sample. *Psychiatry Research*, *273*, 52–57. doi:10.1016/j.psychres.2019.01.016 PMID:30639564

Brandt, A. M. (2012). Inventing conflicts of interest: A history of tobacco industry tactics. *American Journal of Public Health*, *102*(1), 63–71. doi:10.2105/AJPH.2011.300292 PMID:22095331

Brandtzæg, P. B., & Heim, J. (2009). Why People Use Social Networking Sites. In A. A. Ozok & P. Zaphiris (Eds.), Lecture Notes in Computer Science: Vol. 5621. *Online Communities and Social Computing. OCSC 2009*. Springer. doi:10.1007/978-3-642-02774-1_16

Brandtzaeg, P., & Følstad, A. (2017). Trust and Distrust in Online Fact-Checking Services. *Communications of the ACM*, *60*(9), 65–71. doi:10.1145/3122803

Bravo, R. B., & Del Valle, M. E. (2017). Opinion leadership in parliamentary twitter networks: A matter of layers of interaction? *Journal of Information Technology & Politics*, *14*(3), 263–276. doi:10.1080/19331681.2017.1337602

Breuer, A., Landman, T., & Farquhar, D. (2015). Social media and protest mobilization: Evidence from the Tunisian revolution. *Democratization*, *22*(4), 764–792. doi:10.1080/13510347.2014.885505

Bright, L. F., Logan, K., English, A., Kingman, J., & Lyons, K. (2019). *Social media fatigue and the advertising industry: How are consumers, clients, and content creators dealing with the pressure to be constantly connected?* Paper presented at the American Academy of Advertising Conference, Dallas, TX.

Britt, R. K., Hayes, J. L., Britt, B. C., & Park, H. (2020). Too big to sell? A computational analysis of network and content characteristics among mega and micro beauty and fashion social media influencers. *Journal of Interactive Advertising*, *20*(2), 111–118. doi:10.1080/15252019.2020.1763873

Bronner, F., & de Hoog, R. (2014). Social media and consumer choice. *International Journal of Market Research*, *56*(1), 51–71. doi:10.2501/IJMR-2013-053

Brooks, S., & Califf, C. (2017). Social media-induced technostress: Its impact on the job performance of it professionals and the moderating role of job characteristics. *Computer Networks*, *114*, 143–153. doi:10.1016/j.comnet.2016.08.020

Brown, K. M. (2017). *Anteil der mehrmals täglichen Nutzer von ausgewählten soizalen Netzwerken nach Altersgruppen weltweit im Jahr 2016.* Retrieved from https://de.statista.com/statistik/daten/studie/680253/umfrage/mehrmals-taegliche-nutzung-von-sozialen-netzwerken-nach-altersgruppen/

Brown, S. S., & Hermann, M. G. (2020). *Black Spots in Cyberspace?* doi:10.1057/978-1-137-49670-6_7

Brummette, J., & Fussell Sisco, H. (2018). Holy guacamole! Framing and the Chipotle contamination issue. *Journal of Communication Management, 22*(3), 280–295. doi:10.1108/JCOM-08-2017-0085

Bruns, A., & Burgess, J. (2012). Researching News Discussion on Twitter. *Journalism Studies, 13*(5-6), 801–814. doi:10.1080/1461670X.2012.664428

Bullock, L. (2018, July 31). How to evaluate and partner with social media influencers *Social Media Examiner.* https://www.socialmediaexaminer. com/partner-social-media-influencers/

Burke, M., Marlow, C., Lento, T., Fitzpatrick, G., Hudson, S., Edwards, K., & Rodden, T. (2010). proceedings of the SIGCHI Conference on Human Factors in Computing Systems. *Social Network Activity and Social Well-Being,* 1909-1912.

Burkell, J., Fortier, A., Yeung, L. L., Wong, C., & Simpson, J. L. (2014). Facebook: Public space, or private space? *Information Communication and Society, 17*(8), 974–985. doi:10.1080/1369118X.2013.870591

Burkhardt, J. M. (2017). History of Fake News. *Library Technology Reports, 53*(8), 5–9.

Burton, P., & Mutongwizo, T. (2009). Inescapable violence: Cyber bullying and electronic violence against young people in South Africa. *Centre for Justice and Crime Prevention, 8,* 1–12.

Burton, S., Dadich, A., & Soboleva, A. (2013). Competing voices: Marketing and counter-marketing alcohol on Twitter. *Journal of Nonprofit & Public Sector Marketing, 25*(2), 186–209. doi:10.1080/10495142.2013.787836

BuzzFeed News. (2016). *Hyperpartisan Facebook Pages Are Publishing False And Misleading Information At An Alarming Rate.* Retrieved from https://www.buzzfeednews.com/article/craigsilverman/partisan-fb-pages-analysis#.pulP7wZbl

Calderaro, A. (2018). Social Media and Politics. In The SAGE Handbook of Political Sociology. Sage. doi:10.4135/9781526416513.n46

Çam, E., & Isbulan, O. (2012). A new addiction for teacher candidates: Social networks. *The Turkish Online Journal of Educational Technology, 11,* 14–19.

Campbell, H. (2010, July 4). *Visualizing Email Communications using NodeXL.* Retrieved June 01, 2020, from http://ichromatiq.blogspot.com/2010/07/visualizing-email-communications-using.html

Campbell, J. P. (1990). M*odeling the performance prediction problem in industrial and organizational psychology.* Academic Press.

Campbell, J. P., Gasser, M. B., & Oswald, F. L. (1996). The substantive nature of job performance variability. *Individual Differences and Behavior in Organizations, 258,* 299.

Campbell, C., & Farrell, J. R. (2020). More than meets the eye: The functional components underlying influencer marketing. *Business Horizons, 63*(4), 469–479. doi:10.1016/j.bushor.2020.03.003

Cao, C., & Caverlee, J. (2015). Detecting Spam URLs in Social Media via. *The Behavior Analyst,* 703–714. doi:10.1007/978-3-319-16354-3_77

Cao, X., Wang, P., Chaudhry, S., Li, L., Guo, X., Vogel, D., & Zhang, X. (2016). Exploring the influence of social media on employee work performance. *Internet Research, 26*(2), 529–545. doi:10.1108/IntR-11-2014-0299

Cao, X., Yu, L., Liu, Z., & Wang, J. (2018). Excessive social media use at work. *Information Technology & People*.

Caplan, S. E. (2002). Problematic Internet use and psychosocial well-being: Development of a theory-based cognitive-behavioral measurement instrument. *Computers in Human Behavior, 18*(5), 553–575. doi:10.1016/S0747-5632(02)00004-3

Caplan, S. E. (2003). Preference for online social interaction: A theory of problematic Internet use and psychosocial well-being. *Communication Research, 30*(6), 625–648. doi:10.1177/0093650203257842

Caprara, G. V., Barbaranelli, C., Borgogni, L., & Perugini, M. (1993). The "Big Five Questionnaire": A new questionnaire to assess the five factor model. *Personality and Individual Differences, 15*(3), 281–288. doi:10.1016/0191-8869(93)90218-R

Caprara, G. V., Barbaranelli, C., & Livi, S. (1994). Mapping personality dimensions in the Big Five model. *European Review of Applied Psychology, 44*(1), 9–15.

Cárdenas, A., Ballesteros, C. & Jara, R. (2017). Redes Sociales y Campañas Electorales en Iberoamérica. Un Análisis Comparativo de los Casos de España, México y Chile. *Cuadernos.info: Comunicación y Medios en Iberoamérica*, (41), 19-40. doi:10.7764/cdi.41.1259

Cardoso, G. (2008). From mass to networked communication: Communicational models and the informational society. *International Journal of Communication, 2*, 587–630.

Cardoso, G., Coelho, A. R., & Costa, A. F. (2015). *A sociedade em rede em Portugal: Uma década de transição*. Campo de Letras.

Cardoso, G., Costa, A. F., Conceição, M., & Gomes, A. (2003). *A sociedade em rede em Portugal*. Campo de Letras.

Carlisle, J., & Patton, R. (2013). Is Social Media Changing How We Understand Political Engagement? An Analysis of Facebook and the 2008 Presidential Election. *Political Research Quarterly, 66*(4), 883–895. doi:10.1177/1065912913482758

Carter, D. (2016). Hustle and brand: The sociotechnical shaping of influence. *Social Media & Society, 2*(3), 1–12.

Casaló, L. V., Flavián, C., & Ibáñez-Sánchez, S. (2020). Influencers on Instagram: Antecedents and consequences of opinion leadership. *Journal of Business Research, 117*, 510–519. doi:10.1016/j.jbusres.2018.07.005

Castells, E. (2003). *A galáxia da internet*. Jorge Zahar.

Castells, M. (2009). *A sociedade em rede. A era da informação: Economia, sociedade e cultura*. Paz e Terra.

Castells, M. (2012). *Networks of outrage and hope: Social movements in the internet age*. Wiley.

Cennamo, C., & Santalo, J. (2013). Platform competition: Strategic trade-offs in platform markets. *Strategic Management Journal, 34*(11), 1331–1350. doi:10.1002mj.2066

Cetinkaya, A. S., & Rashid, M. (2018). *The Effect of Social Media on Employees' Job Performance: The mediating Role of Organizational Structure*. Academic Press.

Ch'ng, E. (2015). The bottom-up formation and maintenance of a twitter community: Analysis of the# freejahar twitter community. *Industrial Management & Data Systems, 115*(4), 612–624. doi:10.1108/IMDS-11-2014-0332

Cha, M., Haddadi, H., Benevenuto, F., & Gummadi, K. P. (Eds.). (2010). Measuring user influence in twitter: The million follower fallacy. *Fourth international AAAI conference on weblogs and social media*.

Chakraborty, P., Pria, U., Rony, M., & Majumdar, M. (2017). Predicting stock movement using sentiment analysis of Twitter feed. *2017 6th International Conference on Informatics, Electronics and Vision & 2017 7th International Symposium in Computational Medical and Health Technology (ICIEV-ISCMHT)*. 10.1109/ICIEV.2017.8338584

Cha, M., Haddadi, H., Benevenuto, F., & Gummadi, P. K. (2010). Measuring User Influence in Twitter: The Million Follower Fallacy. *Proceedings of the Fourth International Conference on Weblogs and Social Media (ICWSM 2010).*

Chapple, C., & Cownie, F. (2017). An investigation into viewers' trust in and response towards disclosed paid-for-endorsements by YouTube lifestyle vloggers. *Journal of Promotional Communications, 5*, 110–136.

Charbonnier, A., Silva, C. A., & Roussel, P. (2007). *Vers une mesure de la performance contextuelle au travail de l'individu: étude exploratoire.* XVIIIème congrès de l'AGRH.

Charbonnier-Voirin, A., & Roussel, P. (2012). Adaptive performance: A new scale to measure individual performance in organizations. *Canadian Journal of Administrative Sciences/Revue Canadienne des Sciences de l'Administration, 29*(3), 280-293.

Charles-Pauvers, B., Comeiras, N., Peyrat-Guillard, D., & Roussel, P. (2006). *Les déterminants psychologiques de la performance au travail.* Un bilan des connaissances et proposition de voies de recherche.

Charney, T., & Greenberg, B. S. (2002). Uses and gratification of the Internet: Communication, technology and science. In C. Lin & D. Atkin (Eds.), *Communication, technology and society: New media adoption and use* (pp. 379–407). Hampton Pres.

Charoensukmongkol, P. (2014). Effects of support and job demands on social media use and work outcomes. *Computers in Human Behavior, 36*, 340–349. doi:10.1016/j.chb.2014.03.061

Chatora, A. (2012). *Encouraging Political Participation in Africa The Potential of Social Media Platforms.* Academic Press.

Chavoshi, N., Hamooni, H., & Mueen, A. (2017). DeBot: Twitter bot detection via warped correlation. *Proceedings - IEEE International Conference on Data Mining, ICDM.* 10.1109/ICDM.2016.86

Chen, I. Y. (2008). A social network-based system for supporting interactive collaboration in knowledge sharing over peer-to-peer network. *International Journal of Human-Computer Studies, 66*(1), 36–50. doi:10.1016/j.ijhcs.2007.08.005

Chen, S., Zhang, H., Lin, M., & Lv, S. (2011, December). Comparision of microblogging service between Sina Weibo and Twitter. In *Proceedings of 2011 International Conference on Computer Science and Network Technology* (Vol. 4, pp. 2259-2263). IEEE. 10.1109/ICCSNT.2011.6182424

Chen, W. J., Boase, J., & Wellman, B. (2002). The Global villagers: Comparing Internet users and uses around the world. In B. Wellman & C. Haythornthwaite (Eds.), *The Internet in Everyday Life* (pp. 74–113). Blackwell. doi:10.1002/9780470774298.ch2

Cheong, Y., Kim, K., & Zheng, L. (2010). Advertising appeals as a reflection of culture: A cross-cultural analysis of food advertising appeals in China and the US. *Asian Journal of Communication, 20*(1), 1–16. doi:10.1080/01292980903440848

Chesney, T., & Su, D. K. S. (2010). The impact of anonymity on weblog credibility. *International Journal of Human-Computer Studies, 68*(10), 710–718. doi:10.1016/j.ijhcs.2010.06.001

Chevrin, V. (2006). *L'interaction Usagers/Services, multimodale et multicanale: une première proposition appliquée au domaine du e-Commerce* (Doctoral dissertation). Lille 1.

Chiew, K. L., Yong, K. S. C., & Tan, C. L. (2018). A survey of phishing attacks: Their types, vectors and technical approaches. In *Expert Systems with Applications* (Vol. 106, pp. 1–20). Elsevier Ltd., doi:10.1016/j.eswa.2018.03.050

Chiu, C., Lin, D., & Silverman, A. (2012). *China's social-media boom.* McKinsey & Company.

Choi, M., Sang, Y., & Woo, H. (2014). Exploring political discussions by Korean twitter users A look at opinion leadership and homophily phenomenon. *ParkAslib Journal of Information Management, 66*(6), 582–602. doi:10.1108/AJIM-11-2012-0089

Choi, N. G., & Dinitto, D. M. (2013). Internet use among older adults: Association with health needs, psychological capital, and social capital. *Journal of Medical Internet Research, 15*(5), e97. doi:10.2196/jmir.2333 PMID:23681083

Choi, S. M., & Ferle, C. L. (2004). Convergence across American and Korean young adults: Socialisation variables indicate the verdict is still out. *International Journal of Advertising, 23*(4), 479–506. doi:10.1080/02650487.2004.11072896

Choi, S. M., & Rifon, N. J. (2012). It is a match: The impact of congruence between celebrity image and consumer ideal self on endorsement effectiveness. *Psychology and Marketing, 29*(9), 639–650. doi:10.1002/mar.20550

Choi, Y. (2018). Narcissism and social media addiction in workplace. Journal of Asian Finance. *Economics and Business, 5*(2), 95–104.

Chopik, W. J. (2016). The benefits of social technology use among older adults are mediated by reduced loneliness. *Cyberpsychology, Behavior, and Social Networking, 19*(9), 551–556. doi:10.1089/cyber.2016.0151 PMID:27541746

Chou, H. T. G., Hammond, R. J., & Johnson, R. (2013). How Facebook might reveal users' attitudes toward work and relationships with coworkers. *Cyberpsychology, Behavior, and Social Networking, 16*(2), 136–139. doi:10.1089/cyber.2012.0321 PMID:23276260

Chung, D., & Nam, C. S. (2007). An analysis of the variables predicting instant messenger use. *New Media & Society, 9*(2), 212–234. doi:10.1177/1461444807072217

Chung, W., & Paynter, J. (2002). Privacy Issues on the Internet. *Proceedings of the 35th Hawaii International Conference on System Sciences.* 10.1109/HICSS.2002.994191

Church, K., & de Oliveira, R. (2013). What's up with WhatsApp?: Comparing mobile instant messaging behaviors with traditional SMS. *Proceedings of the 15th International Conference on Human-Computer Interaction with Mobile Devices and Services,* 352-361. 10.1145/2493190.2493225

Cialdini, R. B., Kallgren, C. A., & Reno, R. R. (1991). A focus theory of normative conduct: A theoretical refinement and reevaluation of the role of norms in human behavior. In Advances in Experimental Social Psychology (Vol. 24, pp. 201–234). Academic Press. doi:10.1016/S0065-2601(08)60330-5

Cigref. (2004). MUSTIC - Métiers et usages des TIC. *La recherche au Cigref, 1,* 17-35.

CIPESA. (2019). Despots and Disruptions: Five Dimensions of Internet Shutdowns in Africa. *CIPESA: Collaboration on International ICT Policy for East and Southern Africa.*

Clauset, A., Newman, M. E. J., & Moore, C. (2004). Finding community structure in very large networks. *Physical Review. E, 70*(6), 066111. doi:10.1103/PhysRevE.70.066111

Clayton, R. B., Osborne, R. E., Miller, B. K., & Oberle, C. D. (2013). Loneliness, anxiousness, and substance use as predictors of Facebook use. *Computers in Human Behavior, 29*(3), 687–693. doi:10.1016/j.chb.2012.12.002

Cleveland, C. (2013) *Disunity in Christ: Uncovering the Hidden Forces that Keep Us Apart.* InterVarsity Press.

Coccia, M. (2018). An introduction to the theories of institutional change. *Journal of Economics Library, 5*(4), 337–344.

Coëffé. (2019). *Le média des professionnels du digital.* https://www.blogdumoderateur.com/chiffres-facebook/

Coelho, A. R. (2019). *Seniores 2.0: Inclusão digital na sociedade em rede* [Unpublished doctoral dissertation]. Lisbon University Institute, Lisbon, Portugal.

Comegys, C., Hannula, M., & Väisänen, J. (2006). Longitudinal comparison of Finnish and US online shopping behavior among university students: The five-stage buying decision process. *Journal of Targeting. Measurement and Analysis for Marketing, 14*(4), 336–356. doi:10.1057/palgrave.jt.5740193

Çömlekçi, M. F. (2019). Sosyal Medyada Dezenformasyon Ve Haber Doğrulama Platformlarının Pratikleri (Disinformation On Social Media And Practices Of Fact-Checking Platforms). *Gümüşhane Üniversitesi İletişim Fakültesi Elektronik Dergisi, 7*(3), 1549–1563.

Çömlekçi, M. F. (2020). *Combating Fake News Online: Turkish Fact-Checking Services. In Navigating Fake News, Alternative Facts, and Misinformation in a Post-Truth World.* IGI Global.

Cooley, D., & Parks-Yancy, R. (2019). The effect of social media on perceived information credibility and decision making. *Journal of Internet Commerce, 18*(3), 249–269. doi:10.1080/15332861.2019.1595362

Corchia, L. (2019). Political Communication in Social Networks Election Campaigns and Digital Data Analysis: A Bibliographic Review. *Rivista Trimestrale di Scienza dell'Administrazione. Studi di Teoria e Ricerca Sociale.* http://www.rtsa.eu/

Corcoran, K. (2018, March 28). Facebook is overhauling its privacy settings in response to the Cambridge Analytica scandal. *Business Insider.* Retrieved on March 31, 2018 from https://www.businessinsider.com/facebook-overhauls-privacy-settings-after-cambridge-analytica-scandal-2018-2013

Corduan, A. (2018). *Social media als instrument der kundenkommunikation.* Springer. doi:10.1007/978-3-658-22317-5

Corre, M. (2011). *Les réseaux sociaux dans une stratégie de communication d'une grande entreprise.* Academic Press.

Coto, M. C., Lizano, F., Rivera, S. M., & Fuentes, J. (2017). Social media and elderly people: Research trends. In G. Meiselwitz (Ed.), *Social computing and social media: Applications and analytics* (pp. 65–81). Springer International Publishing. doi:10.1007/978-3-319-58562-8_6

Cotter, K. (2019). Playing the visibility game: How digital influencers and algorithms negotiate influence on Instagram. *New Media & Society, 21*(4), 895–913. doi:10.1177/1461444818815684

Coursaris, C. K., Van Osch, W., & Kourganoff, C. (2018). Designing the medium and the message for sponsorship recognition on social media: The interplay of influencer type, disclosure type, and consumer culture. SIGCHI 2018 Proceedings.

Coursaris, C. K., Yun, Y., & Sung, J. (2010). *Twitter Users vs. Quitters: A Uses and Gratifications and Diffusion of Innovations approach in understanding the role of mobility in microblogging.* Paper presented at the Mobile Business and 2010 Ninth Global Mobility Roundtable (ICMB-GMR), 2010 Ninth International Conference. 10.1109/ICMB-GMR.2010.44

Coyne, C. J., & Leeson, P. T. (2009). Media as a Mechanism of Institutional Change and Reinforcement. *Kyklos. International Review for Social Sciences, 1*(62), 1–14.

Crane, C. (2020). *The Definitive Cyber Security Statistics Guide for 2020 - Security Boulevard.* https://securityboulevard.com/2020/05/the-definitive-cyber-security-statistics-guide-for-2020/

Cresci, S., Spognardi, A., Petrocchi, M., Tesconi, M., & Di Pietro, R. (2017). The paradigm-shift of social spambots: Evidence, theories, and tools for the arms race. *26th International World Wide Web Conference 2017, WWW 2017 Companion,* 963–972. 10.1145/3041021.3055135

Cresci, S., Di Pietro, R., Petrocchi, M., Spognardi, A., & Tesconi, M. (2018). Social Fingerprinting: Detection of Spambot Groups Through DNA-Inspired Behavioral Modeling. *IEEE Transactions on Dependable and Secure Computing, 15*(4), 561–576. doi:10.1109/TDSC.2017.2681672

Cutillo, L. A., Manulis, M., & Strufe, T. (2010). Security and Privacy in Online Social Networks. In *Handbook of Social Network Technologies and Applications*. doi:10.1007/978-1-4419-7142-5_23

Daft, R. L., & Lengel, R. H. (1986). Organizational information requirements, media richness and structural design. *Management Science, 32*(5), 554–571. doi:10.1287/mnsc.32.5.554

Daka, H., Jacob, W. J., Kakupa, P., & Mwelwa, K. (2017). *The Use of Social Networks in Curbing HIV in Higher Education Institutions: A Case Study of the University of Zambia*. Academic Press.

Danziger, J. N., & Kraemer, K. L. (1985). Computarized Data-Based Systems and Productivity Among Professional Workers: The Case of Detectives. *Public Administration Review, 45*(1), 196-209. https://www.jstor.org/stable/3110149?seq=1

Daugherty, T., & Hoffman, E. (2014). eWOM and the importance of capturing consumer attention within social media. *Journal of Marketing Communications, 20*(1-2), 82–102. doi:10.1080/13527266.2013.797764

Davis, C. A., Varol, O., Ferrara, E., Flammini, A., & Menczer, F. (2016). *BotOrNot: A system to evaluate social bots*. doi:10.1145/2872518.2889302

Davis, F. (1989). Perceived usefulness, perceived ease of use, and user acceptance of information technology. *Management Information Systems Quarterly, 13*(3), 319–339. doi:10.2307/249008

Davis, R. A. (2001). A cognitive–behavioral model of pathological Internet use. *Computers in Human Behavior, 17*(2), 187–195. doi:10.1016/S0747-5632(00)00041-8

De Cock, R., Vangeel, J., Klein, A., Minotte, P., Rosas, O., & Meerkerk, G. J. (2014). Compulsive use of social networking sites in Belgium: Prevalence, profile, and the role of attitude toward work and school. *Cyberpsychology, Behavior, and Social Networking, 17*(3), 166–171. doi:10.1089/cyber.2013.0029 PMID:24111599

De Mooij, M. (2003). Convergence and divergence in consumer behaviour: Implications for global advertising. *International Journal of Advertising, 22*(2), 183–202. doi:10.1080/02650487.2003.11072848

De Mooij, M., & Beniflah, J. (2017). Measuring cross-cultural differences of ethnic groups within nations: Convergence or divergence of cultural values? The case of the United States. *Journal of International Consumer Marketing, 29*(1), 2–10. doi:10.1080/08961530.2016.1227758

De Veirman, M., Cauberghe, V., & Hudders, L. (2017). Marketing through Instagram influencers: The impact of number of followers and product divergence on brand attitude. *International Journal of Advertising, 36*(5), 798–828. doi:10.1080/02650487.2017.1348035

Demerouti, E., Bakker, A. B., & Leiter, M. (2014). Burnout and job performance: The moderating role of selection, optimization, and compensation strategies. *Journal of Occupational Health Psychology, 19*(1), 96–107. doi:10.1037/a0035062 PMID:24447224

Demunter, C. (2006). How skilled are Europeans in using the computers and the internet? *Statistics in Focus, 17*, 1–8.

Dennis, A. R., & Kinney, S. T. (1998). Testing media richness theory in the new media: The effects of cues, feedback, and task equivocality. *Information Systems Research, 9*(3), 256–274. doi:10.1287/isre.9.3.256

Desjarlais, M., & Willoughby, T. (2010). A longitudinal study of the relation between adolescent boys and girls' computer use with friends and friendship quality: Support for the social compensation or the rich-get-richer hypothesis? *Computers in Human Behavior, 26*(5), 896–905. doi:10.1016/j.chb.2010.02.004

Dessart, L. (2017). Social media engagement: A model of antecedents and relational outcomes. *Journal of Marketing Management, 33*(5-6), 375–399. doi:10.1080/0267257X.2017.1302975

Dey, A. (2016). Machine learning algorithms: A review. *International Journal of Computer Science and Information Technologies, 7*(3), 1174–1179.

Dhaha, I. S. Y. (2013). Predictors of Facebook addiction among youth: A structural equation modeling (SEM). *Journal of Social Sciences (COES&RJ-JSS), 2*(4), 186-195.

Dhaha, I. S. Y., & Igale, A. B. (2013). Facebook usage among Somali youth: A test of uses and gratifications approach. *International Journal of Humanities and Social Science, 3*(3), 299–313.

Dhir, A., Yossatorn, Y., Kaur, P., & Chen, S. (2018). Online social media fatigue and psychological wellbeing—A study of compulsive use, fear of missing out, fatigue, anxiety and depression. *International Journal of Information Management, 40*, 141–152. doi:10.1016/j.ijinfomgt.2018.01.012

Dias, I. (2012). O uso das tecnologias digitais entre os seniores: Motivações e interesses. Sociologia. *Problemas e Práticas, 68*, 51–77.

Diener, E. D., Emmons, R. A., Larsen, R. J., & Griffin, S. (1985). The satisfaction with life scale. *Journal of Personality Assessment, 49*(1), 71–75. doi:10.120715327752jpa4901_13 PMID:16367493

Diermeier, D. (2015). Institutionalism and the Normative Study of Politics: From Rational Choice to Behavioralism. *The Good Society, 24*(1), 15-29.

Djafarova, E., & Rushworth, C. (2017). Exploring the credibility of online celebrities' Instagram profiles in influencing the purchase decisions of young female users. *Computers in Human Behavior, 68*, 1–7. doi:10.1016/j.chb.2016.11.009

Dobra, A. (2012). The Democratic Impact of ICT in Africa. *Africa Spectrum, 1*(1), 73–88. doi:10.1177/000203971204700104

Drury, G. (2008). Opinion piece: Social media: Should marketers engage and how can it be done effectively? *Journal of Direct, Data and Digital Marketing Practice, 9*(3), 274–277. doi:10.1057/palgrave.dddmp.4350096

Duan, J., & Dholakia, N. (2015). The reshaping of Chinese consumer values in the social media era: Exploring the impact of Weibo. *Qualitative Market Research, 18*(4), 409–426. doi:10.1108/QMR-07-2014-0058

Dubow, T., Devaux, A., & Manville, C. (2017). Civic Engagement: How Can Digital Technology Encourage Greater Engagement in Civil Society? *Rand Europe: Perspective, Expert Insights on a Timely Policy Issue*, 1-11. https://www.rand.org/content/dam/rand/pubs/perspectives/PE200/PE253/RAND_PE253.pdf

Duffett, R. (2017). Influence of social media marketing communications on young consumers' attitudes. *Young Consumers, 18*(1), 19–39. doi:10.1108/YC-07-2016-00622

Duffy, B. E. (2017). *(Not) getting paid to do what you love*. Yale University Press. doi:10.12987/yale/9780300218176.001.0001

Dutton, W. (2001). Computers and Society. International Encyclopedia of the Social & Behavioral Sciences, 2480-2487.

Dwyer, M., & Molony, T. (2019). Mapping the Study of Politics and Social Media Use in Africa. In *Social Media and Politics in Africa: Democracy, Censorship and Security* (pp. 1–17). Zed Books.

Ebersole, S. (2000). Uses and gratifications of the Web among students. *Journal of Computer-Mediated Communication, 6*(1), 0. doi:10.1111/j.1083-6101.2000.tb00111.x

e-Clincher. (2015). *43 Of The Best Social Media Marketing Quotes.* Retrieved from https://eclincher.com/blog/43-of-the-best-social-media-quotes/

Edelman, D. C. (2015). How to launch your digital platform. *Harvard Business Review, 93*(4), 91–97.

Edosomwan, S., Prakasan, S. K., Kouame, D., Watson, J., & Seymour, T. (2011). The history of social media and its impact on business. *The Journal of Applied Management and Entrepreneurship, 16*(3), 79–91.

Eggermont, S., Vandebosch, H., & Steyaert, S. (2005). Towards the desired future of the elderly and ICT: Policy recommendations based on a dialogue with senior citizens. *Poiesis & Praxis: International Journal of Ethics of Science and Technology Assessment, 4*(3), 199–217. doi:10.100710202-005-0017-9

El-Jawad, M. H. A., Hodhod, R., & Omar, Y. M. K. (2018). Sentiment Analysis of Social Media Networks Using Machine Learning. *2018 14th International Computer Engineering Conference (ICENCO).* doi: 10.1109/icenco.2018.8636124

Ellison, N. B., Steinfield, C., & Lampe, C. (2007). The benefits of Facebook "friends:" Social capital and college students' use of online social network sites. *Journal of Computer-Mediated Communication, 12*(4), 1143–1168. doi:10.1111/j.1083-6101.2007.00367.x

eMarketer.com. (2020, March 2). *How Privacy Concerns Are Changing the World of Location Data.* Retrieved on March 22, 2020 from https://www.emarketer.com/content/how-privacy-concerns-are-changing-the-world-of-location-data

Engelstad, F. (2017). Strategic Communication and Institutional Change. In *Institutional Change in the Public Sphere: Views on the Nordic Model* (pp. 139–159). De Gruyter. doi:10.1515/9783110546330-008

Enke, N., & Borchers, N. S. (2018). Von den zielen zur umsetzung: Planung, organisation und evaluation von influencer-kommunikation [From objectives to implementation: Planning, organizing and evaluating influencer communication]. In A. Schach & T. Lommatzsch (Eds.), *Influencer relations: Marketing und PR mit digitalen meinungsführern* (pp. 177–200). Springer. doi:10.1007/978-3-658-21188-2_12

Enterprising Ideas. (n.d.). *What is a Social Entrepreneur.* PBS Foundation. Retrieved from http://www.pbs.org/now/enterprisingideas/what-is.html

Ephraim, P. E. (2013). African youths and the dangers of social networking: A culture-centered approach to using social media. *Ethics and Information Technology, 15*(4), 275–284. doi:10.100710676-013-9333-2

Eraslan-Capan, B. (2015). Interpersonal sensitivity and problematic Facebook use in turkish university students. *The Anthropologist, 21*(3), 395–403. doi:10.1080/09720073.2015.11891829

Erdmann, G., Elischer, S., & Stroh, A. (2011). Can Historical Institutionalism Be Applied to Political Regime Development in Africa? *German Institute for Global and Area Studies.* www.jstor.org/stable/resrep07620

Erdogan, B. Z. (1999). Celebrity endorsement: A literature review. *Journal of Marketing Management, 15*(4), 291–314. doi:10.1362/026725799784870379

Erickson, L. B. (2011), Social media, social capital, and seniors: The impact of Facebook on bonding and bridging social capital of individuals over 65. *Proceedings of the 17th Americas Conference on Information Systems (AMCIS 2011).*

Ertekin, Z., & Atik, D. (2012). Word-of-mouth communication in marketing: An exploratory study of motivations behind opinion leadership and opinion seeking. *ODTÜ Gelisme Dergisi, 39,* 323–345.

European Commission. (2019). *Demography.* https://data.europa.eu/euodp/pt/data/

Eurostat. (2010). *Internet access and use in 2010.* https://ec.europa.eu/eurostat/documents/2995521/5042418/4-14122010-BP-EN.PDF/2276f2ef-a45b-49ef-90ea-8987cbb8cddd

Eurostat. (2019). *Are you using social networks?* https://ec.europa.eu/eurostat/web/products-eurostat-news/-/EDN-20190629-1

Evans, N. J., Phua, J., Lim, J., & Jun, H. (2017). Disclosing Instagram influencer advertising: The effects of disclosure language on advertising recognition, attitudes, and behavioral intent. *Journal of Interactive Advertising*, *17*(2), 138–149. doi:10.1080/15252019.2017.1366885

Fashoro, I., & Barnard, L. (2017, July). Motivations for Adopting Social Media as a Tool for Public Participation and Engagement in Nelson Mandela Bay Municipality. In *Proceedings of the 4th European Conference on Social Media ECSM* (pp. 106-114). Academic Press.

Feinstein, B. A., Bhatia, V., Hershenberg, R., & Davila, J. (2012). Another venue for problematic interpersonal behavior: The effects of depressive and anxious symptoms on social networking experiences. *Journal of Social and Clinical Psychology*, *31*(4), 356–382. doi:10.1521/jscp.2012.31.4.356

Ferguson, D., & Perse, E. (2000). The World Wide Web as a functional alternative to television. *Journal of Broadcasting & Electronic Media*, *44*(2), 155–174. doi:10.120715506878jobem4402_1

Ferrag, M. A., Maglaras, L., Derhab, A., & Janicke, H. (2020). *Authentication schemes for smart mobile devices: threat models, countermeasures, and open research issues.* doi:10.100711235-019-00612-5

Ferra, I., & Nguyen, D. (2017). #Migrantcrisis: "Tagging" the European migration crisis on Twitter. *Journal of Communication Management*, *21*(4), 411–426. doi:10.1108/JCOM-02-2017-0026

Ferrara, E. (2019). The history of digital spam. In Communications of the ACM (Vol. 62, Issue 8, pp. 82–91). Association for Computing Machinery. doi:10.1145/3299768

Ferreira, A., & Du Plessis, T. (2009). Effect of online social networking on employee productivity. *South African Journal of Information Management*, *11*(1), 1–11. doi:10.4102ajim.v11i1.397

Fioretos, O., Falleti, T., Sheingate, A., Fioretos, O., Falleti, T., & Sheingate, A. (2016). Historical Institutionalism in Political Science. In *The Oxford Handbook of Historical Institutionalism* (pp. 3–17). Oxford University Press. https://www.oxfordhandbooks.com/view/10.1093/oxfordhb/9780199662814.001.0001/oxfordhb-9780199662814-e-1

Fire, M., Goldschmidt, R., & Elovici, Y. (2014). Online social networks: Threats and solutions. *IEEE Communications Surveys and Tutorials*, *16*(4), 2019–2036. doi:10.1109/COMST.2014.2321628

Fishbein, M., & Ajzen, I. (1975). *Belief, attitude, intention, and behavior: An introduction to theory and research.* Addison-Wesley.

Fleetwood, S. (2008). Institutions and Social Structures. *Journal for the Theory of Social Behaviour*, *38*(3). 241-265. http://citeseerx.ist.psu.edu/viewdoc/download?doi=10.1.1.464.8152&rep=rep1&type=pdf

Fleming, S. (2002). Information and Communication Technologies (ICTs) and Democracy Development in the South: Potential and Current Reality. *EJISDC*, *10*(3), 1–10.

Flores-Gomes, G. (2019). *Efeitos de um programa de inclusão digital nas funções cognitivas e qualidade de vida de idosos.* Universidade Federal do Paraná.

Forbes, K. (2016). Examining the beauty industry's use of social influencers. *Elon Journal of Undergraduate Research in Communications*, *7*(2), 78–87.

Forgas, J. P., & Laham, S. M. (2017). Halo effects. In R. F. Pohl (Ed.), *Cognitive illusions* (2nd ed., pp. 276–290). Routledge.

Fountain, J. E. (2004). *Prospects for the Virtual State*. Working papers. http://www.j.u-tokyo.ac.jp/coeps/pdf/040710.pdf

Fountain, J. E. (1995). *Enacting Technology: An Institutional Perspective*. John F. Kennedy School of Government, Harvard University.

Fourati Ennouri, M. (2016). Usages de la banque en ligne et qualité des échanges Entreprises–Banques. In AIMS, XXVe Conférence Internationale de Management Stratégique.

Foxwell, B. (2020, February 17). *A guide to social media influencers: Mega, macro, micro, and nano.* https://blog.iconosquare.com/guide-to-social-media-influencers/

Francalanci, C., & Hussain, A. (2017). Influence-based Twitter browsing with NavigTweet. *Information Systems, 64,* 119–131. doi:10.1016/j.is.2016.07.012

Francis, T., & Hoefel, F. (2018, November). *'True Gen': Generation Z and its Implications for Companies.* Retrieved from https://www.mckinsey.com/industries/consumer-packaged-goods/our-insights/true-gen-generation-z-and-its-implications-for-companies

Frankl, V. E. Quotes. (n.d.). BrainyQuote.com. Retrieved from https://www.brainyquote.com/quotes/viktor_e_frankl_160380

Freberg, K., Graham, K., McGaughey, K., & Freberg, L. A. (2011). Who are the social media influencers? A study of public perceptions of personality. *Public Relations Review, 37*(1), 90–92. doi:10.1016/j.pubrev.2010.11.001

Friedland, G., & Sommer, R. (2010, August). Cybercasing the Joint: On the Privacy Implications of Geo-Tagging. *HotSec'10: Proceedings of the 5th USENIX conference on Hot topics in security.*

Friemel, T. N. (2016). The digital divide has grown old: Determinants of a digital divide among seniors. *New Media & Society, 18*(2), 313–331. doi:10.1177/1461444814538648

Fuchs, C., & Horak, E. (2008). Africa and the Digital Divide. *Telematics and Informatics, 25*(2), 99–116. doi:10.1016/j.tele.2006.06.004

Fuentes, A. (2000). Won't you be my neighbor? *American Demographics, 22*(6), 60–62.

FullFact. (2019). *Who is most likely to believe and to share misinformation?* Retrieved from https://fullfact.org/media/uploads/who-believes-shares-misinformation.pdf

Fulton, J. M., & Kibby, M. D. (2017). Millennials and the normalization of surveillance on Facebook. *Continuum: Journal of Media & Cultural Studies, 31*(2), 189-199. Advance online publication. doi:10.1080/10304312.10302016.11265094

Fu, Q., Feng, B., Guo, D., & Li, Q. (2018). Combating the evolving spammers in online social networks. *Computers & Security, 72,* 60–73. doi:10.1016/j.cose.2017.08.014

Gabriel, R. (n.d.). *What Is Oneness?* Retrieved from https://chopra.com/article/what-oneness

Gaia, A., Sala, E., & Cerati, G. (2020). Social networking sites use and life satisfaction: A quantitative study on older people living in Europe. *European Societies,* 1–21. doi:10.1080/14616696.2020.1762910

Gal-Or, E., Gal-Or, R., & Penmetsa, N. (2018, September). The Role of User Privacy Concerns in Shaping Competition Among Platforms. *Information Systems Research, 29*(3), 698–722. doi:10.1287/isre.2017.0730

Gamal, D., Alfonse, M., El-Horbaty, E.-S. M., & Salem, A.-B. M. (2019). Implementation of Machine Learning Algorithms in Arabic Sentiment Analysis Using N-Gram Features. *Procedia Computer Science, 154,* 332–340. doi:10.1016/j.procs.2019.06.048

Gámez-Guadix, M. (2014). Depressive symptoms and problematic Internet use among adolescents: Analysis of the longitudinal relationships from the cognitive–behavioral model. *Cyberpsychology, Behavior, and Social Networking, 17*(11), 714–719. doi:10.1089/cyber.2014.0226 PMID:25405784

Gangavarapu, T., Jaidhar, C. D., & Chanduka, B. (2020). Applicability of machine learning in spam and phishing email filtering: Review and approaches. *Artificial Intelligence Review*, 1–63. doi:10.100710462-020-09814-9

Ge, J., & Herring, S. C. (2018). Communicative functions of emoji sequences on Sina Weibo. *First Monday*.

Geertz, C. (1973). *The Interpretation of Cultures*. Basic Books.

Geier, A., & Gottschling, M. (2019). Wissenschaftskommunikation auf Twitter? Eine Chance für die Geisteswissenschaften! *Mitteilungen des Deutschen Germanistenverbandes, 66*(3), 282–291. doi:10.14220/mdge.2019.66.3.282

Genç, Z. A., Lenzini, G., & Sgandurra, D. (2019). On deception-based protection against cryptographic ransomware. Lecture Notes in Computer Science, 11543, 219–239. doi:10.1007/978-3-030-22038-9_11

Gibbs, J. L., Ellison, N. B., & Heino, R. D. (2006). Self-presentation in online personals: The role of anticipated future interaction, self-disclosure, and perceived success in Internet dating. *Communication Research, 33*(2), 152–177. doi:10.1177/0093650205285368

Gil, H. (2019). A pertinência de uma cidadania digital 65. In *Atas do Seminário Internacional Cidadania Digital*. Instituto de Educação da Universidade de Lisboa.

Girard, A., & Fallery, B. (2009). *Réseaux Sociaux Numériques: revue de littérature et perspectives de recherche*. Université Montpellier.

Global Web Index. (2019). *Digital vs. Traditional Media Consumption'2019*. Retrieved February 28, 2020, from Global web index: https://www.globalwebindex.com/hubfs/Downloads/Digital_vs_Traditional_Media_Consumption-2019.pdf

Goel, A., Gautam, J., & Kumar, S. (2016). Real time sentiment analysis of tweets using Naive Bayes. *2016 2nd International Conference on Next Generation Computing Technologies (NGCT)*. doi: 10.1109/ngct.2016.7877424

Goldberg, I. (1996). *Internet addiction disorder*. Retrieved March 3, 2008, from http//www.cog.brown.edu/brochures/people/duchon/humor/internet.addiction.html

Gómez-Hernández, J. A., Álvarez-González, L., & García-Teodoro, P. (2018). R-Locker: Thwarting ransomware action through a honeyfile-based approach. *Computers & Security, 73*, 389–398. doi:10.1016/j.cose.2017.11.019

Gomez, J. (2014). Social Media Impact on Malaysia's 13th General Election. *Asia Pacific Media Educator, 24*(1), 95–105. doi:10.1177/1326365X14539213

Gondwe, G. (2017). Are Late Night TV Shows Polarizing Society? Examining the Ambivalence of New Version of Political Partisanship in the United States. *Global Media Journal*, 15.

Gondwe, G. (2018). News Believability & Trustworthiness on African Online Networks: An Experimental Design. *International Communication Research Journal, 53*(2), 51–74.

Gong, Q., Chen, Y., He, X., Zhuang, Z., Wang, T., Huang, H., Wang, X., & Fu, X. (2018). DeepScan: Exploiting Deep Learning for Malicious Account Detection in Location-Based Social Networks. *IEEE Communications Magazine, 56*(11), 21–27. Advance online publication. doi:10.1109/MCOM.2018.1700575

Gonzales, A. L., & Hancock, J. T. (2011). Mirror, mirror on my Facebook wall: Effects of exposure to Facebook on self-esteem. *Cyberpsychology, Behavior, and Social Networking, 14*(1-2), 79–83. doi:10.1089/cyber.2009.0411 PMID:21329447

Gopaldas, R. (2019). Digital Dictatorship versus Digital Democracy in Africa. *Policy Insights*, *75*, 1–18.

Gorbach, J. (2018). Not Your Grandpa's Hoax: A Comparative History of Fake News. *American Journalism*, *35*(2), 236–249. doi:10.1080/08821127.2018.1457915

Gorry, G. A., & Westbrook, R. A. (2009). Academic research: Winning the internet confidence game. *Corporate Reputation Review*, *12*(3), 195–203. doi:10.1057/crr.2009.16

Grandio, M., & Bonaut, J. (2012). Transmedia audiences and television fiction: A comparative approach between skins (UK) and El Barco (Spain). *Participations*, *9*(2), 558.

Grandjean, M. (2016). A social network analysis of Twitter: Mapping the digital humanities community. *Cogent Arts & Humanities*, *3*(1), 1171458. doi:10.1080/23311983.2016.1171458

Granik, M., & Mesyura, V. (2017, May). *Fake news detection using naive Bayes classifier*. Paper presented at the meeting of First Ukraine Conference on Electrical and Computer Engineering (UKRCON). 10.1109/UKRCON.2017.8100379

Gräve, J.-F. (2017). Exploring the perception of influencers vs. traditional celebrities: Are social media stars a new type of endorser? In *Proceedings of the 8th International Conference on Social Media & Society* (#SMSociety17). Association for Computing Machinery. 10.1145/3097286.3097322

Graves, L., & Cherubini, F. (2016). *The rise of fact-checking sites in Europe*. Reuters Institute, University of Oxford.

Greenwood, D. N. (2013). Fame, Facebook, and Twitter: How attitudes about fame predict frequency and nature of social media use. *Psychology of Popular Media Culture*, *2*(4), 222–236. doi:10.1037/ppm0000013

Grewal, L., Stephen, A. T., & Coleman, N. V. (2019). When posting about products on social media backfires: The negative effects of consumer identity signaling on product interest. *JMR, Journal of Marketing Research*, *56*(2), 197–210. doi:10.1177/0022243718821960

Griffiths, M. (1998). Internet addiction: does it really exist? In J. Gackenbach (Ed.), *Psychology and the Internet: Interpersonal, interpersonal and intranspersonal applications* (pp. 61–75). Academic Press.

Griffiths, M. D. (2010). The role of context in online gaming excess and addiction: Some case study evidence. *International Journal of Mental Health and Addiction*, *8*(1), 119–125. doi:10.100711469-009-9229-x

Griffiths, M. D., Kuss, D. J., & Demetrovics, Z. (2014). Social networking addiction: An overview of preliminary findings. In K. P. Rosenberg & L. C. Feder (Eds.), *Behavioral addictions: Criteria, evidence, and treatment* (pp. 119–141). Academic Press. doi:10.1016/B978-0-12-407724-9.00006-9

Grinberg, N., Joseph, K., Friedland, L., Swire-Thompson, B., & Lazer, D. (2019). Fake news on Twitter during the 2016 US presidential election. *Science*, *363*(6425), 374–378. doi:10.1126cience.aau2706 PMID:30679368

Grunbaum, J. A., Tortolero, S., Weller, N., & Gingiss, P. (2000). Cultural, social, and intrapersonal factors associated with substance use among alternative high school students. *Addictive Behaviors*, *25*(1), 145–151. doi:10.1016/S0306-4603(99)00006-4 PMID:10708330

Guan, W., Gao, H., Yang, M., Li, Y., Ma, H., Qian, W., Cao, Z., & Yang, X. (2014). Analyzing user behavior of the micro-blogging website Sina Weibo during hot social events. *Physica A*, *395*, 340–351. doi:10.1016/j.physa.2013.09.059

Gudykunst, W. B. (2004). Bridging differences: *Effective intergroup communication. Sage (Atlanta, Ga.)*.

Guess, A., Nagler, J., & Tucker, J. (2019). Less than you think: Prevalence and predictors of fake news dissemination on Facebook. *Science Advances, 5*(1), eaau4586.

Guess, A., Nyhan, B., & Reifler, J. (2018). Selective exposure to misinformation: Evidence from the consumption of fake news during the 2016 US presidential campaign. *European Research Council, 9*.

Guo, Z., Cho, J., Chen, I., Sengupta, S., Hong, M., & Mitra, T. (2020). Online Social Deception and Its Countermeasures for Trustworthy Cyberspace: A Survey. *ACM Computing Surveys, 1*(1). http://arxiv.org/abs/2004.07678

Habermas, J. (1984). The Theory of Communicative Action.: Vol. 1. *Reason and the Rationalization of Society*. Beacon Press.

Hahn, D. (2012). *The New Brand Culture Model*. Retrieved from https://www.liquidagency.com/brand-exchange/new-brand-culture-model/Whitepaper

Hair, J. F., Black, W. C., Babin, B. J., Anderson, R. E., & Tatham, R. L. (2006). *Multivariate data analysis* (Vol. 6). Pearson Prentice Hall.

Hakim, C. (1983). *Secondary analysis in social research: A guide to data sources and methods with examples*. Allen & Unwin.

Halachmi, A., & Greiling, D. (2014). Transparency, E-Government, and Accountability. *Public Performance & Management Review, 36*(4), 562–584.

Hall, E. T., & Hall, M. R. (2001). Key concepts: Underlying structures of culture. *International HRM: Managing diversity in the workplace*, 24-40.

Hall, E. T. (1973). *The slient language*. Anchor.

Hall, E. T. (1989). *Beyond culture*. Anchor.

Ham, C.-D., Lee, J., Hayes, J. L., & Bae, Y. H. (2019). Exploring sharing behaviors across social media platforms. *International Journal of Market Research, 61*(2), 157–177. doi:10.1177/1470785318782790

Hamjoda, A. (2016). Embracing New Media in Political Communication: A Survey of Parliamentarians' Attitude and Practices in a Changing Media Landscape in West Africa. *The Electronic Journal on Information Systems in Developing Countries, 7*(77), 1–10. doi:10.1002/j.1681-4835.2016.tb00566.x

Hampton, K. N., & Wellman, B. (2003). Neighboring in netville: How the Internet supports community and social capital in a wired suburb. *City & Community, 2*(4), 277–311. doi:10.1046/j.1535-6841.2003.00057.x

Hanchard, S. (2019, April 24). *PR and communications network analysis with NodeXL and Netlytic*. Retrieved June 01, 2020, from http://www.dataviz.my/2019/04/24/pr-and-communications-network-analysis-with-nodexl-and-netlytic/

Hanson, G., & Haridakis, P. (2008). Users Watching and Sharing the News: A Uses and Gratifications Approach. *The Journal of Electronic Publishing: JEP, 11*(3). Advance online publication. doi:10.3998/3336451.0011.305

Harel, D., & Koren, Y. (2001). A Fast Multi-Scale Method for Drawing Large Graphs. *Graph Drawing*, 183–196.

Hargittai, E. (2002). The second-level digital divide: Differences in people's online skills. *First Monday, 7*(4). Advance online publication. doi:10.5210/fm.v7i4.942

Hargittai, E. (2003). Informed web surfing: The social context of user sophistication. In P. E. N. Howard & S. Jones (Eds.), *Society online* (pp. 257–274). Sage.

Hargittai, E., & Hsieh, Y. P. (2013). Digital inequality. In W. H. Dutton (Ed.), *The Oxford handbook of internet studies* (pp. 129–150). Oxford University Press.

Hassan, H., Nevo, D., & Wade, M. (2015). Linking dimensions of social media use to job performance: The role of social capital. *The Journal of Strategic Information Systems*, *24*(2), 65–89. doi:10.1016/j.jsis.2015.03.001

Hastie, T., Tibshirani, R., Friedman, J., & Franklin, J. (2005). The elements of statistical learning: Data mining, inference and prediction. *The Mathematical Intelligencer*, *27*(2), 83–85. doi:10.1007/BF02985802

Havinga, M., Hoving, M., & Swagemakers, V. (2016). Alibaba: a case study on building an international imperium on information and E-Commerce. In R. T. Eden (Ed.), *Multinational Management: a casebook ons Asis's global market leaders* (pp. 13–32). Springer. doi:10.1007/978-3-319-23012-2_2

Hayati, P., Chai, K., Potdar, V., & Talevski, A. (2009). HoneySpam 2.0: Profiling web spambot behaviour. Lecture Notes in Computer Science, 5925, 335–344. doi:10.1007/978-3-642-11161-7_23

Hays, R. D., & DiMatteo, M. R. (1987). A short-form measure of loneliness. *Journal of Personality Assessment*, *51*(1), 69–81. doi:10.120715327752jpa5101_6 PMID:3572711

Hearn, A., & Schoenhoff, S. (2016). From celebrity to influencer: Tracing the diffusion of celebrity value across the data stream. In P. D. Marshall & S. Redmond (Eds.), A companion to celebrity (pp. 194-212). Wiley.

Hedman, U., & Djerf-Pierre, M. (2013). The social journalist: Embracing the social media life or creating a new digital divide? *Digital Journalism*, *1*(3), 368–385. doi:10.1080/21670811.2013.776804

Heidemann, J., Klier, M., & Probst, F. (2012). Online social networks: A survey of a global phenomenon. *Computer Networks*, *56*(18), 3866–3878. doi:10.1016/j.comnet.2012.08.009

Heiden, A. (2015). *Sponsoring im Profifußball: Das Beispiel adidas*. Bacherol Master Publishing.

Helbig, N., Gil-García, J. R., & Ferro, E. (2009). Understanding the complexity of electronic government: Implications from the Digital Divide Literature. *Government Information Quarterly*, *26*(1), 89–97. doi:10.1016/j.giq.2008.05.004

Herring, S. C., Scheidt, L. A., Wright, E., & Bonus, S. (2005). Weblogs as a bridging genre. *Information Technology & People*, *18*(2), 142–171. doi:10.1108/09593840510601513

Herrmann, D. (2019). Cyber Espionage and Cyber Defence. In Information Technology for Peace and Security (pp. 83–106). Springer Fachmedien Wiesbaden. doi:10.1007/978-3-658-25652-4_5

Hettler, U. (2012). *Social media marketing: Marketing mit Blogs, sozialen Netzwerken und weiteren Anwendungen des Web 2.0*. Gebundenes Buch.

He, W., Wang, F. K., Chen, Y., & Zha, S. (2017). An exploratory investigation of social media adoption by small businesses. *Information Technology Management*, *18*(2), 149–160. doi:10.100710799-015-0243-3

Hewage, T. N., Halgamuge, M. N., Syed, A., & Ekici, G. (2018, February). Review: Big data techniques of Google, Amazon, Facebook and Twitter. *Journal of Communication*, *13*(2), 94–100. doi:10.12720/jcm.13.2.94-100

He, X., & Pedraza, R. (2015). Chinese social media strategies: Communication key features from a business perspective. *El Profesional de la Información*, *24*(2), 200–209. doi:10.3145/epi.2015.mar.14

Heyman, R., Wolf, R. D., & Pierson, J. (2014). Evaluating social media privacy settings for personal and advertising purposes. *Info*, *16*(4), 18-32.

Hill, R., Betts, L. R., & Gardner, S. E. (2015). Older adults' experiences and perceptions of digital technology: (Dis) empowerment, wellbeing, and inclusion. *Computers in Human Behavior*, *48*, 415–423. doi:10.1016/j.chb.2015.01.062

Hinsch, C., & Sheldon, K. M. (2013). The impact of frequent social Internet consumption: Increased procrastination and lower life satisfaction. *Journal of Consumer Behaviour, 12*(6), 496-505. doi:10.1002/cb.1453

Hiremath, B. K., & Kenchakkanavar, A. Y. (2016). An alteration of the web 1.0, web 2.0 and web 3.0: A comparative study. *Imperial Journal of Interdisciplinary Research, 2*(4), 705–710.

Hirshcheim, R. (2008). Some Guidelines for the Critical Reviewing of Conceptual Papers. *Journal of the Association for Information Systems, 9*(8), 432–441. doi:10.17705/1jais.00167

Hitesh, S., Hayden, W., Lei, C. & Carl, R. (2018). A New Framework for Securing, Extracting and Analyzing Big Forensic Data. *Journal of Digital Forensics, Security and Law, 13*(2), Article 6.

Hlee, S., Cheng, A., Koo, C., & Kim, T. (2017). The difference of information diffusion for Seoul tourism destination according to user certification on Sina Weibo: Through data crawling method. *International Journal of Tourism Sciences, 17*(4), 262–275. doi:10.1080/15980634.2017.1384131

Hofstede, G. (2011). Dimensionalizing cultures: The Hofstede model in context. *Online Readings in Psychology and Culture, 2*(1), 8. doi:10.9707/2307-0919.1014

Hofstede, G. H. (1991). *Cultures and organizations: Software of the mind.* McGraw-Hill.

Hormes, J. M., Kearns, B., & Timko, C. A. (2014). Craving F acebook? Behavioral addiction to online social networking and its association with emotion regulation deficits. *Addiction (Abingdon, England), 109*(12), 2079–2088. doi:10.1111/add.12713 PMID:25170590

Hosmer, D. W., & Lemeshow, S. (2000). *Applied Logistic Regression.* John Wiley & Sons, Inc., doi:10.1002/0471722146

Hou, Y., & Lampe, C. (2015, April). Social media effectiveness for public engagement: Example of small nonprofits. In *Proceedings of the 33rd annual ACM conference on human factors in computing systems* (pp. 3107-3116). 10.1145/2702123.2702557

Howard, P. N., Duffy, A., Freelon, D., Hussain, M. M., Mari, W., & Maziad, M. (2011). *Opening closed regimes: what was the role of social media during the Arab Spring?* Available at SSRN 2595096

Hsu, C. L., & Lin, J. C. (2008). Acceptance of blog usage: The roles of technology acceptance, social influence and knowledge sharing motivation. *Information & Management, 45*(1), 65–74. doi:10.1016/j.im.2007.11.001

Hsu, H. Y., & Tsou, H. T. (2011). Understanding customer experiences in online blog environments. *International Journal of Information Management, 31*(6), 510–523. doi:10.1016/j.ijinfomgt.2011.05.003

Huang, Y., & Su, F. S. (2018). Motives for Instagram Use and Topics of Interest among Young Adults. *Future Internet, 10*, 77.

Huang, L. Y., Hsieh, Y. J., & Wu, Y. C. J. (2014). Gratifications and social network service usage: The mediating role of online experience. *Information & Management, 51*(6), 774–782. doi:10.1016/j.im.2014.05.004

Huete-Alcocer, N. (2017). A literature review of word of mouth and electronic word of mouth: Implications for consumer behavior. *Frontiers in Psychology, 8*, 1256. doi:10.3389/fpsyg.2017.01256 PMID:28790950

Hughes, D. J., Rowe, M., Batey, M., & Lee, A. (2012). A tale of two sites: Twitter vs. Facebook and the personality predictors of social media usage. *Computers in Human Behavior, 28*(2), 561–569. doi:10.1016/j.chb.2011.11.001

Humayun, M., Niazi, M., Jhanjhi, N. Z., Alshayeb, M., & Mahmood, S. (2020). Cyber Security Threats and Vulnerabilities: A Systematic Mapping Study. *Arabian Journal for Science and Engineering, 45*(3), 3171–3189. doi:10.100713369-019-04319-2

Hunter, G. L., & Taylor, S. A. (2020). The relationship between preference for privacy and social media usage. *Journal of Consumer Marketing, 37*(1), 43–54. doi:10.1108/JCM-11-2018-2927

Hunt, M. G., Marx, R., Lipson, C., & Young, J. (2018). No more FOMO: Limiting social media decreases loneliness and depression. *Journal of Social and Clinical Psychology, 37*(10), 751–768. doi:10.1521/jscp.2018.37.10.751

Hutto, C. J., Bell, C., Farmer, S., Fausset, C., Harley, L., Nguyen, J., & Fain, B. (2015). Social media gerontology: Understanding social media usage among older adults. *Web Intelligence, 13*(1), 69–87. doi:10.3233/WEB-150310

Hwang, H. S., & Choi, E. K. (2016). Exploring Gender Differences in Motivations for Using Sina Weibo. *Transactions on Internet and Information Systems (Seoul), 10*(3), 1429–1441.

IACE. (2016). *La Tunisie en transformation: l'impératif Digital*. les journées de l'entreprise.

IDEA. (2019). *The Global State of Democracy 2019: Addressing the Ills*. Reviving the Promise.

Ifinedo, P. (2016). Applying uses and gratifications theory and social influence processes to understand students' pervasive adoption of social networking sites: Perspectives from the Americas. *International Journal of Information Management, 36*(2), 192–206. doi:10.1016/j.ijinfomgt.2015.11.007

Ignacio Criado, J., Martı'nez-Fuentes, G., & Silva'n, A. (2011). Social media for political campaigning. Theuse of Twitter by Spanish Mayors in 2011 local elections. In C. G. Reddick & S. K. Aikins (Eds.), *Web 2.0 Technologies and Democratic Governance, Public Administration and Information Technology* (pp. 219–232). Springer.

IJCF. (2018). *A short guide to the history of 'fake news' and disinformation*. Retrived from https://www.icfj.org/sites/default/files/2018-07/A%20Short%20Guide%20to%20History%20of%20Fake%20News%20and%20Disinformation_ICFJ%20Final.pdf

Impelman, K. (2007). *How does personality relate to contextual performance, turnover, and customer service?* University of North Texas.

Ingólfsdóttir, H. R. (2017). *The relationship between social media use and self-esteem: gender difference and the effects of parental support* (Doctoral dissertation).

Internet World Stats. (2017, June). Facebook users in the world. *Internet World Stats*. Retrieved on March 20, 2020 from https://internetworldstats.com/facebook.htm

Ioannou, A., Blackburn, J., Stringhini, G., De Cristofaro, E., Kourtellis, N., & Sirivianos, M. (2018). From risk factors to detection and intervention: A practical proposal for future work on cyberbullying. *Behaviour & Information Technology, 37*(3), 258–266. doi:10.1080/0144929X.2018.1432688

Irion, K., & Helberger, N. (2017). Smart TV and the online media sector: User privacy in view of changing market realities. *Telecommunications Policy, 41*(3), 170–184. doi:10.1016/j.telpol.2016.12.013

Ismail, K. (2018, December 10). *Social media influencers: Mega, macro, micro or nano*. https://www.cmswire.com/digital-marketing/social-media-influencers-mega-macro-micro-or-nano/

Jaakonmäki, R., Müller, O., & Vom Brocke, J. (2017). The impact of content, context, and creator on user engagement in social media marketing. *Proceedings of the 50th Hawaii International Conference on System Sciences*. 10.24251/HICSS.2017.136

Jackson, N. (2006). Dipping their big toe into the blogosphere: The use of weblogs by the political parties in the 2005 general election. *Aslib Proceedings, 58*(4), 292–303. doi:10.1108/00012530610687678

Jackson, N., & Lilleker, D. (2011). Microblogging, constituency service and impression management: UK MPs and the use of Twitter. *Journal of Legislative Studies*, *17*(1), 86–105. doi:10.1080/13572334.2011.545181

Jacobs, R. N., & Li, M. (2017). Culture and comparative media research: Narratives about Internet privacy policy in Chinese, U.S., and UK newspapers. *Communication Review*, *20*(1), 1–25. doi:10.1080/10714421.2016.1271641

Jahn, B., & Kunz, W. (2012). How to transform consumers into fans of your brand. *Journal of Service Management*, *23*(3), 344–361. doi:10.1108/09564231211248444

Jalil, S. W., Achan, P., Mojolou, D. N., & Rozaimie, A. (2015). Individual characteristics and job performance: Generation Y at SMEs in Malaysia. *Procedia: Social and Behavioral Sciences*, *170*, 137–145. doi:10.1016/j.sbspro.2015.01.023

James, M. L., Wotring, C. E., & Forrest, E. J. (1995). An exploratory study of the perceived benefits of electronic bulletin board use and their impact on other communication activities. *Journal of Broadcasting & Electronic Media*, *39*(1), 30–50. doi:10.1080/08838159509364287

Jang, S. M., Geng, T., Li, J. Y. Q., Xia, R., Huang, C. T., Kim, H., & Tang, J. (2018). A computational approach for examining the roots and spreading patterns of fake news: Evolution tree analysis. *Computers in Human Behavior*, *84*, 103–113. doi:10.1016/j.chb.2018.02.032

Jia, J., Wang, B., & Gong, N. Z. (2017). Random Walk Based Fake Account Detection in Online Social Networks. *Proceedings - 47th Annual IEEE/IFIP International Conference on Dependable Systems and Networks, DSN 2017*, 273–284. 10.1109/DSN.2017.55

Ji, M. F., & McNeal, J. U. (2001). How Chinese children's commercials differ from those of the United States: A content analysis. *Journal of Advertising*, *30*(3), 79–92. doi:10.1080/00913367.2001.10673647

Jin, Z., Cao, J., Zhang, Y., Zhou, J., & Tian, Q. (2016). Novel visual and statistical image features for microblogs news verification. *IEEE transactions on multimedia*, *19*(3), 598-608.

Ji, Y. G., Hwangbo, H., Yi, J. S., Rau, P. P., Fang, X., & Ling, C. (2010). The influence of cultural differences on the use of social network services and the formation of social capital. *International Journal of Human-Computer Interaction*, *26*(11-12), 1100–1121. doi:10.1080/10447318.2010.516727

Jobs, S. Quotes (n.d.). *Quotable Quotes*. Goodreads.com. Retrieved from https://www.goodreads.com/quotes/988332-some-people-say-give-the-customers-what-they-want-but

Johansen, I. K., & Guldvik, C. S. (2017). *Influencer marketing and purchase intentions: How does influencer marketing affect purchase intentions?* [Unpublished master thesis]. Norwegian School of Economics, Bergen, Norway.

Johansson, J. K. (1994). The sense of "nonsense": Japanese TV advertising. *Journal of Advertising*, *23*(1), 17–26. doi:10.1080/00913367.1994.10673428

John, B., & Opdycke, L. M. (2011). The evolution of an idea. *Journal of Communication Management*, *15*(3), 223–235. doi:10.1108/13632541111150998

Johnson, W. (2015). *Floating Sangha Takes Root Early days in Plum Village with ThichNhatHanh*. Retrieved from https://tricycle.org/magazine/floating-sangha-takes-root/

Johnston, M. P. (2014). Secondary Data Analysis: A Method of which the Time Has Come. *Qualitative and Quantitative Methods in Libraries*, *3*, 619–626.

Joinson, A. N. (2008). Looking at, 'looking up' or 'keeping up with' people? Motives and uses of Facebook. *Proceeding of the SIGCHI Conference on Human Factors in Computing System*.

Joinson, A. M. (2008). Looking at, looking up or keeping up with people?: Motives and use of Facebook. *Proceedings of the Twenty-Sixth Annual SIGCHI Conference on Human Factors in Computing Systems 2008*, 1027-1036. 10.1145/1357054.1357213

Jose, R., & Chooralil, V. S. (2016). Prediction of election result by enhanced sentiment analysis on twitter data using classifier ensemble Approach. *2016 International Conference on Data Mining and Advanced Computing (SAPIENCE)*. 10.1109/SAPIENCE.2016.7684133

Jouët, J. (1993). Pratiques de communication et figures de la médiation. Réseaux. *Communication-Technologie-Société*, *11*(60), 99–120.

Junco, R. (2012). Too much face and not enough books: The relationship between multiple indices of Facebook use and academic performance. *Computers in Human Behavior*, *28*(1), 187–198. doi:10.1016/j.chb.2011.08.026

Junco, R., & Cotten, S. R. (2012). No A 4 U: The relationship between multitasking and academic performance. *Computers & Education*, *59*(2), 505–514. doi:10.1016/j.compedu.2011.12.023

Jung, E. H., & Sundar, S. S. (2016). Senior citizens on Facebook: How do they interact and why? *Computers in Human Behavior*, *61*, 27–35. doi:10.1016/j.chb.2016.02.080

Kahle, L. R., & Homer, P. M. (1985). Physical attractiveness of the celebrity endorser: A social adaptation perspective. *The Journal of Consumer Research*, *11*(4), 954–961. doi:10.1086/209029

Kalogeras, S. (2014). *Transmedia Storytelling and the New Era of Media Convergence in Higher Education*. Palgrave Macmillan. doi:10.1057/9781137388377

Kalpidou, M., Costin, D., & Morris, J. (2011). The relationship between Facebook and the well-being of undergraduate college students. *Cyberpsychology, Behavior, and Social Networking*, *14*(4), 183–189. doi:10.1089/cyber.2010.0061 PMID:21192765

Kamau, S. C. (2017). Democratic Engagement in the Digital Age: Youth, Social Media and Participatory Politics in Kenya. *Communicatio*, *2*(43), 128–146. doi:10.1080/02500167.2017.1327874

Kamhoua, G. A., Pissinou, N., Iyengar, S. S., Beltran, J., Kamhoua, C., Hernandez, B. L., Njilla, L., & Makki, A. P. (2017). Preventing Colluding Identity Clone Attacks in Online Social Networks. *Proceedings - IEEE 37th International Conference on Distributed Computing Systems Workshops, ICDCSW 2017*, 187–192. 10.1109/ICDCSW.2017.64

Kamran, S. (2016). Privacy in the age of social networking. In *Information Security Management Handbook* (6th ed., Vol. 5, pp. 55–66). CRC Press. doi:10.1201/b11250-8

Kane, O. (2013). *Les usages des TIC entre analyse sociotechnique et théories de l'appropriation: état de la littérature*. Les enjeux de la communication. Libreville: Presses universitaires du Gabon, 23-42.

Kang, S. (2007). Disembodiment in online social interaction: Impact of online chat on social support and psychosocial well-being. *Cyberpsychology & Behavior*, *10*(3), 475–477. doi:10.1089/cpb.2006.9929 PMID:17594274

Kantar China. (2018, September 5). China social media landscape 2018. *Kantar China*. Retrieved on March 20, 2020 from https://www.chinainternetwatch.com/26502/social-media-22018/

Kaplan, A. M., & Haenlein, M. (2010). Users of the World, Unite! The Challenges and Opportunities of Social Media. *Business Horizons*, *53*(1), 59–68. doi:10.1016/j.bushor.2009.09.003

Kaplan, A. M., & Haenlein, M. (2011). The early bird catches the news: Nine things you should know about microblogging. *Business Horizons*, *54*(2), 105–113. doi:10.1016/j.bushor.2010.09.004

Kapoor, K. K., Tamilmani, K., Rana, N. P., Patil, P., Dwivedi, Y. K., & Nerur, S. (2018). Advances in social media research: Past, present and future. *Information Systems Frontiers*, *20*(3), 531–558. doi:10.100710796-017-9810-y

Karaiskos, D., Tzavellas, E., Balta, G., & Paparrigopoulos, T. (2010). P02-232-Social network addiction: A new clinical disorder? *European Psychiatry*, *25*, 855. doi:10.1016/S0924-9338(10)70846-4

Karanja, J. M. (2016). *Using Blogs to Create a Competitive Advantage: A Case of the Blogging Industry in Kenya* (MBA thesis). USIU-Africa, Nairobi, Kenya. Retrieved from http://erepo.usiu.ac.ke/11732/2826

Karapanos, E., Teixeira, P., & Gouveia, R. (2016). Need fulfillment and experiences on social media: A case on Facebook and WhatsApp. *Computers in Human Behavior*, *55*, 888–897. doi:10.1016/j.chb.2015.10.015

Karekwaivanane, G., & Mare, A. (2019). 'We are not just voters, we are citizens': Social media, the #ThisFlag campaign and insurgent citizenship in Zimbabwe. In Social Media and Politics in Africa: Democracy, Censorship and Security. London: Zed Books.

Karoui, M., Dudezert, A., & Leidner, D. E. (2015). Strategies and symbolism in the adoption of organizational social networking systems. *The Journal of Strategic Information Systems*, *24*(1), 15–32. doi:10.1016/j.jsis.2014.11.003

Karunian, A. Y., Halme, H., & Söderholm, A. M. (2019). Data Profiling and Elections: Has Data-Driven Political Campaign Gone Too Far? *Economic Perspectives*, *28*(2), 6.

Katz, J. E., & Aspden, P. (1997). A nation of strangers? *Communications of the ACM*, *40*(12), 81–86. doi:10.1145/265563.265575

Kaur, S., & Rashid, E. M. (2016). Web news mining using Back Propagation Neural Network and clustering using K-Means algorithm in big data. *Indian Journal of Science and Technology*, *9*(41). Advance online publication. doi:10.17485/ijst/2016/v9i41/95598

Kaushal, P., Bagga, A., & Sobti, R. (2017). Evolution of bitcoin and security risk in bitcoin wallets. *2017 International Conference on Computer, Communications and Electronics (Comptelix)*. 10.1109/COMPTELIX.2017.8003959

Kaye, B. K., & Johnson, T. J. (2004). Web for all reasons: Uses and gratifications of Internet components for political information. *Telematics and Informatics*, *21*(3), 197–223. doi:10.1016/S0736-5853(03)00037-6

Kayes, I., & Iamnitchi, A. (2017). Privacy and security in online social networks: A survey. *Online Social Networks and Media*, *3–4*(4), 1–21. doi:10.1016/j.osnem.2017.09.001

Kay, S., Mulcahy, R., & Parkinson, J. (2020). When less is more: The impact of macro and micro social media influencers' disclosure. *Journal of Marketing Management*, *36*(3-4), 248–278. doi:10.1080/0267257X.2020.1718740

Keepers, G. A. (1990). Pathological preoccupation with video games. *Journal of the American Academy of Child and Adolescent Psychiatry*, *29*(1), 49–50. doi:10.1097/00004583-199001000-00009 PMID:2295578

Keib, K., Himelboim, I., & Han, J. Y. (2018). Important tweets matter: Predicting retweets in the #BlackLivesMatter talk on Twitter. *Computers in Human Behavior*, *85*, 106–115. doi:10.1016/j.chb.2018.03.025

Kemp, S. (2020). *Digital around the world in April 2020 - We Are Social*. https://wearesocial.com/blog/2020/04/digital-around-the-world-in-april-2020

KentonW. (2018). *Consumerism*. Retrieved from https://www.investopedia.com/terms/c/consumerism.asp

Kenya Audience Research Foundation. (2020). *KARF Media Establishment Survey Highlights*. https://www.karf.or.ke/research/

Kenya National Bureau of Statistics. (2016). *Kenya Integrated Household Budget Survey (KIHBS) March 2016.* http://www.knbs.or.ke/

Kersting, N. (2012). The Future of Electronic democracy. In *Electronic Democracy* (pp. 11-54). Verlag Barbara Budrich. https://www.jstor.org/stable/j.ctvddzwcg.5?seq=1#metadata_info_tab_contents

Khamis, S., Ang, L., & Welling, R. (2017). Self-branding, 'micro-celebrity' and the rise of Social Media Influencers. *Celebrity Studies, 8*(2), 191–208. doi:10.1080/19392397.2016.1218292

Khanna, S., & Verma, A. K. (2018). Classification of SQL injection attacks using fuzzy tainting. *Advances in Intelligent Systems and Computing, 518*, 463–469. doi:10.1007/978-981-10-3373-5_46

Khoros. (2020). *The 2020 social media demographics guide.* https://khoros.com/resources/social-media-demographics-guide

Khosravi, P., Rezvani, A., & Wiewiora, A. (2016). The impact of technology on older adults' social isolation. *Computers in Human Behavior, 63*, 594–603. doi:10.1016/j.chb.2016.05.092

Kim, H., Coyle, J. R., & Gould, S. J. (2009). Collectivist and individualist influences on website design in South Korea and the US: A cross-cultural content analysis. *Journal of Computer-Mediated Communication, 14*(3), 581–601. doi:10.1111/j.1083-6101.2009.01454.x

Kim, J., & Haridakis, P. M. (2009). The role of Internet user characteristics and motives in explaining three dimensions of Internet addiction. *Journal of Computer-Mediated Communication, 14*(4), 988–1015. doi:10.1111/j.1083-6101.2009.01478.x

Kim, M., & Park, H. (2012). Measuring Twitter-based political participation and deliberation in the South Korean context by using social network and Triple Helix indicators. *Scientometrics, 90*(1), 121–140. doi:10.100711192-011-0508-5

Kim, Y., Sohn, D., & Choi, S. M. (2011). Cultural difference in motivations for using social network sites: A comparative study of American and Korean college students. *Computers in Human Behavior, 27*(1), 365–372. doi:10.1016/j.chb.2010.08.015

Kinder, M. (1991). *Playing with Power in Movies, Television, and Video Games: From Muppet Babies to Teenage Mutant Ninja Turtles.* University of California Press. doi:10.1525/9780520912434

Kiranda, Y., Mugisha, M., & Ojok, D. (2016). Social media, Political Communication and Campaigning in Uganda: Opportunity or Challenge? In Assessing the Impact of Social Media on Political Communication and Civic Engagement in Uganda. Konrad-Adenauer-Stiftung, Uganda Programme.

Kırcaburun, K., Kokkinos, C. M., Demetrovics, Z., Király, O., Griffiths, M. D., & Çolak, T. S. (2019). Problematic online behaviors among adolescents and emerging adults: Associations between cyberbullying perpetration, problematic social media use, and psychosocial factors. *International Journal of Mental Health and Addiction, 17*(4), 891–908. doi:10.100711469-018-9894-8

Kirschner, P. A., & Karpinski, A. C. (2010). Facebook® and academic performance. *Computers in Human Behavior, 26*(6), 1237–1245. doi:10.1016/j.chb.2010.03.024

Kishokumar, R. (2016). Influence of social networking in the work place on individual job performance: Special reference to the financial sector in Batticaloa District. *International Journal of Engineering Research and General Science, 4*(6), 22–34.

Klobas, J. E., McGill, T. G., Moghavvemi, S., & Paramanathan, T. (2018). Compulsive YouTube usage: A comparison of use motivation and personality effects. *Computers in Human Behavior, 87*, 129–139. doi:10.1016/j.chb.2018.05.038

Kluemper, D. H., & Rosen, P. A. (2009). Future employment selection methods: Evaluating social networking web sites. *Journal of Managerial Psychology, 24*(6), 567–580. doi:10.1108/02683940910974134

KMPG International. (2016). *Creepy or cool? Staying on the right side of the consumer privacy line.* Retrieved on March 22, 2020 from https://home.kpmg.com/sg/en/home/insights/2016/2011/crossing-the-line.html

KMPG. (2016, November 7). *Companies that fail to see privacy as a business priority risk crossing the 'creepy line'.* KMPG. Retrieved on June 23, 2019 from https://home.kpmg/sg/en/home/media/press-releases/2016/2011/companies-that-fail-to-see-privacy-as-a-business-priority-risk-crossing-the-creepy-line.html

Koch, O. (2015). Les médias dans les «transitions démocratiques»: état des lieux et prospective. *Questions de communication,* (28), 211-229.

Koc, M., & Gulyagci, S. (2013). Facebook addiction among Turkish college students: The role of psychological health, demographic, and usage characteristics. *Cyberpsychology, Behavior, and Social Networking, 16*(4), 279–284. doi:10.1089/cyber.2012.0249 PMID:23286695

Köffer, S., Ortbach, K. C., & Niehaves, B. (2014). Exploring the relationship between IT consumerization and job performance: A theoretical framework for future research. *Communications of the Association for Information Systems, 35*(1), 14. doi:10.17705/1CAIS.03514

Kolb, G. (2008, May 29). Social media as a global phenomenon: Recent discoveries. *Corporate Communications Compass.* Retrieved on March 20, 2020 from http://ccc.georgkolb.com/?p=2020

Koohang, A., Paliszkiewicz, J., & Goluchowski, J. (2018). Social media privacy concerns: Trusting beliefs and risk beliefs. *Industrial Management & Data Systems, 118*(6), 1209–1228. doi:10.1108/IMDS-12-2017-0558

Koopmans, L., Bernaards, C. M., Hildebrandt, V. H., Schaufeli, W. B., de Vet Henrica, C. W., & van der Beek, A. J. (2011). Conceptual frameworks of individual work performance: A systematic review. *Journal of Occupational and Environmental Medicine, 53*(8), 856–866. doi:10.1097/JOM.0b013e318226a763 PMID:21775896

Korshunov, P., & Marcel, S. (2018). *DeepFakes: a New Threat to Face Recognition? Assessment and Detection.* http://arxiv.org/abs/1812.08685

Kotler, P., Keller, K. L., Brady, M., Goodman, M., & Hansen, T. (2019). *Marketing management* (4th European Ed.). Pearson Education Limited.

Kranzberg, M. (1986). Technology and History: Kranzberg's Laws. *Technology and Culture, 27*(3), 547. doi:10.2307/3105385

Kraut, R., Kiesler, S., Boneva, B., Cummings, J., Helgeson, V., & Crawford, A. (2002). Internet Paradox Revisited. *The Journal of Social Issues, 58*(1), 49–74. doi:10.1111/1540-4560.00248

Kraut, R., Patterson, M., Landmark, V., Kielser, S., Mukophadhyaya, T., & Scherlis, W. (1998). Internet paradox: A social technology that reduces social involvement and psychological well-being? *The American Psychologist, 53*(9), 1017–1031. doi:10.1037/0003-066X.53.9.1017 PMID:9841579

Kreutzer, R. T. (2018). *Social-Media-Marketing kompakt: Ausgestalten, Plattformen finden, messen, organisatorisch verankern.* Springer Gabler. doi:10.1007/978-3-658-21147-9

Krishnaveni, K., Pai, R., & Iyer, V. (2017). Faculty rating system based on student feedbacks using sentimental analysis. *2017 International Conference on Advances in Computing, Communications and Informatics (ICACCI).* 10.1109/ICACCI.2017.8126079

Kross, E., Verduyn, P., Demiralp, E., Park, J., Lee, D. S., Lin, N., ... Sueur, C. (2013). Facebook use predicts declines in subjective well-being in young adults. *PLoS One*, *8*(8), e69841. doi:10.1371/journal.pone.0069841 PMID:23967061

Kubey, R. W., Lavin, M. J., & Barrows, J. R. (2001). Internet use and collegiate academic performance decrements: Early findings. *Journal of Communication*, *51*(2), 366–382. doi:10.1111/j.1460-2466.2001.tb02885.x

Kubheka, B. (2017). Ethical and legal perspectives on use of social media by health professionals in South Africa. *South African Medical Journal*, *107*(5), 386–389. doi:10.7196/SAMJ.2017.v107i5.12047 PMID:28492116

Kumar, R., Reganti, A. N., Bhatia, A., Maheshwari, T., & Rao, B. (2018). Aggression-annotated Corpus of Hindi-English Code-mixed Data. *Proceedings of the Eleventh International Conference on Language Resources and Evaluation (LREC 2018)*. https://www.aclweb.org/anthology/L18-1226

Kuss, D. J., & Griffiths, M. D. (2011). Online social networking and addiction—A review of the psychological literature. *International Journal of Environmental Research and Public Health*, *8*(9), 3528–3552. doi:10.3390/ijerph8093528 PMID:22016701

Kwahk, K. Y., & Park, D. H. (2016). The effects of network sharing on knowledge-sharing activities and job performance in enterprise social media environments. *Computers in Human Behavior*, *55*, 826–839. doi:10.1016/j.chb.2015.09.044

Lagacé, M., Charmarkeh, H., Zaky, R., & Firzly, N. (2016). From psychological to digital disengagement: Exploring the link between ageism and the 'grey digital divide'. *Romanian Journal of Communication and Public Relations*, *18*(1), 65–75. doi:10.21018/rjcpr.2016.1.202

Lakkysetty, N., Deep, P., & Balamurugan, J. (2018). Social Media and its Impact on Politics. *International Journal of Advance Research. Ideas and Innovations in Technology*, *4*(2), 2108–2118.

Lalitha, L. A., Hulipalled, V. R., & Venugopal, K. R. (2018). Spamming the mainstream: A survey on trending Twitter spam detection techniques. *Proceedings of the 2017 International Conference On Smart Technology for Smart Nation, SmartTechCon 2017*, 444–448. 10.1109/SmartTechCon.2017.8358413

Lammers, M. (2018). Wie unternehmen aus micro-influencern co-marketer machen. In M. Jahnke (Ed.), *Influencer marketing* (pp. 107–126). Springer Gabler. doi:10.1007/978-3-658-20854-7_6

Lampe, C., Ellison, N. B., & Steinfield, C. (2006). A face(book) in the crowd: Social searching vs. Social browsing. In *Proceedings of the 2006 20th Anniversary Conference on Computer Supported Cooperative Work* (pp. 167–170). 10.1145/1180875.1180901

Lange, C., Bojars, U., Groza, T., Breslin, J., & Handschuh, S. (2008). Expressing argumentative discussions in social media sites. *Social Data on the Web (SDoW2008), Workshop at the 7th Int. Semantic Web Conference.*

Lansing, J. B., & Heyns, R. W. (1959). Need affiliation and frequency of four types of communication. *Journal of Abnormal and Social Psychology*, *58*(3), 365–372. doi:10.1037/h0045906 PMID:13653887

Larsson, A. O., & Hallvard, M. (2012). Studying political microblogging: Twitter Users in the 2010 Swedish Election Campaign. *New Media & Society*, *14*(5), 729–747. doi:10.1177/1461444811422894

Lau, W. W. (2017). Effects of social media usage and social media multitasking on the academic performance of university students. *Computers in Human Behavior*, *68*, 286–291. doi:10.1016/j.chb.2016.11.043

Lazer, D. M. J., Baum, M. A., Benkler, Y., Berinsky, A. J., Greenhill, K. M., Menczer, F., & Zittrain, J. L. (2018). The science of fake news. *Science*, *359*(6380), 1094–1096. doi:10.1126cience.aao2998 PMID:29590025

Lee, C. S., & Ma, L. (2011). News sharing in social media: The effects of gratifications and prior experience. *Computers in Human Behavior, 28*(2), 331–339. doi:10.1016/j.chb.2011.10.002

Lee, E. B. (2015). Too much information: Heavy smartphone and Facebook utilization by African American young adults. *Journal of Black Studies, 46*(1), 44–61. doi:10.1177/0021934714557034

Lee, M. S., Geistfeld, L. V., & Stoel, L. (2007). Cultural differences between Korean and American apparel web sites. *Journal of Fashion Marketing and Management, 11*(4), 511–528. doi:10.1108/13612020710824571

Lee, S., & Kim, J. (2013). Warning bird: A near real-time detection system for suspicious URLs in twitter stream. *IEEE Transactions on Dependable and Secure Computing, 10*(3), 183–195. doi:10.1109/TDSC.2013.3

Leetaru, K. H. (2015, August 27). Who's doing the talking on Twitter? *The Atlantic.* Retrieved on March 20, 2020 from https://www.theatlantic.com/international/archive/2015/2008/twitter-global-social-media/402415/

Leftheriotis, I., & Giannakos, M. N. (2014). Using social media for work: Losing your time or improving your work? *Computers in Human Behavior, 31*, 134–142. doi:10.1016/j.chb.2013.10.016

Leidner, D., Koch, H., & Gonzalez, E. (2010). Assimilating Generation Y IT New Hires into USAA's Workforce: The Role of an Enterprise 2.0 System. *MIS Quarterly Executive, 9*(4).

Lei, K., Liu, Y., Zhong, S., Liu, Y., Xu, K., Shen, Y., & Yang, M. (2018). Understanding user behavior in sina weibo online social network: A community approach. *IEEE Access: Practical Innovations, Open Solutions, 6*, 13302–13316. doi:10.1109/ACCESS.2018.2808158

Lemon, J. (2002). Can we call behaviors addictive? *Clinical Psychologist, 6*(2), 44–49. doi:10.1080/13284200310001707411

Leonardi, P. M. (2015). Ambient awareness and knowledge acquisition: Using social media to learn 'who knows what' and 'who knows whom'. *Management Information Systems Quarterly, 39*(4), 747–762. doi:10.25300/MISQ/2015/39.4.1

Leung, L. (2004). Net-generation attributes and seductive properties of the Internet as predictors of online activities and Internet addiction. *Cyberpsychology & Behavior, 7*(3), 333–348. doi:10.1089/1094931041291303 PMID:15257834

Levenson, J. C., Shensa, A., Sidani, J. E., Colditz, J. B., & Primack, B. A. (2016). The association between social media use and sleep disturbance among young adults. *Preventive Medicine, 85*, 36–41. doi:10.1016/j.ypmed.2016.01.001 PMID:26791323

LévyP. (1999). *Cibercultura.* Editora 34.

Lewis, O. A., & Steinmo, S. (2012). How Institutions Evolve: Evolutionary Theory and Institutional Change. *Polity, 44*(3), 314–339. doi:10.1057/pol.2012.10

Li, C, & Bernoff, J. (2008 April 21). *Harvard Business School Press (1805) Groundswell: Winning in a World Transformed by Social Technologies.* Academic Press.

Libicki, M. C. (2018). Drawing inferences from cyber espionage. *International Conference on Cyber Conflict, CYCON*, 109–121. 10.23919/CYCON.2018.8405013

Liebowitz, J., & Beckman, T. (1998). *Knowledge Organizations: What Every Manager Should Know.* St. Lucie Press.

Lien, H. C., & Cao, Y. (2014). Examining WeChat users' motivations, trust, attitudes, and positive word-of-mouth: Evidence from China. *Computers in Human Behavior, 41*, 104–111. doi:10.1016/j.chb.2014.08.013

Liew, S. W., Sani, N. F. M., Abdullah, M. T., Yaakob, R., & Sharum, M. Y. (2019). An effective security alert mechanism for real-time phishing tweet detection on Twitter. *Computers & Security, 83,* 201–207. doi:10.1016/j.cose.2019.02.004

Lim, X. J., Radzol, A. R., Cheah, J., & Wong, M. W. (2017). The impact of social media influencers on purchase intention and the mediation effect of customer attitude. *Asian Journal of Business Research, 7*(2), 19–36. doi:10.14707/ajbr.170035

Lin, C., Varadharajan, V., Wang, Y., & Mu, Y. (2004). On the design of a new trust model for mobile agent security. Lecture Notes in Computer Science, 3184, 60–69. doi:10.1007/978-3-540-30079-3_7

Lin, L. Y., Sidani, J. E., Shensa, A., Radovic, A., Miller, E., Colditz, J. B., & Primack, B. A. (2016). Association between social media use and depression among U.S. young adults. *Depression and Anxiety, 33*(4), 323-331. . doi:10.1002/da.22466

Lindsey-Mullikin, J., & Borin, N. (2017). Why strategy is key for successful social media sales. *Business Horizons, 60*(4), 473–482. doi:10.1016/j.bushor.2017.03.005

Lin, J.-S., Lee, Y.-I., Jin, Y., & Gilbreath, B. (2017). Personality Traits, Motivations, and Emotional Consequences of Social Media Usage. *Cyberpsychology, Behavior, and Social Networking, 20*(10), 615–623. doi:10.1089/cyber.2017.0043 PMID:29039699

Lin, S.-H., & Chou, W. H. (2014). Developing a social media system for the Taiwanese elderly by participatory design. *Bulletin of Japanese Society for the Science of Design, 60*(3), 39–48.

Lips, A. M. B., & Eppel, E. A. (2017). Understanding and explaining online personal information-sharing behaviours of New Zealanders: A new taxonomy. *Information Communication and Society, 20*(3), 428–443. doi:10.1080/136911 8X.2016.1184697

Litvin, S. W., Goldsmith, R. E., & Pan, B. (2008). Electronic word-of-mouth in hospitality and tourism management. *Tourism Management, 29*(3), 458–468. doi:10.1016/j.tourman.2007.05.011

Liu, I. L. B., Cheung, C. M. K., & Lee, M. K. O. (2010). Understanding Twitter usage: What drive people continue to tweet. PACIS 2010 Proceedings, 928–939.

Liu, B. F., Jin, Y., & Austin, L. L. (2013). The tendency to tell: Understanding publics' communicative responses to crisis information form and source. *Journal of Public Relations Research, 25*(1), 51–67. doi:10.1080/1062726X.2013.739101

Liu, M. T., Shi, G., Wong, I. A., Hefel, A., & Chen, C.-Y. (2010). How physical attractiveness and endorser–product match-up guide selection of a female athlete endorser in China. *Journal of International Consumer Marketing, 22*(2), 169–181. doi:10.1080/08961530903476238

Liu, Y. (2016). *Social Media in China.* Springer Gabler. doi:10.1007/978-3-658-11231-8

Livingstone, D. W. (1999). Exploring the icebergs of adult learning: Findings of the first Canadian survey of informal learning practices. *Canadian Journal for the Study of Adult Education, 13*(2), 49–72.

Li, Y.-M., Lee, Y.-L., & Lien, N.-J. (2014). Online social advertising via influential endorsers. *International Journal of Electronic Commerce, 16*(3), 119–153. doi:10.2753/JEC1086-4415160305

Lokare, R., Kumari, K. W. S. N., Yadav, U., Borge, S., & Shinkar, D. V. (2016). *FRAppE Detecting Malicious Facebook Applications.* Academic Press.

Lokithasan, K., Simon, S., Jasmin, N. Z., & Othman, N. A. (2019). Male and female social media influencers: The impact of gender on emerging adults. *International Journal of Modern Trends in Social Sciences, 2*(9), 21–30. doi:10.35631/IJMTSS.29003

Long, G. (2007). *Transmedia Storytelling. Business, aesthetics and production at the Jim Henson Company* (Master's dissertation). MIT. Retrieved from http://cms.mit.edu/research/thesis/GeoffreyLong2007.pdf

Longstreet, P., & Brooks, S. (2017). Life satisfaction: A key to managing internet & social media addiction. *Technology in Society*, *50*, 73–77. doi:10.1016/j.techsoc.2017.05.003

Loos, E. (2012). Designing for dynamic diversity: Representing various senior citizens in digital information sources. *The Observatory Journal*, *7*(1), 21–45.

Loos, M. D. (2002). The synergy of depravity and loneliness in alcoholism: A new conceptualization, and old problem. *Counseling and Values*, *46*(3), 199–212. doi:10.1002/j.2161-007X.2002.tb00213.x

Lorenzo-Romero, C., Constantinides, E., & Alarcón-del-Amo, M.-C. (2011). Consumer adoption of social networking sites: Implications for theory and practice. *Journal of Research in Interactive Marketing*, *5*(5), 170–188. doi:10.1108/17505931111187794

Lou, C., & Yuan, S. (2019). Influencer marketing: How message value and credibility affect consumer trust of branded content on social media. *Journal of Interactive Advertising*, *19*(1), 58–73. doi:10.1080/15252019.2018.1533501

Luna, M. D. (2020, July 14). Should you delete TikTok? Why some experts think the app is a privacy threat. *Houston Chronicle*. Retrieved on July 14, 2020 from https://www.chron.com/news/houston-texas/article/Should-you-delete-TikTok-Is-the-popular-app-a-15407966.php

Luoma-aho, V., Pirttimäki, T., Maity, D., Munnukka, J., & Reinikainen, H. (2019). Primed authenticity: How priming impacts authenticity perception of social media influencers. *International Journal of Strategic Communication*, *13*(4), 352–365. doi:10.1080/1553118X.2019.1617716

Lutkenhaus, R. O., Jansz, J., & Bouman, M. P. (2019). Tailoring in the digital era: Stimulating dialogues on health topics in collaboration with social media influencers. *Digital Health*, *5*, 1–11. doi:10.1177/2055207618821521 PMID:30729023

Lynch, G., Willis, J., & Cheeseman, N. (2018). Claims about Cambridge Analytica's role in Africa Should be Taken with a Pinch of Salt. *The Conversation*.

Maarit, M. & Kuira, M. W. (2008). Social Media and Post-Election Crisis in Kenya. *Information & Communication Technology-Africa*, 13.

Madzova, V., Sajnoski, K., & Davcev, L. (2013, June). E-Government as an Efficient Tool towards Good Governance: Trends and Comparative Analysis throughout Worldwide Regions and within West Balkan Countries. *Balkan Social Science Review*, *1*, 157–174.

Mahmoudi, A., Yaakub, M. R., & Bakar, A. A. (2018). New time-based model to identify the influential users in online social networks. *Data Technologies and Applications*, *52*(2), 278–290. doi:10.1108/DTA-08-2017-0056

Makinen, M & Kuira, W. M. (2008). Social Media and Post-Election Crisis in Kenya. *Information & Communication Technology – Africa*, 13.

Malik, M. E., Ghafoor, M. M., Iqbal, H. K., Ali, Q., Hunbal, H., Noman, M., & Ahmad, B. (2013). Impact of brand image and advertisement on consumer buying behavior. *World Applied Sciences Journal*, *23*(1), 117–122.

Malik, S., & Khan, M. (2015). Impact of facebook addiction on narcissistic behavior and self-esteem among students. *JPMA. The Journal of the Pakistan Medical Association*, *65*(3), 260–263. PMID:25933557

Mallouli, M., Hachicha, Z. S., & Chaabouni, J. (n.d.). Management Research on Social Networking Sites: State of the Art and Further Avenues of Research. *EJISE*, *20*(2), 128–141.

Mallouli, M., Hachicha, Z. S., & Chaabouni, J. (2016). *Réseaux Sociaux Numériques: état de l'art*. AIM.

Mambwe, E. (2014). 20 years of internet in Zambia-how has journalism been impacted? African trends. *Rhodes Journalism Review, 2014*(34), 77–80.

Mambwe, E. (2019). Investigating the use and impact of social media in Zambian newsrooms between 2011-2013. *International Journal of Multidisciplinary Research and Development, 6*(4), 30–37.

Manchanda, P., Dubé, J.-P., Goh, K. Y., & Chintagunta, P. K. (2006). The effect of banner advertising on internet purchasing. *JMR, Journal of Marketing Research, 43*(1), 98–108. doi:10.1509/jmkr.43.1.98

Manglic, A. (2017). *Artificial Intelligence and Machine/ Deep Learning*. Retrieved from http://arun-aiml.blogspot.com/2017/07/k-means-clustering.html

Mann, L., & Berry, M. (2015). Understanding the political motivations that shape Rwanda's emergent developmental state. *New Political Economy, 21*(1), 119-144.

Manning, J. (2014). Definition and Classes of Social Media. In K. Harvey (Ed.), *Encyclopedia of Social Media and Politics* (pp. 1158–1162). Sage.

Mano, W., & Ndlela, M. N. (2020). Introduction: Social Media, Political Cultures and Elections in Africa. In M. Ndlela & W. Mano (Eds.), *Social Media and Elections in Africa* (Vol. 2, pp. 1–7). Palgrave Macmillan. doi:10.1007/978-3-030-32682-1_1

Mäntymäki, M., & Islam, A. K. M. N. (2016). The Janus face of Facebook: Positive and negative sides of social networking site use. *Computers in Human Behavior, 61*, 14–26. doi:10.1016/j.chb.2016.02.078

Maraz, A., Eisinger, A., Hende, B., Urbán, R., Paksi, B., Kun, B., Kökönyei, G., Griffiths, M. D., & Demetrovics, Z. (2015). Measuring compulsive buying behaviour: Psychometric validity of three different scales and prevalence in the general population and in shopping centres. *Psychiatry Research, 225*(3), 326–334. doi:10.1016/j.psychres.2014.11.080 PMID:25595336

March, J. G., & Olsen, J. P. (1984). The New Institutionalism: Organizational Factors in Political Life. *The American Political Science Review, 78*(3), 734–749. doi:10.2307/1961840

March, J. G., & Olsen, J. P. (1989). *Rediscovering Institutions: The Organizational Basis of Politics*. The Free Press.

Marcus, S. R. (2015). 'Picturing' ourselves into being: Assessing identity, sociality and visuality on Instagram. *Proceedings of the International Communication Association Conference*.

Mare, A. (2014). Social Media: The New Protest Drums in Southern Africa? In B. Pătruț & M. Pătruț (Eds.), *Social Media in Politics. Public Administration and Information Technology* (Vol. 13, pp. 315–335). Springer. doi:10.1007/978-3-319-04666-2_17

Marino, C., Gini, G., Vieno, A., & Spada, M. M. (2018). A comprehensive meta-analysis on problematic Facebook use. *Computers in Human Behavior, 83*, 262–277. doi:10.1016/j.chb.2018.02.009

Marino, C., Vieno, A., Moss, A. C., Caselli, G., Nikčević, A. V., & Spada, M. M. (2016). Personality, motives and metacognitions as predictors of problematic Facebook use in university students. *Personality and Individual Differences, 101*, 70–77. doi:10.1016/j.paid.2016.05.053

Marlatt, G. A., Baer, J. S., Donovan, D. M., & Kivlahan, D. R. (1988). Addictive behaviors: Etiology and treatment. *Annual Review of Psychology, 39*(1), 223–252. doi:10.1146/annurev.ps.39.020188.001255 PMID:3278676

Marshall, T. C., Lefringhausen, K., & Ferenczi, N. (2015). The Big Five, self-esteem, and narcissism as predictors of the topics people write about in Facebook status updates. *Personality and Individual Differences*, *85*, 35–40. doi:10.1016/j. paid.2015.04.039

Marwick, A. (2010). *Status update: Celebrity, publicity and self-branding in Web 2.0* [Unpublished doctoral dissertation]. New York University.

Marwick, A. (2016). You may know me from Youtube: (Micro-)celebrity in social media. In P. D. Marshall & S. Redmond (Eds.), A companion to celebrity (pp. 333-350). Wiley.

Marwick, A., & boyd. (2011). To see and be seen: Celebrity practice on Twitter. *Convergence*, *17*(2), 139–158. doi:10.1177/1354856510394539

Massit-Folléa, F. (2002). Usages des Technologies de l'Information et de la Communication: acquis et perspectives de la recherche. *Le Français dans le monde*, 8-14.

Masur, P. K., Reinecke, L., Ziegele, M., & Quiring, O. (2014). The interplay of intrinsic need satisfaction and Facebook specific motives in explaining addictive behavior on Facebook. *Computers in Human Behavior*, *39*, 376–386. doi:10.1016/j.chb.2014.05.047

Matthes, J., Potter, R., & Davis, C. (2017). *Empirical and Non-Empirical Methods*. Retrieved from: https://www.researchgate.net/publication/309922961_Empirical_and_Non-Empirical_Methods

Mauritti, R. (2004). Padrões de vida na velhice. *Analise Social*, *39*(171), 339–363.

Maxwell, M. E. (2012). *Motivations to tweet: a uses and gratifications perspective of twitter use during a natural disaster* (Master's thesis). Department of Advertising and Public Relations, University of Alabama.

Mazza, M., Cresci, S., Avvenuti, M., Quattrociocchi, W., & Tesconi, M. (2019). *RTbust: Exploiting Temporal Patterns for Botnet Detection on Twitter*. http://arxiv.org/abs/1902.04506

Mazzoni, E., & Iannone, M. (2014). From high school to university: Impact of social networking sites on social capital in the transitions of emerging adults. *British Journal of Educational Technology*, *45*(2), 303–315. doi:10.1111/bjet.12026

McCracken, G. (1989). Who is the celebrity endorser? Cultural foundations of the endorsement process. *The Journal of Consumer Research*, *16*(3), 310–321. doi:10.1086/209217

McDonough, C. C. (2016). Determinants of a digital divide among able-bodied older adults: Does "feeling too old" play a role? *International Journal of Aging Research*, *3*, 60.

McDougall, M. A., Walsh, M., Wattier, K., Knigge, R., Miller, L., Stevermer, M., & Fogas, B. S. (2016). The effect of social networking sites on the relationship between perceived social support and depression. *Psychiatry Research*, *246*, 223–229. doi:10.1016/j.psychres.2016.09.018 PMID:27721061

McIntyre, S. (2020). *Key Concept - What is Transmedia Storytelling?* Retrieved from: https://www.coursera.org/lecture/transmedia-storytelling/key-concept-what-is-transmedia-storytelling-sRicJ?authMode=signup&redirectTo=%2Flearn%2Ftransmedia-storytelling%3Faction%3Denroll

McKenna, K. Y. A., & Bargh, J. A. (2000). Plan 9 from cyberspace: The implication of the Internet for personality and social psychology. *Personality and Social Psychology Review*, *4*(1), 57–75. doi:10.1207/S15327957PSPR0401_6

McKinsey & Company. (2011, May). *The world gone digital: Insights from McKinsey's Global iConsumer Research*. New York: McKinsey & Company.

McKinsey & Company. (2012, January). *The Young and the Digital: A Glimpse into Future Market Evolution*. New York: McKinsey & Company.

Media Council of Kenya. (2016). *The Impact of Digital Technologies and Internet on Media and Journalism in Kenya*. United Nations Office at Nairobi.

Medora, N. P., & Woodward, J. C. (1991). Factors associated with loneliness among alcoholics in rehabilitation centers. *The Journal of Social Psychology, 131*(6), 769–779. doi:10.1080/00224545.1991.9924664 PMID:1667810

Mehmood, A., On, B. W., Lee, I., Ashraf, I., & Sang Choi, G. (2018). Spam comments prediction using stacking with ensemble learning. *Journal of Physics: Conference Series, 933*(1). Advance online publication. doi:10.1088/1742-6596/933/1/012012

Meier, A., Reinecke, L., & Meltzer, C. E. (2016). "Facebocrastination"? Predictors of using Facebook for procrastination and its effects on students' well-being. *Computers in Human Behavior, 64*, 65–76. doi:10.1016/j.chb.2016.06.011

Mendoza, M., Poblete, B., & Castillo, C. (2010, July). Twitter under crisis: Can we trust what we RT? In *Proceedings of the first workshop on social media analytics* (pp. 71-79). 10.1145/1964858.1964869

Mesch, G. S. (2001). Social relationships and Internet use among adolescents in Israel. *Social Science Quarterly, 82*(2), 329–339. doi:10.1111/0038-4941.00026

Mfumbusa, B. F. (2006). Media accountability challenges in sub-Saharan Africa: the limits of self-regulation in Tanzanian newsrooms. *Cross connections: Interdisciplinary communication studies at the Gregorian University*, 259-270.

Mhlomi, Y., & Osunkule, O. (2017). Social Media and Youth Political Participation in South Africa's 2014 General Election. *Communitas, 12*(22), 149–158.

Mihajlović, G., Hinić, D., Damjanović, A., Gajić, T., & Dukić-Dejanović, S. (2008). Excessive internet use and depressive disorders. *Psychiatria Danubina, 20*, 5–14. PMID:18376325

Miladi, N. (2016). Social Media and Social Change. *DOMES. Digest of Middle East Studies., 1*(25), 36–51. doi:10.1111/dome.12082

Milakovich, M. E. (2010). The Internet and Increased Citizen Participation in Government. *JeDEM - eJournal of eDemocracy and Open Government, 2*(1), 1-9. https://www.jedem.org/index.php/jedem/article/view/22

Miles, M. B., & Huberman, A. M. (2003). *Analyse des données qualitatives*. De Boeck Supérieur.

Millerand, F. (2008). *Usages des NTIC: Les approches de la diffusion, de l'innovation et de l'appropriation* (1ère partie). *Commposite, 2*(1), 1–19.

Minnich, A., Chavoshi, N., Koutra, D., & Mueen, A. (2017). BotWalk: Efficient adaptive exploration of twitter bot networks. *Proceedings of the 2017 IEEE/ACM International Conference on Advances in Social Networks Analysis and Mining, ASONAM 2017*. 10.1145/3110025.3110163

Miranda, S., Antunes, A. C., Machado, A. T., & Gama, A. (2020). Age 2.0: Motivations and brand engagement. *Proceedings of 7th European Conference on Social Media*.

MITRE Corporation. (2019). *Matrix - Enterprise | MITRE ATT&CK®*. https://attack.mitre.org/matrices/enterprise/

Mitry, D. J., & Smith, D. E. (2009). Convergence in global markets and consumer behaviour. *International Journal of Consumer Studies, 33*(3), 316–321. doi:10.1111/j.1470-6431.2009.00746.x

Mkono, M. (2018). The age of digital activism in tourism: Evaluating the legacy and limitations of the Cecil anti-trophy hunting movement. *Journal of Sustainable Tourism, 26*(9), 1608–1624. doi:10.1080/09669582.2018.1489399

Mkono, M., & Tribe, J. (2017). Beyond reviewing: Uncovering the multiple roles of tourism social media users. *Journal of Travel Research, 56*(3), 287–298. doi:10.1177/0047287516636236

Monacis, L., De Palo, V., Griffiths, M. D., & Sinatra, M. (2017). Social networking addiction, attachment style, and validation of the Italian version of the Bergen Social Media Addiction Scale. *Journal of Behavioral Addictions, 6*(2), 178–186. doi:10.1556/2006.6.2017.023 PMID:28494648

Monty, S. Brand Quarterly. (2018 July 27). *Reclaiming Humanity In Business.* http://www.brandquarterly.com/reclaiming-humanity-business

Mooij, M. (2018). *Global marketing and advertising: Understanding cultural paradoxes* (5th ed.). SAGE Publications Limited.

Moore, C., & Chuang, L. (2017). Redditors Revealed: Motivational Factors of the Reddit Community. *Proceedings of the 50th Hawaii International Conference on System Sciences*, 2313-2322. 10.24251/HICSS.2017.279

Moqbel, M., & Kock, N. (2018). Unveiling the dark side of social networking sites: Personal and work-related consequences of social networking site addiction. *Information & Management, 55*(1), 109–119. doi:10.1016/j.im.2017.05.001

Moqbel, M., Nevo, S., & Kock, N. (2013). Organizational members' use of social networking sites and job performance. *Information Technology & People, 26*(3), 240–264. doi:10.1108/ITP-10-2012-0110

Morar, D. D. (2013). An overview of the consumer value literature – perceived value, desired value. *Marketing From Information to Decision, 6*, 169–186.

Moravec, P., Minas, R., & Dennis, A. R. (2018). *Fake News on Social Media: People Believe What They Want to Believe When it Makes No Sense at All.* Kelley School of Business Research Paper (18-87).

Moreau, A., Laconi, S., Delfour, M., & Chabrol, H. (2015). Psychopathological profiles of adolescent and young adult problematic Facebook users. *Computers in Human Behavior, 44*, 64–69. doi:10.1016/j.chb.2014.11.045

Moreno, M. A., Jelenchick, L. A., Egan, K. G., Cox, E., Young, H., Gannon, K. E., & Becker, T. (2011). Feeling bad on Facebook: Depression disclosures by college students on a social networking site. *Depression and Anxiety, 28*(6), 447–455. doi:10.1002/da.20805 PMID:21400639

Morgan, E. (2016, September 6). *Homogenization of social media.* Retrieved on March 9, 2020 from https://morganandco.com/homogenization-social-media/

Morth, D. (2014). 89% of British internet users are worried about online privacy: report. *eConsultancy.* Retrieved on March 16, 2020 from https://econsultancy.com/2089-of-british-internet-users-are-worried-about-online-privacy-report/

Mostafa, M. M. (2013). More than words: Social networks' text mining for consumer brand sentiments. *Expert Systems with Applications, 40*(10), 4241–4251. doi:10.1016/j.eswa.2013.01.019

Mostert, C. (2016). Determining the motivating factors for the general use of social media amongst tourists to South Africa. *International Journal of Business and Management Studies, 8*(2), 84–101.

Motowidlo, S. J., & Van Scotter, J. R. (1994). Evidence that task performance should be distinguished from contextual performance. *The Journal of Applied Psychology, 79*(4), 475–480. doi:10.1037/0021-9010.79.4.475

Mthokozisi E. N & Teferra, D. (2017). Implications of Social Media on Student Activism: The South African Experience in a Digital Age. *JHEA/RESA, 15*(2), 63-80.

Mubaris, N. K. (2017). *Support Vector Machines for Classification*. Retrieved from https://mubaris.com/posts/svm

Mulenga, F. K. (2017). *Factors that influence mobile applications (apps) usage in mobile banking in Zambia* (Unpublished Master's thesis). University of Cape Town, Cape Town, South Africa.

Mull, I. R., & Lee, S. E. (2014). "PIN" pointing the motivational dimensions behind Pinterest. *Computers in Human Behavior*, *33*, 192–200. doi:10.1016/j.chb.2014.01.011

Munene, A. G., & Nyaribo, Y. M. (2013). Effect of social media pertication in the workplace on employee productivity. *International Journal of Advances in Management and Economics*, *2*(2), 141–150.

Murray, H. A. (1938). *Explorations in Personality*. Oxford University Press.

Murungi, K. M. (2018). Influence of Social Media to Community Development: Lessons from Kenya. *International Journal of Social Science and Technology*, *3*(6), 1–18.

Mustafaraj, E., & Metaxas, P. (2010). From obscurity to prominence in minutes: political speech and real-time search. *Proceedings of the WebSci10: Extending the Frontiers of Society On-Line*.

Mustapha, L. K., Azeez, A. L., & Wok, S. (2011, September). *Globalization, Global Media and Homogenization of Global Culture: Implications for Islam and Muslims*. Paper presented at the National Seminar on New Media and Islamic Issues: Challenges and Opportunities, Organized by Department of Communication, CERDAS & ISTAC, IIUM.

Mutahi, P., & Kimari, B. (2017). The impact of social media and digital technology on electoral violence in Kenya. *IDS*.

Mwalimu, E. C., Mulauzi, F., & Mwiinga, T. M. (2017). *Use of social media among University of Zambia lecturers in teaching and learning*. Academic Press.

Mwangi, M. W., & Wagok, J. (2016). Effect of Social Media on Performance of Advertisement Business in the Mainstream Media in Kenya: A Survey of Leading Media Groups in Kenya. *International Journal of Economics. Commerce and Management*, *IV*(4), 159–177.

Mwiya, B., Chikumbi, F., Shikaputo, C., Kabala, E., Kaulung'ombe, B., & Siachinji, B. (2017). *Examining Factors influencing e-banking adoption: evidence from bank customers in Zambia*. Available at SSRN 2987982

Myhre, J. W., Mehl, M. R., & Glisky, E. L. (2017). Cognitive benefits of online social networking for healthy older adults. *Journal of Gerontology*, *72*(5), 752–760. PMID:26984523

Myrick, J. G. (2015). Emotion regulation, procrastination, and watching cat videos online: Who watches Internet cats, why, and to what effect? *Computers in Human Behavior*, *52*, 168–176. doi:10.1016/j.chb.2015.06.001

Nanda, C., Dua, M., & Nanda, G. (2018). Sentiment Analysis of Movie Reviews in Hindi Language Using Machine Learning. *2018 International Conference on Communication and Signal Processing (ICCSP)*. 10.1109/ICCSP.2018.8524223

Nandan, S. (2005). An exploration of the brand identity-brand image linkage: A communications perspective. *Journal of Brand Management*, *12*(4), 264–278. doi:10.1057/palgrave.bm.2540222

NapoleonCat. (2019). *Instagram users in India*. https://napoleoncat.com/stats/instagram-users-in-india/2019/01

Narula, S., & Jindal, N. (2015). Use of social network sites by AUMP students: A comparative study on Facebook, Twitter and Instagram usage. *Journal of Advanced Research*, *2*(2), 20–24.

Navlani, A. (2018). *KNN Classification using Scikit-learn*. Retrieved from https://www.datacamp.com/community/tutorials/k-nearest-neighbor-classification-scikit-learn

Nawaz, S. S., & Mubarak, K. M. (2015). Adoption of Social Media Marketing By Tourism Product Suppliers: A Study in Eastern Province Of Sri Lanka. *European Journal of Business and Management*, *7*(7), 448–455.

Nazir, Iqbal, & Kanwal, Nasir & Abid. (2016). Effect of Social Media on Employee's Performance: A Study, in Corporate Sector of Pakistan. *International Review of Basic and Applied Sciences*, *4*(9).

Naz, S., Sharan, A., & Malik, N. (2018). Sentiment Classification on Twitter Data Using Support Vector Machine. *2018 IEEE/WIC/ACM International Conference on Web Intelligence (WI)*. 10.1109/WI.2018.00-13

Ndavula, J. O., & Mueni, J. (2014). New Media and Political Marketing in Kenya: The Case of 2013 General Elections. *International Journal of Arts and Commerce*, *6*(3), 69–84.

Ndlela, M. N. (2020). Social Media Algorithms, Bots and Elections in Africa. In Social Media and Elections in Africa, Volume 1. Theoretical Perspectives and Election Campaigns. Palgrave Macmillan.

Ndlela, M. N., & Mulwo, A. (2017). Social media, youth and everyday life in Kenya. *Journal of African Media Studies*, *9*(2), 277–290. doi:10.1386/jams.9.2.277_1

Nendo. (2020). *Nendo 2020 Digital Report*. https://www.nendo.co.ke/2020dtr

NETSCOUT. (2019). *Threat Intelligence Report - Powered by ATLAS | NETSCOUT*. https://www.netscout.com/threatreport?ls=PR-MKTG&lsd=pr-021820-5

Neves, B. B., Waycott, J., & Malta, S. (2018). Old and afraid of new communication technologies? Reconceptualising and contesting the 'age-based digital divide.'. *Journal of Sociology (Melbourne, Vic.)*, *54*(2), 236–248. doi:10.1177/1440783318766119

Neves, B., & Amaro, F. (2012). Too old for technology? How the elderly of Lisbon use and perceive ICT. *The Journal of Community Informatics*, *8*(1), 1–12.

Nimrod, G. (2014). Seniors' online communities: A quantitative content analysis. *The Gerontologist*, *50*(3), 382–392. doi:10.1093/geront/gnp141 PMID:19917645

Nimrod, G. (2017). Older audiences in the digital media environment. *Information Communication and Society*, *20*(2), 233–249. doi:10.1080/1369118X.2016.1164740

Njeri, M. W. (2014). *Effect of Social Media Interactions on Financial Performance of Commercial Banks in Kenya* (Master Thesis). School of Business, Department of Finance, University of Nairobi.

Njoroge, C., & Koloseni, D. (2015). Adoption of Social Media as Full-Fledged Banking Channel: An Analysis of Retail Banking Customers in Kenya. *International Journal of Information and Communication Technology Research*, *5*(2), 1–12.

Nkwe, N., & Cohen, J. (2017). *Impact Of Social Network Sites On Psychological And Behavioural Outcomes In The Work-Place: A Systematic Literature Review. Association for Information Systems AIS Electronic Library (AISeL)*, 6-10.

Nooruddin, Z., & Zhang, L. (2012). *7 Steps to Weibo Success*. Retrieved from https://www.chinabusinessreview.com/7-steps-to-weibo-success/

Norris, P. (2001). *Digital Divide: Civic Engagement, Information Poverty, and the Internet Worldwide*. Cambridge University Press. doi:10.1017/CBO9781139164887

North, M. (2010). An evaluation of employees' attitudes toward social networking in the workplace. *Issues in Information Systems*, *11*(1), 192–197.

Nyagah, V. W., Asatsa, S., & Mwania, J. M. (2015). Social Networking Sites and their Influence on the Self Esteem of Adolescents in Embu county, Kenya. *Journal of Educational Policy and Entrepreneurial Research, 2*(1), 87–92.

Nyamboga, E. N. (2014). Social Media in Kenyan Journalism: Benefits, Opportunities and Challenges. *IOSR Journal of Humanities and Social Science, 19*(12), 89–94. doi:10.9790/0837-191248994

Nyamnjoh, F. (2015). *New media and religious transformations in Africa.* Indiana University Press.

O'Brien, D., & Torres, A. M. (2012, April). Social networking and online privacy: Facebook users' perceptions. *Irish Journal of Management, 31*(2), 63.

Obar, J. A., & Wildman, S. S. (2015). Social media definition and the governance challenge: An introduction to the special issue. *Telecommunications Policy, 39*(9), 745–750. doi:10.1016/j.telpol.2015.07.014

Oginni, S. O., & Moitui, J. N. (2015). Social Media and Public Policy Process in Africa: Enhanced Policy Process in Digital Age. *Consilience. The Journal of Sustainable Development Vol., 2*(14), 158–172.

Ogola, G. (2019). What would Magufuli do? Kenya's digital "practices" and "individuation" as a (non) political act. *Journal of Eastern African Studies: the Journal of the British Institute in Eastern Africa, 13*(1), 124–139. doi:10.1080/17531055.2018.1547263

Ogri, E. U., Mboso, A. G. & Adomi, K. O. (2016). Social Media and Participatory Democracy in Africa: A Study of Democratic Transitions in Nigeria and Uganda. *International Journal of Linguistics and Communication, 3*(2), 25-49.

Olenski, S. (2018). *Storytelling, Brands And Some Words Of Wisdom.* Retrieved from https://www.forbes.com/sites/steveolenski/2018/04/06/storytelling-brands-and-some-words-of-wisdom/#6c3335cb5ae1

Olowu, A. O., & Seri, F. O. (2012). A study of social network addiction among youths in Nigeria. *Journal of Social Science and Policy Review, 4*, 62–71.

Omnicore. (2020). *YouTube by the numbers: Stats, demographics & fun facts.* https://www.omnicoreagency.com/youtube-statistics/

Ones, D. S., Viswesvaran, C., & Schmidt, F. L. (1993). Comprehensive meta-analysis of integrity test validities: Findings and implications for personnel selection and theories of job performance. *The Journal of Applied Psychology, 78*(4), 679–703. doi:10.1037/0021-9010.78.4.679

Orford, J. (2001). *Excessive appetites: A psychological view of addictions* (2nd ed.). Wiley.

Oukemeni, S., Rifà-Pous, H., & Puig, J. M. M. (2019). Privacy analysis on microblogging online social networks: A survey. In ACM Computing Surveys (Vol. 52, Issue 3, pp. 1–36). Association for Computing Machinery. doi:10.1145/3321481

Ouni, A. (2008). *L'élaboration de modèles et d'outils pour l'analyse et la conception des usages des outils de travail collaboratif en entreprise* (Doctoral dissertation).

Ozturk, A. (2016, February 26-28). Global Convergence of Consumer Spending Behavior: An Empirical Examination. *2016 AMA Winter Educators' Proceedings.*

Ozturk, A., & Cavusgil, S. T. (2019). Global convergence of consumer spending: Conceptualization and propositions. *International Business Review, 28*(2), 294–304. doi:10.1016/j.ibusrev.2018.10.002

Paillé, P., & Mucchielli, A. (2016). L'analyse qualitative en sciences humaines et sociales (4th ed.). Armand Colin.

Pantic, I. (2014). Online social networking and mental health. *Cyberpsychology, Behavior, and Social Networking, 17*(10), 652–657. doi:10.1089/cyber.2014.0070 PMID:25192305

Papacharissi, Z., & Rubin, A. M. (2000). Predictors of Internet use. *Journal of Broadcasting & Electronic Media*, *44*(2), 175–196. doi:10.120715506878jobem4402_2

Park, C. S. (2013). Does Twitter motivate involvement in politics? Tweeting, opinion leadership, and political engagement. *Computers in Human Behavior*, *29*(4), 1641–1648. doi:10.1016/j.chb.2013.01.044

Park, H., & Cho, H. (2012). Social network online communities: Information sources for apparel shopping. *Journal of Consumer Marketing*, *29*(6), 400–411. doi:10.1108/07363761211259214

Park, N., Kee, K. F., & Valenzuela, S. B. (2009). Being immersed in social networking environment: Facebook groups, uses and gratifications, and social outcomes. *Cyberpsychology & Behavior*, *12*(6), 729–733. doi:10.1089/cpb.2009.0003 PMID:19619037

Páscoa, G., & Gil, H. (2015). Uma nova forma de comunicação para o cidadão sénior: Facebook. *Revista Kairós Gerontologia*, *18*(1), 9–29.

Paúl, C., & Fonseca, A. (2005). *Envelhecer em Portugal*. Climepsi.

Peele, S. (1985). *The Meaning of Addiction*. Lexington Books.

Permatasari, R. I., Fauzi, M. A., Adikara, P. P., & Sari, E. D. L. (2018). Twitter Sentiment Analysis of Movie Reviews using Ensemble Features Based Naïve Bayes. *2018 International Conference on Sustainable Information Engineering and Technology (SIET)*. 10.1109/SIET.2018.8693195

Perol, A., Gaitan, J., & Ramos, A. (2015). From digital divide to psycho-digital divide: Elders and online social networks. *Media Education Research Journal*, *45*, 57–64.

Persia, F., & D'Auria, D. (2017). A survey of online social networks: Challenges and opportunities. *Proceedings - 2017 IEEE International Conference on Information Reuse and Integration, IRI 2017*, 614–620. 10.1109/IRI.2017.74

Peteraf, M. A., & Barney, J. B. (2003). Unraveling the resource-based tangle. *Managerial and Decision Economics*, *24*(4), 309–323. doi:10.1002/mde.1126

Peter, J., & Valkenburg, P. M. (2006). Adolescents' exposure to sexually explicit material on the Internet. *Communication Research*, *33*(2), 178–204. doi:10.1177/0093650205285369

Peters, B. G. (2019). *Institutional Theory in Political Science: The New Institutionalism*. Edward Elgar Publishing.

Petersen, M. B., & Aarøe, L. (2015). Evolutionary Theory and Political Behavior. In R. Scott & S. Kosslyn (Eds.), *Emerging Trends in the Social and Behavioral Sciences* (pp. 1–15). John Wiley & Sons, Inc. doi:10.1002/9781118900772.etrds0125

Petracca, M. P. (1991). The Rational Choice Approach to Politics: A Challenge to Democratic Theory. *The Review of Politics*, *2*(53), 289–319. doi:10.1017/S0034670500014637

Pew Research Centre. (2019). *Social media fact sheet*. https://www.pewresearch.org/internet/fact-sheet/social-media/

Pew Research Internet Project. (2019, June 12). *Mobile Technology Fact Sheet*. Washington, DC: Pew Research Internet Project. Retrieved on March 14, 2020 from https://www.pewresearch.org/internet/fact-sheet/mobile/

Pfeffer, J., & Carley, K. M. (2012). Social Networks, Social Media, Social Change. In Advances in Design for Cross-Cultural Activities Part II. Boca Raton: CRC Press.

Phiri, M., & Junior, B. M. (2018). *PA 19-4-0723 Use of social media to provide awareness about medical and social service aid to victims of gender-based violence in Zambia*. Academic Press.

Phiri, M. N., & Banda, D. E. (2019). Investigating Mobile Money Usage Patterns in Zambia: A Case of Mobile Network Operator Systems. *International Journal of Advanced Studies in Computers Science and Engineering, 8*(2), 13–20.

Piccirillo, R. A. (2010). *The Lockean Memory Theory of Personal Identity: Definition, Objection, Response.* Retrieved from: http://www.inquiriesjournal.com/articles/1683/the-lockean-memory-theory-of-personal-identity-definition-objection-response

Pinheiro, O. D., & Areosa, S. (2018). A importância de políticas públicas para idosos. *Revista Brasileira de Assuntos Regionais e Urbanos, 4*(2), 183–193. doi:10.18224/baru.v4i2.6724

Poe, E. A. (1844). *"The Balloon Hoax," published 1844, reprinted in PoeStories.com.* Retrived from https://poestories.com/read /balloonhoax

Pollay, R. W. (1983). Measuring the cultural values manifest in advertising. *Current Issues and Research in Advertising, 6*(1), 71-92.

Pontes, H. M., Kuss, D. J., & Griffiths, M. D. (2015). Clinical psychology of Internet addiction: A review of its conceptualization, prevalence, neuronal processes, and implications for treatment. *Neuroscience and Neuroeconomics, 4*, 11–23.

Pope, W. (1975). Durkheim as a Functionalist. *The Sociological Quarterly, 16*(3), 361–379. doi:10.1111/j.1533-8525.1975.tb00954.x

Porteous, J. (2018, June 20). *Micro influencers vs macro influencers, what's best for your business?* https://www.socialbakers.com/blog/micro-influencers-vs-macro-influencers

Portugal, I., Alencar, P., & Cowan, D. (2018). The use of machine learning algorithms in recommender systems: A systematic review. *Expert Systems with Applications, 97*, 205–227. doi:10.1016/j.eswa.2017.12.020

Pourghomi, P., Safieddine, F., Masri, W., & Dordevic, M. (2017, May). How to stop spread of misinformation on social media: Facebook plans vs. right-click authenticate approach. In *2017 International Conference on Engineering & MIS (ICEMIS)* (pp. 1-8). IEEE.

Poushter, J., Bishop, C., & Chwe, H. (2018). Social media use continues to rise in developing countries but plateaus across developed ones. Pew Research Center, 22.

Pöyry, E. I., Pelkonen, M., Naumanen, E., & Laaksonen, S.-M. (2019). A call for authenticity: Audience responses to social media influencer endorsements in strategic communication. *International Journal of Strategic Communication, 13*(4), 336–351. doi:10.1080/1553118X.2019.1609965

Pozzoli, T., & Gini, G. (2013). Why do bystanders of bullying help or not? A multidimensional model. *The Journal of Early Adolescence, 33*(3), 315–340. doi:10.1177/0272431612440172

Prasad, R., & Rohokale, V. (2020a). *BOTNET.* doi:10.1007/978-3-030-31703-4_4

Prasad, R., & Rohokale, V. (2020b). Cyber Threats and Attack Overview. In *Cyber Security: The Lifeline of Information and Communication Technology. Springer Series in Wireless Technology* (pp. 15–31). Springer. doi:10.1007/978-3-030-31703-4_2

Prensky, M. (2001). Digital natives, digital immigrants part 1. *On the Horizon, 9*, 1–6.

Prensky, M. (2001). Digital natives, digital immigrants. *On the Horizon, 9*(5-6), 1–6.

Priyadarshiny, U. (2019). *How to create a Perfect Decision Tree.* Retrieved from https://dzone.com/articles/how-to-create-a-perfect-decision-tree

Proulx, S. (2001). Usages des technologies d'information et de communication: reconsidérer le champ d'étude. *Émergences et continuité dans les recherches en information et communication*, 10-13.

Przepiorka, A., & Blachnio, A. (2016). Time perspective in Internet and Facebook addiction. *Computers in Human Behavior*, *60*, 13–18. doi:10.1016/j.chb.2016.02.045

Przybylski, A. K., Murayama, K., DeHaan, C. R., & Gladwell, V. (2013). Motivational, emotional, and behavioral correlates of fear of missing out. *Computers in Human Behavior*, *29*(4), 1841–1848. doi:10.1016/j.chb.2013.02.014

Quinkert, F., Holz, T., Hossain, K. T., Ferrara, E., & Lerman, K. (2018). *RAPTOR: Ransomware Attack PredicTOR*. http://arxiv.org/abs/1803.01598

Quinn, K. (2018). Cognitive effects of social media use: A case of older adults. *Social Media and Society*, *4*(3), 1–9. doi:10.1177/2056305118787203

Raacke, J., & Bonds-Raacke, J. (2008). MySpace and Facebook: Applying the uses and gratifications theory to exploring friend-networking sites. *Cyberpsychology & Behavior*, *11*(2), 169–174. doi:10.1089/cpb.2007.0056 PMID:18422409

Rabaa'i, A. A., Bhat, H., & Al-Maati, S. A. (2018). Theorising social networks addiction: An empirical investigation. *International Journal of Social Media and Interactive Learning Environments*, *6*(1), 1–24. doi:10.1504/IJSMILE.2018.092363

Racherla, P., & Friske, W. (2012). Perceived 'usefulness' of online consumer reviews: An exploratory investigation across three services categories. *Electronic Commerce Research and Applications*, *11*(6), 548–559. doi:10.1016/j.elerap.2012.06.003

Rahman, M. S., Huang, T. K., Madhyastha, H. V., & Faloutsos, M. (2012a). FRAppE: Detecting malicious facebook applications. *CoNEXT 2012 - Proceedings of the 2012 ACM Conference on Emerging Networking Experiments and Technologies*, 313–324. 10.1145/2413176.2413213

Rahman, M. S., Huang, T. K., Madhyastha, H. V., & Faloutsos, M. (2012b). Efficient and scalable socware detection in online social networks. *Proceedings of the 21st USENIX Security Symposium*, 663–678.

Rahman, S. U., Saleem, S., Akhtar, S., Ali, T., & Khan, M. A. (2014). Consumers' adoption of apparel fashion: The role of innovativeness, involvement, and social values. *International Journal of Marketing Studies*, *6*(3), 49–64. doi:10.5539/ijms.v6n3p49

Ralston, D. A. (2008, January-February). The crossvergence perspective: Reflections and projections. *Journal of International Business Studies*, *39*(1), 27–40. doi:10.1057/palgrave.jibs.8400333

Ramalingam, D., & Chinnaiah, V. (2018). Fake profile detection techniques in large-scale online social networks: A comprehensive review. *Computers & Electrical Engineering*, *65*(3), 165–177. doi:10.1016/j.compeleceng.2017.05.020

Ramkumar, G., Vigneshwari, S., & Roodyn, S. (2016, August 2). An enhanced system to identify mischievous social malwares on Facebook applications. *Proceedings of IEEE International Conference on Circuit, Power and Computing Technologies, ICCPCT 2016*. 10.1109/ICCPCT.2016.7530271

Rampersad, G., & Althiyabi, T. (2020). Fake news: Acceptance by demographics and culture on social media. *Journal of Information Technology & Politics*, *17*(1), 1–11. doi:10.1080/19331681.2019.1686676

Rane, A., & Kumar, A. (2018). Sentiment Classification System of Twitter Data for US Airline Service Analysis. *2018 IEEE 42nd Annual Computer Software and Applications Conference (COMPSAC)*. doi: 10.1109/compsac.2018.00114

Rashid, M., Hamid, A., & Parah, S. A. (2019). Analysis of Streaming Data Using Big Data and Hybrid Machine Learning Approach. In *Handbook of Multimedia Information Security: Techniques and Applications* (pp. 629–643). Springer. doi:10.1007/978-3-030-15887-3_30

Rathi, M., Malik, A., Varshney, D., Sharma, R., & Mendiratta, S. (2018). Sentiment Analysis of Tweets Using Machine Learning Approach. *2018 Eleventh International Conference on Contemporary Computing (IC3)*. 10.1109/IC3.2018.8530517

Razis, G., Anagnostopoulos, I., & Zeadally, S. (2020). Modeling Influence with Semantics in Social Networks: A Survey. *ACM Computing Surveys*, *53*(1), 7.

Rebelo, A. R. (2013). *Seniores em rede: Motivações para o uso da internet e do Facebook pelos mais velhos* [Unpublished master thesis]. Lisbon University Institute, Lisbon, Portugal.

Rebelo, C. (2015). Utilização da internet e do Facebook pelos mais velhos em Portugal: Estudo exploratório. *Observatorio (OBS*), 9*(3), 129-153.

Reed, M. S., Evely, A. C., Cundill, G., Fazey, I., Glass, J., Laing, A., Newig, J., Parrish, B., Prell, C., Raymond, C., & Stringer, L. C. (2010). What is Social Learning? *Ecology and Society*, *15*(4), r1. doi:10.5751/ES-03564-1504r01

Reid Chassiakos, Y., Radesky, J., Christakis, D., Moreno, M. A., & Cross, C. (2016). Children and Adolescents and Digital Media. *Pediatrics*, *138*(5), 1–18. doi:10.1542/peds.2016-2593 PMID:27940795

Reporters Lab. (2014). *Duke Study Finds Fact-Checking Growing Around the World*. Retrieved from https://reporterslab.org/duke-study-finds-fact-checking-growing-around-the-world/

Reporters Lab. (2018). *Fact-Checking Triples Over Four Years*. Retrieved from https://reporterslab.org/fact-checking-triples-over-four-years/

Reporters Lab. (2019). *Number Of Fact-Checking Outlets Surges To 188 İn More Than 60 Countries*. Retrieved from https://reporterslab.org/tag/fact-checking-census/

Reporters Lab. (2020). *Global Fact-Checking sites*. Retrieved from https://reporterslab.org/fact-checking/

Rheingold, H. (1993). *The virtual community: Homesteading on the electronic frontier*. Addison Wesley.

Riley, E. (2019). Social media, activism and democracy in Senegal. In Social Media and Politics in Africa: Democracy, Censorship and Security. London: Zed Books.

Riquelme, F., & Cantergiani, P. G. (2016). Measuring user influence on Twitter. *Information Processing & Management*, *52*(5), 949–975. doi:10.1016/j.ipm.2016.04.003

Rispal, M. H. (2002). *La méthode des cas*. De Boeck Supérieur. doi:10.3917/dbu.hlady.2002.01

Roberto, M., Fidalgo, A. & Buckingham, D. (2015). De que falamos quando falamos de infoexclusão e literacia digital? *Perspetivas dos nativos digitais. Observatorio (OBS*), 9*(1), 43-54.

Robertson, S. (2018). *Generation Z Charactertistics & Traits That Explain The Way They Learn*. Retrieved from https://info.jkcp.com/blog/generation-z-characteristics

Robertson, P. J., & Tang, S.-Y. (1995). The Role of Commitment in Collective Action: Comparing the Organizational Behavior and Rational Choice Perspectives. *Public Administration Review*, *55*(1), 67–80. doi:10.2307/976829

Rodríguez, G. E., Torres, J. G., Flores, P., & Benavides, D. E. (2020). Cross-site scripting (XSS) attacks and mitigation: A survey. *Computer Networks*, *166*, 106960. doi:10.1016/j.comnet.2019.106960

Rogers, E. M. (1995). *Diffusion of innovations* (4th ed.). Free Press.

RohrR. (2019a, June 2). *One in Love*. Retrieved from https://cac.org/one-in-love-2019-06-02/

RohrR. (2019b, May 20). *The Psalms*. Retrieved from https://cac.org/the-psalms-2018-05-20/

Roper, W. (2020, March 3). *Privacy concerns fuel facebook exodus*. Statista. Retrieved on July 14, 2020 from https://www.statista.com/chart/21018/top-reasons-people-leave-facebook/

Rosa, M. J. (2012). *O envelhecimento da sociedade portuguesa*. Fundação Francisco Manuel dos Santos.

Rosenthal, S. (2014). Detecting influencers in social media discussions. *XRDS: Crossroads, 21*(1), 40–45. doi:10.1145/2659889

Rosenthal, S. (2018). Motivations to seek science videos on YouTube: Free-choice learning in a connected society. *International Journal of Science Education, 8*(1), 22–39.

Rosenthal, S., & Mckeown, K. (2017). Detecting Influencers in Multiple Online Genres. *ACM Transactions on Internet Technology, 17*(2), 12. doi:10.1145/3014164

Ross, C., Orr, E. S., Sisic, M., Arseneault, J. M., Simmering, M. G., & Orr, R. R. (2009). Personality and motivations associated with Facebook use. *Computers in Human Behavior, 25*(2), 578–586. doi:10.1016/j.chb.2008.12.024

Roudaut, K., & Jullien, N. (2017). Les usages des outils de réseau social par des salariés: Des registres privés et professionnels individualisés. Terminal. *Technologie de l'information, culture & société,* (120).

Ruchansky, N., Seo, S., & Csi, Y. L. (2017). A hybrid deep model for fake news detection. In *Proceedings of the 2017 ACM on Conference on Information and Knowledge Management*, (pp. 797–806). ACM. 10.1145/3132847.3132877

Ruiz-Gomez, A. (2019). Digital fame and fortune in the age of social media: A classification of social media influencers. *aDResearch ESIC, 19*, 8-29.

Rütten, L. (2016). Facebook user perceptions of privacy and security on Facebook, between Millennials and Non-Millennials. *Political Science*. Retrieved on July 14, 2020 from https://www.semanticscholar.org/paper/Facebook-user-perceptions-of-privacy-and-security-R%C3%BCtten/f878ebd1ffb358a2068e88ffa9a84c71769a924e

Ryan, T., Chester, A., Reece, J., & Xenos, S. (2014). The uses and abuses of Facebook: A review of Facebook addiction. *Journal of Behavioral Addictions, 3*(3), 133–148. doi:10.1556/JBA.3.2014.016 PMID:25317337

Ryan, T., Reece, J., Chester, A., & Xenos, S. (2016). Who gets hooked on Facebook? An exploratory typology of problematic Facebook users. *Cyberpsychology (Brno), 10*(3). Advance online publication. doi:10.5817/CP2016-3-4

S˘kilters, J., Kreile, M., Bṵja‾rs, U., Briks˘e, I., Pencis, J., & Uzule, I.. (2012). The pragmatics of political messages in Twitter communication. In The Semantic Web: ESWC 2011 Workshops. Springer.

Sabir, E., Cheng, J., Jaiswal, A., AbdAlmageed, W., Masi, I., & Natarajan, P. (2019). Recurrent Convolutional Strategies for Face Manipulation Detection in Videos. *Proceedings of the IEEE Conference on Computer Vision and Pattern Recognition Workshops*, 80–87. http://arxiv.org/abs/1905.00582

Sadeghian, A., Zamani, M., & Abdullah, S. M. (2013). A taxonomy of SQL injection attacks. *Proceedings - 2013 International Conference on Informatics and Creative Multimedia, ICICM 2013*, 269–273. 10.1109/ICICM.2013.53

Sadik, J. (2008). Technology adoption, convergence, and divergence. *European Economic Review, 52*(2), 338–355. doi:10.1016/j.euroecorev.2007.02.005

Sæbø, Ø. (2011). Understanding twittere use among parliament representatives: a genre analysis. In *Proceedings of the Third IFIP WG 8.5 International Conference on Electronic Participation*. Springer.

Sagioglou, C., & Greitemeyer, T. (2014). Facebook's emotional consequences: Why Facebook causes a decrease in mood and why people still use it. *Computers in Human Behavior, 35*, 359-363. . doi:10.1016/j.chb.2014.03.003

Sakaki, T., Okazaki, M., & Matsuo, Y. (2010). Earthquake shakes Twitter users: Real-time event detection by social sensors. *World Wide Web (Bussum)*, 851–860.

Salahdine, F., & Kaabouch, N. (2019). Social engineering attacks: A survey. In Future Internet (Vol. 11, Issue 4, p. 89). MDPI AG. doi:10.3390/fi11040089

Sanawi, J., Samani, M. C., & Taibi, M. (2017). #Vaccination: Identifying Influencers in the Vaccination Discussion on Twitter Through Social Network Visualisation. *International Journal of Business and Society, 8*(S4), 718–726.

Sánchez-Villar, J., Bigné, E., & Aldás-Manzano, J. (2017). Blog influence and political activism: An emerging and integrative model. *Spanish Journal of Marketing, 21*(2), 102–116. doi:10.1016/j.sjme.2017.02.002

Sanders, C. E., Field, T. M., Diego, M., & Kaplan, M. (2000). The relationship of Internet use To depression and social isolation among adolescents. *Adolescence, 35*, 237–242. PMID:11019768

SanMiguel, P., Guercini, S., & Sádaba, T. (2018). The impact of attitudes towards influencers amongst millennial fashion buyers. *Studies in Communication Sciences, 18*, 439–460.

Saravanakumar, M., & SuganthaLakshmi, T. (2012). Social media marketing. *Life Science Journal, 9*(4), 4444–4451.

Satici, S. A., & Uysal, R. (2015). Well-being and problematic Facebook use. *Computers in Human Behavior, 49*, 185-190. doi:10.1016/j.chb.2015.03.005

Saunders, M. (2018). *Ecology is Not a Dirty Word. How do you review a conceptual paper?* Retrieved from https://ecologyisnotadirtyword.com/2018/06/21/how-do-you-review-a-conceptual-paper

Savci, M., & Aysan, F. (2017). Technological addictions and social connectedness: Predictor effect of internet addiction, social media addiction, digital game addiction and smartphone addiction on social connectedness. *Dusunen Adam: Journal of Psychiatry & Neurological Sciences, 30*(3), 202–216. doi:10.5350/DAJPN2017300304

Sawyer, R. (2011). The Impact of New Social Media on Intercultural Adaptation. *Senior Honors Projects*. Paper 242. http://digitalcommons.uri.edu/srhonorsprog/242http://digitalcommons.uri.edu/srhonorsprog/242

Scharpf, F. W. (1991). Political Institutions, Decision Styles, and Policy Choices. In A. Windhoff-Héritier & R. Czada (Eds.), *Political Choice: Institutions, Rules, and the Limits of Rationality* (pp. 53–86). Westview Press.

Schewe, K.-D., & Thalheim, B. (2019). Web Information Systems Engineering. In Design and Development of Web Information Systems (Vol. 2). Springer International Publishing. doi:10.1007/978-3-662-58824-6_12

Schmidt, F. L., & Hunter, J. (2004). General mental ability in the world of work: Occupational attainment and job performance. *Journal of Personality and Social Psychology, 86*(1), 162–173. doi:10.1037/0022-3514.86.1.162 PMID:14717634

Schneider, F., Feldmann, A., Krishnamurthy, B., & Willinger, W. (2009, November). Understanding online social network usage from *a* network perspective. In *Proceedings of the 9th ACM SIGCOMM conference on Internet measurement* (pp. 35-48). 10.1145/1644893.1644899

Schouten, A. P., Janssen, L., & Verspaget, M. (2019). Celebrity vs. influencer endorsements in advertising: The role of identification, credibility, and product-endorser fit. *International Journal of Advertising, 39*(2), 258–281. doi:10.1080/02650487.2019.1634898

Schroder, J. E., & Saltzer-Morling, M. (2006). *Brand Culture*. Routledge. doi:10.4324/9780203002445

Scolari, C. (2009). Transmedia Storytelling: Implicit consumers, narrative worlds, and branding in contemporary media production. *International Journal of Communication*, *3*, 586–606.

Scott, W. R. (2008). Lords of the dance: Professionals as institutional agents. *Organization Studies*, *29*(2), 219–238. doi:10.1177/0170840607088151

Scott, W. R. (2014). *Institutions and Organizations: Ideas, Interests and Identities*. Sage Publications Ltd.

Segaard, S. B. (2017). The Institutional Anchoring of Social Media Venues as Arenas for Local Political Communication. Perceptions by Voters and Politicians. In F. Engelstad, H. Larsen, J. Rogstad, K. Steen-Johnsen, D. Polkowska, A. S. Dauber-Griffin, & A. Leverton (Eds.), *Institutional Change in the Public Sphere: Views on the Nordic Model* (pp. 118–138). De Gruyter. doi:10.1515/9783110546330-007

Selligent Markteting Cloud. (2020). *Selligent Global Connected Consumer Index* (2nd ed.). Selligent Markteting Cloud. Retrieved on March 19, 2020 from Retrieved on March 19, 2020 from https://www.selligent.com/resources/analyst-reports/selligent-global-connected-consumer-index/arconsumerindexus

Sertoglu, A. E., Catli, O., & Korkmaz, S. (2014). Examining the effect of endorser credibility on the consumers' buying intentions: An empirical study in Turkey. *International Review of Management and Marketing*, *4*(1), 66–77.

Sethna, Z., & Blythe, J. (2016). *Consumer behavior*. Sage (Atlanta, Ga.).

Shaffer, H. J. (1996). Understanding the means and objects of addiction: Technology, the Internet and gambling. *Journal of Gambling Studies*, *12*(4), 461–469. doi:10.1007/BF01539189 PMID:24234163

Shami, N. S., Nichols, J., & Chen, J. (2014). Social media participation and performance at work: a longitudinal study. In Proceedings of the SIGCHI conference on human factors in computing systems (pp. 115-118). doi:10.1145/2556288.2557417

Shan, Z., Cao, H., Lv, J., Yan, C., & Liu, A. (2013). Enhancing and identifying cloning attacks in online social networks. *Proceedings of the 7th International Conference on Ubiquitous Information Management and Communication, ICUIMC 2013*, 1–6. 10.1145/2448556.2448615

Shao, C., Ciampaglia, G. L., Varol, O., Flammini, A., & Menczer, F. (2017). *The spread of fake news by social bots*. arXiv preprint arXiv:1707.07592

Sharifah, S. S., Omar, S. Z., Bolong, J., & Osman, M. N. (2011). Facebook addiction among female university students. *Revista De Administratie Publica Si Politici Sociale*, *3*(7), 95.

Sharma, V. D., Yadav, S. K., Yadav, S. K., & Singh, K. N. (2020). Social media ecosystem: Review on social media profile's security and introduce a new approach. In *Lecture Notes in Networks and Systems* (Vol. 119, pp. 229–235). Springer. doi:10.1007/978-981-15-3338-9_27

Shaw, L. H., & Gant, L. M. (2002). In defense of the internet: The relationship between internet communication and depression, loneliness, self-esteem, and perceived social support. *Cyberpsychology & Behavior*, *5*(2), 157–171. doi:10.1089/109493102753770552 PMID:12025883

Sheldon, P. (2009). Maintain or develop new relationships. Gender differences in Facebook use. *Rocky Mountain Communication Review*, *6*(1), 51–56.

Shen, C., Kasra, M., Pan, W., Bassett, G. A., Malloch, Y., & O'Brien, J. F. (2019). Fake images: The effects of source, intermediary, and digital media literacy on contextual assessment of image credibility online. *New Media & Society*, *21*(2), 438-463.

Shen, C., & Williams, D. (2011). Unpacking time online: Connecting internet and massively multiplayer online game use with psychosocial well-being. *Communication Research, 38*(1), 123–149. doi:10.1177/0093650210377196

Shensa, A., Escobar-Viera, C. G., Sidani, J. E., Bowman, N. D., Marshal, M. P., & Primack, B. A. (2017). Problematic social media use and depressive symptoms among US young adults: A nationally-representative study. *Social Science & Medicine, 182*, 150–157. doi:10.1016/j.socscimed.2017.03.061 PMID:28446367

Sherchan, W., Nepal, S., & Paris, C. (2013). A survey of trust in social networks. *ACM Computing Surveys, 45*(4), 1–33. doi:10.1145/2501654.2501661

Sheth, J. N., Sisodia, R. S., & Sharma, A. (2000). The antecedents and consequences of customer-centric marketing. *Journal of the Academy of Marketing Science, 28*(1), 55–66. doi:10.1177/0092070300281006

Shuen, A. (2018). *Web 2.0: A Strategy Guide: Business thinking and strategies behind successful Web 2.0 implementations.* O'Reilly Media.

Shu, K., Sliva, A., Wang, S., Tang, J., & Liu, H. (2017). Fake News Detection on Social Media. *ACM SIGKDD Explorations Newsletter, 19*(1), 22–36. doi:10.1145/3137597.3137600

Silva, N. F. D., Hruschka, E. R., & Hruschka, E. R. (2014). Tweet sentiment analysis with classifier ensembles. *Decision Support Systems, 66*, 170–179. doi:10.1016/j.dss.2014.07.003

Silverman, C., & Alexander, L. (2016). *Fake news had more share on Facebook than mainstream news, How teens in the balkans are duping trump supporters with fake news.* Buzzfeed News.

Silverstone, R. (2003). *Media and technology in the everyday life of European societies.* Routledge.

Silvia, F., Scortegagna, S. A., & De Marchi, A. C. B. (2018). Facebook as a social support environment for older adults. *Universitas Psychologica, 17*(3), 1–11. doi:10.11144/Javeriana.upsy.17-3.fsse

SimilarWeb. (2019). *Twitter.com - Visits weltweit 2019 | Statista.* Retrieved from https://de.statista.com/statistik/daten/studie/1021439/umfrage/anzahl-der-visits-pro-monat-von-twittercom/

Sims, T., Reed, A. E., & Carr, D. C. (2017). Information and communication technology use is related to higher well-being among the oldest-old. *The Journals of Gerontology: Series B, 72*(5), 761-770.

Singh, V., Varshney, A., Akhtar, S. S., Vijay, D., & Shrivastava, M. (2019). Aggression Detection on Social Media Text Using Deep Neural Networks. *October*, 43–50. doi:10.18653/v1/w18-5106

Singh, A., Halgamuge, M. N., & Mouess, B. (2019). An Analysis of Demographic and Behaviour Trends using Social Media: Facebook, Twitter and Instagram. In *Social Network Analytics: Computational Research Methods and Techniques.* Elsevier. doi:10.1016/B978-0-12-815458-8.00005-0

Smith, D. (2014). Internet Use on Mobile Phones in Africa Predicted to Increase 20-fold. *The Guardian.* Retrieved from http://www.theguardian.com/world/2014/jun/05/internet-use-mobilephones-africa-predicted-increase-20-fold

Smith, M. A., Rainie, L., Shneiderman, B., & Himelboim, I. (2014). Mapping Twitter topic networks: From polarized crowds to community clusters. *Pew Research Center, 20*, 1–56.

Smock, A. D., Ellison, N. B., Lampe, C., & Wohn, D. Y. (2011). Facebook toolkit: A uses and gratification approach to unbundling feature use. *Computers in Human Behavior, 27*(6), 2322–2329. doi:10.1016/j.chb.2011.07.011

Social, W. A. (2019). Global Social Media Users Pass 3.5 Billion. *Global Digital Reports.* https://wearesocial.com/blog/2019/07/global-social-media-users-pass-3-5-billion

Sokoloff, W. W. (2017). *Confrontational Citizenship: Reflections on Hatred, Rage, Revolution, and Revolt*. State University of New York Press.

Sokolova, K., & Kefi, H. (2020). Instagram and YouTube bloggers promote it, why should I buy? How credibility and parasocial interaction influence purchase intentions. *Journal of Retailing and Consumer Services*, 53.

Solomon, M. (2018). *Consumer behavior: Buying, having, and being* (12th ed.). Pearson Education.

Some, E., Gondwe, G., & Rowe, E. W. (2019, October). Cybersecurity and Driverless Cars: In Search for a Normative Way of Safety. In *2019 Sixth International Conference on Internet of Things: Systems, Management and Security (IOTSMS)* (pp. 352-357). IEEE.

Song, I., LaRose, R., Eastin, M., & Lin, C. (2004). Internet gratifications and Internet addiction: On the uses and abuses of new media. *Cyberpsychology & Behavior*, *7*(4), 384–394. doi:10.1089/cpb.2004.7.384 PMID:15331025

Song, S., & Yoo, M. (2016). The role of social media during the pre-purchasing stage. *Journal of Hospitality and Tourism Technology*, *7*(1), 84–99. doi:10.1108/JHTT-11-2014-0067

Sonnentag, S., & Frese, M. (2002). Performance concepts and performance theory. *Psychological Management of Individual Performance*, *23*(1), 3-25.

Sophia Van Zyl, A. S. (2009). The impact of Social Networking 2.0 on organisations. *The Electronic Library*, *27*(6), 906–918. doi:10.1108/02640470911004020

Spenkuch, J. L., & Toniatti, D. (2016). *Political advertising and election outcomes*. Kilts Center for Marketing at Chicago Booth–Nielsen Dataset Paper Series, 1-046.

Sriwilai, K., & Charoensukmongkol, P. (2016). Face it, don't Facebook it: Impacts of social media addiction on mindfulness, coping strategies and the consequence on emotional exhaustion. *Stress and Health*, *32*(4), 427–434. doi:10.1002mi.2637 PMID:25825273

Statista. (2018). *Fake news in Europe - Statistics & Facts*. Retrieved from https://www.statista.com/topics/5833/fake-news-in-europe/

Statista. (2018). *Media Usage*. Retrieved from https://www.statista.com/statistics/649234/fake-news-exposure-usa/

Statista. (2018). *Social media usage in Europe - Statistics & Facts*. https://www.statista.com/topics/4106/social-media-usage-in-europe/

Statista. (2018, May). *Number of global social media users 2010-2021*. Statista. Retrieved on March 19, 2020 from https://www.statista.com/statistics/278414/number-of-worldwide-social-network-users/

Statista. (2019). *Apps - Top 20 nach Anzahl der Unique Devices in China 2019 | Statista*. Retrieved from https://dc.statista.com/statistik/daten/studie/894126/umfrage/beliebteste-apps-nach-anzahl-der-unique-visitors-in-china/

Statista. (2019). *Médias sociaux et contenu généré par les utilisateurs*. https://fr.statista.com/statistiques/570930/reseaux-sociaux-mondiaux-classes-par-nombre-d-utilisateurs/

Statista. (2019a). *Opinions on social media bans to prevent fake news in Europe 2019*. Retrieved from https://www.statista.com/statistics/1088148/fake-news-and-social-media-bans-in-europe/

Statista. (2019b). *Daily time spent on social networking by internet users worldwide from 2012 to 2019*. Retrived from https://www.statista.com/statistics/433871/daily-social-media-usage-worldwide/

Statista. (2020). *Number of internet users in China from December 2008 to December 2018*. Retrieved from http:// https://www.statista.com/statistics/265140/number-of-internet-users-in-china/

Statista. (2020, January). *Countries with the most Twitter users 2020*. Statista. Retrieved on March 20, 2020 from https://www.statista.com/statistics/242606/number-of-active-twitter-users-in-selected-countries/

Statista. (2020a). *Average Number of Social Media Accounts per Internet User as of July 2019, by Age Group* [Graph illustration]. https://www.statista.com/statistics/381964/number-of-social-media-accounts/

Statista. (2020b). *Most Popular Social Networks Worldwide as of April 2020, Ranked by Number of Active Users* [Graph illustration]. https://www.statista.com/statistics/272014/global-social-networks-ranked-by-number-of-users/

Statista. (2020c). *Distribution of Facebook Users Worldwide as of April 2020, by Age and Gender* [Graph illustration]. https://www.statista.com/statistics/376128/facebook-global-user-age-distribution/

Statista. (2020d). *Distribution of Instagram Users Worldwide as of April 2020, by Age and Gender* [Graph illustration]. https://www.statista.com/statistics/248769/age-distribution-of-worldwide-instagram-users/

Statista. (2020e). *Distribution of Facebook Users in Brazil as of January 2018, by Age group and Gender* [Graph illustration]. https://www.statista.com/statistics/198923/age-distribution-of-users-facebook-brazil/

Statista. (2020f). *Distribution of Instagram Users in Brazil as of January 2018, by Age Group and Gender* [Graph illustration]. https://www.statista.com/statistics/866268/instagram-user-share-brazil-age/

Statista. (2020g). *Penetration Rate of YouTube among People in Japan as of March 2019, by Age Group* [Graph illustration]. https://www.statista.com/statistics/1071780/japan-youtube-penetration-rate-by-age-group/

Statista. (2020h). *Share of YouTube Users in Latin America in 2018, by Age* [Graph illustration]. https://www.statista.com/statistics/754376/latin-america-usage-penetration-youtube-age/

Steinfield, C., Ellison, N. B., & Lampe, C. (2008). Social capital, self-esteem, and use of online social network sites: A longitudinal analysis. *Journal of Applied Developmental Psychology*, *29*(6), 434–445. doi:10.1016/j.appdev.2008.07.002

Steinmo, S. (2008). Historical institutionalism. In D. Della Porta & M. Keating (Eds.), *Approaches and Methodologies in the Social Sciences: A Pluralist Perspective,* (pp. 118-138). Cambridge: Cambridge University Press. https://www.cambridge.org/core/books/approaches-and-methodologies-in-the-social-sciences/historical-institutionalism/B6482BAC0D68CE27AC1DBF6A3AE5A1B9

Stenger, T., & Coutant, A. (2010). Les réseaux sociaux numériques: des discours de promotion à la déðnition d'un objet et d'une méthodologie de recherche. *HERMES-Journal of Language and Communication in Business,* (44), 209-228.

Stolee, G., & Caton, S. (2018). Twitter, Trump, and the Base: A Shift to a New Form of Presidential Talk? *Signs and Society (Chicago, Ill.)*, *6*(1), 147–165. doi:10.1086/694755

Stoll, C. (1995). *Silicon snake oil*. Doubleday.

Struweg, I. (2018). # Liberty breach: an exploratory usage case of NodeXL Pro as a social media analytics tool for Twitter. *ICMBD Conference Proceedings*, 153-163.

Such, J. M., & Criado, N. (2018, August). Multiparty privacy in social media. *Communications of the ACM*, *61*(8), 74–81. doi:10.1145/3208039

Sudha, M., & Sheena, K. (2017). Impact of influencers in consumer decision process: The fashion industry. *Journal of Indian Management*, *14*(3), 14–30.

Sui, Y., & Yang, X. (2010, June). Article. In *Second International Conference on Communication Systems, Networks and Applications* (*Vol. 1*, pp. 164-167). IEEE.

Sullivan, J. (2012). A tale of two microblogs in China. *Media Culture & Society*, *34*(6), 773–783. doi:10.1177/0163443712448951

Svensson, M. (2014). Voice, power and connectivity in China's microblogosphere: Digital divides on SinaWeibo. *China Information*, *28*(2), 168–188. doi:10.1177/0920203X14540082

Swann Jr, W. B. (1996). *Self-traps: The elusive quest for higher self-esteem*. WH Freeman/Times Books/Henry Holt & Co.

Tacchini, E., Ballarin, G. D., Vedova, M. L., Moret, S., & de Alfaro, L. (2017). *Some like it hoax: Automated fake news detection in social networks*. arXiv preprint arXiv:1704.07506

Talwar, S., Dhir, A., Kaur, P., Zafar, N., & Alrasheedy, M. (2019). Why do people share fake news? Associations between the dark side of social media use and fake news sharing behavior. *Journal of Retailing and Consumer Services*, *51*, 72–82. doi:10.1016/j.jretconser.2019.05.026

Tandoc Jr, E. C., Lim, Z. W., & Ling, R. (2018). Defining "fake news" A typology of scholarly definitions. *Digital Journalism, 6*(2), 137-153.

Tang, J. H., Chen, M. C., Yang, C. Y., Chung, T. Y., & Lee, Y. A. (2016). Personality traits, interpersonal relationships, online social support, and Facebook addiction. *Telematics and Informatics*, *33*(1), 102–108. doi:10.1016/j.tele.2015.06.003

Tan, L. K.-W., & Na, J.-C. (2013). Bloggers' Influence Style within Blog. *Journal of Information Science Theory and Practice*, *1*(2), 36–57. doi:10.1633/JISTaP.2013.1.2.3

Tartari, E. (2015). Facebook usage among Albanian Students: A Test of uses and Gratifications Theory. *EDULEARN15 Proceedings*, 3774-3779.

Teyit.org. (2020). Retrieved from https://teyit.org/about/

Thejas, G. S., Boroojeni, K. G., Chandna, K., Bhatia, I., Iyengar, S. S., & Sunitha, N. R. (2019). Deep learning-based model to fight against Ad click fraud. *ACMSE 2019 - Proceedings of the 2019 ACM Southeast Conference*, 176–181. 10.1145/3299815.3314453

Thelen, K. (1999). Historical Institutionalism in Comparative Politics. *Annual Review of Political Science*, *2*(1), 369–404. doi:10.1146/annurev.polisci.2.1.369

Thompson, R. L. (2012). Radicalization and the Use of Social Media. *Journal of Strategic Security*, *4*(4), 167–190. doi:10.5038/1944-0472.4.4.8

Thorne, J., Chen, M., Myrianthous, G., Pu, J., Wang, X., & Vlachos, A. (2017). Fake news stance detection using stacked ensemble of classifiers. *Proceedings of the 2017 EMNLP Workshop: Natural Language Processing meets Journalism*, 80–83. 10.18653/v1/W17-4214

Tierney, B. (2018). *Random Forest Machine Learning in R, Python and SQL - Part 1*. Retrieved fromhttps://blog.toad-world.com/2018/08/31/random-forest-machine-learning-in-r-python-and-sql-part-1

Till, B. D., & Busler, M. (1998). Matching products with endorsers: Attractiveness versus expertise. *Journal of Consumer Marketing*, *15*(6), 576–586. doi:10.1108/07363769810241445

Till, B. D., & Busler, M. (2000). The match-up hypothesis: Physical attractiveness, expertise, and the role of fit on brand attitude, purchase intent, and brand beliefs. *Journal of Advertising*, *29*(3), 1–13. doi:10.1080/00913367.2000.10673613

Tofler, A. (1980). *The third wave*. Think Review.

Tolson, A. (2010). A new authenticity? Communicative practices on YouTube. *Critical Discourse Studies*, *7*(4), 277–289. doi:10.1080/17405904.2010.511834

Torres, P., Augusto, M., & Matos, M. (2019). Antecedents and outcomes of digital influencer endorsement: An exploratory study. *Psychology and Marketing*, *36*(12), 1267–1276. doi:10.1002/mar.21274

Trepte, S., Reinecke, L., Ellison, N. B., Quiring, O., Yao, M. Z., & Ziegele, M. (2017, January-March). *A Cross-Cultural perspective on the privacy calculus. Social Media + Society*, 1-13.

Triki, A. (2010). *Epistémologie & méthodologie de la recherche: théories et applications en marketing et en gestion*. Academic Press.

Tsai, W.-H., & Men, L. R. (2012). Cultural values reflected in corporate pages on popular social network sites in China and the United States. *Journal of Research in Interactive Marketing*, *6*(1), 42–58. doi:10.1108/17505931211241369

Tully, M., & Ekdale, B. (2014). Sites of playful engagement: Twitter hashtags as spaces of leisure and development in Kenya. *Information Technologies and International Development*, *10*(3), 67–82.

Tumasjan, A., Sprenger, T. O., Sandner, P. G., & Welpe, I. M. (2011). Election forecasts with Twitter – how 140 characters reflect the political landscape. *Social Science Computer Review*, *29*(4), 402–418. doi:10.1177/0894439310386557

Turcotte, J., York, C., Irving, J., Scholl, R. M., & Pingree, R. J. (2015). News recommendations from social media opinion leaders: Effects on media trust and information seeking. *Journal of Computer-Mediated Communication*, *20*(5), 520–535. doi:10.1111/jcc4.12127

Turel, O., He, Q., Xue, G., Xiao, L., & Bechara, A. (2014). Examination of neural systems sub-serving Facebook "addiction". *Psychological Reports*, *115*(3), 675–695. doi:10.2466/18.PR0.115c31z8 PMID:25489985

Turkle, S. (1996). Virtuality and its discontents: Searching for community in cyberspace. *The American Prospect*, *24*, 50–57.

Turner, G. (2006). The mass production of celebrity: 'Celetoids', reality TV and the 'demotic turn'. *International Journal of Cultural Studies*, *9*(2), 153–165. doi:10.1177/1367877906064028

Tuten, T. L., & Solomon, M. R. (2017). Social media marketing. *Sage (Atlanta, Ga.)*.

Twitter. (2019). *Anzahl der monatlich aktiven Nutzer von Twitter weltweit vom 1. Quartal 2010 bis zum 1. Quartal 2019 (in Millionen)*. Retrieved from https://de.statista.com/statistik/daten/studie/232401/umfrage/monatlich-aktive-nutzer-von-twitter-weltweit-zeitreihe/

United Nations. (2020). *World population prospects 2020: Highlights*. https://population.un.org/wpp/Publications/Files/WPP2019_Highlights.pdf

Uzunoğlu, E., & Kip, S. M. (2014). Brand communication through digital influencers: Leveraging blogger engagement. *International Journal of Information Management*, *34*(5), 592–602. doi:10.1016/j.ijinfomgt.2014.04.007

Valente, T. W. (2010). *Social Networks and Health: Models, Methods, and Applications*. Oxford University. doi:10.1093/acprof:oso/9780195301014.001.0001

Valentine, O. A. (2013). Uses and gratifications of Facebook members 35 years and older. In *The Social Media Industries* (pp. 188–212). Routledge.

Valkenburg, P. M., & Peter, J. (2009). Social consequences of the Internet for adolescents: A decade of research. *Current Directions in Psychological Science*, *18*(1), 1–5. doi:10.1111/j.1467-8721.2009.01595.x

Valkenburg, P. M., Peter, J., & Schouten, A. P. (2006). Friend networking sites and their relationship to adolescents' well-being and social self-esteem. *Cyberpsychology & Behavior*, *9*(5), 584–590. doi:10.1089/cpb.2006.9.584 PMID:17034326

Van der Meer, T. G. L. A., Gelders, D., & Rotthier, S. (2014). E-Democracy: Exploring the Current Stage of e-Government. *Journal of Information Policy*, *4*, 489–506. doi:10.5325/jinfopoli.4.2014.0489

Van Deursen, A. J. A. M., Bolle, C. L., Hegner, S., & Kommers, P. A. M. (2015). Modeling habitual and addictive smartphone behavior: The role of smartphone usage types, emotional intelligence, social stress, self-regulation, age, and gender. *Computers in Human Behavior*, *45*, 411–420. doi:10.1016/j.chb.2014.12.039

Van Deursen, A. J. A. M., & Helsper, E. J. (2015). The third level digital divide: Who benefits most from being online? In L. Robinson, S. R. Cotten, & J. Schulz (Eds.), *Communication and information technologies annual* (Vol. 9, pp. 29–52). Emerald. doi:10.1108/S2050-206020150000010002

Van Deursen, A. J. A. M., & Van Dijk, J. A. G. M. (2014). The digital divide shifts to differences in usage. *New Media & Society*, *16*(3), 507–526. doi:10.1177/1461444813487959

Van Dijk, J. (2005). The deepening divide: Inequality in the information society. *Sage (Atlanta, Ga.)*.

Van Dijk, J. A. G. M., & Hacker, K. (2003). The digital divide as a complex and dynamic phenomenon. *The Information Society*, *19*(4), 315–326. doi:10.1080/01972240309487

Van Dyne, L., Koh, C., Ng, K. Y., Templer, K. J., Tay, C., & Chandrasekar, N. A. (2007). Cultural intelligence: Its measurement and effects on cultural judgment and decision making, cultural adaptation and task performance. *Management and Organization Review*, *3*(3), 335–371. doi:10.1111/j.1740-8784.2007.00082.x

Van Rensburg, A. H. J. (2012). Using the Internet for Democracy: A Study of South Africa, Kenya and Zambia. Global Media Journal African Edition, 6(1), 93-117.

Velankar, S., Valecha, S., & Maji, S. (2018). Bitcoin price prediction using machine learning. *2018 20th International Conference on Advanced Communication Technology (ICACT)*.

Venkatesh, V., Morris, M. G., Davis, G. B., & Davis, F. D. (2003). User acceptance of information technology. *Management Information Systems Quarterly*, *27*(3), 425–478. doi:10.2307/30036540

Vermeir, I., & Sompel, D. (2014). Assessing the what is beautiful is good stereotype and the influence of moderately attractive and less attractive advertising models on self-perception, ad attitudes, and purchase intentions of 8–13-year-old children. *Journal of Consumer Policy*, *37*(2), 205–233. doi:10.100710603-013-9245-x

Veroff, J., Reuman, D., & Feld, S. (1984). Motive in American men and women across the adult life span. *Developmental Psychology*, *20*(6), 1142–1158. doi:10.1037/0012-1649.20.6.1142

Vicario, M. D., Quattrociocchi, W., Scala, A., & Zollo, F. (2019). Polarization and Fake News. *ACM Transactions on the Web*, *13*(2), 1–22. doi:10.1145/3316809

Virmani, C., Pillai, A., & Juneja, D. (2014). Study and analysis of social network aggregator. *ICROIT 2014 - Proceedings of the 2014 International Conference on Reliability, Optimization and Information Technology*, 145–148. 10.1109/ICROIT.2014.6798314

Vishwakarma, K. D., Varshney, D., & Yadav, A. (2019). Detection and Veracity analysis of Fake News via Scrapping and Authenticating the Web Search. *Cognitive Systems Research*, *58*, 217–229. Advance online publication. doi:10.1016/j.cogsys.2019.07.004

Vissers, S., & Stolle, D. (2014). The Internet and New Modes of Political Participation: Online Versus Offline Participation. *Information Communication and Society*, *17*(8), 937–955. doi:10.1080/1369118X.2013.867356

Vodak, J., Cakanova, L., Pekar, M., & Novysedlak, M. (2019). Influencer marketing as a modern phenomenon in reputation management. *Managing Global Transitions*, *17*(3), 211–220.

Vogel, E. A., Rose, J. P., Roberts, L. R., & Eckles, K. (2014). Social comparison, social media, and self-esteem. *Psychology of Popular Media Culture*, *3*(4), 206–222. doi:10.1037/ppm0000047

Voramontri, D., & Klieb, L. (2019, January). Impact of social media on consumer behaviour. *International Journal of Information and Decision Sciences, 11*(3), 209-233. Advance online publication. doi:10.1504/IJIDS.2019.101994

Vosoughi, S., Roy, D., & Aral, S. (2018). The spread of true and false news online. *Science*, *359*(6380), 1146–1151. doi:10.1126cience.aap9559 PMID:29590045

Vyawahare, M., & Chatterjee, M. (2020). Taxonomy of Cyberbullying Detection and Prediction Techniques in Online Social Networks. *Advances in Intelligent Systems and Computing*, *1049*, 21–37. doi:10.1007/978-981-15-0132-6_3

Wacheux, F. (1996). Méthodes qualitatives et recherche en gestion. *Economica.*

Wahila, R., Mwape, L., Lyambai, K., & Kabinga-Makukula, M. (2018). Use of social media to support nursing students' learning in Zambia. *Creative Education*, *9*(08), 1237–1251. doi:10.4236/ce.2018.98092

Walden, I., & Woods, L. (2011). Broadcasting privacy. *Journal of Medicine and Law*, *3*(1), 117–141. doi:10.5235/175776311796471323

Wamuyu, P. K. (2017). Closing the digital divide in low-income urban communities: A domestication approach. *Interdisciplinary Journal of e-Skills and Lifelong Learning, 13,* 117-142.

Wamuyu, P. K. (2017). Bridging the digital divide among low income urban communities. Leveraging use of Community Technology Centers. *Telematics and Informatics*, *34*(8), 1709–1720. doi:10.1016/j.tele.2017.08.004

Wamuyu, P. K. (2017, September). Exploring the Use of Global Positioning System (GPS) for Identifying Customer Location in M-Commerce Adoption in Developing Countries. In *International Conference on Information and Communication Technology for Develoment for Africa* (pp. 99-111). Springer.

Wamuyu, P. K. (2018). Leveraging Web 2.0 technologies to foster collective civic environmental initiatives among low-income urban communities. *Computers in Human Behavior*, *85*, 1–14. doi:10.1016/j.chb.2018.03.029

Wang, Y., & Ma, J. (2014). *Mobile Social Networking and Computing: A Multidisciplinary Integrated Perspective*. CRC Press. https://dl.acm.org/doi/book/10.5555/2721424

Wang, B., Zhang, L., & Gong, N. Z. (2017). SybilSCAR: Sybil detection in online social networks via local rule based propagation. *Proceedings - IEEE INFOCOM*. Advance online publication. doi:10.1109/INFOCOM.2017.8057066

Wang, C. W., Ho, R. T., Chan, C. L., & Tse, S. (2015). Exploring personality characteristics of Chinese adolescents with internet-related addictive behaviors: Trait differences for gaming addiction and social networking addiction. *Addictive Behaviors*, *42*, 32–35. doi:10.1016/j.addbeh.2014.10.039 PMID:25462651

Wang, T., Wang, G., Li, X., Zheng, H., & Zhao, B. Y. (2013). Characterizing and detecting malicious crowdsourcing. *Computer Communication Review*, *43*(4), 537–538. doi:10.1145/2534169.2491719

Wang, X. (2016). *Social media in industrial China*. UCL Press. doi:10.2307/j.ctt1g69xtj

Wankhede, R., & Thakare, A. (2017). Design approach for accuracy in movies reviews using sentiment analysis. *2017 International conference of Electronics, Communication and Aerospace Technology (ICECA)*. 10.1109/ICECA.2017.8203652

Wasserman, H. (2020). Fake news from Africa: Panics, politics and paradigms. *Journalism, 21*(1), 3-16.

Wasserman, H., & Madrid-Morales, D. (2019). An exploratory study of "fake news" and media trust in Kenya, Nigeria and South Africa. *African Journalism Studies, 40*(1), 107-123.

Wasserman, H. (2020). Fake news from Africa: Panics, politics and paradigms. *Journalism, 21*(1), 3–16. doi:10.1177/1464884917746861

Wasserman, H., & Madrid-Morales, D. (2019). *An Exploratory Study of "Fake News" and Media Trust in Kenya*. African Journalism Studies. doi:10.1080/23743670.2019.1627230

Wasserman, S., & Faust, K. (1994). *Social network analysis: Methods and applications*. Cambridge University Press. doi:10.1017/CBO9780511815478

Waszak, P. M., Kasprzycka-Waszak, W., & Kubanek, A. (2018). The spread of medical fake news in social media–the pilot quantitative study. *Health Policy and Technology, 7*(2), 115-118.

Watson, C., & Zaw, T. (2018). *OWASP Automated Threat Handbook*. doi:10.1023/A:1020392231924

We Are Flint. (2018). *Social 2018 main findings*. https://castfromclay.co.uk/main-findings-social-media-demographics-uk-usa-2018

We are Social. (2019). *Digital in 2019*. Retrieved from https://wearesocial.com/blog/2019/01/digital-2019-global-internet-use-accelerates

Weinberg, T., Ladwig, W., & Pahrmann, C. (2012). *Social Media Marketing: Strategien für Twitter, Facebook & Co*. O'Reilly.

Weiss, R. (2014). Influencer marketing: How word-of-mouth marketing can strengthen your organization's brand. *Marketing Health Services, 34*(1), 16–17. PMID:24741762

White, D., & Cornu, A. (2011). Visitors and residents: A new typology for online engagement. *First Monday, 16*(9). Advance online publication. doi:10.5210/fm.v16i9.3171

White, J. E. (2017). *Meet Generation Z: Understanding and Reaching the New Post-Christian World*. Baker Books.

Whiting, A., & Williams, D. (2013). Why people use social media: A uses and gratifications approach. *Qualitative Market Research, 16*(4), 362–369. doi:10.1108/QMR-06-2013-0041

Whiting, A., Williams, D. L., & Hair, J. (2019). Guest editorial. *Qualitative Market Research, 22*(2), 90–93. doi:10.1108/QMR-08-2018-0098

Wickramasinghe, V., & Nisaf, M. S. M. (2013). Organizational policy as a moderator between online social networking and job performance. *Vine, 43*(2), 161–184. doi:10.1108/03055721311329945

Widyanto, L., & McMurran, M. (2004). The psychometric properties of the internet addiction test. *Cyberpsychology & Behavior, 7*(4), 443–450. doi:10.1089/cpb.2004.7.443 PMID:15331031

Williams, H. T. P., McMurray, J. R., Kurz, T., & Lambert, T. H. (2015). Network analysis reveals open forums and echo chambers in social media discussions of climate change. *Global Environmental Change, 32*, 126–138. doi:10.1016/j.gloenvcha.2015.03.006

Wilson, F., & Umar, M. A. (2019). The Effect of Fake News on Nigeria's Democracy within the Premise of Freedom of Expression. *Global Media Journal, 17*(32), 1–12.

Wilson, K., Fornasier, S., & White, K. M. (2010). Psychological predictors of young adults' use of social networking sites. *Cyberpsychology, Behavior, and Social Networking, 13*(2), 173–177. doi:10.1089/cyber.2009.0094 PMID:20528274

Wilson, R. E., Gosling, S. D., & Graham, L. T. (2012). A review of Facebook research in the social sciences. *Perspectives on Psychological Science, 7*(3), 203–220. doi:10.1177/1745691612442904 PMID:26168459

Windhoff-Héritier, A., & Czada, R. (1991). Introduction. In A. Windhoff-Héritier & R. Czada (Eds.), *Political Choice: Institutions, Rules, and the Limits of Rationality* (pp. 9–26). Westview Press.

Winner, L. (2009). Do Artifacts have Politics. In *Readings in the Philosophy of Technology* (pp. 251–263). Rowman & Littlefield Publishers.

Witte, J., & Mannon, S. (2010). *The internet and social inequalities.* Routledge. doi:10.4324/9780203861639

Witting, M. (2006). *Relations Between organizational identity, identification, and organizational objectives: An empirical study in municipalities.* Academic Press.

Wolf, J. (2017). *Ransomware Detection.* Academic Press.

Woods, H. C., & Scott, H. (2016). # Sleepyteens: Social media use in adolescence is associated with poor sleep quality, anxiety, depression and low self-esteem. *Journal of Adolescence, 51*, 41–49. doi:10.1016/j.adolescence.2016.05.008 PMID:27294324

Wright, S. A. (2016). Reinvestigating the endorser by product matchup hypothesis in advertising. *Journal of Advertising, 45*(1), 26–32. doi:10.1080/00913367.2015.1077360

Wu, S., Hofman, J. M., Mason, W. A., & Watts, D. J. (2011). Who says what to whom on twitter. In *Proceedings of the 20th International Conference on World Wide Web in Hyderabad.* ACM. 10.1145/1963405.1963504

Wu, T., Liu, S., Zhang, J., & Xiang, Y. (2017). Twitter spam detection based on deep learning. *ACM International Conference Proceeding Series.* 10.1145/3014812.3014815

Wu, T., Wen, S., Xiang, Y., & Zhou, W. (2018). Twitter spam detection: Survey of new approaches and comparative study. *Computers & Security, 76*, 265–284. doi:10.1016/j.cose.2017.11.013

Wu, Y., & Ren, F. (2011). Learning Sentimental Influence in Twitter. *2011 International Conference on Future Computer Sciences and Application.* 10.1109/ICFCSA.2011.34

Wyche, S., & Baumer, E. P. (2017). Imagined Facebook: An exploratory study of non-users' perceptions of social media in rural Zambia. *New Media & Society, 19*(7), 1092–1108. doi:10.1177/1461444815625948

Xu, H., Dinev, T., Smith, J., & Hart, P. (2011, December). Information privacy concerns: Linking individual perceptions with institutional privacy assurances. *Journal of the Association for Information Systems, 12*(12), 798–824. doi:10.17705/1jais.00281

Xu, W. W., Sang, Y., Blasiola, S., & Park, H. W. (2014). Predicting opinion leaders in twitter activism networks: The case of the Wisconsin recall election. *The American Behavioral Scientist, 58*(10), 1278–1293. doi:10.1177/0002764214527091

Yadav, M. S., Valck, K. D., Hennig-Thurau, T., Hoffman, D. L., & Spann, M. (2013). Social commerce: A contingency framework for assessing marketing potential. *Journal of Interactive Marketing, 27*(3), 311–323. doi:10.1016/j.intmar.2013.09.001

Yang, Y., Zheng, L., Zhang, J., Cui, Q., Li, Z., & Yu, P. S. (2018). *TI-CNN: Convolutional neural networks for fake news detection.* arXiv preprint arXiv:1806.00749

Yang, J. (2019). Cheap Wheat Adidas-apmkingstrack. com. *American Journal of Industrial and Business Management, 9*(3), 720–726.

Yang, Y., Yuan, Y., Archer, N. P., & Ryan, E. (2016). Adoption of social media and the quality of life of older adults. In *Proceedings of the 49th Hawaii International Conference on System Sciences (HICSS).* IEEE Computer Society. 10.1109/HICSS.2016.394

Yen, D., & Dey, B. (2019). Acculturation in the Social Media: Myth or reality? Analysing social-media-led integration and polarisation. *Technological Forecasting and Social Change, 145,* 426–427. doi:10.1016/j.techfore.2019.04.012

Yep, J., & Shulman, J. (2014). Analyzing the library's Twitter network Using NodeXL to visualize impact. *ACRL Tech-Connect, 75*(4), 177–186.

Yin, R. K. (1994). *Case study research Design and methods* (2nd ed.). Sage Publications.

Younes, F., Halawi, G., Jabbour, H., El Osta, N., Karam, L., Hajj, A., & Khabbaz, L. R. (2016). Internet addiction and relationships with insomnia, anxiety, depression, stress and self-esteem in university students: A cross-sectional designed study. *PLoS One, 11*(9), e0161126. doi:10.1371/journal.pone.0161126 PMID:27618306

Young, J. A. (2017). Facebook, Twitter, and blogs: The adoption and utilization of social media in nonprofit human service organizations. *Human Service Organizations, Management, Leadership & Governance, 41*(1), 44–57. doi:10.1 080/23303131.2016.1192574

Young, K. S. (2004). Internet addiction: A New Clinical Phenomenon and Its Consequences. *The American Behavioral Scientist, 48*(4), 402–415. doi:10.1177/0002764204270278

Young, K. S., & Rogers, R. C. (1998). The relationship between depression and Internet addiction. *Cyberpsychology & Behavior, 1*(1), 25–28. doi:10.1089/cpb.1998.1.25

YouTube. (n.d.). *YouTube for press.* https://www.youtube.com/about/press/

Zare, M., Khasteh, S. H., & Ghafouri, S. (2020). Automatic ICA detection in online social networks with PageRank. *Peer-to-Peer Networking and Applications,* 1–15. doi:10.100712083-020-00894-6

Zhang, K., & Kizilcec, R. F. (2014, May). *Anonymity in social media: Effects of content controversiality and social endorsement on sharing behavior.* Paper presented at the meeting of Eighth International AAAI Conference on Weblogs and Social Media.

Zhang, X., Gao, Y., Chen, H., Sun, Y., & de Pablos, P. O. (2015). Enhancing Creativity or Wasting Time?: The Mediating Role of Adaptability on Social Media-Job Performance Relationship. In PACIS (p. 230). Academic Press.

Zhang, C., Gupta, A., Kauten, C., Deokar, A. V., & Qin, X. (2019). Detecting Fake News for Reducing Misinformation Risks Using Analytics Approaches. *European Journal of Operational Research, 279*(3), 1036–1052. Advance online publication. doi:10.1016/j.ejor.2019.06.022

Zhang, J., & Mao, E. (2016). From online motivations to ad clicks and to behavioral intentions: An empirical study of consumer response to social media advertising. *Psychology and Marketing, 33*(3), 155–164. doi:10.1002/mar.20862

Zhang, J., Zhang, R., Zhang, Y., & Yan, G. (2018). The rise of social botnets: Attacks and countermeasures. *IEEE Transactions on Dependable and Secure Computing, 15*(6), 1068–1082. doi:10.1109/TDSC.2016.2641441

Zhang, L., & Pentina, I. (2012). Motivations and Usage Patterns of Weibo. *Cyberpsychology, Behavior, and Social Networking, 6*(15), 312–317. doi:10.1089/cyber.2011.0615 PMID:22703037

Zhang, Y., & Leung, L. (2015). A review of social networking service (SNS) research in communication journals from 2006 to 2011. *New Media & Society, 17*(7), 1007–1024. doi:10.1177/1461444813520477

Zhao, Z., Zhao, J., Sano, Y., Levy, O., Takayasu, H., Takayasu, M., & Havlin, S. (2018). *Fake news propagate differently from real news even at early stages of spreading.* arXiv preprint arXiv:1803.03443

Zhenqiang Gong, N., & Liu, B. (2018). Attribute Inference Attacks in Online Social Networks. *ACM Trans. Priv. Secur, 21*(3). Advance online publication. doi:10.1145/3154793

Zivnuska, S., Carlson, J. R., Carlson, D. S., Harris, R. B., & Harris, K. J. (2019). Social media addiction and social media reactions: The implications for job performance. *The Journal of Social Psychology, 159*(6), 746–760. doi:10.1080/002 24545.2019.1578725 PMID:30821647

Zulli, D. (2018). Capitalizing on the look: Insights into the glance, attention economy, and Instagram. *Critical Studies in Media Communication, 35*(2), 137–150. doi:10.1080/15295036.2017.1394582

About the Contributors

Patrick Kanyi Wamuyu is the coordinator of the SIMElab Africa (Social Media Lab Africa), and an Associate Professor of Information Technology at United States International University-Africa, Nairobi, Kenya. Dr. Wamuyu earned his Ph.D. degree in Information Systems and Technology from the University of KwaZulu-Natal, Durban, South Africa. He completed his postdoc research at the Indian Institute of Information Technology, Allahabad, India and the Freie Universität, Berlin, Germany. His research focuses on a broad range of topics related to Information and Communication Technologies for Development (ICT4D), Social Media Use and Consumption, E-business Infrastructures, ICT Innovations and Entrepreneurship, Wireless Sensor Networks and Databases. His academic publications include a book, book chapters, peer reviewed journal articles, and conference proceedings. He has over twenty years of experience in the computing and information technology industry that have taken him from software development, running his own Information Technology Enterprise to the academic world. He has advised many graduate (Masters and Ph.D.) and undergraduate students. In his spare time, he enjoys traveling.

* * *

Asli Elif Aydin earned her Ph.D. in Marketing at Bogazici University, Istanbul, Turkey in 2013. Currently she is an assistant professor at Istanbul Bilgi University, Istanbul, Turkey. Her primary research interests are in consumer decision making and brand management.

Marwa Mallouli Bouzouitina is currently a university teacher in Business School ESC of Sfax and member of the PRISME Research Laboratory. She received her Master's Degree (Research Master) in Management from Faculty of Economics and Management of Sfax – Tunisia (FSEGS) in 2014. Marwa is a regular contributor to scientific rearches in both French and English languages. she participated in international conferences and a english journal . Her research interests include Social Networking Sites usage and management. Since 2015, she has been a doctoral student on the thematic "Social Networking Sites and individual performance" at the faculty of Economics and Management of Sfax.

Tarunpreet Bhatia is working as an Assistant Professor in CSED, TIET, Patiala, Punjab, India. She received her Ph.D and M.E. degree in Computer Science & Engineering from Thapar Institute of Engineering & Technology and B.E. (with Honors) in Computer Science and Engineering from Kurukshetra University. She received the Gold Medal in Master of Engineering. Her research interests include Network and Information Security, Mobile Computing, Cloud Computing, Internet of Things and Soft Computing. She has more than 30 research publications in reputed journals and conferences.

She is member of various program committees for different International/National Conferences and reviewer of various International/National journals. She is Vice President, Computer Society of India (CSI), TIET, Patiala, Punjab, India.

Esra Bozkanat holds her PhD degree in Public Relations and Publicity, Istanbul University. Her research interests new media studies, social media researches, and political communications.

Jamil Chaabouni is Honorary Professor at SESAME University in Tunis and a member of the National Statistics Council. He was until 2017 Professor of Management at the University of Sfax where he leads the Research Unit in Business Management (URGE). He received a Ph.D. degree in management science, in 1980, from the University Philipp of Marburg / Germany. His research interests include governance, strategy, organisation and information management. He served as vice dean of the Faculty of Economics and Management of Sfax. He leads several cooperative research projects with the universities of Toulouse, Marseille in France and Technical University Berlin. He performed consultancy work and expertise with, among others, the UNDP, the ILO, the UNECA, the National Center for Informatics, the IGL group, the Tunisian Institute for Strategic Studies, the Gesellschaft für Technische Zusammenarbeit (GTZ).

Gregory Gondwe studies contemporary media ecosystems in Africa and their role in shaping society. His current works focus on the role of new media and the implications it poses to the multi-party media that emerged in the wake of democratic mandates.

S. K. Gupta received his B.Tech in Electronics and Telecommunication Engineering from National Institute of Technology, Raipur (Chhattisgarh, India in 2008 and M.Tech & Ph.D. with Specialization in Systems Engineering, Department of Electrical Engineering from Indian Institute of Technology (Banaras Hindu University), Varanasi (UP), India in 2011 & 2016, respectively. Previously, he was the former research fellow in Mobile Computing and Broadband Networking Lab, Department of Computer Science, National Chiao Tung University, Hsinchu, Taiwan, and IIT Jodhpur, India. Currently, he is working as Assistant Professor in the School of Electronics and Communication Engineering, Shri Mata Vaishno Devi University, Kakryal, Katra, (J&K), India. His research interest includes cryptography and network security, networking, etc. He has published many articles in the reputed international/national journals and prestigious conference proceedings, and an author of many book chapters as well. He has supervised seven master research scholars till date. Currently, he is supervising three master research scholars and two PhD research scholars in the domain of network security and networking. He has organized the number of faculty development programs, short term courses, workshops, conference, etc in the capacity of coordinator and organizing secretary. Also, served as organizing committee members, session chairs of the various workshop, seminars, and conferences. Moreover, he has delivered expert talks in the domain of cryptography and network security and networking in many organizations.

Stavroula Kalogeras is a television and film professional with experience in marketing communications, film licensing, programming, and production. She holds a Bachelor of Arts in Communication, a Master of Business Administration in Telecommunications, a Ph.D. in Media Culture and Society, and a Postgraduate Certificate in Research Training (eLearning). Kalogeras is a media-education convergence theorist who pioneered transmedia storytelling edutainment. She uses design thinking and neuroscience to understand learners to generate compelling learning experiences. She is an expert in higher education teaching strategies (traditional and digital), and a subject matter expert in marketing communication and media management. Her innovative research papers have been published in a variety of academic journals. Her visionary books are Transmedia Storytelling and the New Era of Media Convergence in Higher Education and Illuminating the Heart: Finding meaning and purpose in life through higher education, transmedia storytelling, and moral character. Dr. Kalogeras has worked for leading entertainment conglomerates, such as E! Entertainment Television, Paramount Pictures, and DirecTV. In 2001, TBWA\Chiat\Day recruited her, and she relocated to Athens, Greece, to head up the company's television division. Kalogeras collaborated with two of the leading television networks in Greece - Mega Channel and Antenna TV - where she was responsible for creating their most successful branding campaigns. Most recently, Dr. Kalogeras teaches courses in marketing, management, and communications with the Business College of Athens in conjunction with Plymouth University, UK. In the USA, she teaches online graduate courses in the Department of Humanities at Tiffin University.

Yowei Kang (Ph.D.) is Assistant Professor at Bachelor Degree Program in Oceanic Cultural Creative Design Industries, National Taiwan Ocean University, TAIWAN. His research interests focus on new media design, digital game research, visual communication, and experiential rhetoric. Some of his works have been published in International Journal of Strategic Communication, and Journal of Intercultural Communication Studies. He has received government funding to support his research in location-based advertising and consumer privacy management strategies.

Ozge Kirezli recieved her M.A. degree in Production Management and Marketing from Marmara University in 2010. In 2015 she received her Ph.D. degree in Production Management and Marketing from Marmara University. She started her academic career as a Teaching Assistant at Business Administartion Department of İstanbul Bilgi University in 2010, and worked till 2018. She is now currently working as an Assistant Prof. at Yeditepe University, lecturing Marketing Management, Marketing Research and Consumer Behavior courses. She has articles in The Journal of World Intellectual Property and Journal of Innovation Economics & Management and book chapters about Green Marketing and Corporate Social Responsilbility in Global IGI books.

Abhishek Kumar is working as an Assistant Professor in School of Computer Science and IT, Jain University, Bangalore,India. He has been awardedwith Ph.D., Doctorate in Computer Application (Research Interests: Stereoscopy, 3D Animation, Design, Computer Graphics & visual effects) and Dual Master Degree in Computer Science and Animation. Dr. Abhishek Kumar is Apple Certified Associate (USA), Adobe Certified Educator (USA) & Certified by Autodesk. Dr. Abhishek holding 2 Patent in the field of VR and IOT & Published 20+ Research papers Scopus/WOS indexed. Dr. Abhishek has trained over 50,000+ students across the globe from 153 Countries, top 5 countries are India, Germany, United States, Spain & Australia. He has completed their professional studies related to Animation, computer graphics, Virtual reality, Stereoscopy, Filmmaking, Visual Effects & photography form Norwich University of Arts, University of Edinburg, Wizcraft MIME & FXPHD, Australia.

Steffen Mayer is an MBA-Student in International Management at the Universities of Applied Science in Aschaffenburg (Germany) and Seinäjoki (Finnland). Several years of professional sales experience in the German Automotive Industry.

Roberta Muchangwe is a Media and Communication Studies Lecturer at the University of Zambia and a current Fulbright-Scholar-In-Residence at Texas Southern University.

Japhet Mwaya is a Catholic Priest and Assistant Lecturer at St. Augustine University of Tanzania (SAUT).

Ishrat Nazeer is currently Research Scholar in School of Computer Science & Engineering, Lovely Professional University, Jalandhar, India. She has completed her Bachelors in Engineering from University of Kashmir. Her area of interest is Machine learning, Deep Learning and Sentiment Analysis.

Hasitha Ranasinghe has completed his Masters degree at the School of Computing and Mathematics, Charles Sturt University, Melbourne, Australia.

Sanjeev Rao is working as Assistant Professor in CSED, TIET, Patiala, Punjab, India. He received his B.Tech and M.Tech in year 2007 and 2012 respectively, majoring in Computer Science and Engineering. He is an Oracle Certified Professional (OCP) from Oracle University. He is also pursuing Ph.D. in the domain of security issues in Online Social Networks at CSED, TIET, Patiala, Punjab, India. His area of interests are data-mining, social network analysis and security in social networks. He has published and presented many papers in Conferences and Journals. He is also a member of IEEE, ACM, and IAENG.

Mamoon Rashid is currently working as an Assistant Professor in School of Computer Science & Engineering, Lovely Professional University, India. He has published many papers in Journals and Conferences of International repute. He is a regular contributor to monthly Editorial of CSI Communications and serves as an Editorial Review Board Member in Journals of International Journal of E-Health and Medical Communications (IJEHMC), International Journal of End-User Computing and Development (IJEUCD), International Journal of Distributed Artificial Intelligence (IJDAI) and International Journal of Patient-Centered Healthcare (IJPCH).His research interests include Big Data Analytics, Machine Learning, Neuro Imaging.

José Duarte da Rocha Santos received his PhD in Management from the University of Vigo, Spain. He is also Master of Marketing and has a Bachelor degree in Business Sciences. Additionally, he obtained the title Specialist in Marketing and Advertising in accordance with Portuguese Decree-Law No. 206/August 31, 2009. Between 1987 and 2002, he has played various roles in sales, marketing, and management of companies in the information technologies sector. From 2003, he has performed functions of management and marketing consultant. Since 1999, he has been a professor in higher education in Portugal in the field of management and marketing. He is currently a professor at the Instituto Superior Politécnico Gaya (ISPGaya) and at the Instituto Superior de Contabilidade e Administração do Porto (ISCAP). He is also research at the Centre for Organisational and Social Studies of Polytechnic of Porto (CEOS.PP). His current research areas include, social media marketing, social customer relationship management and social selling.

Zouhour Smaoui Hachicha is an Associate Professor in management in the Faculty of Economics and Management of Sfax – Tunisia (FSEGS) and member of the PRISME Research Laboratory. Her PhD thesis is obtained from University of Sfax and deals with e-commerce development influencing factors in the hospitality field in Tunisia. In addition to her experience as professor, Dr. Smaoui Hachicha is a regular contributor to scientific conferences and Journals in both French and English languages. Her research interests include e-commerce in hotels, social network sites use, social entrepreneurship, resilience and transitional contexts. She is head of PRISME Research Laboratory at FSEGS.

Anil Kumar Verma is currently a Professor in CSED, TIET, Patiala. He received his B.S., M.S. and Ph.D. in 1991, 2001 and 2008, respectively, majoring in Computer Science and Engineering. He has published over 150 papers in referred journals and conferences (India and Abroad). He has chaired various sessions in the International and National Conferences. He is active member of MIEEE, MACM, MISCI, LMCSI, MIETE, GMAIMA. He is a certified software quality auditor by MoCIT, Govt. of India. His research interests include Security in Online Social Networks, Mobile computing, wireless networks, routing algorithms and mobile clouds.

Kenneth C. C. Yang (Ph.D.) is Professor in the Department of Communication at the University of Texas at El Paso, USA. His research focuses on new media advertising, consumer behavior, and international advertising. Some of his many works have been published in Cyberpsychology, Journal of Strategic Communication, International Journal of Consumer Marketing, Journal of Intercultural Communication Studies, Journal of Marketing Communication, and Telematics and Informatics. He has edited or co-edited three books, Asia.com: Asia encounters the Internet (Routledge, 2003), Multi-Platform Advertising Strategies in the Global Marketplace (IGI Global, 2018), and Cases on Immersive Virtual Reality Techniques (IGI Global, 2019).

Index

Recommended Reference Books

ISBN: 978-1-5225-8491-9
© 2019; 454 pp.
List Price: $295

ISBN: 978-1-5225-7458-3
© 2019; 356 pp.
List Price: $195

ISBN: 978-1-5225-6023-4
© 2019; 384 pp.
List Price: $195

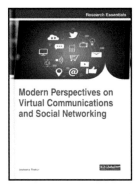

ISBN: 978-1-5225-5715-9
© 2019; 273 pp.
List Price: $175

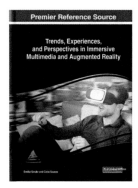

ISBN: 978-1-5225-5696-1
© 2019; 277 pp.
List Price: $185

ISBN: 978-1-5225-9369-0
© 2019; 358 pp.
List Price: $205

Do you want to stay current on the latest research trends, product announcements, news and special offers?
Join IGI Global's mailing list today and start enjoying exclusive perks sent only to IGI Global members.
Add your name to the list at **www.igi-global.com/newsletters.**

Publisher of Peer-Reviewed, Timely, and Innovative Academic Research

www.igi-global.com   ✉ Sign up at www.igi-global.com/newsletters   f facebook.com/igiglobal   t twitter.com/igiglobal   in linkedin.com/igiglobal

Ensure Quality Research is Introduced to the Academic Community

Become an IGI Global Reviewer for Authored Book Projects

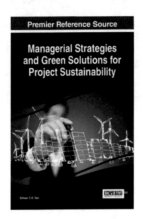

The overall success of an authored book project is dependent on quality and timely reviews.

In this competitive age of scholarly publishing, constructive and timely feedback significantly expedites the turnaround time of manuscripts from submission to acceptance, allowing the publication and discovery of forward-thinking research at a much more expeditious rate. Several IGI Global authored book projects are currently seeking highly-qualified experts in the field to fill vacancies on their respective editorial review boards:

Applications and Inquiries may be sent to:
development@igi-global.com

Applicants must have a doctorate (or an equivalent degree) as well as publishing and reviewing experience. Reviewers are asked to complete the open-ended evaluation questions with as much detail as possible in a timely, collegial, and constructive manner. All reviewers' tenures run for one-year terms on the editorial review boards and are expected to complete at least three reviews per term. Upon successful completion of this term, reviewers can be considered for an additional term.

If you have a colleague that may be interested in this opportunity, we encourage you to share this information with them.

www.igi-global.com

Publisher of Peer-Reviewed, Timely, and
Innovative Academic Research Since 1988

IGI Global's Transformative Open Access (OA) Model:
How to Turn Your University Library's Database Acquisitions Into a Source of OA Funding

In response to the OA movement and well in advance of Plan S, IGI Global, early last year, unveiled their OA Fee Waiver (Read & Publish) Initiative.

Under this initiative, librarians who invest in IGI Global's InfoSci-Books (5,300+ reference books) and/or InfoSci-Journals (185+ scholarly journals) databases will be able to subsidize their patron's OA article processing charges (APC) when their work is submitted and accepted (after the peer review process) into an IGI Global journal. *See website for details.

How Does it Work?

1. When a library subscribes or perpetually purchases IGI Global's InfoSci-Databases and/or their discipline/subject-focused subsets, IGI Global will match the library's investment with a fund of equal value to go toward subsidizing the OA article processing charges (APCs) for their patrons.

   Researchers: **Be sure to recommend the InfoSci-Books and InfoSci-Journals to take advantage of this initiative.**

2. When a student, faculty, or staff member submits a paper and it is accepted (following the peer review) into one of IGI Global's 185+ scholarly journals, the author will have the option to have their paper published under a traditional publishing model or as OA.

3. When the author chooses to have their paper published under OA, IGI Global will notify them of the OA Fee Waiver (Read and Publish) Initiative. If the author decides they would like to take advantage of this initiative, IGI Global will deduct the US$ 2,000 APC from the created fund.

4. This fund will be offered on an annual basis and will renew as the subscription is renewed for each year thereafter. IGI Global will manage the fund and award the APC waivers unless the librarian has a preference as to how the funds should be managed.

Hear From the Experts on This Initiative:

"I'm very happy to have been able to make one of my recent research contributions, "Visualizing the Social Media Conversations of a National Information Technology Professional Association" featured in the *International Journal of Human Capital and Information Technology Professionals*, freely available along with having access to the valuable resources found within IGI Global's InfoSci-Journals database."

– **Prof. Stuart Palmer**,
Deakin University, Australia

For More Information, Visit: www.igi-global.com/publish/contributor-resources/open-access/read-publish-model
or contact IGI Global's Database Team at eresources@igi-global.com.

Printed in the United States
By Bookmasters